InDesign® CS3 For Dummies®

Cheat Sheet

W9-CFK-280

Most Useful InDesign Keyboard Shortcuts

	Macintosh	Windows
File import/export		
Export document	⌘+E	Ctrl+E
Place text and graphics	⌘+D	Ctrl+D
Viewing		
Zoom in	⌘+=	Ctrl+=
Zoom out	⌘+− (hyphen)	Ctrl+− (hyphen)
Fit page/spread in window	⌘+0	Ctrl+Alt+=
Display actual size	⌘+1	Ctrl+1
Display at 50%	⌘+5	Ctrl+5
Display at 200%	⌘+2	Ctrl+2
Show/hide rulers	⌘+R	Ctrl+R
Show hidden characters	Option+⌘+I	Ctrl+Alt+I
Guides		
Show/hide guides	⌘+; (semicolon)	Ctrl+; (semicolon)
Lock/unlock guides	Option+⌘+; (semicolon)	Ctrl+Alt+; (semicolon)
Snap to guides on/off	Shift+⌘+; (semicolon)	Ctrl+Shift+; (semicolon)
Show/hide baseline grid	Option+⌘+"	Ctrl+Alt+"
Show/hide document grid	⌘+"	Ctrl+"
Moving objects		
Bring object to front	Shift+⌘+]	Ctrl+Shift+]
Bring object forward	⌘+]	Ctrl+]
Send object to back	Shift+⌘+[	Ctrl+Shift+[
Send object backward	⌘+[	Ctrl+[
Object commands		
Paste into	Option+⌘+V	Ctrl+Alt+V
Paste in place	Option+Shift+⌘+V	Ctrl+Alt+Shift+V
Step and repeat	Shift+⌘+U	Ctrl+Shift+U
Fit graphics into frame proportionally	Option+Shift+⌘+E	Ctrl+Alt+Shift+E
Transform again	Option+⌘+3	Ctrl+Alt+3

For Dummies: Bestselling Book Series for Beginners

InDesign® CS3 For Dummies®

Cheat Sheet

	Macintosh	Windows
Text alignment and spacing		
Align left	Shift+⌘+L	Ctrl+Shift+L
Align right	Shift+⌘+R	Ctrl+Shift+R
Align center	Shift+⌘+C	Ctrl+Shift+C
Justify left	Shift+⌘+J	Ctrl+Shift+J
Justify right	Option+Shift+⌘+R	Ctrl+Alt+Shift+R
Justify center	Option+Shift+⌘+C	Ctrl+Alt+Shift+C
Align to grid on/off	Option+Shift+⌘+G	Ctrl+Alt+Shift+G
Table editing		
Insert table	Option+Shift+⌘+T	Ctrl+Alt+Shift+T
Insert column	Option+⌘+9	Ctrl+Alt+9
Insert row	⌘+9	Ctrl+9
Special characters		
Bullet (•)	Option+8	Alt+8
Copyright (©)	Option+G	Alt+G
Registered trademark (®)	Option+R	Alt+R
Trademark (™)	Option+2	Alt+2
Em dash (—)	Option+Shift+− (hyphen)	Alt+Shift+− (hyphen)
En dash (–)	Option+− (hyphen)	Alt+− (hyphen)
Discretionary hyphen	Shift+⌘+− (hyphen)	Ctrl+Shift+− (hyphen)
Em space	Shift+⌘+M	Ctrl+Shift+M
En space	Shift+⌘+N	Ctrl+Shift+N
Insert current page number	Option+Shift+⌘+N	Ctrl+Alt+Shift+N
Miscellaneous		
Print document	⌘+P	Ctrl+P
Undo	⌘+Z	Ctrl+Z
Redo	Shift+⌘+Z	Ctrl+Shift+Z

For Dummies: Bestselling Book Series for Beginners

InDesign® CS3 FOR DUMMIES®

by Galen Gruman

BICENTENNIAL
1807
WILEY
2007
BICENTENNIAL

Wiley Publishing, Inc.

InDesign® CS3 For Dummies®

Published by
Wiley Publishing, Inc.
111 River Street
Hoboken, NJ 07030-5774

www.wiley.com

WILEY

About the Author

Galen Gruman is the principal at The Zango Group, an editorial and marketing consulting firm. Currently a regular contributor to *Macworld, Layers Magazine, CIO,* and *InfoWorld,* he has also been editor of *Macworld* and *M-Business,* executive editor of *Upside,* West Coast bureau chief of *Computerworld,* and vice president of content for ThirdAge.com. He is co-author of 20 other books on desktop publishing. Gruman led one of the first successful conversions of a national magazine to desktop publishing in 1986 and has covered publishing technology since then for several publications, including the trade weekly *InfoWorld,* for which he began writing in 1986, *Macworld,* whose staff he joined in 1991, and, most recently, *Layers Magazine.*

Dedication

To Rick, Karen, and Kyle Bull, for many years of wonderful holidays and cordial visits.

Publisher's Acknowledgments

We're proud of this book; please send us your comments through our online registration form located at www.dummies.com/register/.

Some of the people who helped bring this book to market include the following:

Acquisitions, Editorial, and Media Development

Project Editor: Linda Morris

Acquisitions Editor: Bob Woerner

Copy Editor: Linda Morris

Technical Editor: Jonathan Woolson

Editorial Manager: Jodi Jensen

Media Development Manager: Laura VanWinkle

Editorial Assistant: Amanda Foxworth

Sr. Editorial Assistant: Cherie Case

Cartoons: Rich Tennant
(www.the5thwave.com)

Composition Services

Project Coordinator: Jennifer Theriot

Layout and Graphics: Joyce Haughey, Stephanie D. Jumper, Barbara Moore, Alicia B. South, Ronald Terry

Proofreaders: Debbye Butler, Susan Moritz

Indexer: Aptara

Anniversary Logo Design: Richard J. Pacifico

Publishing and Editorial for Technology Dummies

Richard Swadley, Vice President and Executive Group Publisher

Andy Cummings, Vice President and Publisher

Mary Bednarek, Executive Acquisitions Director

Mary C. Corder, Editorial Director

Publishing for Consumer Dummies

Diane Graves Steele, Vice President and Publisher

Joyce Pepple, Acquisitions Director

Composition Services

Gerry Fahey, Vice President of Production Services

Debbie Stailey, Director of Composition Services

Contents at a Glance

Table of Contents

Introduction

● ●

*W*hat is Adobe InDesign and what can it do for you? InDesign is a power-ful publishing application that lets you work the way *you* want to work. You can use InDesign as a free-form but manual approach to layout, or as a structured but easily revised approach. The fact that you can choose which way to work is important for both novice and experienced users because there isn't a single, correct way to lay out pages. Sometimes (for example, if your project is a single-instance publication), creating a layout from scratch — almost as if you were doing it by hand on paper — is the best approach. And sometimes using a highly formatted template that you can modify as needed is the way to go: There's no need to reinvent the wheel for documents that have a structured and repeatable format.

InDesign can handle sophisticated tasks, such as magazine and newspaper page layout, but its simple approach to publishing also makes it a good choice for smaller projects, such as one-off ads and fliers. InDesign is also a good choice for corporate publishing tasks, such as proposals and annual reports. Plug-in software from other vendors adds extra capabilities.

But that's not all. InDesign was designed from the ground up as an *electronic* publishing tool. That means that you can easily send documents to service bureaus and printing presses for direct output, which saves you lots of time and money. It also means that you can create documents for electronic distri-bution, particularly using the Adobe Acrobat Portable Document Format (PDF). These electronic files can include interactive features, such as buttons to play sounds or a movie.

After you get the hang of it, InDesign is quite easy to use. At the same time, it's a powerful publishing program with a strong following among the ranks of professional publishers — and the latest InDesign CS3 version is certain to reinforce that position. Part of its success is due to the fact that its interface is like that of its sister applications, Adobe Illustrator and Adobe Photoshop, which are also components of the Adobe Creative Suite.

If you are just getting started with InDesign, welcome! I hope you'll find the information in these pages to be helpful in getting you started.

How to Use This Book

Although this book has information that any level of publisher needs to know to use InDesign, this book is primarily for those of you who are fairly new to the field, or who are just becoming familiar with the program. I try to take the mystery out of InDesign and give you some guidance on how to create a bunch of different types of documents. Here are some conventions used in this book:

- ✔ **Menu commands** are listed like this: Window⇨Pages.

- ✔ **Key combinations:** If you're supposed to press several keys together, I indicate that by placing plus signs (+) between them. Thus, Shift+⌘+A means press and hold the Shift and ⌘ keys, and then press A. After you've pressed the A key, let go of all the keys. I also use the plus sign to join keys to mouse movements. For example, Alt+drag means to hold the Alt key when dragging the mouse.

  Note that the Macintosh sequence comes first, followed by the Windows equivalent.

- ✔ **Pointer:** The small graphic icon that moves on the screen as you move your mouse is a pointer (also called a cursor). The pointer takes on different shapes depending on the tool you select, the current location of the mouse, and the function you are performing.

- ✔ **Click:** This means to quickly press and release the mouse button once. On most Mac mice, there is only one button, but on some there are two or more. All PC mice have at least two buttons. If you have a multi-button mouse, click the leftmost button when I say to click the mouse.

- ✔ **Double-click:** This tells you to quickly press and release the mouse button twice. On some multi-button mice, one of the buttons can function as a double-click. (You click it once, the mouse clicks twice.) If your mouse has this feature, use it; it saves strain on your hand.

- ✔ **Right-click:** A Windows feature, this means to click the right-hand mouse button. On a Mac's one-button mouse, hold the Control key when clicking the mouse button to do the equivalent of right-clicking in programs that support it. On multi-button Mac mice, assign one of the buttons to the Control+click combination.

- ✔ **Dragging:** Dragging is used for moving and sizing items in an InDesign document. To drag an item, position the mouse pointer on the item, press and hold down the mouse button, and then slide the mouse across a flat surface.

How This Book Is Organized

I've divided this book into eight parts, not counting this introduction. Note that the book covers InDesign on both Macintosh and Windows. Because the application is almost identical on both platforms, I only point out platform-specific information when I need to, when I remember to, or both.

I have also included some bonus content on the InDesignCentral Web site (www.InDesignCentral.com).

Part 1: Before You Begin

Designing a document is a combination of science and art. The science is in setting up the structure of the page: How many places will hold text, and how many will hold graphics? How wide will the margins be? Where will the page numbers appear? And so on. The art is in coming up with creative ways of filling the structure to please your eyes and the eyes of the people who will be looking at your document.

In this part, I tell you how to navigate your way around InDesign using the program's menus, dialog boxes, panels, and panes. I also explain how to customize the preferences to your needs.

Part II: Document Essentials

Good publishing technique is about more than just getting the words down on paper. It's also about opening, saving, adding, deleting, numbering, and setting layout guidelines for documents. This part shows you how to do all that and a lot more, including tips on setting up master pages that you can use over and over again. You'll also find out how to create color swatches for easy reuse in your documents.

Part III: Object Essentials

This part of the book shows you how to work with *objects:* the lines, text frames, graphics frames, and other odds and ends that make up a publication. And you'll discover how to apply some really neat special effects to them.

Part IV: Text Essentials

When you think about it, text is a big deal when it comes to publishing documents. After all, how many people would want to read a book with nothing but pictures? In this part, I show you how to create and manipulate text, in more ways than you can even imagine.

Part V: Graphics Essentials

Very few people would want to read a book with nothing but text, so this part is where I show you how to handle graphics in InDesign.

Part VI: Getting Down to Business

InDesign — especially with some of the enhancements in its latest version — is really good at handling the many kinds of documents that tend to be used in businesses, such as manuals, annual reports, and catalogs. This part shows you how to create tables, handle footnotes, create indexes, manage page numbering across multiple chapters in a book, and use text variables to make InDesign update text as needed based on the document's current context.

Part VII: Printing and Output Essentials

Whether you're printing a publication or simply creating a PDF file for readers to download from a Web site, you still need to understand the basics of outputting an InDesign document. This part is where I show you how to set up your output files, manage color, and work with service bureaus.

Part VIII: The Part of Tens

This part of the book is like the chips in the chocolate chip cookies; you could eat the cookies without them, but you'd be missing a really good part. It's a part that shows you some important resources that will help you make the most of InDesign. It also gives some pointers on switching to InDesign from QuarkXPress and Adobe PageMaker.

Icons Used in This Book

So that you can pick out parts that you really need to pay attention to (or, depending on your taste, to avoid), I've used some symbols, or *icons*, in this book.

When you see this icon, it means I am pointing out a feature that's new to InDesign CS3.

If you see this icon, it means that I'm mentioning some really nifty point or idea that you may want to keep in mind as you use the program.

This icon lets you know something you'll want to keep in mind. If you forget it later, that's fine, but if you remember it, it will make your InDesign life a little easier.

If you skip all the other icons, pay attention to this one. Why? Because ignoring it could cause something really, really bad or embarrassing to happen, like when you were sitting in your second-grade classroom waiting for the teacher to call on you to answer a question, and you noticed that you still had your pajama shirt on. I don't want that to happen to you!

This icon tells you that I am about to pontificate on some remote technical bit of information that might help explain a feature in InDesign. The technical info will definitely make you sound impressive if you memorize it and recite it to your friends.

Part I
Before You Begin

The 5th Wave   By Rich Tennant

"It says, 'Seth — Please see us about your idea
to wrap newsletter text around company logo.
Signed, the Production Department.'"

In this part . . .

You have your copy of InDesign and you'd like some basic information on how to get started, right? Well, you have come to the right place. Read along and, before you know it, you'll be sailing smoothly through InDesign. This part of the book gives you a general idea of what InDesign can do. I explain the layout approaches you can take and how to set up InDesign to work the way you work. Along the way, you'll find out how to navigate the plethora of panels, menus, tools, and shortcuts that can seem overwhelming at first but that soon become second nature as you gain experience using the program. Welcome aboard!

Chapter 1

Understanding InDesign Ingredients

Starting to use a new software application is not unlike meeting a new friend for the first time. You take a long look at the person, maybe ask a few questions, and begin the process of becoming acquainted. Just as it's worthwhile to learn the likes and dislikes of a new friend, it's also worth your time to wrap your head around InDesign's unique style and approaches. When you do so, you'll find it much easier to start using InDesign to get work done.

This chapter explains where to look in InDesign for the features and capabilities you need to master. I introduce you to the process that InDesign assumes you use when laying out documents, explain some of the terms you'll encounter throughout the book, describe the unique interface elements in the document window, survey the most commonly used tools, and explain how InDesign packages much of its functionality through an interface element called a *panel*.

The InDesign Approach

Publishing programs have some similarities and some differences in their various approaches to the publishing task. One way to describe a program's approach to publishing is to talk about its *metaphor,* or the overall way that it handles publishing tasks.

Some programs use a *free-form* metaphor, which means that the method used to craft a document is based on assembling page elements as you would if they were placed on a traditional pasteboard until you were ready to use them. This is also called the *pasteboard* metaphor, which is an imprecise term because software that uses other metaphors can still include a pasteboard. The now-defunct PageMaker is the best-known example of the free-form approach.

Other programs approach page layout by using a *frame-based* metaphor, in which frames (or boxes) hold both the page elements and the attributes that control the appearance of those elements. QuarkXPress is the best-known example of the frame-based approach.

InDesign offers the best of both worlds because it incorporates both the free-form and the frame-based metaphors.

The frame-based metaphor

When you work with a frame-based metaphor, you build pages by assembling a variety of frames that will contain your text and graphics. First, you set up the basic framework of the document — the page size and orientation, margins, number of columns, and so on. You then fill that framework with text, graphics, and lines.

These frames and lines need not be straight or square. With InDesign, you can create frames that are shaped by *Bézier curves.* (In the 1970s, French engineer Pierre Bézier created the mathematics that make these adjustable curves work.)

Why would you want to use frames? Publishers find several reasons why frames come in handy:

- **To create a template for documents, such as newsletters and magazines, that use the same basic layout elements across many articles.** You create the frames and then add the text and graphics appropriate for each specific article, modifying, adding, and deleting frames as necessary for each article.

- **To get a sense of how you want your elements to be placed and sized before you start working with the actual elements.** This is similar to sketching a rough layout on paper with a pen or pencil before doing a formal layout with InDesign.

- **To set up specific size and placement of elements up front.** You often work with a template or with guidelines that limit the size and placement of elements. In many cases, you can copy an existing frame because its size is the same as what you use in several locations of your layout. For structured or partly structured documents, such as newsletters and magazines, it is usually easier to set up documents up front so that elements are sized and placed correctly; the less favorable alternative is resizing elements one at a time later on.

Whether you start by creating frames to hold graphics or text or you simply place the text and graphics directly on your page, you're using frames. When you directly place elements on the page, InDesign creates a frame automatically for each element. The frame that InDesign creates is based on the amount of text or the size of the graphic, rather than on your specific frame specifications. Of course, in either case, you can modify the frames and the elements within them.

The free-form metaphor

Working under a free-form metaphor, you draw a page's content as if you're working on paper. If you've been in the publishing business for a while, you might once have used wax to stick strips of type, camera-ready line drawings, and halftone pictures to a pasteboard. You would then assemble and reassemble all those pieces until you got the combination that looked right to you. The free-form metaphor encourages a try-as-you-go, experimental layout approach, which is particularly well suited to one-of-a-kind documents such as ads, brochures, annual reports, and some marketing materials.

If you use a frame-based approach to page layout, you can experiment with using the frames as placeholders for actual text and graphics. Visual thinkers like to work with actual objects, which is why the free-form metaphor works much better for them. With InDesign, you pick the metaphor that works for your style, your current situation, and your mood. After all, both approaches can lead to the same great design.

Understanding Global and Local Control

The power of desktop publishing in general, and InDesign in particular, is that it lets you automate time-consuming layout and typesetting tasks while at the same time letting you customize each step of the process according to your needs.

This duality of structure and flexibility — implemented via the dual use of the frame-based and free-form layout metaphors — carries over to all operations, from typography to color. You can use global controls to establish general settings for layout elements, and then use local controls to modify those elements to meet specific publishing requirements. The key to using global and local tools effectively is to know when each is appropriate.

Global tools include

- ✔ General preferences and application preferences (see Chapter 2)
- ✔ Master pages and libraries (see Chapter 6)
- ✔ Character and paragraph styles (see Chapter 14)
- ✔ Table and cell styles (see Chapter 20)
- ✔ Object styles (see Chapter 10)
- ✔ Sections and page numbers (see Chapter 4)
- ✔ Color definitions (see Chapter 7)
- ✔ Hyphenation and justification (see Chapter 15)

Styles and master pages are the two main global settings that you can expect to override locally throughout a document. You shouldn't be surprised to make such changes often because, although the layout and typographic functions that styles and master pages automate are the fundamental components of any document's look, they don't always work for all the specific content within a publication. (If they did, who'd need human designers?!)

Local tools include

- ✔ Frame tools (see Part III, as well as Chapter 17)
- ✔ Character and paragraph tools (see Chapters 15 and 16)
- ✔ Graphics tools (see Part V)

Keep your bearings straight

A powerful but confusing capability in InDesign is something called a control point. InDesign lets you work with objects from nine different reference points — any of the four corners, the middle of any of the four sides, or the center — such as when positioning the object precisely or rotating the object. You choose the active reference point, or *control point,* in the Control panel or Transform panel, using the grid of nine points arranged in a square.

By default, InDesign uses the central reference point as the control point, which is great for rotating an object, but can lead to confusion when you enter in the X and Y coordinates to place it precisely. That's because most people use the upper-left corner of an object when specifying its coordinates, not the center of the object. Be sure to change the control point to the upper-left reference point whenever entering X and Y coordinates in the Control or Transform panels.

How do you change the control point? That's easy: Just click the desired reference point in that preview grid. The control point will be black, whereas the other reference points will be white.

Choosing the right tools for the job

Depending on what you're trying to do with InDesign at any given moment, you may or may not immediately know which tool to use. If, for example, you maintain fairly precise layout standards throughout a document, using master pages is the way to keep your work in order. Using styles is the best solution if you want to apply standard character and paragraph formatting throughout a document. When you work with one-of-a-kind documents, on the other hand, it doesn't make much sense to spend time designing master pages and styles — it's easier just to format elements as you create them.

For example, you can create *drop caps* (large initial letters set into a paragraph of type, like the drop cap that starts each chapter in this book) as a character option in the Character panel, or you can create a *paragraph style* (formatting that you can apply to whole paragraphs, ensuring that the same formatting is applied each time) that contains the drop-cap settings, and then apply that style to the paragraph containing the drop cap. Which method you choose depends on the complexity of your document and how often you need to perform the action. The more often you find yourself taking a set of steps, the more often you should use a global tool (like character and paragraph styles) to accomplish the task.

Fortunately, you don't need to choose between global and local tools while you're in the middle of designing a document. You can always create styles from existing formatting later. You can also add elements to a master page if you start to notice that you need them to appear on every page.

What to do when you make a mistake

InDesign is a very forgiving program. If you make a mistake, change your mind, or work yourself into a complete mess, you don't have to remain in your predicament or save your work. InDesign offers several escape routes. You can

✔ **Undo your last action by choosing Edit➪Undo or pressing ⌘+Z or Ctrl+Z.** (Some actions, particularly actions such as scrolling that do not affect any items or the underlying document structure, cannot be undone.) You can undo multiple actions in the reverse order in which they were done

by repeatedly choosing Edit➪Undo or pressing ⌘+Z or Ctrl+Z; each time you undo, the previous action is undone.

✔ **Redo an action you've undone by choosing Edit➪Redo or pressing Shift+⌘+Z or Ctrl+Shift+Z.** Alternatively, choosing Undo and Redo is a handy way of seeing a before/after view of a particular change. As with undo, you can redo multiple undone actions in the reverse of the order in which they were undone.

Specifying measurement values

Another situation in which you can choose between local or global controls is specifying measurement values. Regardless of the *default measurement unit* you set (that is, the measurement unit that appears in all dialog boxes and panels), you can use any unit when entering measurements in an InDesign dialog box. For example, if the default measurement is picas, but you're new to publishing and are more comfortable with working in inches, go ahead and enter measurements in inches.

InDesign accepts any of the following codes for measurement units. Note that the *x* in the items listed below indicates where you specify the value, such as **2i** for 2 inches. It doesn't matter whether you put a space between the value and the code. Typing **2inch** and typing **2 inch** are the same as far as InDesign is concerned:

- ✔ *x*i or *x* inch or *x*" (for inches)
- ✔ *x*p (for picas)
- ✔ *x*pt or 0p*x* (for points)
- ✔ *x*c (for ciceros)
- ✔ *x*ag (for agates)
- ✔ *x*cm (for centimeters)
- ✔ *x*mm (for millimeters)

The ability to specify measurements in agates is new to InDesign CS3. Agates are typically used in newspaper publishing.

You can enter fractional picas in two ways: in decimal format (as in **8.5p**) and in picas and points (as in **8p6**). Either of these settings results in a measurement of 8½ picas (there are 12 points in a pica).

Basic InDesign Vocabulary

Not too long ago, only a few publishing professionals knew — or cared about — what the words *pica, kerning, crop,* and *color model* meant. Today, these words are becoming commonplace because almost everyone who wants to produce a nice-looking report, a simple newsletter, or a magazine encounters these terms in the menus and manuals of their layout programs. Occasionally, the terms are used incorrectly or are replaced with general terms to make nonprofessional users feel less threatened, but that substitution ends up confusing professional printers, people who work in service bureaus, and Internet service providers. Throughout this book, I define other publishing terms as they come up.

Altered keystrokes: Revised shortcuts

InDesign CS3 has changed a few shortcuts that users of previous versions of InDesign should know, so they can adapt accordingly:

- Type⇨Paragraph Styles: The new shortcut is ⌘+F11 on the Mac, but the old shortcut of F11 still works (though the Mac OS X's Exposé program also uses this shortcut and thus may appear instead). In Windows, the shortcut remains F11, but Ctrl+F11 also works.

- Type⇨Character Styles: The new shortcut is Shift+⌘+F11 on the Mac, but the old shortcut of Shift+F11 still works. In Windows, the shortcut remains Shift+F11, but Ctrl+Shift+F11 also works.

- Type⇨Paragraph: The new Windows shortcut is now Ctrl+Alt+T, no longer Ctrl+M, to match the Mac's Option+⌘+T. Adobe let Ctrl+Alt+T work as an alternative in InDesign CS2; now the menu has changed to make Ctrl+Alt+T the official shortcut. But the old Ctrl+M continues to work if you want to still use it.

- View⇨Show/Hide Frame Edges: The new shortcut for the Mac only is Control+⌘+H. The Windows shortcut remains Ctrl+H.

- View⇨Display Performance⇨Fast Display: The new shortcut is Option+Shift+⌘+Z or Ctrl+Alt+Z, replacing Shift+⌘+0 or Ctrl+Shift+0.

- View⇨Display Performance⇨High Quality Display: The new shortcut, for the Mac only, is Control+Option+⌘+H. The Windows shortcut remains Ctrl+Alt+H.

- Window⇨Effects: The new shortcut to the renamed Transparency panel is Shift+⌘+F10 on the Mac, but the old shortcut of Shift+F10 still works. In Windows, the shortcut remains Shift+F10, but Ctrl+Shift+F10 also works.

- Window⇨Pages: The new shortcut is ⌘+F12 on the Mac, but the old shortcut of F12 still works. In Windows, the shortcut remains F12, but Ctrl+F12 also works.

- Window⇨Stroke: The new shortcut is ⌘+F10 on the Mac, but the old shortcut of F10 still works. In Windows, the shortcut remains F10, but Ctrl+F10 also works.

For consistency, this book uses the new shortcut for both Mac and Windows for the new shortcuts involving the F10, F11, and F12 keys, such as ⌘+F10 and Ctrl+F10 for opening the Stroke panel. They changed to accommodate Mac OS X's Exposé program, which uses the F10, F11, and F12 keys in its shortcuts, causing it to launch when InDesign users entered shortcuts using them. The new InDesign shortcuts don't step on Exposé's toes.

New shortcuts include the following:

- Type⇨Glyphs: Option+Shift+F11 or Alt+Shift+F11.

- Type⇨Insert Special Character⇨Quotation Marks⇨Straight Double Quotation Marks: Command+Shift+' or Alt+Shift+'.

- Type⇨Insert Special Character⇨Quotation Marks⇨Straight Single Quotation Mark (Apostrophe): Command+' or Alt+'.

- Notes⇨Notes Mode: ⌘+F8 or Ctrl+F8.

- Window⇨Automation⇨Scripts: Option+⌘+F11 or Ctrl+Alt+F11.

Like all great human endeavors, InDesign comes with its own terminology, much of it adopted from other Adobe products. Some general terms to know include the following:

- ✔ **Frame:** The container for an object. A frame can hold text, a graphic, or a color fill.

- ✔ **Link:** The connection to a file that you import, or *place* (defined below), into an InDesign document. The link contains the file's location and its last modification date and time. A link can reference any graphics or text file that you have imported into a layout. InDesign can notify you when a source text or graphics file has changed so you can choose whether to update the version in your layout.

- ✔ **Package:** The collection of all files needed to deliver a layout for printing.

- ✔ **PDF:** The Adobe Portable Document Format, which has become the standard for sharing electronic documents. No matter what kind of computer it is viewed on (Windows, Macintosh, Palm, or Unix), a PDF document displays the original document's typography, graphics representation, and layout. With InDesign, you can place PDF files as if they were graphics, and you can also export its InDesign pages to PDF format.

- ✔ **Place:** To import a graphics or text file.

- ✔ **Plug-in:** A piece of software that loads into, and becomes part of, InDesign to add capabilities to the program.

- ✔ **Stroke:** The outline of an object (whether a graphic, line, or individual text characters) or frame.

- ✔ **Thread:** The connections between text frames that let a story flow from one frame to another.

Discovering the Document Window

In InDesign, you spend lots of time working in document windows — the "containers" for your documents. Each document, regardless of its size, is contained within its own document window.

The best way to get familiar with the InDesign document window is by opening a blank document. Simply choosing File⇨New⇨Document, or pressing ⌘+N or Ctrl+N, and clicking OK opens a new document window. Don't worry about the settings for now — just explore.

Figure 1-1 shows all the standard elements of a new document window. I won't bore you by covering interface elements that are standard to all programs. Instead, the rest of this section focuses on InDesign-specific elements.

Control panel

Tools dock

Tools panel

Reference points   Restore button   Panel flyout menu

Close button   Minimize button   Main dock

Zero point (ruler origin)   Title bar   Panel tab   Panel group

Rulers   Panel

Figure 1-1:
The document window is where you work on documents.

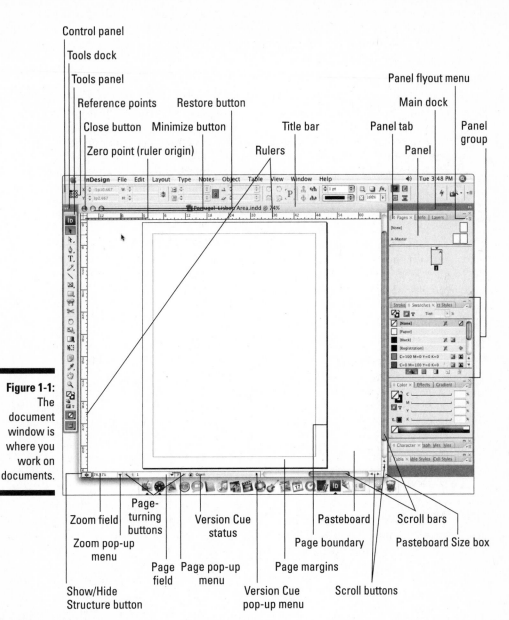

Zoom field   Page-turning buttons   Version Cue status   Pasteboard   Scroll bars

Zoom pop-up menu   Page boundary   Pasteboard Size box

Page field   Page pop-up menu   Page margins

Show/Hide Structure button   Version Cue pop-up menu   Scroll buttons

The Version Cue pop-up menu lets you see the current status of a document in a shared workgroup setup. This is an expert feature you can ignore.

Rulers

Document windows display a horizontal ruler across the top and a vertical ruler down the left side. As shown in Figure 1-1, the horizontal ruler measures from the top-left corner of the page across the entire spread, and the vertical ruler measures from the top to the bottom of the current page. These rulers are handy for judging the size and placement of objects on a page. Even experienced designers often use the rulers while they experiment with a design.

Both rulers display increments in picas unless you change the measurement system for each ruler in the Units & Increments pane of the Preferences dialog box. Choose InDesign⇨Preferences⇨Units & Increments or press ⌘+K on the Mac, or choose Edit⇨Preferences⇨Units & Increments or press Ctrl+K in Windows, to open the Preferences dialog box. Your choices include inches, picas, points, decimal inches, ciceros, agates, millimeters, and centimeters. If you change the ruler measurement system when no documents are open, the rulers in all new documents will use the measurement system you selected. If a document is open when you make the change, the rulers are changed only in that document.

You can also create your own measurement system by choosing Custom. Most people should ignore this option, but sometimes it can make sense, such as setting the ruler to match the line spacing, so you can measure number of lines in your ruler.

If your computer has a small monitor and the rulers start to get in your way, you can hide them by choosing View⇨Hide Rulers or by pressing ⌘+R or Ctrl+R.

Zero point

The point where the rulers intersect in the upper-left corner of the page is called the *zero point.* This is the starting place for all horizontal and vertical measurements. If you need to place items in relation to another spot on the page (for example, from the center of a spread rather than from the left-hand page), you can move the zero point by clicking and dragging it to a new location. Notice that the X: and Y: values in the Control panel update as you drag the zero point so you can place it precisely. If you change the zero point, it changes for all pages or spreads in the document. You can reset the zero point to the upper-left corner of the left-most page by double-clicking the intersection of the rulers in the upper-left corner.

If you move the zero point, all the objects on the page display new X: and Y: values even though they haven't actually moved. Objects above or to the left of the zero point will show negative X: and Y: values, and the X: and Y: values of other objects will not relate to their actual position on the page or spread.

You can lock the ruler origin (the zero point), making it more difficult to accidentally change it. Control+click or right-click the ruler origin and choose Lock Zero Point from the menu that appears. (The Unlock Zero Point command is right there as well, so you can just as easily unlock it.) Locking the zero point is a good idea because it will remind anyone working on your document that you prefer that they not fiddle with the zero point.

Pasteboard

The white area that surrounds the page is called the *pasteboard.* It is a workspace for temporarily storing objects. Above and below each page or spread is about an inch of pasteboard, and on the left and right a pasteboard space as wide as a page. For example, a spread of two 8-inch-wide pages will have 8 inches of pasteboard to the left and 8 inches of pasteboard to the right.

Pages and guides

Pages, which you can see onscreen surrounded by black outlines, reflect the page size you set up in the New Document dialog box (File⇨New⇨Document, or ⌘+N or Ctrl+N). If it looks like two or more pages are touching, you're looking at a *spread.*

InDesign uses nonprinting guides, lines that show you the position of margins and that help you position objects on the page. *Margins* are the spaces at the outside of the page, whereas *columns* are vertical spaces where text is supposed to go by default. Magenta lines across the top and bottom of each page show the document's top and bottom margins. Violet lines show left and right columns (for single-page documents) or inside and outside columns (for spreads).

You can change the location of margin and column guides by choosing Layout⇨Margins and Columns. You can create additional guides — such as to help you visually align objects — by holding down your mouse button on the horizontal or vertical ruler and then dragging a guide into the position you want.

Zoom field and pop-up menu

At the lower-left corner of the document window dwells the Zoom field, which shows the current zoom percentage. You can type in a new value any time. Immediately to its right is the Zoom pop-up menu, which also lets you change the document's view. The view can be between 5 percent and 4,000 percent in 0.01-percent increments.

To change the view without taking your hands off the keyboard, press Option+⌘+5 or Ctrl+Alt+5, enter a new zoom value, and press Return or Enter. Or press ⌘+= or Ctrl+= to zoom in, or ⌘+– or Ctrl+– to zoom out.

Page controls

If you feel like flipping through pages of the document you are creating, InDesign makes it easy with page-turning buttons and the Page field and pop-up menu. Controls for entering prefixes for the page numbers of sections, and for indicating absolute page numbers in a document that contains multiple sections, are also handy. (An absolute page number indicates a page's position in the document, such as +1 for the first page, +2 for the second page, and so on.)

Next to the Zoom pop-up menu is a combined page-number field and pop-up menu encased by two sets of arrows. These arrows are page-turning buttons that take you to, from left to right, the first page, the previous page, the next page, and the last page. Just click an arrow to get where you want to go.

You can also jump directly to a specific page or master page. To jump to a specific page, highlight the current number in the page number field (by selecting it with your cursor, or by pressing ⌘+J or Ctrl+J), enter a new page number, and press Return or Enter. (To jump to a master page, select the Page Number field and enter the first few characters of the master page's name.)

Opening Multiple Document Windows

If you like to work on more than one project at once, you've come to the right program. InDesign lets you open several documents at once. It also lets you open multiple windows simultaneously for individual documents. A large monitor (or having multiple monitors connected) makes this multi-window feature even more useful. By opening multiple windows, you can

✔ **Display two (or more) different pages or spreads at once.** You still have to work on the documents one at a time, but no navigation is required — you have only to click within the appropriate window.

✔ **Display multiple magnifications of the same page.** For example, you can work on a detail at high magnification in one window and display the entire page — and see the results of your detail work — at actual size in another window.

✔ **Display a master page in one window and a document page based on that master page in another window.** When you change the master page, the change is reflected in the window in which the associated document page is displayed.

To open a new window for the active document, choose Window⇨Arrange⇨ New Window. The new window is displayed in front of the original window. To show both windows at once, choose Window⇨Arrange⇨Tile. When you choose the Tile command, all open windows are resized and displayed side by side. (If you choose Window⇨Arrange⇨Cascade, all open windows are displayed stacked and staggered on top of each other. The front-most document window is visible; the title bars of the other windows are visible above the front-most document.)

When multiple windows are open, you activate a window by clicking on a window's title bar or anywhere within the window. Also, the names of all open documents are displayed at the bottom of the Window menu. Choosing a document name from the Window menu brings that document to the front. If multiple windows are open for a particular document, each window is displayed (they're displayed in the order in which you created them) in the Window menu.

To close all windows for the currently displayed document, press Shift+⌘+W or Ctrl+Shift+W. To close all windows for all open documents, press Option+Shift+⌘+W or Ctrl+Alt+Shift+W.

Tooling around the Tools Panel

You can move the InDesign Tools panel — the control center for 32 of InDesign's 33 tools, as well as for 13 additional functions — by clicking and dragging it into position. The Tools panel usually appears to the left of a document (see Figure 1-2).

The one tool not directly accessible from the Tools panel is the Marker tool. But you can switch to it from the Eyedropper tool by holding Option or Alt. (Chapter 7 explains its use.)

To discover each tool's "official" name, hover the mouse pointer over a tool for a few seconds, and a Tool Tip will appear, telling you the name of that tool. If the Tool Tips do not display, make sure that the Tool Tips pop-up menu is set to Normal or Fast in the Interface pane of the Preferences dialog box (choose InDesign⇨Preferences⇨Interface or press ⌘+K on the Mac, or choose Edit⇨Preferences⇨Interface or press Ctrl+K in Windows).

The Interface pane is new to InDesign CS3. In previous versions, the Tool Tips control was in the General pane of the Preferences dialog box.

InDesign gives you one — and only one — tool for each specific job. The Tools panel includes tools for creating and manipulating the objects that make up your designs. The tools in the Tools panel are similar to those in other Adobe products (such as Photoshop, Illustrator, and Dreamweaver). I cover what each tool does in the following sections.

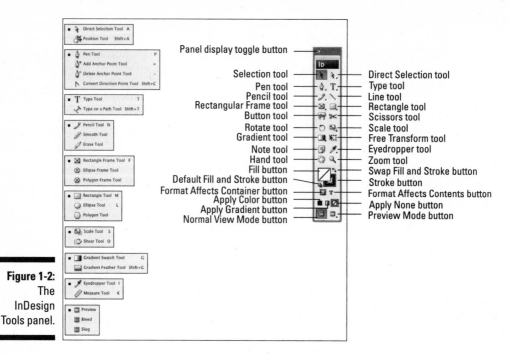

Direct Selection Tool A
Position Tool Shift+A

Pen Tool P
Add Anchor Point Tool =
Delete Anchor Point Tool -
Convert Direction Point Tool Shift+C

Type Tool T
Type on a Path Tool Shift+T

Pencil Tool N
Smooth Tool
Erase Tool

Rectangle Frame Tool F
Ellipse Frame Tool
Polygon Frame Tool

Rectangle Tool M
Ellipse Tool L
Polygon Tool

Scale Tool S
Shear Tool O

Gradient Swatch Tool G
Gradient Feather Tool Shift+G

Eyedropper Tool I
Measure Tool K

Preview
Bleed
Slug

Panel display toggle button

Selection tool — Direct Selection tool
Pen tool — Type tool
Pencil tool — Line tool
Rectangular Frame tool — Rectangle tool
Button tool — Scissors tool
Rotate tool — Scale tool
Gradient tool — Free Transform tool
Note tool — Eyedropper tool
Hand tool — Zoom tool
Fill button — Swap Fill and Stroke button
Default Fill and Stroke button — Stroke button
Format Affects Container button — Format Affects Contents button
Apply Color button — Apply None button
Apply Gradient button — Preview Mode button
Normal View Mode button

Figure 1-2:
The
InDesign
Tools panel.

The small arrow in its lower-right corner of some tools is a pop-out menu indicator. A tool that displays this arrow is hiding one or more similar tools. To access these "hidden" tools, click and hold a tool that has the pop-out menu indicator, as shown in Figure 1-3. When the pop-out displays, click one of the new tools. (Figure 1-2 shows all the pop-out tools.)

You don't need to worry about all the tools, so I highlight just those that you'll need to know to start using InDesign. You'll likely come across the others as you work on specific tasks, so I cover those in the chapters that introduce those functions.

Using the Selection tools

To work with objects, you have to select them. InDesign provides three tools to do that, letting you select different aspects of objects.

Selection tool

This is perhaps the most-used tool in InDesign. With the Selection tool, you can select objects on the page and move or resize them. You might want to think of this tool as the Mover tool because it's the only tool that lets you drag objects around on-screen.

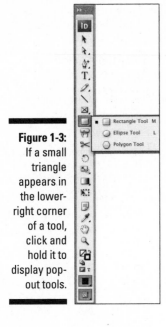

Figure 1-3:
If a small triangle appears in the lower-right corner of a tool, click and hold it to display pop-out tools.

After you've selected the Selection tool, here's how it works:

- ✔ **To select any object on a document page,** click it. If you can't seem to select it, the object might be placed by a master page (a preformatted page used to format pages automatically), or the object might be behind another object.

- ✔ **To select an object placed by a master page,** press Shift+⌘ or Ctrl+Shift while you click.

- ✔ **To select an object that is completely behind another object,** ⌘+click it or Ctrl+click it.

Direct Selection tool

The Direct Selection tool is what you use to work on the contents of a frame, not the frame itself. For example, you can use the Direct Selection tool to select individual handles on objects to reshape them, or to move graphics within their frames.

Here's how the Direct Selection tool works:

- ✔ **To select an object to reshape it,** click the object to display anchor points on the edges (the anchor points are hollow handles that you can select individually, as shown in Figure 1-4). You can drag the anchor points to reshape the object.

✔ **To select objects placed by a master page,** Shift+⌘+click or Ctrl+Shift+ click, as with the Selection tool. The Direct Selection tool lets you easily select objects behind other objects and select items within groups.

✔ **To move a graphic within its frame,** click inside the frame and drag the graphic.

✔ **To move a frame but leave the graphic in place,** click an edge of the frame and drag it.

Figure 1-4:
Reshape an item with the Direct Selection tool by clicking and dragging an anchor point.

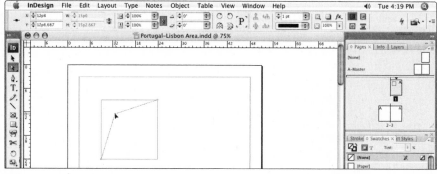

Position tool

Meant to mimic PageMaker's Crop tool to help former PageMaker users adjust to InDesign, the Position tool, which you access from the pop-out menu in the Direct Selection tool, combines some aspects of the Selection tool with some aspects of the Direct Selection tool:

✔ As with the Selection tool, you can resize an object's frame by dragging its handles.

✔ As with the Direct Selection tool, you can click a graphic and reposition it within the frame by dragging — and that has the effect of cropping the graphic.

Using the Type tool

A very frequently used tool, the Type tool lets you enter, edit, and format text. The Type tool also lets you create rectangular text frames.

Here's how the Type tool works:

✔ **To create a rectangular text frame,** click and drag; hold the Shift key to create a perfect square.

✔ **To begin typing or editing text,** click in a text frame or in any empty frame and type away.

I explain stories and threaded text frames in Chapter 12.

Using the object-creation tools

InDesign has a bunch of tools for creating shapes. Part V covers them in more depth, but you should know about a few of them now because they create objects that can contain either text or graphics. Plus, you can also use them to draw your own shapes that you then color or otherwise embellish in your layout.

Pen tool

With the Pen tool, you can create simple illustrations. You use the Pen tool, which is modeled after the pen tools in Illustrator and Photoshop, to create paths (both open, such as lines, and closed, such as shapes) consisting of straight and curved segments. Give it a try — it's fun!

Here's how the Pen tool works:

✔ **To create straight lines,** click to establish an anchor point, and then move the mouse to the next location, click again, and so on. To move an anchor point after clicking, press the spacebar and drag the anchor point.

✔ **To create curved lines,** click and drag, and then release the mouse button to end the segment.

✔ **To close a path and create a frame,** click the first anchor point created (the hollow one).

✔ **To leave a path open and create a line,** ⌘+click or Ctrl+click away from the path or select another tool.

Type tool

The Type tool lets you draw rectangular text frames, as well as type text inside them.

Line tool

The Line tool lets you draw freestanding lines (paths) on your page. After selecting this tool, simply click and drag the mouse to draw the line. Holding the Shift key while you click and drag constrains the line angle to 45-degree increments, which is useful for creating straight horizontal and vertical lines.

Frame and shape tools

InDesign has three frame tools — Rectangle Frame, Ellipse Frame, and Polygon Frame — and three shape tools — Rectangle, Ellipse, and Polygon. The frame and shape tools are redundant because both frames and shapes can hold text or graphics or be empty.

Because the frame and shape tools really do the same thing, you might use the frame tool when creating frames that will have their content added later. Why? Because they display with a big X through them, making them easier to spot when looking for frames to fill. The shape tools create frames without that X, so it's easier to overlook them.

To create a rectangle or ellipse, choose the appropriate tool, click somewhere in the document window, and drag the mouse to another location. The rectangle or ellipse fills the area. But creating a polygon works differently:

1. **Double-click the Polygon or Polygon Frame tool to display the Polygon Settings dialog box, shown in Figure 1-5.**

2. **Enter a value between 3 and 100 in the Number of Sides field to specify the number of sides on your polygon.**

3. **To create a star shape, use the Star Inset field to specify the size of the spikes.**

   The percent value specifies the distance between the polygon's bounding box and the insides of the spikes (for example, entering **50%** creates spikes that are halfway between the bounding box and the center of the polygon).

4. **Click OK to close the Polygon Settings dialog box.**

   The settings are saved with the active document for the next time you use the Polygon or Polygon Frame tool.

5. **Click and drag to create the polygon, using the rulers or the Transform panel or Control panel to judge the size and placement.**

   To create a symmetrical polygon in which all the sides are the same size, press the Shift key while you click and drag the Polygon or Polygon Frame tool.

Using the navigation tools

Several tools help you navigate your document, which means moving around your pages, moving your pages around the screen, and changing the degree of magnification to see just part of a page or to see several pages at once.

Figure 1-5:
Double-clicking the Polygon or Polygon Frame tool displays the Polygon Settings dialog box, which you can use to specify the number of sides on a polygon.

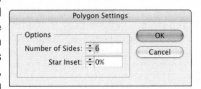

Hand tool

The Hand tool lets you move a page around to view different portions of it or another page entirely. After selecting the Hand tool, click and drag in any direction. You can access the Hand tool temporarily without actually switching tools by pressing Option+spacebar or Alt+Spacebar.

Zoom tool

With the Zoom tool, you increase and decrease the document view scale. You can highlight a specific area on a page to change its view or you can click on-screen to change the view scale within InDesign's preset increments, which is the same as pressing ⌘+= or Ctrl+= to zoom in.

View buttons

The very bottom of the Tools panel has two view buttons: Normal View Mode and Preview Mode. The first shows the document's pasteboard, margins, and guidelines; the second hides those so you can get a better idea of how the document will look when it's printed or saved as a PDF.

A pop-up menu in the Preview Mode button has two preview options: Bleed mode and Slug mode. Bleed mode shows any objects that bleed (extend) beyond the page boundaries, whereas Slug mode shows the space reserved for information such as crop marks and color separation names used in final output. You can read more about these in Chapter 3. You set these options when you create new documents or by choosing File➪Document Setup.

Using contextual menus

InDesign's contextual menu interface element is very useful. By Ctrl+clicking or right-clicking the document, an object, elements listed in a panel (such as a list of files or styles), the rulers, and so on, you can display a menu of options for modifying whatever it is you clicked. InDesign provides a lot of options this way, and it is often easier to use the contextual menus to access InDesign functions than to hunt through the many regular menu options and panels.

Working with Panels, Docks, and Workspaces

InDesign has so many controls and features that its designers have long ago stopped relying on menu commands to access them all. Instead, most of InDesign's features are presented as sort of miniature dialog boxes, called *panels*, that are "windows" of readily accessible options to consider when working in InDesign.

Working with panels

Panels provide an interactive method of working with features, one that lets you access the controls quickly. In many cases, panels offer the only method for performing many tasks. Figure 1-1 shows the panels that appear on-screen by default. Note that you can access all panels — except Quick Apply and Tabs — via the Window menu, whether or not the panel is displayed on-screen at the moment.

Panels typically have two — but sometimes three — controls:

✔ All panels but the Tools, Attributes, Script Label, and Command Bar panels have a flyout menu (formerly called the palette menu), which provides a pop-up menu of controls relevant to that panel. Figure 1-6 shows an example of a flyout menu.

✔ Any active panel — meaning it is displayed in front of any others in its panel group, so you can actually modify its settings — has a close control to remove the panel from the panel group. This is not a way to switch to another panel in that panel group — to do that, just click the tab of the panel you want to work with. (If you remove a panel by mistake, go to the Window menu to open it again.)

✔ *Some* panels have an expand/collapse control. Click the control to show more or fewer options (if all options are displayed, clicking the control will shorten the panel and hide some of the advanced options; if only the basic options are displayed, clicking the control lengthens the panel and show all the options.) Figure 1-7 shows examples of collapsed and expanded panels.

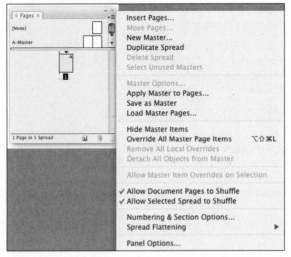

Figure 1-6:
An sample
flyout menu
(for the
Pages
panel).

Figure 1-7:
An example
of a panel
collapsed
(top) and
expanded
(bottom).

InDesign CS3 has seriously revamped the floating palettes that give you quick access to so many InDesign features. In previous versions of InDesign, these floating palettes contained one or more tabbed panes, and you could group and separate most of them as you preferred. What used to be called a pane is now called a *panel*. Panels now also have a consistent appearance: The tab is always on top, not either on the top or at left depending on whether it was free-floating or docked to the side of your monitor. Like the panes of yore, panels can be combined and separated into groups.

Adobe has also changed how panels are arranged on screen. By default, InDesign CS3 comes with two docks, one that holds only the Tools panel, and one that holds all the other panels, which I call the main dock. (Well, almost. The Control panel also displays separately, though it's not in a dock, just by itself at the top of the screen unless you move it.) Note that the main dock cannot be moved from the right side of the screen.

To better suit your working style, you can drag panels by their tabs to move them from one panel group to another, drag them out of a dock so they are free-floating, or drag them into a dock so they are no longer free-floating. The new dock feature lets you keep panel groups in one contained area, which helps keep the interface from getting too cluttered. But you're not forced to work this way: You can still drag panels outside the main dock so they are free-floating on screen.

Not all panels display in the main dock; less-used panels such as Data Merge will show up in a free-floating panel group when you open it via the Window menu. Of course, you can always add such panels to the main dock if you use them a lot.

All but four panels have a tab, which contains its name, to help you select the desired panel without having to go to the Window menu. To quickly select a panel, just click its tab. The four special panels (without tabs) are the Tools, Control, Command Toolbar, and Quick Apply panels. Unlike the rest of InDesign's panels, they can't be grouped with other panels, so there's no need for a tab to select them. (And for some reason, the Tools panel resides in a dock of its own, whereas the other three do not.)

When a panel is active, its controls have the following characteristics:

- ✔ **To display and select an option,** click a pop-up menu or an iconic button; the changes take effect immediately.

- ✔ **To place a new value in a field,** highlight the value that's already in the field and enter the new value. Note that fields accept values in all supported measurement systems, as described earlier in this chapter. To implement the new value, press Shift+Return or Shift+Enter. To get out of a field you've modified, leaving the object unchanged, press Esc.

- ✔ **To increase or decrease the value in the field,** use the clickable up and down arrows where available.

- ✔ **To use math to perform changes,** enter calculations in the field. You can add, subtract, multiply, and divide values in fields by using the following operators: +, –, * (multiply), and / (divide). For example, to reduce the width of a frame by half, type **/2** after the current value in the Width field. Or, to increase the length of a line by 6 points, you can type **+6** next to the current value in the Length field. You can also use percentages in fields, such 50%, which adjusts the current value by that percentage.

You can tell that the developers of InDesign have a passion for panels. Because there are so many of them, you might want to consider hooking up a second monitor for displaying them. As with the tools, if you make sure Tool Tips are enabled in the Interface panel of the Preferences dialog box (choose InDesign⇨Preferences⇨Interface or press ⌘+K on the Mac, or choose Edit⇨Preferences⇨Interface or Ctrl+K in Windows), you'll get some ideas as to what the panel iconic buttons and fields do.

InDesign CS3 adds the Assignments panel, which provides access to the optional InCopy CS3 program's features; these expert features are beyond the scope of this book. InDesign CS3 also adds the Cell Styles and Table Styles panels, which provide additional control over table formatting, as covered in Chapter 20. The new Notes panel lets you insert nonprinting reminders in your text, as explained in Chapter 13.

If panels are getting in your way, you can make them all disappear by pressing Tab — as long as the Type tool is not active and the text cursor is active within a text frame, of course. Press Tab to get your panels back.

Working with docks

Docks have controls to collapse and expand them — a new approach in InDesign CS3. Click the double-arrow iconic button at a dock's upper corner to collapse or expand the dock; you can also click the dark depression at the top of the main dock to collapse it. The main dock also can be resized by dragging the resize handle. Figure 1-8 shows the dock controls and what they look like when expanded and collapsed.

Working with workspaces

Although you can rearrange InDesign's panels to suit your needs, doing this again and again as you switch from one task to another can be a real chore. For example, you may open several of the table- and text-oriented panels when working on text, but then close them and open the graphics- and positioning-oriented panels when refining layout placement. That's why InDesign lets you create workspaces, which are essentially memorized panel collections. Display the panels you want, where you want them, and create a new workspace by choosing Window⇨Workspace⇨Save Workspace. Give the workspace a name that makes sense, such as Text Panels. That workspace is now available via Window⇨Workspace⇨*workspace name,* automatically displaying just those saved panels in their saved locations.

Dock resize handle

Collapse Dock buttons Panel group close button

Main dock Panel group minimize button

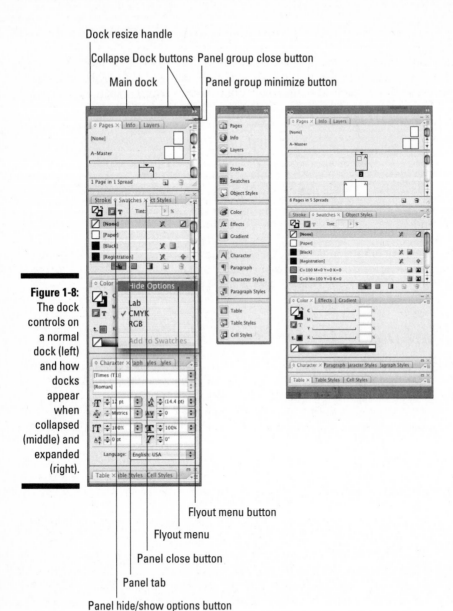

Figure 1-8:
The dock
controls on
a normal
dock (left)
and how
docks
appear
when
collapsed
(middle) and
expanded
(right).

Flyout menu button

Flyout menu

Panel close button

Panel tab

Panel hide/show options button

Surveying the Menus

Although InDesign relies heavily on its panels to present its rich capabilities, it also uses traditional menus. In some cases, you can use menus instead of panels; in others, you must use a menu command; in still others, you must use a panel (such as for the data merge and object alignment features).

There are 10 menus in InDesign for Windows and 11 in InDesign for Macintosh:

- **InDesign (Macintosh only):** This menu contains the Preferences menu, where you set much of InDesign's behavioral defaults. You can also configure plug-ins here. Other functions are standard for all Mac programs, including hiding and quitting the program. Note that none of these menu items' functions are available in panels.

- **File:** This menu is where you open, create, close, save, export, and set up documents and books; where you import text and graphics; where you print documents and prepare them for commercial printing; and where you set basic user information. Note that none of these menu items' functions are available in panels.

- **Edit:** This menu lets you cut, copy, and paste elements; edit, spell-check, and do search-and-replace operations across entire stories and set up story for the InCopy add-on program; adjust and manage color settings; set up and change keyboard shortcuts and menu preferences; apply various styles to selected objects and text; and undo and redo recent actions. In Windows, you also set preferences and quit the program from this menu. Note that these menu items' functions, except for Quick Apply, are not available in panels.

- **Layout:** With this menu, you add, delete, rearrange, and navigate pages; change margins and guides; automatically resize a page and its objects; set up page numbering and sections; and create and format tables of contents. Note that these menu options' functions — except for the Pages, page-navigation, and Numbering & Section Options menus — are not available in panels.

- **Type:** With this menu, you adjust typographic attributes such as size and font, insert special characters, work with footnotes, add placeholder text; and control the on-screen display of special characters such as spaces. Note that the Find Font, Change Case, Type on a Path, Document Footnote Options, Text Variables, Insert Character, Fill with Placeholder text, and Show Hidden Characters menu items' functions are not available though panels.

- **Notes:** This new menu lets you insert and manage notes in your layout that do not print. This feature used to be available only if you bought the InCopy add-on software.

- **Object:** You use this menu to change the shape, size, location, and other attributes of objects such as frames and lines; to apply special effects to objects; to insert multimedia effects such as buttons; and control display redraw speed. Note that the Text Frame Options, Anchored Object, Corner Options, Clipping Path, and Convert Shape menu items' functions are not available through panels.

- **Table:** Use this menu to create, change, and format tables and cells. Note that this menu's functions are available through panels.

✔ **View:** This menu lets you control the display of your document, from zoom level to whether guides, rulers, and frame edges appear. Note that none of these menu items' functions, except for Screen Mode and the zoom controls, are available in panels.

✔ **Window:** This menu is where you manage the display of document windows and panels, as well as where you set up and work with workspaces. The window display and workspace functions are not available via panels.

✔ **Help:** Use this menu to access InDesign's help system and manage product activation and registration. In Windows, this menu also lets you manage plug-ins. Note that none of these menu items' functions are available in panels.

Among the new menu options in InDesign are InCopy and Menus in the Edit menu; Text Variables and Bulleted & Numbered Lists in the Type menu; Show/Hide Assigned Frames and Show/Hide Notes in the View menu; and Assignment and Notes in the Window menu. Also, the Effects option replaces the Drop Shadow and Feather options in the InDesign CS2 Object menu, and the Compound Paths menu item in InDesign CS3's Object menu used to be submenu items in the InDesign CS2 Paths menu.

Chapter 2

Making It Work Your Way

*I*t's safe to say that the nice people who created InDesign did their best: They put their heads together and made educated guesses about how most people would like to work and, in doing so, established defaults for various settings in the program. When you're just starting out, it's not a bad idea to simply stick with the default settings and see how they work for you. But after you become more familiar with InDesign and start putting it through its paces, you can change default preferences, views, and measurements, making them better suited to your way of working.

Preferences are program settings that dictate how InDesign will act in certain instances. InDesign provides extensive preference settings for everything from how objects appear on-screen to how text is managed for spelling and hyphenation.

Setting InDesign to work your way is easy, and this chapter explains how. And I promise not to numb you by covering every single option. Instead, I focus on just those preferences you are likely to change. As for the rest, feel free to explore their effects once you've gotten more comfortable using InDesign. (And in other chapters, I sometimes recommend specific preferences changes for the specific actions explained there.)

InDesign stores some preferences in the documents that govern how the document works as you work on it, or as it is transferred to other users. Other preference settings reside on your computer. Knowing how InDesign manages preferences is important if you share preferences with others or want to make sure that all your documents are updated with a new preference setting.

Setting Document Preferences

Preferences are settings that affect an entire document — such as what measurement system you use on rulers, what color the guides are, and whether substituted fonts are highlighted. To access these settings, open the Preferences dialog box by choosing InDesign⇨Preferences⇨*desired pane name* or pressing ⌘+K on the Mac, or by choosing Edit⇨Preferences⇨*desired pane name* or pressing Ctrl+K in Windows.

When you open the Preferences dialog box using the keyboard shortcut (⌘+K or Ctrl+K), InDesign automatically opens the General pane, as shown in Figure 2-1. To access one of the other 16 preferences panes, just click its name from the list at the left of the dialog box.

The Interface pane is new, taking settings formerly found in the General pane as well as adding collapse options for docks (sometimes called *icon panels* in the InDesign documentation and user interface). Likewise, the Clipboard Handling pane is new, taking settings formerly in the File Handling and Type panes. The Notes pane is completely new, providing controls over the non-printing notes feature that used to be available only if you bought the InCopy add-on program.

InDesign has two methods for changing preferences: You can change preferences when no documents are open to create new settings for all future documents, or you can change preferences for the active document, which affects only that document. Either way, after you've changed the desired preferences settings, just click OK to save those settings.

You cannot reverse changes to preferences by using the Undo command (Edit⇨Undo or ⌘+Z or Ctrl+Z). If you change your mind about a preference setting, reopen the Preferences dialog box and change the setting again.

Type preferences

The Type pane of the Preferences dialog box, shown in Figure 2-2, includes settings that affect character formats, controls whether you use typographer's quotes, and manages how text appears on-screen. You're likely to adjust these settings, so here's a quick review of the main ones:

✔ If Use Typographer's Quotes is checked, InDesign inserts the correct typographer's quotes (often called *curly quotes*) for the current language in use whenever you use quotation marks. For example, for U.S. English, InDesign inserts typographic single quotes (') or double quotes (") rather than straight quotes. For French, Catalan, Polish, and other languages, InDesign inserts guillemets (« »).

✔ Check Triple Click to Select a Line if you want to be able to select an entire line of text by triple-clicking it.

✔ When the Apply Leading to Entire Paragraph box is checked, changes to leading (the space between lines) apply to the entire paragraph, as opposed to the current line. In most cases, you want the leading to be applied to all paragraphs, so it's a good idea to check this box.

✔ Adjust Spacing Automatically When Cutting and Pasting Words, which is checked by default, will add or delete spaces around words when you cut and paste.

✔ When Font Preview Size is checked, menus let you preview how your font choice looks before you actually select it. The pop-up menu at right of the check box lets you select the size of the preview.

✔ The options in the Drag and Drop Text Editing section of the Type pane control whether you can drag and drop text selections within a document. By default, Enable in Story Editor is checked and Enable in Layout View is unchecked, which means that you can drag and drop text in the Story Editor but not when working on a layout. You'll probably want to check them both.

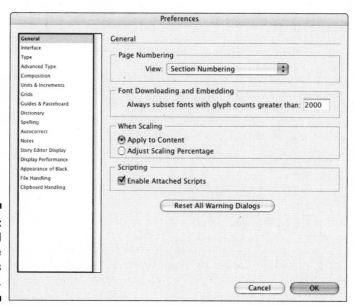

Figure 2-1:
The General pane of the Preferences dialog box.

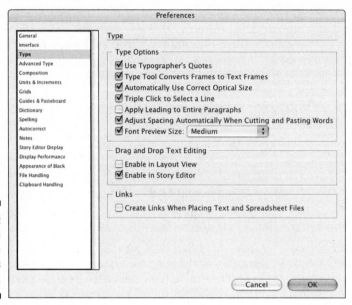

Figure 2-2:
The Type
pane of the
Preferences
dialog box.

The Advanced Type pane includes additional typographic settings, as
Figure 2-3 shows.

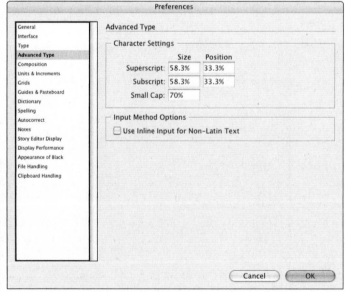

Figure 2-3:
The
Advanced
Type pane
of the
Preferences
dialog box.

In the Character Settings section of the Advanced Type pane, you control precisely how superscript, subscript, and small-caps characters are placed and sized:

- The Size fields let you specify the percentages to which superscript and subscript characters are reduced (or even enlarged). The default is 58.3 percent, but you can enter a value between 1 and 200 percent. I prefer 60 or 65 percent, depending on the type size and font.

- The Position fields let you specify how much to shift superscript characters up and subscript characters down. The default is 33.3 percent, but you can enter a value between –500 and 500 percent. I prefer 30 percent for subscripts and 35 percent for superscripts. Note that negative values move text in the opposite directions: down for superscripts and up for subscripts. The percentage is relative to the top of a lowercase letter (the *x height*) for superscripts and to the baseline for subscripts.

- The Small Cap field lets you specify the scale of Small Caps characters in relation to the actual capital letters in the font. The default is 70 percent, but you can enter a value between 1 and 200 percent.

The Clipboard Preferences pane includes one text-oriented preference that used to be in the Type pane: Use the When Pasting Text and Tables from Other Applications setting to choose how formatting is handled when you paste textual objects from other applications. The default is Text Only, which means that you want copied text to assume the formatting of the destination location's text in InDesign. The All Information option retains the original formatting when you copy the text into InDesign.

Typographic terminology 101

Publishing tools like InDesign use specialized terms, some of which appear in the Preferences dialog box:

- **Baseline:** This term refers to the invisible line that text sits on in each line. Except for a few characters like *g* and *p* that poke below it, all characters rest on this baseline.

- **Kerning:** This refers to an adjustment of the space between two letters. You kern letters to accommodate their specific shapes. For example, you probably would use tighter kerning in the letter pair *to* than in *oo* because *to* looks better if the *o* fits partly under the cross of the *t*.

- **Leading:** This term, also called line spacing, refers to the space from one baseline to another.

- **Tracking:** Tracking determines the overall space between letters within a word.

Composition preferences

Preferences in the Composition pane, shown in Figure 2-4, do two things: highlight potential problems on-screen while you're working, and establish the behavior of text wrap in certain situations.

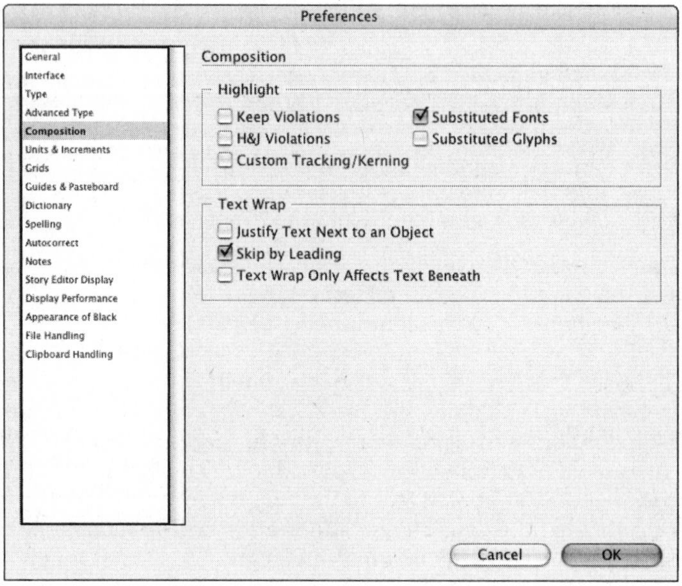

Figure 2-4:
The Composition pane of the Preferences dialog box.

Highlighting potential problems

The Highlight check boxes control whether InDesign calls attention to possible typesetting problems by drawing a highlighter pen effect behind the text. All are unchecked by default unless indicated otherwise below:

- ✔ Keep Violations highlights the last line in a text frame when it cannot follow the rules specified in the Keep Options dialog box in the Paragraph panel's flyout menu (Type⇨Paragraph, or Option+⌘+T or Ctrl+Alt+T), as explained in Chapter 15. For example, if the Keep Options settings require at least three lines of text in the text frame, but only two lines fit and thus bump all the text in a frame to the next text frame in the chain, the Keep Options rules are violated, and the last line of text is highlighted.

- ✔ When H&J Violations is checked, InDesign uses three shades of yellow (the darker the shade, the worse the problem) to mark lines that might be too loose or too tight due to the combination of spacing and hyphenation settings. (H&J refers to hyphenation and justification.) Chapter 15 covers this, too.

✔ Custom Tracking/Kerning, if checked, highlights custom tracking and kerning (essentially, anywhere you overrode the defaults) in a bluish green. Chapter 16 covers kerning and tracking in more detail.

✔ Substituted Fonts, which is checked by default, uses pink highlights to indicate characters in fonts that are not available and thus for which InDesign has substituted a different font. For output purposes, it's important that you have the correct fonts, so you typically want to leave this checked.

✔ Substituted Glyphs highlights, in pink, any glyphs (special characters) that were substituted. This usually occurs when you have multiple versions of the same font, with different special characters in each version. For example, a file that uses the euro (€) currency symbol might have been created in the newest version of a font, but a copy editor working on the same file may have an older version of the font that is missing the euro symbol.

Setting text-wrap rules

The three options in the Text Wrap area affect how text flows (wraps) around images and other frames:

✔ Selecting the Justify Text Next to an Object check box overrides any local justification settings to make text wrapping around an object justified. That means the text will smoothly follow the object's shape, rather than keep any ragged margins that can make the wrap look strange. This option comes into play when you wrap ragged (left-aligned or right-aligned) text around objects.

✔ Skip by Leading, if checked, uses the text's leading to determine how much space follows an object around which text wraps. This effect is used only if you choose the Jump Object text-wrap option in the Text Wrap panel (Window➪Text Wrap, or Option+⌘+W or Ctrl+Alt+W).

✔ Text Wrap Only Affects Text Beneath, if checked, causes only text below (behind) an object to wrap around that object.

Chapter 17 covers text wrap in detail.

Measurement preferences

The Units & Increments pane, shown in Figure 2-5, is where you choose the measurement systems for positioning items.

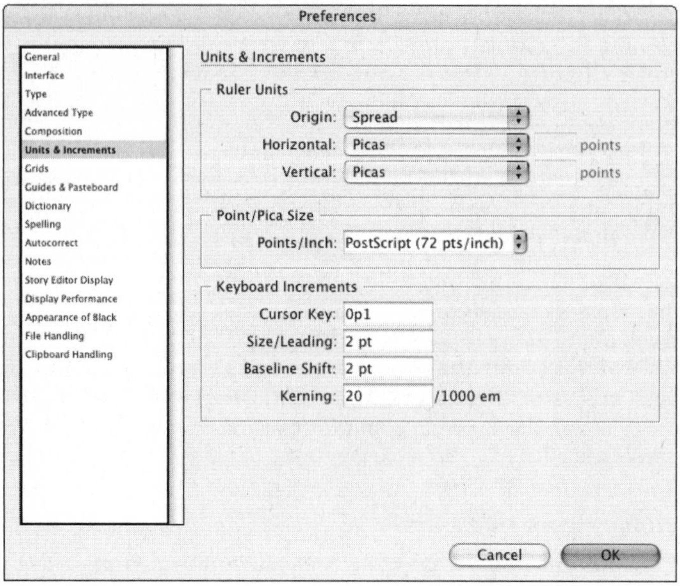

Figure 2-5:
The Units &
Increments
pane of the
Preferences
dialog box.

Ruler Units area

The Ruler Units area affects three things: the origin point (by page, by spread, or by the spine), the measurement system displayed on the horizontal and vertical rulers in the document window, and the default values in fields used for positioning objects.

The Origin pop-up menu determines the zero point (typically, the upper-left corner of the page) for object positions. If you choose Page, the positions of objects are relative to each page's upper-left corner. If you choose Spread, the positions of objects are relative to the current spread's upper-left corner. If you choose Spine, objects' positions are relative to the binding spine of each spread — the very top and center of where the two pages meet.

With the Vertical and Horizontal pop-up menus, you specify one measurement system for the horizontal ruler and measurements, and the same or different measurement system for the vertical ruler and measurements. For example, you might use points for horizontal measurements and inches for vertical measurements.

To specify the measurement systems you want to use, choose an option from the Horizontal pop-up menu and from the Vertical pop-up menu. You have the following options:

✔ **Points:** A typesetting measurement equal to ¹⁄₇₂ of an inch (or ¹⁄₁₂ of a pica). To enter values in points, type a **p** before the value or **pt** after the value (for example, **p6** or **6 pt**).

✔ **Picas:** A typesetting measurement equal to ⅙ of an inch. To enter values in picas, type a **p** after the value (for example, **6p**).

You can combine measurements using both picas and points. Keeping in mind that 1 pica is equal to 12 points, you can enter 1½ picas as either **1.5p** or **1p6**.

✔ **Inches:** An English measurement system that is divided into 16ths. To enter values in inches, type **i**, **in**, **inch**, or **"** after the value. For example, **3i**, **3in**, **3 inch**, and **3"** are all read by InDesign as "3 inches."

✔ **Inches decimal:** Inches divided into 10ths on the ruler rather than 16ths. To enter values in inches decimal, include a decimal point as appropriate and type **i**, **in**, **inch**, or **"** after the value.

✔ **Agates:** Typically used in newspapers, an agate is ¼₄ of an inch, usually the depth of a line in the small type of classified ads, stock tables, and sports statistics boxes. To enter values in agates, type **ag** after the value. For example, **10ag**.

✔ **Millimeters:** A metric measurement that is ¹⁄₁₀ of a centimeter. To enter values in millimeters, type **mm** after the value. For example, **14mm**.

✔ **Centimeters:** A metric measurement that is about ⅓ of an inch. To enter values in centimeters, type **cm** after the value. For example, **2.3cm**.

✔ **Ciceros:** A European typesetting measurement that is slightly larger than a pica. To enter values in ciceros, type **c** after the value. For example, **2c**.

✔ **Custom:** This option lets you set a customer number of points as your measurement unit, placing a labeled tick mark at every point increment you specify. You get to customize the number of tick marks between the labeled marks by entering a value in the Points field. For example, if you enter **12** in the field, you get a tick mark at each pica because there are **12** points in a pica. A good way to use this is if you need to have the rulers show tick marks at whole-line increments; in that case, if your leading is 8 points, you'd set the Custom field to **8**.

Keyboard Increments area

This area lets you customize the way the keyboard arrow keys work. You can use the arrow keys to move selected objects right, left, up, or down. You can also use the arrow keys and other keyboard shortcuts to change some text formatting. The options are

✔ **Cursor Key field:** When you select an object with the Selection tool or the Direct Selection tool, you can move it up, down, left, or right by using the arrow keys on the keyboard. By default, the item moves 1 point with each key press. You can change the increment to a value between 0.001 and 8p4 (1.3888 inches). If you use a document grid, you might change the increment to match the grid lines.

- **Size/Leading field:** The value in this field specifies by how many points the leading or font size is increased or decreased when done with keyboard commands. You can enter a value between 0.001 and 100 (the default is 2).

- **Baseline Shift field:** To shift the baseline of highlighted text up or down, you can click in the Baseline Shift field on the Character panel, and then click the up or down arrow on the keyboard. The default for the Baseline Shift increment value is 2 points, which you can change to any value between 0.001 and 100.

- **Kerning field:** To kern text with keyboard commands, you position the cursor between two letters and then Option+press or Alt+press the right arrow button to increase kerning or the left arrow to decrease kerning. By default, each click changes kerning by ⅟₅₀ of an em — shown on screen as 20/1000 em. You can change this value to anything between 1 and 100, in increments of ⅟₁₀₀₀ of an em. (An em is a space the width of a capital *M*, a commonly used space in professional typography.)

Document defaults

InDesign also lets you change the default page size, margins, and columns in new documents; the default attributes of guides; and the way layouts are adjusted. You don't modify these settings in the Preferences dialog box; instead, to modify document defaults, first make sure that no documents are open and then choose the following:

- **File⇨Document Setup (Option+⌘+P or Ctrl+Alt+P).** The Document Setup dialog box lets you change the default settings in the New Document dialog box for the Number of Pages, Page Size, Facing Pages, and Master Text Frame, as well as for bleeds and slugs if you click the More Options button.

- **Layout⇨Margins and Columns.** The Margins and Columns dialog box lets you change the default settings in the New Document dialog box for the Margins and Columns areas.

- **Layout⇨Ruler Guides.** This opens the Ruler Guides dialog box where you adjust the View Threshold and Color for all new guides.

- **Layout⇨Layout Adjustment.** The Layout Adjustment dialog box lets you resize entire layouts and modify how they are resized.

If you are unhappy with the preferences and defaults you have established, you can revert InDesign to all its default settings. To revert all preferences and defaults, press Control+Option+Shift+⌘ or Ctrl+Alt+Shift when launching InDesign.

Working with stored preferences

Some preferences in InDesign are stored in files that you can share with other users, so the preferences can be consistently used in a workgroup. These include keyboard shortcut sets, color swatch libraries, document setups, workspaces, and scripts.

Some of these stored preferences — such as document setups and printing setups — are called *presets,* and the files that store them reside in the Presets folder within the InDesign application folder. When you save a preset, InDesign automatically updates the presets file. You can then copy that preset file to another user's Presets folder.

To create presets, look for menu items with the word *preset* in them — examples are Adobe PDF Presets, Document Presets, and Print Presets in the File menu; and Transparency Flattener Presets in the Edit menu. Also look for the Save Preset option in some dialog boxes. To use a preset, look for a pop-up menu with the word *preset* in them in dialog boxes; for example, you would use the Document Preset pop-up menu in the New Document dialog box to create a new document using a specific preset's settings.

InDesign has other types of stored preferences whose settings are also stored in separate files, also stored in the Presets folder. But you won't see options labeled *Presets* in the InDesign user interface to work with them. These stored preferences include Keyboard Shortcuts, Menus, and Color Profiles options in the Edit menu and the Workspace option in the Window menu. You can share these settings by copying them to other users' Presets folders.

Another kind of preference is typically stored as part of a document: master pages, text variable, color swatches, and the various types of text, stroke, and object styles available through a series of panels. These preferences can be imported from other documents using the Load command in the various panels' flyout menus and in some dialog boxes. Most presets — such as document presets, print presets, trap presets, and Adobe PDF presets — can also be loaded and saved this same way. In addition, color swatches can be saved to files to be shared with other Adobe applications using a Save Swatches command in the Swatches panel's flyout menu.

Modifying Defaults for Text and Objects

When you create a new document, start typing, or create a new object, your work conforms to default settings. You can change these settings. For example, by default, a new document is always letter-sized, but if you design only posters, you can change the default.

You may need to work with InDesign for a while to figure out which settings you prefer. When you identify a problem — for example, you realize that you always end up changing the inset for text frames — jot down a note about it or close all documents right then. When no documents are open, change the setting for all future documents.

Text defaults

When you start typing in a new text frame, the text is formatted with default formats and attributes. You can also choose to show invisible characters such as spaces and tabs by default; otherwise, you need to manually activate character visibility in each text-heavy document. To modify text defaults:

- **Choose default options for character formats** such as Font Family, Font Size, and Leading from the Character panel. Choose Type➪Character (⌘+T or Ctrl+T).

- **Choose defaults for paragraph formats,** such as alignment, indents, spacing, and so on, from the Paragraph panel. Choose Type➪Paragraph (Option+⌘+T or Ctrl+Alt+T).

- **Choose defaults for the [Basic Paragraph] style,** which is what all unstyled imported text, as well as text entered in a new text frame in InDesign, will use. Choose Type➪Paragraph Styles (⌘+F11 or Ctrl+F11).

- **Activate Optical Margin Alignment.** Choose Type➪Story. This adjusts the left position of characters along the left margin to make the left edges look more pleasing, by letting the top of a *T*, for example, hang slightly to the left of the margin, even if that means the characters aren't strictly aligned. (Because Optical Margin Alignment works best for display type rather than body type, it's unlikely that you'll activate optical margin alignment as your default setting.)

- **Show Hidden Characters** is a good thing to activate if you always end up turning on Show Hidden Characters when you are editing a document. Choose Type➪Show Hidden Characters (⌘+Option+I or Ctrl+Alt+I). Hidden characters are spaces, tabs, and so forth that print "blank" but that you may want to see on-screen to make sure you have the right character in use. InDesign has a unique on-screen symbol for every kind of space, tab, indent-to-here, and other such "blank" characters.

Object defaults

When you create new objects, they're based on default settings. For example, you can specify how text wraps around objects. To modify object defaults, use the following commands:

- **Specify the default Columns, Inset Spacing, First Baseline, and Ignore Text Wrap settings** for new text frames using the Text Frame Options dialog box. Choose Object➪Text Frame Options (⌘+B or Ctrl+B).

- **Choose defaults for the [Normal Graphics Frame] and [Normal Text Frame] styles,** which are what all new frames created in InDesign will use. Choose Window➪Object Styles (⌘+F7 or Ctrl+F7).

- **Specify how text will wrap around all new objects.** Choose Window⇨ Text Wrap (⌘+Option+W or Ctrl+Alt+W).

- **Choose a style for the corners of all new frames except those created with the Type tool.** Choose Object⇨Corner Options (⌘+Option+R or Ctrl+Alt+R).

- **Specify the default attributes of clipping paths imported into graphics frames.** Choose Object⇨Clipping Path.

- **Specify other default properties of objects.** For example, if all objects you create are stroked (framed), specify a weight in the Stroke panel. Choose Window⇨Stroke (⌘+F10 or Ctrl+F10), Window⇨Swatches (F5), Window⇨Gradient (F6), or Window⇨Attributes.

- **Specify the default number of sides and the inset for the first new polygon in a new document.** Double-click the Polygon or Polygon Frame tool to open the Polygon Settings dialog box (there is no menu command or keyboard shortcut).

Modifying Defaults for Views

You can also control which layout tools display by default. Selections in the View menu let you do this. If you prefer not to view the edges of frames, you can hide them by default. Or if you always want to start with a document-wide grid (see Chapter 11), you can show that by default. Other defaults you can modify in the View menu include

- **Show the links between text frames.** Choose View⇨Show Text Threads (Option+⌘+Y or Ctrl+Alt+Y).

- **Hide the edges of frames.** Choose View⇨Hide Frame Edges (Control+⌘+H or Ctrl+H).

  The Mac shortcut for showing and hiding text frames has changed to Control+⌘+H in InDesign CS3, from just ⌘+H in previous versions. The Windows shortcut (Ctrl+H) is unchanged.

- **Hide the horizontal and vertical ruler.** Choose View⇨Hide Rulers (⌘+R or Ctrl+R).

- **Hide margin, column, and layout guides.** View⇨Grids & Guides⇨Hide Guides (⌘+; [semicolon] or Ctrl+; [semicolon]).

- **Show the baseline grid established in the Grids pane of the Preferences dialog box.** Choose View⇨Grids & Guides⇨Show Baseline Grid (Option+ ⌘+' [apostrophe] or Ctrl+Alt+' [apostrophe]).

- **Show the document-wide grid established in the Grids pane of the Preferences dialog box.** Choose View⇨Grids & Guides⇨Show Document Grid (⌘+' [apostrophe] or Ctrl+' [apostrophe]).

InDesign has another place to set view settings: in the Pages panel's flyout menu, choose View⇨Show/Hide Master Items. When you choose Show Master Items, any objects on the currently displayed document page's master page are displayed. When you choose Hide Master Items, master objects on the currently displayed page are hidden. This command is page-specific, so you can show or hide master objects on a page-by-page basis.

Adding Default Colors and Styles

If you are a creature of habit, you may find yourself creating the same colors, paragraph styles, character styles, and object styles over and over again. Save yourself some steps by creating these features when no documents are open; when you do so, the features will be available to all future documents.

To set up these often-used items, use the New command in the flyout menus for the following panels: Swatches (F5), Character Styles (Shift+⌘+F11 or Ctrl+Shift+F11), Paragraph Styles (⌘+F11 or Ctrl+F11), and Object Styles (⌘+F7 or Ctrl+F7). You can also use the flyout menus' Load commands to import colors and styles from existing documents instead of creating them from scratch.

Chapter 7 covers color swatches, Chapter 10 covers object styles, and Chapter 14 covers character and paragraph styles in more detail.

Part II

Document Essentials

The 5th Wave   By Rich Tennant

"Remember, your Elvis should appear bald and slightly hunched. Nice Big Foot, Brad. Keep your two-headed animals in the shadows and your alien spacecrafts crisp and defined."

In this part . . .

The reader sees your text and images, but as a layout artist, you know there's a lot more going on behind the scenes. Your documents contain all sorts of elements — the publishing equivalent of the girders and beams and so forth of a building — that are essential to delivering the final text and graphics. This part covers those document essentials, showing you how to work with the document files, pages, layers, templates, libraries, and sections — the basic organizing elements and containers. You'll also discover how to create colors that you can use over and over again.

Chapter 3

Opening and Saving Your Work

In This Chapter

▶ Creating a new document

▶ Opening documents

▶ Saving and exporting documents

▶ Exporting document content

▶ Recovering information after a crash

*Y*ou're eager to create a new document and get started with InDesign. So you launch InDesign, create or open a new document, and begin working. Right? Wrong, sort of. You can just plunge in, but you're best served if you have an idea before you start of what you want to accomplish. That way, you won't be staring at a blank screen with no brilliant ideas in mind.

After you have an idea of what you want to do, you need to create the document that will hold those brilliant ideas. InDesign lets you apply those ideas from the very start of creating the document, and also lets you make changes later on, as you refine your ideas.

This chapter shows you the basics of working with document files, from creating and opening them to saving them.

Setting Up a New Publication

After you launch InDesign, you have two options: You can choose File⇨Open (or press ⌘+O or Ctrl+O) to open a previously created document or template, or you can choose File⇨New⇨Document (or press ⌘+N or Ctrl+N) to create a new document.

Creating a new document is where all the fun is because you get to create something yourself, from scratch. Here's how to create a new document:

1. **Choose File⇨New⇨Document or press ⌘+N or Ctrl+N.**

   The New Document dialog box appears, as shown in Figure 3-1. It is here that you will have to make many up-front decisions about how you want your new document set up — including page size, number of pages, number of columns, and margin width. Although you're free to change your mind later, you'll save yourself time and potential headaches by sticking with the basic page parameters you establish in the New Document dialog box.

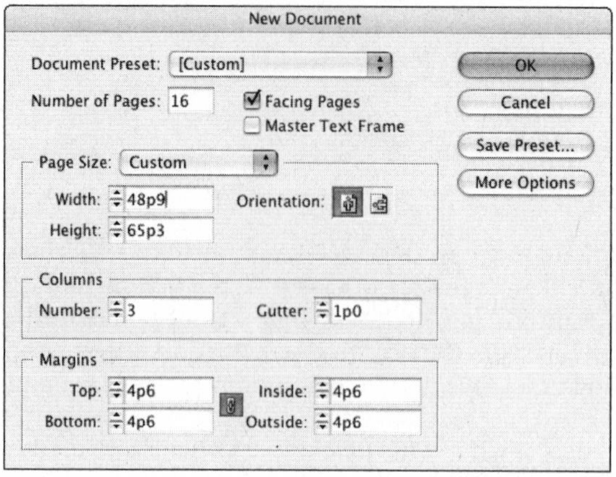

Figure 3-1:
The New Document dialog box establishes the basic framework for your pages.

2. **If you know exactly how many pages your publication will have, enter the number in the Number of Pages field.**

   If you don't know for sure, you can always add or delete pages later. Just guesstimate: It's easy to add or delete pages later.

3. **Decide whether to lay out your documents in a spread or as separate pages.**

   - If you're creating a multi-page publication that will have a spine, such as a book, catalog, or magazine, select Facing Pages.

   - If you're creating a one-page document, such as a business card, an ad, or a poster, don't select Facing Pages.

   - Some publications, such as flip charts, presentations, and three-ring bound documents, have multiple pages but use only one side of the page. For such documents, don't check Facing Pages, either.

4. **If you want to flow text from page to page in a multi-page document, such as a book or a catalog, check Master Text Frame.**

    If you check this box, InDesign automatically adds a text frame to the document's master page and to all document pages based on this master page. Doing this saves you the work of creating a text frame on each page and manually threading text through each frame. (See Chapter 6 for more information about using master text frames.)

5. **In the Page Size area, you can choose one of the predefined sizes from the pop-up menu.**

6. **Specify margin values in the Margins area.**

    If Facing Pages is checked, Inside and Outside fields are available in the Margins area. Designers often specify larger inside margins for multi-page publications to accommodate the fold at the spine. If Facing Pages is not checked, Left and Right fields replace the Inside and Outside fields. You can also specify margin values by clicking the up/down arrows associated with the fields.

7. **To specify how many columns your pages have, enter a value in the Columns field.**

    You can also specify the number of columns by clicking the up/down arrows associated with the Column field.

8. **Specify a gutter distance (the gutter is the space between columns) in the Gutter field.**

    You can also specify a gutter width value by clicking the up/down arrows associated with the Gutter field.

9. **Click the More Options button to access the Bleed and Slug area of the New Document dialog box (refer to Figure 3-1 to see the Bleed and Slug area).**

    Clicking the More Options button provides options to set bleed and slug areas. (Note that the button then changes to Fewer Options.) A *bleed area* is a margin on the outside of the page for objects you want to extend past the edge of the page — you want them to extend at least ⅛ inch so if there is any shifting of the paper during printing, there's no white space where the image should be (touching the edge of the page). The slug area is an area reserved for printing crop marks, color plate names, and other such printing information — some output devices will cut these off during printing unless a slug area is defined. For both bleed and slug areas, you can set the top, bottom, left, and right margins independently.

10. **Click OK to close the New Document dialog box.**

    Your new, blank document appears in a new document window. Figure 3-2 shows the window of a newly created document that uses the settings shown in Figure 3-1.

You can bypass the New Document dialog box by pressing Shift+⌘+N or Ctrl+Shift+N. When you use this method, the most recent settings in the New Document dialog box are used for the new document.

Opening documents

Opening documents with InDesign is pretty much the same as opening documents with any program. Simply choose File⇨Open (or press ⌘+O or Ctrl+O), select the document you want to work on, and then click the Open button. But InDesign offers a few options for opening documents that you don't find in every program. For example, you can

✔ **Open more than one document at a time.**

✔ **Open a copy of a document instead of the original.** This keeps the original file from being overwritten accidentally — very helpful if you're making several variations of one document.

✔ **Open a template under its own name.** This makes editing templates easier than it is with other programs, specifically QuarkXPress.

✔ **Open documents created with Versions 6.0, 6.5, and 7.0 of PageMaker and Versions 3.3, 4.0, and 4.1 of both QuarkXPress and QuarkXPress Passport.**

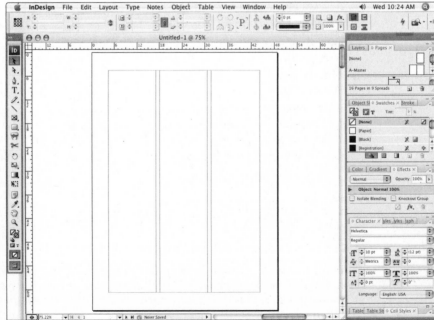

Figure 3-2:
The results of the settings in the New Document dialog box shown in Figure 3-1.

Banishing Version Cue

Adobe's Version Cue feature is meant to help people collaborate in a workgroup, so you can share a master file with multiple people, each working on it in turn. Version Cue even lets you save different versions of a file, so you can experiment and then decide which one to keep. But Version Cue is complicated and difficult to use for beginners. If you find it unwieldy, you can accomplish its basic functions simply by saving common files to a network server and saving new versions with slightly different names, so you can later choose the version you want.

InDesign turns Version Cue on for you automatically within InDesign. But that won't really affect you unless Version Cue is also turned on for your computer — when it's turned on in both places, you'll see Version Cue options in your Open a File, Export, and Save dialog boxes; you'll also see the Check In menu option become available in the File menu. To get rid of Version Cue, just choose InDesign⇨Preferences⇨File Handling or press ⌘+K on the Mac, or choose Edit⇨Preferences⇨File Handling or press Ctrl+K in Windows, and then uncheck the Enable Version Cue option. Click OK. Voilà! Version Cue is disabled within all your Adobe Creative Suite 3 software.

If other people in your workgroup are using Version Cue, you might also go to the Macintosh System Preferences dialog box (⌘⇨System Preferences) or the Windows Control Panel (Start⇨Control Panel⇨Classic View in the

Windows XP and Windows Vista interface, or Start⇨Settings⇨Control Panels in the Classic Start menu interface) and double-click the Adobe Version Cue CS3 iconic button. Clicking that button opens a pane that has an option to turn off the Version Cue server. (Click Stop to disable the server immediately, and uncheck the Turn On Server When the Computer Starts option to keep it off when you next start up your computer.) This prevents your computer from being a server to other Version Cue users on the network, so they cannot work on your files.

In some cases, you might want to leave Version Cue on (maybe because you use it occasionally in a workgroup setting) but not use its unique dialog boxes for opening, saving, exporting, and importing until you're ready to use the Version Cue tools. That's also easy: First, make sure Version Cue is turned on within InDesign and for your computer. Then click the Use OS Dialog button in the Open a File, Save As, Export As, Load, and other dialog boxes that work with filenames. Clicking OS Dialog brings you to the standard Mac or Windows dialog boxes, which will continue to display until you later click Use Adobe Dialog button in any of those dialog boxes. Clicking the Use Adobe Dialog button in any of those dialog boxes brings back the Version Cue interface for all of those dialog boxes. Note that these dialog box changes affect only InDesign CS3, not your other Adobe software.

Opening InDesign files

To open an InDesign file (any version from 1.0 to CS3), follow these steps:

1. **Choose File⇨Open, or press ⌘+O or Ctrl+O.**

   The Open a File dialog box, shown in Figures 3-3 and 3-4, appears. The Open a File dialog box will differ based on whether you are using Adobe's Version Cue file-management system or the standard Mac or Windows interface. The sidebar "Banishing Version Cue" later in this chapter explains how to turn Version Cue off.

This book's screen shots assume that you are not using Version Cue, so this is the only time I'll show you the Version Cue interface.

When I do show Windows screens, I'll show them in Windows XP only, unless the Windows Vista screen is radically different. In practically every case, though, InDesign in Windows Vista looks just like it does in Windows XP, except for colors and slight adjustments where elements are placed in some dialog boxes such as Open a File and Save.

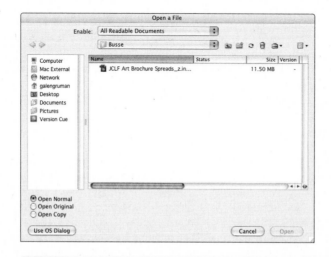

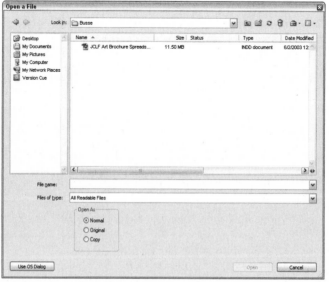

Figure 3-3: The Open a File dialog box with Version Cue enabled (Mac at top, Windows XP at bottom).

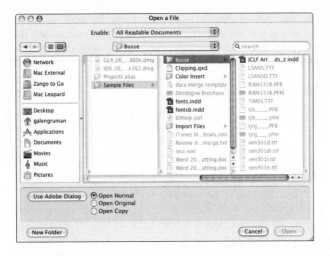

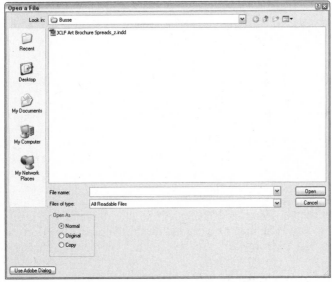

Figure 3-4:
The Open a
File dialog
box with
Version Cue
disabled
(Mac top,
Windows
XP at
bottom).

2. Locate and open the folder that contains the document(s) you want to open.

Select a single filename or hold down the ⌘ or Ctrl key and select multiple filenames.

In Windows, the Files of Type pop-up menu offers several options: PageMaker 6.0–7.0 files, QuarkXPress 3.3–4.1 files, InDesign files, InDesign Interchange, Adobe PDF Creation Settings Files, and All Formats. Choose any of these options to display a specific file format in the file list. (The Adobe PDF Creation Settings Files option is for experts, so don't worry about it for now.)

On a Mac, the Open a File dialog box will display any supported file formats that have a filename extension, and the dialog box includes a Preview pane that displays a thumbnail version of the selected file or, more commonly, its icon. Use All Documents in the Enable pop-up menu to display files without the expected filename extensions (typically, those transferred or copied from a computer running Mac OS 9).

In Windows, the Open a File dialog box will display any supported file formats that have a supported filename extension. Use All Files in the Files of Type pop-up menu to display files with no filename extensions (typically, these are files created on an older version of the Mac OS).

3. **Select Open Normal at the bottom of the dialog box to open the original version of the document or a copy of a template; click Open Original to open the original version of the document or of a template; click Open Copy if you just want to open a copy of it.** (Chapter 6 covers templates.)

In Windows, the options are labeled simply Normal, Original, and Copy, and appear under the Open As label.

When you open a copy of a document, it's assigned a default name (Untitled-1, Untitled-2, and so on).

4. **Click OK to close the dialog box.**

Each document you opened is displayed in a separate document window. The page and view magnification used when the document was last saved is also used when you open the document. (Chapter 1 covers document views.)

An alternative approach is to choose File⇨Browse to open the Adobe Bridge program, which provides an alternative way to find files on your computer. Bridge is an expert feature that most InDesign users — even advanced ones — never use. Its biggest attraction is that it lets you see previews of almost all files you'd be working with in your layouts. But if you're a Photoshop user, you may be a big fan and therefore be comfortable using it for InDesign files as well.

Opening foreign formats

One of InDesign's hallmarks is its ability to open documents from other programs and convert them into InDesign documents. You can open documents created in PageMaker 6.0, 6.5, and 7.0 as well as QuarkXPress and QuarkXPress Passport 3.3, 4.0, and 4.1. (Chapters 28 and 29 cover conversion issues in greater detail.)

But beware: InDesign's ability to open a foreign-format file doesn't mean you get a perfect translation. The other programs' formats and capabilities are so different from InDesign's that you should expect to spend time cleaning up the converted files by hand. In some cases, you might find that the amount of cleanup work is greater than if you simply re-create the document from scratch in InDesign — don't panic when this is the case. And be happy when your documents convert effortlessly. The good news is that InDesign will alert you to any import issues of PageMaker and QuarkXPress files with a dialog box that appears after the import is complete, as Figure 3-5 shows.

Figure 3-5:
InDesign shows a Warnings dialog box if there are any issues in importing foreign file formats.

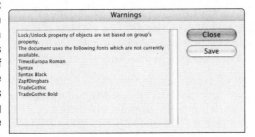

Saving documents

When you open a new document, it's assigned a default name — Untitled-1, Untitled-2, and so on — and the first page is displayed in the document window. At this point, you're like a painter in front of a blank canvas. You can work on your layout without giving it a name, but it's best to give it a name by saving it as soon as possible so you don't lose any changes to a power outage or other system problem.

The second group of commands in InDesign's File menu — Close, Save, Save As, Save a Copy, Check In, and Revert — provide options for saving the active (frontmost) document. Here's a rundown of what each command does:

✔ **Close** (⌘+W, or Ctrl+W or Ctrl+F4) closes the active document. If the document has never been saved or if it has been changed since it was last saved, a dialog box lets you save, close without saving, or cancel and return to the document.

To close multiple windows at once, use the shortcuts Option+Shift+⌘+F4 or Ctrl+Alt+Shift+W.

✔ **Save** (⌘+S or Ctrl+S) saves changes you've made to the active document since you last saved. (If you choose Save for a document that hasn't yet been saved, the Save As dialog box is displayed.)

✔ **Save As** (Option+⌘+S or Ctrl+Alt+S) lets you save a copy of the active document using a different name (or with the same name in a different folder). When you choose Save As — and when you choose Save for an unsaved document — the Save As dialog box, shown in Figure 3-6, appears. This dialog box lets you create or choose a folder for the document, as well as name the document.

✔ **Check In** saves the current document as a version within a Version Cue project. This latest save will be considered a version of the previously saved file. (This expert option is available only if Version Cue is enabled. It had been called Save a Version in previous versions of InDesign.)

✔ **Save a Copy** lets you create a copy of the active document in a different (or in the same) folder using a different (or the same) name. When you use the Save a Copy command, the original document remains open and retains its original name. It differs from Save As only in that it keeps the original document open.

✔ **Revert** undoes all changes you've made to a document since you last saved it.

Exporting document content

InDesign's Save commands (Save, Save As, and Save a Copy) let you save documents and templates in InDesign's native file format. But the Export command (File⇨Export) lets you save the stories — and in some cases stories and whole layouts — from InDesign documents in several formats: InDesign Interchange, Rich Text Format (RTF), Text Only, InDesign Tagged Text, Encapsulated PostScript (EPS), Portable Document Format (PDF), JPEG, and Scalable Vector Graphics (SVG).

Note that when exporting a file, you need to choose a format from the Format menu (Mac) or Save as Type menu (Windows).

Figure 3-6: The Mac version of the Save As dialog box (top) and the Windows version (bottom) are slightly different.

Here are your format options in more detail:

- ✔ **InDesign Interchange format:** You can make your InDesign CS3 files readable by InDesign CS2 users by saving your files in the InDesign Interchange format. (Only InDesign CS2 and CS3 can open InDesign CS3's Interchange files. Similarly, InDesign CS3 can open only InDesign CS2 Interchange and CS3 Interchange files, as well as any version of regular InDesign document files.)

- ✔ **Word-processing formats:** If you place the text cursor into a story, you can export its text (select a range of text if you want to export only that selection) into one of two formats: RTF, for import into word processors with only basic formatting retained; and Text Only, for import into word processors that don't support RTF (with Text Only, note that no formatting is retained).

You can save only one text file at a time. If you need to export several stories from the same document, you must do so one at a time.

- ✔ **InDesign workflow formats:** If text is selected via the Type tool, you can save the story in the InDesign Tagged Text format (for editing in a word processor and later reimporting into InDesign CS3 with all InDesign formatting retained) or in the InDesign CS Interchange format (for import into InDesign CS2).

- ✔ **Production formats:** If text or a frame is selected via the Type tool or the Direct Selection tool, you can save the document — not just the story — in EPS or PDF formats for use by prepress tools and service bureaus or for import into other applications as pictures.

- ✔ **Online formats:** If text or a frame is selected via the Type tool or the Direct Selection tool, you can save the document — not just the story — in XML format for use in online database-oriented content-management systems, as well as a specific page, spread, or text selection into JPEG or SVG formats for use as online graphics.

Two separate options are available for the entire document (no matter what tool is active) or for whatever objects are selected. One is File➪Cross-Media Export➪XHTML/Dreamweaver, which lets you export InDesign layouts to the structured HTML format for use in Web creation programs such as (but not limited to) Adobe Dreamweaver. The other is File➪Cross-Media-Export➪XHTML/Digital Editions, which lets you create a new type of online multimedia document, called an e-book. You can also export XML files by choosing File➪Cross-Media-Export➪XML, as well as by using the regular Export dialog box (File-.Export). All three are expert features that are beyond the scope of this book.

Recovering from Disaster

Make sure that when you work on InDesign documents, you follow the first rule of safe computing: Save early and often.

InDesign includes an automatic-recovery feature that protects your documents in the event of a power failure or a system crash. As you work on a document, any changes you make after saving it are stored in a separate, temporary file. Under normal circumstances, each time you choose Save, the information in the temporary file is saved to the document file. The data in the temporary file is important only if you aren't able to save a document before a crash. (A word of warning: Although InDesign's automatic recovery feature is a nice safety net, you should still be careful to save your work often.) If you suffer a system crash, follows these steps to recover your most recent changes:

1. **Relaunch InDesign or, if necessary, restart your computer and then launch InDesign.**

2. **If automatic-recovery data is available, InDesign automatically opens the recovered document and displays the word "Recovered" in the document's title bar.**

   This lets you know that the document contains changes that were not included in the last saved version.

3. **If you want to save the recovered data, choose File⇨Save; "Recovered" is removed as part of the filename, and InDesign asks if you want to overwrite the old file.**

   Overwriting the old file is easier than using File⇨Save As and entering a name — unless you do want to save a copy of the file in case you want to go back to the old version later. If you want to use the last saved version of the document (and disregard the recovered data), close the file (File⇨Close, or ⌘+W or Ctrl+W) without saving, and then open the file (File⇨Open, or ⌘+O or Ctrl+O).

Sometimes, InDesign can't automatically recover the documents for you. Instead, it gives you the choice of recovering any files open during a crash or power outage, saving the recovery data for later, or deleting the recovery data. You typically want to recover the files immediately.

For more information about using the Pages panel to work on master pages, see Chapter 6.

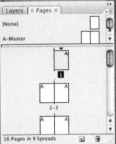

Figure 4-1:
The Pages
panel and
its flyout
menu
showing a
facing-
pages
document.

Keep in mind that the overwhelming majority of multi-page documents are facing-pages publications such as books, catalogs, and magazines. Some exceptions are flip charts and three-hole-punched publications printed on only one side. In this chapter, the figures show examples of a facing-pages document. If you create a single-sided multi-page document, the techniques are the same as for facing-pages documents, but the icons in the Pages panel show only single-sided page icons (the icons aren't dog-eared).

Adding pages

A document can contain as many as 9,999 pages — more than anyone would ever want to have in one file. In general, try to break up long publications into logical pieces. For example, if you're creating a book, it's a good idea to create separate documents for the front matter, each chapter, the index, and any other parts (appendixes and so on). Also, if you're producing a long document, you want to take advantage of master pages (covered in Chapter 6), which save you the work of building each page from scratch.

When you create a multi-page document, you're free to add however many pages you want. But be careful: Even though InDesign will let you create a seven-page newsletter, in real life, facing-page publications always have an even number of pages — usually a multiple of 4 and often a multiple of 16 — because of the way printers arrange multiple pages on a single sheet of paper before folding and cutting them into the final document.

Chapter 4

Discovering How Pages Wo

In This Chapter

▶ Adding and removing document pages

▶ Adjusting page numbers and creating sections

▶ Navigating through a document

▶ Adjusting page layouts and objects

*I*t's a rare InDesign user who creates only one-page documents
spend your time working on business cards, ads, and posters.
bly produce at least a few multi-page documents. And if you crea
ters, newspapers, books, catalogs, or any other such multi-page
you must know how to add pages to your document, move page:
you change your mind, and delete pages if necessary. InDesign a
divide multi-page documents into independently numbered sect

As documents grow in size, getting around can be a real drag —
that is. The longer you spend getting to the page you want, the l
have to work on it. Fortunately, InDesign provides several naviga
that make it easy to move around on a page or in a document.

Understanding the Pages Panel

The Pages panel is where you do most of your page actions, so y
know it better as you use InDesign more.

If you intend to create a multi-page document, you want to displ
panel (Window⇨Pages, or ⌘+F12 or Ctrl+F12), shown in Figure 4
provides the controls that let you add pages (both document an
delete and move pages, apply master pages to document pages,
through a document.

The shortcut for accessing the Pages panel has changed to ⌘+F
in InDesign CS3 from just F12 in previous versions. But you can :
F12, though that might conflict with Apple's Exposé software on

Here's how to add pages to a document:

1. **If it's not displayed, open the Pages panel by choosing Window⇨Pages or pressing ⌘+F12 or Ctrl+F12.**

2. **From the Pages panel's flyout menu, choose Insert Pages.**

   The Insert Pages dialog box, shown in Figure 4-2, appears.

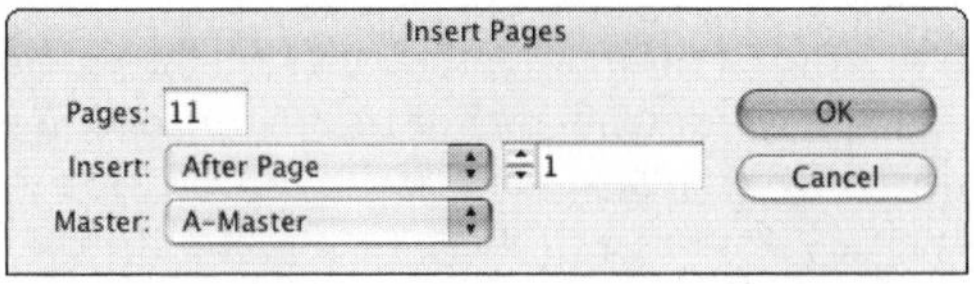

Figure 4-2:
The Insert
Pages
dialog box.

Insert Pages	
Pages: 11	OK
Insert: After Page ⇕ ⇕ 1	Cancel
Master: A–Master ⇕	

3. **In the Pages field, type the number of pages you want to add.**

4. **Select an option from the Insert pop-up menu: After Page, Before Page, At Start of Document, or At End of Document.**

   Be careful: If you've already started working on page 1, for example, make sure you add new pages *after* page 1. Otherwise, it won't be page 1 anymore, and you'll have to move the objects you already created.

5. **Type a page number in the field next to Insert or use the arrows to increase or decrease the value in one-page increments.**

6. **From the Master pop-up menu, select the master page you want to apply to the new pages.**

7. **When you're finished, click OK to close the dialog box.**

InDesign offers a faster way to add and manipulate pages if you don't happen to have the Pages panel already open: Choose Layout⇨Pages, and then select the appropriate option, such as Add Pages, from the submenu. The resulting dialog boxes match those accessed from the Pages panel.

If you want to quickly add just one page after the current page, click Layout⇨ Pages⇨Add Page or just press Shift+⌘+P or Ctrl+Shift+P.

You can also add new pages or spreads one at a time at the end of a document by clicking the Create New Page iconic button at the bottom of the Pages panel. (Spreads are added if a spread is selected in the Pages panel.) When you use this method, the master page applied to the last document page is applied to each new page. Pages are added after the currently selected page in the panel.

You can also click and drag a master page icon (or both pages in a facing-pages spread to add a spread) from the top of the Pages panel to add a page using a master page's settings (use the [None] page for a plain page) between any pair of document page spreads or to the right of the last document spread. If a vertical bar appears when you release the mouse button, the spread is placed between the spreads on either side of the bar. If a vertical bar does not appear between document page spreads when you release the mouse button, the new spread is placed at the end of the document.

When you insert an uneven number of new pages into a facing-pages document, existing pages are automatically changed from left-hand pages to right-hand pages, and vice versa. You can prevent this for selected spreads by first selecting them in the Pages panel and then clicking Keep Spread Together in the flyout menu. You might do this for a spread, such as a two-page table, that you don't want to have broken apart when other pages are added or deleted. Of course, for proper printing, you might need to move that spread when you're done adding or deleting pages so that it follows a complete spread.

Selecting pages

InDesign offers several choices for selecting pages from a document, so you can move, delete, copy, or otherwise manipulate them:

- ✔ Click a page's icon in the Pages panel to select it.
- ✔ To select both pages in a spread, the easiest way is to click a spread's page numbers to select both pages.
- ✔ To select a range of pages, you can click a page icon or spread number beneath it and then Shift+click another page icon or spread number.
- ✔ To select multiple, noncontiguous pages, hold down the ⌘ or Ctrl key and click page icons or spread numbers.

InDesign CS3 now shows a preview image of your pages in the Pages panel. You can control the display by choosing Panel Options from the panel's flyout menu. In the Panel Options dialog box, select the desired icon size and make sure Show Thumbnails is checked. You can also set separate view settings for master pages.

Copying pages

You can copy pages from one document to another by clicking and dragging the page icon(s) from the source document's Pages panel to the target document's Pages panel. Any master page(s) associated with the copied document pages(s) are copied as well.

You can also duplicate the current spread within the current document by clicking Duplicate Spread from the Pages panel's flyout menu or by choosing Layout⇨Pages⇨Duplicate Spread.

Deleting pages

The fastest way to delete selected pages is either click and drag them to the pane's Delete Selected Pages button (the trashcan icon) or simply click the Delete Selected Pages button.

Moving pages within documents

To move a page within a document, drag its icon between two spreads or between the pages of a spread inside the Pages panel. A vertical bar indicates where the selected page will be placed. Release the mouse button when the vertical bar is where you want to move the page. To move a spread, drag the page numbers beneath the icons (rather than the page icons themselves).

InDesign now automatically scrolls the Pages panel's pages as you move pages up or down. Before, you had to enlarge the panel so the location you wanted to drag the pages to was visible. That was a real pain that thankfully has gone away.

Alternatively, you can select the pages you want to move in the Pages panel and then choose Move Pages from the Pages panel's flyout menu. (If you don't want to work through the Pages panel, you can also choose Layout⇨Pages⇨Move Pages.) In that dialog box, you can specify where to move the pages: after a specific page, before a specific page, at the beginning of the document, or at the end of the document.

Although you can move pages around in a document, do so only with great care — if at all. Generally, if you want to move the objects on one page to another page, it's safer to cut (Edit⇨Cut or ⌘+X or Ctrl+X) or copy (Edit⇨Copy, or ⌘+C or Ctrl+C) the objects than to move the page, which might cause subsequent pages to shuffle.

What's the big deal about shuffling? Shuffling will move pages around to make space for the moved page, and that can move what had been left-hand pages to the right-hand side of the spread and vice versa. If you have different alignments on left and right pages — such as having page numbers on the outside of pages — this shuffling can wreak havoc with that alignment.

If you absolutely must move a single page, it's safer to move its spread. (Of course, if you're working on a single-sided facing-page document, shuffling is not an issue.)

Moving pages among documents

You can also copy or move pages to other documents. Select the page in the Pages panel, and then drag its icon to the document you want to copy or move it to.

New to InDesign CS3 is the Insert Pages dialog box that appears, giving you a choice of where to insert the page in the new document as well as whether to copy or move the page into the new document. (In previous versions, InDesign just copied the page in front of the current one.) To move a page rather than copy it, be sure to check the Delete Pages After Inserting option.

Alternatively you can copy or move pages among documents by choosing Layout⇨Pages⇨Move Pages, or by choosing Move Pages from Pages panel's flyout menu, either of which opens the Move Pages dialog box. Here, you also can select the destination (at which page number to insert the new pages) and — new in InDesign CS3 — which document you want to move the page into via the Move to pop-up menu. (The document must be open to display in that pop-up menu.) To move a page rather than copy it, be sure to check the Delete Pages After Moving option.

Figure 4-3 shows both the Insert Pages and Move Pages dialog boxes.

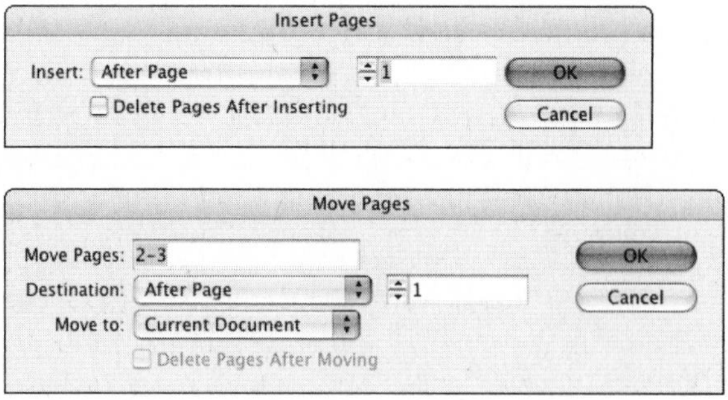

Figure 4-3:
The Insert Pages dialog box (top) displays when you drag pages between documents, while the Move Pages dialog box (bottom) displays through a menu option.

Insert Pages		
Insert: After Page	1	OK
☐ Delete Pages After Inserting		Cancel

Move Pages		
Move Pages: 2–3		OK
Destination: After Page	1	Cancel
Move to: Current Document		
☐ Delete Pages After Moving		

Starting documents on a left page

By default, InDesign starts all documents on the right page, which makes sense because the first sheet in a document is always a right-hand page. But sometimes you want documents to start on a left-hand page, particularly if they are a chapter or section in a larger document. For example, magazine articles often start on a left page, giving the introduction a full spread. To start a document on a left page:

1. **Select the first page in the Pages panel and then choose Numbering & Section Options from the panel's flyout menu or choose Layout⇨Numbering & Section Options.**

2. **Select the Start Section option.**

3. **Select the Start Page Numbering At option and enter an even number in the field.**

4. **Click OK.**

    The Pages panel will update, showing the start page on the left of the spine.

    You may not want to assign a starting page number (for example, if the starting page number is unknown because the number of pages that precede this document is unknown and you let the book feature determine the page numbers later). In this case, repeat Step 1, but deselect Start Section. Doing so leaves the page as a left-hand page but let the book feature figure out the page number.

See Chapter 23 for more information on the book feature and long-document creation. Sections are covered later in this chapter.

Working with Page Numbers

By default, pages are numbered automatically starting at 1, but you can change the page numbering from Arabic numerals to Roman numerals or letters, as well as change the start page to something other than 1. To do so, select the first page in the document in the Pages panel and choose Layout⇨Numbering & Sections or choose Numbering & Section Options from the Pages panel's flyout menu. You get the dialog box shown in Figure 4-4. (If the current page is not the first page in the document and if a section had not been applied to this page previously, the dialog box is called New Section. Its options are identical.)

To change the initial page number, select the Start Page Numbering At option and type a new starting page number in its field. To change the page numbering style from the default of Arabic numerals (1, 2, 3, 4 . . .), use the Style pop-up menu and choose from I, II, III, IV . . . ; i, ii, iii, iv . . . ; A, B, C, D . . . ; and a, b, c, d . . . .

To have a facing-pages document start on a left-hand page, the starting page number must be even.

Figure 4-4:
The
Numbering
& Section
Options
dialog box
lets you
change the
starting
page
number and
the types of
numerals
used.

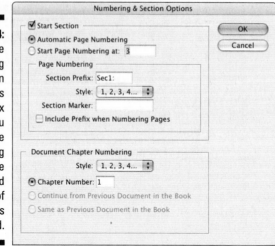

Numbering & Section Options

☑ Start Section

⦿ Automatic Page Numbering

◯ Start Page Numbering at: 3

Page Numbering

Section Prefix: Sec1:

Style: 1, 2, 3, 4...

Section Marker:

☐ Include Prefix when Numbering Pages

OK

Cancel

Document Chapter Numbering

Style: 1, 2, 3, 4...

⦿ Chapter Number: 1

◯ Continue from Previous Document in the Book

◯ Same as Previous Document in the Book

Dividing a document into sections

Some long documents are divided into parts that are numbered separately. For example, the page numbers of book introductions often use Roman numerals, while standard Arabic numerals are used for the body of the book. If the book has appendixes, a separate numbering scheme could be applied to these pages. In InDesign, such independently numbered parts are referred to as *sections*.

A multi-page document can contain as many sections as you want (a section has to contain at least one page). If each section of a document uses a different page layout, you probably want to create a different master page for each section. Here's how to create a section:

1. **If it's not displayed, open the Pages panel by choosing Window⇨ Pages or pressing ⌘+F12 or Ctrl+F12.**

2. **Click the icon of the page where you want to start a section.**

3. **Choose Numbering & Section Options from the panel's flyout menu.**

   If you've selected the document's first page, the Numbering & Section Options dialog box appears (refer to Figure 4-4). Otherwise, the identical New Section dialog box appears. By default, the Start Section option is selected. Leave it selected.

   You can also create a section starting at the current page in your document by choosing Layout⇨Numbering & Section Options.

4. **In the Section Prefix field, type up to eight characters that identify the section in the page-number box at the lower-left corner of the document window.**

   For example, if you type **Sec2**, the first page of the section will be displayed as Sec2:1 in the page-number box. This prefix won't appear as part of the actual page numbers when you print — it's really just a way for you to keep track of sections while you work.

5. **From the Style menu, choose the Roman numeral, Arabic numeral, or alphabetic style you want to use for page numbers.**

6. **For Page Numbering, select the Automatic Page Numbering option if you want the first page of the section to be one number higher than the last page of the previous section.**

   The new section will use the specified style; the previous section may use this style or another style.

7. **Select the Start Page Numbering At option and type a number in the accompanying field to specify a different starting number for the section.**

   For example, if a book begins with a section of front matter, you could begin the body section of a book on page 1 by choosing Start At and typing **1** in the field. If you select Continue from Previous Section, the first page of the body section begins one number higher than the numeral on the last page of the front matter.

8. **In the Section Marker field, type a text string that you can later automatically apply to pages in the section.**

   You might want to enter something straightforward like **Section 2** or, if the section is a chapter, the name of the chapter.

   You can insert the section marker name so it prints in folios, chapter headings, and story text by choosing Type⇨Insert Special Character⇨Markers⇨Section Marker. This is a great way to get a chapter name (if you use it as the section marker) in your folio or to have cross-references in text to a section whose name might later change. (A *folio* is the collection of a page number, magazine or chapter name, section name, or issue date, and so forth that usually appears at the top or bottom of pages.)

9. **Click OK to close the dialog box.**

When you create a section, it's indicated in the Pages panel by a small, black triangle over the icon of the first page in the section, as shown in Figure 4-5. (If you move the mouse pointer over the black triangle, the name of the section appears.) The page-numbering scheme you specify is reflected in the page numbers below the page icons. When you begin a section, it continues until the end of the document or until you begin a new section.

TIP

By default, the Pages panel displays section numbers beneath the icons of document pages. If you want to display absolute page numbers — the first page is page 1 and all other pages are numbered sequentially — you can do so by choosing InDesign➪Preferences➪General or pressing ⌘+K on the Mac, or by choosing Edit➪Preferences➪General or press Ctrl+K in Windows. Then choose Absolute Numbering from the General pane's View pop-up menu.

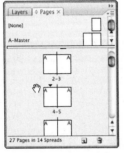

Figure 4-5:
The small triangle above a page icon represents a section start.

Removing a section start

If you decide that you want to remove a section start, navigate to the page that begins the section, choose Numbering & Section Options from the Pages panel's flyout menu, or choose Layout➪Numbering & Section Options, and deselect the Section Start option. That's it! The pages in the former section remain, but their numbering now picks up from the previous pages.

Navigating Documents and Pages

Moving from page to page in a long document and scrolling around a large or magnified page are among the most common tasks you perform in InDesign. The more time you spend navigating to the page or page area you want to work on, the less time you have to do the work you need to do. Like most trips, the less time you spend between destinations, the better.

For navigating through the pages of a document, the Pages panel (Window➪Pages, or ⌘+F12 or Ctrl+F12) offers the fastest ride. For navigating within a page, you may want to switch to the Navigator panel (Window➪Object & Layout➪Navigator).

Navigating with the Pages panel

When the Pages panel appears, you can use it to quickly move from page to page in a multi-page document and to switch between displaying master pages and document pages. To display a particular document page, double-click its icon. The selected page is centered in the document window. To display a master spread, double-click its icon in the lower half of the panel. (Note that you can reverse the order of master pages and regular pages in the Pages panel by choosing the Panel Options option in the flyout menu.)

The Fit Page in Window command (View⇨Fit Page in Window, or ⌘+0 or Ctrl+0) and Fit Spread in Window command (View⇨Fit Page in Window or Option+⌘+0 or Ctrl+Alt+0) let you enlarge or reduce the display magnification to fit the selected page or spread in the document window. Related view options are View⇨Fit Spread in Window (Option+⌘+0 or Ctrl+Alt+0) and View⇨Entire Pasteboard (Option+Shift+⌘+0 or Ctrl+Alt+Shift+0). (Note that the shortcuts use the numeral *0,* not the letter *O.*)

Navigating with the menus and shortcuts

InDesign also offers several menu commands and keyboard shortcuts to quickly navigate your layout, as Table 4-1 details.

Table 4-1	Page Navigation Menus and Shortcuts		
Navigation	*Menu Sequence*	*Macintosh Shortcut*	*Windows Shortcut*
Go to first page	Layout⇨First Page	Shift+⌘+PgUp	Ctrl+Shift+Page Up
Go back one page	Layout⇨Previous Page	Shift+PgUp	Shift+Page Up
Go forward one page	Layout⇨Next Page or Layout⇨Go Forward	Shift+PgDn or ⌘+PgDn	Shift+Page Down or Ctrl+keypad PgDn
Go to last page	Layout⇨Last Page	Shift+⌘+PgDn	Ctrl+Shift+Page Down
Go to last page viewed	Layout⇨Go Back	⌘+PgUp	Shift+Page Up or Ctrl+keypad PgUp
Go forward one spread	Layout⇨Next Spread	Option+PgDn	Alt+Page Down
Go back one spread	Layout⇨Previous Spread	Option+PgUp	Alt+Page Up

Using the Navigator panel

Although it's possible to use the Navigator panel (Window⇨Object & Layout⇨ Navigator) to move from page to page in a long document, the Pages panel is better for this task. The Navigator panel is more useful for scrolling within a page, particularly for doing detail work on a page that's displayed at a high magnification. If you're an Illustrator, PageMaker, or Photoshop user, you may already be familiar with the Navigator panel, which works the same in all three applications.

Figure 4-6 shows the Navigator panel and its flyout menu.

Figure 4-6:
The
Navigator
panel and
its flyout
menu.

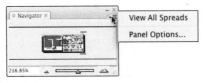

You can also use the scroll bars at the right and bottom of the document window to move to different areas of a page or to a different page in a document.

Adjusting Page Layouts and Objects

If you've ever created and worked with a document all the way to the finishing touches and then discovered that the page size was wrong from the beginning, you know the meaning of frustration. Manually adjusting the size and placement of all the objects in a document is an ugly chore: one you want to avoid at all costs. However, should the unthinkable happen — you have to modify the size, orientation, or margins of a document that is partially or completely finished — InDesign can automatically resize and reposition objects when you change its basic layout.

For example, maybe you created a magazine for an American audience that subsequently needs to be converted for publication in Europe. Most newsletters in the United States use letter-sized pages (8½ × 11 inches), while in Europe the standard page size for such publications is A4 (210 × 297 mm), which is slightly narrower and slightly taller than U.S. letter size. Of course, you have to change *color* to *colour, apartment* to *flat,* and so on, but you also have to both squeeze (horizontally) and stretch (vertically) every item on every page to accommodate the A4 page's dimensions.

The Layout Adjustment command (Layout⇨Layout Adjustment) gives you the option of turning this chore over to InDesign, which automatically adjusts object shape and position according to the new page size, column guides, and margins.

The Layout Adjustment dialog box lets you turn layout adjustment on or off and specify the rules used to adjust objects when you change page size or orientation, margins, or columns. To adjust a layout, follow these steps:

1. **Choose Layout⇨Layout Adjustment to display the Layout Adjustment dialog box, shown in Figure 4-7.**

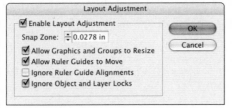

Figure 4-7:
The Layout
Adjustment
dialog box.

2. **Select the Enable Layout Adjustment option to turn on the feature; deselect it to turn it off.**

3. **In the Snap Zone field, type the distance within which an object edge will automatically snap to a guideline when layout adjustment is performed.**

4. **Select the Allow Graphics and Groups to Resize option if you want InDesign to resize objects when layout adjustment is performed.**

   If you don't select this option, InDesign will move objects but not resize them (the preferred option, so you don't get awkward sizes).

5. **Select the Allow Ruler Guides to Move option if you want InDesign to adjust the position of ruler guides proportionally according to a new page size.**

   Generally, ruler guides are placed relative to the margins and page edges, so you probably want to select this option.

6. **Select the Ignore Ruler Guide Alignments option if you want InDesign to ignore ruler guides when adjusting the position of objects during layout adjustment.**

   If you think that objects might snap to ruler guides that you don't want them to snap to during layout adjustment, select this option. If selected, InDesign will still snap object edges to other margin and column guides.

7. **Select the Ignore Object and Layer Locks option to let InDesign move locked objects (either objects locked directly via Object⇨Lock Position or ⌘+L or Ctrl+L, or objects that reside on a locked layer).**

   Otherwise, locked objects will not be adjusted.

8. **When you're done, click OK to close the dialog box.**

The Layout Adjustment feature works best when there's not much work for it to do. Otherwise, it usually creates more work than it saves. For example, the switch from a U.S. letter-sized page to an A4-sized page is a relatively minor change and the layout adjustments will probably be barely noticeable. But if you decide to change a tabloid-sized poster into a business card in midstream, well, you're probably better off starting over.

Here are a few things to keep in mind if you decide to use InDesign's Layout Adjustment feature:

- ✔ If you change page size, the margin widths (the distance between the left and right margins and the page edges) remain the same.

- ✔ If you change page size, column guides and ruler guides are repositioned proportionally to the new size.

- ✔ If you change the number of columns, column guides are added or removed accordingly.

- ✔ If an object edge is aligned with a guideline before layout adjustment, it remains aligned with the guideline after adjustment. If two or more edges of an object are aligned with guidelines, the object is resized so that the edges remain aligned with the guidelines after layout adjustment.

- ✔ If you change the page size, objects are moved so that they're in the same relative position on the new page.

- ✔ If you used margin, column, and ruler guides to place objects on pages, layout adjustment will be more effective than if you placed objects or ruler guides randomly on pages.

- ✔ Check for text reflow when you modify a document's page size, margins, or column guides. Decreasing a document's page size can cause text to overflow a text frame whose dimensions have been reduced.

- ✔ Check *everything* in your document after the adjustment is complete. Take the time to look over every page of your document. You never know what InDesign has actually done until you see it with your own eyes.

If you decide to enable layout adjustment for a particular publication, you might want to begin by using the Save As command (File⇨Save As or Shift+⌘+S or Ctrl+Shift+S) to create a copy. That way, if you ever need to revert back to the original version, you can simply open the original document.

Chapter 5

Layers and Layers

*I*f you've ever seen a series of clear plastic overlays in presentations, understanding layers is easy. In one of those old overhead presentations, the teacher could choose to start with one overlay containing a graphic, add another overlay with descriptive text, and then add a third overlay containing a chart. Each overlay contained distinct content, but you could see through each one to the others to get the entire message. InDesign's layers are somewhat like this, letting you isolate content on slices of a document. You can then show and hide layers, lock objects on layers, rearrange layers, and more.

And unlike those old overhead slides, you can selectively turn layers on or off, so you can use layers for other purposes as well, such as having multiple languages in one document, with each language's text frames on their own layers. Or you could have production notes on their own layer, so you can see them when desired but otherwise keep them out of the way.

What Layers Can Do for You

You could do your work in InDesign without ever once taking a look at the Layers panel. But take a look at the possibilities and see whether they fit into your workflow. In the long run, using layers can save you time and help you prevent mistakes that can result when you need to track changes across multiple documents. It's the kind of feature that, once discovered, can help you work much easier.

Say you've created an ad with the same copy in it but a different headline and image for each city where the ad runs. You can place the boilerplate information on one layer and the information that changes on other layers. If any of the boilerplate information changes, you need to change it only once. To print different versions of the ad, you control which layers print.

You might use layers in the following situations (and in many others):

- **A project with a high-resolution background image:** For example, a background such as a texture might take a long time to redraw. You can hide that layer while designing other elements, and then show it occasionally to see how it works with the rest of the design.

- **A document that you produce in several versions:** For example, a produce ad may have different prices for different cities, or a clothing catalog may feature different coats depending on the climate in each area. You can place the content that changes on separate layers, and then print the layers you need.

- **A project that includes objects you don't want to print:** If you want to suppress printout of objects for any reason, the only way you can do this is to place them on a layer and hide the layer. You might have a layer that's used for nothing but adding editorial and design comments, which can be deleted when the document is final. (Even though InDesign CS3 now adds support for nonprinting notes, they can only be inserted into text, so having a design-comments layer is still useful to be able to make annotations for frames, images, and other nontextual elements.)

- **A publication that is translated into several languages:** Depending on the layout, you can place all the common objects on one layer, and then create a different layer for each language's text. Changes to the common objects need to happen only once — unlike creating copies of the original document and flowing the translated text into the copies, which you would need to do for each language's version.

- **To ensure folios and the like are never overprinted.** This book's tech editor and overall production guru, Jonathan Woolson, places folios (the document's page numbers, running headings, and so forth) on their own layer, uppermost in the layer stack. This ensures that they are never accidentally obscured by other objects.

- **To help text print properly over transparent elements.** Woolson also finds layers useful to isolate text above other objects with transparency effects. This avoids the rasterizing of text during output to plate or film — something that can make the text quality look poor.

Layer Basics

Each document contains a default layer, Layer 1, which contains all your objects until you create and select a new layer. Objects on the default layer — and any other layer for that matter — follow the standard *stacking order* of InDesign. (What's the stacking order? Well, the first object you create is the backmost, the last one you create is the frontmost, and all the other objects fall somewhere in between. This is how InDesign knows what to do with overlapping objects.)

Like the clear plastic overlays, the order of the layers also affects the stacking order of the objects. Objects on the bottom layer are behind other objects, and objects on the top layer are in front of other objects. For example, for a business card, the Default layer would contain the business card's standard graphics and the main text. An additional layer would contain a different set of contact information — in separate text frames — for a different person. Each new person would have his or her information on his or own new layer. Each layer has its own color, and frames will display in that color if frame edges are visible (choose View⇨Show Frame Edges or press Control+⌘+H or Ctrl+H).

Note that the new Mac shortcut for View⇨Show Frame Edges is Control+⌘+H; the Windows shortcut (Ctrl+H) is unchanged.

Although people often compare layers to plastic overlays, one big difference exists: Layers aren't specific to individual pages. Each layer encompasses the entire document, which doesn't make much difference when you're working on a one-page ad but makes a significant difference when it comes to a 16-page newsletter. When you create layers and place objects on them, you must consider all the pages in the document.

The Layers panel (choose Window⇨Layers or press F7) is your gateway to creating and manipulating layers (see Figure 5-1).

Eye icon (indicates visible layer)

Lock icon (indicates locked layer)

Pen icon
(indicates active layer)

Object icon (indicates layer
associated with selected object)

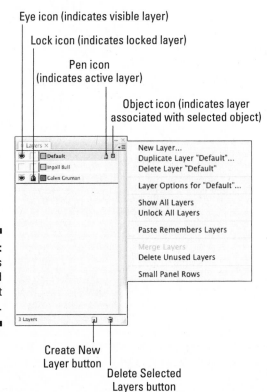

Figure 5-1:
The Layers
panel and
its flyout
menu.

Create New
Layer button

Delete Selected
Layers button

Working with Layers

Each document contains a default layer, Layer 1, that contains all the objects you place on master pages and document pages. You can create as many layers as you need. After you create a new layer, it's activated automatically so you can begin working on it.

Creating a layer

The Layers panel (choose Window⇨Layers or press F7) provides several methods for creating new layers. It doesn't matter which document page is displayed when you create a layer because the layer encompasses all the pages in the document. To create a layer, do one of the following:

- ✔ **To create a new layer on top of all existing layers,** click the New Layer button on the Layers panel to open the New Layer dialog box. The layer receives the default name of Layer *x*.

- ✔ **To create a layer above the selected layer,** ⌘+click or Ctrl+click the New Layer button. The layer receives the default name of Layer *x*.

- ✔ **To create a new layer on top of all existing layers but customize its name and identifying color,** Option+click or Alt+click the New Layer iconic button, or choose New Layer from the Layers panel's flyout menu. Use the New Layer dialog box to specify options for the layer. (The New Layer dialog box — set with a custom name and color — is shown in Figure 5-2.)

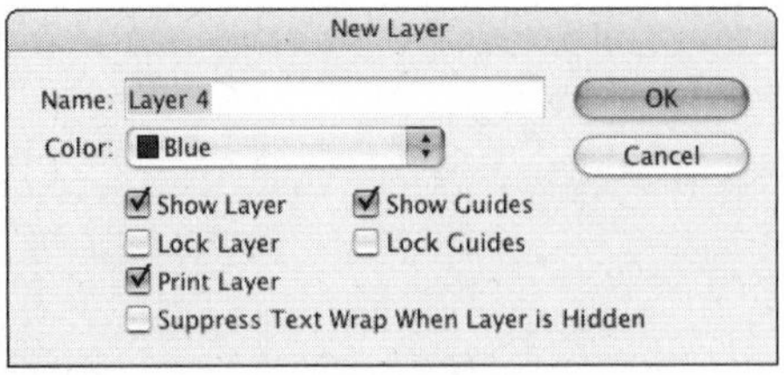

Figure 5-2:
The New
Layer dialog
box.

New Layer

Name: Layer 4   OK
Color: ■ Blue   Cancel
☑ Show Layer   ☑ Show Guides
☐ Lock Layer   ☐ Lock Guides
☑ Print Layer
☐ Suppress Text Wrap When Layer is Hidden

Customizing layers

You can customize the name, identifying color, guides, and lock status of objects on a new or existing layer. If you choose to customize the layer when you create it (by Option+clicking or Alt+clicking the New Layer iconic button or by choosing New Layer from the Layers panel's flyout menu), the New

Layer dialog box appears. If you choose to customize an existing layer, double-click it to display the Layer Options dialog box. (You can also choose Layer Options for *Layer Name* from the flyout menu on the Layers panel.)

Whether you're using the New Layer dialog box shown in Figure 5-2 or the nearly identical Layer Options dialog box, the options all work the same:

- **Name field:** Type a descriptive name for the layer. For example, if you're using layers for multilingual publishing, you might have a United States English layer, a French layer, and a German layer. If you're using layers to hide background objects while you're working, you might have a Background Objects layer.

- **Color pop-up menu:** Choose a color from the menu. A layer's color helps you identify which layer an object is on. The color appears to the left of the layer name in the Layers panel and appears on each object on that layer. The color is applied to frame edges, selection handles, bounding boxes, text ports, and text wraps. By default, InDesign applies a different color to each new layer, but you can customize it to something meaningful for your document and workflow.

- **Show Layer check box:** Selected by default, this control lets you specify whether objects on a layer display onscreen. Hidden layers also do not print. The Show Layer option has the same effect as clicking the eye icon on the Layers panel.

- **Lock Layer check box:** Deselected by default, this option lets you control whether objects on a layer can be edited. You might lock a layer that contains boilerplate text or a complex drawing that you don't want altered. Locking and unlocking layers is easy, so you might lock one layer while focusing on another, and then unlock it. Select Lock Layer if you don't want to be able to select items and modify them. For example, in a document containing multiple versions of text on different layers, you might lock the layer containing background images and other objects that stay the same. The Lock Layer option has the same effect as clicking the lock icon on the Layers panel. There are additional locking options in the Layers panel's flyout menu to, for example, unlock all layers and lock all layers but the active one.

  The lock icon had been the pencil icon in previous versions of InDesign.

  When you lock an object to a page (by choosing Object⇨Lock Position, or ⌘+L or Ctrl+L), the object's position stays locked regardless of its layer's lock status.

- **Print Layer check box:** Selected by default, this option lets you control whether the layer prints or exports to PDF. You might use this option for a layer containing design comments, for example. (In previous versions of InDesign, deselecting Show Layer also prevented the layer from printing. That remains true, but now you can control whether unhidden layers print or not as well.) You can also override whether nonprinting layers print in the Print dialog box, as explained in Chapter 25.

✔ **Suppress Text Wrap When Layer Is Hidden check box:** Deselected by default, this option prevents text wrapping around the layer's objects when the layer is hidden. Be sure to select this option when you use multiple layers for variations of the same content, such as multilingual text or different contacts for business cards. Otherwise, your layer's text can't display because it's wrapping around a hidden layer with an object of the same size in the same place.

✔ **Show Guides check box:** This check box lets you control the display of guides that were created while the selected layer was active. When selected, as it is by default, you can create guides while any layer is active and view those guides on any layer. When deselected, you can't create guides. Any guides you create while that layer is active are not displayed, but you can still see guides that you created while other layers were active. Note that when guides are hidden entirely (choose View⇔Grids & Guides⇔Hide Guides, or press ⌘+; [semicolon] or Ctrl+; [semicolon]), this command has no apparent effect.

✔ **Lock Guides check box:** This works similarly to Show Guides in that it affects only the guides that you created while the layer is active. When deselected, as it is by default, you can move guides on any layer for which Lock Guides is deselected. When selected, you cannot move guides created while that layer was active. You can, however, move guides on other layers for which Lock Guides is deselected. Note that when all guides are locked (choose View⇔Grids & Guides⇔Lock Guides, or Option+⌘+; [semicolon] or press Ctrl+Alt+; [semicolon]), this command has no apparent effect.

You can select multiple layers and customize them all at once. However, because each layer must have a different name, the Name field isn't available in the Layer Options dialog box when multiple layers are selected.

Working with Objects on Layers

Whether you're designing a magazine template from the ground up or modifying an existing ad, you can isolate specific types of objects on layers. You can create objects on a layer, move objects to a layer, or copy objects to a layer.

The active layer

The *active layer* is the one on which you're creating objects — whether you're using tools, importing text or graphics, clicking and dragging objects in from a library, or pasting objects from other layers or other documents. A pen icon to the right of a layer's name means it's the active layer. Although more than one layer can be selected at a time, only one can be active. To switch the active layer to another layer, click to the right of the layer name that you want to be active; the pen icon moves, making that the new active layer. Keep in mind that to activate a layer, it must be visible.

Selecting objects on layers

Regardless of the active layer, you can select, move, and modify objects on any visible, unlocked layer. You can even select objects on different layers and manipulate them.

The Layers panel (choose Window⇨Layers or press F7) helps you work with selected objects in the following ways:

- To determine which layer an object belongs to, match the color on its bounding box to the color that appears to the left of a layer name.
- To determine which layers contain active objects, look to the right of the layer names. A small square — the object icon — to the right of a layer name indicates that you have selected an object on that layer.
- To select all the objects on a layer, Option+click or Alt+click the layer's name in the Layers panel. The layer must be active, unlocked, and visible.

To select master-page objects as well as document-page objects on a layer, you need to Option+Shift+click or Alt+Shift+click the layer name.

Placing objects on layers

To place objects on a layer, the layer must be active as indicated by the pen icon. Anything you copy, import, or create in InDesign goes on the active layer.

When you create objects on master pages, they are placed on the default layer and are therefore behind other objects on document pages. To create objects on master pages that are in front of other objects, place the objects on a different layer while the master page is displayed.

You can cut and paste objects from one page to another, but have the objects remain on their original layer — without concern about the active layer. To do this, be sure the Paste Remembers Layers check box is selected in the Layers panel's flyout menu before choosing Edit⇨Paste or pressing ⌘+V or Ctrl+V.

Moving objects to different layers

When an object is on a layer, it isn't stuck there. You can copy and paste objects to selected layers, or you can move them by using the Layers panel. When you move an object to a layer, it's placed in front of all other objects on a layer. To select multiple objects, remember to Shift+click them, and then move them in one of the following ways:

- **Paste objects on a different layer.** First cut or copy objects to the Clipboard. Activate the layer on which you want to put the objects, and then use the Paste command (by choosing Edit⇨Paste or by pressing ⌘+V or Ctrl+V). This method works well for moving objects that are currently on a variety of layers.

- **Move objects to a different layer.** Click and drag the object icon for the selected objects (to the right of a layer's name) to another layer. When you use this method, it doesn't matter which layer is active. However, you can't move objects from several different layers to the same layer using this method. (If you select multiple objects that reside on different layers, dragging the box moves only objects that reside on the first layer on which you selected an object.)

- **Move objects to a hidden or locked layer.** Press ⌘ or Ctrl while you click and drag the selected objects' object icon.

- **Copy rather than move objects to a different layer.** Press Option or Alt while you click and drag the selected objects' object icon.

- **Copy objects to a hidden or locked layer.** Press Option+⌘ or Ctrl+Alt while you drag the selected objects' object icon.

Manipulating Entire Layers

In addition to working on objects and their layer positions, you can also select and manipulate entire layers. These changes affect all the objects on the layer — for example, if you hide a layer, all its objects are hidden; if you move a layer up, all its objects appear in front of objects on lower layers. Functions that affect an entire layer include hiding, locking, rearranging, merging, and deleting. You work on entire layers in the Layers panel.

Selecting layers

The active layer containing the pen icon is always selected. You can extend the selection to include other layers the same way you multiple-select objects: Shift+click for a continuous selection and ⌘+click or Ctrl+click for a noncontiguous selection.

Rearranging layers

Each layer has its own front-to-back stacking order, with the first object you create on the layer being its backmost object. You can modify the stacking order of objects on a single layer by using the Arrange commands on the Object menu. Objects are further stacked according to the order in which the layers are listed in the Layers panel. The layer at the top of the list contains the frontmost objects, and the layer at the bottom of the list contains the backmost objects.

If you find that all the objects on one layer need to be in front of all the objects on another layer, you can move that layer up or down in the list. In fact, you can move all currently selected layers up or down, even if the selection is noncontiguous. To move layers, click the selection and drag it up or down. When you move layers, remember that layers are document-wide, so you're actually changing the stacking order of objects on all the pages.

Combining layers

When you're just discovering the power of layers, you might create a document that is unnecessarily complex (for example, you might have put each object on a different layer and realized that the document has become too difficult to work with). The good news is that you can also merge all the layers in a document to *flatten* it to a single layer. To flatten all layers:

1. **Select the *target layer* (the layer where you want all the objects to end up) by clicking it.**

2. **Select the *source layers* (the layers that contain the objects you want to move) in addition to the target layer.**

   Shift+click or ⌘+click or Ctrl+click to add the source layers to the selection.

3. **Make sure the target layer contains the pen icon and that the target and source layers are all selected.**

4. **Choose Merge Layers from the Layers panel's flyout menu.**

   All objects on the source layers are moved to the target layer, and the source layers are deleted.

When you merge layers, the stacking order of objects doesn't change, so the design looks the same, but with one notable exception: If you created objects on a layer while a master page was displayed, those objects go to the back of the stacking order with the regular master-page objects.

Deleting layers

If you carefully isolate portions of a document on different layers and then find that you don't need that portion of the document, you can delete the layer. For example, if you have a United States English and an International English layer and you decide that you can't afford to print the different versions, you can delete the unneeded layer. You might also delete layers that you don't end up using to simplify a document.

When you delete layers, all the objects on the layer throughout the document are deleted.

Using the Layers panel, you can delete selected layers in the following ways:

- ✔ Click and drag the selection to the Delete Selected Layers iconic button.
- ✔ Click the Delete Selected Layers iconic button. The currently selected layers are deleted.
- ✔ Choose Delete Layer from the Layers panel's flyout menu.

If any of the layers contain objects, a warning reminds you that they will be deleted. And, of course, the ubiquitous Undo command (choose Edit➪Undo or press ⌘+Z or Ctrl+Z) lets you recover from accidental deletions.

To remove all layers that don't contain objects, choose Delete Unused Layers from the Layers panel's flyout menu.

Chapter 6

The Joys of Reuse

In This Chapter

▶ Using templates

▶ Using master pages

▶ Using libraries

▶ Working with XML snippets

*U*nless you enjoy continually reinventing the wheel, you'll want to take full advantage of the features that InDesign offers to help you work more productively. After you make some important decisions about elements in your document that will repeat, page after page, in the same spot (such as page numbers, graphics, headers and footers, and so on), you want to set up mechanisms that make the process simple.

Fewer activities in life are less rewarding than doing the same job over and over, and publishing is no exception. Fortunately, InDesign includes some valuable features that let you automate repetitive tasks. In this chapter, I focus on three of them: templates, master pages, and libraries. (Note that there are other ways to reuse InDesign elements, such as exporting to PDF or XHTML files, or exporting stories and graphics. These are covered in Chapter 3.)

Building and Using Templates

A *template* is a pre-built InDesign document that you use as the starting point for creating multiple versions of the same design or publication. For example, if you create a monthly newsletter that uses the same basic layout for each issue, but with different graphics and text, you begin by creating a template that contains all the elements that are the same in every issue — placeholder frames for the graphics and text, guidelines, and so on.

Creating templates

Creating a template is very similar to creating a document. You create character, paragraph, and object styles, master pages, repeating elements (for example, page numbers), and so on. The only thing you don't add to a template is actual content.

Most often, you create a template after building the first iteration of a document. After you have that document set up the way you like, you simply strip out the content (that first issue's stories and graphics in our newsletter example) and save it as a template.

Here are the steps for creating a template:

1. **Choose File➪Save As or press Shift+⌘+S or Ctrl+Shift+S to display the Save As dialog box.**
2. **Choose a folder and specify a name for the file.**
3. **Choose InDesign CS3 Template in the Format pop-up menu (Mac) or Save as Type pop-up menu (Windows).**
4. **Click Save to close the Save As dialog box and save the template.**

If you're designing a template that will be used by others, you might want to add a layer of instructions. When it's time to print a document based on the template, simply hide the annotation layer. (See Chapter 5 for more information about working with layers.)

If you didn't know better, you might think that a template is exactly the same as a regular InDesign document. It is, with one major exception: A template is a bit more difficult to override. When you open a template, it receives a default name (Untitled-1, Untitled-2, and so on). The first time you choose File➪Save or press ⌘+S or Ctrl+S, the Save As dialog box appears.

Modifying templates

As you use a template over time, you might discover that you forgot to include something — perhaps a paragraph style, a repeating element on a particular master page, or an entire master page. To modify a template, you have two options:

✔ Open it as a normal file, make your changes, and then choose File➪Save As (or press Shift+⌘+S or Ctrl+Shift+S) to save it again as a template. To open a file as a normal file, be sure that Open Normal (Mac) or Normal (Windows) is selected at the bottom of the Open a File dialog box — this is the default option.

✔ Open it as an original file (see Chapter 3), make your changes, and then choose File⇨Save (⌘+S or Ctrl+S) to save it again as a template. To open a file as an original file, be sure that Open Original (Mac) or Original (Windows) is selected at the bottom of the Open a File dialog box — it's easy to forget to select this option, so most people end up using the previous technique to resave the template.

Creating documents from templates

It's very easy to create a document from a template: Just open a template file and save it with a new name, making sure that InDesign CS3 Document is selected in the Format pop-up menu (Mac) or Save as Type pop-up menu (Windows) — this the default setting. Work on your document and continue to save changes normally.

A more complicated way to create a document from a template is to choose File⇨New Document from Template. This opens the Adobe Bridge program, which can contain InDesign templates that you open and then save as documents. Bridge is meant as a central place for all Creative Suite documents and many related files such as color libraries to help workgroups have one place for all their Creative Suite needs. I think it's more complicated than it is useful, at least for InDesign users (many Photoshop users love it).

Building and Using Master Pages

A *master page* is a preconstructed page layout that you can use to create new pages — it is the starting point for document pages. Typically, master pages contain text and graphic elements, such as page numbers, headers, footers, and so on, which appear on all pages of a publication. Master pages also include guidelines that indicate page edges, column boundaries, and margins, as well as other manually created guidelines to aid page designers in placing objects. By placing items on master pages, you save yourself the repetitive work of placing the same items one by one on each and every document page.

It may surprise you to know that every InDesign document you create already contains a master page, called A-Master. Whether you use the default master page or create and use additional master pages depends on what kind of document you want to create. If it's a single-page document, such as a flier or an ad, you don't need master pages at all, so you can just ignore them. However, if you want to create a document with multiple pages — a brochure or booklet, for example — master pages save time and help ensure consistent design.

Creating a new master page

When you're ready to create a new master page, here's what you do:

1. **If the Pages panel is not displayed, choose Windows⇨Pages or press ⌘+F12 or Ctrl+F12.**

   The Pages panel is covered in more detail in Chapter 4.

2. **From the Pages panel's flyout menu, choose New Master.**

   You can also hold Option+⌘ or Ctrl+Alt and click the Create New Page iconic button at the bottom of the panel. The New Master dialog box, shown in Figure 6-1, appears.

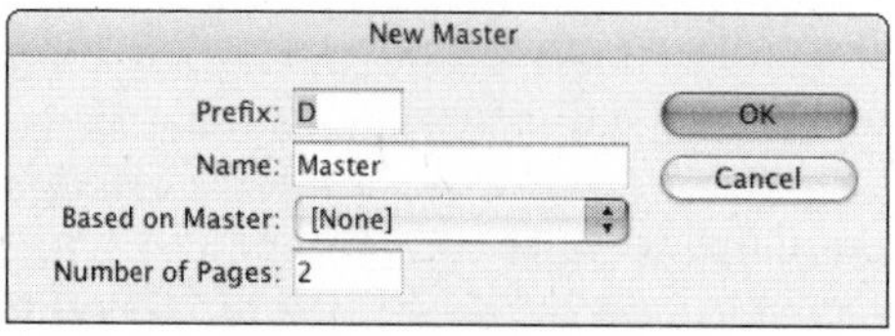

Figure 6-1:
The New
Master
dialog box.

> New Master
> Prefix: D
> Name: Master
> Based on Master: [None]
> Number of Pages: 2
> OK
> Cancel

3. **In the Prefix field, specify a one-character prefix to attach to the front of the master page name and display on associated document page icons in the Pages panel.**

   The default will be a capital letter, such as the *D* in Figure 6-1.

4. **In the Name field, give your new master page a name.**

   It's a good idea to use a descriptive name, such as `Title Page`.

5. **To base the new master page (the *child*) on another master page (the *parent*), choose the parent master page from the Based on Master pop-up menu.**

6. **In the Number of Pages field, enter the number of pages you want to include in the master spread.** For a document with a single-page design, enter **1**; if the document will have facing pages, enter **2**.

7. **Click OK to save the page and close the dialog box.**

Your new master page appears in the document window. The name of the master page appears in the Page Number field in the bottom-left corner of the document window. To make changes to a master page's attributes, simply click its icon at the top of the Pages panel, choose Master Options from the panel's flyout menu, and then change settings in the Master Options dialog box.

Note that you can move master pages to be at the bottom of the Pages panel — rather than at the top — by choosing Panel Options from the flyout menu and enabling the Pages on Top option.

When you're building a master page, you should think more about the overall structure of the page than about details. Keep the following in mind:

✓ **To build a document with facing pages,** create facing-page master spreads. The facing pages are somewhat like mirror images of each other. Typically, the left-hand master page is for even-numbered document pages, and the right-hand master page is for odd-numbered document pages.

✓ **To have page numbers automatically appear on document pages,** add a page number character on each page of your master spreads by drawing a text frame with the Type tool where you want the page number to appear and then choosing Type➪Insert Special Character➪Markers➪Current Page Number or pressing Option+⌘+N or Ctrl+Alt+N. The prefix of the master page (A, B, C, and so on) appears on the master page, but the actual page number is what appears on document pages. Don't forget to format the page number on the master page so that page numbers will look the way you want them to in the document.

✓ **Specify master page margins and columns** by first making sure that the page is displayed in the document window and then choosing Layout➪Margins and Columns. The Margins and Columns dialog box, shown in Figure 6-2, is displayed. The controls in this dialog box let you specify the position of the margins, the number of columns, and the gutter width (space between columns).

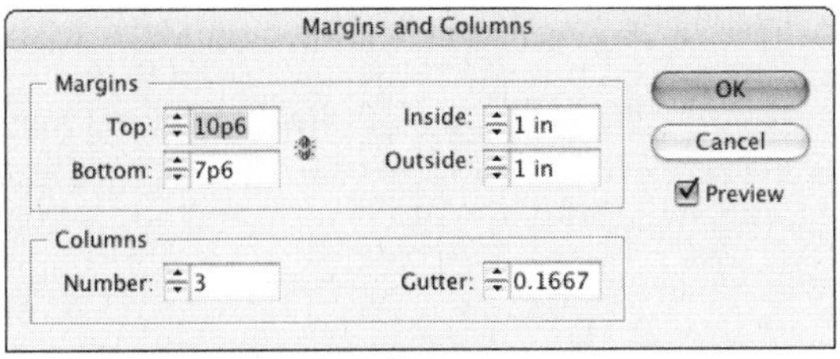

Figure 6-2:
The Margins and Columns dialog box.

Margins and Columns

Margins
Top: 10p6   Inside: 1 in
Bottom: 7p6   Outside: 1 in

Columns
Number: 3   Gutter: 0.1667

OK
Cancel
☑ Preview

You can place additional guidelines on a master page — as many custom guidelines as you want. (Guidelines are covered in Chapter 11.)

Basing one master page on another

Some publications benefit from having more than one master page. If you're building a document with several pages that are somewhat similar in design, it's a good idea to start with one master page and then use it as a basis for additional master pages.

For example, if the brochure you're working on uses both two-column and three-column page layouts, you can create the two-column master spread first and include all repeating page elements. You can then create the three-column master page spread, basing it on the two-column master, and simply specify different column formats. The "child" master page will be identical to the parent except for the number of columns. If you later change an element on the original master page, the change will apply automatically to the child master page.

When you create a new master page, the New Master dialog box provides the option to base it on an existing master page. To help you keep things straight, when you base a master page on another master page, InDesign displays the prefix of the parent page on the icon of the child page.

If you base a master spread on another master spread, you can still modify the master objects (that is, the objects inherited from the parent master) on the child master page. As with regular document pages, you have to Shift+⌘+click or Ctrl+Shift+click the object inherited from a parent master to release it before you can edit it on a child master.

Basing a master spread on a document spread

You might be talented enough to create an effective spread, one that is so handsome that you want to create a master page from it to use on future documents. Simply highlight the spread by clicking the page numbers below the relevant page icons in the Pages panel and choose Save as Master from the Pages panel's flyout menu. The new master is assigned a default name and prefix. To change any of its attributes, click its name in the Pages panel and then choose Master Options from the flyout menu.

Duplicating a master spread

Create a copy of a master spread by selecting its icon and then choosing Duplicate Master Spread from the Pages panel's flyout menu or simply by dragging its icon onto the Create New Page button at the bottom of the panel. Note that if you duplicate a master spread, the duplicate loses any parent/child relationships.

Importing a master page

Sometimes, another document has a master page that you'd like to use in your current layout. InDesign CS3 lets you import those master pages: Just choose Load Master Pages from the Pages panel's flyout menu, select the source document in the dialog box that appears, and click Open. InDesign will import all master pages from that document into your current one. Sorry, there's no way to select specific master pages.

The ability to import master pages is new to InDesign CS3. Before, you had two not-so-great options that required both the source and target documents be open. One option is to create a new master page in your document, and then copy the elements from another document using old-fashioned copy-and-paste. The other option is to drag the name of the master page that you want to copy from the source document's Pages panel to the target document's document window. (You can still use these two approaches if you insist.)

If any of the imported master pages have the same name as your current document's master pages (such as the default name A-Master), a dialog box will appear giving you the choice of replacing the current master pages with the imported ones that use the same name or of renaming the imported master pages, so you keep what you have and add the imported ones. InDesign does the renaming for you.

Note that InDesign will also alert you if the imported master pages use different dimensions than the current document's pages. It won't adjust the imported pages, so some items may appear off the page if the imported master page has larger dimensions than the current document.

Deleting a master page

To delete a master page, select its name and then choose Delete Master Page from the Pages panel's flyout menu. You can also drag the master icon to the Delete Pages iconic button at the bottom of the Pages panel.

So what happens when you delete a master page on which document pages are based? Don't worry — your document pages are unchanged, though they no longer have a master page (in the Pages panel, the page icons won't display the letter of a master page in their upper outside corners).

You can remove a master page from a specific document page without removing the master page from your document (and thus other pages), by applying the [None] master page to the document page using the process described next.

Applying a master page to document pages

After you build a master page, you can apply it to new or existing document pages. (See Chapter 4 for information about adding and removing document pages.) For documents with facing pages, you can apply both pages of a master spread to both pages of the document spread or you can apply one page of a master spread to one page of the document spread. For example, you can apply a master page with a two-column format to the left-hand page of a document spread and apply a master page with a three-column format to the right-hand page.

To apply a master page to a document page, select the name or icon of the page in the top part of the Pages panel and then drag it onto the icon of the document page you want to format. When the target document page is highlighted (framed in a black rectangle, as shown in the left side of Figure 6-3), release the mouse button. If both document pages are highlighted, and if you are applying a master page to the document, both sides of the master spread are applied to the document spread.

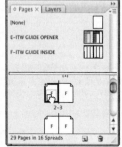

Figure 6-3:
Applying a
single
master page
to a
document
page.

You can also apply a master page to the currently displayed pages by choosing Layout⇨Pages⇨Apply Master to Pages.

Changing master items on document pages

As you work on a document page that's based on a master, you may find that you need to change, move, or delete a master object. Any change you make to a master object on a local page is referred to as a *local override*.

Whenever you remove a master object from a document page, you sever the object's relationship to the master-page object for that document page only. If you subsequently move or modify the object on the master page, it won't affect the deleted object on the document page — it remains deleted on that particular document page.

The Show/Hide Master Items command in the Pages panel's flyout menu lets you show or hide master objects on document pages.

To change a master object on a document page, you must first select it, and doing so can be a bit tricky. To select a master object on a document page, hold down Shift+⌘ or Ctrl+Shift when you click the object with one of the selection tools. (You can also Shift+⌘+drag or Ctrl+Shift+drag to select multiple objects within the selection marquee.) After you select a master object on a document page, you can modify it just as you would objects that are not part of a master page.

If you modify one or more master objects on a document page and then decide you want to revert back to using the original master objects, you can remove the local overrides. To do so, display the document page that contains the master objects you've modified, select the objects, and then choose Remove Selected Local Overrides from the Pages panel's flyout menu. If no objects are selected, the command name changes to Remove All Local Overrides. If the selected spread doesn't have any modified master objects, the command is not available.

Sometimes, you don't want people to have the ability to override a master page object. InDesign CS3 gives you a way to block such overrides: With the master page open and any objects selected that you don't want to be overridden, deselect Allow Master Item Overrides on Selection in the Pages panel's flyout menu. With this option deselected, someone won't be able to override the selected master page objects on any document pages using them — unless of course they reselect the Allow Master Item Overrides on Selections option.

Building and Using Libraries

An InDesign *library* is a file — similar in some ways to a document file — where you can store individual objects (graphics, text, and so forth), groups and nested objects, ruler guides, and grids (see Chapter 11). Once an item is in a library, every time you need a copy, you simply drag one out of the library.

Creating a library

Creating a library is easy:

1. **Choose File⇨New⇨Library.**

   The New Library dialog box appears, with essentially the same options as the Save As dialog box covered in Chapter 3.

2. **Choose a location in which to save the library.**

3. **Give the library a name.**

4. **Click OK.**

You can create as many libraries as you want and store them wherever is most convenient, including on a networked server so that other InDesign users can share them. You can also open libraries created on a Mac from a Windows computer, and vice versa.

Right after you create a new library, you see an empty library panel group. Each library that you create or open will appear as its own panel within that panel group, with its name displayed in its tab, as shown in Figure 6-4. To add items to the library, you simply drag them to the desired panel.

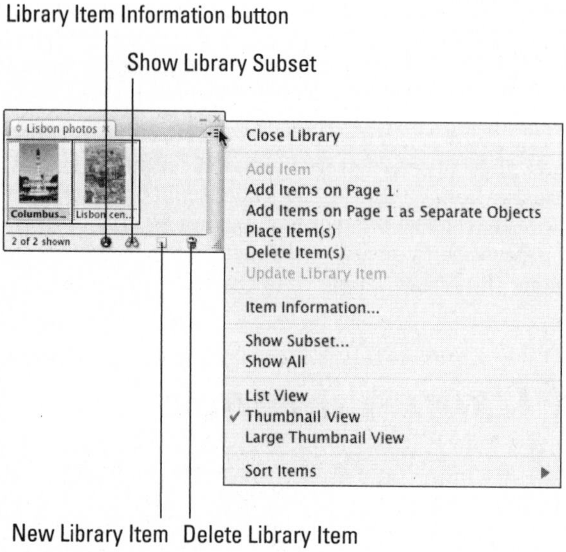

Library Item Information button

Show Library Subset

Figure 6-4:
A library
and its
flyout menu.

New Library Item   Delete Library Item

Here is an explanation of some of the controls and commands shown in Figure 6-4:

- ✔ The numbers in the lower-left corner of the panel indicate the number of items currently displayed in the pane and the number of items in the library.

- ✔ The Library Item Information iconic button displays the Item Information dialog box, as does the Library Item flyout menu option. Here you can give each library item a name, a type (for example, image or text), and a description. Later, you can search for library items based on these attributes.

- ✔ The Show Library Subset iconic button displays a dialog box that lets you locate and display items that meet certain search criteria, as does the Show Subset flyout menu option.

- ✔ The Delete Library Item iconic button lets you delete highlighted items in the library, as does the Delete Item(s) flyout menu option.

Why you'll love snippets

InDesign has a neat option called XML snippets that lets you take pieces of your document and create a file that other InDesign users can bring into their documents, preserving all formatting and effects applied to them.

They're sort of like libraries, with a key exception: Each snippet is a separate file, so they're not as easy or as convenient as libraries when you have lots of document pieces that you want to share or make available for reuse. So snippets are best for sharing specific elements on an as-needed basis, whereas libraries are better for having, well, a library of standard, shared elements.

The process of creating snippets is easy: Select the objects and drag them outside your document window onto the Mac or Windows desktop or onto a folder. InDesign automatically creates the XML snippet file containing those objects and their formatting. You can then send that snippet to other users on storage drives, via e-mail, or over the network — like any other file.

To use the snippet in another document, just drag the snippet into your document window. That's it!

Putting items into a library

You can place individual items, such as text and graphics frames, into a library. You can also place multiple selected objects, groups, nested frames, ruler guides, guidelines, and all items on a document page.

To add items to a library:

- ✔ Select one or more items and then drag them into an open library panel. (Open an existing library by choosing File➪Open or by pressing ⌘+O or Ctrl+O.)
- ✔ Select one or more items and then choose Add Item from the flyout menu of an open Library panel.
- ✔ Choose Add All Items on Page from the flyout menu of an open Library panel to add all items on the current page or spread as *one library item*. Choose Add All Items on Page as Separate Objects to add each object on the page in one step as *separate library items*.
- ✔ Select one or more items and then click the New Library Item iconic button at the bottom of an open Library panel.

If you hold down the Option or Alt key when adding an item to a library, the Item Information dialog box is displayed. This dialog box lets you add searchable attributes to the library item.

If you import a graphic into a document and then place a copy of the graphic into a library, the path to the original graphics file is saved, as are any transformations you've applied to the graphic or its frame (scale, rotation, shear, and so on). If you save text in a library, all formatting, including styles, is retained.

Tagging library items

A library can hold as many items as you want. As a library grows, locating a particular item can become increasingly difficult. To make InDesign library items easier to find, tag them with several searchable attributes.

To tag a library element, select it and then choose Item Information from the library panel's flyout menu. You can also display the Item Information dialog box by double-clicking a library item or by clicking once on a library item and then clicking the Library Item Information iconic button at the bottom of the Library panel. (It's the *i* in a circle.) Specify a Name, Object Type, and/or Description. In the Description field, use a few words that describe the object; this will make it easier to find later. Click OK to close the dialog box and return to the document.

Searching for library items

You can search for library items based on the information specified in the Item Information dialog box. For example, if you place several different icons into a library that includes many other items, and if you use the term *icon* in the Name or Description field, a search of these fields that includes "icon" will find and display those items stored in your library.

Follow these steps to search a library:

1. **Choose Show Subset from a library panel's flyout menu or click the Show Library Subset iconic button at the bottom of the panel.**

2. **Decide whether to search the entire library or only the items currently displayed in the page and select the appropriate radio button.**

3. **In the Parameters area, choose the Item Information category you want to search from the first pop-up menu.**

   Your choices are Item Name, Creation Date, Object Type, and Description.

4. **From the next pop-up menu, choose Contains if you intend to search for text contained in the chosen category; choose Doesn't Contain if you want to exclude items that contain the text you specify.**

5. **In the Parameter's area text-entry field, type the word or phrase you want to search for (if you selected Contains in Step 4) or exclude (if you selected Doesn't Contain).**

6. **Add more search criteria by clicking the More Choices button; reduce the number of search criteria by clicking Fewer Choices.**

    You can create up to five levels of search criteria. If you select two or more levels of search criteria, you will be able to choose whether to display items that match all search criteria (by selecting Match All) or to display items that match any of the search criteria (by selecting Match Any One).

7. **Click OK to conduct the search and close the dialog box.**

The library items that match the search criteria are displayed in the panel (unless no items matched the search criteria). To display all items after conducting a search, choose Show All from the Library panel's flyout menu.

Deleting items from a library

To delete a library item, drag its icon to the trashcan icon at the bottom of the panel or select the item and then choose Delete Item(s) from the library panel's flyout menu. You can select a range of items by clicking the first one and then Shift+clicking the last one. You can select multiple, noncontiguous items by holding down the ⌘ or Ctrl key and clicking each icon.

Copying library items onto document pages

After an item is in a library, you can place copies of that library item into any document or into another library. To place a copy of a library item onto the currently displayed document page, drag the item's icon from the library panel onto the page. As you drag, the outline of the library item is displayed. Release the mouse button when the outline of the item is positioned where you want it to end up. You can also place a library item onto a document by clicking its icon and then choosing Place Item(s) from the flyout menu.

Copy an item from one library to another by dragging its icon from the source library panel onto the target library panel. To move (rather than copy) an item from one library to another, hold down the Option or Alt key when dragging and dropping an item between libraries.

Managing library panels

You can close an individual panel by clicking its close box or choosing Close Library from its flyout menu. You can close all libraries at once by clicking the panel group's close box.

You can move panels into their own panel groups by dragging their tab outside their current panel groups. Likewise, you can combine library panels by dragging them by their tabs into another panel group (including those that contain non-library panels).

Chapter 7

Working with Color

*W*e see the world in glorious color. Yet not all publications take advantage of that fact, typically for budget reasons. But when you do have color available, take advantage of it: It brings a visual dimension that taps into our primal brains, creating a level of raw visual interest unmatched by anything else.

To take advantage of human beings' color "hot buttons," InDesign offers the ability to create and apply colors in many creative ways. But even if you can't use color in every document, some of the techniques described here — especially for tints and gradients — can help a staid black-and-white document get new panache through shades of gray.

Working with Colors

InDesign comes with only a few predefined colors: black, registration (black on each negative for the printing press), paper (white), none (transparent), cyan, magenta, yellow, red, green, and blue. You likely want to add a few of your own.

Creating color swatches

Before you can apply any colors — whether to bitmap images or to layout elements such as strokes, text, frames, and shapes — you must first define the colors, which you do in the Swatches panel (Window⇨Swatches or F5). You can also import colors from other Adobe programs and from some color images.

No matter how you define colors, you have a couple of decisions to make first:

- Do you want to create your own color by mixing basic colors like red, green, and blue (called RGB and typically used for documents like Web pages and PDF files displayed onscreen), or cyan, yellow, magenta, and black (called CMYK, or *process colors,* and typically used for printing presses and by inkjet printers)?

- Do you want to use a color from an ink maker like Pantone or Toyo? These colors — called *spot colors* — are typically used as an extra ink on your professionally printed document but can also be converted to the standard four-process colors and so are handy when you know the color you want when you see it.

All of the color-creation tools in InDesign support both process and spot colors, and all have access to the predefined colors like Pantone and Toyo as well as to the free-form color pickers for mixing CMYK or RGB colors. If you plan to print the color on its own plate, you need to use a predefined color so you know the printer can reproduce it. If you plan to color-separate a color into the four CMYK plates, it doesn't matter whether you use a predefined color or make one of your own. One advantage to using a predefined color is that it's easy to tell other designers what the color is; another is that you will get very close matches if you start with a predefined color and then end up having it color-separated in some documents and kept as a spot color in others.

All colors in the Swatches panel receive a unique name and are tracked by InDesign. That means each color is available to be used on any object in your document, with no risk of having slightly different variants. Plus, you can modify a swatch and ensure that all objects using that swatch are updated. You can also delete a swatch and tell InDesign which color to use in its place. Furthermore, when you print, you have control over how each color is handled (whether it is printed to its own plate, whether it is printed at all, and whether there should be any adjustments to its ink density or screening angle). Figure 7-1 shows the Swatches panel.

If no document is open when you create, edit, or delete colors, the new color palette becomes the default for all future documents.

To create your own color, go to the Swatches panel and select New Color Swatch from the flyout menu. The New Color Swatch dialog box shown in Figure 7-2 appears. Now follow these steps:

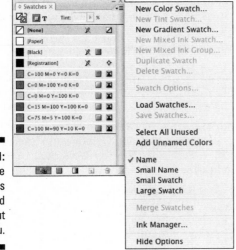

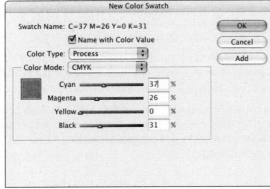

1. **In the Swatch Name field, give your color a name that describes it, such as** Lemon Yellow **or** Blood Red.

   You can also select the Name with Color Value option, which uses the color values to make up the color name, as done for the colors under [Registration] in Figure 7-1. This option is the default setting for CMYK, RGB, and LAB colors; it is not available for swatch-based colors such as Pantone.

2. **In the Color Type pop-up menu, choose from Process or Spot.**

   The difference between process colors and spot colors is discussed later in this chapter; leave the color type at Process if you're not sure.

3. **In the Color Mode pop-up menu, choose the mixing system or swatch library (both are considered to be *color models*) you will use:**

   - **CMYK:** Cyan, magenta, yellow, and black are the colors used in professional printing presses and many color printers.

   - **RGB:** Red, green, and blue are the colors used on a computer monitor, for CD-based or Web-based documents, and for some color printers.

   - **Lab:** Luminosity, *A* axis, *B* axis, is a way of defining colors created by the international standards group Commission Internationale de l'Éclairage (the CIE, which translates to *International Commission on Illumination* in English).

   - **A swatch-based model:** Sets of premixed colors from various vendors, including ANPA, DIC, Focoltone, HKS, Pantone, Toyo Ink, and Trumatch for print documents, as well as a Web-specific set and sets specific to Windows and the Mac OS for onscreen documents.

   - **Other Library:** InDesign also has the Other Library option from which you can select any color, tint, or gradient swatch library file in the old Adobe Illustrator 8 format. (You can't use Illustrator's patterned swatches, but don't worry if the swatch file contains them: InDesign will simply ignore them.)

4. **For the CMYK, RGB, and Lab models, use the sliders to create your new color. (A preview appears in the box on the left.) For the swatch-based models, scroll through the lists of colors and select one.**

5. **If you want to create multiple colors, click Add after each color definition and then click Done when you're finished. To create just one color, click OK instead of Add. You can also click Cancel to abort the current color definition.**

The most popular swatch libraries used by North American professional publishers are those from Pantone, whose Pantone Matching System (PMS) is the de facto standard for most publishers in specifying spot-color inks. The Pantone swatch libraries come in several variations, of which InDesign includes 13. Most of the time, you'll use one of the following four:

- ✔ **Pantone Process Coated:** Use this library when you color-separate Pantone colors and your printer uses the standard Pantone-brand process-color inks. (These colors reproduce reliably when color-separated, while the other Pantone swatch libraries' colors often do not.)

- ✔ **Pantone Solid Coated:** Use this library when your printer will use actual Pantone inks (as spot colors) when printing to coated paper stock.

- ✔ **Pantone Solid Matte:** Use this library when your printer will use actual Pantone inks (as spot colors) when printing to matte-finished paper stock.

- ✔ **Pantone Solid Uncoated:** Use this library when your printer will use actual Pantone inks (as spot colors) when printing to uncoated paper stock.

The bad way to create colors

Many people try to use the Color panel (Window⇨Color or F6) to define colors, which can be a mistake. At first, you might not realize that you can create colors from the Color panel. It shows a gradation of the last color used and lets you change the tint for that color on the current object. But if you go to its flyout menu and choose a color model (RGB, CMYK, or Lab), you get a set of mixing controls.

So what's the problem? Colors created through the Color panel won't appear in your Swatches panel, so they can't be used for other objects. They are called *unnamed colors* because they don't appear in the Swatches panel, but may be used by objects in a document, which can cause problems for when you print. (Adobe added them to InDesign to be consistent with how Illustrator defines colors — a foolish consistency.)

Fortunately, there is a way to prevent unnamed colors: If you go to the Color panel and modify a color without thinking about it, choose Add Unnamed Colors from the Swatches panel's flyout menu to add the modified color to the Swatches panel. Of course, if you forget to do this, you have an unnamed color, so it's best to think *Swatches panel* when you think about adding or editing colors instead of the more obvious *Color panel*. Even better, close the Color panel so you're not tempted to use it in the first place.

Similarly, don't use this InDesign feature: the ability to create colors by double-clicking the Stroke and Fill buttons on the Tools panel, using a Photoshop-style color picker. As with colors created in the Color panel, you can rectify this sin by adding any colors created this way to the Swatches panel by using the Swatches panel's Add Unnamed Colors menu item. Otherwise, you run the same risk as creating colors through the Color panel.

Color swatches based on the CMYK colors — such as Focoltone, Pantone Process, and Trumatch — will accurately color-separate and thus print accurately on a printing press because a printing press uses the CMYK colors. Other swatches' colors often do not color-separate accurately because they are supposed to represent special inks that may have added elements like metals and clays designed to give metallic or pastel appearances that simply can't be replicated by combining cyan, magenta, yellow, and black. Similarly, some colors (like several hues of orange and green) can't be accurately created using the CMYK colors.

Creating mixed colors

InDesign offers another type of color: mixed-ink color. Essentially, a mixed-ink color combines a spot color with the default process colors (cyan, magenta, yellow, and black) to create new color swatches. For example, you can combine 38 percent black with 100 percent Pantone 130C to get a darker version of Pantone 130C (called a *duotone*, though InDesign doesn't limit you to mixing spot colors with just black, as traditional duotones do).

To create a mixed-ink swatch, follow these steps:

1. **Select the spot color you want to begin with and then choose New Mixed Ink Swatch from the Swatches panel's flyout menu.**

   The New Mixed Ink Swatch dialog box appears, as shown in Figure 7-3.

Figure 7-3:
The New Mixed Ink Swatch dialog box lets you mix a selected spot color with any or all of the default process colors to create new shades and variations.

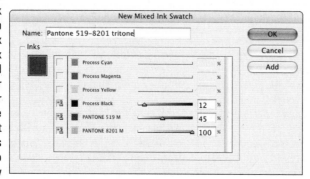

2. **Select the percentages of the spot color and any or all of the default process colors you want to mix and give the new color a name.**

3. **Click Add to add another mixed-ink swatch based on the current spot color.**

   If you're creating just one color, click OK instead of Add. You can click Cancel to abort the current mixed-ink color definition.

4. **Click OK when you're finished.**

There's a related option in the Swatches panel's flyout menu called New Mixed Ink Group. This lets you create a set of colors from the same mix. You get to set the initial percentage of each color you want in the mix and the final value, as well as how many increments of each color you want. InDesign then takes all this information and creates a bunch of color swatches that combine each of the colors at each level so you get a whole range of colors. The idea is to get a set of related colors created for you, such as a set of blue-green hues that range from light aqua to dark marine. Experiment with this expert feature to see what it can do for you.

Defining Tints

A *tint* is simply a shade of a color. InDesign lets you create such tints as separate color swatches — like any other color — so they're easy to use for multiple items. The process is easy:

1. **In the Swatches panel, select a color from which you want to create a tint.**

2. **Using the Swatches panel's flyout menu, select New Tint Swatch.**

   The New Tint Swatch dialog box, shown in Figure 7-4, appears.

3. **Click and drag the slider to adjust the tint, or type a value in a field on the right.**

4. **Click Add to create another tint from the same base color, and then click OK when you're finished. (If you're adding a single tint, there's no need to click Add; just click OK when done.)**

   Click Cancel if you change your mind about the current tint. Any new tint will have the same name as the original color and the percentage of shading, such as Sky Blue 66%.

You can create a tint from a tint, which can be confusing. Fortunately, InDesign goes back to the original color when letting you create the new tint. Thus, if you select Sky Blue 66% and move the slider to 33%, you get a 33 percent tint of the original Sky Blue, not a 33 percent tint of the Sky Blue 66% (which would be equivalent to a 22 percent tint of the original Sky Blue).

You modify and delete tint swatches like any other color swatch, using the Swatches panel's flyout menu.

Figure 7-4:
The New Tint Swatch dialog box lets you define colors; a nearly identical dialog box named Swatch Options lets you edit them.

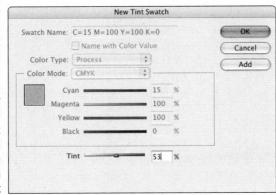

You can also apply tints to objects without creating a separate swatch for each tint. After applying the color (described later in this chapter), select the object and change the value in the Tint field of the Swatches panel, or use its pop-up menu's predefined tint values. Easy as pie!

Working with Gradients

A long-popular design technique is the gradient (also called a *blend* or *graduated fill*), which blends two or more colors in a sequence, going smoothly from, say, green to blue to yellow to orange. InDesign has a powerful gradient-creation feature that lets you define and apply gradients to pretty much any object in InDesign, including text, lines, frames, shapes, and their outlines (strokes).

Creating gradient swatches

In the Swatches panel, where you define colors and tints, you can also define gradients. Just select the New Gradient Swatch option in the flyout menu. You get the dialog box shown in Figure 7-5. The first two options are straightforward:

- ✔ Type a name for the gradient in the Swatch Name field. Picking a name is a bit more difficult than for a color, but use something like "Blue to Red" or "Bright Multihue" or "Logo Gradient" that has a meaning specific to the colors used or to its role in your document.

- ✔ In the Type pop-up menu, choose Linear or Radial. A linear blend goes in one direction, while a radial blend radiates out in a circle from a central point.

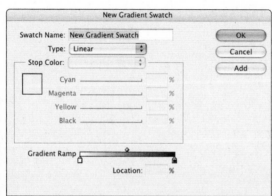

Figure 7-5:
The New
Gradient
Swatch
dialog box.

Now it gets a little tricky. Follow these steps:

1. **Select a stop point — one of the squares at the bottom of the dialog box on either end of the gradient ramp that shows the gradient as you define it.**

   The stop points essentially define the start color (the stop point on the left) and the end color (the stop point on the right). With a stop point selected, you can now define its color.

2. **Choose what color model you want to use — select from CMYK, RGB, LAB, and Swatches in the Stop Color pop-up menu.**

   The area directly beneath the pop-up menu changes accordingly, displaying sliders for CMYK, RGB, or LAB, or a list of all colors from the Swatches panel for Swatches, depending on which model you choose.

3. **Create or select the color you want for that stop point.**

   You can select the [Paper] swatch — essentially, transparency or no color — as a stop point in a gradient. You can also click and drag swatches from the Swatches panel to the gradient ramp.

4. **Repeat Steps 1 to 3 for the other stop point.**

   Note that the color models for the two stop points don't have to be the same — you can blend from a Pantone spot color to a CMYK color, for example. (If a gradient mixes spot colors and process colors, InDesign converts the spot colors to process colors.)

You now have a simple gradient. But you don't have to stop there. Here are your other options:

✔ You can change the rate at which the colors transition by sliding the diamond icons at the top of the gradient ramp.

✔ You can create additional stop points by clicking right below the gradient ramp. By having several stop points, you can have multiple color transitions in a gradient. (Think of them like tab stops in text — you can define as many as you need.) You delete unwanted stop points by clicking and dragging them to the bottom of the dialog box.

Notice that there's a diamond icon between each pair of stop points — that means each pair can have its own transition rate.

When you create a new gradient, InDesign uses the settings from the last one you created. If you want to create a gradient similar to an existing one, click that existing gradient before selecting New Gradient Swatch from the flyout menu. InDesign copies the selected gradient's settings to the new one, which you can then edit. One reason to use this is to create, say, a radial version of an existing linear gradient.

The Swatches panel shows the actual gradient next to its name. The pattern also appears in the Fill button or Stroke button in the Tools panel if that gradient is currently selected as a fill or stroke, as well as in the Gradient button in that panel, whether or not it's currently applied as a fill or stroke.

Understanding the Gradient panel

Just as it does with unnamed colors, InDesign lets you create *unnamed gradients* — gradients that have no swatches. Unlike unnamed colors, you can use these to your heart's content because all colors in a gradient are converted to process colors and/or use defined spot-color swatches — so there are no unnamed colors in their output. The process is pretty much the same as creating a gradient swatch, except that you select an object and then open the Gradient panel (Window⊃Gradient). In that panel, you select a stop point and then choose a color to apply to it by clicking a color in the Swatches panel or in the Color panel. You create and adjust stop points here just as you do when defining a gradient swatch.

The difference? Gradients in the Swatches panel can be reused, whereas gradients applied through the Gradient panel cannot be. But you can add them to the Swatches panel by right-clicking or Control+clicking the gradient in the Tools panel's Fill or Stroke button, and then choosing Add to Swatches in the contextual menu that appears.

The Gradient panel can also manipulate gradient swatches: After you apply a linear gradient — whether via a gradient swatch or as an unnamed gradient — you can change the angle of the gradient, rotating the gradient within the object. Just type the desired degree of rotation in the Angle field to rotate the gradient's direction by the value. Negative values rotate counterclockwise, whereas positive values rotate clockwise.

Note that you can't rotate a radial gradient because it's circular and, thus, any rotation has no effect. That's why InDesign grays out the Angle field for radial gradients.

But you can still adjust the location of a radial gradient — as well as that of a linear gradient — by using the Gradient tool in the Tools panel. After applying a gradient to an object, select the Gradient tool and draw a line in the object, as shown in Figure 7-6:

- For a linear gradient, the start point of your line corresponds to where you want the first stop point of the gradient to be; the end point of the line corresponds to the last stop point. This lets you stretch or compress the gradient, as well as offset the gradient within the object. Also, the angle at which you draw the line becomes the angle for the gradient.

- For a radial gradient, the line becomes the start and end point for the gradient, in effect offsetting it.

Figure 7-6:
At left: The
Gradient
tool lets you
set the
offset, adjust
the gradient
length, and
(for gradient
blends)
adjust the
gradient
angle. At
right: The
Gradient
Feather tool
acts like the
Gradient
tool but
starts with
transparent
as the color.

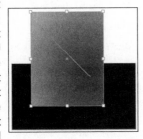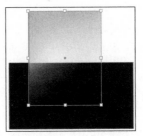

The new Gradient Feather tool — accessed through the Gradient tool's pop-out menu or via the shortcut Shift+G — acts just like the Gradient tool except that it starts with transparency as the initial "color," as shown in Figure 7-6. See Chapter 9 for more on gradient feather and other lighting effects.

Managing Swatches

When you create colors, tints, and gradients, it's easy to go overboard and make too many. You'll also find that different documents have different colors, each created by different people, and you'll likely want to move colors from one document to another. InDesign provides basic tools for managing colors in and across documents.

Editing swatches

It's easy to modify a swatch to change its settings: Just double-click it in the Swatches panel. (You can also choose Swatch options from the Swatches panel's flyout menu.) The Swatch options dialog box will appear, a clone of the New Color Swatch, New Tint Swatch, or New Gradient Swatch dialog box (based on what kind of swatch you double-clicked).

There is a slight difference between the New Swatch dialog boxes and the Swatch Option dialog boxes: The Swatch Option dialog boxes include the Preview option, which lets you see your changes in a selected object (if it's visible on-screen, of course) as you make changes in the Swatch Options dialog box.

Copying swatches

To duplicate a swatch, so you can create a new one based on it, use the Duplicate Swatch option in the Swatches panel. The word *copy* will be added to the name of the new swatch. You edit it — including its name — as you would any swatch.

When selecting swatches for deletion or duplication, you can ⌘+click or Ctrl+click multiple swatches to work on all of them at once. Note that Shift+clicking selects all swatches between the first swatch clicked and the swatch that you Shift+click, whereas ⌘+click or Ctrl+click lets you select specific swatches in any order and in any location in the panel.

Deleting swatches

InDesign makes deleting swatches easy: Just select the color, tint, or gradient in the Swatches panel. Then choose Delete Swatch from the flyout menu, or click the trash can iconic button at the bottom of the Swatches panel.

Well, that's not quite it. You then get the Delete Swatch dialog box, which lets you either assign a new color to anything using the deleted swatch (the Defined Swatch option) or leave the color on any object that is using it but delete the swatch from the Swatches panel (the Unnamed Swatch option). (As explained earlier in this chapter, unnamed colors should be avoided, so if your document uses a color, keep its swatch.)

If you delete a tint and replace it with another color, any object using that tint will get the full-strength version of the new color, not a tint of it. Likewise, if you delete a color swatch that you've based one or more tints on, those tints will also be deleted if you replace the deleted swatch with an unnamed swatch. However, if you delete a color swatch and replace it with a defined swatch, any tints of that deleted swatch will retain their tint percentages of the replacement-defined swatch.

InDesign offers a nice option to quickly find all unused colors in the Swatches panel — the palette menu's Select All Unused option. With this option, you can delete all the unused colors in one fell swoop. Note that you don't get the option to assign each deleted color separately to another color in the Delete Swatch dialog box — they all are replaced with the color you select or are made into unnamed colors. Because no object uses these colors, choosing Unnamed Swatch in essence is the same as replacing them with a color using the Defined Swatch option.

Sampling colors

You may wonder how you can use colors in your imported graphics for which InDesign can't find any swatch information, such as in TIFF files or photos embedded in a PDF file. As you might expect, InDesign provides a way to capture these colors: the Eyedropper tool. Here's how it works:

1. **In the Tools panel or Swatches panel, choose the Fill iconic button or Stroke iconic button.** It doesn't really matter which unless you will immediately create a shape or enter text after capturing the desired color; in that case, choose whichever aspect you'll want the new object or text to have the color applied to.

2. **Select the Eyedropper tool and then click on the graphic where the desired color is used.** The Fill or Stroke iconic button will now have that color. (If the Eyedropper tool is not visible in the Tools panel, look for the Measure tool, then click and hold down its icon to get the pop-up menu that lets you select the Eyedropper tool.)

3. **The Eyedropper tool changes to the Marker tool.** Any object you select with the Marker tool will have the color applied to its fill or stroke, depending on whether the Fill or Stroke iconic button is active. Note you can switch between the Eyedropper and Marker tools to select different colors and apply them by holding the Option or Alt key to get the Eyedropper tool back, then releasing it to switch to the Marker tool.

4. **To add the new, unnamed color to the Swatches panel, Control+click or right-click the Fill iconic button or Stroke iconic button (whichever has the captured color) and choose Add to Swatches from the contextual menu that appears.** Now you can edit and apply the captured color like any other color swatch.

The figure below shows a composite image that highlights the Eyedropper tool at center left and the Marker tool at right.

If you delete a swatch and replace it with an unnamed swatch, you can recapture that deleted swatch later by choosing the Add Unnamed Colors menu item in the Swatches panel's flyout menu.

Importing swatches

A quick way to import specific colors from another InDesign document or template is to click and drag the colors from that other file's Swatches panel into your current document or template.

You can import colors from other Creative Suite programs from which you have saved Adobe Swatch Exchange color library files, choosing Load Swatches from the Swatches panel's flyout menu. You can also import swatches directly from other InDesign documents. From the resulting dialog box, navigate to the file that contains the colors you want to import, select that file, and click Open.

When you import color swatches from other documents or Adobe Swatch Exchange files, InDesign brings in *all* the colors. You cannot choose specific colors to import.

Also, when you import a graphic file in PDF or EPS format, any named colors (swatches) in that file are automatically added to the Swatches panel.

Exporting swatches

You can do more than import swatches. InDesign also lets you save swatches into color library files for use by other Creative Suite 2 or 3 users. Just select the colors you want to save and then choose Save Swatches from the Swatches panel's flyout menu. You are asked to give the color library file a name before you save it.

InDesign does not include mixed-ink colors when you save swatches for use by other Creative Suite programs. Any selected such swatches are simply ignored.

Applying Swatches

Applying colors, tints, and gradients to objects in InDesign is easy. Select the object, click the Formatting Affects Text button or Formatting Affects Container iconic button in the Swatches or Gradient panel as appropriate. If you're using the Swatches panel, click the appropriate swatch; if you're using the Gradient panel, adjust the gradient as desired.

When it comes to coloring graphics in InDesign, you can apply color and tints to grayscale and black-and-white bitmapped images, such as those in the TIFF and Photoshop formats. But you cannot color vector-based graphics (such as those in the Illustrator and EPS formats) or color bitmapped images.

Another way to apply colors, tints, and gradients is by selecting the object and using the Formatting Affects Text, Formatting Affects Content, Fill, or Stroke iconic buttons in the Tools panel to define what part of the object you want to color. You can use the Swatches or Gradients panels to select a swatch, or pick the last-used color and gradient from the Apply Color and Apply Gradient iconic buttons on the Tools panel, shown in Figure 7-7.

For tints, you can use a tint swatch, or you can simply apply a color from the Swatches panel and enter a tint value in the panel's Tint field.

Figure 7-7:
The Tools panel lets you choose what part of an object you want to color, as well as apply the last-used color or gradient.

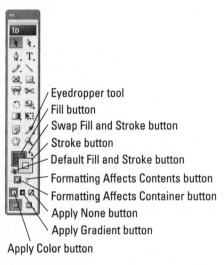

Eyedropper tool
Fill button
Swap Fill and Stroke button
Stroke button
Default Fill and Stroke button
Formatting Affects Contents button
Formatting Affects Container button
Apply None button
Apply Gradient button
Apply Color button

When applying color to text, you can apply it to all the text in the frame by using the Formatting Affects Text iconic button (which is what the Formatting Affects Contents iconic button is renamed when you select text), or to specific text by highlighting that text with the Type tool.

You can also apply color as part of your character and paragraph styles in the Character Color pane when creating or editing styles. See Chapter 14 for more on styles, and Chapters 15 through 17 for more on text formatting.

You can also apply colors and tints to gaps in strokes by using the Stroke panel's flyout menu (select Show Options and select a gap color). Open the Stroke panel by choosing Window⇨Stroke or by pressing ⌘+F10 or Ctrl+F10.

Part III
Object Essentials

The 5th Wave   By Rich Tennant

Principal

"I found these two in the multimedia lab morphing faculty members into farm animals."

In this part . . .

The rubber really hits the road when you've got your basic layout structure in place. Now you can focus on the meat of your documents: the objects that contain your text and graphics. It's amazing all objects you can create — from simple rectangles to complex curves. And it's equally amazing all the things you can do to objects, such as rotate them, align them, and apply special effects like drop shadows and directional feathers (you'll just have to read on to see what these are!). And you can even save a lot of these settings so you can apply them consistently to other objects later — a real timesaver that also ensures quality results. You'll find out about all that and more in this part.

Note that you can apply most of these effects to objects whether or not they already contain their graphics and text — so if you're a really structured kind of person, you'll probably create your basic object containers first and apply your effects to them and then bring in the text and graphics. But if you're more free-form in your approach, you'll likely bring in all your text and graphics and then start arranging the objects that contain them to produce your final layout. Either way, you'll apply the techniques you discover here.

Chapter 8

Creating Essential Elements

· ·

· ·

*T*he fundamental components of any layout are its objects. An *object* is a container that can (but doesn't have to) hold text or graphics, as well as display attributes such as color, strokes, and gradients. This chapter explains how to create these building blocks: frames, shapes, lines, and paths, as well as the strokes you apply to them.

Creating Frames and Shapes

When an object contains an imported graphic or text, or if an object is created as a placeholder for a graphic or text, it's referred to as a *frame* in InDesign. Otherwise, it is called a *shape*.

The difference between frames and shapes is artificial, and because a shape can easily become a frame simply by placing text or graphics into it, it's easiest to think of shapes and frames as the same thing. I tend to use the word "frame" to mean either frames or shapes.

Designing pages in InDesign is largely a matter of creating and modifying frames and shapes, as well as modifying the text and graphics that the frames contain.

As Figure 8-1 shows, the Tools panel contains several tools for creating both shapes and frames:

✔ The Rectangle, Ellipse, and Polygon shape tools (the Ellipse and Polygon tools are available through the pop-up menu that appears if you click and hold on the Rectangle tool).

✔ The Rectangle Frame, Ellipse Frame, and Polygon Frame tools (the Ellipse Frame and Polygon Frame tools are available through the pop-up menu that appears if you click and hold on the Rectangle Frame tool).

✔ The Type tool (which can create rectangular text frames in addition to letting you work with text).

Frame tool

Type tool

Line tool

Shape tools

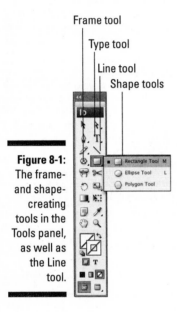

Figure 8-1: The frame- and shape- creating tools in the Tools panel, as well as the Line tool.

Here's how to create a frame (or shape):

1. **Select the desired tool from the Tools panel.**

   For the Polygon and Polygon Frame tools, you can set the shape and number of sides by double-clicking the tool and then using the dialog box that appears. Figure 8-2 shows that dialog box and example starburst.

2. **Move the mouse pointer anywhere within the currently displayed page or on the pasteboard.**

3. **Click and drag in any direction.**

   As you drag, a crosshair pointer appears in the corner opposite your starting point; a colored rectangle indicates the boundary of the frame. (The color will be blue for objects on the default layer; objects on other layers will have that layer's color. See Chapter 5 for more on layers.) You can look at the width and height values displayed in the Control panel or the Transform panel as you drag to help you get the size you want. Holding down the Shift key as you drag limits the tool to creating a frame or shape within a square bounding box.

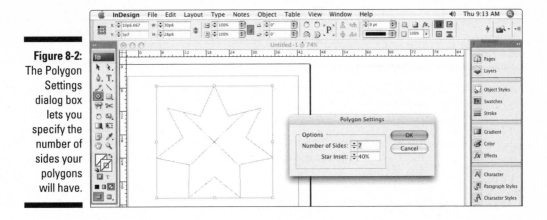

Figure 8-2:
The Polygon
Settings
dialog box
lets you
specify the
number of
sides your
polygons
will have.

4. **When the frame is the size and shape you want, release the mouse button.**

Pretty easy, huh? At this point, you can begin typing in the frame, paste text or a graphic into it, or import a text or a graphics file, as Chapters 11 and 17 explain.

If you create a text frame with the Type tool, be sure not to click in an existing text frame when your intention is to create a new one. If you click within an existing frame when the Type tool is selected, the flashing cursor appears, and InDesign thinks you want to type text.

When any of the frame-creation tools is selected, you can create as many new frames as you want. Simply keep clicking, dragging, and releasing. After you create a graphics frame, you can modify it (without changing tools) by adding a border or a colored background or by applying any of the effects — such as rotation, shear, and scale — in the Control panel. You can also move or resize a graphics frame, but you have to switch to the Selection tool or the Direct Selection tool to do so. Chapter 9 explains how to resize, move, delete, and otherwise manipulate frames and other objects.

Reshaping Frames and Shapes

Sometimes, a frame or shape needs to be more than resized or moved. It needs to be reshaped. InDesign makes it easy to change an object's shape:

✔ The simplest way is to select an object with the Direct Selection tool, and then drag any of the handles or frame edges. Notice how the frame's shape actually changes, as show in Figure 8-3.

✔ To change a shape more radically, choose the desired shape from Object➪Convert Shape's submenu. Your choices are Rectangle, Rounded Rectangle, Beveled Rectangle, Inverse Rounded Rectangle, Ellipse, Triangle, Polygon, Line, and Orthogonal Line. (Note that if you choose Polygon, InDesign will use whatever the last polygon settings were, which you can see by double-clicking the Polygon or Polygon Frame tool. Also, if you try to convert a text frame into a line, InDesign will abort the action, telling you it can't do the conversion.)

✔ You can manually edit a shape by adding or removing anchor points — the points in a shape's edges that you can adjust, as described in the next section.

InDesign CS3 introduces a quick new way to switch between the Selection tool and the Direct Selection tool: Just double-click an object.

Figure 8-3: Reshaping a frame by dragging its handle with the Direct Selection tool.

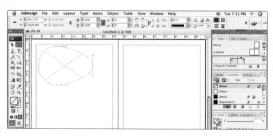

Creating Lines and Paths

When you're drawing the old-fashioned way, with pen and paper, you typi-cally use one tool to draw straight lines, curved lines, and free-form objects. InDesign is less flexible, using different tools for different kinds of lines. InDesign lets you create straight lines with the Line tool and zigzag lines, curved lines, and free-form shapes with the Pen and Type on a Path tools. (Those non-straight lines and free-form shapes are called *paths* in InDesign.)

Drawing a straight line

Although they're not as flashy or versatile as shapes and paths, lines can serve many useful purposes in well-designed pages. For example, you can use plain ol' vertical rules to separate columns of text in a multicolumn page or the rows and columns of data in a table. Dashed lines are useful for indicating folds and cut lines on brochures and coupons. And lines with arrowheads are handy if you have to create a map or a technical illustration.

Follow these steps to draw a simple, straight line:

1. **Select the Line tool (or press \).**

   (Figure 8-1 shows the Line tool.)

2. **Move the pointer anywhere within the currently displayed page or on the pasteboard.**

3. **Click and drag the mouse in any direction.**

   As you drag, a thin, blue line appears from the point where you first clicked to the current position of the cross-hair pointer. Holding down the Shift key as you drag constrains the line to a horizontal, vertical, or 45-degree diagonal line.

4. **When the line is the length and angle you want, release the mouse button.**

   Don't worry too much about being precise when you create a line. You can always go back later and fine-tune it.

When you release the mouse button after creating a line, the line is active. As illustrated in Figure 8-4, if the Selection tool was previously selected, the line appears within a rectangular bounding box, which contains eight resizing handles. If the Direct Selection tool was previously selected, moveable anchor points appear at the ends of the line. In either case, you have to choose the right tool if you want to change the shape or size of the bounding box or the line:

✔ The Selection tool lets you change the shape of the line's bounding box (which also changes the angle and length of the line) by dragging any of the resizing handles.

✔ The Direct Selection tool lets you change the length and angle of the line itself by moving anchor points on the frame.

Figure 8-4:
A line selected with the Selection tool (left) and the Direct Selection tool (right).

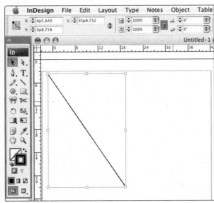 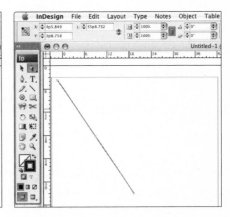

As long as the Line tool is selected, you can create as many new lines as you want. Simply keep clicking, dragging, and releasing.

When you create a line, it takes on the characteristics specified in the Stroke panel (Window⇨Stroke, or ⌘+F10 or Ctrl+10), covered later in this chapter. When you first open a document, the default line width is 1 point. If you want to change the appearance of your lines, double-click the Line tool and adjust the Weight setting in the Stroke panel that appears. If you make this adjustment when no document is open, all new documents will use the new line settings.

Understanding paths

Paths are a lot more complex than lines, so it's important that you understand some of the theory behind paths because that knowledge will help you create and manipulate them more easily.

Every object you create with InDesign's object-creation tools is a *path*. Regardless of the tool you use to create a path, you can change its appearance by modifying any of four properties that all paths share:

- ✔ **Closure:** A path is either open or closed. Straight lines created with the Line tool and curved and zigzag lines created with the Pen tool are examples of open paths. Basic shapes created with the Ellipse, Rectangle, and Polygon tools and free-form shapes created with the Pen and Pencil tools are examples of closed shapes. A closed free-form shape is an uninterrupted path with no end points.

- ✔ **Stroke:** If you want to make a path visible, you can apply a stroke to it by selecting it with a selection tool, entering a Weight value in the Stroke panel (covered later in this chapter) (Window⇨Stroke or ⌘+F10 or Ctrl+F10), and selecting a color from the Swatches panel (see Chapter 7). (An unselected, unstroked path is not visible.)

- ✔ **Fill:** A color, color tint, or gradient applied to the background of a path is called a *fill*. You apply fills by using the Swatches panel.

- ✔ **Contents:** You can place a text file or a graphics file in any path except a straight line. When a path is used to hold text or a graphic, the path functions as a frame. Although InDesign can place text or graphics in an open path, placing text and pictures in closed paths is far more common than placing them in open paths. In addition to putting text inside paths, you can also have text on the path itself, following its shape, as Chapter 17 explains.

No matter how simple or complicated, all paths are made up of the same components. Figure 8-5 shows the parts that make up a path:

- ✔ A path contains one or more straight or curved *segments*.

- ✔ An anchor point is located at each end of every segment. The anchor points at the ends of a closed path are called *end points*. When you create a path of any kind, anchor points are automatically placed at the end of each segment. After you create a path, you can move, add, delete, and change the direction of corner points.

- ✔ InDesign has two kinds of anchor points: *smooth points* and *corner points*. A smooth point connects two adjoining curved segments in a continuous, flowing curve. At a corner point, adjoining segments — straight or curved — meet at an angle. The corners of a rectangular path are the most common corner points.

- ✔ A *direction line* runs through each anchor point and has a handle at both ends. You can control the curve that passes through an anchor point by dragging a direction line's handles, as I explain a little later on.

Figure 8-5:
Anchor points can be corner or smooth, resulting in angular (top) or curved (bottom) connections between segments.

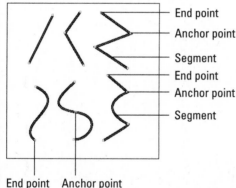

End point
Anchor point
Segment
End point
Anchor point
Segment

End point   Anchor point

Drawing your own paths

Even if you're an artistic master with a piece of charcoal or a Number 2 pencil, you need to practice with the Pen tool for a while before your drawing skills kick in. The good news is that after you get comfortable using the Pen tool, you can draw any shape you can imagine. (Of course, if you can't draw very well in the first place, using the Pen tool won't magically transform you into a master illustrator!) If this is new terrain for you, start simply and proceed slowly.

When creating paths, use as few anchor points as possible. As you become more comfortable creating free-form paths, you should find yourself using fewer anchor points to create paths.

For an easy way to draw free-form shapes, use the Pencil tool. This tool simply traces the movement of your mouse (or pen tablet) as you move it, much like a pencil works on paper. Although not as exact as the Pen tool, the Pencil tool creates Bézier curves that you can later edit. Note that the Pencil tool is not meant for creating straight lines — unless you are capable of drawing perfectly straight lines by hand, that is.

Straight and zigzag lines

Follow these steps to draw lines with straight segments, such as a zigzag:

1. **Select the Pen tool.**

2. **Move the Pen pointer to where you want to start your line segment.**

3. **Click and release the mouse button. (Make sure you don't drag before you release the mouse button.)**

   An anchor point appears; it looks like a small, filled-in square.

4. **Move the Pen pointer to where you want to place the next anchor point.**

5. **Click and release the mouse button.**

   InDesign draws a straight line between the two anchor points. The first anchor point changes to a hollow square, and the second anchor point is filled in, which indicates that it is the active anchor point.

6. **Repeat Steps 4 and 5 for each additional anchor point.**

   To reposition an anchor point after you click the mouse button but before you release it, hold down the spacebar and drag. Otherwise, you need to select it with the Direct Selection tool after you finish drawing the line and then click and drag it to its new location.

7. **To complete the path, ⌘+click or Ctrl+click elsewhere on the page or simply choose another tool.**

   If you ⌘+click or Ctrl+click, the Pen tool remains active, so you can continue creating new paths.

Curved lines

Knowing how to draw zigzag lines is fine, but chances are, you want to draw curved shapes as well. The basic process is similar to drawing straight segments, but drawing curved paths (technically called *Bézier paths*) is more complicated and will take you some time to get the hang of.

How smooth and corner points work

Bézier paths have two kinds of points to join segments: corner and smooth.

The two segments that form a smooth point's direction line work together as a single, straight line. When you move a handle, the line acts like a teeter-totter; the opposite handle moves in the opposite direction. If you shorten one of the segments, the length of the other segment doesn't change. The angle and length of direction lines determine the shape of the segments with which they're associated.

A corner point that connects two curved segments has two direction lines; a corner point that connects two straight segments has no direction lines; and a corner point that connects a straight and curved segment has one direction line. If you drag a corner point's direction line, the other direction line, if there is one, is not affected.

If you want to draw a continuously curvy path that contains no corner points and no straight segments, you should create only smooth points as you draw. Here's how:

1. **Select the Pen tool.**

2. **Move the Pen pointer to where you want to start the curve segment.**

3. **Click and hold down the mouse button.**

   The arrowhead pointer appears.

4. **Drag the mouse in the direction of the next point you intend to create and then release the mouse button.**

   As you drag, the anchor point, its direction line, and the direction line's two handles are displayed, as shown in Figure 8-6.

   If you hold down the Shift key as you drag, the angle of the direction line is limited to increments of 45 degrees.

Figure 8-6:
To create a smooth point when beginning a path, click and hold the mouse and drag in the direction of the next point.

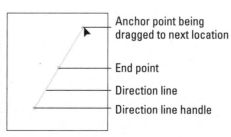

Anchor point being dragged to next location

End point

Direction line

Direction line handle

5. **Move the Pen pointer to where you want to place the next anchor point — and end the first segment — and then drag the mouse.**

    If you drag in roughly the same direction as the direction line of the previous point, you create an S-shaped curve; if you drag in the opposite direction, you create a C-shaped curve.

6. **When the curve between the two anchor points looks how you want it to look, release the mouse button.**

    Alternatively, when you want to connect curved segments to corner points (shown in Figure 8-7), move the Pen pointer to where you want to place the next anchor point — and end the first segment — and then press and hold Option or Alt as you click and drag the mouse. As you drag, the anchor point's handle moves, and the direction line changes from a straight line to two independent segments. The angle of the direction line segment that you create when you drag the handle determines the slope of the next segment.

7. **Repeat Steps 5 and 6 for each additional desired curved segment.**

8. **To complete the path, ⌘+click or Ctrl+click elsewhere on the page or simply choose another tool.**

    If you ⌘+click or Ctrl+click, the Pen tool remains active, so you can create new paths.

    You can also complete the path by clicking on the first point you created. This creates a closed path.

Figure 8-7:
Three corner points join four curved segments. The direction handles of the two right-most segments are visible.

Closed paths

A *closed path* is simply a path that ends where it began. When it comes to creating closed paths with the Pen tool, the process is exactly the same as for creating open paths, as explained earlier in this section, with one difference at the end:

✔ To create a straight segment between the end point and the last anchor point you created, click and release the mouse button.

✔ To create a curved segment, click and drag the mouse in the direction of the last anchor point you created, and then release the mouse button.

Just like an open path, a closed path can contain straight and/or curved segments and smooth and/or corner anchor points. All the techniques explained earlier in this chapter for drawing lines with curved and straight segments and smooth and corner points apply when you draw closed paths.

You can also, of course, edit and adjust your curves in InDesign. But this requires some more expertise with drawing tools such as those in Adobe Illustrator and is beyond the scope of this book. Check out *Illustrator CS3 For Dummies* by Ted Alspach or *Adobe InDesign CS3 Bible* by Galen Gruman (both by Wiley Publishing) for more details.

Applying Strokes

All objects have a stroke with a width of 0 built in, so you never really have to add strokes. But to use them, you need to modify them so they have some thickness onto which you can apply attributes such as colors and gradients.

Adding fills

The option to add a stroke to any shape becomes even more powerful when combined with the option to fill any shape with a color or tint. For example, adding a fill to a text frame is an effective way to draw attention to a sidebar.

Adding a fill to a shape is much like adding a stroke, and the options available for specifying color and tint are identical. The only difference is that you click the Fill button in the Tools panel or Swatches panel rather than the Stroke button.

Setting stroke appearance

The Stroke panel is where you give the stroke its width, as well as apply the type of stroke and other attributes:

The shortcut for the Stroke panel has changed in InDesign CS3: It is now ⌘+F10 or Ctrl+F10, no longer just F10. (F10 still works, though it may conflict with the Mac's Exposé software.)

1. **Select either of the selection tools and click the object whose stroke you want to modify.**

2. **If the Stroke panel is not displayed, show it by choosing Window⇨Stroke or by pressing ⌘+F10 or Ctrl+F10.**

   Figure 8-8 shows the panel.

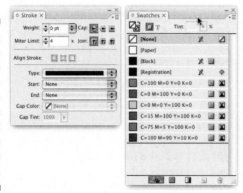

Figure 8-8:
The Stroke panel (top) and the Swatches panel that is often used at the same time (bottom).

3. **To change the width of the stroke, enter a new value in the Weight field.**

   You can also change the Weight value by choosing a new value from the field's pop-up menu or by clicking the up and down arrows. (Each click increases or decreases the stroke by 1 point.)

4. **Set the Miter Limit.**

   The default of 4 is fine for almost all frames. You rarely need to use this feature, so don't worry about it.

5. **Click any of the three Cap iconic buttons to specify how dashes will look if you create a dashed stroke (covered in Step 9).**

   Experiment with them in your objects to see which looks best for your situation.

6. **Click any of the three Join iconic buttons to specify how corners are handled.**

   Again, experiment with these to see what works best for you.

7. **Choose an Align Stroke option.**

   The default is the first button, Align Stroke to Center, which has the stroke straddle the frame. You can also choose Align Stroke to Inside, which places the entire thickness inside the frame boundary, or Align Stroke to Outside, which places the entire thickness outside the frame boundary.

8. **You can also choose end points for your strokes (this only affects lines, not rectangles, ellipses, and other closed-loop shapes) by using the Start and End pop-up menus.**

   Figure 8-9 shows the options.

Figure 8-9: The Start options in the Stroke panel. (The End options are identical.)

9. **To create a dashed line instead of a solid line, choose an option from the Type pop-up menu.**

   (These are also available from the Control panel.) Choose from 18 types of predefined dashes and stripes. The Gap Color and Gap Tint fields at the bottom of the Stroke panel become active as well, to let you choose a specific color and tint for the gaps in dashes and stripes.

Now that you have a visible stroke, you want to color it. Here's how:

1. **Select either of the selection tools and click the frame to which you want to add a stroke.**

2. **Click the Stroke button in the Swatches panel or Tools panel.**

3. **You now can click a color, tint, or gradient from the Swatches panel, or click one of the three boxes at the bottom of the Tools panel, which let you use (from left to right) the last-selected color, last-selected gradient, or None. (This removes the stroke's color, tint, or gradient.)**

For information about adding colors to the Swatches panel and applying colors to objects, see Chapter 7.

Creating stroke styles

InDesign lets you create custom strokes, known as *stroke styles,* in any of three types: dashed, dotted, and striped. To create custom dashes or stripes, choose the Stroke Styles option in the Stroke panel's flyout menu. In the resulting Stroke Styles dialog box, you can create new strokes, edit or delete existing ones, and import strokes from a stroke styles file, which you create by saving a document's strokes as a separate file for import into other documents. Stroke style files have the filename extension .inst.

Note that you cannot edit or delete the seven default stripe patterns shown in the Stroke Styles dialog box, nor can you edit or delete the default dash patterns — they're not even available in the dialog box. When you edit or create a stroke pattern, you get the New Stroke Style dialog box, shown in Figure 8-10. In the Name field, enter a name for your stroke. In the Type pop-up menu, you can choose to create (or convert a stripe you are editing to) a dashed, dotted, or striped stroke.

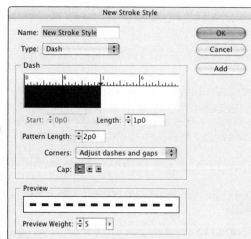

Figure 8-10:
The dashes version of the New Stroke Style dialog box.

For dashes, you can resize the dash component by dragging the down-pointing triangle at the end of the dash in the ruler section. You can add dash segments by simply clicking the ruler and dragging a segment to the desired width. Or you can use the Start and Length fields to manually specify them. The Pattern Length field is where you indicate the length of the segment that will be repeated to create a dashed line.

In the Corners pop-up menu, you tell InDesign whether to adjust how the dashes and gaps are handled at corners; the default is Adjust Dashes and Gaps, a setting you should keep — it will make sure your corners have dash segments that extend along both sides of the corner, which looks neater. (Your other options are Adjust Dashes, Adjust Gaps, and None.) You can also choose a cap style and the stroke weight. The preview section of the pane lets you see your dash as you create or edit it.

For dots, you get a similar dialog box as for dashes. The Start and Length fields disappear, replaced with the Center field that determines where any added dots are placed on the ruler. (The initial dot, shown as a half-circle, starts at 0 and cannot be moved or deleted.) The Caps field is also gone.

To delete a dash or dot segment, just drag it to the left, off the ruler.

For stripes, you also get a similar dialog box. The principle is the same as for dashes: You create segments (in this case vertical, not horizontal) for the stripes by dragging on the ruler. However, the stripes version of the dialog box expresses its values in percentages because the actual thickness of each stripe is determined by the stroke weight — the thicker the stroke, the thicker each stripe is in the overall stroke.

In all three versions of the New Stroke Style dialog box, you click Add to add the stroke to your document, and then you can create a new stroke. When you're done creating strokes, click OK. (When editing a stroke, the Add button won't be available.)

Be sure to use the Preview Weight slider shown in Figure 8-10. This is available in all three versions of the New Stroke Style dialog box. It lets you increase or decrease the preview size so you can better see thin or small elements in your stroke.

Chapter 9

Manipulating Objects

● ●

In This Chapter

▶ Selecting objects

▶ Resizing and scaling objects

▶ Moving and deleting objects

▶ Keeping objects from printing

▶ Rotating, shearing, and flipping objects

▶ Replacing object attributes

▶ Applying corner options

▶ Using transparency and lighting effects

● ●

*F*rames, shapes, lines, and paths are the building blocks of your layout. But as anyone who ever played with Legos or Tinkertoys knows, it's how you manipulate the building blocks that results in a unique creation, whether it be a Lego house, a Tinkertoys crane, or an InDesign layout.

InDesign provides a lot of control over layout objects so that you can create really interesting, dynamic publications suited to any purpose. In this chapter, I explain the controls that apply to all objects.

This chapter focuses on various effects and actions that apply to any frame or path. Chapter 17 covers various actions specific to text frames and paths, while Chapter 19 covers actions specific to graphics frames. Chapter 8 explains how to add frames, shapes, lines, and paths in the first place. Chapter 11 explains how to align objects and precisely position them.

Selecting Objects

Before you can manipulate an object, you have to select it so that InDesign knows what you want to work on. To select an object (rather than its contents), use the Selection tool. Selected items will display their item boundary (a rectangle that encompasses the object) as well as eight small resizing handles (one at each of the four corners and one midway between each side of the item boundary). Figure 9-1 shows an example.

Figure 9-1:
When you
select a
frame with
the
Selection
tool, the
bounding
box is
displayed
with eight
resizing
handles.

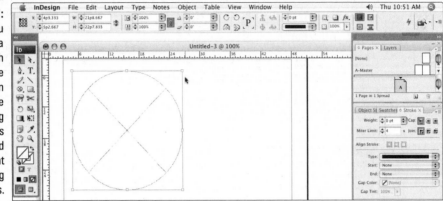

To select an individual object, just click it with the Selection tool. To select multiple objects, you have several options:

- ✔ Click the first object and Shift+click each additional object.

- ✔ Click and drag the mouse to create a selection rectangle (called a *marquee*) that encompasses at least part of each desired object. When you release the mouse, all objects that this marquee touches are selected.

- ✔ Choose Edit⇨Select All or press ⌘+A or Ctrl+A to select all objects on the current spread.

If an object is on a master page and you're working on a document page, you must Shift+⌘+click or Ctrl+Shift+click the object to select it. How do you know whether an object is on a master page? Easy: If you try to select it by clicking and it doesn't become selected, it must be on a master page.

Choose View⇨Show Frame Edges or press Control+⌘+H or Ctrl+H to see object edges if they aren't already visible.

The shortcut for View⇨Show Frame Edges has changed in InDesign CS3 for Mac: It is now Control+⌘+H (the Windows shortcut, Ctrl+H, is unchanged).

These options are pretty easy, but it can get tricky when you want to select objects that overlap or are obscured by other objects (see Chapter 11 for more details on object stacking). So how do you select them?

One way is to use the Select Previous Object or Select Next Object iconic buttons in the Control panel. (If you Shift+click either button, InDesign jumps past four objects and selects the fifth one. If you ⌘+click or Control+click either button, InDesign selects to the bottommost or topmost object, respectively.)

If you use the Select Previous Object or Select Next Object iconic buttons and reach the top or bottom of the object stack, InDesign CS3 now cycles back. For example, if you reach the topmost object and click Select Previous Object, InDesign CS3 now moves to the bottommost object. In previous versions, you had to go all the way back to the bottom by using the Select Next Object button — there was no way to just loop around.

Another way to select buried objects is by using the Select submenu option in the Object menu.

The first four options in the Select submenu let you select another object relative to the currently selected object:

- ✔ First Object Above (Option+Shift+⌘+] or Ctrl+Alt+Shift+]) selects the topmost object.

- ✔ Next Object Above (Option+⌘+] or Ctrl+Alt+]) selects the object immediately on top of the current object.

- ✔ Next Object Below (Option+⌘+[or Ctrl+Alt+[) selects the object immediately under the current object.

- ✔ Last Object Below (Option+Shift+⌘+[or Ctrl+Alt+Shift+[) selects the bottommost object.

If no objects are selected, InDesign bases its selection on the order in which the objects were created, the topmost object being the one that was most recently created.

You can also access these four selection options by Control+clicking or right-clicking an object and choosing the Select menu from the contextual menu that appears.

The Select submenu has four other options:

- ✔ If you select an object's content (text or graphic), choose Object⇨ Select⇨Container to choose the frame or path. Using this option is the same as selecting the object with the Selection tool.

- ✔ If an object has content (text or graphic) and you select it, choose Object⇨Select⇨Content to choose the content within the object. This is basically the same as selecting the frame with the Direct Selection tool (which I explain later in this chapter).

- ✔ If you select an object in a group of objects by using the Direct Selection tool, choose Object⇨Select⇨Previous Object in Group to navigate to the previous object in the group.

- ✔ Similarly, if you select an object in a group of objects by using the Direct Selection tool, choose Object⇨Select⇨Next Object in Group to navigate to the next object in the group.

Object creation order determines what is "previous" or "next" in a group.

The Control panel also provides iconic buttons to select the next or previous object, as well as to select the content or container (frame). These last two buttons appear only if you have selected a group. The buttons for selecting the next or previous object appear only if you are using the Direct Selection tool, while the buttons for selecting the content or container appear whether you are using the Selection or Direct Selection tool. (Yes, this is very confusing!) Figure 9-2 shows the buttons.

Figure 9-2:
The Control
panel
buttons for
selecting
the next and
previous
objects in a
group, as
well as for
selecting
contents
versus
containers.

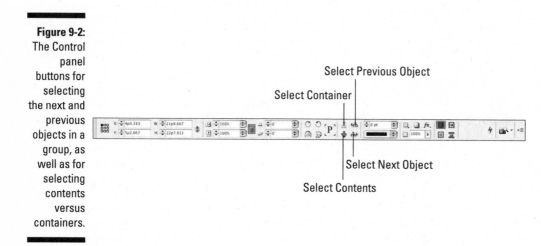

Select Previous Object

Select Container

Select Next Object

Select Contents

To deselect objects, just click another object, an empty part of your page, or the pasteboard. To deselect individual objects after you have selected multiple objects, Shift+click those you want to deselect.

The Direct Selection tool lets you select any of the individual anchor points (and direction handles of free-form shapes and curved lines) on an object. If you use the Direct Selection tool to click an object that has a bounding box, the shape within is selected, and the bounding box is deselected. You use this tool to work on the contents independently of its container frame. You can also move a graphic within its frame by clicking within the object (see Chapter 19).

Resizing and Scaling Objects

Two closely related features are resizing and scaling. What's the difference? Resizing affects just the container — the frame or path — whereas scaling affects both the container and its contents.

Resizing objects

You resize objects in pretty much the same way you move them: by using the mouse for inexact sizes or the Control panel for precise sizes.

To resize an object with the mouse, click and drag one of the frame's (or path's) handles with the Selection tool. (Hold the Shift key as you drag to maintain the proportions of the frame.) Drag a corner handle to resize both the width and height or a side handle to resize just the height or width. This will leave the contents' size unchanged but change the size of the frame or path.

You can also enter new values in the W: and H: fields (for *width* and *height*) of the Control panel. This action also does not change the contents' size.

Remember those reference points for positioning an object from Chapter 1? They come into play for resizing objects as well. Basically, the object will grow or shrink starting from the selected reference point, called the *control point*. So if the upper-left reference point is selected and you enter greater W: and H: values, the object will add the extra width to the right and the extra height below. But if you choose the center reference point, it will grow on both sides as well as on the top and bottom, spreading the extra size evenly.

Another way to resize a frame — this doesn't apply to paths — is to choose Object⇨Fit Frame to Content or press Option+⌘+C or Ctrl+Alt+C. For a graphic, this makes the frame the same size as the graphic itself. For text, this increases or decreases the depth of the text frame to match the depth of the text; it does not widen or narrow the frame.

Double-clicking one of a frame's four handles — the squares at the midpoints of each side — will resize the frame to the content in that axis. For example, double-clicking the left or right handles will fit the frame to the contents' width, while double-clicking the top or bottom handle will fit the frame to the contents' height. Likewise, double-clicking a corner handle will resize the frame in both directions.

Scaling objects

InDesign offers several ways to *scale* an object, resizing both its contents and its frame (or path):

✔ Enter percentage values in the Scale X Percentage and Scale Y Percentage fields of the Control panel. If the icon to the right of these fields shows a solid chain, adjusting one field automatically adjusts the other by the same percentage, creating proportional resizing. If the icon shows a broken chain, the two dimensions will be resized independently, distorting the contents. Click the iconic button to toggle between the unbroken chain and broken chain icons.

✔ You can also scale an object using the mouse. Select the object with the Selection tool, make sure the desired control point is active to control where the scaling operation starts, and then select the Scale tool. Now drag the mouse away from the object to enlarge it or into the object to reduce it. Objects scaled this way are scaled unproportionally; to scale the object proportionally, hold the Shift key when moving the mouse. (You can also use the Free Transform tool in the same way.)

✔ For graphics frames, use the content-fitting options in the Object menu and Control panel, described in Chapter 19.

Moving Objects

The easiest way to move an object is by using the mouse. With the Selection tool, click an object and drag it to a new location. When you release the mouse, the object will be deposited in the new location.

If you want to more precisely move an object, you can enter specific X: and Y: coordinates in the Control panel, as explained in Chapter 11.

Be sure to select the correct reference point to be used as the control point when entering coordinates. The little squares at the top-left of the Control panel and Transform panel represent the object's reference points (corners, side midpoints, and center). Click a reference point to make it the control point (it will turn black, the others will turn white); all coordinates are now based on this point.

Deleting Objects

Alas, not all the objects you create will survive all the way to the final version of your publication. Some will wind up on the cutting room floor. You can always move an object to the pasteboard if you're not sure whether you want to get rid of it altogether (objects on the pasteboard don't print). But when it's time to ax an object, oblivion is just a keystroke or two away.

If you delete a text or graphics frame or path, the contents are removed as well as the frame.

Here's how to delete objects: Using any selection tool, select the object or objects you want to delete and then press the Delete key or Backspace key. You can also delete a selected item by choosing Edit➪Clear.

Choosing Edit⇨Cut or pressing ⌘+X or Ctrl+X also removes a selected object. However, in this case a copy of the object is saved to the Clipboard and can be pasted elsewhere (by choosing Edit⇨Paste or by pressing ⌘+V or Ctrl+V) until you cut or copy something else or you shut down your computer.

Preventing Objects from Printing

InDesign lets you prevent a specific object from printing. To do so, select the object with the Selection or Direct Selection tool, open the Attributes panel (Window⇨Attributes), and then select the Nonprinting check box. (The other settings in this panel duplicate stroke settings covered in Chapter 8.)

You use this feature for comments and other elements that should not print but that the designer needs to have visible on-screen. Another approach to nonprinting objects is to place them all on a layer and make the entire layer nonprinting, as explained in Chapter 5.

Transforming Objects

InDesign offers several tools and methods for transforming objects. I discuss resizing, scaling, and moving earlier in this chapter, but there are several other useful transformation tools, including rotating, shearing (skewing), flipping, and reshaping.

Rotating is just spinning an object around. Shearing is a little more complicated: Shearing skews an object (slanting it in one direction) while also rotating the other axis at the same time. Regardless of whether you use the mouse or numeric controls to apply rotation and/or shearing to graphics, you first need to follow these steps:

1. **Select the Selection tool.**

2. **Click the object you want to modify.**

3. **If you want, change the object's control point (by default it's the upper-left corner of a frame or shape).**

    You can change the control point by clicking one of the little black boxes — the reference points — in the upper-left corner of the Control panel.

4. **Choose the appropriate tool — Rotate, Shear, or Free Transform — or use the flip options in the Control panel.**

    Figure 9-3 shows the Tools panel and Control panel iconic buttons for these controls.

TIP

If you hold down the Option or Alt key while using a transformation tool, the modification will be performed on a copy of the selected object, rather than on the object itself.

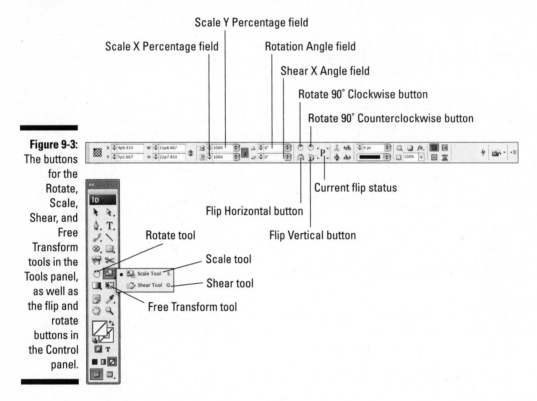

Figure 9-3:
The buttons for the Rotate, Scale, Shear, and Free Transform tools in the Tools panel, as well as the flip and rotate buttons in the Control panel.

Scale Y Percentage field

Scale X Percentage field Rotation Angle field

Shear X Angle field

Rotate 90° Clockwise button

Rotate 90° Counterclockwise button

Current flip status

Flip Horizontal button

Flip Vertical button

Rotate tool

Scale tool

Shear tool

Free Transform tool

Rotating objects

After you have selected the Rotate tool, click and drag a selected object to rotate it — the object will rotate following your mouse movement. (Holding down the Shift key while dragging limits rotation increments to multiples of 45 degrees.)

For more precise rotation, use the Control panel. You can change the angle of a selected object by entering a value in the Rotation field. If you choose to enter a value in the Rotation field, positive values rotate the selected item counterclockwise around the control point; negative values rotate it clockwise.

Or you can choose one of the predefined angles from the Rotation Angle field's pop-up menu, or choose any of the three rotation options — Rotate 180°, Rotate 90° CW, and Rotate 90° CCW — in the Control panel's flyout menu.

Using the Free Transform tool

Advanced users will like the Free Transform tool. When you select this tool, InDesign lets you scale, rotate, and resize — but not shear — selected objects — as follows:

✔ If you click within the frame, you can move the object by dragging it.

✔ If you select a frame handle (whether corner or midpoint), you can resize the object by dragging.

✔ Finally, if you move the mouse very close to a frame handle, you will see a curved arrow, which indicates that you can rotate the object around that object's center point.

Having a tool that does more than one thing can be confusing, but once you get the hang of it, it sure beats constantly changing tools!

If you choose one of these flyout menu options, the current angle of the selected object is added to the applied angle. For example, if you choose Rotate 90° CCW (counterclockwise), an object that's currently rotated 12 degrees will end up with a rotation angle of 102 degrees.

No matter what method you choose to rotate an object, the center of rotation will be whatever control point is selected in the Control panel.

To "unrotate" an object, enter a Rotation Angle value of **0**.

Shearing objects

After you have selected the Shear tool, click and drag a selected object to shear it. (Holding down the Shift key constrains the selected object's rotation value to increments of 45 degrees.) If you drag the mouse in a straight line parallel with one set of edges (such as the top and bottom), you skew the graphic (just slant it in one direction). But if you move the mouse in any other direction, you slant the object's edges closest to the direction that you move the mouse the furthest and rotate the rest of the graphic. Give it a few tries to see what happens.

As with other functions, you can also use the Control panel for more precise control. Just enter a Shear X Angle value in the Control panel or choose a predefined value from the field's pop-up menu. Positive shear values slant an object to the right (that is, the top edge of the object is moved to the right), whereas negative values slant an object to the left (the bottom edge is moved to the right). You can enter shear values between 1 and 89 (although values above 70 cause considerable distortion).

Note that when you use the Shear tool, you change the selected object's angle of rotation *and* skew angle simultaneously. If you use the mouse, you can in effect get different skew and rotation angles based on how you move the mouse, but if you use the Control panel, both the skew and rotation will have the same angles applied.

To "unshear" an object, enter a Shear X Angle value of **0**.

Flipping objects

The Object menu has two flipping commands: Object⇨Transform⇨Flip Horizontal and Object⇨Transform⇨Flip Vertical. They are also available in the Control panel as iconic buttons.

These controls let you make a mirror image of a selected object and its contents. If you choose Flip Horizontal, the graphic is flipped along a vertical axis (that is, the right edge and left edge exchange places); if you choose Flip Vertical, the object is flipped upside down. (You're not making a flipped copy of the select object, but actually flipping the selected object.)

As with other tools, the invisible line over which an object is flipped is based on what reference point is currently active as the control point for that object.

In InDesign CS3, the Control panel now displays iconic buttons for Flip Vertical and Flip Horizontal, as well as a preview of the current object's flip status (look for the large *P* in the panel when an object is selected; it's to the right of the two flip buttons). The *P* changes appearance so it is flipped the same way as the selected object.

Repeating transformations

Whatever transformations you use, you can apply them repeatedly. InDesign remembers the effects that you apply to frames via the Control panel, Transform panel, and transform tools. Choose Object⇨Transform Again⇨ Transform Again (Option+⌘+3 or Ctrl+Alt+3) to repeat the last transformation on the selected object (it can be a different object than you last applied a transformation to).

Or choose Object⇨Transform Again⇨Transform Sequence Again (Option+ ⌘+4 or Ctrl+Alt+4) to apply all recent transformations to a selected object. That sequence of transactions stays in memory until you perform a new transformation, which then starts a new sequence, so you can apply the same transformation to multiple objects.

Two other transform-again options are available through the Object⇨ Transform Again menu option's submenu: Transform Again Individually and Transform Sequence Again Individually. You use these on groups; they work like the regular Transform Again and Transform Sequence Again options but apply any effects to each object individually within the group. For example, choosing Transform Again to a group might rotate the entire group as if it were one unit, but choosing Transform Again Individually would rotate each object in the group separately, not the group as a unit. Try it and see exactly what it does!

Replacing Object Attributes

A really painstaking task in any layout is going through it to fix formatting to frames, lines, or other objects once the design standards have changed. InDesign has a very handy way to apply object formatting consistently to objects — the object styles feature described in Chapter 10 — but even if you use these styles, you will still have local formatting applied to at least some objects.

That's where the Object pane of the Find/Replace dialog box comes in, letting you replace attributes throughout your document, no matter what they are applied to. Figure 9-4 shows that pane.

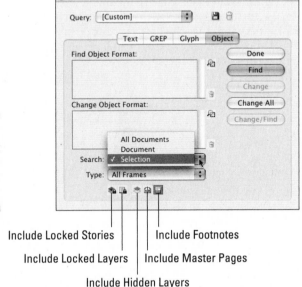

Figure 9-4:
The Object
pane of the
Find/Change
dialog box.

Include Locked Stories
Include Locked Layers
Include Hidden Layers
Include Footnotes
Include Master Pages

Here's how it works:

1. **Open the Find/Change dialog box by choosing Edit⇨Find/Change, and then go to the Object pane.**

2. **Select the desired object attributes by clicking the Object Find Format Settings iconic button to the left of the Find Object Format list. In the dialog box that displays (refer to Figure 9-5), select the attributes to search (choose one category at a time from the list at left and then set the desired parameters in the pane that appears), and click OK when you're done.**

   This dialog box is nearly identical to the New Object Style dialog box covered in Chapter 10. They'll appear in that Find Object format list. (Highlight an attribute in the list and click the Clear Object Find Format Settings iconic button — the trashcan icon — if you want to remove an attribute from your search.)

3. **If you're replacing attributes, click the Object Format Settings iconic button to the right of the Change Object Format list.**

   These controls work like the Find Object Format controls.

4. **Limit or expand the search range by choosing an option from the Search pop-up menu: Selection, Document, and All Documents. Also choose the type of frames to search in the Type pop-up menu: All Frames, Text Frames, Graphic Frames, and Unassigned Frames. Finally, to determine the scope of your search, select or deselect any of the six buttons at the bottom of the pane.**

   From left to right, the five buttons are Include Locked Layers, Include Locked Stories, Include Hidden Layers, Include Master Pages, and Include Footnotes. Note that the first two buttons apply only to finds; you cannot change the formatting of locked objects. (If an icon's background darkens, it is selected.)

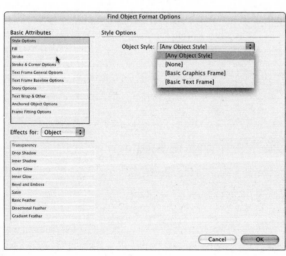

Figure 9-5:
The Find Object Format Options dialog box (the Change Object Format dialog box is identical).

   5. **Click Find, Change, Change All, or Change/Find as desired to perform
      your search and/or replace operation.**

   6. **Click Done when done.**

Making Fancy Corners

Anytime you're working on an object that has any sharp corners, you have
the option to add a little pizzazz to those corners via InDesign's Corner
Options feature (Object⇨Corner Options). Five built-in corner options,
shown in Figure 9-6, are available. Note that if the shape contains only
smooth points, any corner option you apply won't be noticeable.

Figure 9-6:
The Corner
Options
dialog box
lets you
apply any of
five effects
to frame
and path
corners.
From left to
right: None,
Fancy,
Bevel, Inset,
Inverse
Rounded,
and
Rounded.

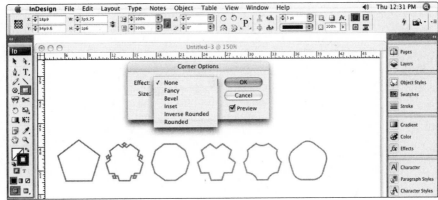

To add a corner option:

   1. **Select either of the selection tools and click the object to which you
      want to add a corner effect.**

   2. **Choose Object⇨Corner Options to display the Corner Options
      dialog box.**

      Select the Preview check box to view changes as you make them.

   3. **Choose an option from the Effect pop-up menu.**

4. **Enter a distance in the Size field.**

   The Size value determines the length that the effect extends from the corner.

5. **Click OK to close the dialog box and apply your changes.**

If you can't see a corner effect after applying one, make sure that a color is applied to the stroke or try making the object's stroke thicker. Increasing the Size value in the Corner Options dialog box can also make a corner effect more visible.

The Corner Options menu option and dialog box had been called Corner Effects in previous versions of InDesign.

Using Transparency and Lighting Effects

InDesign was a pioneer in the use of transparency effects on objects. These effects let you overlay objects without having them completely be obscured, allowing for very interesting visual effects such as fades and shadows.

InDesign CS3 takes the next step by adding much richer controls over transparency and lighting, so you can now create effects such as embossing and beveled edges *and* control the intensity and direction of shadows and light. As part of these enhancements, you'll find a significantly revised interface for transparency and related controls, not the least of which is the renaming of the Transparency panel to the Effects panel.

Basic transparency

One of InDesign's most sophisticated tools is its set of transparency options, which let you make objects partially transparent. You apply transparency with the Effects panel (Window⇨Effects or Shift+F10), by choosing Object⇨Effects⇨Transparency, or by clicking the Effects iconic button in the Control panel and choosing Transparency from its pop-up menu.

The first option displays the Effects panel, which takes the least screen space and is best used for simple operations. The other options open the more complex and larger Effects dialog box. (Be sure that the Transparency pane is visible in the Effects dialog box; if not, click the Transparency option in the option list at left.)

Figure 9-7 shows the panel as well as a text title that uses transparency as it overprints a background photo. Notice how the semi-transparent text fades away toward the top and is brighter toward the bottom. Figure 9-8 shows the dialog box.

Figure 9-7:
The Effects panel and its flyout menu (right), as well as transparency applied to the image and text (the original objects are at left).

Figure 9-8:
The Effects dialog box.

In the Opacity field of the Effects panel or Effects dialog box's Transparency pane, enter a value or choose one from the pop-up menu. A value of 0 is completely invisible, whereas a value of 100 is completely solid.

You cannot apply transparency to text selections or to entire layers, but InDesign CS3 now lets you apply different transparency settings to an object's contents, fill, and stroke, as well as to the object itself. You do so by choosing the desired component in the list in the Effects panel or using the Settings For pop-up menu in the Effects dialog box. (If you see only Object listed in the Effects panel, click the right-facing triangle to its left to display the rest.)

If you want more than basic transparency, you'll find a lot of other options. Most are for experts, but a few are worth describing. One is the set of 16 transparency types — called *blending modes*. (Photoshop and Illustrator users will recognize these expert options.) You access these in the pop-up menu in the Effects panel or via the Mode pop-up menu on the Effects dialog box's Transparency pane. The differences among them can be subtle or extreme, depending on a variety of issues. You should experiment with them to see what effect works best in each case.

The Difference, Exclusion, Hue, Saturation, Color, and Luminosity modes do not blend spot colors — only process colors.

You have two other options in the Effects panel and in the Transparency pane of the Effects dialog box:

- ✔ **Isolate Blending** restricts the blending modes to the objects in a group, instead of also applying them to objects beneath the group. This can prevent unintended changes to those underlying objects.

- ✔ **Knockout Group** obscures any objects below the selected group. But those objects are still affected by any blend mode settings applied to the group, unless Isolate Blending is also checked.

Using drop shadows and inner shadows

The Effects panel and dialog box, as well as the Object➪Effects menu command, now give you access to a bunch of other lighting features, including drop shadows. In the panel, choose Effects➪Drop Shadow from the flyout menu, or choose Drop Shadow from the *fx* iconic button's pop-up menu. In the Effects dialog box, select Drop Shadow from the option list at left. Or just press Option+⌘+M or Ctrl+Alt+M. No matter how you get there, you'll see the following options in the Drop Shadow pane, shown in Figure 9-9:

Figure 9-9:
The Drop Shadow pane of the Effects dialog box.

Choose what component of the object to apply the drop shadow to by using the Settings For pop-up menu. (You can apply multiple drop shadows, one to each component of an object.)

- ✔ Select the Drop Shadow check box option to turn on the drop shadow function for the selected component.

- Select a lighting type (technically, a *blend mode*) by choosing one of the 16 options in the Mode pop-up menu. (These are the same blending modes used in transparencies.)

- Specify the opacity by entering a value in the Opacity field — 0% is invisible, whereas 100% is completely solid.

- Specify the shadow's position relative to the object by using the X Offset and Y Offset fields. A positive X Offset moves the shadow to the right; a positive Y Offset moves the shadow down. Negative values go in the other direction.

- Specify the shadow's size by entering a value in the Distance field (formerly named Blur in previous versions of InDesign) — this blurs a copy of the text used in the drop shadow to make it look like it was created by shining light on solid letters.

- Choose a lighting angle in the Angle field or use the mouse to move the direction within the circle to determine the direction of the shadow. You can also select the Use Global Light option, which then uses whatever settings you define in the Global Light dialog box — a handy way to have consistent settings for all objects. (Choose Object➪Effects➪Global Light, or choose Global Light from the Effects panel's flyout menu, to open the Global Light dialog box.)

- Choose a color source — Swatches, RGB, CMYK, or Lab — from the Color pop-up menu in the Effect Color dialog box, which you get by clicking the color swatch to the right of the Mode pop-up menu, and then select a color from the sliders or swatches below that menu. You get sliders for RGB, CMYK, and Lab colors, or a set of previously defined color swatches if you selected Swatches in the Color pop-up menu.

- Adjust the other settings, if desired, to control other, expert drop shadow characteristics: Size, Spread, Noise, Object Knocks Out Shadow, and Shadow Honors Other Effects.

- To see the effects of your various setting adjustments in the actual layout, check the Preview option. (Because the Effects dialog box is so big, you'll likely need a big monitor to have room for both the dialog box and the object you're applying the effects to.)

There's a new shadow option in InDesign CS3: inner shadows. It works pretty much like drop shadows, with a nearly identical pane in the Effects dialog box. The visual difference is that an inner shadow is contained within the object, as if the frames were a wall blocking the shadow, whereas a drop shadow occurs outside the frame, as if the frame were casting a shadow outside.

Using feathering and other lighting effects

A similar option to drop shadows is feathering, which essentially softens the edges of objects. There are three types of feathering available:

✔ **Basic feathering:** These are the options that previous versions of InDesign offered.

✔ **Directional feathering:** This adds the ability to control the direction of the feathering as well as separate feather widths for each side, creating a smeared-border effect.

✔ **Gradient feathering:** This adds a gradient effect to the feathered area.

The other new effects are outer glow, inner glow, bevel and emboss, and satin. Figure 9-10 shows examples of each.

You apply them the same ways as you do drop shadows, selecting the object component in the Settings For pop-up menu and modifying the various controls such as opacity, light angle and distance, blending mode, and effect size, as appropriate for the specific effect. Once you get a hang for transparency and drop shadows, it's easy to use the other effects.

Figure 9-10:
Various effects applied to a set of objects. Top row: The original object, drop shadow, and inner shadow. Second row: Basic feather, directional feather, and gradient feather. Third row: Outer glow and inner glow. Bottom row: Bevel and emboss, and satin.

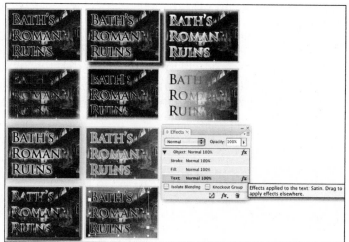

Chapter 10

Organizing Objects

*Y*ou use objects throughout your layout: lines, text frames, graphics frames, shapes, and so forth. A big part of working with them involves organizing them — deciding when to group them together, when to lock them in location, how to arrange objects with others, and so on. That's where this chapter comes in.

Then I discuss a powerful new feature called *object styles* that lets you save object attributes. Object styles let you organize your settings so you can apply them to other objects for consistent, easy formatting.

Finally, I show you how to manage objects' relations with their source files, so you can make sure you're using the correct version of your graphics and text.

Combining Objects into a Group

Groups have many uses. For example, you might create a group to

✔ Combine several objects that make up an illustration so that you can move, modify, copy, or scale all objects in a single operation.

✔ Keep a graphics frame and its accompanying caption (text) frame together so that, if you change your mind about their placement, you can reposition both objects at once.

✔ Combine several vertical lines that are used to separate the columns of a table so that you can quickly change the stroke, color, length, and position of all lines.

InDesign lets you combine several objects into a group. A group of objects behaves like a single object, which means that you can cut, copy, move, or modify all the objects in a group in a single operation.

To create a group, select all the objects (which can include other groups) that you want to include in your group and then choose Object⇨Group or press ⌘+G or Ctrl+G.

Keep in mind the following when creating groups:

- ✔ If you create a group from objects on different layers, all objects are moved to the top layer and stacked in succession beneath the topmost object.

- ✔ You cannot create a group if some of the selected objects are locked and some are not locked. All selected objects must be locked or unlocked before you can group them. (Locking and unlocking objects are covered in the following section.)

If you want to manipulate a group, choose the Selection tool and then click any object in the group. The group's bounding box appears. Any transformation you perform is applied to all objects in the group.

If you want to manipulate a specific object in a group, use the Direct Selection tool to select that object. If you want to change something that requires the Selection tool be active, switch to it by selecting the Selection tool or simply by double-clicking the object. (See Chapter 9 for more details on selecting objects.)

If you remove an object from a group that had transparency applied (via cut and paste or copy and paste), that pasted object will not retain the group's transparency settings.

After creating a group, you may eventually decide that you want to return the objects to their original, ungrouped state. To do so, simply click any object in the group with the Selection tool and then choose Object⇨Ungroup or press Shift+⌘+G or Ctrl+Shift+G. If you ungroup a group that contains a group, the contained group is not affected. To ungroup this group, you must select it and choose Ungroup again.

Locking Objects

If you're certain that you want a particular object to remain exactly where it is, you can select Object⇨Lock Position or press ⌘+L or Ctrl+L to prevent the object from being moved. Generally, you want to lock repeating elements such as headers, footers, folios, and page numbers so that they're not accidentally moved. (Such repeating elements are usually placed on a master page; you can lock objects on master pages, too.)

A locked object can't be moved whether you click and drag it with the mouse or change the values in the X: and Y: fields in the Control panel or Transform panel. Not only can you *not* move a locked object, but you can't delete it, either. However, you can change other attributes of a locked object, including its stroke and fill.

To unlock a selected object, choose Object⇨Unlock Position or press Option+⌘+L or Ctrl+Alt+L.

You can also lock entire layers, as described in Chapter 5.

Working with Object Styles

I suspect that object styles are underappreciated and underused, rarely used in real-world documents. That's a pity, because the use of styles for object formatting — not just text formatting — makes your work easier by automatically and reliably applying time-consuming settings to multiple objects and ensuring that your object formatting is both consistent and easily managed.

Creating object styles

You create object styles by using the Object Styles panel (Window⇨Object Styles or ⌘+F7 or Ctrl+F7), shown in Figure 10-1. You can also click the New Object Style iconic button at the bottom of the panel.

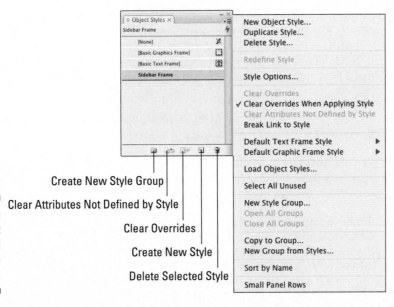

Figure 10-1: The Object Styles panel and its flyout menu.

Create New Style Group

Clear Attributes Not Defined by Style

Clear Overrides

Create New Style

Delete Selected Style

The simplest way to create an object style is to select an already-formatted object with any selection tool, then choose New Object Style from the Object Style panel's flyout menu. InDesign records all the settings automatically from the selected object, so they're in place for the new object style.

Whether you start with an existing object or create a new object style completely from scratch, you use the New Object Style menu option that opens the New Object Style dialog box shown in Figure 10-2.

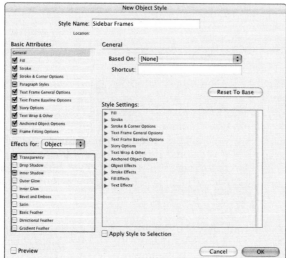

Figure 10-2:
The New Object Style dialog box and its General pane.

At the left side of the dialog box is a list of types of attributes that are or can be set. The checked items are in use for this style — you can uncheck an item so InDesign doesn't apply its settings to objects using the style. For example, if Fill is unchecked, the object style won't apply any Fill settings to objects using that style (and won't change any fill settings that have been applied to that object locally).

To switch from one type of attribute to another, simply click the item name for the type of attribute that you want to adjust, such as Stroke or Transparency.

Be sure to select the Preview option to see the results of object styles on the currently selected object. Of course, you need to make sure that the object is visible on-screen to see those effects.

When you open the New Object Style dialog box, you see the General pane, which lets you create a new style based on an existing object style (by using the Based On pop-up menu), and which lets you assign a keyboard shortcut for fast application of this style (by using the Shortcuts field).

You can use the Based On feature to create families of object styles. For example, you can create a style called *Photo-Standard* for the bulk of your placed photographs, and then create variations such as *Photo-Sidebar* and *Photo-Author*. The Photo-Standard style might specify a hairline black stroke around the photo, while Photo-Sidebar might change that to a white stroke. But if you later decide you want the stroke to be 1 point and change it in Photo-Standard, Photo-Sidebar automatically gets the 1-point stroke while retaining the white color.

The General pane also lets you see the current style settings. Click any of the arrows in the Style Settings section to get more details on how they are set for this object style.

The other panes in the New Object Styles dialog box provide the same capabilities that you find elsewhere in InDesign, brought into one convenient place so you can use them in styles. Because there are so many panes, the New Object Style dialog box now breaks them into two sections. The panes in the first section — Basic Attributes — are

- ✔ **The Fill pane** lets you set colors for fills using whatever colors are defined in the Swatches panel. You can also set the tint and, if you select a gradient fill, the angle for that gradient. Finally, you can choose to have the fill overprint the contents of the frame by selecting the Overprint Fill option.

- ✔ **The Stroke pane** is identical to the Fill pane except that options specific to fills are grayed out, and options available to strokes are made available. The color, tint, and gradient angle options are the same as for the Fill pane. You can also choose the type of stroke (solid line, dashed line, or dotted line) by using the Type pop-up menu, and adjust the thickness by filling in the Weight field. You can also choose to overprint the stroke over underlying content, plus determine — if your stroke is a dotted or dashed line — the color, tint, and overprint for the gap.

- ✔ **The Stroke & Corner Options pane** lets you set stroke position and how corners and line ends are handled. It also lets you apply fancy corners to frames. The Stroke Options section is where you align the strokes to the frame edges, determine how lines join at corners, and decide what line endings are applied. The Corner Options section is where you select from five fancy corners, such as Bevel and Rounded, by using the Effect pop-up menu, and where you specify the radius, or reach, of the corner by using the Size field. (See Chapter 8 for the low-down on strokes and Chapter 9 for the skinny on corner options.)

- ✔ **The Paragraph Styles pane** controls what paragraph style, if any, is applied to text in the frame. Chances are you won't use this setting except for frames that contain only consistent, very simple text, such as pull-quotes or bios. (See Chapter 13 for details.)

- ✔ **The Text Frame General Options pane** controls how text is handled within a frame. This essentially replicates the controls in the General pane of the Text Box Options dialog box (Object⇨Text Frame Options or

⌘+B or Ctrl+B), including number of columns, column width, gutter settings, inset spacing (how far from the frame edge text is placed), vertical justification (how text is aligned vertically in the frame), and whether text wrap settings are ignored when this frame overlaps other frames. (See Chapter 12 for details.)

✔ **The Text Frame Baseline Options pane** controls how text is handled within a frame. This essentially replicates the controls in the Baseline Options pane of the Text Box Options dialog box (Object⇨Text Frame Options or ⌘+B or Ctrl+B), including how the text baseline is calculated for the frame and whether the text frame gets its own baseline grid. (See Chapter 11 for details.)

✔ **The Story Options pane** enables optical margin alignment — its controls are the same as in the Story panel (Type⇨Story), detailed in Chapter 17. Optical margin alignment adjusts the placement of text along the left side of a frame so the text alignment is more visually pleasing.

✔ **The Text Wrap & Other pane** lets you set text wrap, mirroring the features of the Text Wrap panel (Window⇨Text Wrap or Option+⌘+W or Ctrl+Alt+W, explained in Chapter 17), as well as make an object nonprinting (normally handled through the Attributes panel by choosing Window⇨Attributes).

✔ **The Anchored Object Options pane** lets you set the attributes for inline and anchored frames, mirroring the controls in the Anchored Object Options dialog box (Object⇨Anchored Object⇨Options), which I explain in Chapter 11.

The second set of panes all relate to the features found in the Effects dialog box and panel, as covered in Chapter 9: Transparency, Drop Shadow, Inner Shadow, Outer Glow, Inner Glow, Bevel and Emboss, Satin, Basic Feather, Directional Feather, and Gradient Feather.

Managing object styles

The Object Styles panel's flyout menu (refer to Figure 10-1) has several options for managing object styles:

✔ **Duplicate Style:** Click an object style's name and then choose this menu option to create an exact copy. If you want to create an object style that's similar to one you already created, you might want to choose New Object Style rather than Duplicate Style, and then use the Based On option to create a child of the original. If you choose Duplicate Style, the copy is identical to, but not based on, the original; if you modify the original, the copy is not affected.

✔ **Delete Style:** Choose this to delete selected object styles. To select multiple styles, press and hold ⌘ or Ctrl as you click their names. To select a range of styles, click the first one, and then press and hold Shift and click the last one. You can also delete styles by selecting them in the pane and then clicking the Delete Selected Styles iconic button (the trashcan icon) at the bottom of the panel.

✔ **Redefine Style:** To modify an existing object style, first make changes to an object that already has an object style defined for it, and then select Redefine Style. The newly applied formats are applied to the object style.

✔ **Style Options:** This option lets you modify an existing object style. When a style is highlighted in the Object Styles panel, choosing Style Options displays the Object Style Options dialog box, which is identical to the New Object Style dialog box covered earlier.

✔ **Load Object Styles:** Choose this option if you want to import object styles from another InDesign document. After selecting the document from which to import the styles, you will get a dialog box listing the styles in the chosen document, so you can decide which ones to import. Note the Incoming Style Definitions window at the bottom of the dialog box; it lists the style definitions to help you decide which to import, as well as which to overwrite or rename.

✔ **Select All Unused:** Select this option to highlight the names of all object styles that have not been applied to any objects in the current document. This is a handy way of identifying unused styles in preparation for deleting them (by choosing the Delete Style menu option).

✔ **Sort by Name:** This option alphabetizes your object styles for easier access. (InDesign adds styles to the Object Styles panel in the order in which they were created.)

✔ **Small Panel Rows:** Select this option to reduce the text size in the Object Styles panel. Although harder to read, a panel with this option selected lets you access more styles without having to scroll. To return the panel to its normal text size, deselect this option.

InDesign comes with three predefined object styles — [Normal Text Frame], [Normal Graphics Frame], and [Normal Grid] — that you can modify as desired.

Applying object styles

After you create an object style, applying it is easy. Just click an object and then click the object style name in the Object Styles panel or press its keyboard shortcut. (Windows users must make sure Num Lock is on when using shortcuts for styles.)

You can set which object styles are automatically used for new text and graphics frames: In the Object Styles panel's flyout menu, choose Default Text Frame Style and select the desired style from the submenu to set a default text frame; choose Default Graphic Frame Style and select the desired style from the submenu to set a default graphics frame. To no longer have object styles automatically applied to new objects, choose [None] in the Default Text Frame and/or Default Graphic Frame submenus.

How existing formatting is handled

When you apply an object style to selected objects, all local formats are retained. All other formats are replaced by those of the applied style — that is, unless you do one of the following:

- ✔ If you press and hold Option or Alt when clicking a name in the Object Styles panel, any local formatting that has been applied to the objects is removed. You can achieve the same effect by choosing Clear Attributes Not Defined by Style from the Object Styles panel's flyout menu or by clicking the Clear Attributes Not Defined by Style iconic button at the bottom of the Object Styles panel.

- ✔ If you want to override any local changes with the settings in the object style, choose Clear Overrides in the flyout menu or click the Clear Overrides iconic button at the bottom of the Object Styles panel. The difference is that Clear Attributes Not Defined by Style removes all attributes for which the object style contains no settings, whereas Clear Overrides imposes the object style's settings over conflicting attributes that you set manually.

- ✔ To have InDesign CS3 automatically override local changes when applying a style, be sure the new Clear Overrides When Applying Style flyout menu option is checked. Choosing the item toggles between selecting (checking) and deselecting (unchecking) this option.

If a plus sign (+) appears to the right of an object style's name, it means that the object has local formats that differ from those of the applied object style. This can occur if you apply an object style to object text to which you've done some manual formatting, or if you modify formatting for an object after applying an object style to it. (For example, you may have changed the fill color; that is a local change to the object style and causes the + to appear.)

Removing an object style from an object

To remove a style from an object, choose Break Link to Style from the Object Styles panel's flyout menu. The object's current formatting won't be affected, but it will no longer be updated when the object style is changed.

Managing object styles

InDesign also lets you manage your styles, such as creating groups of styles to make it easier to find relevant ones, and bring in styles from other documents. Because these features work the same for paragraph, character, table, and cell styles as well, I've covered these features in one place: Chapter 14.

Managing Links

The Links panel (Window⇨Links, or Shift+⌘+D or Ctrl+Shift+D) is a handy place to manage the links to your graphics and text, particularly when you need to update them. (Figure 10-3 shows the Links panel.)

InDesign always creates links for graphics files. But it will create links to source text files (including spreadsheets) only if the Create Links When Placing Text and Spreadsheet Files option is checked in the Type pane of the Preferences dialog box (InDesign⇨Preferences⇨Type or ⌘+K on the Mac, or Edit⇨Preferences-Type or Ctrl+K in Windows). This option is *not* checked by default because many designers don't want to have text files be easily updated in their layouts. That's because all the formatting they have done to the file in InDesign is removed when the link to the source file is updated, causing the text to be replaced.

The first five commands in the Links panel's flyout menu let you reestablish links to missing and modified files, display an imported graphic or text file in the document window, open the program used to create a graphic or text file, and work on copies and versions of the source graphics and text:

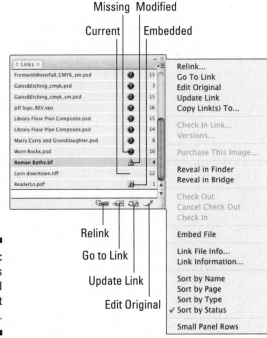

Figure 10-3:
The Links panel and its flyout menu.

✔ **Relink:** This command, and the Relink iconic button (the leftmost at the bottom of the panel), lets you reestablish a missing link or replace the original file you imported with a different file. When you choose Relink or click the button, the Relink dialog box is displayed and shows the original pathname and filename. You can enter a new pathname and filename in the Location field, but it's easier to click Browse, which opens a standard Open a File dialog box. Use the controls to locate and select the original file or a different file, and then click OK. (You can also drag and drop a file icon from the Mac OS Finder or Windows Explorer directly into the Relink dialog box.) If you want to restore broken links to multiple files simultaneously, highlight their filenames in the scroll list, and then choose Relink or click the Update Link button.

InDesign CS3 now lets you relink all instances of a file in your layout, so you only have to do the operation once. Here's the trick: In the Relink dialog box, be sure to check the new Relink All Instances option.

✔ **Go to Link:** Choose this option, or click the Go to Link iconic button (second from left) in the panel to display the highlighted file in the document window. InDesign will, if necessary, navigate to the correct page and center the frame in the document window. You can also display a particular graphic or text file by double-clicking its name in the scroll list while holding down the Option or Alt key.

✔ **Edit Original:** If you want to modify an imported graphic or text file, choose Edit Original from the flyout menu or click the Edit Original button (far right) at the bottom of the panel. InDesign will try to locate and open the program used to create the file. This may or may not be possible, depending on the original program, the file format, and the programs available on your computer.

✔ **Update Link:** Choose this option or click the Update Link iconic button (third from the left) at the bottom of the panel to update the link to a modified graphic or text file. Highlight multiple filenames, and then choose Update Link or click the Update Link button to update all links at once.

When you update missing and modified graphics, any transformations — rotation, shear, scale, and so on — that you've applied to the graphics or their frames are maintained, unless you've deselected the new Relink Preserves Dimensions option in the File Handling pane of the Preferences dialog box (InDesign➪Preferences➪File Handling or ⌘+K on the Mac, or Edit➪Preferences➪File Handling or Ctrl+K in Windows).

✔ **Copy Link To:** Choose this option to copy the source graphic or text file to a new location and update the link so that it refers to this new copy.

Other useful flyout menu options include

✓ **Reveal in Finder (Macintosh) and Reveal in Explorer (Windows):** This menu option opens a window displaying the contents of the folder that contains the source file, so you can perhaps move, copy, or rename it. (The Reveal in Bridge option is a similar feature for the expert Adobe Bridge companion program not covered in this book.)

✓ **Embed File (for graphics only):** This option lets you embed the complete file of any imported graphics file. (InDesign normally imports only a low-resolution screen preview when you place a graphic that is 48K or larger.) If you want to ensure that the graphics file will forever remain with a document, you can choose to embed it — however, by embedding graphics, you'll be producing larger document files, which means it will take you longer to open and save them. If you do use this option, an alert is displayed and informs you about the increased document size that will result. Click Yes to embed the file. Note that this menu option changes to Unembed File, so you can re-enable the original link at any time.

✓ **Unlink (for text files only):** This option removes the link to the source text file, so it can't be updated. Note that this option cannot be undone from the Links panel; you have choose Edit⇨Undo, or press ⌘+Z or Ctrl+Z.

✓ **Link Information:** This option displays the Link Information dialog box, which actually doesn't let you do much. (The Previous and Next buttons let you display information about the previous and next files in the list, but that's about it.) But it does display 11 sometimes-useful bits of information about the highlighted file, including its name, status, creation date, file type, and location.

✓ **Sort by Name:** This option lists all files in alphabetical order.

✓ **Sort by Page:** This option lists imported files on page 1 first, followed by imported files on page 2, and so on.

✓ **Sort by Type:** This option lists all files grouped by type of file (such as Word, JPEG, and TIFF).

✓ **Sort by Status:** This option lists files with missing links first, followed by files that have been modified, and finally files whose status is okay.

✓ **Small Panel Rows:** This option lets you reduce the size of text in the panel and decrease the space between entries so that you can see more entries at once. Of course, the reduced rows are also harder to read. To go back to the normal display size, simply select this option again.

The other options in the flyout menu — Save Link Version, Versions, Purchase This Image, Check Out, Cancel Check Out, Check In, and Link File Info — are expert features not covered in this book.

Chapter 11

Aligning and Arranging Objects

*W*hen you draw objects like frames or lines, they appear where you draw them. That's what you expect, right? But sometimes you want them to appear where you meant to draw them, not where you actually did. Working with the mouse is inexact, but you can overcome that.

This chapter shows you how to use a variety of InDesign features to precisely control the placement of objects, including the ability to enter actual coordinates for objects, to use grids and guidelines features to ensure that your objects and text line up where you want them to, and to use the Align panel and related commands to make sure objects line up relative to each other, so your layouts are all neat and tidy.

The other part of keeping your layouts neat and tidy is managing the arrangements of objects. In addition to the grouping and locking functions covered in Chapter 10, InDesign also lets you control the stacking order of objects that overlap and tie objects to spots in text so they stay close to the text that references them.

Precise Positioning with Coordinates

The most precise way to position objects is by entering the object's desired coordinates in the X: and Y: fields of the Control panel or the Transform panel. (You can also precisely change the object's size by entering values in the W: and H: fields.) The Control panel is visible by default at the top of the document window. If it's not visible, open the Control panel by choosing Window⇨Control or by pressing Option+⌘+6 or Ctrl+Alt+6.

The Control panel is more powerful than the Transform panel, which is a holdover from older versions of InDesign, but if you want to use the Transform panel, choose Window⇨Object & Layout⇨Transform. Figure 11-1 shows both the Control panel and Transform panel, their flyout menus, and a selected frame.

Everyone should use the Control panel's coordinates to make sure that objects are consistently placed from page to page. Many designers place objects by eye, using the mouse, but that typically means there are small position and size variations from page to page that shouldn't be there. Many readers won't notice if the differences are slight, but even small differences make small adjustments to text flow that can add up over pages. And it's all so unnecessary.

You usually want to enter coordinates based on the upper-left corner, so be sure that the upper-left reference point is made into the control point (just click it if it is not). How do you know which reference point is the current control point? The control point is black, while the other reference points are white. (Chapter 1 provides the deeper details.)

Figure 11-1:
The Control panel (top) and Transform panel let you enter precise coordinates for an object's position.

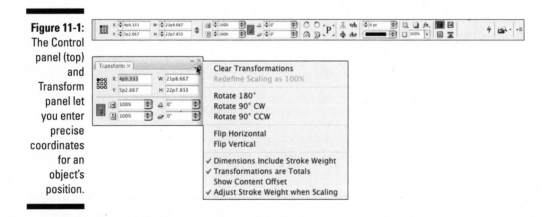

Lining Up Objects with Guidelines and Grids

If you've ever seen a carpenter use a chalked string to snap a temporary line as an aid for aligning objects, you understand the concept behind ruler guidelines and grids. They're not structurally necessary and they don't appear in the final product, yet they still make your work easier.

InDesign provides several types of grids and guidelines:

✔ **Ruler guides** are moveable guidelines that are helpful for placing objects precisely and for aligning multiple items.

✔ **Margin and column guides** are part of your page setup when you create or modify a document (see Chapter 3), providing the default margin around the sides of the page and the space between the default text frame's columns.

✔ A **baseline grid** is a series of horizontal lines that help in aligning lines of text and objects across a multicolumn page. When a document is open and it has a baseline grid showing, the page looks like a sheet of lined paper.

✔ A **document grid** is a set of horizontal and vertical lines that help you place and align objects.

✔ A **frame-based grid** is similar to a baseline grid except that it is just for a specific text frame.

You won't need all the grids and guidelines at once. You'll most likely use a combination of guides and grids, but using all four at once is more complicated than necessary.

Using ruler guides

InDesign lets you create individual ruler guides manually. You can also set ruler guides automatically with the Create Guides command (Layout⇨Create Guides).

Manually creating ruler guides

To create ruler guides on an as-needed basis, follow these steps:

1. **Go to the page or spread onto which you want to place ruler guides.**

2. **If the rulers are not displayed at the top and left of the document window, choose View⇨Show Rulers or press ⌘+R or Ctrl+R.**

3. **Drag the pointer (and a guideline along with it) from the horizontal ruler or vertical ruler onto a page or the pasteboard.**

4. **When the guideline is positioned where you want it, release the mouse button.**

   If you release the mouse when the pointer is over a page, the ruler guide extends from one edge of the page to the other (but not across a spread). If you release the mouse button when the pointer is over the pasteboard, the ruler guide extends across both pages of a spread and the pasteboard. If you want a guide to extend across a spread and the pasteboard, you can also hold down the ⌘ or Ctrl key as you drag and release the mouse when the pointer is over a page.

TIP

Place both a horizontal and vertical guide at the same time by pressing ⌘ or Ctrl and dragging the *ruler intersection point* (where the two rulers meet) onto a page. You can also place a guide that extends across the page or spread and pasteboard by double-clicking the vertical or horizontal ruler.

Ruler guides are cyan in color (unless you change the color by choosing Layout⇨Ruler Guides) and are associated with the layer onto which they're placed. You can show and hide ruler guides by showing and hiding the layers that contain them. You can even create layers that contain nothing but ruler guides and then show and hide them as you wish. (See Chapter 5 for more information about layers.)

TIP

To create ruler guides for several document pages, create a master page, add the ruler guides to the master page, and then apply the master to the appropriate document pages.

Automatically creating ruler guides

Here's how to create a set of ruler guides automatically:

1. **If the documents contain multiple layers, display the Layers panel (Window⇨Layers or F7) and click the name of the layer to which you want to add guides.**

2. **Choose Layout⇨Create Guides to display the Create Guides dialog box, shown in Figure 11-2. (To see the guides on the page while you create them, check Preview.)**

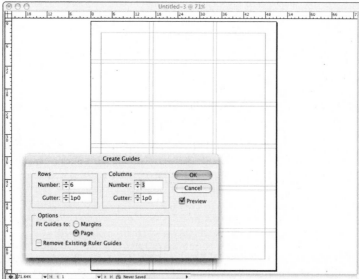

Figure 11-2:
The Create Guides dialog box and the guides it created.

3. **In the Rows and Columns areas, specify the number of guides you want to add in the Number fields and, optionally, specify a Gutter width between horizontal (Rows) and vertical (Columns) guides. Enter 0 (zero) in the Gutter fields if you don't want gutters between guides.**

4. **In the Options area, click Margins to fit the guides in the margin boundaries; click Page to fit the guides within the page boundary.**

5. **Remove any previously placed ruler guides by checking Remove Existing Ruler Guides.**

6. **When you finish specifying the attributes of the ruler guides, click OK to close the dialog box.**

Working with ruler guides

You can show and hide, lock and unlock, select and move, copy and paste, and delete ruler guides. Here are a few pointers for working with ruler guides:

- **Display or hide ruler guides** by choosing View➪Grids & Guides➪Show/Hide Guides or by pressing ⌘+; (semicolon) or Ctrl+; (semicolon).

- **Lock or unlock all ruler guides** by choosing View➪Grids & Guides➪Lock Guides or by pressing Option+⌘+; (semicolon) or Ctrl+Alt+; (semicolon). Ruler guides are locked when Lock Guides is checked.

- **Select a ruler guide** by clicking it with a selection tool. To select multiple guides, hold down the Shift key and click them. The color of a guide changes from cyan to the color of its layer when it is selected. To select all ruler guides on a page or spread, press Option+⌘+G or Ctrl+Alt+G.

- **Move a guide** by clicking and dragging it as you would any object. To move multiple guides, select them and then drag them. To move guides to another page, select them, choose Edit➪Cut or press ⌘+X or Ctrl+X (or choose Edit➪Copy or press ⌘+C or Ctrl+C), display the target page, and then choose Edit➪Paste or press ⌘+V or Ctrl+V. If the target page has the same dimensions as the source page, the guides are placed in their original positions.

- **Delete ruler guides** by selecting them and then pressing Delete or Backspace.

- **Change the color of the ruler guides and the view percentage above which they're displayed** by choosing Layout➪Ruler Guides. The Ruler Guides dialog box, shown in Figure 11-3, appears. Modify the View Threshold value, choose a different color from the Color pop-up menu, and then click OK. If you change the settings in the Ruler Guides dialog box when no documents are open, the new settings become defaults and are applied to all subsequently created documents.

- **Display ruler guides behind — instead of in front of — objects** by choosing InDesign➪Preferences➪Guides & Pasteboard or pressing ⌘+K on the Mac, or by choosing Edit➪Preferences➪Guides & Pasteboard or by pressing Ctrl+K in Windows. Then select the Guides in Back option in the Guide Options section of the dialog box.

✔ **Make object edges snap (align) to ruler guides when you drag them into the snap zone** by selecting the Snap to Guides option (View⇨Grids & Guides⇨Snap to Guides, or press Shift+⌘+; [semicolon] or Ctrl+Shift+; [semicolon]). To specify the snap zone (the distance — in pixels — at which an object will snap to a guide), choose InDesign⇨Preferences⇨ Guides & Pasteboard or press ⌘+K on the Mac, or choose Edit⇨ Preferences⇨Guides & Pasteboard or press Ctrl+K in Windows, and enter a value in the Snap to Zone field in the Guide Options section of the dialog box.

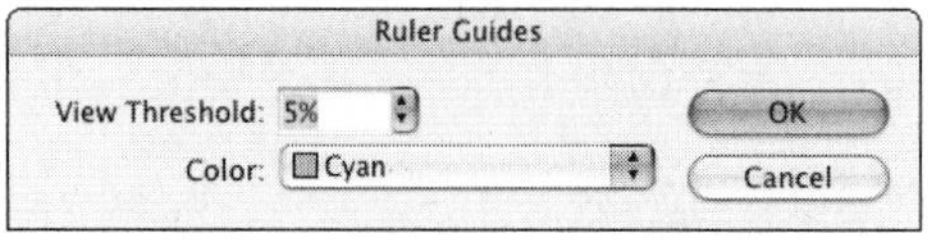

Figure 11-3:
The Ruler
Guides
dialog box.

Ruler Guides

View Threshold: 5%

Color: ☐ Cyan

OK

Cancel

Working with column guides

You can also adjust column guides if your document has them, though you don't get the same flexibility in adjusting column guides as you do ruler guides. Column guides are created when you create a new document and set it up as having multiple columns (see Chapter 3).

By default, column guides are locked. To unlock them (or relock them) choose View⇨Grids & Guides⇨Lock Column Guides. (If the menu option has a check mark to its left, the column guides are locked.)

To move a column guide, click and drag it. Note that the color of a selected column guide does not change as the color of a selected ruler guide does. Also note that you cannot select multiple column guides or move them to other pages. The only way to add or delete column guides is to change the number of guides in the Margins and Columns dialog box (choose Layout⇨Margins and Columns); adjusting the number of columns undoes any custom moves applied to column guides.

Using document grids

A document grid is like the grid paper you used in school, a visual crutch to help ensure that the objects you draw and reposition are placed at desired increments. Using a grid can help ensure that objects align and are sized consistently.

If you plan to use a grid, set it up before you start working in the document. Because documents tend to have different grid settings based on individual contents, you probably want to set Grids preferences with a specific document open so that the grid will apply only to that document. The Grids pane of the Preferences dialog box (InDesign⇨Preferences⇨Grids or ⌘+K on the Mac, or Edit⇨Preferences⇨Grids or Ctrl+K in Windows) is shown in Figure 11-4.

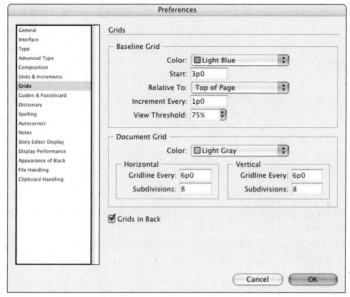

Figure 11-4:
The Grids
pane of the
Preferences
dialog box.

You have the following options:

- ✔ **Color:** The default color of the document grid is Light Gray. You can choose a different color from the Color pop-up menu or choose Other to create your own.

- ✔ **Gridline Every:** The major gridlines, which are slightly darker, are positioned according to this value. The default value is 6p0; in general, you want to specify a value within the measurement system you're using. For example, if you work in inches, you might enter **1 inch** in the Gridline Every field. You set the horizontal and vertical settings separately.

- ✔ **Subdivisions:** The major gridlines established in the Gridline Every field are subdivided according to the value you enter here. For example, if you enter **1 inch** in the Gridline Every field and **4** in the Subdivisions field, you get a gridline at each quarter-inch. The default number of subdivisions is 8. You set the horizontal and vertical settings separately.

By default, the document grid appears on every spread behind all objects. You can have grids display in front by deselecting the Grids in Back check box.

To make object edges snap (align) to the grid when you drag them into the snap zone, select the Snap to Document Grid option (View⇨Grids & Guides⇨ Snap to Document Grid, or press Shift+⌘+' [apostrophe] or Ctrl+Shift+' [apostrophe]). To specify the snap zone (the distance — in pixels — at which an object will snap to a gridline), InDesign will use whatever settings you specified for guidelines, as explained earlier in this chapter.

To display the document grid, choose View⇨Grids & Guides⇨Show Document Grid or press ⌘+' (apostrophe) or Ctrl+' (apostrophe).

Using baseline grids

You may not already know this, but each and every new document you create includes a baseline grid. A baseline grid can be helpful for aligning text baselines across columns and for ensuring that object edges align with text baselines.

But chances are that the default settings for the baseline grid won't match the baselines (leading) for the majority of your text. The default baseline grid begins ½ inch from the top of a document page; the default gridlines are light blue, are spaced 1 pica apart, and appear at view percentages above 75 percent. If you change any of these settings when no documents are open, the changes are applied to all subsequently created documents; if a document is open, changes apply only to that document.

So here's how to modify the baseline grid:

1. **Choose InDesign⇨Preferences⇨Grids or press ⌘+K on the Mac, or choose Edit⇨Preferences⇨Grids or press Ctrl+K in Windows.**

   The Grids pane, shown in Figure 11-4, appears. (If you used the shortcuts, then select the Grids pane from the list at left.)

2. **Pick a color for the baseline from the Color pop-up menu in the Baseline Grid area.**

3. **In the Start field, enter the distance between the top of the page and the first gridline.**

   If you enter **0**, the Increment Every value determines the distance between the top of the page and the first gridline.

4. **In the Increment Every field, enter the distance between gridlines.**

   If you're not sure what value to use, enter the leading value for the publication's body text.

5. **Choose a View Threshold percentage from the pop-up menu or enter a value in the field.**

   You probably don't want to display the baseline grid at reduced view percentages because gridlines become tightly spaced.

6. **Click OK to close the dialog box and return to the document.**

The Show/Hide Baseline Grid command (View⇨Grids & Guides⇨Show/Hide Baseline Grid, or Option+⌘+' [apostrophe] or Ctrl+Alt+' [apostrophe]) lets you display and hide a document's baseline grid.

When you set a baseline grid, it applies to the entire document. Gridlines are displayed behind all objects, layers, and ruler guides. To get text to line up to the baseline grid, you need to ensure that the Align to Grid pop-up menu is set to either First Line Only or All Lines in your paragraph style or that the Align to Baseline Grid check box is selected in the Paragraph panel or Control panel. Chapter 13 covers such paragraph formatting in detail.

A document-wide baseline grid is all fine and dandy, but often it's not enough. The document-wide baseline grid is basically useful for your body text and often your headline text, assuming that the baseline grid's increments match the leading for that text. But what if you have other elements, like sidebars, that have different leading?

The answer is to use text frame–specific baseline grids. You set the grid as part of text frame options by choosing Object⇨Text Frame Options or by pressing ⌘+B or Ctrl+B and then going to the Baseline Options pane. Its options are almost identical to those in the Grids pane of the Preferences dialog box. A baseline grid established for a text frame affects only the text in that frame.

Aligning Objects to Each Other

InDesign lets you align and distribute objects, saving you the hassle of manually moving and placing each element, or figuring out the correct locations in the Control panel or Transform panel to do so. The Align panel is where InDesign offers these timesaving abilities.

The Align panel (Window⇨Object & Layout⇨Align or Shift+F7), shown in Figure 11-5, has several iconic buttons that let you manipulate the relative position of multiple objects in two ways. (The buttons show the alignments they provide.) You can

✔ **Line up objects along a horizontal or vertical axis.** For example, if you've randomly placed several small graphic frames onto a page, you can use the alignment buttons in the Align panel to align them neatly — either horizontally or vertically.

✔ **Distribute space evenly among objects along a horizontal or vertical axis.** Here's a typical problem that's easily solved by using this feature: You've carefully placed five small pictures on a page so that the top edges are aligned across the page and there is equal space between each picture. Then you find out one of the pictures needs to be cut. After deleting the unneeded picture, you could use the Align panel to redistribute the space among the remaining pictures so that they're again equally spaced.

The Align buttons don't work with objects that have been locked with the Lock Position command (Object⇨Lock Position, or ⌘+L or Ctrl+L). If you need to align a locked object, you must first unlock it (Object⇨Unlock Position, or Option+⌘+L or Ctrl+Alt+L). If the objects are on a locked layer, you need to unlock the layer.

When you click an iconic button in the Align panel, selected objects are repositioned in the most logical manner. For example, if you click the Horizontal Align Left button, the selected objects are moved horizontally (to the left, in this case) so that the left edge of each object is aligned with the left edge of the leftmost object. Along the same lines, if you click the Vertical Distribute Center button, the selected objects are moved vertically so that there's an equal amount of space between the vertical center of each object.

Spacing can appear uneven if you click the Horizontal or Vertical Distribute buttons when objects of various sizes are selected. For objects of different sizes, you'll usually want to use the Distribute Spacing buttons (which make the space between objects even) rather than space objects based on their centers or sides (which is how the Distribute Object buttons work).

If the two Distribute Spacing icons do not appear at the bottom of the panel and you want to distribute objects, choose Show Options from the flyout menu.

Figure 11-5:
The Align panel contains 14 iconic buttons that let you control the alignment and space among selected objects.

Stacking Objects

As I mentioned at the beginning of this chapter, arranging your objects is as key to having neat and tidy layouts as using grids and so forth to align objects.

Each time you begin work on a new page, you start with a clean slate (unless the page is based on a master page, in which case the master objects act as the page's background; see Chapter 6 for more on master pages). Every time you add an object to a page — either by using any of InDesign's object-creation tools or with the Place command (File⇨Place or ⌘+D or Ctrl+D) — the new object occupies a unique place in the page's object hierarchy, or *stacking order*.

The first object you place on a page is automatically positioned at the bottom of the stacking order; the next object is positioned one level higher than the first object (that is, in front of the backmost object); the next object is stacked one level higher; and so on for every object you add to the page. (It's not uncommon for a page to have several dozen or even several hundred stacks.)

Although each object occupies its own stack level, if the objects on a page don't overlap, the stacking order is not an issue. But some of the most interesting graphic effects you can achieve with InDesign involve arranging several overlapping objects, so it's important to be aware of the three-dimensional nature of a page's stacking order.

You may change your mind about what you want to achieve in your layout after you've already placed objects in it. To change an object's position in a page's stacking order, use the Arrange command (Object⇨Arrange), which offers four choices:

 ✔ **Bring to Front** (Shift+⌘+] or Ctrl+Shift+])

 ✔ **Bring Forward** (⌘+] or Ctrl+])

 ✔ **Send Backward** (⌘+[or Ctrl+[)

 ✔ **Send to Back** (Shift+⌘+[or Ctrl+Shift+[)

To select an object that's hidden behind one or more other objects, press and hold ⌘ or Ctrl and then click anywhere within the area of the hidden object. The first click selects the topmost object; each successive click selects the next lowest object in the stacking order. When the bottom object is selected, the next click selects the top object. If you don't know where a hidden object is, you can simply click the object or objects in front of it, then send the object(s) to the back. (See Chapter 9 for more on selecting stacked objects.)

Creating Inline and Anchored Frames

In most cases, you want the frames you place on your pages to remain precisely where you put them. But sometimes, you want to place frames relative to related text in such a way that the frames move when the text is edited.

The simplest way is to use inline graphics. For example, if you're creating a product catalog that's essentially a continuous list of product descriptions and you want to include a graphic with each description, you can paste graphics within the text to create inline graphics frames.

A close cousin to the inline frame is the anchored frame, in which a frame follows a point in the text, but that frame is not actually in the text. For example, you might have a "For More Information" sidebar that you want to appear to the left of the text that first mentions a term. By using an anchored frame, you can have that sidebar move with the text so it always appears to its left, perhaps in an adjacent column or in the page margins.

Figure 11-6 shows examples of both an inline frame and an anchored frame.

Note that the process of creating inline and anchored frames — especially anchored frames — can appear overwhelming. It does require thinking through the frame's placement and visualizing that placement so you pick the right options in the various dialog boxes. But relax: You can experiment until you get the hang of it. That's why InDesign lets you undo your work.

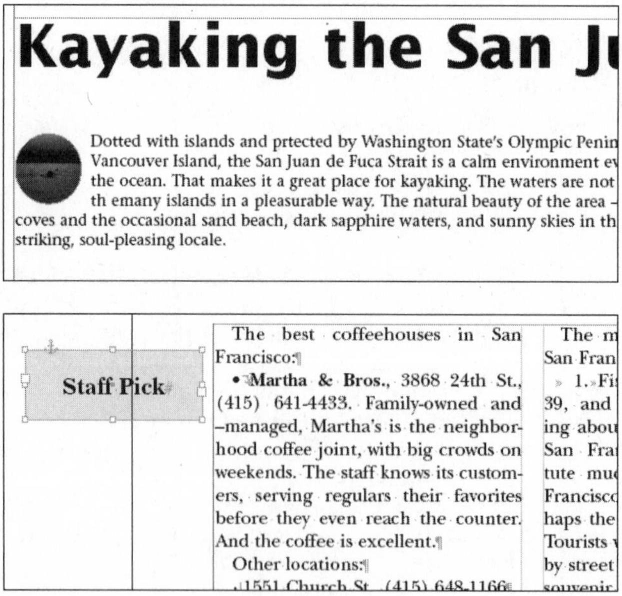

Figure 11-6:
An inline frame (at top) and an anchored frame (the "Staff Pick" box is anchored to the word "Martha").

Kayaking the San Ju

Dotted with islands and prtected by Washington State's Olympic Penin Vancouver Island, the San Juan de Fuca Strait is a calm environment ev the ocean. That makes it a great place for kayaking. The waters are not th emany islands in a pleasurable way. The natural beauty of the area – coves and the occasional sand beach, dark sapphire waters, and sunny skies in th striking, soul-pleasing locale.

Staff Pick

The best coffeehouses in San Francisco:¶
• **Martha & Bros.**, 3868 24th St., (415) 641-4433. Family-owned and –managed, Martha's is the neighborhood coffee joint, with big crowds on weekends. The staff knows its customers, serving regulars their favorites before they even reach the counter. And the coffee is excellent.¶
  Other locations:¶
  ,1551 Church St. (415) 648-1166¶

The m
San Fran
» 1.»Fi
39, and
ing abou
San Fra
tute mu
Francisc
haps the
Tourists
by street
souvenir

Working with inline frames

An inline frame is treated like a single character. If you insert or delete text that precedes an inline frame, the frame moves forward or backward along with the rest of the text that follows the inserted or deleted text. Although inline frames usually contain graphics, they can just as easily contain text or nothing at all.

Inline frames may interfere with line spacing in paragraphs that have automatic leading. If the inline frame is larger than the point size in use, the automatic leading value for that line is calculated from the inline frame. This leads to inconsistent line spacing in the paragraph. To work around this, you can apply a fixed amount of leading to all characters in the paragraph, adjust the size of inline frames, place inline frames at the beginning of a paragraph, or place inline frames in their own paragraphs.

There are three ways to create inline frames: pasting the frame into text, placing the frame into text, and using the new Anchored Object menu option. The first two are the simplest, but the third gives you more control over the inline frame when you create it. The third way also lets you create anchored frames, which are covered later in this chapter.

Using the Paste command

If you want to create an inline frame from an object you already created, all you have to do is copy or cut the object and then paste it into text as you would a piece of highlighted text. Here's how:

1. **Use the Selection tool to select the object you want to paste within text.**

   Any type of object can be used: a line, an empty shape, a text or picture frame, even a group of objects.

2. **Choose Edit⇨Copy or press ⌘+C or Ctrl+C.**

   If you don't need the original item, you can use the Cut command (Edit⇨ Cut or ⌘+X or Ctrl+X) instead of the Copy command.

3. **Select the Type tool and then click within the text where you want to place the copied object.**

   Make sure the cursor is flashing where you intend to place the inline frame.

4. **Choose Edit⇨Paste or press ⌘+V or Ctrl+V.**

Inline frames often work best when placed at the beginning of a paragraph. If you place an inline frame within text to which automatic leading has been applied, the resulting line spacing can be inconsistent. To fix this problem, you can resize the inline frame.

Using the Place command

You can also use the Place command to create an inline graphics frame from an external picture file. (You can't use this technique for inline text frames.) Here's how:

1. **Select the Type tool and then click within a text frame to establish the insertion point.**

2. **Choose File⇨Place or press ⌘+D or Ctrl+D.**

3. **Locate and select the graphics file you want to place within the text; choose Open.**

To delete an inline frame, you can select it and then choose Edit⇨Clear or Edit⇨Cut, or you can position the text cursor next to it and press Delete or Backspace.

Adjusting inline frames

After you create an inline frame, you can adjust its position vertically or horizontally. Again, there are several methods.

Two quick-and-dirty methods to move an inline frame vertically are as follows:

✔ Use the Type tool to highlight the inline frame as you would highlight an individual text character. In the Character panel or Control panel, type a positive value in the Baseline Shift field to move the inline frame up; type a negative value to move the frame down.

✔ Use the Selection tool or Direct Selection tool to select the inline frame; drag the frame up or down.

A quick way to move an inline frame horizontally is to follow these steps:

1. **With the Type tool selected, click between the inline frame and the character that precedes it.**

2. **Use the kerning controls in the Character panel or Control panel to enlarge or reduce the space between the inline frame and the preceding character.**

You can more precisely control the position of inline frames by using the Anchored Object Options dialog box, covered in the next section.

Of course, you can also adjust its other attributes as needed, such as strokes, fills, dimensions, rotation, and skew, by using the Tools panel, Control panel, and other panels.

Working with anchored frames

Anchored frames give you a whole new way of organizing objects. Essentially, they follow the relevant text within the parameters you specify, such as staying to the left of the text or staying at the top of the page that contains the text.

Note that an inline frame is a type of anchored frame, one where the frame stays within the text it is linked to. For simplicity, I'm using the term *anchored frame* to mean only those frames that are outside the text frame but remain linked to a specific point in the text.

In addition to preserving anchored framed in imported Microsoft Word files, InDesign lets you create anchors in your layout. To create anchored frames, do the following:

1. **Select the Type tool and then click within a text frame to establish the insertion point.**

2. **Choose Object⇨Anchored Object⇨Insert.**

   The Insert Anchored Object dialog box appears.

3. **In the Object Options section of the dialog box, specify the anchored frame's settings.**

   You can choose the type of content (text, graphics, or unassigned) with the Content pop-up menu, apply an object style by using the Object Style pop-up menu, apply a paragraph style via the Paragraph Style pop-up menu (if Content is set to Text), and set the anchored frame's dimensions in the Height and Width fields. Note that the paragraph style you choose, if any, applies to the anchored frame, not to the paragraph in which the anchored frame is linked.

4. **In the Position pop-up menu, choose what kind of frame you are creating: Inline or Above Line (both are inline frames) or Custom (an anchored frame).**

   The dialog box will show different options based on that choice, as Figure 11-7 shows.

Anchored frames that you add by choosing Object⇨Anchored Object⇨ Insert do not have text automatically wrapped around them. Use the Text Wrap panel (Window⇨Text Wrap or Option+⌘+W or Ctrl+Alt+W) to open this panel and set text wrap. But anchored frames created by pasting a graphic into text *do* automatically have text wrap around them.

Selecting the Prevent Manual Positioning option ensures that the positions of individual anchored frames can't be adjusted by using InDesign's other text and frame controls (such as Baseline Shift). This forces users to use this dialog box to change the anchored frame's position, reducing the chances of accidental change.

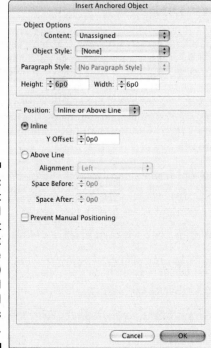

Figure 11-7:
The Insert
Anchored
Object
dialog box
for inline
frames (left)
and
anchored
frames
(right).

5. **Decide whether to select the Relative to Spine option.**

   If this option is *not* selected, the anchored frame is placed on the same side of the text frame on all pages, whether those pages are left-facing or right-facing. If the Relative to Spine option is selected, InDesign places the text frame on the outside of both pages or inside of both pages, depending on how the anchored position is set.

6. **In the Anchored Object section of the dialog box, click one of the positioning squares to set up the text frame's relative position.**

   Note that you need to think about both the horizontal and vertical position you desire. For example, if you want the anchored frame to appear to the right of the text reference, click one of the right-hand squares. (Remember that selecting the Relative to Spine option overrides this, making the right-hand pages' positions mirror that of the left-hand pages, rather than be identical to them.) If you choose the topmost right-hand square, the anchored frame is placed to the right of the text reference and vertically appears at or below that text reference. But if you choose the bottommost right-hand square, you're telling InDesign you want the anchored frame to appear vertically above the text reference. Experiment with your layout to see what works best in each case.

7. **In the Anchored Position section of the dialog box, click one of the positioning squares to set up the text reference's relative position.**

   Although there are nine squares shown, the only three that matter are those in the middle row. Typically, you place the text reference on the opposite side of the anchored frame — if you want the anchored frame to be to the left, you would indicate that the text reference is to the right. (If you set the text reference on the same side as the anchored frame, InDesign places the anchored frame over the text.) The reason there are three squares (left, middle, and right) is to accommodate layouts in which you want some anchored frames to appear to the left of the text and some to the right; in that case, choose the middle position here and select the right- or left-hand position in the Anchored Object section as appropriate to that object.

8. **There are three options in the Anchored Position section that give InDesign more precise instructions on how to place the anchored frames:**

   • **The X Relative To pop-up menu** tells InDesign from where the horizontal location is calculated, using the following options: Anchor Marker, Column Edge, Text Frame, Page Margin, and Page Edge. The right option depends both on where you want the anchored frames placed and whether you have multicolumn text boxes (in which case Text Frame and Column Edge result in different placement, while in a single-column text frame they do not). You can also specify a specific amount of space to place between the chosen X Relative To point and the anchored frame by typing a value in the X Offset field.

   • **The Y Relative To pop-up menu** tells InDesign from where the vertical location is calculated, using the following options: Line (Baseline), Line (Cap-height), Line (Top of Leading), Column Edge, Text Frame, Page Margin, and Page Edge. As you expect, you can also indicate a specific amount of space to place between the chosen Y Relative To point and the anchored frame by typing a value in the Y Offset field.

   • **The Keep Within Top/Bottom Column boundaries check box** does exactly what it says.

9. **Click OK to insert the anchored frame.**

You can create inline frames using the same basic process as above, choosing Inline or Above Line in Step 4. You'll get most of the same controls as for anchored objects, such as the frame size and type, but of course there are no controls for the relative position because an inline frame goes at the text-insertion point. But it's easier to use the techniques described in the previous section for creating inline frames: copying or placing a frame into text.

Anchoring caveats

There are several caveats to consider when creating anchored frames:

✓ Because an anchored frame follows its text as it flows throughout a document, you need to ensure that your layout retains clear paths for those anchored objects to follow. Otherwise, anchored frames could overlap other frames as they move.

✓ Anchored frames should generally be small items and/or used sparingly. The more items you have anchored to text, the greater the chance that they will interfere with each other's placement. Likewise, large items can be moved only so far within a page, so the benefit of keeping them close to their related text disappears.

✓ Items such as pull-quotes are obvious candidates for use as anchored frames. But in many layouts, you want the pull-quotes to stay in specific locations on the page for good visual appearance. The InDesign anchored-frame function can accommodate that need for specific positioning on a page, but you need to be careful as you add or delete text so that you do not end up with some pages that have no pull-quotes at all because there is so much text between the pull-quotes' anchor points. Conversely, you need to make sure you don't have too many pull-quotes anchored close to each other, which could result in overlapping.

Typically, you use anchored frames for small graphics or icons that you want to keep next to a specific paragraph (such as the Tip and Warning icons used in this book). Another good use would be for cross-reference ("For More Information") text frames.

Converting existing frames to anchored frames

After you get the hang of when and how to use anchored frames, you'll likely want to convert some frames in existing documents into anchored frames. There's no direct way to do that in InDesign, but there is a somewhat circuitous path you can take:

1. **Use the Selection or Direct Selection tool to cut the existing frame that you want to make into an anchored frame by choosing Edit⇨Cut or by pressing ⌘+X or Ctrl+X.**

   You can also copy an existing frame by choosing Edit⇨Copy or by pressing ⌘+C or Ctrl+C.

2. **Switch to the Type tool and click in a text frame at the desired location to insert the text reference to the anchored frame.**

3. **Paste the cut or copied frame into that insertion point by choosing Edit⇨Paste or by pressing ⌘+V or Ctrl+V.**

   You now have an inline frame.

4. **Select the frame with the Selection tool, and then choose Object⇨ Anchored Object⇨Options to display the Anchored Object Options dialog box.**

   This dialog box looks like the Insert Anchored Options dialog box, shown in Figure 11-7, except that it doesn't include the top Object Options section.

5. **Choose Custom from the Position pop-up menu.**

   This converts the frame from an inline frame to an anchored frame.

6. **Adjust the position for the newly minted anchored frame as described in the previous section.**

7. **Click OK when you're done.**

Adjusting anchored frames

After you create an anchored frame, you can adjust its position.

A quick-and-dirty method is simply to click and drag anchored frames or use the Control panel to adjust their position. If the text the frame is anchored to moves, however, InDesign overrides those changes. (You can't manually move an anchored frame if the Prevent Manual Positioning option is selected in the Insert Anchored Object dialog box or Anchored Object Options dialog box. This option is deselected by default.)

For the most control of an anchored frame's position, choose Object⇨ Anchored Object⇨Options. The resulting Anchored Object Options dialog box is identical to the Insert Anchored Object dialog box (covered previously in this section and shown in Figure 11-7) but without the Object Options section.

And, of course, you can adjust the frame's other attributes as needed, such as strokes, fills, dimensions, rotation, and skew.

Releasing and deleting anchored frames

If you no longer want an anchored frame to be anchored to a text location, you can release the anchor. To do so, select the anchored frame with the Selection or Direct Selection tool and then choose Object⇨Anchored Object⇨Release.

It's also easy to delete an anchored frame: Select the frame with the Selection or Direct Selection tool and then choose Edit⇨Clear or press Delete or Backspace. If you want to remove the object but keep it on the Clipboard for pasting elsewhere, choose Edit⇨Cut or press ⌘+X or Ctrl+X.

Part IV
Text Essentials

The 5th Wave   By Rich Tennant

"Well, shoot! This eggplant chart is just as confusing as the butternut squash chart and the gourd chart. Can't you just make a pie chart like everyone else?"

In this part . . .

Getting words on the page is an important part of what you do with InDesign. After you have the words in place, you want to tweak the letters and lines, and the space between them, to make your pages sparkle. This part shows you how to arrange words on the page, including words made up of exotic characters. You find out how to set text in columns and how to add bullets and numbers to that text. You also find out how to stretch, squeeze, rotate, and add special effects to text. Additionally, you see how to become skilled at using character and paragraph styles to make your life easier and to speed up your publishing workflow.

Chapter 12

Putting Words on the Page

*T*ext is more than words — it's also a layout element that flows through your pages in the locations that you need. Much of the work you do in InDesign will be controlling that flow and working with the text as blocks that need to have the right arrangement to fit your layout's goals.

This chapter helps you manage that flow and arrangement, showing you how to deftly maneuver the text through your layout, just as you would move your way through the dance floor.

After you have the steps nailed down, you can do the dance: bringing in text from your source files.

Working with Text Frames

When you're creating a simple layout, such as a single-page flier or a magazine advertisement, you will probably create text frames — the containers for text — as you need them. But if you're working on a book or a magazine, you'll want your text frames placed on master pages so your text will be consistently framed automatically when it appears on document pages. And you'll still have individual text frames you create for specific elements like sidebars.

Chapter 8 shows you how to create frames (including text frames), whereas Chapter 6 shows you how to create master pages. This chapter brings those two concepts together to show you how to work with text frames, both those in master pages and those you create in your document pages.

Creating master text frames

Master pages — predesigned pages that you can apply to other pages to automate layout and ensure consistency — can contain several types of text frames:

- Text frames containing standing text, such as page numbers or page headers.

- Text frames containing placeholder text for elements such as figure captions or headlines.

- One master text frame (an automatically placed text frame for flowing text throughout pages), which you create in the New Document dialog box (File➪New➪Document, or ⌘+N or Ctrl+N).

Think of a master text frame as an empty text frame on the default master page that lets you automatically flow text through a document. When you create a new document, you can create a master text frame at the same time. Here's how it works:

1. **Choose File➪New➪Document or press ⌘+N or Ctrl+N.**

2. **Check the Master Text Frame check box at the top of the New Document dialog box.**

3. **Specify the size and placement of the master text frame by entering values in the Margins area for Top, Bottom, Inside, and Outside (or Left and Right if Facing Pages is unchecked) fields.**

   InDesign places guides according to these values and places a text frame within the guides. The text frame fits within the boundaries of these values and those of the guides on the master page.

4. **To specify the number of columns in the master text frame, enter a value in the Number field in the Columns area.**

   You can also specify the amount of space between the columns by entering a value in the Gutter field.

5. **Establish any other needed settings as described in Chapter 3.**

   Check the Facing Pages check box if your pages will have different inside and outside margins (for example, a book might have different inside and outside margins for left-hand and right-hand pages).

6. **Click OK to create a new document containing a master text frame.**

After you create a document with a master text frame, you'll see guides on the first document page that indicate the placement of the frame.

Creating individual text frames

Although the master text frame is helpful for containing body text that flows through a document, there's a good chance you'll need additional text frames on both master pages and document pages. Generally, these are smaller text frames that hold text such as headlines, sidebars, or captions.

To add text frames to a master page for repeating elements such as headers and footers, first display the master page. Choose Window⇨Pages or press ⌘+F12 or Ctrl+F12 to display the Pages panel. Then double-click the A-Master icon in the upper portion of the panel, as shown in Figure 12-1. That displays the A-Master master page. (If you have multiple master pages in your document, you can follow these instructions to add text frames to any of them. Just choose the desired master page.)

To add text frames to a document page, first go to the page. You can use any of the techniques described in Chapter 4 to move among pages.

Now draw the desired frame using any of the frame or shape tools, or the Type tool, as described in Chapter 8. Modify them with the Control panel (or Transform panel) or by using the mouse, also as described in that chapter.

Text frames you add to a master page will show up on any document pages based on that master page.

Figure 12-1:
To access a master page so you can add or modify text frames and other objects, double-click its master-page icon in the upper portion of the Pages panel.

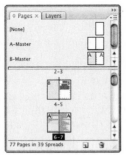

If you're working on a document page and want to type inside a text frame placed on the page by a master page, select the Type tool and then Shift+⌘+click or Ctrl+Shift+click the frame.

Making changes to text frames

You're not confined to the settings you originally established when you set up a master text frame or an individual text frame — you may change the size, shape, and/or number of columns in the text frame later. Use the Selection tool to click the desired text frame and then modify it with the following options (the first six are covered in detail in Chapter 8):

- ✔ Change the placement of a selected master text frame by using the X: and Y: fields in the Control panel.
- ✔ Change the size of the master text frame by using the W: and H: fields.
- ✔ Change the angle by using the Rotation field.
- ✔ Change the skew by using the Shear X field.
- ✔ Enter values in the Scale fields to increase or decrease, by percentage amounts, the width and height of the text frame.
- ✔ Use the General pane of the Text Frame Options dialog box (Object➪Text Frame Options, or ⌘+B or Ctrl+B, shown in Figure 12-2) to make further modifications:
  - • Change the number of columns and the space between them.
  - • Specify how far text is inset from each side of the frame.
  - • Align text vertically within the frame.
  - • Control the placement of the first baseline.
- ✔ Use the Baseline Options pane of the Text Frame Options dialog box to set a baseline grid, if desired, for the text to align to. Chapter 11 describes this feature in more detail.

If you don't want the text inside this text frame to wrap around any items in front of it, check Ignore Text Wrap at the bottom of the dialog box.

If you open the Text Frame Options dialog box with no document open, any changes you make will become the default for all new documents.

- ✔ Specify character styles, paragraph styles, object styles, Story panel settings, text-wrap settings, and other text attributes to apply in the text frame to the document text you flow into that frame. (You can always override those attributes by applying other styles or formatting to the text later.) The rest of Part IV covers these other settings.

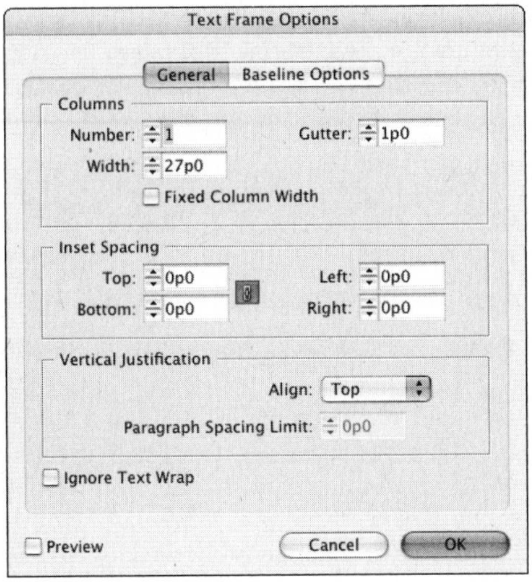

Figure 12-2:
Change the
properties
of a text
frame using
the Text
Frame
Options
dialog box.

Additionally, if you select the frame with the Direct Selection tool, you can change its shape by dragging anchor points on the frame to other positions, as described in Chapter 9.

Importing Text

You can import text from a word processor file (Word 97/98 or later, RTF, ASCII (text-only), or InDesign Tagged Text files) into an InDesign text frame using the Place dialog box (File⇨Place, or ⌘+D or Ctrl+D). You can also import Microsoft Excel spreadsheets (version 97/98 or later). Many of the text's original styles will remain intact, although you will want to review the imported text carefully to see if any adjustments need to be made.

Follow these steps to place imported text:

1. **Choose File⇨Place, or press ⌘+D or Ctrl+D to open the Place dialog box.**

2. **Locate the text file you want to import.**

3. **To specify how to handle current formatting in the file, check the Show Import Options check box.**

   This opens the appropriate Import Options dialog box for the text file's format. (Note that there are no import options for ASCII text.) Then click OK to return to the Place dialog box.

4. **Click the Open button to import the text.**

5. **If you selected an empty frame with the Type tool, InDesign will flow the text into that frame. If you selected a text frame with the Type tool, InDesign will flow the text at the text-insertion point in that frame, inserting the new text within the existing text.**

   If you hadn't already selected a frame before starting to import the text, specify where to place it by clicking and dragging the loaded-text icon to create a rectangular text frame, clicking in an existing frame, or clicking in any empty frame.

You can now select multiple files — text and/or graphics — by Shift+clicking a range or ⌘+clicking or Ctrl+clicking multiple files one by one. InDesign will let you place each file in a separate frame. Just click once for each file imported, or Shift+⌘+click or Ctrl+Shift+click to have InDesign place all files on the page in separate frames. The loaded-text icon will show the number of files to be placed, as well as a mini preview of each file, as Figure 12-3 shows. When placing files, you can use the keyboard left- and right-arrow keys to move through the thumbnail previews before clicking to place the one whose thumbnail preview is currently displayed, so you can place the files in any order you want.

You can't click on a master text frame — a text frame that is placed on the page by the master page in use — and simply start typing. To select a master text frame and add text to it, Shift+⌘+click or Ctrl+Shift+click it. (For more on master pages, see Chapter 6.)

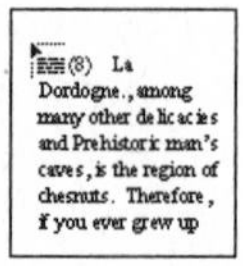

Figure 12-3:
The new
loaded-text
icon
showing
multiple files
have been
selected
and showing
a preview of
the first
document.

```
|------
|▦▦ (8)  La
Dordogne., among
many other delicacies
and Prehistoric man's
caves, is the region of
chestnuts. Therefore,
if you ever grew up
```

Import options for Microsoft Word and RTF files

InDesign offers a comprehensive set of import options for Word and RTF files. With these options, you can control how these files will import into InDesign.

To save time on future imports, you can save your import preferences as a preset file for repeat use.

Figure 12-4 shows the Microsoft Word Import Options dialog box. The import options for RTF files are identical.

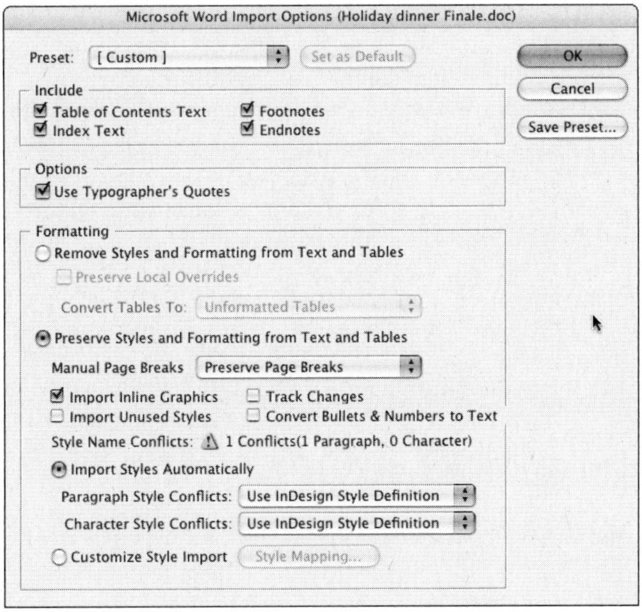

Figure 12-4:
The Import
Options
dialog box
for a
Word file.

The Preset pop-up menu, at the top of the page, lets you select from saved sets of import options. You can save the current settings by clicking the Save Preset button. And you can set a preset as the default import behavior by clicking the Set as Default button; these settings will be used for all Word file imports unless you choose a new default or make changes in this dialog box. This lets you avoid using the Import Options dialog box for your routine imports.

The Include section of the Import Options dialog box is where you decide whether to strip out specific types of text (Table of Contents Text, Index Text, Footnotes, and Endnotes) from the Word file. If you check items, their corresponding text will be imported. You probably won't want to import table-of-contents or index text because you can create much nicer-looking tables of contents and indexes in InDesign.

The third section, Options, has just one option: Use Typographer's Quotes. If this box is checked, InDesign converts keyboard quotes from your source file (' and ") to "curly" typographic quotes (', ', ", and ").

The fourth section, Formatting, is fairly complex, so take it one step at a time. Start with deciding whether to remove or retain the formatting in your imported text.

To *remove* text formatting during import so that you can do the formatting in InDesign, select the Remove Styles and Formatting from Text and Tables option. You have two additional controls for this option:

- ✔ Preserve Local Overrides, which retains local formatting such as italics and boldface while ignoring the paragraph style attributes. You'd usually want this option checked so that meaning-related formatting is retained.

- ✔ You also can choose how tables are "unformatted" during import via the Convert Tables To pop-up menu. Unformatted Tables retains the table's cell structure but ignores text and cell formatting, while Unformatted Tabbed Text converts the table to tabbed text (with a tab separating what used to be cells and a paragraph return separating what used to be rows) and strips out any formatting. If you intend to keep tables as tables but format them in InDesign, choose Unformatted Tables.

To *retain* text formatting during import, so that the InDesign document at least starts out using the settings used in Word, choose the Preserve Styles and Formatting from Text and Tables option. This option includes several controls and bits of information:

- ✔ The Manual Page Breaks pop-up menu lets you retain any page breaks entered in Word, convert them to column breaks, or strip them out.

- ✔ Checking the Import Inline Graphics check box will enable the import of any graphics in the Word text.

- ✔ Checking the Import Unused Styles check box means that all Word style sheets will transfer into InDesign, rather than just the ones you actually applied to text in the file. Unless you want all those extra Word styles, keep this box unchecked.

- ✔ Checking the Track Changes check box preserves the revisions tracking information from Word so you can see it in the companion Adobe InCopy editing program. But InDesign itself does not display or let you use that tracking information. This book does not cover the expert InCopy add-on software.

- ✔ Checking Convert Bullets & Numbers to Text removes any automatic bullet and numbering lists in Word, converting the bullets and numbers into the actual characters. If you select this option, and insert an item in an imported numbered list, the list won't renumber automatically, as it would if you leave this unchecked. (In previous versions of InDesign, bullets and numbers were converted, eliminating the automatic aspect.)

✔ If InDesign detects that the Word file has a style with the same name as your InDesign document, it will note how many to the right of the Style Name Conflicts label. You have choices in how to handle these conflicts:

  • Use InDesign Style Definition preserves the current InDesign style sheets and applies them to any text in Word that uses a style sheet of the same name. Redefine InDesign Style causes the Word style sheet's formatting to permanently replace that of InDesign's style sheet. Auto Rename renames the Word file's style sheet and adds it to the Paragraph Styles or Character Styles panel. This preserves your existing InDesign style sheets while also preserving those imported from the Word file.

  • Customize Style Import lets you decide which specific InDesign styles override same-name Word styles, which Word styles override same-name InDesign styles, and which Word styles are renamed during import to prevent any overriding.

Import options for Microsoft Excel files

When importing Excel spreadsheets, you have several options, as Figure 12-5 shows.

In the Options section, you can control the following settings:

✔ The Sheet pop-up menu lets you choose which sheet in an Excel workbook to import. The default is the first sheet, which is usually named Sheet1 unless you renamed it in Excel. (If you want to import several sheets, you'll need to import the same spreadsheet several times, choosing a different sheet each time.)

✔ The View pop-up menu lets you import custom views that are defined in Excel for that spreadsheet. If the spreadsheet has no custom views, this pop-up menu is grayed out. You can also ignore any custom views by choosing [Ignore View] from the pop-up menu.

✔ In the Cell Range pop-up menu, you specify a range of cells using standard Excel notation $Sx:Ey$, where S is the first row, x the first column, E the last row, and y the last column, such as A1:G35. You can enter a range directly in the pop-up menu, which also acts as a text-entry field, or choose a previously entered range from the pop-up menu.

✔ Checking the Import Hidden Cells Not Saved in View check box will import hidden cells. Be careful when doing so, because these cells are usually hidden for a reason (typically, they show interim calculations and the like).

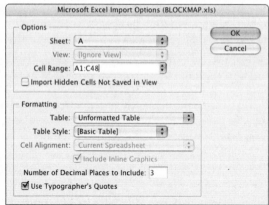

Figure 12-5:
The Import
Options
dialog box
for an Excel
file.

In the Formatting section, you can control the following settings:

- ✔ In the Table pop-up menu, you choose from Formatted Table, which imports the spreadsheet as a table and retains text and cell formatting; Unformatted Table, which imports the spreadsheet as a table but does not preserve formatting; and Unformatted Tabbed Text, which imports the spreadsheet as tabbed text (tabs separate cells and paragraph returns separate rows) with no formatting retained.

- ✔ In the Table Style pop-up menu, you choose an InDesign table style to apply to the imported table, or leave it alone (by choosing [No Table Style]).

- ✔ In the Cell Alignment pop-up menu, you tell InDesign how to align the text in cells. You can retain the spreadsheet's current alignment settings by choosing Current Spreadsheet, or override them by choosing Left, Right, or Center.

- ✔ Checking the Include Inline Graphics check box imports any graphics placed in the Excel cells.

- ✔ The Number of Decimal Places to Include field is where you enter how many decimal places to retain for numbers.

- ✔ Check the Use Typographer's Quotes check box to convert keyboard quotes (' and ") to the "curly" typographic quotes (', ', ", and "). It's a good idea to keep this box checked.

Pasting text into an InDesign document

As you probably already know, you can hold text on the Mac or Windows Clipboard by cutting it or copying it from its original location. After you've captured some text on the Clipboard, you can paste it into an InDesign document at the location of the cursor. You can also replace highlighted text with the text that's on the Clipboard. If no text frame is active when you do the pasting, InDesign creates a new text frame to contain the pasted text.

InDesign uses standard menu commands and keyboard commands for cutting/copying text to the Clipboard, and for pasting text. On the Mac, press ⌘+X to cut, ⌘+C to copy, and ⌘+V to paste. In Windows, press Ctrl+X to cut, Ctrl+C to copy, and Ctrl+V to paste.

Text that is cut or copied from InDesign normally retains its formatting, whereas text pasted from other programs loses its formatting. But you can specify whether pasted text from other programs always retains its formatting. Go to the Clipboard Handling pane in the Preferences dialog box (choose InDesign⇨Preferences⇨Clipboard Handling or press ⌘+K on the Mac, or choose Edit⇨Preferences⇨Clipboard Handling or press Ctrl+K in Windows) and select the All Information option in the When Pasting Text and Tables from Other Applications section. If you select this option, you can still tell InDesign to *not* preserve the formatting on a case-by-case basis by choosing Edit⇨Paste without Formatting (Shift+⌘+V or Ctrl+Shift+V).

Dragging and dropping text

You can drag highlighted text from other programs — or even text files from the desktop or a folder — into an InDesign document. Text that you drag and drop is inserted at the location of the cursor, replaces highlighted text, or is placed in a new rectangular text frame.

Keep characters to a minimum

When you're working with text in a professional publishing application, such as InDesign, you need to keep in mind some differences between the professional method and traditional way of typing:

✔ Remember that you don't need to type two spaces after a period or colon; books, newspapers, magazines, and other professional documents all use just one space after such punctuation.

✔ Don't enter extra paragraph returns for space between paragraphs and don't enter tabs to indent paragraphs — instead, set up this formatting using InDesign's paragraph attributes (Type⇨Paragraph, or Option+⌘+T or Ctrl+Alt+T).

✔ To align text in columns, don't enter extra tabs; place the same number of tabs between each column, and then align the tabs (Type⇨Tabs, or Shift+⌘+T or Ctrl+Shift+T).

To see where your InDesign document has tabs, paragraph breaks, spaces, and other such invisible characters, use the command Option+⌘+I or Ctrl+Alt+I, or choose Type⇨ Show Hidden Characters.

When you drag and drop a text selection, its original formatting is usually retained — unless you hold the Shift key when dragging. If you hold the Shift key, the text takes on the attributes of the text you drag it into.

When you drag and drop a text *file*, the process is more like a text import: The text retains its formatting and styles. Unlike the Place command (File⇔Place, or ⌘+D or Ctrl+D) that imports text, drag and drop does not give you the option to specify how some of the formatting and styles in the imported text file are handled.

Threading Text Frames

The text that flows through a series of frames is what InDesign considers a *story,* and the connections among those frames are called *threads.* When you edit text in a threaded story, the text reflows throughout the text frames. You can also spell-check and do a find/change operation for an entire story, even though you have just one of the story's text frames active on-screen.

When you have threaded text frames, you'll see visual indicators on your text frame, assuming you choose View⇔Show Text Threads (Option+⌘+Y or Ctrl+Alt+Y) and have selected the frame with one of the selection tools. At the lower right of the text frame is a small square, called the *out port,* that indicates the outflow status:

- ✔ If the square is empty, that means there is no text flowing to another frame, and not enough text to flow to another frame.

- ✔ If the square is red and has a plus sign in it, that means there is more text than fits in the selected frame but that it is *not* flowing to another frame. This is called *overset text.*

- ✔ If the square has a triangle icon, that means the text is flowing to another frame. That doesn't mean that text *is* flowing, just that if there is more text than the current frame can hold, it *will* flow.

Similarly, there's an *in port* at the upper left of a text frame that indicates whether text is flowing from another frame into the current frame:

- ✔ If the square is empty, that means there is no text flowing from another frame, making this frame the first (and perhaps only) frame in a story.

- ✔ If the square has a triangle icon, that means the text is flowing from another frame. That doesn't mean that text *is* flowing, just that if there is more text than the other frame can hold, it *will* flow into this frame.

So how do you thread the frames in the first place? You have three options in InDesign: manual, semi-autoflow, and autoflow. Each of these options has its own icon. The method you choose depends on the amount of text you're dealing with and the size and number of your text frames:

✔ To link two text frames across several pages (for example, for an article that starts on page 2 and continues on page 24), you might use the manual method, in which you click the first text frame's out port and then click on the second text frame.

✔ To link a succession of text frames, you might want to use the semi-autoflow method, which allows you to click a series of text frames to flow text from one frame to the next.

✔ To import text that is intended for long documents (such as a book chapter or brochure), you might want to use the autoflow method to add text frames and pages that accommodate the text you're importing.

For a quick glance at your text threads while you're threading text across pages, simply change the document view briefly to 20 percent or so.

Text flows in the order in which you select frames. If you move a frame, its order in the text flow remains unchanged. If you're not careful, you could, for example, accidentally have text flow from a frame at the top of the page to a frame at the bottom of a page and then to one in the middle of a page.

Threading frames manually

To thread text frames manually, you simply use a selection tool to link out ports to in ports. You can pre-thread existing text frames by linking empty text frames and add text later, or you can create threads from a text frame that contains text.

Always switch to a selection tool when you're threading frames. Oddly, you cannot thread frames while the Type tool is selected. Oh well.

To thread text frames, follow these steps:

1. **Create a series of text frames that will hold the text you import.**

   These text frames do not need to be on the same page.

2. **Click either the Selection tool or the Direct Selection tool.**

3. **Click the out port of the first text frame in the thread.**

   The pointer becomes the loaded-text icon.

4. **Click the in port of the second text frame in the thread.**

   You can also click any empty frame or click and drag to draw a new text frame. How text flow behaves depends on the text frame's status:

   - If the first frame held no text, any text placed or typed in later will flow into the second frame if it doesn't all fit in the first text frame.

   - If the first frame held text but was not already linked to another text frame, any overset text will flow into the existing text frame.

   - If the first text frame was already linked to another text frame, the text will now be redirected to the text frame you just selected.

5. **Use the Pages panel to add or switch pages while you continue clicking out ports and in ports until your chain of threaded text frames is complete.**

   You can also switch pages using the page controls at the bottom of the document window, by choosing Layout⇨Go to Page, or pressing ⌘+J or Ctrl+J.

6. **When you're finished threading text frames, select another object on the page or select another tool.**

   A story imported into any text frame in this chain will start in the upper-right corner of the first frame and flow through the frames in the same order as the threads.

Threading frames with the semi-autoflow method

InDesign includes a *semi-autoflow* method of threading text frames, which incorporates a few automatic shortcuts but varies only slightly from the manual method. Follow the same steps for threading text frames manually, except hold down the Option or Alt key each time you click in the next text frame. Doing so lets you bypass the in ports and out ports and simply click from text frame to text frame to establish links.

If you want to begin a semi-autoflow process when you place a word-processing file for the first time, you can Option+click or Alt+click in the first text frame that will hold the placed text.

As you're threading frames, Option+click or Alt+click each text frame, or you'll revert to manual threading.

Threading frames and automatically adding pages

You can flow a lengthy story quickly through a document using the autoflow method for threading frames. You can either autoflow text into the master text frame or into automatically created text frames that fit within the column guides. InDesign flows the text into any existing pages, and then adds new pages based on the current master page. You can initiate autoflow before or after placing a word processing file.

Placing text while autoflowing

If you haven't imported text yet, you can place a file and have it automatically flow through the document. This method works well for flowing text into pages that are all formatted the same way (as in a book). Here's how it works:

1. **Before you begin, check your master page.**

   Make sure that the master page you're using includes a master text frame or appropriate column guides.

2. **With no text frames selected, choose File⇨Place or press ⌘+D or Ctrl+D.**

3. **Locate and select the word-processing file you want to import, and then click Open.**

4. **When you see the loaded-text icon, Shift+click in the first column that will contain the text. Be sure to Shift+click near the upper-left corner of the master text frame, so InDesign uses that frame rather than create a new one.**

   InDesign adds all the necessary text frames and pages, and flows in the entire story.

Autoflowing after placing text

Even if you've already placed a text file into a single text frame or a threaded chain of text frames, you can still autoflow text from the last text frame. To do this, click the out port, and then Shift+click any page to indicate where to start the autoflow.

You might use this method if you're placing the introduction to an article in an elaborately designed opener page. Then you can flow the rest of the article into standard pages.

Breaking and rerouting threads

After text frames are threaded, you have three options for changing the threads: You can break threads to stop text from flowing, insert a text frame into an existing chain of threaded text frames, and remove text frames from a thread. Here are the techniques in a nutshell:

- Break the link between two text frames by double-clicking either an out port or an in port. The thread between the two text frames is removed, and all text that had flowed from that point is sucked out of the subsequent text frames and stored as overset text.

- Insert a text frame after a specific text frame in a chain by clicking its out port. Then, click and drag the loaded-text icon to create a new text frame. That new frame is automatically threaded to both the previous and the next text frames.

- Reroute text threads — for example, to drop the middle text frame from a chain of three — by clicking the text frame with the Selection tool and then pressing Delete or Backspace. This deletes the text frame and reroutes the threads. You can also Shift+click to multiple-select text frames to remove. Note that you cannot reroute text threads without removing the text frames.

Working with Columns

Where you place columns on the page — and the amount of space you allow between columns — has a big impact on readability. Used with a little know-how, column width works with type size and leading to make text easier to read. Columns help you keep from getting lost from one line to the next, and from getting a headache as you're trying to read the words on the page.

Generally, as columns get wider, the type size and leading increase. For example, you might see 9-point text and 15-point leading in 2½-inch columns, whereas 15-point text and 13-point leading might work better in 3½-inch columns.

InDesign lets you place columns on the page automatically, create any number of columns within a text frame, and change columns at any time.

Specifying columns in master frames

You can specify the number of columns at the same time you create a *master text frame* — a text frame placed automatically within the margin guides.

In the Columns area in the New Document dialog box, use the Number field to specify how many columns, and the Gutter field to specify how much space to place between the columns. (The gutter is the space between columns.) Whether or not you check Master Text Frame (which makes the frame appear on all pages), guides for these columns will still be placed on the page and can be used for placing text frames and other objects.

Changing columns in text frames

You can change the number of columns in a text frame (whether an individual text frame or a master text frame), even after you've flown text into the frame — and doing so isn't difficult. First, select the text frame with a selection tool or the Type tool (or Shift+click to select multiple text frames and change all their columns at once). Then choose Object⇨Text Frame Options, or press ⌘+B or Ctrl+B, and set the desired Number and Gutter values in the General pane of the Text Frame Options dialog box, shown in Figure 12-2.

You can also use the Control panel to quickly change the number of columns, but note that this control will not display on a monitor set below 1152-x-870-pixel resolution unless you customize the Control panel interface (to disable other controls to make room for this one) using the Customize command in its flyout menu.

Some designers like to draw each column as a separate frame. I strongly recommend against this practice; it's too easy to create columns of slightly different widths and slightly different positions, so text doesn't align properly. Instead, specify columns in your text frames so you won't have to worry about sloppy layouts.

Note that the options in the Columns area of the Text Frame Options dialog box work differently depending on whether Fixed Column Width is checked or unchecked:

- ✔ If Fixed Column Width is unchecked, InDesign subtracts from the text frame the space specified for the gutters, and then divides the remaining width by the number of columns to figure out how wide the columns can be. For example, if you specify a 10-inch-wide text frame with three columns and a gutter of ½ inch, you end up with three 3-inch columns and two ½-inch gutters. The math is $(10–[2 \times 0.5]) \div 3$.

- ✔ If Fixed Column Width is checked, InDesign resizes the text frame to fit the number of columns you selected at the indicated size, as well as the gutters between them. For example, suppose you're using a 10-inch-wide text frame with a column width of 5 inches and a gutter of ½ inch, and you choose three columns: You end up with a 15-inch-wide text frame containing three 5-inch columns and two ½-inch gutters. The math is $(5 \times 3) + (2 \times 2)$.

Check Preview to see the effects of your changes before finalizing them.

Wrapping Text around Objects

In the days before personal computers and page-layout software, wrapping text around a graphic or other object was a time-consuming and expensive task. Text wraps were rare, found only in the most expensively produced pub-lications. Not any more. Not only do all page-layout programs let you create text runarounds, most programs — including InDesign — provide several options for controlling how text relates to graphics and other objects that obstruct its flow.

When a frame is positioned in front of a text frame, InDesign provides the fol-lowing options. You can

- ✔ Ignore the frame and flow the text behind it.
- ✔ Wrap the text around the frame's rectangular bounding box.
- ✔ Wrap the text around the frame itself.
- ✔ Jump the text around the frame (that is, jump the text from the top of the frame to the bottom).
- ✔ Jump the text to the next column or page when the text reaches the top of frame.
- ✔ Specify the amount of distance between the text and the edge of the obstructing shape.
- ✔ Flow text within the obstructing shape rather than outside it.

InDesign lets you wrap text around frames on hidden layers — as well as remove text wrap for objects on hidden layers. This is handy when you want to hide images or other distracting items but preserve the layout. See Chapter 5 for details on using layers.

If you want to wrap text around only a portion of a graphic — perhaps you need to isolate a face in a crowd — the best solution is to open the graphics file in its original program, create a clipping path around that portion, and then resave the file and import it and its clipping path into an InDesign docu-ment (clipping paths are explained in Chapter 19).

The Text Wrap panel

The controls in the Text Wrap panel (see Figure 12-6) let you specify how a selected object will affect the flow of text behind it. Remember, the flow of text around an obstructing object is determined by the text wrap settings applied to the obstructing object.

You can override the text-wrap settings of objects that are in front of a text frame by telling the text frame to ignore them. To do so, click a text frame, and then choose Object⇨Text Frame Options or press ⌘+B or Ctrl+B. In the Text Frame Options dialog box's General pane, select Ignore Text Wrap, and then click OK. Text in the frame will now flow behind any obstructing items regardless of the text-wrap settings applied to them.

The Text Wrap panel has three options that may not display when you open it: Wrap Options, Contour Options, and Include Inside Edges. You can more easily hide/show these functions by double-clicking the double-arrow symbol to the left of the Text Wrap label in the panel's tab or by choosing Hide Options/Show Options from the flyout menu.

Here's how to apply text-wrap settings to a frame or other object:

1. **If the Text Wrap panel is not displayed, choose Window⇨Text Wrap or press Option+⌘+W or Ctrl+Alt+W.**

2. **Click any of the selection tools.**

3. **Click the object to which you want to apply text-wrap settings.**

   The object can be anywhere, but you'll probably want to position it on top of a text frame that contains text so you can see the results of the settings you apply.

4. **Click one of the five text-wrap iconic buttons at the top of the Text Wrap panel.**

   The iconic buttons show you what each wrap does conceptually.

5. **If you want, adjust the space between the surrounding text and the obstructing shape by typing values in the Top Offset, Bottom Offset, Left Offset, and Right Offset fields.**

   These fields are not available if you click the No Text Wrap button. If the object is a rectangle, all four fields are available if you click the Wrap around Bounding Box button or Wrap around Object Shape. Only the Top Offset field is available if you click the Wrap around Object Shape button for a free-form shape or the Jump to Next Column button. The Top Offset and Bottom Offset fields are available if you click the Jump Object button.

   If the Make All Settings the Same iconic button displays a chain, then changing any of the offset values will cause the other offset values to match. If the icon shows a broken chain, each offset value is independent of the others. Click the button to switch between these two modes.

6. **Select Invert if you want to flow the text in the obstructing shape.**

7. **If you choose the Wrap around Object Shape button and there is a graphic in the frame, you can also select from the Contour Options's Type pop-up menu.**

   There are six options:

   • Bounding Box is the same as clicking the Wrap around Bounding Box button.

   • Detect Edges tries to determine the graphic's outside boundary by ignoring white space — you would use this for bitmapped images that have a transparent or white background.

- Alpha Channel uses the image's alpha channel, if any, to create a wrapping boundary (see Chapter 19).

- Photoshop Path uses the image's clipping path, if any, to create a wrapping boundary (see Chapter 19).

- Graphic Frame uses the frame's boundary rather than the bounding box.

- Same as Clipping uses the clipping path for the graphic created in InDesign (see Chapter 19).

8. **You can control how text wraps around an object that splits a column by choosing an option from the Wrap To pop-up menu.**

The options are Right Side, Left Side, Both Left and Right Sides, Side Towards Spine, Side Away from Spine, and Largest Area. You'll rarely choose Both Left and Right Sides, because unless the object is small, readers' eyes will stop at the interposed object and not see the rest of the text on the other side of it. Use either of the spine options to have the text stay on the outside or inside of a page, relative to the object, based on whether the page is right-facing or left-facing. You'll often choose Largest Area because that gives the text the most space next to the interposed object, which tends to be what looks good in many situations.

9. **By selecting the Include Inside Edges option, InDesign lets text appear inside any interior "holes" in the graphic.** You'll rarely use this technique because in most cases it's hard for the reader to follow text that wraps around an image, flows inside it, and then continues to flow outside it. But if the interior is large enough and not too distant from the text that flows on the outside, this effect might be readable.

Figure 12-6:
The Text Wrap panel and its flyout menu, with a wrap applied to the object at left.

If you specify text-wrap settings when no objects are selected, the settings are automatically applied to all new objects.

To apply text-wrap settings to a master item on a document page, press and hold Shift+⌘ or Ctrl+Shift to select the item, and then use the controls in the Text Wrap panel as just described. If you don't want the text wrap applied to existing document items, just to new ones, choose Apply to Master Page Only in the flyout menu.

Setting text-wrap preferences

There are several global text-wrap options you should be aware of, all of which are accessed via the Composition pane of the Preferences dialog box (choose InDesign⇨Preferences⇨Composition or press ⌘+K on the Mac, or choose Edit⇨Preferences⇨Composition or press Ctrl+K in Windows). Here are the options:

✔ **Justify Text Next to an Object.** This option is useful when you have left-aligned text that wraps around an object at the right. (It also works if you have right-aligned text that wraps around an object at the left.) This can lead to an awkward wrap, however, because InDesign won't try to make the text align precisely to the wrap's contour (because the text isn't justified). Use this option to justify the text just around the wrap, and then continue using the text's specified non-justified alignment.

✔ **Skip by Leading.** This option makes text wrap below or above an object based on the text's leading, so there's at least a full line space between the text and the object, even if the object's text-wrap settings would allow less space.

✔ **Text Wrap Only Affects Text Beneath.** This option, if selected, prevents text frames placed on top of an object from wrapping, while those behind the graphic frame will still be allowed to wrap. This option allows some text to overlap the graphic and other text to wrap around it. Note this is a global setting, affecting all objects. To override wrap settings of individual text frames, choose Object⇨Text Frame Options, or press ⌘+B or Ctrl+B, and enable the Ignore Text Wrap option in the General pane.

Chapter 13

The Ins and Outs of Text Editing

*W*hether you import text or type it into text frames directly in InDesign, you'll appreciate the tools that let you edit that text, search and replace, spell-check, and hyphenate your text. You'll find out all about these capabilities in this chapter.

To do anything with text, you need to use the Type tool. When the Type tool is selected, you can click in any empty frame. (If it's not already a text frame, it will become one automatically when you click it with the Type tool.) Or you can click and drag to create a new text frame. You can even click in an existing block of text. From this point, start typing to enter text.

Chapter 8 gets into more of the nitty-gritty of creating frames. And you can discover all about importing text in Chapter 12.

Editing Text

InDesign offers basic editing capabilities, not unlike those found in a word processor: cutting and pasting, deleting and inserting text, searching and replacing of text and text attributes, and spell checking. (Cutting, pasting, inserting, and deleting text works just like it does for any standard Mac or Windows program, so I won't repeat those details for you here.)

Controlling text view

In many layout views, the text is too small to work with. Generally, you zoom in around the block of text using the Zoom tool. Select the tool, and then click to zoom in. To zoom out, hold the Option or Alt key when clicking.

Another way to zoom in is to use the keyboard shortcut ⌘+= or Ctrl+=. Each time you use it, the magnification increases. (Zoom out via ⌘+– [hyphen] or Ctrl+– [hyphen].)

In addition to seeing the text larger, zooming in also helps you see the spaces, tabs, and paragraph returns that exist in the text. Choose Type⇨Show Hidden Characters or press Option+⌘+I or Ctrl+Alt+I to have the nonprinting indicators for those characters display.

Navigating through text

To work at a different text location in your InDesign document, click in a different text frame or another location in the current text frame. You can also use the four arrow (cursor) keys on the keyboard to move one character to the right, one character to the left, one line up, or one line down. Hold ⌘ or Ctrl when pressing the arrow keys to jump one word to the right or left, or one paragraph up or down. The Home and End keys let you jump to the beginning or end of a line; hold ⌘ or Ctrl when pressing those keys to jump to the beginning or end of a story. (A *story* is text within a text frame or that is linked across several text frames.)

Highlighting text

To highlight (or select) text, you can click and drag. Or you can use some keyboard options. For example, Shift+⌘+right arrow or Ctrl+Shift+right arrow highlights the next word to the right. Likewise, Shift+⌘+End or Ctrl+Shift+End highlights all the text to the end of the story.

To highlight a word, double-click (this will not select its punctuation) and triple-click to select the entire paragraph. If you're highlighting a word and also want to include the punctuation that follows the word, double-click, and then press Shift+⌘+right arrow or Ctrl+Shift+right arrow to extend the selection.

To select an entire story, choose Edit⇨Select All, or press ⌘+A or Ctrl+A.

To deselect text, choose Edit➪Deselect All or press Shift+⌘+A or Ctrl+Shift+A. An even easier way to deselect text is simply to select another tool or click another area of the page.

Undoing text edits

It's nice to know that InDesign makes it easy for you to change your mind about text edits. Choose Edit➪Undo and Edit➪Redo any time you change your mind about edits. The Undo and Redo keyboard commands are definitely worth remembering: ⌘+Z and Shift+⌘+Z or Ctrl+Z and Ctrl+Shift+Z.

Using the Story Editor

The Story Editor is a window that lets you see your text without the distractions of your layout. In it, you see your text without line breaks or other nonessential formatting — you just see attributes like boldface and italics, as well as the names of the paragraph styles applied in a separate pane to the left (see Figure 13-1). After clicking in a text frame, you open the Story Editor by choosing Edit➪Edit in Story Editor or by pressing ⌘+Y or Ctrl+Y.

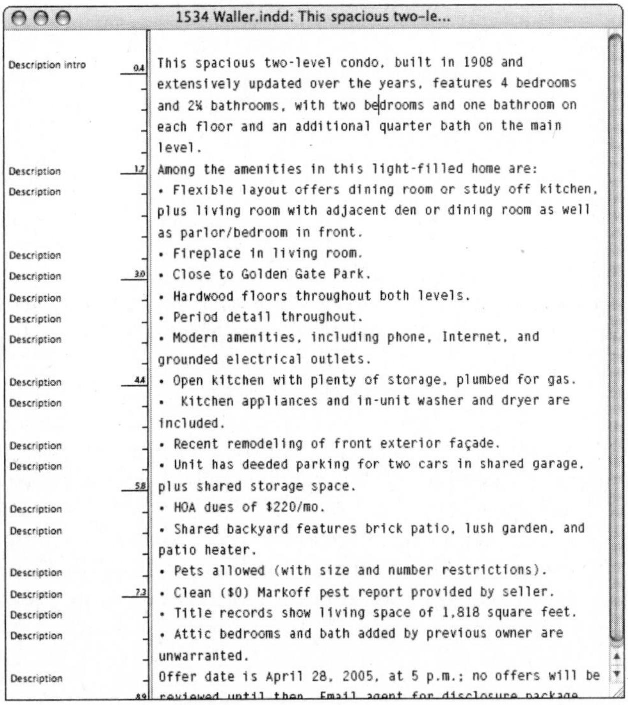

Figure 13-1: The Story Editor.

In the Story Editor, you use the same tools for selection, deletion, copying, pasting, and search and replace as you would in your layout. The Story Editor is not a separate word processor; it's simply a way to look at your text in a less distracting environment for those times when your mental focus is on the meaning and words, not the text appearance.

The Story Editor also shows you the column depth for text, using a ruler along the left side of the text, just to the right of the list of currently applied paragraph styles. Overset text (text that goes beyond the text frame, or beyond the final text frame in a threaded story) is indicated by a depth measurement of *OV* and is furthermore noted with a red line to the right of the text.

Searching and Replacing Text

InDesign has a handy Find/Change feature (Edit➪Find/Change, or ⌘+F or Ctrl+F) that is similar to the search-and-replace features with which you may already be familiar if you've used any word processor or page-layout application. With the Find/Change dialog box, you can find and change text or you can extend the search to include attributes. Before starting a Find/Change operation, first determine the scope of your search:

- ✔ To search within a text selection, highlight the selection.
- ✔ To search from one point in a story to its end, click the cursor at that beginning location.
- ✔ To search an entire story, select any frame or click at any point in a frame containing the story.
- ✔ To search an entire document, simply have that document open.
- ✔ To search multiple documents, open all of them (and close any that you don't want to search).

Then choose the appropriate search scope — InDesign's term for *range* — using the Search pop-up menu and the scope iconic buttons below it.

Figure 13-2 shows the Find/Change dialog box.

InDesign CS3 adds a lot of new features to the Find/Change dialog box, including a new interface, the ability to search for special characters (glyphs), the ability to search for object attributes (see Chapter 9), and the ability to save search/replace queries so you can use them repeatedly. (It also lets you use the Unix grep syntax for conducting criteria-based searches; this feature is for experts familiar with grep searching and so is not covered in this book.)

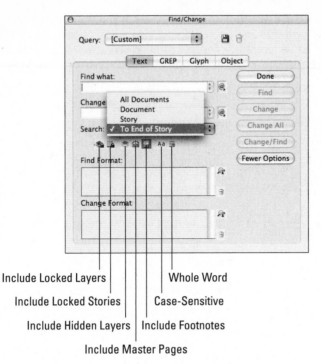

Figure 13-2:
The Find/
Change
dialog box.

Include Locked Layers
Include Locked Stories
Include Hidden Layers
Include Master Pages

Whole Word
Case-Sensitive
Include Footnotes

Replacing text

To search for text, follow these steps:

1. **Determine the scope of your search, open the appropriate documents, and insert the text cursor at the appropriate location.**

2. **Choose Edit⇨Find/Change or press ⌘+F or Ctrl+F.**

   Go to the Text pane if it's not already displayed.

3. **Use the Search pop-up menu, as shown in Figure 13-2, to specify the scope of your search by choosing All Documents, Document, Story, To End of Story, or Selection.**

   Unavailable options won't display, such as Selection in Figure 13-2.

4. **Type or paste the text you want to find in the Find What field.**

   To use special characters, use the Special Characters for Search pop-up list (the icon to the right of the Find What field) to select from a menu of special characters (see Figure 13-3).

5. **Type or paste the replacement text into the Change To field.**

   To use special characters, use the Special Characters for Replace pop-up list (to the right of the Find What field).

6. Specify any additional parameters for your search by selecting or deselecting the seven iconic buttons at the bottom of the pane: Include Locked Layers, Include Locked Stories, Include Hidden Layers, Include Master Pages, Include Footnotes, Case Sensitive, and Whole Word.

If an icon's background darkens, it is selected.

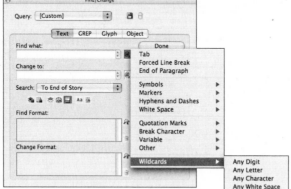

Figure 13-3:
The special characters pop-up list in the Find/Change dialog box.

7. To search for or replace with specific formatting, use the Format buttons.

These buttons are available only if you had clicked the More Options button. (Look for details later in this section.)

8. Click the Find button to start the search.

After the search has begun, click the Find Next button (it changes from the Find button after you start the search) to skip instances of the Find What text, and click the Change, Change All, or Change/Find buttons as appropriate. (Clicking the Change button simply changes the found text, clicking the Change All button changes every instance of that found text in your selection or story, and clicking the Change/Find button changes the current found text and moves on to the next occurrence of it — it basically does in one click the actions of clicking Change and then Find Next.)

If you use the Change All feature, InDesign reports how many changes were made. If the number looks extraordinarily high and you suspect the Find/Change operation wasn't quite what you wanted, remember that you can use InDesign's undo function (Edit⇨Undo, or ⌘+Z or Ctrl+Z) to cancel the search and replace, and then try a different replace strategy.

9. Click the Done button when you're finished doing the finding and replacing.

The solution to missing fonts

Sometimes, when you open a document, InDesign tells you that it can't find the fonts used in the documents on your computer. You get the option of finding the missing fonts, which opens the Find Fonts dialog box. This dialog box shows the names of all missing fonts; if you select one, you can change all occurrences of that font to one that you do have by selecting a new font family and font style from the menus at the bottom of the dialog box and then clicking Change All. New to InDesign CS3 is the Redefine Style When Changing All check box, which, if selected, ensures that any font replaced is also replaced in any paragraph and character styles that used the original font.

Of course, another — often preferable — solution is to get the fonts installed on your computer. After all, the design shouldn't change just because you don't happen to have the needed fonts on your computer.

Replacing formatting

To find and change formatting or text with specific formatting, use the expanded Find/Change dialog box. For example, you might find all the words in 14-point Futura Extra Bold and change them to 12-point Bodoni.

To replace text formatting, follow these steps:

1. **To add formats to a Find/Change operation for text, click the More Options button in the Find/Change dialog box (if it was not clicked earlier).**

   The dialog box expands to include the Find Format Settings and Change Format Settings areas.

2. **Use the Format buttons to display the Find Format Settings and Change Format Settings dialog boxes, which let you specify the formats you want to find.**

   Your options are Style Options (paragraph and character styles), Basic Character Formats, Advanced Character Formats, Indents and Spacing, Keep Options, Bullets and Numbering, Character Color, OpenType Features, Underline Options, Strikethrough Options, and Drop Caps and Other. You can change multiple attributes at once by making selections from as many panes as needed.

   Open one of these dialog boxes, select the desired formatting to search or replace, and then click OK when done. Now open the other dialog box to select its formatting, and then click OK when done.

3. **Click Find Next and then Change to change the next occurrence, or click Change All to change all occurrences. Click Done when you are finished with the search and replace.**

To search and replace formatting only — regardless of the text to which it is applied — leave the Find What and Change To fields blank.

Changing special characters

InDesign CS3 also lets you replace special characters (glyphs) through a separate Glyph pane in the Find/Change dialog box. This makes it easier to actually enter the desired characters. The process is mostly straightforward (just ignore the parts of the pane not described below):

1. **In the Find Glyph section, choose the font of the desired character in the Font Family pop-up menu, and its style in the Font Style pop-up menu.**

2. **To choose the character itself, click the unnamed pop-up menu to the right of the Glyph field.**

   You'll get a dialog box that mimics the Glyphs panel (see Chapter 16); choose the character from the panel by double-clicking it.

3. **Repeat steps 1 and 2 using the controls in the Change Glyph section to select the replacement glyph.**

4. **Set the scope of your search using the Search pop-up menu and the Include Locked Layers, Include Locked Stories, Include Hidden Layers, Include Master Pages, and Include Footnotes buttons, as described earlier in this chapter.**

5. **Execute the search and/or replace using the Find, Change, Change All, and Change/Find buttons as described earlier in this chapter.**

6. **Click Done when done.**

If you want to quickly wipe out the selected glyphs, click the Clear Glyphs button.

Working with saved queries

If you plan to do the same search and/or replace operation repeatedly, you can now save queries in InDesign CS3. After entering the find and search information, click the Save Query iconic button, enter a name in the Save Query dialog box that appears, and click OK. That query will now appear in the Query pop-up menu in the Find/Change dialog box.

To run a saved query, just choose it from the Query pop-up menu. To delete a saved query, choose it from the Query pop-up menu and then click Delete Query iconic button.

That's all there is to it!

Checking Spelling

The spell-check feature not only helps you eradicate spelling errors, but it also catches repeated words, as well as words with odd capitalization such as internal capitalization (called *intercaps*). InDesign also flags words not found in the spelling dictionary. You can customize the spelling dictionary, and you can purchase additional spelling dictionaries.

Checking spelling as you type

You can have InDesign check your spelling as you type by simply choosing Edit⇨Spelling⇨Dynamic Spelling. If that menu option is checked, your spelling will be checked as you type, as will the spelling of any text already in the document. Suspected errors are highlighted with red squiggle underlining, so that you can correct them as needed. If you want InDesign to suggest proper spelling, you'll need to use the Check Spelling dialog box, covered in the next section.

Correcting mistakes on the fly

If you use a word processor, chances are it is one that corrects mistakes as you type. Microsoft Word, for example, has a feature called AutoCorrect that lets you specify corrections to be made as you type, whether those be common typos you make or the expansion of abbreviations to their full words (such as having Word replace *tq* with *thank you*).

InDesign offers much of the same functionality, which it calls *Autocorrect*. Unlike Word, you cannot use this feature to replace symbols, such as having InDesign convert *(R)* to the (r) symbol as you type. Note that — like Word — Autocorrect works only for text entered in InDesign after Autocorrect is turned on; it will not correct imported or previously typed text.

You enable Autocorrect in the Autocorrect pane of the Preferences dialog box (choose InDesign⇨Preferences⇨Autocorrect or press ⌘+K on the Mac, or choose Edit⇨Preferences⇨Autocorrect or press Ctrl+K in Windows). If you want InDesign to automatically fix capitalization errors, check the Autocorrect Capitalization Errors check box. Typically, this finds typos involving capitalizing the second letter of a word in addition to the first. For example, InDesign would replace *FOrmat* with *Format*.

To add your own custom corrections, click the Add button. This opens the Add to Autocorrect List dialog box, where you can enter the typo text or code that you want InDesign to be alert for in the Misspelled Word field, as well as the corrected or expanded text you want InDesign to substitute in the Correction field.

Using the Check Spelling dialog box

The Check Spelling dialog box not only lets you choose what part of the document to spell check, but it also provides suggestions on correct spelling. Plus, you can use the dialog box to add correctly spelled words to InDesign's spelling dictionary. Even if you use the new dynamic spell-checking feature, you'll still want to do a final spell-checking pass with the Check Spelling dialog box.

Specifying the text to check is a two-step process: First set up the spell check's scope in the document, and then specify the scope in the Search menu.

To set up the scope for the spell check, highlight text, click in a story to check from the cursor forward, select a frame containing a story, or open multiple documents.

Next, open the Check Spelling dialog box (Edit⇨Spelling⇨Check Spelling, or ⌘+I or Ctrl+I) and choose an option from the Search pop-up menu: Document, All Documents, Story, To End of Story, and Selection. Figure 13-4 shows the dialog box. You may not see all the options in the Search pop-up menu; the list of options depends on how you set up the scope. For example, if you didn't highlight text, the Selection option will not be available. However, you can change the scope setup in the document while the Check Spelling dialog box is open — for example, you can open additional documents to check.

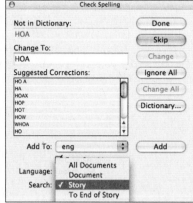

Figure 13-4: In the Check Spelling dialog box, use the Search pop-up menu to specify which text to spell-check.

When you first open the Check Spelling dialog box, if text is selected or the text cursor is active, it immediately begins checking the spelling, going to the first suspect word.

Otherwise, the dialog box displays "Ready to Check Spelling" at the top. To begin checking the text, click Start.

You can adjust the scope of the spell-check by using the Search pop-up menu and choosing All Documents, Document, Story, and To End of Story. You can also make the spell-check case-sensitive by checking the Case Sensitive check box.

When the spell checker encounters a word without a match in the dictionary or a possible capitalization problem, the dialog box displays "Not in Dictionary" at the top and shows the word. When the spell checker encounters a duplicate word, such as *of of,* the dialog box displays "Duplicate Word" and shows which word is duplicated. Use the buttons along the right side of the dialog box to handle flagged words as follows:

- ✔ Click the Skip button (this appears only after the spell-check has started) to leave the current instance of a Not in Dictionary word or Duplicate Word unchanged. To leave all instances of the same problem unchanged, click the Ignore All button.

- ✔ To change the spelling of a Not in Dictionary word, click a word in the Suggested Corrections list or edit the spelling or capitalization in the Change To field. To make the change, click the Change button.

- ✔ To correct an instance of a Duplicate Word, edit the text in the Change To field, and then click the Change button.

- ✔ To change all occurrences of a Not in Dictionary word or a Duplicate Word to the information in the Change To field, click the Change All button.

- ✔ To add a word flagged as incorrect — but that you know is correct — to InDesign's spelling dictionary, click the Add button. (If you have multiple dictionaries, first choose the dictionary to add it to using the Add To pop-up menu.)

- ✔ To add a word flagged as incorrect to a specific dictionary, click the Dictionary button. A Dictionary dialog box appears, which lets you choose the dictionary to which you want to add the word, as well as what language to associate it with.

- ✔ After you've finished checking spelling, click the Done button to close the Check Spelling dialog box.

Changing the spelling and hyphenation dictionaries

The spelling dictionary that comes with InDesign is pretty extensive, but it's very likely that you will need to add words to it. For example, your company might use words that are company-specific terms. Or you might use some product or individuals' names that would not typically be found in the dictionary. Additionally, you might have some words that you prefer not to hyphenate, others that you want to hyphenate in a specific manner. To address these issues, you can customize InDesign's spelling and hyphenation dictionaries. InDesign handles both spelling and hyphenation in one dictionary for each language, so you use the same controls to modify both spelling and hyphenation.

Changes made to a dictionary file are saved only in the dictionary file, not with an open document. So if you add words to the English: USA dictionary, the modified dictionary is used for spell checking and hyphenating all text in documents that use the English: USA dictionary.

If you're in a workgroup, be sure to share the edited dictionary file so that everyone is using the same spelling and hyphenation settings. (The file is located in the Dictionaries folder inside the Plug-ins folder inside your InDesign folder.) You can copy it for other users, who must then restart InDesign or press Option+⌘+/ or Ctrl+Alt+/ to reflow the text according to the new dictionary's hyphenation.

Customizing the spelling dictionary

When you add a word to the spelling dictionary, this word will no longer be flagged when you check spelling, and you can be sure that when it's used, it is spelled as it is in the dictionary.

When you add words to the dictionary, you can specify their capitalization. For example, InDesign's dictionary prefers *E-mail*. You can add *e-mail* if you prefer a lowercase *e* or *email* if you prefer to skip the hyphen. To add words to the dictionary, follow these steps:

1. **Choose Edit⇨Spelling⇨Dictionary.**

   The Dictionary dialog box, shown in Figure 13-5, appears.

2. **Choose whether the addition to the dictionary affects just this document or all documents.**

   The Target pop-up menu lists the current document name as well as the name of the user dictionary.

3. **Choose the dictionary that you want to edit from the Language pop-up menu.**

4. **Type or paste a word in the Word field.**

   The word can have capital letters if appropriate, and it can include special characters such as accents and hyphens.

5. **To have the added word accepted as being spelled correctly only with the capitalization specified in the Word field, check the Case Sensitive check box.**

6. **To edit the hyphenation of the word, click the Hyphenate button.**

   I cover hyphenation in the next section.

7. **Click the Add button.**

8. **To import a word list or export one for other users to import into their copies of InDesign, click the Import or Export button.**

   You will then navigate to a folder and choose a filename in a dialog box. Note that when you click the Export button, InDesign will export all selected words from the list. If no words are selected, it will export all the words in the list.

9. **When you're finished adding words, click the Done button.**

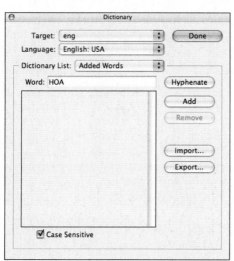

Figure 13-5:
Use the Dictionary dialog box to add words to the spelling dictionary and to customize how words are hyphenated.

To delete a word that you added to the dictionary, select it in the list and click the Remove button. To change the spelling of a word you added, delete it and then re-add it with the correct spelling. You can see all deleted words — just those deleted since you opened the dialog box — by selecting Removed Words from the Dictionary List pop-up menu, so you can add back any deleted by error.

Customizing hyphenation points

People can be particular about how to hyphenate words. Fortunately, InDesign lets you modify the hyphenation dictionary by specifying new, hierarchical hyphenation points.

Follow these steps to specify hyphenation points:

1. **Choose Edit⇨Spelling⇨Dictionary.**

2. **In the Language pop-up menu, pick the dictionary that you want to edit.**

3. **Type or paste the word in the Word field; you can also double-click a word in the list.**

4. **To see InDesign's suggestions for hyphenating the word, click the Hyphenate button.**

   If you want to change the hyphenation, continue on to Step 5.

5. **Type a tilde (~, obtained by pressing Shift+`, the open single keyboard quote at the upper left of the keyboard) at your first preference for a hyphenation point in the word.**

   If you don't want the word to hyphenate at all, type a tilde in front of it.

6. **To indicate an order of preference, use two tildes for your second choice, three tildes for your third choice, and so on.** InDesign will first try to hyphenate your top preferences (single tildes), and then it will try your second choices if the first ones don't work out, and so on.

7. **Click the Add button.**

8. **Continue to add words until you're finished, and then click the Done button.**

To revert a word to the default hyphenation, select it in the list and click the Remove button. To change the hyphenation, double-click a word in the list to enter it in the Word field, change the tildes, and then click the Add button. When you're adding variations of words, you can double-click a word in the list to place it in the Word field as a starting place.

Chapter 14

The Styles of Text

*I*t's the dirty secret of desktop publishing: Most users avoid using styles, even though they know they should. Instead, they apply formatting locally to text, hoping it's the same as a few pages back. It's a lot like not eating your vegetables — even though we know that they're good for us (and they even taste good), it's easier to get something already made, never mind what's in it.

So, I'm going to tell you about styles before I get to the other ways to format text. Styles really are good for you: They will save you lots of work, help you avoid embarrassingly inconsistent formatting, and give you more time to indulge in the guilty pleasure of local formatting.

A *style* is a simple but powerful concept: It's a collection of formatting attributes that you can apply to text all at once, saving you time. Even better, if you change the style, all text that uses it is automatically updated, saving you time *and* ensuring consistency. That's got to be appealing!

I cover the particulars of paragraph and character formatting in Chapters 15 and 16, respectively. The formats themselves are the same whether you apply them directly (locally) or through a style (globally). I cover table styles and cell styles in Chapter 20 and object styles in Chapter 10, although the basic creation and management methods are the same for all styles.

Text in your layout may already have styles applied, using styles defined in Microsoft Word, as explained in Chapter 12.

If you have a smallish monitor, set at 1024 by 768 pixels — the norm for a 17-inch display — the Character Styles and Paragraph Styles panels are shoved to the bottom of the panel dock, and, when they're selected, the only thing you'll see is their panel tab and flyout menu icon. You have a few choices: Shorten other panel groups in the dock to make room for them, remove other panel groups to make room for them, or drag them out of the dock and make them floating.

Creating Styles

InDesign gives you two kinds of styles for text: paragraph and character. Paragraph styles apply formatting to entire paragraphs, while character styles apply formatting to text selections. Unless you're doing a one-page ad, the formatting of which won't be repeated, you should have paragraph styles for all different types of paragraphs in your layout. You would also have character styles for places where you consistently want to override your paragraph styles, such as for the lead-in of a bulleted paragraph that might have the first few words in a different font or color.

Whether you're creating styles for paragraphs or characters, the basic process is the same.

The easiest way is to format your text using the Paragraph and Character panels, as described in Chapters 15 and 16, and then make sure you've selected the text you want to use as the model for your new style. Next, create the appropriate type of new style:

✔ For paragraph styles, open the Paragraph Styles panel by choosing Type⇨Paragraph Styles or pressing ⌘+F11 or Ctrl+F11. Then choose New Paragraph Style from the flyout menu to open the New Paragraph Style dialog box shown in Figure 14-1.

✔ For character styles, open the Character Styles panel by choosing Type⇨Character Styles or pressing Shift+⌘+F11 or Ctrl+Shift+F11. Then choose New Character Style from the flyout menu to open the New Character Style dialog box shown in Figure 14-2.

The shortcut for accessing the Paragraph Styles panel has changed to ⌘+F11 or Ctrl+F11 in InDesign CS3 from just F11 in previous versions. Similarly, the shortcut for the Character Styles has changed to Shift+⌘+F11 or Ctrl+Shift+F11 from the previous Shift+F11. But the old shortcuts continue to work, though they may interfere with Mac OS X's Exposé software.

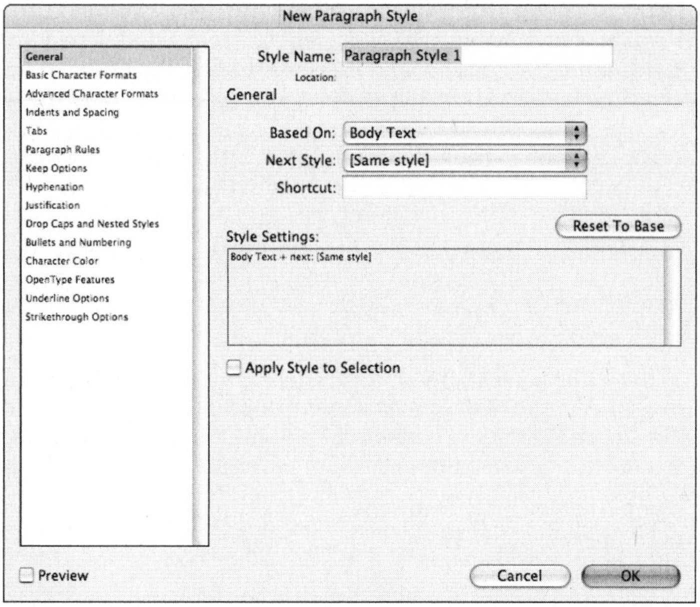

Figure 14-1:
The New Paragraph Style dialog box's General pane.

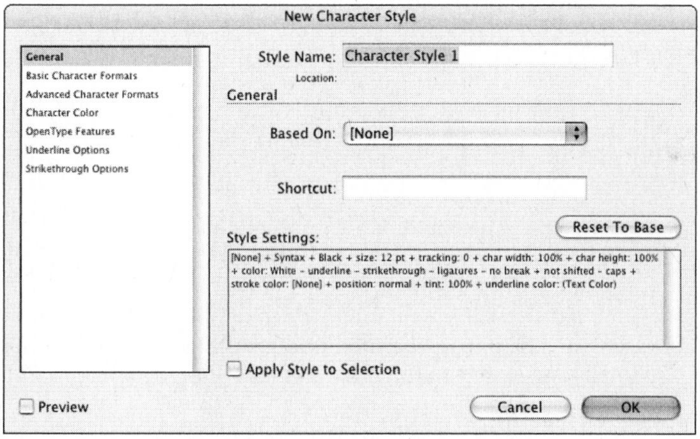

Figure 14-2:
The New Character Style dialog box's General pane.

In both cases, the style will pick up the selected text's formatting. Adjust the style further if desired, give the style a name using the Style Name field in the General pane, and then click OK.

Of course, you can specify all the formatting directly in the new-style dialog boxes rather than having InDesign pick it up from existing text. Create the new styles as just described, and then go through each of the panes (selecting each from the list at the left of the dialog box) and choose your settings.

In the General pane of the New Paragraph Style and New Character Style dialog boxes, there are several controls that make styles work more intelligently:

- ✔ The Based On pop-up menu displays the names of other styles. You use this feature to create families of styles. Thus, if you change a style that other styles are based on, all those styles are updated with the new settings.

- ✔ In the Shortcut field, hold down any combination of ⌘, Option, and Shift, or Ctrl, Alt, and Shift, and press any number on the keypad. (Letters and non-keypad numbers cannot be used for keyboard shortcuts. And Windows users need to make sure that Num Lock is on.)

- ✔ If you want to apply a new style to text that is selected, be sure to check the Apply Style to Selection check box before clicking OK to save the new style.

InDesign comes with a predefined default paragraph style called [Basic Paragraph] that text in a new frame automatically has applied to it. You can edit [Basic Paragraph] like any other style. Similarly, there's a predefined character style called [Basic Character].

There are several things to keep in mind when creating paragraph styles. (Character styles are pretty straightforward, so I'm not presenting a similar list for them.)

- ✔ To have InDesign automatically apply a different style to the next paragraph when you type in text, choose a style name from the Next Style pop-up menu while defining a style. For example, when you define a style named Headline, you might choose Byline as the next style, so after you type in a headline, the next paragraph will be formatted for a byline. Obviously, you need to have the Byline style available.

- ✔ If you want your paragraph style to use a character style, you must define that character style first. (Drop caps and nested styles use character styles.)

A special function available to paragraph styles is something called a *nested style*. Basically, a nested style is a way of applying a series of character styles within a paragraph style based on a set of parameters you specify. For example, in a numbered list, you might want one character style applied to the numeral, and another to the first sentence, and then have the paragraph style's text formatting applied to the rest of the paragraph. With nested styles, you build all that into the paragraph style and let InDesign do the heavy lifting. Here's how it works:

1. **Define any character styles that you'll apply to text through a nested style.**

   Even if all you're doing is making text italic, you need to define a character style to do so. The Nested Styles feature cannot apply any attributes other than those available in a character style.

2. **Open the Paragraph panel (Type⇨Paragraph Styles, or ⌘+F11 or Ctrl+F11), choose Style Options from the flyout menu to open the Paragraph Style Options dialog box, and go to the Drop Caps and Nested Styles pane.**

3. **Click New Nested Style.**

   An entry appears in the Nested Styles section of the dialog box. This is what will be applied to text.

4. **Click the style name in the Nested Styles section of the pane to choose from an existing character style.**

   When you click the style name, a list of other styles appears, including [None], which uses the paragraph style's default formatting.

   You also have the [Repeat] option, which, if selected, lets you repeat a sequence of previous styles (you choose the number in the third column).

5. **Click in the second column to determine the scope end point.**

   Your choices are Through or Up To. For example, if you choose Through for a nested style that is set for four words, all four words will get the nested style. If you choose Up To, the first three words will get the style and the fourth will not.

6. **In the third column, specify how many items you want InDesign to count in determining the scope's end point.**

   For example, if you want to have the first seven characters have the style applied, choose 7. If you want to have the style applied up to the first tab, choose 1.

7. **Click the item in the fourth column to specify the scope of text to which you're applying the nested styles.**

   Figure 14-3 shows the options. They break into three groups: a number of items (characters, words, and so on), a specific character (tab, em space, and so on), and a specific marker character (inline graphic marker, auto page number, and section marker). Whatever you choose needs to be consistent in all your text because InDesign will follow these rules slavishly.

8. **Create multiple nested styles in one paragraph with different rules for each.**

   Obviously, you may not need to do this, but the option exists. InDesign applies the styles in the order in which they appear in the dialog box, and each starts where the other ends. Use the up and down arrow buttons to change the order of nested styles.

9. **Select the Preview option to preview the formatting if you selected sample text before opening the dialog box.**

10. **Click OK when you're done.**

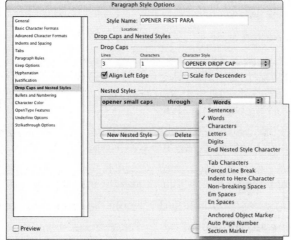

Figure 14-3: You can use a nested style to, for example, set the first words in a paragraph (in this case, the eight that follow the drop cap) as small caps.

Managing Styles

InDesign provides lots of ways to manage your styles. In this section, I cover the common ones. Note that the options described here also apply to object styles, table styles, and cell styles — so, for example, the Load Paragraph Styles menu option will have a counterpart in the Object Styles, Table Styles, and Cell Styles panels' flyout menus.

Updating styles

If you've already created a style and want to change it, just go to the appropriate styles panel and choose Style Options from its flyout menu. If you've selected text that has the formatting you want the style to use in place of its current formatting, just choose Redefine Style from the flyout menu. Remember that all text using the style will be automatically be updated when the style changes.

What's that Quick Apply panel?

Another way to apply paragraph and character styles (and object styles, scripts, menu commands, and other elements) is by using the Quick Apply feature. Quick Apply is a consolidated list of styles that you access by choosing Edit⇨Quick Apply, by clicking the Quick Apply iconic button (the lightning-bolt icon) in many panels, or by pressing ⌘+Return or Ctrl+Enter.

If you have selected text or have the text-insertion point active, the Quick Apply panel presents all stored formatting attributes available. You can scroll down to the one you want, or you can type the first few letters of the style name in the text field at the top to jump to styles beginning with those letters and then navigate to the one you want. Then press Return or Enter, which brings you back to where you were working with your text. Pressing ⌘+Return or Ctrl+Enter again closes the Quick Apply panel.

For users who are working on layouts from their keyboards — perhaps a layout artist who's working on a notebook while commuting — Quick Apply can be handy because you can switch to it, apply the style, and return to your text without touching the mouse.

InDesign CS3 adds a lot more attributes to the Quick Apply panel, so it can quickly get overwhelming. (InDesign CS2 just had styles in this panel.) To remove attributes you likely will never use in this panel — such as scripts and menu customizations — choose the unnamed pop-up menu at the top of the panel, and deselect unwanted attributes (the check marks indicate attributes that *will* display). (You can also choose what attributes display in the Quick Apply panel by choosing Customize from its flyout menu.)

Sharing styles with others

The Load Paragraph Styles or Load Character Styles menu option (based on which styles panel is open) and the Load All Text Styles menu option let you import styles from another InDesign document. (Load All Text Styles imports paragraph and character styles at the same time.) You will get a dialog box listing the styles in the chosen document, so you can decide which ones to import.

If you import styles whose names match those in the current document, InDesign gives you a chance to let the imported style overwrite the current style or to leave the current style as is and give the imported style a new name. If there is an entry in the Conflict with Existing Style, you can click that entry for a pop-up menu that provides two choices: Auto-Rename and Use Incoming Style Definition. Figure 14-4 shows this Load Styles dialog box.

Note that at the bottom of the dialog box is the Incoming Style Definitions window, which lists the style definitions to help you decide which to import, as well as which to overwrite or rename.

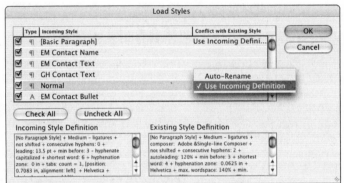

Figure 14-4:
The Load
Styles
dialog box.

Using style groups

To help you find the desired style in documents that have dozens of them, InDesign lets you create style groups, which create a folder in the styles panel's style list that you can open and close as desired. To create a group, choose New Style Group from the panel's flyout menu or click the Create New Style Group iconic button (folder icon) on the bottom of the panel. Enter a name in the dialog box that appears and click OK.

When working with style groups (which have a folder icon to the left of their names in the panel list), you have several options to add styles:

- ✔ You can drag any desired styles into the group.

- ✔ You can copy a selected style to the group by choosing Copy to Group and then selecting the target group in the dialog box that appears.

- ✔ If multiple styles are selected, you can create a group and move them into it in one fell swoop by choosing New Group from Styles in the flyout menu. (Note that this option is grayed out if any of the predefined styles — [None] and either [Basic Paragraph] or [Basic Character] — are selected.)

To quickly open all groups, choose Open All Groups in the panel's flyout menu. To quickly close them all, choose Close All Groups.

Other management options

The styles panels' flyout menus have several other options to manage your styles:

- ✔ Duplicate Style copies the currently selected style, so you can work on the copy.

- ✔ Delete Style — no surprise! — deletes selected styles.

✔ Select All Unused selects all styles not used in the document, so you can delete them all at once with the Delete Style menu option — part of keeping your document neat and tidy.

✔ Sort by Name alphabetizes the list of style names. (You can change the order of style names by dragging them within the list.)

Applying Styles

There are some subtle differences between applying paragraph styles and character styles, so I'll cover those particulars a little later in this section. But two techniques work the same for both types of style:

✔ If your text selection uses more than one paragraph style or more than one character style, the styles panel will display the text (Mixed) at the upper left to let you know that.

✔ InDesign has a neat new capability that lets you apply multiple styles at once to selected text. First, define the various styles, and be sure that each style has a different style selected in the Next Style pop-up menu in the Paragraph Style Options or New Paragraph Style dialog boxes. For example, if you have Headline, Byline, and Body Copy styles, make sure that Headline has Byline selected in Next Style and that Byline has Body Copy selected in Next Style. Then highlight *all* the text that uses this sequence of styles. Now Control+click or right-click Headline and select Apply "Headline" Then Next Style from the contextual menu. InDesign applies Headline to the first paragraph, Byline to the second paragraph, and Body Copy to the rest.

Paragraph particulars

To apply a paragraph style, just click within a paragraph or highlight text in a range of paragraphs and then click the style name in the Paragraph Styles panel or press its keyboard shortcut. (Windows users must make sure Num Lock is on when using shortcuts for styles.)

When you apply a style to selected paragraphs, all local formats and applied character styles are retained. All other formats are replaced by those of the applied style. If you want to override those attributes, choose Clear Overrides from the Paragraph Styles panel's flyout menu or hold the Option or Alt key when clicking the style name in the panel.

If you want to remove a style from a paragraph, so it's not changed if the style is later changed, choose Break Link to Style from the flyout menu. The upper left of the panel will display the text (No Style).

Character characteristics

To apply a character style, just highlight text and then click the style name in the Character Styles panel or press its keyboard shortcut. (Windows users must make sure Num Lock is on when using shortcuts for styles.)

If you want to remove a style from a text selection so that it's not changed if the character style is later changed, choose Break Link to Style from the flyout menu or simply apply the [None] style. Note that if you later apply a paragraph style to text with [None] character style, the text will take on the paragraph style's formatting rather than retaining its local formatting.

Chapter 15

Fine-Tuning Paragraph Details

*P*aragraphs are more than lines of text; they are chunks of information that themselves help convey meaning by organizing that information into related bits. Various types of paragraph formatting let you both make those chunks clearly distinguishable from each other and highlight certain chunks, such as lists or long quotes, from others.

This chapter explains what you need to know about formatting paragraphs, from setting indents and alignment — the two most commonly used paragraph attributes.

Applying Paragraph Formats

InDesign provides three ways to apply paragraph formats:

✔ Use the controls in the Paragraph panel, shown in Figure 15-1, or their keyboard shortcuts. This method is great for working on individual paragraphs, although it's not the best method when working with lots of paragraphs you want to have the same formatting. There are three ways to open the Paragraph panel: Choose Type⇨Paragraph, choose Window⇨Type & Tables⇨Paragraph, or press Option+⌘+T or Ctrl+Alt+T.

✔ Use the controls in the Control panel (be sure that the Type tool is active and that the ¶ iconic button is selected in the panel to display paragraph-oriented functions). These controls mirror those in the

Paragraph panel, and using them instead of the Paragraph panel can reduce screen clutter. If the Control panel is not visible (it almost always is), display it by choosing Window⇨Control or pressing Option+⌘+6 or Ctrl+Alt+6.

✔ Create and apply paragraph styles, as covered in Chapter 14. Paragraph styles let you apply consistent formatting — and easily change it to all affected paragraphs — throughout your document.

Whichever method you use — and you'll use them all — the types of formatting available to you are the same.

The Paragraph panel and Control panel provide access to most of InDesign's paragraph-formatting options. Also, several of the options have keyboard shortcuts, as shown in the menus. But to set tabs, you must open the Tabs panel, as covered in Chapter 20.

Figure 15-1 shows the Paragraph panel. If you choose Hide Options from the flyout menu, the Space Before, Space After, Drop Cap Number of Lines, Drop Cap Number of Characters, Hyphenate, and Align/Do Not Align to Baseline Grid controls are not displayed. You can use the double-arrow iconic button to the left of the panel name to toggle among showing the panel title, the basic options, and all options.

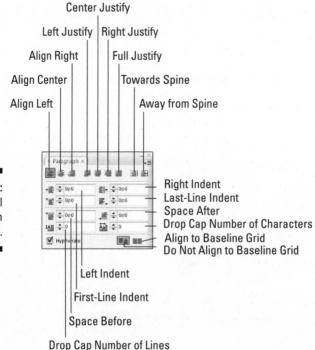

Figure 15-1:
The full
Paragraph
panel.

If you have a smallish monitor, set at 1024 by 768 pixels — the norm for a 17-inch display — the Paragraph and Paragraph Styles panels are shoved to the bottom of the panel dock, and, when they're selected, the only thing you'll see is their panel tab and flyout menu icon. You have a few choices: Shorten other panel groups in the dock to make room for them, remove other panel groups to make room for them, or drag them out of the dock and make them floating.

Specifying Alignment and Indents

Alignment and indents give paragraphs their fundamental appearance. Indentation helps readers visually separate paragraphs — the indent acts as the separator, like the blank lines used to separate paragraphs in typewritten documents — while alignment provides visual texture.

Controlling alignment

The alignment buttons at the top of the Paragraph panel control how a selected paragraph begins and ends relative to the left and right margins. To apply a paragraph alignment to selected paragraphs, click one of the buttons. You can also use the keyboard shortcuts described in the following list. Here's a description of each alignment option (the icons themselves illustrate what they do):

- **Align Left** (Shift+⌘+L or Ctrl+Shift+L): This alignment places the left edge of every line at the left margin (the margin can be the frame edge, frame inset, left indent, or column edge) and fits as many words (or syllables, if the hyphenation is turned on) on the line as possible. In left-aligned paragraphs, the right margin is said to be *ragged* because the leftover space at the right end of each line differs from line to line and produces a ragged edge.

- **Align Center** (Shift+⌘+C or Ctrl+Shift+C): This alignment makes both the left and right edges of the paragraphs equally ragged.

- **Align Right** (Shift+⌘+R or Ctrl+Shift+R): This is a mirror opposite of Align Left. The right edge is straight; the left edge is ragged.

- **Justify, Last Line Aligned Left** (Shift+⌘+J or Ctrl+Shift+J): In justified text, the left and right ends of each line are flush with the margins. (There's more about justification later in this chapter.) Justified text is nearly always hyphenated — if you don't hyphenate justified text, spacing between letters and words is very inconsistent. Aligning the last line flush left is the traditional way of ending a paragraph.

- **Justify, Last Line Aligned Center:** This produces justified text with the last line centered.

- **Justify, Last Line Aligned Right:** This produces justified text with the last line aligned to the right.

- **Justify All Lines** (Shift+⌘+F or Ctrl+Shift+F): This produces justified text with the last line forcibly justified. This option can produce last lines that are very widely spaced. The fewer the number of characters on the last line, the greater the spacing.

  The previous three alignment options are rarely used, and for good reason. People expect justified text to have the last line aligned left; the space at the end of the line marks the end of the paragraph. By changing the position of that last line, you can confuse your reader.

- **Align Toward Spine:** Essentially, this option automatically creates right-aligned text on left-hand pages and left-aligned text on right-hand pages. InDesign chooses a left or right alignment based on the location of the spine in a facing-pages document.

- **Align Away from Spine:** This option is the same as Align Toward Spine except that the alignment is reversed: Text aligns to the left on left-hand pages and to the right on right-hand pages.

When creating paragraph styles, all the above controls are available in the Indents and Spacing pane of the New Paragraph Styles dialog box.

Adjusting indent controls

The indent controls in the Paragraph panel let you both move the edges of paragraphs away from the left and/or right margins and indent the first line.

Your options are as follows:

- **Left Indent:** Moves the left edge of selected paragraphs away from the left margin by the amount you specify in the field. You can also click the up and down arrows. Each click increases the value by 1 point; holding down the Shift while clicking increases the increment to 1 pica.

- **Right Indent:** Moves the right edge of selected paragraphs away from the right margin by the amount you specify in the field. You can also use the up and down arrows.

- **First-Line Left Indent:** Moves the left edge of the first line of selected paragraphs away from the left margin by the amount you specify in the field. You can also click the up and down arrows to adjust the indentation. The value in the First-Line Left Indent field is added to any Left Indent value. Using a tab or spaces to indent the first line of a paragraph, which is what was done in the age of typewriters, is usually *not* a good idea. You're better off specifying a First-Line Left Indent.

 ✔ **Last-Line Right Indent:** Moves the right edge of the last line of selected paragraphs away from the right margin by the amount you specify in the field. You can also click the up and down arrows.

When creating paragraph styles, all the above controls are available in the Indents and Spacing pane of the New Paragraph Styles dialog box.

Inserting space between paragraphs

To format a lengthy chunk of text with multiple paragraphs, you can indicate a new paragraph by indenting the paragraph's first line (by specifying a First-Line Left Indent value, as covered earlier). Or you can insert some extra space between the new paragraph and the preceding one. Although no rule states that you can't use both of these spacing methods, it's a good idea to use one or the other — not both:

 ✔ To insert space before selected paragraphs, enter a value in the Space Before field in the Paragraph panel or Control panel. You can also use the up and down arrow buttons; each click increases the value by 1 point and holding down Shift key increases the increment to 1 pica.

 ✔ The Space After field works the same as the Space Before field but inserts space below selected paragraphs. If you use Space Before to space paragraphs, you won't need to use Space After, and vice versa; combining both can be confusing.

What you don't want to do is insert extra paragraph returns between paragraphs. Doing so makes it harder to ensure that columns begin with text (as opposed to blank lines).

Controlling space between lines

Leading (pronounced "ledding") is the space between lines of text *within* a paragraph. Even though leading is traditionally an attribute of the paragraph, InDesign treats it as a character format, which you specify by using the Leading control in the Character panel or Control panel.

To change this character-oriented approach to affect entire paragraphs, select the Apply Leading to Entire Paragraphs option in the Type pane of the Preferences dialog box (choose InDesign⇨Preferences⇨Type or press ⌘+K on the Mac, or choose Edit⇨Preferences⇨Type or press Ctrl+K in Windows).

Another way to control space between lines of text is to use baseline grids, as described in Chapter 11. Essentially, a baseline grid overrides the leading specified for paragraphs — you choose whether it overrides the spacing of every line in the paragraph or just the first line. To align to baseline grids, you must click the Align to Baseline iconic button in the Paragraph panel (the rightmost iconic button on the bottom of the panel) for the selected paragraphs. To prevent such locking to the baseline, click the Do Not Align to Baseline iconic button to its immediate left. These same buttons also exist on the right side of the Control panel.

Controlling where paragraphs break

InDesign's Keep Options feature lets you prevent widows and orphans; it also lets you keep paragraphs together when they would otherwise be broken at the bottom of a column. A *widow* is the last line of a paragraph that falls at the top of a column. (The poor thing has been cut off from the rest of the family, the last survivor.) An orphan is the first line of a paragraph that falls at the bottom of a column. (It, too, has become separated from its family, the only survivor.)

When you choose Keep Options from the Paragraph panel's flyout menu, the Keep Options dialog box, shown in Figure 15-2, is displayed.

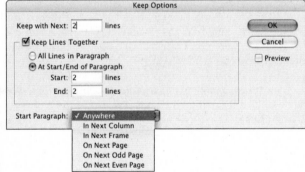

Figure 15-2:
The Keep
Options
dialog box.

The Keep Options dialog box holds several options for how paragraphs are managed as text breaks across columns and pages:

✔ **Keep with Next Lines:** This option applies to two consecutive paragraphs and controls the number of lines of the second paragraph that must stay with the first paragraph if a column or page break occurs within the second paragraph.

✔ **Keep Lines Together:** If you click this check box, it will prevent paragraphs from breaking. When this box is checked, the two radio buttons below it become available. The radio buttons present an either/or choice. One must be selected; At Start/End of Paragraph is selected by default.

✓ **All Lines in Paragraph:** This option prevents a paragraph from being broken at the end of a column or page. When a column or page break occurs within a paragraph to which this setting has been applied, the entire paragraph moves to the next column or page.

✓ **At Start/End of Paragraph:** Select this check box to control widows and orphans. When this button is selected, the two fields below it become available:

- **Start *x* Lines:** This field controls orphans. The value you enter is the minimum number of lines at the beginning of a paragraph that must be placed at the bottom of a column when a paragraph is split by a column ending.

- **End *x* Lines:** This field controls widows. The value you enter is the minimum number of lines at the end of a paragraph that must be placed at the top of a column when a paragraph is split by a column ending.

✓ **Start Paragraph:** From this pop-up menu, choose Anywhere to let the paragraph begin where it would fall naturally in the sequence of text (no forced break). Choose In Next Column to force a paragraph to begin in the next column; choose In Next Frame to make it begin in the next frame in the story chain; choose On Next Page to force a paragraph to begin on the next page (such as for chapter headings). Your other choices are similar: On Next Odd Page and On Next Even Page.

When creating paragraph styles, all the above controls are available in the Keep Options pane of the New Paragraph Styles dialog box.

Adding Drop Caps

Drop caps are enlarged capital letters that are often used to embellish paragraphs (usually the first paragraph of a chapter or story) and to draw attention to paragraphs. In the Paragraph panel or Control panel, InDesign lets you specify the number of letters you want to include in a drop cap and the number of lines you want to drop them down into.

To add one or more drop caps to selected paragraphs, enter a number in the Drop Cap Number of Characters field in the Paragraph panel or Control panel. The number you enter determines how many characters in a selected paragraph will be made into drop caps. To specify the number of lines a drop cap will extend into a paragraph (and therefore the height of the drop cap), enter a number in the Drop Cap Number of Lines field.

After you create a drop cap, you can modify it by highlighting it and changing any of its character formats — font, size, color, and so on — by using the Character panel or Control panel, as well as other panes such as Stroke and Swatches. Even better: Apply a character style to it that has all the desired attributes stored in one place. Figure 15-3 shows two examples of drop caps.

When creating paragraph styles, the above controls are available in the Drop Caps and Nested Styles pane of the New Paragraph Styles dialog box. (See Chapter 14 for details on nested styles.)

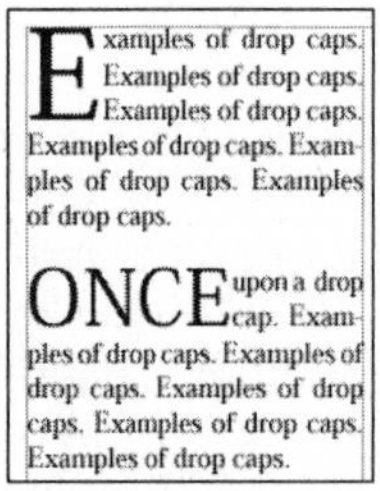

Figure 15-3:
A one-character drop cap three lines deep (top), and a two-line, four-character drop cap with the first word set in small caps (bottom).

Examples of drop caps. Examples of drop caps. Examples of drop caps. Examples of drop caps. Examples of drop caps. Examples of drop caps.

ONCE upon a drop cap. Examples of drop caps. Examples of drop caps. Examples of drop caps. Examples of drop caps. Examples of drop caps.

Controlling Hyphenation and Justification

Hyphenation is the placement of hyphens between syllables in words that won't fit at the end of a line of text. A hyphen is a signal to the reader that the word continues on the next line. InDesign gives you the option to turn paragraph hyphenation on or off. If you choose to hyphenate, you can customize the settings that determine when and where hyphens are inserted.

Justification is the addition or removal of space between words and/or letters that produces the flush-left/flush-right appearance of justified paragraphs. InDesign's justification controls let you specify how space is added or removed when paragraphs are justified. If you justify paragraphs, you almost certainly want to hyphenate them, too. If you opt for left-aligned paragraphs, whether to hyphenate is a personal choice.

InDesign offers both manual and automatic hyphenation.

Manual hyphenation

To break a particular word in a specific place, you can place a *discretionary hyphen* in the word. If the word won't entirely fit at the end of a line in a hyphenated paragraph, InDesign will use the discretionary hyphen to split the word if the part of the word before the hyphen fits on the line. To insert a discretionary hyphen, use the shortcut Shift+⌘+– (hyphen) or Ctrl+Shift+– (hyphen) in the text where you want the hyphen to appear.

If a word has a discretionary hyphen, and hyphenation is necessary, InDesign breaks the word *only* at that point. But you can place multiple discretionary hyphens within a single word. If a word needs to be hyphenated, InDesign will use the hyphenation point that produces the best results.

You can prevent a particular word from being hyphenated either by placing a discretionary hyphen in front of the first letter or by highlighting the word and choosing No Break from the flyout menu of the Control panel or Character panel. (You need to select the A iconic button in the Control panel to get this option in its flyout menu.) But be careful: If you select more than a line's width of text and apply No Break, InDesign will not know what to do, and so it won't display the rest of the story.

To prevent hyphenation for an entire paragraph, click anywhere inside of it and uncheck Hyphenate from the Paragraph panel or Control panel (be sure the ¶ button is selected in the Control panel).

Automatic hyphenation

To have InDesign automatically hyphenate selected paragraphs, all you have to do is check the Hyphenate check box in the Paragraph panel or Control panel. (A reminder that, in the Paragraph panel, the Hyphenate check box is displayed only if you choose Show Options from the flyout menu.)

You can control how InDesign actually performs the hyphenation via the Hyphenation option in the flyout menu. When you choose Hyphenation, the Hyphenation Settings dialog box, shown in Figure 15-4, appears.

The options in the Hyphenation Settings dialog box include

- **Hyphenate:** This is a duplicate of the Hyphenate check box in the Paragraph panel and Control panel. If you didn't check it before opening the Hyphenation Settings dialog box, you can check it here.

- **Words with at Least *x* Letters:** This is where you specify the number of letters in the shortest word you want to hyphenate.

- **After First *x* Letters:** In this field, enter the minimum number of characters that can precede a hyphen.

- **Before Last *x* Letters:** The number entered in this field determines the minimum number of characters that can follow a hyphen.

- **Hyphen Limit: *x* Hyphens:** In this field, you specify the number of consecutive lines that can be hyphenated. Several consecutive hyphens produce an awkward, ladder-like look, so consider entering a small number, such as **2** or **3**, in this field.

- **Hyphenation Zone:** The entry in this field applies only to nonjustified text and only when the Adobe Single-Line Composer option is selected (in the Paragraph panel's flyout menu). A hyphenation point must fall within the distance specified in this field in relation to the right margin in order to be used. Acceptable hyphenation points that do not fall within the specified hyphenation zone are ignored. You can also use the Better Spacing/Fewer Hyphens slider below the field to pick a value rather than entering a value in the Hyphenation Zone field.

- **Hyphenate Capitalized Words:** If you check this box, InDesign will hyphenate, when necessary, capitalized words. If you don't check this box, a capitalized word that would otherwise be hyphenated will get bumped to the next line, which may cause excessive spacing in the previous line.

✔ **Hyphenate Last Word:** Check this box to allow InDesign to break the last word in a paragraph. Otherwise, InDesign moves the entire word to the last line and spaces the preceding text as necessary.

✔ **Hyphenate Across Column:** Check this box to let text hyphenate at the end of a column.

When creating paragraph styles, all the above controls are available in the Hyphenation pane of the New Paragraph Styles dialog box — except for the composer setting, covered in the next sections.

Controlling justification

To control how justification is achieved, you can

✔ Condense or expand the width of spaces between words.

✔ Add or remove space between letters.

✔ Condense or expand the width of characters.

The options in the Justification dialog box, shown in Figure 15-5, let you specify the degree to which InDesign will adjust normal word spaces, character spacing, and character width to achieve justification. Access this dialog box via the flyout menu in the Control panel or in the Paragraph panel, or by pressing Option+Shift+⌘+J or Ctrl+Alt+Shift+J. When specifying values in the Justification dialog box, Minimum values must be smaller than Desired values, which in turn must be smaller than Maximum values.

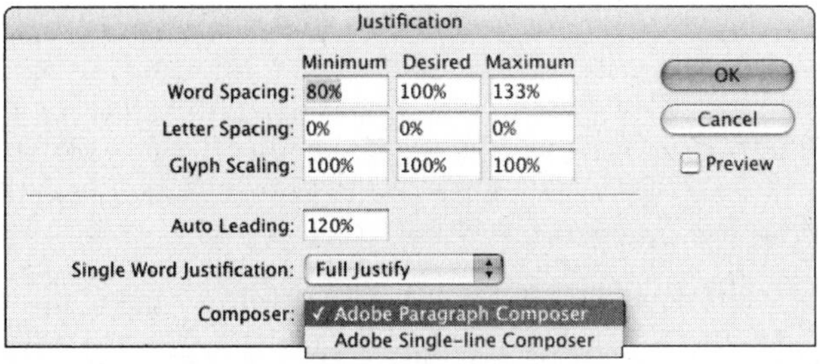

	Justification		
	Minimum	Desired	Maximum
Word Spacing:	80%	100%	133%
Letter Spacing:	0%	0%	0%
Glyph Scaling:	100%	100%	100%
Auto Leading:	120%		
Single Word Justification:	Full Justify		
Composer:	✓ Adobe Paragraph Composer		
	Adobe Single-line Composer		

[OK] [Cancel] ☐ Preview

Figure 15-5:
The
Justification
dialog box.

The Justification dialog box lets you specify the following options:

✔ **Word Spacing:** Enter the percentage of a character that you want to use whenever possible in the Desired field. (The default value is 100%, which uses a font's built-in width.) Enter the minimum acceptable percentage in the Minimum field; enter the maximum acceptable percentage in the Maximum field. The smallest value you can enter is 0%; the largest is 1000%.

- ✔ **Letter Spacing:** The default value of 0% in this field uses a font's built-in letter spacing. In the Desired field, enter a positive value to add space (in increments of 1% of an en space) between all letter pairs; enter a negative value to remove space. Enter the minimum acceptable percentage in the Minimum field; enter the maximum acceptable percentage in the Maximum field.

- ✔ **Glyph Scaling:** The default value of 100% uses a character's normal width. In the Desired field, enter a positive value to expand all character widths; enter a negative value to condense character widths. Enter the minimum acceptable percentage in the Minimum field and the maximum acceptable percentage in the Maximum field. If you do apply glyph scaling, it's best to keep it to a range of 97 to 103 percent at most.

If you use the Adobe Paragraph Composer option (explained in the following section) for justified paragraphs, specifying a narrow range between minimum and maximum Word Spacing, Letter Spacing, and Glyph Scaling will generally produce good-looking results. However, if you choose the Adobe Single-Line Composer option, a broader range between Minimum and Maximum gives the composer more leeway in spacing words and letters and hyphenating words and can produce better-looking results. The best way to find out what values work best is to experiment with several settings. Print out hard copies and let your eyes decide which values produce the best results.

When creating paragraph styles, all the above controls are available in the Justification pane of the New Paragraph Styles dialog box.

Composing text

The Paragraph panel's flyout menu offers two options for implementing the hyphenation and justification settings you establish: the Adobe Single-Line Composer and the Adobe Paragraph Composer. (These options are also available in the Justification dialog box, covered in the previous section.)

Adobe Single-Line Composer

In single-line composition, hyphenation, and justification settings are applied to each line in a paragraph, one line at a time. The effect of modifying the spacing of one line on the lines above and below it is not considered in single-line composition, so it can cause poor spacing.

Adobe Paragraph Composer

InDesign's Adobe Paragraph Composer is selected by default. It takes a broader approach to composition than the Adobe Single-Line Composer by looking at the entire paragraph at once. If a poorly spaced line can be fixed by adjusting the spacing of a previous line, the Adobe Paragraph Composer will reflow the previous line.

The Adobe Paragraph Composer is more sophisticated than the Single-Line Composer, offering better overall spacing because it will sacrifice optimal spacing a bit on one line to prevent really bad spacing on another, something the single-line method does not do.

Ruling Your Paragraphs

If you want to place a horizontal line within text so that the line moves with the text when editing causes the text to reflow — an often effective highlighting device — you need to create a paragraph rule. A paragraph rule looks much like a line created with the line tool but behaves like a text character. Here's how to create paragraph rules:

1. **Select the paragraphs to which you want to apply a rule above and/or a rule below and then choose Paragraph Rules from the Paragraph panel's or Control panel's flyout menu; alternatively, you can use the shortcut Option+⌘+J or Ctrl+Alt+J.**

   You can also specify rules as part of a paragraph style. The Paragraph Rules dialog box, shown in Figure 15-6, is displayed.

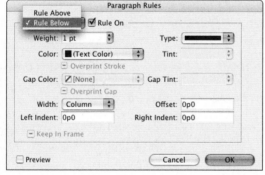

Figure 15-6: The Paragraph Rules dialog box.

2. **Choose Rule Above or Rule Below and then click Rule On.**

   To add rules both above and below, click Rule On for both options and specify their settings separately. To see the rule while you create it, select the Preview option.

3. **Choose a predefined thickness from the Weight pop-up menu or enter a value in the Weight field.**

4. **Choose a rule type from the Type pop-up menu.**

   You can choose from 17 types, including dashed, striped, dotted, and wavy lines.

5. **Choose a color for the rule from the Color pop-up menu.** This menu lists the colors displayed in the Swatches panel (Window➪Swatches or F5).

6. **From the Width pop-up menu, choose Column to have the rule extend from the left edge of the column to the right edge of the column; choose Text to have the rule extend from the left edge of the frame or column to the right.**

7. **To indent the rule from the left and/or right edges, enter values in the Left Indent and/or Right Indent fields.**

8. **Control the vertical position of the rule by entering a value in the Offset field.**

   For a rule above, the offset value is measured upward from the baseline of the first line in a paragraph to the bottom of the rule; for a rule below, the offset is measured downward from the baseline of the last line in a paragraph to the top of the rule.

9. **Check the Overprint Stroke box if you want to print a rule on top of any underlying colors.**

   This ensures that any misregistration during printing will not result in white areas around the rule where the paper shows through. There's a similar Overprint Gap check box for lines that have a Gap Color.

10. **To ensure that a rule over a paragraph at the top of a frame displays within the frame, check the Keep in Frame option.**

11. **Click OK to close the dialog box, implement your changes, and return to the document.**

To remove a paragraph rule, click in the paragraph to which the rule is applied, choose Paragraph Rules from the Paragraph panel's flyout menu, uncheck the Rule On box, and then click OK.

When creating paragraph styles, all the above controls are available in the Paragraph Rules pane of the New Paragraph Styles dialog box.

Chapter 16

Finessing Character Details

*W*hen you create documents, you have lots of opportunities to make decisions about how the text appears. With its comprehensive set of character-formatting tools, InDesign lets you change the look of type so it can precisely match the communication needs of your publications. You can control not just the font and size of type, but also many other variations.

Decisions about type matter. A document relies on good typography to allow others to easily read and understand it. The appearance of type supports the message you're conveying, and doing a good job of character formatting is worth your time.

Specifying Character Formats

InDesign lets you modify the appearance of highlighted characters or selected paragraphs with the following options:

✔ **Character panel:** Highlight the text and open the Character panel (Type➪Character, or ⌘+T or Ctrl+T), which is shown in Figure 16-1. (You can also choose Window➪Type & Tools➪Character.) Be sure Show Options is visible in the flyout menu in order to see all the possible options. You can also use the double-arrow iconic button to the left of the panel name to toggle among showing the panel title, the basic options, and all options.

The Character panel provides access to most of InDesign's character formatting options. Three of the options — Font Family, Font Style, and Font Size — are also available via the Type menu, and several options have keyboard shortcuts.

✔ **Paragraph panel:** Select a paragraph and open the Paragraph panel (Type➪Paragraph, or Option+⌘+T or Ctrl+Alt+T). Chapter 15 covers these settings in detail.

✔ **Control panel:** The Control panel offers all the formatting options of the Character panel plus others. If the Control panel doesn't show all the character formatting options, select the text and then click the A iconic button on the panel. If the Control panel is not visible (it almost always is), display it by choosing Window➪Control or pressing Option+⌘+6 or Ctrl+Alt+6.

 To change the default character formats — the settings that InDesign will use when you type text into an empty frame — make changes in the Character panel or Control panel when no text is selected or when the text-insertion cursor isn't flashing. That'll save you the hassle of having to reformat new text.

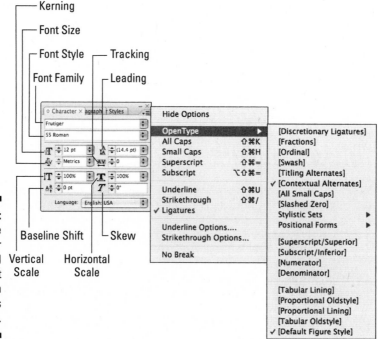

Figure 16-1:
The Character panel and its flyout menu with all options shown.

You can choose to apply character formats to highlighted text in two ways:

✔ Create and apply character styles. Character styles offer an important advantage: A character style's settings are stored, so you can apply the exact same settings easily to other text. When you change a character style's settings, any text based on that style is automatically changed to reflect the new settings. (Chapter 14 covers styles in detail.)

✔ Use the local controls in the Character panel, the Control panel, the Type menu, or their keyboard shortcuts, which I cover in the upcoming sections.

Even when you do use character styles, you'll probably also do some local formatting from time to time. For example, you would probably use the Character panel to format the type on the opening spread of a feature magazine article, and then use character styles to quickly format the remainder of the article.

If you have a smallish monitor, set at 1024 by 768 pixels — the norm for a 17-inch display — the Character and Character Styles panels are shoved to the bottom of the panel dock, and, when they're selected, the only thing you'll see is their panel tab and flyout menu icon. You have a few choices: Shorten other panel groups in the dock to make room for them, remove other panel groups to make room for them, or drag them out of the dock and make them floating.

Modifying Font, Type Style, and Size

Many people use typographic terms — *font, face, typeface, font family,* and *type style* — inconsistently. Which terms you use doesn't matter as long as you make yourself understood, but I recommend becoming familiar with the font-related terms in InDesign's menus and panels:

✔ **Font or typeface:** A collection of characters — including letters, numbers, and special characters — that share the same overall appearance, including stroke width, weight, angle, and style.

For example, Helvetica Regular and Adobe Garamond Semibold Italic are well-known fonts.

✔ **Font family:** A collection of several fonts that share the same general appearance but differ in stroke width, weight, and/or stroke angle.

For example, Helvetica and Adobe Garamond are font families.

✔ **Font style:** Each of the fonts that make up a font family. When you choose a font family from the Character panel's Font Family menu, InDesign displays the family's font style variations — what most of the design world calls *type styles* — in the accompanying Font Style pop-up menu.

For example, Regular and Semibold Italic are examples of font styles.

Changing font family and font style

When you change from one font to another in InDesign, you can choose a new font family and font style independently in the Character panel. For example, changing from Arial Bold to Times Bold or from Arial Regular to Berthold Baskerville Regular is a simple change of font family (Arial to Berthold Baskerville). However, if you switch from, say, Bookman Light to Century Schoolbook Bold Italic, you're changing both family and style (Bookman to Century, then Light to Bold Italic).

InDesign can display previews of fonts when you select fonts via the Control panel, various text-oriented panels, and the Type menu. You turn on this capability in the Type pane of the Preferences dialog box (choose InDesign⇨ Preferences⇨Type or press ⌘+K on the Mac, or choose Edit⇨Preferences⇨ Type or press Ctrl+K in Windows). But doing so makes your menus huge, often so much that they are unwieldy to use. Although it can help you get familiar with your fonts, its unwieldy nature may not be worth that benefit. Only you can decide, but if you do use it, I recommend keeping the preview size small to limit its size.

Whether you use the Control panel or Character panel, you can choose between two methods for changing the font family:

✔ Choose the Font Family menu, and then select a name from the list of available font families.

✔ Place the cursor in front of or highlight the font name displayed in the Font Family field, type the first few letters of the font family you want to apply, and then press Return or Enter. For example, entering **Cas** selects Caslon (if it's available on your computer).

If you choose only a font family when font styles are available in an accompanying submenu, no changes are applied to the selected text. So be sure to select a font style from the submenu.

When creating character styles, the above controls are available in the Basic Character Formats pane of the New Character Styles and New Paragraph Styles dialog boxes.

Changing type size

You can be very precise with type sizes (what InDesign calls *font size*). InDesign supports sizes from 0.1 point to 1,296 points (108 inches) in increments as fine as 0.001 point. Of course, you want to use good judgment when choosing type sizes. For example, headlines should be larger than subheads, which in turn are larger than body text, which is larger than photo credits, and so on.

Change the type size of highlighted text with the following methods:

✔ Choose Type⇨Size, and then choose one of the predefined sizes listed in the Size submenu. If you choose Other from the submenu, the Font Size field is highlighted in the Character panel. Enter a custom size, and then press Return or Enter.

✔ Use the Character panel or Control panel:

- Choose one of the predefined sizes from the Font Size menu.

- Highlight the currently applied type size displayed in the accompanying editable field, enter a new size, and then press Return or Enter.

- Make sure the Font Size field is selected, and then use the up and down arrow keys to increase or decrease the size in 1-point increments. Pressing Shift multiplies the increment to 10.

✔ Control+click or right-click a text selection, and then choose a size from the Size submenu. If you choose Other from the submenu, the Font Size field is highlighted in the Character panel. Enter a custom size, and then press Return or Enter.

If text is highlighted and the Font Size field is empty, more than one type size is used in the selected text.

When creating character styles, the Font Size control is available in the Basic Character Formats pane of the New Character Styles dialog box.

Using Other Character Formats

In the Control panel, you can adjust other character formats, including all caps, small caps, superscript, subscript, underline, strikethrough, kerning, tracking, horizontal and vertical scale, baseline shift, skew, font style, and language. Through the flyout menu, you can also set ligatures, modify underline and strikethrough settings, control whether text may break (be hyphenated), select its case (such as all caps and small caps), and select OpenType features. (OpenType fonts can have a dozen kinds of special formatting. These are expert features, so I don't get into the details here, but feel free to explore the options for any OpenType fonts you have.)

In the Character panel, you can adjust kerning, tracking, horizontal and vertical scale, baseline shift, skew, and language. Through its flyout menu (refer to Figure 16-1), you can also set all caps, small caps, superscript, subscript, underline, strikethrough, ligatures, and underline and strikethrough settings, as well as control whether text may break (be hyphenated) and select OpenType features. (InDesign also lets you create custom underlines and strikethroughs, as described in Chapter 17.)

When creating character styles, the kerning, tracking, subscript, superscript, case, ligature, underlining, break, and strikethrough controls are available in the Basic Character Formats pane of the New Character Styles and New Paragraph Styles dialog boxes. The scale, baseline shift, skew, and language controls are in the Advanced Character Formats pane. OpenType controls are in the OpenType Features pane. Custom underline and strikethrough options, covered in Chapter 17, are available in the Underline Options and Strikethrough Options panes, respectively.

You must choose Show Options from the Character panel's flyout menu to display the Vertical Scale, Horizontal Scale, Baseline Shift, Skew, and Language options in the panel.

The Control panel has the same functions as the Character panel, except the all caps, small caps, superscript, subscript, underline, and strikethrough options are in the panel itself rather than in its flyout menu.

Figure 16-2 shows the various effects in action. In its top row, *InDesign* has a different font style applied, *incredible* has been scaled horizontally, and *control* is in all caps, while *over* has had each letter's baseline shifted by a different amount. In the middle row, the word *text* has been skewed, the word *with* is in small caps, a gradient and underline are applied to *typographic*, a custom underline has been applied to *capabilities*, and the word *formatting* has been vertically scaled. In the bottom row, compare the baseline shifts in the top row to the true superscript and subscript following the words *most* and *people*. The word *never* has a custom strikethrough applied, while *even* uses a standard one. The word *heard* has a colored stroke applied and a fill of white.

Figure 16-2:
Various
character
formatting
options
applied
to text.

> InDesign *has incredible* CONTROL ᵒᵛₑᵣ
> ᴛᴇxᴛ *formatting,* ᴡɪᴛʜ *typographic* capabilities
> *most*[1] *people*[2] have ~~never even~~ heard *of!*

Horizontal and Vertical Scale options

InDesign's Horizontal Scale option lets you condense and expand type by
squeezing or stretching characters. Similarly, the Vertical Scale option lets
you shrink or stretch type vertically.

Typographers tend to agree that excessive scaling should be avoided. If you
need to make text bigger or smaller, your best bet is to adjust font size; if you
need to squeeze or stretch a range of text a bit, use InDesign's kerning and
tracking controls (covered later in this chapter) because the letter forms
aren't modified — only the space between letters changes when you kern or
track text.

Unscaled text has a horizontal and vertical scale value of 100 percent. You
can apply scaling values between 1 percent and 1,000 percent. If you apply
equal horizontal and vertical scale values, you're making the original text
proportionally larger or smaller. In this case, changing font size is a simpler
solution.

To change the scale of highlighted text, enter new values in the Horizontal
and/or Vertical Scale fields in the Character panel or Control panel. If a value
is highlighted in the Horizontal Scale or Vertical Scale field, you can also use
the up and down arrow keys to increase and decrease the scaling in 1-percent
increments; press Shift to increase or decrease in 10-percent increments.

Baseline shift

The *baseline* is an invisible horizontal line on which a line of characters rests.
The bottom of each letter sits on the baseline (except descenders, such as in
y, p, q, j, and g). When you perform a *baseline shift,* you move highlighted
text above or below its baseline. This feature is useful for carefully placing
such characters as trademark and copyright symbols and for creating
custom fractions.

To baseline-shift highlighted text, enter new values in the Baseline Shift field in the Character panel or Control panel. You can also use the up and down arrow keys to increase the baseline shift in 1-point increments, or press Shift with the arrow keys to increase or decrease it in 10-point increments.

Skew (false italic)

For fonts that don't have an italic type style, InDesign provides the option to skew, or slant, text to create an artificial italic variation of any font. Like horizontal and vertical text scaling, skewing is a clunky way of creating italic-looking text. Use this feature to create special typographic effects, as shown in Figure 16-3, or in situations where a true italic style is not available. Skewing works better for sans-serif typefaces than for serif typefaces because the characters are simpler and have fewer embellishments that can get oddly distorted when skewed.

To skew highlighted text, you have three options:

- ✔ Enter an angle value between –85 and 85 in the Skew field in the Character panel or Control panel. Positive values slant text to the left; negative values slant text to the right.

- ✔ Press the accompanying up/down arrow keys when the cursor is in the Skew field to skew text in 1-degree increments. Pressing the Shift key with an arrow key changes the increment 4 degrees.

- ✔ You can also skew all the text in a text frame using the Shear tool or by changing the value in the Shear X Angle field in the Control panel after selecting the frame. Slanting text by shearing a text frame does not affect the skew angle of the text. You can specify a skew angle for highlighted text independently from the frame's shear angle.

Figure 16-3:
Characters in skewed text can slant forward, like italics, or backward, as in this example.

Skewed shadow

Capitalization options

When you choose All Caps, the uppercase version of all highlighted characters is used: Lowercase letters are converted to uppercase, and uppercase letters remain unchanged.

Similarly, the Small Caps option affects just lowercase letters. When you choose Small Caps, InDesign automatically uses the Small Caps font style if one is available for the font family (few font families include this style). If a Small Caps type style is not available, InDesign generates small caps from uppercase letters using the scale percentage specified in the Advanced Type pane of the Preferences dialog box (choose InDesign⇨Preferences⇨ Advanced Type or press ⌘+K on the Mac, or choose Edit⇨Preferences⇨ Advanced Type or press Ctrl+K in Windows). The default scale value used to generate small caps text is 70% (of uppercase letters).

Another handy way to change the case of text is to highlight the text and then choose Type⇨Change Case, and then select from the appropriate submenu option: Uppercase, Lowercase, Title Case, and Sentence Case. Title Case capitalizes the first letter in each word, whereas Sentence Case capitalizes the first letter in the beginning of each sentence.

Superscript and Subscript

When you apply the Superscript and Subscript character formats to highlighted text, InDesign applies a baseline shift to the characters, lifting them above (for superscript) or lowering them below (for subscript) their baseline, and reduces their size.

The amount of baseline shift and scaling that's used for the Superscript and Subscript formats is determined by the Position and Size fields in the Advanced Type pane of the Preferences dialog box (choose InDesign⇨ Preferences⇨Advanced Type or press ⌘+K on the Mac, or choose Edit⇨ Preferences⇨Advanced Type or press Ctrl+K in Windows). The default Position value for both formats is 33.3%, which means that characters are moved up or down by one-third of the applied leading value. The default Superscript and Subscript Size value is 58.3%, which means that superscripted and subscripted characters are reduced to 58.3% of the applied font size. The Advanced Type pane lets you specify separate default settings for Superscript and Subscript.

To apply the Superscript or Subscript format to highlighted text, choose the appropriate option from the Character panel's flyout menu. Figure 16-2 shows examples of characters to which the default Superscript and Subscript settings have been applied.

Underline and Strikethrough

Underline and Strikethrough formats are typographically considered to be unacceptable for indicating emphasis in text, which is better accomplished by using bold and/or italic font styles.

Underlines can be useful in kickers and other text above a headline, as well as in documents formatted to look as if they are typewritten. Strikethrough can be used in cases where you want to indicate incorrect answers, eliminated choices, or deleted text.

If you use underlines and strikethrough, InDesign lets you specify exactly how they look through the Underline Options and Strikethrough Options dialog boxes available in the flyout menus of the Character panel and Control panel.

InDesign lets you create your own underlines and strikethroughs, in addition to using the standard ones, as Chapter 17 explains.

Ligatures

A *ligature* is a special character that combines two letters. Most fonts include just two ligatures — fi and fl. When you choose the Ligature option, InDesign automatically displays and prints a font's built-in ligatures — instead of the two component letters — if the font includes ligatures.

One nice thing about the Ligature option is that, even though a ligature looks like a single character on-screen, it's still fully editable. That is, you can click between the two-letter shapes and insert text if necessary. Also, a ligature created with the Ligature option doesn't cause InDesign's spell checker to flag the word that contains it.

To use ligatures within highlighted text, choose Ligatures from the Character panel's or Control panel's flyout menu (Ligatures is set to On by default). Figure 16-4 shows an example of text with a ligature.

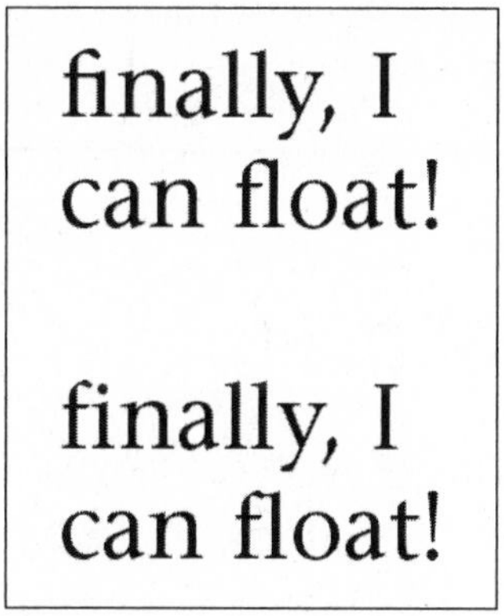

Figure 16-4:
Ligatures
are used
between the
fi and *fl*
letter pairs
in the two
words.

finally, I
can float!

finally, I
can float!

You can also insert ligatures manually:

✔ On the Mac, press Option+Shift+5 to insert the fi ligature and
Option+Shift+6 to insert the fl ligature. You can also use the Mac OS X's
Character Palette utility or InDesign's Glyphs panel (Type⇨Glyphs,
or Option+Shift+F11 or Alt+Shift+F11) to choose them visually.

✔ In Windows, you have to use a program such as the Character Map utility
that comes with Windows. Choose Start⇨All Programs⇨Accessories⇨
System Tools⇨Character Map; if you have the Classic Start menu interface enabled, choose Start⇨Programs⇨Accessories⇨System Tools⇨
Character Map.

However, if you do enter ligatures yourself, InDesign's spell checker flags any
words that contain them. For this reason, you'll typically want InDesign to
handle the task of inserting ligatures automatically.

Turning off hyphenation and other breaks

You can prevent individual words from being hyphenated or a string of words
from being broken at the end of a line. For example, you may decide that you
don't want to hyphenate certain product names, such as *InDesign.* The No
Break option was created for situations such as these.

To prevent a word or a text string from being broken, highlight it, and then
choose No Break from the Character panel's flyout menu or the Control
panel's flyout menu. You can also prevent a word from being hyphenated by
placing a discretionary hyphen (Shift+⌘+– [hyphen] or Ctrl+Shift+– [hyphen])
in front of the first letter. (See Chapter 15 for more on hyphenation controls.)

Controlling Space between Characters and Lines

The legibility of a block of text depends as much on the space around it — called *white space* — as it does on the readability of the font. InDesign offers two ways to adjust the space between characters:

- ✔ *Kerning* is the adjustment of space between a pair of characters. Most fonts include built-in kerning tables that control the space between character pairs, such as *LA, Yo,* and *WA,* that otherwise could appear to have a space between them even when there isn't one. For large font sizes — for example, a magazine headline — you may want to manually adjust the space between certain character pairs to achieve consistent spacing.

- ✔ *Tracking* is the process of adding or removing space among all letters in a range of text.

You can apply kerning and/or tracking to highlighted text in $\frac{1}{1,000}$-em increments, called units. An em is as wide as the height of the current font size (that is, an em for 12-point text is 12 points wide), which means that kerning and tracking increments are relative to the applied font size.

Leading (rhymes with sledding) controls the vertical space between lines of type. It's traditionally an attribute of paragraphs, but InDesign lets you apply leading on a character-by-character basis. To override the character-oriented approach, ensuring that leading changes affect entire paragraphs, check the Apply Leading to Entire Paragraphs option in the Type pane of the Preferences dialog box (choose InDesign⇨Preferences⇨Type or press ⌘+K on the Mac, or choose Edit⇨Preferences⇨Type or press Ctrl+K in Windows).

Kerning

The Kerning controls in the Character panel and Control panel provide three options for kerning letter pairs:

- ✔ **Metrics:** Controls the space between character pairs in the highlighted text using a font's built-in kerning pairs.

- ✔ **Optical:** Evaluates each letter pair in highlighted text and adds or removes space between the letters based on the shapes of the characters.

- ✔ **Manual:** Adds or removes space between a specific letter pair in user-specified amounts.

When the flashing text cursor is between a pair of characters, the Kerning field displays the pair's kerning value. If Metrics or Optical kerning is applied, the kerning value is displayed in parentheses.

To apply Metrics or Optical kerning to highlighted text, choose the appropriate option from the Kerning pop-up menu. To apply manual kerning, click between a pair of letters, and then enter a value in the Kerning field or choose one of the predefined values. Negative values tighten; positive values loosen.

When letter shapes start to collide, you've tightened too far.

Tracking

Tracking is uniform kerning applied to a range of text. You might use tracking to tighten character spacing for a font that you think is too spacey or loosen spacing for a font that's too tight. Or you could track a paragraph tighter or looser to eliminate a short last line or a *widow* (the last line of a paragraph that falls at the top of a page or column).

To apply tracking to highlighted text, enter a value in the Character panel's or Control panel's Tracking field or choose one of the predefined values. Negative values tighten; positive values loosen (in 0.001-em increments).

You might wonder how tracking is different than kerning. They're essentially the same thing, with this difference: Tracking applies to a selection of three or more characters, whereas kerning is meant to adjust the spacing between just two characters. You use tracking to change the overall tightness of character spacing; you use kerning to improve the spacing between letters that just don't quite look right compared to the rest of the text.

Leading

Leading refers to the vertical space between lines of type as measured from baseline to baseline. Leading in InDesign is a character-level format, which means that you can apply different leading values within a single paragraph. InDesign looks at each line of text in a paragraph and uses the largest applied leading value within a line to determine the leading for that line.

By default, InDesign applies Auto Leading to text, which is equal to 120 percent of the type size. As long as you don't change fonts or type sizes in a paragraph, Auto Leading works pretty well. But if you do change fonts or sizes, Auto Leading can result in inconsistent spacing between lines. For this reason, specifying an actual leading value is safer.

In most cases, using a leading value that is slightly larger than the type size is a good idea. When the leading value equals the type size, text is said to be set *solid.* That's about as tight as you ever want to set leading, unless you're trying to achieve a special typographic effect or working with very large text sizes in ad-copy headlines. As is the case with kerning and tracking, when tight leading causes letters to collide — ascenders and descenders are the first to overlap — you've gone too far.

You can change InDesign's preset Auto Leading value of 120%. To do so, choose Type⇨Paragraph, or press Option+⌘+T or Ctrl+Alt+T, to display the Paragraph panel. Choose Justification in the flyout menu, enter a new value in the Auto Leading field, and then click OK. (Why a character format setting is accessed via the Paragraph panel and what Auto Leading has to do with Justification are both mysteries.)

To modify the leading value applied to selected text, choose one of the predefined options from the Leading pop-up menu in the Character panel or Control panel, or enter a leading value in the field. You can enter values from 0 to 5,000 points in 0.001-point increments. You can also use the up and down arrow keys to change leading in 1-point increments.

Chapter 17

Tricks with Text

*W*ith the myriad of text-formatting techniques available in InDesign, you can create some snazzy and sophisticated effects. You can stretch, skew, rotate, and color text. You can use a wide range of characters for bullets. You can add shadows and feathering effects to give words a dramatic flair. As with all good things, moderation in your use of text effects will keep your documents looking professional. This chapter shows you some InDesign features that can produce typographic special effects and gives some suggestions on when to use them. (Chapters 15 and 16 cover more prosaic formatting controls.)

You can also apply all sorts of transformations to text frames, which affects the text inside of them. Chapter 9 covers these capabilities.

Using Bulleted and Numbered Lists

Automatic bullets and numbering are available as a paragraph format in InDesign. You access these options (after selecting the paragraphs you want to make into automatic lists, of course) by choosing Bullets and Numbering Options from the Paragraph panel's or Control panel's flyout menus. Doing so displays the Bullets and Numbering dialog box shown in Figure 17-1.

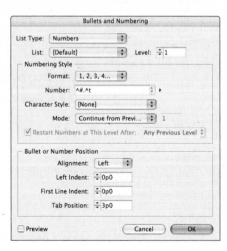

Figure 17-1:
The Bullets
and
Numbering
dialog box
set for
bullets
(left) and
numbering
(right).

To set bullets or numbered lists in the Bullets and Numbering dialog box, first select either Bullets or Numbers from the List Type pop-up menu, and then follow these steps (select the Preview check box to see the results of your choices before you finalize them):

1. **For bullets, choose a bullet character from the Bullet Character area.**

   The area will show bullet characters available for the current font; you can change the selection by changing the selected font or by clicking the Add button.

   For numbered lists, choose a numbering style from the Format pop-up menu, format the numbers' appearance by choosing spaces and number placeholders from the pop-up menu to the right, and choose whether the numbers continue or start anew at this paragraph through the Mode pop-up menu (your choices are Continue from Previous Number and Start At).

   In the Number field (which replaces the previous version's Separator pop-up menu), you can insert all sorts of special spaces and characters, giving you broad control on how numbers display. You can also choose number placeholders, which tell InDesign what numbers to insert in the list. For simple lists, choose Current Level from the Insert Number Placeholder pop-up submenu. The other levels are used when you have sublists, an expert feature. You can also choose Chapter Number to insert the chapter's number as the list item's number.

   The Mode pop-up menu replaces the previous version's Start At field.

2. **Adjust the font settings for the bullets or numbers by using the Character Style pop-up menu to choose a character style.**

   The default setting ([None]) uses the paragraph's current formatting.

The Character Style pop-up menu replaces the previous version's Font Family, Font Style, Size, and Color options.

3. **In the Bullet or Number Position section of the dialog box, set the indentation for the list.** Using the Alignment pop-up menu, choose Left, Center, or Right to determine where the bullet or numeral is positioned within its tab. You can set the hanging indent amount and the bullet's or number's overhang by using the Left Indent, First Line Indent, and Tab Position fields.

This Bullet or Number Position section's settings have changed to provide greater control over the list's indentation and bullet or number position.

4. **When you finish formatting the bulleted or numbered list, click OK.**

InDesign CS3 gives you even more control over bulleted and numbered lists through the new options you get by choosing Type➪Bulleted & Numbered Lists:

- ✔ The Apply/Remove Bullets and Apply/Remove Numbers submenu options quickly let you turn on or off the bullets or numbering for selected paragraphs. You can also use the iconic buttons for these controls on the Control panel.

- ✔ The Restart/Continue Numbering is a handy way to control which paragraphs are numbered, such as when you have an unnumbered paragraph within a list. (These options are also available in the flyout menu of the Paragraph panel and Control panel.)

- ✔ The Convert Bullets to Text and Convert Numbering to Text options remove the automatic bullets or numerals in a paragraph but leave an actual bullet character or numeral at the beginning of the paragraph for you to do as you please.

A more expert option is the Define Lists option (available in two places: by choosing Type➪Bulleted & Numbered Lists➪Define Lists, or by choosing Define Lists from the Paragraph panel's flyout menu). Here, you create list styles with just two options: Continue Numbers Across Stories and Continue Numbers from Previous Document in a Book. These list styles are accessed when you create or edit paragraph styles using the style dialog boxes' Bullets and Numbering pane, or when you apply bullets and numbering through the Paragraph panel's or Control panel's flyout menu. (Either way, choose the appropriate style in the List pop-up menu.)

When you choose the first option, InDesign continues numbering text based on the last number used in the previous story rather than restart the numbering at each story (the normal behavior). When you choose the second option, InDesign continues numbering text based on the last number used in the previous chapter of a book (see Chapter 23) rather than start over again with this document (the normal behavior).

It's possible that the bulleted or numbered list you're working with was first created in a word processor and then placed in InDesign. Perhaps the writer simply used an asterisk followed by a space to indicate a bullet, or used the word processor's automatic bullet or numbering feature. You can deal with imported bulleted and numbered lists as described in Chapter 12.

For the bullets in a list, you're not limited to using the small round bullet (•) included in most typefaces. You can use any character in the body text font, or you can switch to a symbol or pi font and choose a more decorative character. Zapf Dingbats and Wingdings are the most common symbol fonts, offering an array of boxes, arrows, crosses, stars, and check marks.

Labeling Paragraphs

Along with using drop caps, which I cover in Chapter 15, changing the formatting of the first few words in a paragraph as a *label* can serve as a visual indicator that the reader has arrived at the beginning of a story, chapter, or new topic. To experiment with label formatting, use the attributes available via the Character panel or Control panel and their flyout menus, such as font changes, horizontal scale, or small caps. After you decide on the formatting for labels, you can apply it by using character styles after paragraph styles are applied — and after the text is final. You might also be able to use the nested styles feature if the label text follows a specific pattern, such as a specific number of words or characters or an entire sentence.

A real easy way to consistently apply the desired label formatting to text is to use a nested style, as explained in Chapter 14.

The following descriptions show frequently used label formatting:

✔ **Boldface:** Bold type is often used for titles and subheads in magazines, newspapers, and reports. To apply boldface in InDesign, select the bold version of the typeface from the Font Style pop-up menu in the Character panel.

✔ *Italics:* Italic text is a good choice for emphasizing specific words and for applying to tertiary heads. To apply italics in InDesign, select the oblique version of the typeface from the Font Style pop-up menu on the Character panel.

✔ Underlines: Underlined text isn't used as frequently as it once was, simply because page-layout programs such as InDesign offer more sophisticated options for labeling text. Still, you might have occasion to use underlines, such as to emphasize a label. Use the Underline command in the menu on the Character panel or via the iconic button in the

Control panel's character (A) pane. Note that you have no control over the style, thickness, or placement of the underline if you use this option; for custom underlines, use the controls described later in this chapter.

✔ SMALL CAPS: Small caps offer a subtle, classic look that blends well with the rest of the document. You have two choices for applying small caps from the Character pane: Choose a small-caps variation of a typeface from the Font Style pop-up menu or choose the Small Caps command from the Character panel's flyout menu, or via the iconic button in the Control panel's character (A) pane.

✔ Typeface change: Rather than relying on different variations of a font, you can use a different font altogether, such as Futura Medium, for a label. To contrast with serif body text, you might choose a sans-serif typeface that complements the look of your publication. To apply a different typeface, use the Font Family pop-up menu in the Character panel or Control panel.

✔ S c a l e d   t e x t : Scaling text horizontally — up 10 or 20 percent — is a subtle effect that makes the section of text visually distinct. Scaling text vertically, however, can be *too* subtle unless combined with boldface or another style. Use the Horizontal Scale and Vertical Scale fields in the Character panel or Control panel to scale text.

✔ Size change: Bumping the size of a label up a point or two is another subtle design choice. To change the size of type, use the Font Size field in the Character panel or Control panel.

Adding Special Type Treatments

Skilled graphic designers make decisions based on what best serves the content. In doing so, they often rely on special typographic techniques. For example, the use of reverse type helps to break up pages and to organize text, while careful formatting of fractions and hanging punctuation adds a professional touch.

Reversing type out of its background

Reversed type is white type on a black background rather than black type on a white background. Of course, reversed type doesn't have to be white on black; it can be any lighter color on a darker color. You often find reversed type in table headings, kickers (explanatory blurbs following headlines), and decorative layout elements.

To lighten the text, highlight it with the Type tool, click the Fill button on the Tools panel, and choose a light color from the Swatches panel (Window⇨ Swatches or F5). For the dark background, you have three options: filling the text frame with a darker color, making the text frame transparent and placing it on top of darker objects, or placing a thick, dark ruling line behind the text.

For the first two options, select the text frame and then click the Fill iconic button on the Tools panel.

✔ To fill the text frame with a darker color, click a color from the Swatches panel.

✔ To make the text frame transparent, click the Apply None iconic button on the Tools panel. Then place the text frame in front of a darker object or graphic.

To create reversed type that is not in its own text frame, use a ruling line of the appropriate width (at least a couple points larger than the text size). If you use a Ruling Line Above, move the line down behind the text; if you use a Ruling Line Below, move it up. Figure 17-2 shows reversed type used as a heading, as well as the Paragraph Rules dialog box and the settings used to create the effect. (To access this dialog box, choose Paragraph Rules from the flyout menu of the Control panel's ¶ pane or of the Paragraph panel, or press Option+⌘+J or Ctrl+Alt+J.)

I explain how to create and adjust ruling lines in greater detail in Chapter 15.

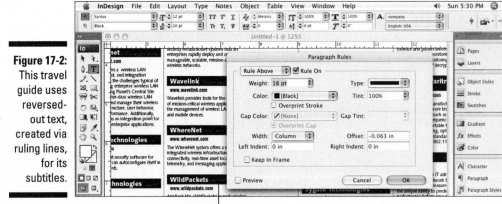

Figure 17-2: This travel guide uses reversed-out text, created via ruling lines, for its subtitles.

Reversed type

Creating sidebars and pull-quotes

A *sidebar* is supplemental text that is often formatted differently from the rest of the document and placed within a shaded or outlined box. Sidebars help break up text-heavy pages and call attention to information that is often interesting but not essential to the main story.

Particularly in text-heavy publications, pulling in-depth information or related text into sidebars can help provide visual relief. To create a sidebar, you usually place the text in its own frame, then stroke the frame and optionally fill it with a tint. To inset the text from the edges of the frame, use the Text Frame Options dialog box (Object➪Text Frame Options or ⌘+B or Ctrl+B).

A *pull-quote* is a catchy one- or two-line excerpt from a publication that is enlarged and reformatted to achieve both editorial and design objectives. Pull-quotes draw readers into articles with excerpts that do everything from summarize the content to provide shock value. From the design perspective, pull-quotes break up static columns and offer opportunities for typographic treatment that emphasizes the content, such as colors and typefaces that support the mood of an article.

To create a pull-quote, copy and paste the relevant text into its own text frame and then reformat the text and frame as you wish. Use the Text Wrap panel (Window➪Text Wrap or Option+⌘+W or Ctrl+Alt+W) to control how text in columns wraps around the pull-quote.

To create sidebars, pull-quotes, or other such elements that stay close to the text that refers to them, use the anchored-object feature described in Chapter 11.

Formatting fractions

Creating fractions that are formatted correctly can be handy. Compare the top line in Figure 17-3, which is not formatted appropriately for a fraction, to the bottom line, which is correctly formatted. Although InDesign doesn't provide an automatic fraction maker, you can use OpenType typefaces, expert typefaces, or character formats to achieve professional-looking fractions.

Applying a fraction typeface

Some expert typefaces include a variation, appropriately called Fractions, that includes a number of common fractions, such as ½, ⅓, ¼, and ¾. Adobe has Expert Collection variants for many of its popular Type 1 PostScript fonts; these collections include true small caps, true fractions, and other typographic characters. You can also use a symbol font, though the numerals may not exactly match the appearance of numerals in the rest of your text because symbol fonts typically use plain fonts like Helvetica as their basis.

To use a true fraction from an Expert Collection font, choose Type⇨Glyph (or press Option+Shift+F11 or Alt+Shift+F11), select the font and face from the pop-up menus at the bottom of the dialog box shown in Figure 17-3, and then select the fraction you want to use.

If you have OpenType fonts, the process can be automated: Be sure that the Fraction option is enabled for the selected text, either as part of its character or paragraph style, or by highlighting the text and adjusting the OpenType options directly:

- ✔ For styles, go to the OpenType Features pane when creating or modifying a paragraph or character style, and check Fractions.

- ✔ For local formatting, highlight the text containing the fraction and then choose OpenType⇨Fraction from the flyout menu of the Character panel or Control panel — be sure that Fraction is checked in the menu.

These OpenType options have no effect on non-OpenType fonts.

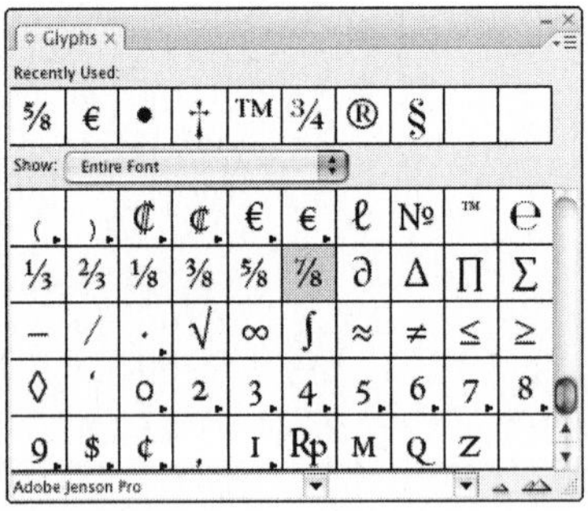

Figure 17-3:
The Glyphs panel lets you choose special characters not accessible easily (or at all) from the keyboard.

Formatting fractions manually

If you're dealing with a wide range of fractions in something like a cookbook, you probably won't find all the fractions you need in your Expert Collection or OpenType font. And regular Type 1 Postscript and TrueType fonts certainly won't have the desired fractions. Because it would be difficult to format fractions such as $\frac{3}{16}$ exactly the same as, say, an expert font's $\frac{1}{4}$, you might opt for formatting all the fractions manually.

The built-in fractions in expert and OpenType fonts are approximately the same size as a single character in that font, and this is your eventual goal in formatting a fraction manually. Usually, you achieve this by decreasing the size of the two numerals, raising the numerator (the first, or top, number in the fraction) using the baseline shift feature, and kerning on either side of the slash as necessary. (Chapter 16 covers these controls.) Figure 17-4 shows examples of an unformatted fraction, an expert font's fraction, an OpenType-generated fraction, and a manually created fraction.

Macintosh PostScript and TrueType fonts (as well as expert fonts and OpenType fonts for both Windows and Macintosh) provide another option for refining fractions: a special kind of slash called a *virgule,* which is smaller and at more of an angle than a regular slash. Press Option+Shift+1 to enter a virgule, then kern around it as you would a slash. (You can see how a virgule differs from a slash in Figure 17-4: The first and fourth fractions use slashes, while the second and third use virgules.)

Unless you rarely use fractions, by all means save your formatting as character styles. You can apply the formats with a keystroke or use Find/Change (Edit➪Find/Change or ⌘+F or Ctrl+F) to locate numbers and selectively apply the appropriate character style.

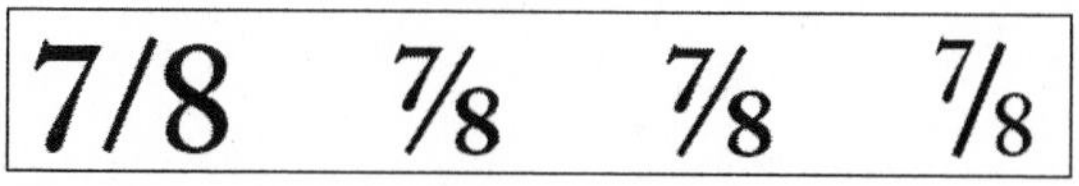

Figure 17-4:
Four ways to make a fraction (from left to right): unformatted, via expert fonts, via OpenType fonts, and via manual formatting.

7/8   ⁷⁄₈   ⁷⁄₈   ⁷⁄₈

Optical margin alignment

When display type, such as a pull-quote or headline type in ads, is left-aligned or justified, the edges can look uneven due to the gaps above, below, or next to quotation marks, other punctuation, and some capital letters. Notice the text frame on the left in Figure 17-5, which does not have hanging punctuation. To correct the unevenness, you can use a technique called *hanging punctuation,* or *optical margin alignment,* which extends the punctuation slightly beyond the edges of the rest of the text.

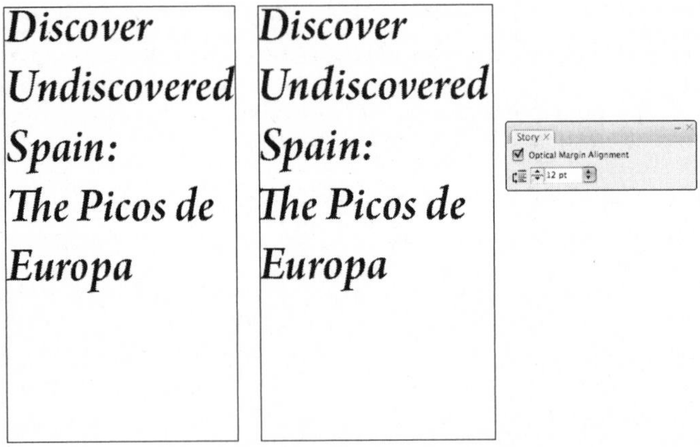
Discover
Undiscovered
Spain:
The Picos de
Europa
Discover
Undiscovered
Spain:
The Picos de
Europa
Story
Optical Margin Alignment
12 pt

Figure 17-5: Notice the difference between the standard alignment on the left and the hanging punctuation on the right.

TECHNICAL STUFF

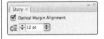

The "edge" of text is defined by the edges of the text frame or any Inset Spacing specified in the Text Frame Options dialog box (Object➪Text Frame Options or ⌘+B or Ctrl+B).

The optical margin alignment feature automates hanging punctuation, extending punctuation and the edges of some glyphs (such as the capital *T*) slightly outside the edges of the text. Unfortunately, you can't control how much the characters "hang" outside the text boundaries — InDesign decides that for you. And optical margin alignment applies to all the text frames in a story, rather than to highlighted text. Therefore, you need to isolate any text for which you want hanging punctuation into its own story.

To specify optical margin alignment, select any text frame in a story and choose Type➪Story. In the Story panel, check the Optical Margin Alignment option, as shown in Figure 17-5

Custom underline and strikethrough options

You can use InDesign to create text with custom underlines and strikethroughs. Although you should use these effects sparingly, they can be effective for signs and other design-oriented text presentations, such as the examples shown in Figure 17-6.

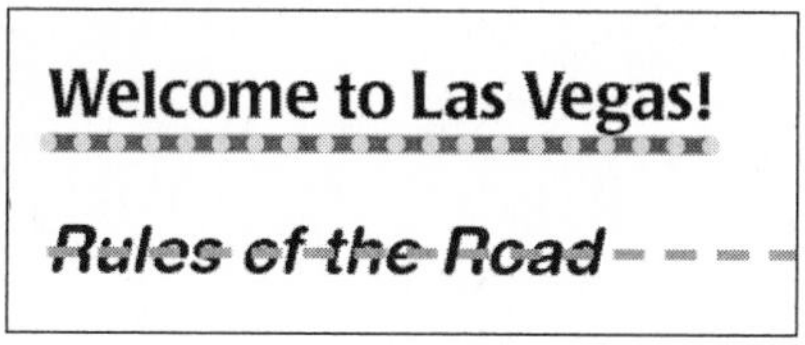

Figure 17-6:
Examples of custom underlines and strike-throughs.

You can find both the Underline Options and Strikethrough Options menu items in the flyout menu of the Character panel's and of the Control panel's A pane, and you can use these menu options to get just the look you're interested in. The process for setting both Underline Options and Strikethrough Options is similar:

1. **Highlight the text to which you want the custom underline or strikethrough.**

2. **Specify the thickness, type, color, and other settings for the line that makes up the underline or the strikethrough line.**

   If you choose an underline or strikethrough line type that has gaps — such as dashed, dotted, or striped lines — you can also choose a gap color. Figure 17-7 shows the Underline Options dialog box; the Strikethrough Options dialog box is almost identical.

3. **Apply the underline style via the Control panel, Character panel, or keyboard shortcut (Shift+⌘+U or Ctrl+Shift+U). Apply the strikethrough style via the Control panel, Character panel, or keyboard shortcut (Shift+⌘+/ or Ctrl+Shift+/).**

Note that a custom underline or strikethrough created and applied this way is in effect only for the first text to which an underline or strikethrough is applied. InDesign reverts to the standard settings the next time you apply an underline or strikethrough. If you want to use a custom underline or strikethrough setting repeatedly, you should define the setting as part of a character style.

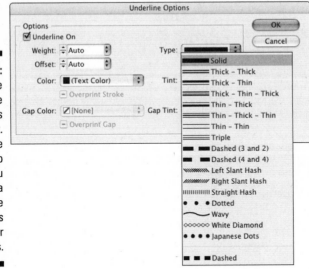

Figure 17-7:
The
Underline
Options
dialog box.
The Type
pop-up
menu
presents a
list of line
types
available for
underlines.

Converting Text into Shapes

If you want to use the shape of a letter or the combined shapes of several letters as a frame for text or a graphic, you could test your skill with the Pen
tool and create the letter shape(s) yourself. But getting hand-drawn characters to look just the way you want them to can take lots of time. A quicker
solution is to use the Create Outlines command to convert text characters
into editable outlines. The Create Outlines command is particularly useful if
you want to hand-tweak the shapes of characters, particularly at display font
sizes, or place text or a graphic within character shapes.

If all you need to do is apply a stroke or fill to characters within text, you
don't have to convert the characters into outlines. Instead, simply highlight
the characters and use the Stroke panel (Window⇔Stroke, or ⌘+F10 or
Ctrl+F10) and Swatches panel (Window⇔Swatches or F5) to change their
appearance. This way you can still edit the text. (See Chapter 8 for more
details.)

When you use the Create Outlines command, you have the choice of creating
an inline compound path that replaces the original text or an independent
compound path that's placed directly on top of the original letters in its own
frame. If you want the text outlines to flow with the surrounding text, create
an inline compound path. If you want to use the outlines elsewhere, create an
independent compound path.

To convert text into outlines:

1. **Use the Type tool to highlight the characters you want to convert into outlines.**

   Generally, this feature works best with large font sizes.

2. **Choose Type⇨Create Outlines or press Shift+⌘+O or Ctrl+Shift+O (that's the letter *O*, not a zero).**

   If you hold down the Option or Alt key when you choose Create Outlines, or if you press Shift+Option+⌘+O or Ctrl+Alt+Shift+O, a compound path is created and placed in front of the text. In this case, you can use either of the selection tools to move the resulting compound path. If you don't hold down Option or Alt when you choose Create Outlines, an inline compound path is created. This object replaces the original text and flows with the surrounding text.

After you create text outlines, you can modify the paths the same as you can modify hand-drawn paths. You can also use the transformation tools, the Control panel (Window⇨Control, or Option+⌘+6 or Ctrl+Alt+6), and the Transform panel (Window⇨Transform) to change the appearance of text outlines. You cannot, however, edit text after converting it to outlines.

Additionally, you can use the Place command (File⇨Place, or ⌘+D or Ctrl+D) or the Paste Into command (Edit⇨Paste Into, or Option+⌘+V or Ctrl+Alt+V) to import text or a graphic into the frames created by converting text to graphics.

Making Text Follow a Path

InDesign lets you have text follow any open or closed path, such as a line or frame. Simply select the path or shape with the Type on a Path tool, which is available from the Type tool's pop-up menu. Now start typing (or paste or place) your text.

Once you have entered the text and formatted it with font, size, color, and so forth, you can apply special effects to it using the Type on a Path Options dialog box, accessed by choosing Type⇨Type on a Path⇨Options and then selecting from its options.

You can also double-click the Type on a Path tool to open the Type on a Path Options dialog box.

Figure 17-8 shows the dialog box and several examples of its formatting. In the dialog box:

- Use the Effect pop-up menu to choose a visual effect.
- Use the Align pop-up menu to choose what part of the text is aligned (baseline, center, ascender, or descender).
- Use the To Path pop-up menu to choose whether to align to the center, bottom, or top of the path.
- Flip the text by selecting the Flip option.
- Change the text's spacing by entering a value in the Spacing field (positive numbers space out the text, while negative ones contract it).

Figure 17-8:
The Type on a Path Options dialog box lets you apply special effects, alignment, and flip to text following a path.

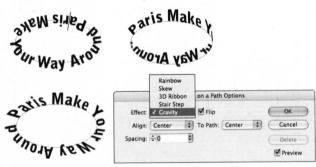

Part V
Graphics Essentials

The 5th Wave   By Rich Tennant

"You know kids — you can't buy them just any web authoring software."

In this part . . .

They say a picture is worth a thousand words. Well, a lot of them are. Graphics make layouts come alive, providing a visceral connection that text by itself just cannot. So it should be no surprise that InDesign has tons of features to work with and even create graphics. This part shows you how to work with imported graphics files, cropping them and making them fit your layout's canvas.

You might wonder why this part is so short, given how many graphical effects InDesign offers. If you skipped Part III, that confusion is understandable: InDesign lets you apply most of its special effects and controls to *any* object, not just those containing graphics, so Part III covers that common razzle-dazzle in one place.

Chapter 18

Importing Graphics

● ●

● ●

*W*hat is a layout without graphics? Boring, that's what. And that's why InDesign lets you import a wide variety of graphics types, so you have a lot of choices and flexibility in the images you use.

And through the Mac and Windows Clipboards (copy and paste), you can import file formats — to a limited degree — that are not directly supported by InDesign.

The terms *graphic* and *picture* are interchangeable, referring to any type of graphic — though InDesign consistently uses the word *graphic* in its user interface and documentation. An *image* is a bitmapped graphic, such as that produced by an image editor, digital camera, or scanner, while an *illustration* or *drawing* is a vector file produced by an illustration program.

Preparing Graphics Files

InDesign offers support for many major formats of graphics files. Some formats are more appropriate than others for certain kinds of tasks. The basic rules for creating your graphics files are as follows:

> ✔ Save line art (drawings) in a format such as EPS, PDF, Adobe Illustrator, Windows Metafile (WMF), Enhanced Metafile (EMF), or PICT. (These object-oriented formats are called *vector* formats. Vector files are composed of instructions on how to draw various shapes.) InDesign works best with EPS, PDF, and Illustrator files.

✔ Save bitmaps (photos and scans) in a format such as TIFF, Adobe Photoshop, PNG, JPEG, PCX, Windows Bitmap (BMP), GIF, Scitex Continuous Tone (SCT), or PICT. (These pixel-oriented formats are called *raster* formats. Raster files are composed of a series of dots, or pixels, that make up the image.) InDesign works best with TIFF and Photoshop files.

InDesign CS3 can also import InDesign files as if they were graphics — in a multi-page document, you choose the page you want to import, as you can with PDF files. Note that InDesign files imported as graphics cannot be edited in your InDesign layout (you must update the original file instead).

Make EPS and TIFF formats your standards because these have become the standard graphics formats in publishing. If you and your service bureau are working almost exclusively with Adobe software, you can add the PDF, Illustrator, and Photoshop formats to this mix. (The Illustrator and PDF formats are variants of EPS.) If you use transparency in your graphics, it's best to save them in Photoshop, Illustrator, or PDF formats, because other formats (particularly EPS and TIFF) remove much of the transparency layering data that will help an imagesetter optimally reproduce those transparent files.

The graphics file formats that InDesign imports include (the text in monofont is the PC filename extension for the format):

✔ **BMP:** The native Windows bitmap format (`.bmp`, `.dib`).

✔ **EPS:** The Encapsulated PostScript file format favored by professional publishers (`.eps`).

✔ **GIF:** The Graphics Interchange Format common in Web documents (`.gif`).

✔ **JPEG:** The Joint Photographers Expert Group compressed bitmap format often used on the Web (`.jpg`).

✔ **Illustrator:** The native format in Adobe Illustrator 5.5 through CS3. This file format is similar to EPS (`.ai`).

✔ **PCX:** The PC Paintbrush format that was very popular in DOS programs and early version of Windows; it has now been largely supplanted by other formats (`.pcx`, `.rle`).

✔ **PDF:** The Portable Document Format that is a variant of EPS and is used for Web-, network-, and CD-based documents. InDesign CS3 supports PDF versions 1.3 through 1.7 (the formats used in Acrobat 4 through 8) (`.pdf`).

✔ **Photoshop:** The native format in Adobe Photoshop 5.0 through CS3 (`.psd`). (Note that InDesign cannot import the Photoshop Raw format.)

- **PICT:** Short for *Picture,* the Mac's native graphics format until Mac OS X (it can be bitmap or vector) that is little used in professional documents and has become rare even for inexpensive clip art (`.pct`).

- **PNG:** The Portable Network Graphics format introduced more than a decade ago as a more capable alternative to GIF (`.png`).

- **QuickTime movie:** For use in interactive documents, InDesign supports this Apple-created, cross-platform format (`.mov`).

- **Scitex CT:** The continuous-tone bitmap format used on Scitex prepress systems (`.ct`).

- **TIFF:** The Tagged Image File Format that is the bitmap standard for professional image editors and publishers (`.tif`, `.tiff`).

- **Windows Metafile:** The format native to Windows but little used in professional documents. Since Office 2000, Microsoft applications create a new version called Enhanced Metafile, also supported by InDesign (`.wmf`, `.emf`).

Spot colors (called spot inks in Photoshop) are imported into InDesign when you place Photoshop, Illustrator, and PDF images into InDesign, as well as for InDesign documents imported as graphics. They appear in the Swatches panel, which is covered in Chapter 7.

Importing and Placing Graphics

It's important to understand that when you import a graphic into a document, InDesign establishes a link between the graphics file and the document file and then sends the original graphics file to the printer when the document is output. (For more details on managing linked files, see Chapter 10.)

InDesign links to graphics because a graphics file, particularly a high-resolution scanned graphic, can be very large. If the entire graphics file is included in an InDesign document when you import it, InDesign documents would quickly become prohibitively large. Instead, InDesign saves a low-resolution preview of an imported graphics file with the document, and it's this file that you see displayed on-screen. InDesign remembers the location of the original file and uses this information when printing.

The Place command (File⇨Place, or ⌘+D or Ctrl+D) is the method you typically use to bring graphics into your InDesign layout. Here's how to use the Place command to import a graphic:

1. **Choose File⇨Place or press ⌘+D or Ctrl+D.**

   If you want to import a graphic into an *existing frame,* select the target frame using either of the selection tools (either before you choose File⇨Place or afterwards). If you want InDesign to create a *new frame* when you import the graphic, make sure no object is selected when you choose Place. Either way, the Place dialog box appears.

   You can import a graphic into any kind of frame or shape (including a curved line created with the Pen tool) except a straight line. Be careful: If the Type tool is selected when you use the Place command to import a graphic into a selected text frame, you'll create an inline graphic at the text cursor's location.

2. **Use the controls in the Place dialog box to locate and select the graphics files you want to import.**

   You can now select multiple files — graphics and/or text — by Shift+clicking a range or ⌘+clicking or Ctrl+clicking multiple files one by one. InDesign will let you place each file in a separate frame. Just click once for each file imported, or Shift+⌘+click or Ctrl+Shift+click to have InDesign place all files on the page in separate frames. The loaded-graphic icon will show the number of files to be placed, as well as a mini preview of each file, as Figure 18-1 shows. You can also navigate through these previews using the keyboard's left and right arrow keys, so you can control more easily which file is placed when.

3. **Specify the desired import options, if any are applicable.** If you want to display import options that let you control how the selected graphics file is imported, either select Show Import Options, and then click Open; or hold down the Shift key and double-click on the filename or Shift+click Open. If you choose to Show Import Options, the EPS Import Options, Place PDF, Place InDesign Document, or Image Import Options dialog box, depending on what kind of graphic you are importing, is displayed. Click OK after selecting the desired options. (These options are covered later in this chapter.)

4. **You can place a graphic in an existing frame or in a new frame, as follows:**

   • If an empty frame is selected, the graphic is automatically placed in the frame. The upper-left corner of the graphic is placed in the upper-left corner of the frame, and the frame acts as the cropping shape for the graphic.

   • If a frame already holding a graphic is selected, InDesign will replace the existing graphic with the new one if you've selected the Replace

Selected Item check box in the Place dialog box. Otherwise, InDesign will assume you want to put the new graphic in a new frame.

- To place the graphic into a new frame, click the loaded-graphic icon on an empty portion of a page or on the pasteboard. The point where you click establishes the upper-left corner of the resulting graphics frame, which is the same size as the imported graphic and which acts as the graphic's cropping shape.

- To place the graphic in an existing, unselected frame, click in the frame with the loaded-graphic icon. The upper-left corner of the graphic is placed in the upper-left corner of the frame, and the frame acts as a cropping shape.

Figure 18-1:
The loaded-graphic icon displays a preview image of the imported graphics, as well as the number of graphics ready to be placed.

After you place a graphic, it's displayed in the frame that contains it, and the frame is selected. If the Selection tool is selected, the eight handles of its bounding box are displayed; if the Direct Selection tool is selected, handles are displayed only in the corners. At this point, you can modify either the frame or the graphic within, or you can move on to another task.

When importing JPEG files, InDesign automatically scales the image to fit in the page. This feature helps deal with digital-camera graphics that tend to be very large in dimension, so when imported end up taking much more than the width of a page. Although you'll likely still need to scale the image to fit your layout, you can at least see the whole image before doing so.

Specifying Import Options

If you've ever used a graphics application — for example, an image-editing program like Adobe Photoshop or an illustration program like Adobe Illustrator or CorelDraw — you're probably aware that when you save a graphics file, you have several options that control such things as file format, image size, color depth, preview quality, and so on. When you save a graphics file, the settings you specify are determined by the way in which the image will be used. For example, you could use Photoshop to save a high-resolution TIFF version of a scanned graphic for use in a slick, four-color annual report or a low-resolution GIF version of the same graphic for use on the company's Web page. Or you could use Illustrator or CorelDraw to create a corporate logo that you'll use in various sizes in many of your printed publications.

If you choose to specify custom import settings when you import a graphics file, the choices you make will depend on the nature of the publication. For example, if it's bound for the Web, there's no need to work with or save graphics using resolutions that exceed a computer monitor's 72-dpi resolution. Along the same lines, if the publication will be printed, the image import settings you specify for a newspaper that will be printed on newsprint on a SWOP (Specifications for Web Offset Publications) press will be different than those you specify for a four-color magazine printed on coated paper using a sheet-fed press.

If you select Show Import Options when you place a graphic, the options displayed in the resulting dialog boxes depend on the file format of the selected graphic. When you set options for a particular file, the options you specify remain in effect for that file format until you change them. If you don't select the Show Import Options check box when you place a graphic, the most recent settings for the file format of the selected graphic are used.

Import options for bitmap graphics

InDesign gives you two sets of import options for the following types of bitmap images: TIFF, GIF, JPEG, Scitex CT, BMP, and PCX. You get three options for PNG files, and a different set of three for Photoshop files. No import options are available for PICT or QuickTime movie files. Figure 18-2 shows three of the four possible panes for bitmap images: The Image and Color panes are for most bitmap formats; PNG files have a third pane, PNG Settings, and Photoshop files also have a third pane, Layers, covered later in this chapter.

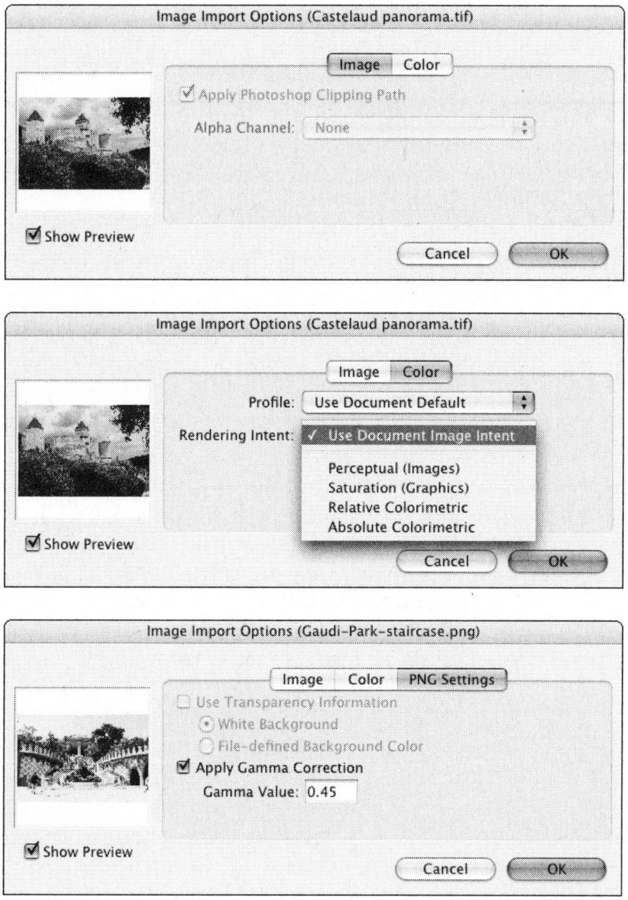

Figure 18-2:
The Image,
Color, and
PNG
Settings
panes in the
Image
Import
Options
dialog box.

If you import a Photoshop, TIFF, or EPS file that contains an embedded clipping path, the Image pane lets you apply any embedded clipping path and/or alpha channel to the image in order to mask, or cut out, part of the image. (Otherwise, these options are grayed out.) Check the Apply Photoshop Clipping Path option to import the clipping path along with the image; select an alpha channel from the Alpha Channel pop-up menu to import the alpha channel along with the image. (Chapter 19 covers clipping paths in more detail.)

Color pane

In the Color pane, you can turn on color management for the image and control how the image is displayed. Check the Enable Color Management option to enable color management. This is an expert feature, so ask your production manager or service bureau whether you should make any adjustments here.

PNG Settings pane

Use the PNG Settings pane — available only if you place a PNG file — to use the transparency information in a PNG file, assuming it has a transparent background. You have two choices for controlling transparency handling: White Background and File-Defined Background. The former forces the transparent portion to display as white in InDesign; the latter uses whatever background color is specified in the PNG file itself.

This pane also lets you adjust the gamma value during import — an expert color-management feature you should leave alone unless told otherwise by a production manager or service bureau.

Import options for vector file formats

If you're importing vector files, selecting the Import Options check box will result in one of two dialog boxes appearing, depending on what the vector file type is. If you import older-version Illustrator or EPS files, you'll get the EPS Import Options dialog box; if you import PDF and newer-version Illustrator files, you'll get the Place PDF dialog box, which has two panes. (Both dialog boxes are shown in Figure 18-3.) No import options are available for Windows Metafile or Enhanced Metafile graphics.

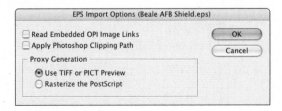

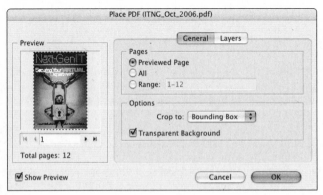

Figure 18-3:
The EPS Import Options and Place PDF dialog boxes.

Illustrator CS through CS3 use PDF as their native file format, even though the filename extension is .ai, so InDesign detects these files as PDF files and provides the PDF options during import. In earlier versions of Illustrator, the native format was actually a variant of EPS.

EPS Import Options dialog box

Use this dialog box to import any clipping paths embedded in images that are in the EPS file. Check the Apply Photoshop Clipping Path option to enable this option.

Also, use this pane to control how the EPS file appears on-screen in InDesign. If you select the Use TIFF or PICT Preview option, InDesign will use the low-resolution proxy image embedded in the EPS file for display on-screen and print the graphic using the embedded high-resolution PostScript instructions. If you select the Rasterize the PostScript option, InDesign will convert the PostScript file into a bitmap image during import. There's rarely a reason to rasterize an imported EPS file — it just takes up some of your valuable time.

Place PDF dialog box

When you use the Place command to import a PDF file and you select the Show Import Options check box, the Place PDF file dialog box, shown in Figure 18-3, is displayed. It provides several controls for specifying how the file is imported. The General pane provides the following options:

✔ In the Pages section, select Previewed Page, All, or Range to determine which page(s) you want to import. You can change the previewed page by using the arrow buttons under the preview image at left or entering a specific page number in the field below the preview image. If you want to import a range, use commas to separate pages and a hyphen to indicate range; for example, **3, 5-9, 13** will import pages 3, 5 through 9, and 13.

When you place the PDF in InDesign, you'll get a separate loaded-graphic icon for each page, so as you place each page, a new loaded-graphic icon will appear for the next page, until there are no more to place. You can tell you're placing multiple pages because the loaded-graphics icon will have a plus sign in it.

✔ In the Options section, select one of the cropping options from the Crop To pop-up menu. If you choose Content, the page's bounding box or a rectangle that encloses all items, including page marks, is used to build the graphics frame. Choosing Art places the area defined by the file's creator, if any, as placeable artwork. For example, the person who created the file might have designated a particular graphic as placeable artwork. Choosing Crop places the area displayed and printed by Adobe

Acrobat. Choosing Trim places the graphic in an area equal to the final, trimmed piece. Choosing Bleed places the page area plus any specified bleed area. Choosing Media places an area defined by the paper size specified for the PDF document, including page marks.

✔ Also in the Options section, select the Transparent Background check box if you want the white areas of the PDF page to be transparent. Uncheck this option if you want to preserve the page's opaque white background.

Import options for placed InDesign files

When you import InDesign files to use as a graphic, you can use exactly the same options as for PDF files. The Place InDesign Document dialog box is identical to the Place PDF dialog box covered in the previous section, except of course, for the dialog box's name.

Working with image layers

InDesign lets you work with individual layers in some imported graphics. What that means is that you have more control over what displays because you can turn on or off individual layers. Of course, to use this capability, the source graphic must be constructed with multiple layers.

Use the Layers pane in the Image Import Options dialog box, the Place PDF, or Place InDesign Document dialog box to select which layer(s) you want visible in InDesign. (The Layers pane is available only if you place an Illustrator, PDF, or Photoshop graphic or InDesign file.) You will see a list of image layers. Any that have the eye icon will display in InDesign, and you can select or deselect layers by clicking the box to the right of the layer name to make the eye icon appear or disappear. (You cannot change their order — you'd need to go back to Photoshop or Illustrator and change the layer order there.) Figure 18-4 shows the Layers pane.

Note that you can adjust which layers are visible later on by selecting the graphic and then choosing Object⇨Object Layers Options.

Although you can save an image file in the TIFF format and preserve any layers, InDesign CS3 does not give you the ability to manage which layers you import from a TIFF file into InDesign.

There's also an option, in the When Updating Link pop-up menu, to control how changes to the file are handled in terms of layer management: If you choose Use Photoshop's Layer Visibility or Use Illustrator's Layer Visibility, InDesign will make all layers that are visible in Photoshop, InDesign or Illustrator visible when you update the link to the graphic from InDesign. If you choose Keep Layer Visibility Overrides in the When Updating Link pop-up menu, InDesign will import only the layers chosen in this dialog box if you later update the graphic in Photoshop, InDesign, or Illustrator.

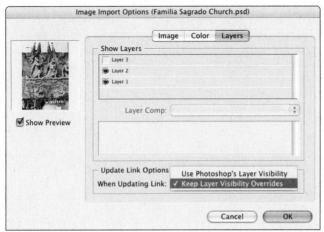

Figure 18-4:
The Layers pane of the EPS Import Options, Place PDF, and Place InDesign Document dialog boxes.

Using Other Ways to Import Graphics

If you want to specify custom import options for an imported graphics file, you must use the Place command. However, if you don't need this level of control, InDesign offers three other options for importing graphics:

✔ You can use your computer's Copy (File➪Copy, or ⌘+C or Ctrl+C) and Paste (File➪Paste, or ⌘+V or Ctrl+V) commands to move a graphics file between two InDesign documents or from a document created with another program into an InDesign document. If you copy an object in an InDesign document and then paste it into a different InDesign document, the copy retains all the attributes of the original, as well as the link to the original graphics file. Otherwise, a link between the original graphics file and the InDesign document is *not* established; the graphic becomes part of the InDesign document, as though you created it using InDesign tools.

✔ You can drag and drop graphics file icons from your computer's desktop into InDesign documents. A link between the original graphics file and the document is established, just as it would be if you had used the Place command.

✔ For Illustrator files, you can drag objects directly from Illustrator into InDesign. Each object becomes a separate, editable InDesign object, as though you had created it in InDesign. (And no links are established to the source file.)

If you use these methods to add a graphic to an InDesign document, some of the attributes of the original graphic may not survive the trip. The operating system, the file format, and the capabilities of the originating application all play roles in determining which attributes are preserved. If you want to be safe, use the Place command.

Chapter 19

Fitting Graphics and Setting Paths

*A*fter you import a graphic into an InDesign document, you can modify either the graphic or the frame that contains it. The most common actions you'll take are cropping, repositioning, and resizing. *Cropping* is a fancy term for deciding what part of the picture to show by altering the dimensions of the frame holding the graphic. *Repositioning* is essentially the same as cropping, except that you move the graphic within its frame. And if you want to get really fancy, you might work with clipping paths to create "masks" around picture portions or even cut the graphic into pieces.

Transformations such as resizing, flipping, rotating, and skewing that you're likely to apply to graphics use the same tools for graphics as for any InDesign objects. So I cover all these transformations in one place, in Chapter 9.

In almost every case, you select graphics with the Direct Selection tool to work with the graphic itself, rather than to the frame. If you use the Selection tool, the work you do will apply to the frame, as Chapter 12 explains.

Cropping and Repositioning

Remember, when you import a graphic using the Place command (File➪Place, or ⌘+D or Ctrl+D) or by dragging a graphics file into a document window, the graphic is contained in a graphics frame — either the frame that was selected when you placed the graphic or the frame that was automatically created if a frame wasn't selected. The upper-left corner of an imported graphic is automatically placed in the upper-left corner of its frame.

The easiest way to crop a graphic is to resize the frame that contains it using the Selection or Position tool. To discover how to resize the frame, go to Chapter 9. Note that resizing the frame does *not* resize the graphic.

You can also click on a graphic with the Direct Selection tool, and then drag the graphic within its frame to reveal and conceal different parts of the graphic. For example, you could crop the top and left edges of a graphic by dragging the graphic above and to the left of its original position (in the upper-left corner of the frame).

You can also crop using the X+ and Y+ options in the Control panel and Transform panel; this is more precise than using the mouse. The advantage of moving the image within the frame is that you don't have to move the frame from its desired position in the layout.

If you want to *mask out* (hide) portions of an imported graphic, you have the option of using an irregular shape as the frame, a graphic's built-in clipping path (if it has one), or a clipping path you generated in InDesign, as covered later in this chapter.

Figuring out the Fitting Commands

If you've placed a graphic in a frame that's either larger or smaller than the graphic, you can use the Fitting options (available by choosing Object⇨ Fitting or by using the appropriate iconic buttons in the Control panel) to scale the graphic to fit the frame proportionately or disproportionately or to scale the frame to fit the graphic. Another option lets you center the graphic in the frame. These are very handy, and a *lot* easier than trying to resize a graphic or frame to fit using the mouse or the Control panel.

Keep in mind that the fitting commands for graphics are available only if you've used the Selection or Position tool to select a graphic's frame. Here's a description of each of the six options:

✔ **Fit Content to Frame:** To scale a graphic to fill the selected frame, choose Object⇨Fitting⇨Fit Content to Frame or press Option+⌘+E or Ctrl+Alt+E. If the frame is larger than the graphic, the graphic is enlarged; if the frame is smaller, the graphic is reduced. If the graphic and the frame have different proportions, the graphic's proportions are changed so that the image completely fills the frame — this can distort the graphic's appearance.

- ✔ **Fit Frame to Content:** To resize a frame so that it wraps snugly around a graphic, choose Fit Frame to Content or press Option+⌘+C or Ctrl+Alt+C. The frame will be enlarged or reduced depending on the size of the graphic, and the frame's proportions will be changed to match the proportions of the graphic.

- ✔ **Center Content:** To center a graphic in its frame, choose Center Content or press Shift+⌘+E or Ctrl+Shift+E. Neither the frame nor the graphic is scaled when you center a graphic.

- ✔ **Fit Content Proportionally:** To scale a graphic to fit in the selected frame while maintaining the graphic's current proportions, choose Object⇨Fitting⇨Fit Content Proportionally or press Option+Shift+⌘+E or Ctrl+Alt+Shift+E. If the frame is larger than the graphic, the graphic is enlarged; if the frame is smaller, the graphic is reduced. If the graphic and the frame have different proportions, a portion of the frame background will show above and below or to the left and right of the graphic. If you want, you can drag frame edges to make the frame shorter or narrower and eliminate any portions of the background that are visible.

- ✔ **Fill Frame Proportionally:** To resize a frame to fit the selected graphic, choose Object⇨Fitting⇨Fill Frame Proportionally or press Option+Shift+⌘+C or Ctrl+Alt+Shift+C. This guarantees that there will be no space between the graphic and the frame. (The Fit Frame to Content option can result in such space at the bottom and/or right sides of a graphic.)

- ✔ **Frame Fitting Options:** To control the default fitting for newly placed graphics, use the new Frame Fitting Options dialog box, shown in Figure 19-1. Here you can set the amount of crop, choose the control point for the imported graphic (see Chapter 1), and automatically apply your choice of the Fit Content to Frame, Fit Content Proportionally, and Fill Frame Proportionally options.

For frames with strokes, the Fitting options align the outer edge of a graphic with the center of the stroke. A stroke obscures a strip along the graphic's edge that's half the width of the stroke. The wider the stroke, the more of the graphic that gets covered up.

You can also use the frame-fitting iconic buttons in the Control panel, shown in Figure 19-2. But note that these may not display in your Control panel; by default, InDesign shows them only if your monitor is set to a resolution whose width is 1,280 or more pixels. You can make room for them at smaller resolutions by customizing the Control panel display: choose Customize from the panel's flyout menu and then deselect some of the Object controls to make room.

Figure 19-1:
The Frame
Fitting
Options
dialog box
lets you set
the default
behavior
for newly
imported
graphics.

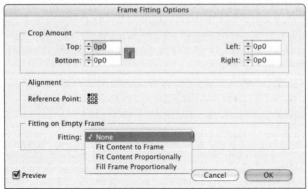

Figure 19-2:
The frame-
fitting iconic
buttons in
the Control
panel.

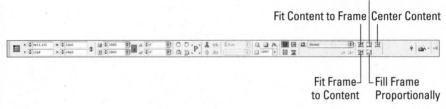

Fit Content Proportionally

Fit Content to Frame | Center Content

Fit Frame ┘ └ Fill Frame
to Content   Proportionally

Working with Graphics in Irregular Shapes

Although most graphics you use will be placed in rectangular frames, InDesign does give you other choices:

✔ You can select any type of frame — oval or polygonal, not just rectangular — to place or copy your graphic into.

✔ You can draw your own shape using the Pencil or Pen tool and then place or copy your graphic into it. When you create the free-form shape, make sure that the default color for the Pen tool is set to None so that the shape you create is transparent. Otherwise, the colored area in the shape will obscure the graphic behind it.

The Pen tool lets you create one shape at a time. The Compound Paths command lets you combine multiple shapes to create more complex objects. For example, you can place a small circle on top of a larger circle, and then use the Compound Paths command to create a doughnut-shaped object. (This is an expert feature not covered in this book.)

If you copy the graphic into a frame or shape, you must use the Paste Into command (Edit⇨Paste Into, or Option+⌘+V or Ctrl+Alt+V) to place the copied graphic inside the selected shape, rather than on top of it.

✔ You can use a clipping path that was defined in the graphic itself when it was created or a clipping path that was created in InDesign.

So what is a clipping path, anyway? A *clipping path* is used to mask certain parts of a graphic and reveal other parts; it's basically an invisible outline placed in the graphic that InDesign can then work with. For example, if you want to create a silhouette around a single person in a crowd, open the file in an image-editing program such as Photoshop, and then create and save a clipping path that isolates the shape of the person. (You can also erase everything except the person you want to silhouette; this can be time-consuming, and if you want to reveal other parts of the graphic later, you're out of luck.) TIFF, Photoshop EPS, and Photoshop-native (.PSD) files can have embedded clipping paths.

Regardless of the method you use to clip an imported graphic, you can modify a clipping path by moving, adding, deleting, and changing the direction of anchor points and by moving direction lines.

You can convert a clipping path — whether imported or created in InDesign — to a frame by choosing Convert Clipping Path to Frame for a selected object using the contextual menu (right-click or Control+click the object).

See the *Photoshop For Dummies* series (Wiley Publishing) for more on creating clipping paths in Photoshop.

Using a graphic's own clipping path

In an ideal world, any graphics that you want to have fit in an irregular shape will come with their own clipping paths. In that wonderful situation, you would first be sure to import the clipping path when you place the graphic and then use InDesign's Text Wrap panel to access that clipping path.

The steps are easy:

1. **Be sure to select the Show Import Options check box in the Place dialog box (File⇨Place, or ⌘+D or Ctrl+D) when you import the graphic and select the Apply Photoshop Clipping Path option in the Image Import Options dialog box.**

2. **Open the Text Wrap panel (Window⇨Text Wrap, or Option+⌘+W or Ctrl+Alt+W).**

3. **Select the graphic.**

4. **Click the Wrap Around Object Shape iconic button (the third one from the left) at the top of the Text Wrap panel.**

5. **If you want, adjust the space between the surrounding text and the obstructing shape by typing values in the Top Offset field.**

6. **Now select the clipping source from the Type pop-up menu in the Contour Options section of the Text Wrap panel. Choose from two relevant options:**

   • Alpha Channel uses the image's alpha channel, if any, to create a wrapping boundary. (An *alpha channel* is another type of clipping path and is also created in the source program such as Photoshop.)

   • Photoshop Path uses the image's clipping path, if any, to create a wrapping boundary. Use the Path pop-up menu to select which path to use, if your image has more than one embedded clipping path.

See Chapter 12 for the basics of text wraps.

Creating a clipping path in InDesign

If you import a graphic that doesn't have a clipping path, you have two sets of options for creating a clipping path.

The easiest is to use the Text Wrap panel as described in the previous section but to instead choose one of the following options from the Type pop-up menu:

✔ Detect Edges tries to determine the graphic's outside boundary by ignoring white space — you would use this for bitmapped images that have a transparent or white background.

✔ Same as Clipping uses the clipping path for the graphic created in InDesign — you would use this when the desired clipping path can't be created through the Detect Edges option. (I cover this method of clipping-path creation shortly.)

You can further modify the clipping path by selecting the graphic with the Direct Selection tool. The text-wrap boundary appears as a blue line — you can make the boundary easier to select by setting offsets in the Text Wrap pane, which moves the boundary away from the frame edge.

A slightly more difficult way to create a clipping path — but one that gives you more control — is to use the Clipping Path command (Object⇨ Clipping Path⇨Options, or Option+Shift+⌘+K or Ctrl+Alt+Shift+K) to generate one automatically:

1. **Select the graphic to which you want to add a clipping path.**

   It's best to use the Direct Selection tool, so that you can see the clipping path within the frame as you work.

2. **Choose Object⇨Clipping Path⇨Options, or press Option+Shift+⌘+K or Ctrl+Alt+Shift+K.**

   The Clipping Path dialog box appears, as shown in Figure 19-3.

3. **To have InDesign detect the likely boundary of the image, as opposed to a white or other light background, choose Detect Edges from the Type pop-up menu.**

   You can use the other options to select Alpha Channel or Photoshop Path as the clipping path for graphics that have one or more of these. (InDesign can only use one alpha channel or Photoshop path as the clipping path, so use the Path pop-up menu to choose the one you want.)

4. **Type a value in the Threshold field or click and drag the field's slider to specify the value below which pixels will be placed outside the clipping path shape (that is, pixels that will become transparent).**

   Pixels darker than the Threshold value remain visible and thus are inside the clipping path shape. The lowest possible Threshold value (0) makes only white pixels transparent. As the value gets higher, less of the graphic remains visible. The lightest areas are removed first, then mid-tones, and so on. (Select the Preview option to see the results of your changes without closing the dialog box.)

5. **Type a value in the Tolerance field.**

   This value determines how closely InDesign looks at variations in adjacent pixels when building a clipping path. Higher values produce a simpler, smoother path than lower values. Lower values create a more complicated, more exact path with more anchor points.

6. **If you want to enlarge or reduce the size of the clipping path produced by the Threshold and Tolerance values, type a value in the Inset Frame field.**

   Negative values enlarge the path; positive values shrink it. (The Inset Frame value is also applied to the path's bounding box.)

7. **Select the Invert option to switch the transparent and visible areas of the clipping path produced by the Threshold and Tolerance values.**

8. **If you want to include light areas in the perimeter shape InDesign generates based on the Threshold and Tolerance values, select the Include Inside Edges option.**

   For example, if you have a graphic of a doughnut and you want to make the hole transparent (as well as the area around the outside of the doughnut), click Include Inside Edges. If you don't click Include Inside Edges, InDesign builds a single shape (in the case of a doughnut, just the outside circle). The portion of the graphic in the shape remains visible; the rest of the graphic becomes transparent.

9. **Select the Restrict to Frame option if you want InDesign to generate a clipping path from just the portion of the graphic visible in the graphic frame, as opposed to the entire graphic (such as if you cropped the graphic).**

10. **Select the Use High Resolution Image option if you want InDesign to use the high-resolution information in the original file instead of using the low-resolution proxy image.**

    Even though using the high-resolution image takes longer, the resulting clipping path is more precise than it would be if you didn't check Use High Resolution Image.

11. **When you've finished specifying clipping path settings, click OK to close the dialog box and apply the settings to the selected graphic.**

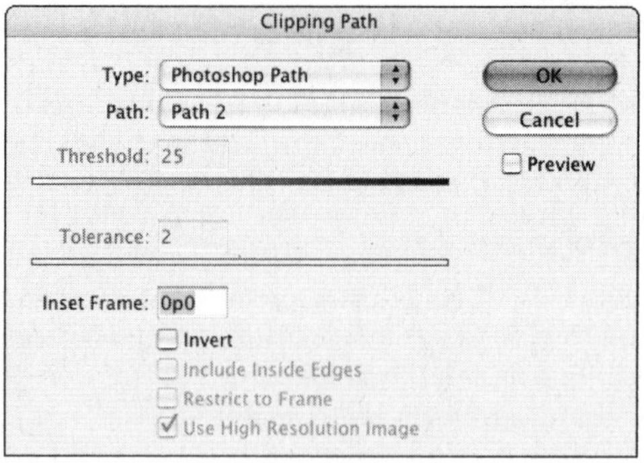

	Clipping Path	
Type:	Photoshop Path	OK
Path:	Path 2	Cancel
Threshold:	25	☐ Preview
Tolerance:	2	
Inset Frame:	0p0	
	☐ Invert	
	☐ Include Inside Edges	
	☐ Restrict to Frame	
	☑ Use High Resolution Image	

Figure 19-3:
The Clipping
Path dialog
box.

If you use the Clipping Path command to generate a clipping path for a graphic that has a built-in clipping path, the one that InDesign generates replaces the built-in path.

Figure 19-4 shows a graphic before and after a clipping path was applied to it using the Clipping Path command. At left is a graphic of coastal France with a graphic of a glider superimposed. At right is the same set of graphics, but with a clipping path applied to the glider so the outside area is masked out, making it transparent.

Figure 19-4:
A super-imposed image before (left) and after applying a clipping path (right).

The Clipping Path command works very well for images that have a white or light background but no clipping path. It's less useful for graphics with back-grounds that contain a broad range of intermingling values.

You can remove a clipping path by choosing None as the Type in the Clipping Path dialog box. You can also select a different path — Detect Edges, Alpha Channel, Photoshop Path, or User-Modified Path — than was selected previously if you decide to change the current clipping path.

InDesign lets you convert a clipping path into a frame, so you get the exact shape as your clipping path to use as a container or silhouette in your layout. Select the clipping path with the Direct Selection tool and choose Object⇨ Clipping Path⇨Convert Clipping Path to Frame. It's as easy as that!

Part VI
Getting Down to Business

The 5th Wave   By Rich Tennant

SINCE INSTALLING InDesign, THE 4th PRECINCT BECAME NOTED FOR ITS CREATIVE WANTED POSTERS

"Ooo—look! Sgt. Rodriguez has the felon's head floating in a teacup!"

In this part . . .

Microsoft Word, move over. It used to be that a word processor did all the business-y stuff like footnotes, tables, tables of contents, indexing, and mail-merge. Not anymore. Over the years, like a slow-moving movie monster nonetheless catching up with the terrorized teens, more and more of these business functions have found their way into InDesign. This version has even *more* such features, such as text variables.

This part shows you how to suit up your documents. But relax — you'll still be a designer at heart!

Chapter 20

Working with Tabs and Tables

*P*erhaps the most common business-oriented formatting done in InDesign involves tabular material, whether financial tables or simple comparative feature lists. InDesign provides two methods for creating tabular material: old-fashioned tabs and more sophisticated tables. Although you can create tables with tabs, you have less control over the formatting and thus can create just basic tables when you use tabs. On the other hand, for simple tables, using tabs is often the faster method. So don't feel you should never use tabs — but do be sure that when you mix methods that you don't let visual consistency suffer as a result.

Tabs and tables in InDesign work somewhat like the same functions in Microsoft Word, so if you're familiar with Word's tabs and tables, it'll be a quick adjustment to InDesign's, at least for the basic capabilities.

Setting Tabs

To set tabs in InDesign, you use the Tabs panel, which floats above your text so that you can keep it open until you're finished experimenting with tabs. To open the Tabs panel, choose Type⇨Tabs or press Shift+⌘+T or Ctrl+Shift+T. Figure 20-1 shows the Tabs panel along with a simple table created using one tab stop.

In InDesign CS3, you can no longer access the Tabs panel by choosing Window⇨Type & Tables⇨Tabs.

You can also set up tabs in the Tabs pane of the New Paragraph Styles and Paragraph Style Options dialog boxes, so tabs are consistently applied to all paragraphs. Chapter 14 covers styles in more detail.

Four buttons — Left, Center, Right, and Align On — on the Tabs panel let you control how the text aligns with the tab you're creating. The Align On option is usually used for decimal tabs, which means that a period in the text aligns on the tab stop. But you can align on any character, not just periods — simply specify the align-on character in the Align On field. (If you enter nothing in the Align On field, InDesign assumes you want to align to periods.) If the Align On field is not visible in the Tabs panel, just widen the panel by dragging one of its sides so the field displays.

The X: field of the Tabs panel lets you specify a position for a new tab stop. You can type a value in this field in 0.01-point increments, and then press Shift+Enter or Shift+Return to create a tab. InDesign positions tabs relative to the left edge of the text frame or column.

Rather than typing values in the X: field, you can position tabs by clicking at the desired location on the ruler at the bottom of the Tabs panel. You can also drag tab stops within the ruler to change their position. And you can reposition left and right indents and indent hangs using the arrow sliders on the tab ruler. (These have the same effects as changing indents using the Paragraph panel or Paragraph Styles panel, as explained in Chapter 15.)

To have the Tabs panel "snap" to your text frame, so you can see exactly where the tab stops will be, click the Position Panel Above Text Frame iconic button (the magnet icon).

If you need a tab flush with the right margin — for example, to position a dingbat at the end of the story — press Shift+Tab. There's no need to use the Tabs panel.

Figure 20-1:
The Tabs panel, its flyout menu, and a table created using tab settings.

		Clear All
		Delete Tab
X: .979 in Leader:	Align On:	Repeat Tab
		Reset Indents

ADOPTION OF INTRUSION DETECTION TOOLS		
Organization Type	2002	2007
North American medium organizations	48%	83%
North American small organizations	38	62
French organizations	27	60
German organizations	20	54
	SOURCE: INFONETICS RESEARCH	

InDesign lets you specify up to eight characters, including special characters that will repeat to fill any white space. These repeating characters are called *leaders*. When you set a leader for a tab stop, the leaders actually fill any space prior to that tab stop (between the previous text and the tab location). To spread out the leader characters, type spaces between the characters you enter. Don't enter spaces before and after a single character though, as that will result in two spaces between the characters when the pattern repeats (unless that's the look you're going for).

In addition to setting tabs in the Tabs panel, InDesign provides four additional options through its flyout menu: Clear All and Repeat Tab.

- ✔ The Clear All command deletes any tabs you've created, and any text positioned with tabs reverts to the position of the default tab stops. (You can delete an individual tab stop by dragging its icon off the ruler.)

- ✔ The Delete Tab command deletes the currently selected tab (just click it in the tab ruler).

  You can also delete tabs by dragging them off the tab ruler using the mouse.

- ✔ The Repeat Tab command lets you create a string of tabs across the ruler that are all the same distance apart. When you select a tab on the ruler and choose this command, InDesign measures the distance between the selected tab and the previous tab (or, if it's the first tab on the ruler, the distance between the selected tab and the left indent/text inset). The program then uses this distance to place new tabs, with the same alignment, all the way across the ruler. InDesign repeats tabs only to the right of the selected tab, but it inserts tabs between other tab stops.

- ✔ The Reset Indents command removes any changes to the left indent, right indent, or indent hang settings defined in the paragraph style currently applied to the text.

Setting Up Tables

You can create tables using tabs. But the more complex the table, the more work that requires. So make your life easier and use InDesign's table editor, which lets you specify almost any attribute imaginable in a table through the Table panel and the Table menu.

InDesign lets you import tables from Microsoft Word, RTF, and Microsoft Excel files, including some of their cell formatting. Likewise, you can convert their tables to tabbed text by using the options in the Import Options dialog box that is accessible when you place a file through the Place dialog box (File⇨Place, or ⌘+D or Ctrl+D), as covered in Chapter 12.

To create a table in InDesign, you first create or select a text frame with the Type tool and then choose Table⇨Insert Table or press Option+Shift+⌘+T or Ctrl+Alt+Shift+T. If you select an existing text frame, the table will be inserted at the cursor's location in the existing text.

That produces the Insert Table dialog box, where you type the number of body rows and columns and the number of header and footer rows. (Header and footer rows repeat on each page for tables that go across multiple pages.) Click OK to have InDesign create the basic table, which will be set as wide as the text frame. The depth will be based on the number of rows, with each row defaulting to the height that will hold 12-point text.

You can also apply a table style to the new table by selecting one from the Table Style pop-up menu. I cover how to create these styles later in this chapter.

With the basic table in place, you now format it using the Table panel and the Table menu. In both, you can increase or decrease the number of rows and columns, set the row and column height, set the text's vertical alignment within selected cells (top, middle, bottom, and justified), choose one of four text-rotation angles, and set the text margin within a cell separately for the top, bottom, left, and right. Note that all the Table panel's options affect only the currently selected cells, except for the Number of Rows and Number of Columns fields. Figure 20-2 shows the Table panel and its flyout menu. Figure 20-3 shows an example table created using these tools.

If you have a smallish monitor, set at 1024 by 768 pixels — the norm for a 17-inch display — the Table, Table Styles, and Cell Styles panels are shoved to the bottom of the panel dock, and, when they're selected, the only thing you'll see is their panel tab and flyout menu icon. You have a few choices: Shorten other panel groups in the dock to make room for them, remove other panel groups to make room for them, or drag them out of the dock and make them floating.

You set cell text's horizontal alignment using the paragraph formatting controls covered in Chapter 15. You can apply character formatting to cell text as described in Chapter 16. You can also apply tabs within cells using the Tabs panel covered earlier in this chapter.

To add items to a table, you can type text in any cell, paste text or graphics into a cell, or place text or graphics into a cell by choosing File⇨Place or pressing ⌘+D or Ctrl+D.

InDesign CS3 lets you paste tabbed text into tables. The tabs are retained, and all the text is pasted into the same cell.

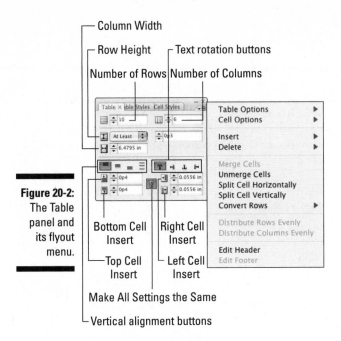

Figure 20-2: The Table panel and its flyout menu.

- Column Width
- Row Height
- Text rotation buttons
- Number of Rows
- Number of Columns
- Table Options
- Cell Options
- Insert
- Delete
- Merge Cells
- Unmerge Cells
- Split Cell Horizontally
- Split Cell Vertically
- Convert Rows
- Distribute Rows Evenly
- Distribute Columns Evenly
- Edit Header
- Edit Footer
- Bottom Cell Insert
- Right Cell Insert
- Top Cell Insert
- Left Cell Insert
- Make All Settings the Same
- Vertical alignment buttons

Figure 20-3: An example table created with the table tools.

WHERE HOT SPOTS ARE AVAILABLE	2001	2002	2003	2004	2005
Airports	85	152	292	378	423
Hotels	569	2,274	11,687	22,021	23,663
Retail Outlets	474	11,109	50,287	82,149	85,567
Enterprise Guesting Areas	84	624	1,762	3,708	5,413
Stations and Ports	—	88	623	2,143	3,887
Community Hot Spots	2	266	5,637	20,561	30,659
Others	—	240	790	1,526	2,156
Total Market	1,214	14,752	71,079	132,486	151,768

SOURCE: GARTNER

Adjusting tables

InDesign lets you add and delete rows and columns, as well as split and join cells using the Insert, Delete, Merge, and Split commands in the Table menu and in the Table panel's flyout menu. You can also select rows, columns, and entire tables using the Table menu. There are also several shortcuts, shown in Table 20-1, to speed things along if you are a keyboard-oriented person.

These commands work intuitively, so I won't bore you with detailed explanations here. For example, to delete a row, select it or a cell within it using the

Type tool, and then choose Table⇨Delete⇨Row. To split a cell vertically, select the cell and choose Table⇨Split Cell Vertically. You get the idea.

Table 20-1	Table-Editing Shortcuts	
Command	*Macintosh Shortcut*	*Windows Shortcut*
Select cell	⌘+/	Ctrl+/
Select row	⌘+3	Ctrl+3
Select column	Option+⌘+3	Ctrl+Alt+3
Select table	Option+⌘+A	Ctrl+Alt+A
Insert cell	Option+⌘+9	Ctrl+Alt+9
Insert row	⌘+9	Ctrl+9
Delete cell	Shift+Backspace	Shift+Backspace
Delete row	⌘+Backspace	Ctrl+Backspace

Formatting tables

For more sophisticated table attributes, use the Table Options dialog box and its five panes (choose Table⇨Table Options and then the desired pane from the submenu. To go straight to the Table Setup pane, you can also just press Option+Shift+⌘+B or Ctrl+Alt+Shift+B.) You'll see the Table Setup pane, shown in Figure 20-4. If you want to go straight to one of the four other panes, you can do so by choosing the desired pane in the submenu after choosing Table⇨Table Options.

When formatting tables, take advantage of the Preview option in most dialog boxes to see the effects of your changes before committing to them.

If you select more than one cell — meaning the entire cell, not just some of its contents — the Control panel's options change to display many of the controls available in the Table panel, as well as some cell-oriented controls such as setting cell boundary line weights and line types.

Here are some of the basics to keep in mind:

✔ The Table Setup pane lets you change the number of rows and columns, as well as footer rows and columns. You also can specify the table border, color, line type, and even tint. Use the Table Spacing options to have space automatically added before and after a table that is in the same text frame as other text.

✔ The Row Strokes pane, shown in Figure 20-5, lets you decide how often rows have an alternating pattern of strokes applied to them. For example, you may want every third row to have a thicker stroke than the first and second rows, because each set of three rows is related to each other and the third row marks the end of that set. You choose how many rows you want the special stroke to skip before being applied in the Alternating Pattern pop-up menu, and then use the rest of the controls to choose the stroke weight, color, type, and so on.

✔ The Column Strokes pane works just like the Row Strokes pane, except it lets you alternate the strokes across columns rather than rows.

✔ The Fills pane works like the Row Strokes pane and Column Strokes pane, except that it applies a fill to the cells in the specified series of rows or columns. The reason that there is just one pane for fills but two for strokes is that you can't have both row fills and column fills automatically applied to the same table — that would usually make for a hard-to-read checkerboard. Of course, you could use horizontal fills to accentuate rows and use strokes on columns to help keep them visually separate.

✔ The Headers and Footers pane lets you change the number of header and footer rows — just like the Table Setup pane — but it also lets you control how often the header and/or footer rows repeat: Every Text Column, Once Per Frame, or Once Per Page.

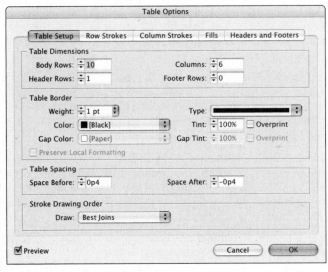

Figure 20-4:
The Table Setup pane of the Table Options dialog box.

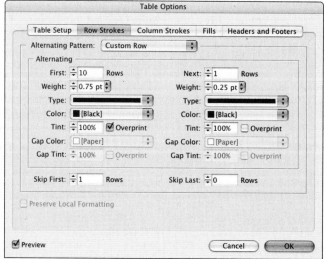

Figure 20-5:
The Row
Strokes
pane of the
Table
Options
dialog box.

InDesign also provides formatting controls over cells, using the Cell Options dialog box. (Choose Table⇨Cell Options and then one of the four desired panes: Text, Strokes and Fills, Rows and Columns, and Diagonal Lines. You can go straight to the Text pane by pressing Option+⌘+B or Ctrl+Alt+B.) After you selected the cells you want to format, use the various panes as desired:

- ✔ The Text pane works very much like the General pane of the Text Frame Options dialog box (covered in Chapter 15). Here, you set how far text is inset from the cell boundaries, how text is vertically aligned within the cell, and where the text baseline begins within the cell. Unique to cells, you can also specify whether the cell grows to fit the text automatically (by unchecking Clip Contents to Cell) and the degree of text rotation (0, 90, 180, and 270 degrees).

- ✔ The Strokes and Fills pane, shown in Figure 20-6, lets you set the stroke and fill for selected cells. You can select which cell boundaries to apply a stroke to, by selecting the sides from the preview image at the top of the pane and then choosing the desired options. You can also set the desired fill color and tint.

- ✔ The Rows and Columns pane lets you set the row height, including its maximum for rows that are allowed to expand automatically as specified in the Text pane, as well as the column width. You also can specify which rows must be kept together and if certain rows should start at a new page, frame, or column.

  You can also adjust column and row heights by dragging on the row and column boundaries with the mouse.

✔ The Diagonal Lines pane lets you place three types of diagonal lines within cells — upper left to lower right, lower right to upper left, or both — and then specify the stroke weight, type, color, and tint. You can also choose whether the diagonal lines overprint the cell contents or vice versa. To remove a diagonal line, just click the No Diagonal Lines iconic button.

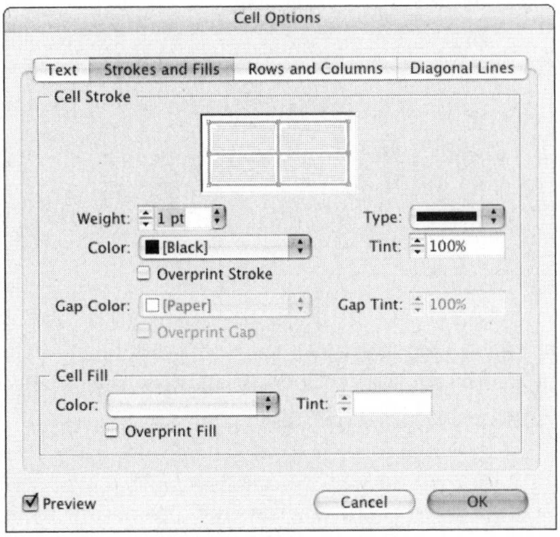

Figure 20-6:
The Strokes and Fills pane of the Cell Options dialog box.

Using table and cell styles

To make it easy to apply and update table formatting across a document, InDesign CS3 adds table and cell styles. They work like paragraph, character, and object styles, taking the table formatting features covered earlier in this section and bringing them together into the New Table Style and New Cell Style dialog boxes.

To work with table styles, open the Table Styles panel by choosing Window⇨ Type & Tables⇨Table Styles. To work with cell styles, open the Cell Styles panel by choosing Window⇨Type & Tables⇨Cell Styles. Choose New Table Style or New Cell Style from the appropriate panel's flyout menu, and then use the various panes to specify the desired formatting. The panes, and their options, are the same as described in the previous section, "Formatting tables." Figure 20-7 shows the New Table Style dialog box's General pane.

Whether creating a new table style or a new cell style, the easiest method is to format an existing table or cell the way you want it, select it, then create a new table or cell style — InDesign will pick up the existing formatting for the new style. Otherwise, you'll have to specify everything in the New Table Style or New Cell Style dialog box, where it's harder to see the effects of your settings. (Even if you enable the Preview option, the dialog boxes are fairly large and tend to obscure most of your document.)

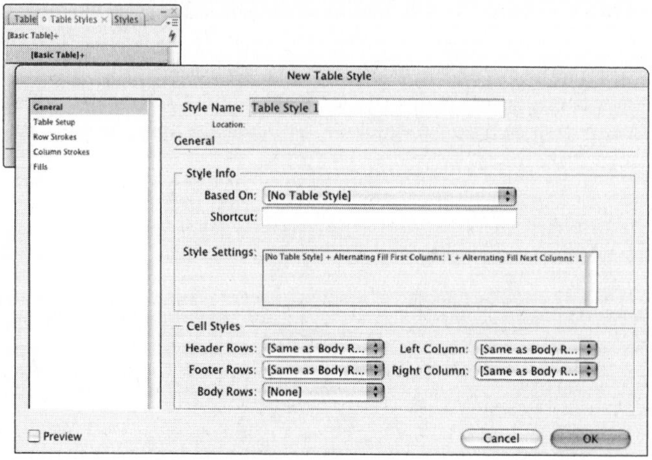

Figure 20-7:
The General
pane of
the New
Table Style
dialog box.

There are a few notes about creating table and cell styles — in the General pane of the New Table Style and New Cell Style dialog boxes — that you should know before getting too far into them:

✔ You give each style its own name. Choose names that will make sense a week or a month later, so you know what they are meant to be used for!

✔ You can base a new table style on an existing one, so changes to the parent style are automatically reflected in the children styles based on it.

✔ You can assign a keyboard shortcut to styles you use frequently.

When creating table styles, you can also have the table style automatically apply the cell styles of your choosing to the following table elements: header rows, footer rows, body rows, the leftmost column, and the rightmost column.

When creating cell styles, you can choose a paragraph style to be automatically applied to text in cells using the style.

To apply styles to selected tables or cells, just choose the desired style from the Table Style or Cell Style panel. To override existing formatting, use the options indicated for paragraph and character styles described in Chapter 13.

Modifying and managing table and cell styles

Modifying styles is easy: Double-click the style name in the Table Styles or Cell Styles panel. This opens the Table Style Options or Cell Style Options dialog box, which is identical to the New Table Styles or New Cell Styles dialog box explained in the previous section. Make your changes, click OK, and your styles and all tables and cells using them are instantly updated!

InDesign also lets you manage your styles, such as creating groups of styles to make it easier to find relevant ones, and bringing in styles from other documents. Because these features work the same for paragraph and character styles as well, I've covered these features in Chapter 14.

Converting Tabs to Tables (and Back)

Often, you'll have a table done using tabs — whether imported from a word processor or originally created in InDesign with tabs — that you want to convert to a real InDesign table. That's easy. Select the tabbed text you want to convert using the Type tool and choose Table⇨Convert Text to Table.

In the Convert Text to Table dialog box, you can choose a Column Separator (Tab, Comma, Paragraph, or a text string you type in the field) or a Row Separator (same options). Although most textual data uses tabs to separate columns and paragraphs to separate rows, you may encounter other data that uses something else. For example, spreadsheets and databases often save data so that commas, rather than tabs, separate columns. That's why InDesign lets you choose the separator characters before conversion.

During the conversion, InDesign formats the table using the standard settings, using the current text formatting and the default cell insets and stroke types. You can then adjust the table using the tools covered earlier in this chapter. Note that the conversion treats all rows as body rows.

You can also convert a table to text by selecting multiple cells or an entire table, as described earlier, and choosing Table⇨Convert Table to Text. InDesign presents the same options as it does in the Convert Text to Table dialog box, so you can determine how the converted data appears.

Chapter 21

Working with Footnotes, Indexes, and TOCs

Many business documents — books, reports, white papers, and so on — use features traditionally associated with academic book publishing: footnotes to cite sources, indexes to provide a map to specific content's location in the document, and tables of contents (TOCs) to provide an overview of the document's structure and contents.

When you're working on any type of document — a report, a magazine, a textbook — you can easily spend more time manually creating tables of contents, keeping footnotes updates, and laboriously managing indexes than you spend designing the publication. InDesign helps reduce this labor while also ensuring that your footnotes, indexes, and tables of content stay automatically updated as your document is revised.

You can extend the power of these tools to book-length projects composed of multiple InDesign documents (covered in Chapter 23), creating consistent indexing and tables of contents in one fell swoop.

Adding Footnotes

Many documents, including academic and technical documents, use footnotes. InDesign lets you add footnotes to your document with very little fuss.

You can import footnotes from Microsoft Word files (see Chapter 12), or you can add footnotes directly in InDesign. With the text-insertion cursor in your text where you want the footnote marker to appear, choose Type➪Insert Footnote to add a footnote to the bottom of the column that contains the footnote marker, as Figure 21-1 shows. You need to manually enter the text that will go with each numbered footnote, but InDesign updates the footnote numbering as you add and delete footnotes.

You cannot insert footnotes into tables. But you can simulate footnotes by adding a superscripted footnote character in the table text and typing your footnote text below the table — note this "footnote" is not linked to the text, will not renumber automatically as a real footnote would, and cannot be formatted with InDesign's footnote formatting controls.

You can control much of the appearance of footnotes by choosing Type➪Document Footnote Options to open the Footnote Options dialog box, shown in Figure 21-2.

The Numbering and Formatting pane controls the formatting of the footnote text and footnote character in the current InDesign document. The Layout pane controls the placement of the footnote relative to the rest of the document.

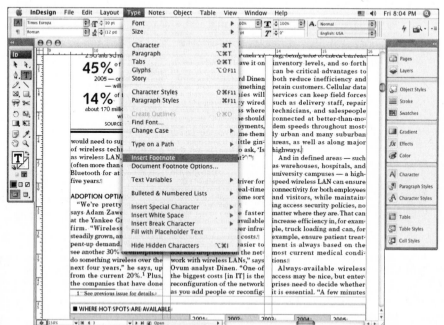

Figure 21-1:
Inserting a
footnote.

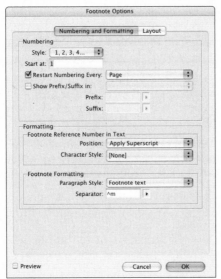 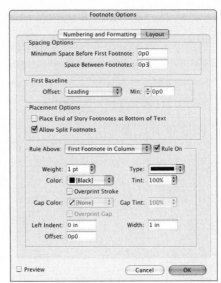

Figure 21-2:
The
Footnote
Options
dialog box
contains
two panes:
Numbering
and
Formatting
and Layout.

Among the features you should note in the Numbering and Formatting pane are

✔ Choose the numbering style — such as 1, 2, 3, 4 ... or I, ii, iii, iv ... — via the Style pop-up menu.

✔ Control whether the footnote numbers start anew (such as at the beginning of a section) or continue from the previous number via the Start At field.

✔ Control whether numbering automatically resets every page, spread, or section via the Restart Numbering Every pop-up menu.

✔ Add a prefix and/or suffix to your footnote numbers via the Prefix and Suffix fields. Note the unnamed pop-up menus that let you add special characters such as a thin space or bracket.

✔ Use the Position and Character Style options in the Footnote Reference Number in Text subsection to determine how the footnote characters appear in text.

✔ Similarly, use the Paragraph Style and Separator options in the Footnote Formatting subsection to determine how the footnote text appears. (Note any Separator options will display after any Suffix options chosen.)

Among the features to note in the Layout pane are

- Set the preferred spacing for the footnote text in the Spacing Options section.

- Convert Word's endnotes (which will appear at the end of a story) to InDesign footnotes (which appear in the column or page that the footnote reference occurs in) by checking the Place End of Story Footnotes at Bottom of Text option.

- Control whether footnotes can break across columns via the Allow Split Footnotes option. Enabling this option can improve the layout when you have long footnotes that otherwise eat up a column of text.

- Control the ruling line above footnotes using the Rule Above options. They work like the paragraph rules covered in Chapter 15.

To change these settings for future documents, open the dialog box while no document is open and set your new defaults.

Creating Indexes

When trying to locate information in a book, nothing is as wonderful as a good index. Once upon a time, book indexing was a labor-intensive process involving piles of index cards. InDesign makes indexing much easier, while still allowing you to make key decisions about how the index is formatted.

But be warned: Indexing is complicated business and is, by and large, an expert feature. So I cover just the basics here.

Choosing an indexing style

Before you begin indexing your document, ask yourself the following questions:

- Do you want to initial-cap all levels of all entries, or do you just want sentence case?

- Should index headings appear in boldface?

- What type of punctuation will you use in your index?

- Will you capitalize secondary entries in the index?

- Should the index be nested or run-in style? (A nested index is an indented list, with each entry on its own line. A run-in index puts all related entries in one paragraph, separated by semicolons.)

After you make these decisions, it's a good idea to make a small dummy index. From the dummy, create a master page for index pages, paragraph styles for index headings (the letters *A, B, C,* and so on), paragraph styles for each level of the index (including indents as appropriate), and character styles for any special formatting you want on page numbers or cross-reference text. InDesign doesn't do any of this for you.

Inside the Index panel

When you want to index a chapter or document, open the Index panel by choosing Window➪Type & Tables➪Index or by pressing Shift+F8. Use this panel to add words to the index in up to four indent levels, edit or delete index entries, or create cross-references. The Index panel is shown in Figure 21-3.

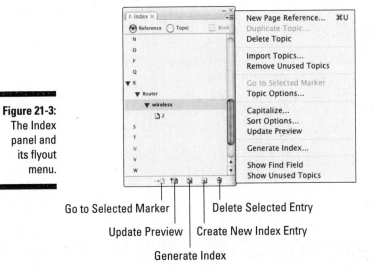

Figure 21-3: The Index panel and its flyout menu.

Go to Selected Marker

Update Preview

Generate Index

Delete Selected Entry

Create New Index Entry

Two radio buttons appear at the top of the Index panel: Reference and Topic. You use Reference mode to add and edit entries from selected text. (Although it is a well-intentioned feature meant to help standardize index entries, the Topic mode's use is not intuitive, and most indexers simply ignore it and add entries manually from selected text or type phrases into the Index pane in Reference mode. You should ignore it, too.)

Select the Book check box if you are creating an index for multiple chapters in a book (see Chapter 23). You must have a book open for this option to be available. If you have a book open and do not select the Book check box, the index is saved with the current document and not opened when you open other chapters of the book.

Adding index items via the Index panel

To add entries to the index, be sure the Type tool is active, then choose New Page Reference from the Index panel's flyout menu, or press ⌘+U or Ctrl+U, to get the dialog box shown in Figure 21-4.

If the Type tool is not active when you open the dialog box, the flyout menu option will be called New Cross-Reference instead, letting you add a cross-reference entry to the index. The resulting New Cross-Reference dialog box is identical to the New Page Reference dialog box, except the various options default to ones appropriate for a cross-reference.

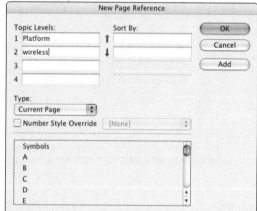

Figure 21-4: The New Page Reference dialog box.

Here's how the controls work:

- ✔ If you selected text first in your document, the text is entered automatically into Topic Level 1. Otherwise, type in the text that you want to add to the index. In Figure 21-4, you can see that I typed **Platform**. The text will be added to the Topic list and to the list of index entries.

- ✔ You can enter text that controls how the entry is sorted in the Sort By column. For example, if the selected text you're indexing is *The A-Team*, but you want it sorted as if it were *A-Team, The* (so it appears with the A entries in the index), enter **A-Team, The** in the Sorted By column.

✔ If you want a more complex index, you might want to use some or all of the four possible entry levels. You may want an index entry to appear under a higher-level topic. For example, you may want *Border Collies* to appear in the index under *Herding Dogs,* in which case you would enter **Herding Dogs** the Topic Level 1 field and **Border Collies** in the Topic Level 2 field. In Figure 21-4, I entered **wireless** in the Topic Level 2 field.

✔ Use the Type pop-up menu to determine the page entries for the index entry. For instance, if you select To End of Section, the page numbers for the selected text in the index will cover the range from the index entry to the end of the section it is in.

✔ To add just the selected text as an index entry, click Add. (If no text is selected, the text will be added to the Topic list, but no index entry will appear for it.) To add all occurrences of the text in the book, click Add All.

✔ To change previously defined index entries, select an entry and then choose Page Reference Options in the Index panel's flyout menu.

✔ At the bottom of the New Page Reference dialog box is a list of letters as well as the entry Symbols (where entries that begin with numbers and other non-letter characters will be grouped in the index). You can scroll through this list of headings to see what is already in the index under each letter. Although you might think clicking a letter would force the current index entry to appear in that letter's section of the index, it does not.

To quickly add a word or text selection to an index, highlight the text and press ⌘+U or Ctrl+U to add the text to the New Page Reference dialog box. To index a word without opening that dialog box, just press Option+Shift+⌘+[or Ctrl+Alt+Shift+[. This adds the text to the index using the index's default settings. (You can always edit them later.) And to enter an index entry as a proper name (last name, first name), use the shortcut Option+Shift+⌘+] or Ctrl+Alt+Shift+].

Polishing and generating the index

The Index panel's flyout menu has several options useful for generating and fine-tuning an index:

✔ **Duplicate Topic** lets you duplicate a topic entry so you can use the settings from one entry without having to re-enter those settings in a new entry.

✔ **Delete Topic** removes a topic (and any associated entries) from the index.

✔ **Import Topics** lets you import topic lists from other InDesign documents.

✔ **Go to Selected Marker** causes InDesign to jump to the text that contains the selected index entry in the Index panel.

✔ **Topic Options** lets you edit the Level and Sort By settings for topic entries; these affect all index entries that use them.

✔ **Capitalize** lets you standardize the capitalization of topic entries — you can choose Selected Topic, Selected Topic and All Subtopics, All Level 1 Topics, and All Topics.

✔ **Update Preview** updates the index entries in the Index panel to reflect page-number changes, new occurrences of index text occurrences, and deleted occurrences of indexed text.

✔ **Generate Index** creates the index via the dialog box shown in Figure 21-5. In this dialog box, you specify the following: a title for the index, the paragraph style for that title, whether a selected index is replaced with the new one, whether an entire book is indexed, whether text on hidden layers is indexed, whether the index is nested or run-in, whether empty index headings and sections are included, what paragraph styles are applied to each level of index entry, what character styles are applied to different portions of index entries, and which characters will be used as separators within index entries. (Click the More Options button to see the nested/run-in and later options.) After you generate an index, you get the standard InDesign loaded-text icon (the paragraph icon); click an existing text frame into which you want to flow the index, or click anywhere else in a document to have InDesign create the text frame for you and flow the index text into it.

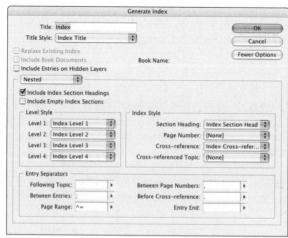

Figure 21-5:
The
Generate
Index dialog
box, with all
options
displayed.

Creating Tables of Contents

A table of contents (TOC) is useful in a long document because it helps readers locate information quickly. A TOC is simply a list of paragraphs that are formatted with the same styles. This means that if you want to use the table of contents feature, you have to use paragraph styles. Not only do styles guarantee consistent formatting, but they also tell InDesign what text you want to include in your TOC.

After you've created a book (or even a single document), InDesign can build a table of contents by scanning pages for the paragraph styles you specify. For example, if you create a book, you might use paragraph styles named *Chapter Title, Section,* and *Subsection.* Using the table of contents feature, InDesign can generate a table of contents that includes all three levels.

TOC styles manage the text that you want in a table of contents, the order in which it appears, how page numbers are added, and how the various TOC elements are formatted. To create a TOC style, choose Layout⇨Table of Contents Styles, which opens the dialog box shown in Figure 21-6.

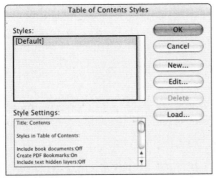

Figure 21-6:
The Table of Contents Styles dialog box.

In the Table of Contents Styles dialog box, click New to create a new TOC style. You can also edit an existing TOC style via the Edit button, delete one via the Delete button, and import one from another InDesign document via the Load button.

Here's how to create a TOC style after clicking the New button:

1. **Enter a name for the TOC style in the TOC Style field (shown in Figure 21-7).**

   The default is TOC Style 1.

2. In the Title field, enter a heading for the TOC.

This text appears in your table of contents.

If you don't want a title, leave the Title field blank, but note that you still get an empty paragraph at the top of your TOC for this title. You can always delete that paragraph.

3. Use the Style pop-up menu to choose the paragraph style that this title will have.

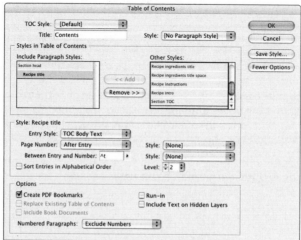

Figure 21-7:
The Table of
Contents
dialog box.

4. In the Styles in Table of Contents section, click a paragraph style that you want to appear in your TOC from the Other Styles list at right.

For example, you might click Chapter Title.

5. Click Add to add it to the Include Paragraph Styles list at left. (Select a style from the Include Paragraph Styles section and click Remove to remove any paragraph styles you don't want to be used in the TOC.)

6. Repeat Steps 4 and 5 until you have added all the paragraph styles that you want to include in the TOC.

7. Use the Entry Style pop-up menu to select a TOC level and then choose the paragraph formatting for that style.

If the Entry Style, Page Number, and other options don't display, click the More Options button to see them.

- Use the Page Number pop-up menu to determine how page numbers are handled: After Entry, Before Entry, and No Page Number. If you want the page numbers to have a character style applied, choose that style from the Style pop-up menu to the right of the Page Number pop-up menu.

- Use the Between Entry and Number field and pop-up menu to choose what appears between the TOC text and the page number. You can enter any characters you want; use the pop-up menu to select special characters such as bullets and tabs. In most cases, you should select a tab; the paragraph style selected earlier for the TOC entry includes leader information, such as having a string of periods between the text and the number. You can also apply a character style to the characters between the text and the page numbers via the Style pop-up menu at right.

- To sort entries at this level alphabetically, such as for a list of products in a brochure, select the Sort Entries in Alphabetical Order check box.

- To change the level of the current TOC entry, use the Level pop-up menu. If you change the level of entries, InDesign will correctly sort them when it creates the TOC, even if the levels seem out of order in the Include Paragraph Styles list.

- In the Options section of the dialog box, choose the appropriate options. Check Create PDF Bookmarks if you're exporting the document to PDF format and want the PDF TOC file to have *bookmarks* (a clickable set of TOC links). Check Run-in if you want all entries at the same level to be in one paragraph. (This is not common for TOCs but is used in indexes and lists of figures.) Check Replace Existing Table of Contents if you want InDesign to automatically replace an existing TOC if the TOC style is changed. Check Include Text on Hidden Layers if you want text on hidden layers to be included in the TOC. Check Include Book Documents if you have a book open and want InDesign to generate a TOC based on all chapters in that book. (InDesign will show the current open book's name.) Finally, control whether numbers are included in the table of contents for numbered paragraphs using the new Numbered Paragraphs pop-up menu.

8. **Continue this process for each paragraph style whose text should be in the TOC.**

Note that the order in which you add these styles determines the initial levels: The first paragraph style added is level 1; the second is level 2, and so on. But you can change the order by changing the Level setting, as described earlier.

To make changes to a TOC style, go to the Edit Table of Contents Style dialog box. Choose Layout⇨Table of Contents Styles, select the TOC style to edit, and click Edit.

With a TOC style in place and your document properly formatted with the paragraph styles that the TOC style will look for when generating a TOC, you're ready to have InDesign create the actual TOC for you.

To generate a TOC, choose Layout⇨Table of Contents. You get a dialog box that is identical to the Table of Contents dialog box shown in Figure 21-7. In this dialog box, you can make changes to the TOC style settings. (If you want to save those TOC style changes, be sure to click the Save Style button.) Then click OK to have InDesign generate the TOC. You might also get a dialog box asking whether you want to include items in *overset text* (text that didn't fit in your document after you placed it) in your TOC. It may take a minute or two for the program to generate the TOC. (See Chapter 13 for more details on overset text.)

Be sure you allow enough space (a single text frame, a series of linked text frames, or one or more empty pages) for the TOC before generating a final TOC because if you end up adding or deleting pages based on the TOC length, the TOC will display the old page numbers. To update page numbering after flowing a TOC, simply rebuild the TOC by selecting the text frame holding the TOC and then choosing Layout⇨Update Table of Contents.

If you select a text frame, InDesign will place the TOC text in it when you generate the TOC. If you don't select a text frame, you see the familiar loaded-text icon (the paragraph pointer) that you see when you place a text file. Click a text frame to insert the TOC text in that frame or click in an empty part of your document to create a text frame in which the TOC text will flow.

The feature that creates TOC is actually a list generator, and you can use it to create other kinds of lists. Basically, anything that is tagged with a paragraph style can be used to create a list. For example, if your figure captions all use their own paragraph style (called Caption Title in this example), you can generate a list of figures by creating a TOC style that includes just the Caption Title paragraph style. An InDesign document can have more than one TOC, so you can include multiple lists in your document.

Chapter 22

Working with Automated Text

A key area of improvement over the years in InDesign is the increased use of automated text. From the very beginning, InDesign offered automatic page numbers so your folios and cross-references would reflect the current pages as your layout changed. Later versions enhanced this with section markers, which let you create variable names in folios for your section titles. Still later came the ability to use data files and merge their contents into a layout to customize your output, similar to how word processors let you customize labels with their mail-merge feature. The newest version of InDesign adds to this mix a new option: variable text, which gives you more flexibility in where and how you can have InDesign update text automatically throughout a document based on your specifications.

Altogether, these features have helped InDesign stake significant ground in reducing the labor and time of manual processes, such as search and replace, for text that changes predictably throughout the document.

Another type of text variable is the hyperlink — the Web address used in Web pages and PDF files so users can just click text to be transported to another page. While the text itself does not change, the underlying hyperlink information can change, and InDesign lets you specify and update these hyperlinks as needed.

Automatic Page Numbers

You'll often want page references in text — the current page number in a folio, for example, or the target page number for a "continued on" reference. You could type in a page number manually on each page of a multipage document, but that can get old fast. As I mentioned in Chapters 4 and 6, if you're working on a multipage document, you should be using master pages. And if you're using master pages, you should handle page numbers on document pages by placing page-number characters on their master pages.

If you want to add the current page number to a page, you can choose Type⇨ Insert Special Character⇨Markers⇨Current Page Number or press Option+ Shift+⌘+N or Ctrl+Shift+Alt+N whenever the Type tool is active and the text-insertion cursor is flashing. If you move the page or the text frame, the page-number character is automatically updated to reflect the new page number.

To create "continued on" and "continued from" lines, choose Type⇨Insert Special Character⇨Markers⇨Next Page Number to have the next page's number inserted in your text, or choose Type⇨Insert Special Character⇨ Markers⇨Previous Page Number to have the previous page's number inserted. (There are no shortcuts for these complex menu sequences.) That next or previous page will be the next or previous page in the *story*, not the next page in the document.

One flaw in InDesign's continued-line approach is that the text frames must be linked for InDesign to know what the next and previous pages are. Thus, you're likely to place your continued lines in the middle of your text. But if the text reflows, so do the continued lines. Here's a way to avoid that: Create separate text frames for your continued-on and continued-from text frames. Now link just those two frames, not the story text. This way, the story text can reflow as needed without affecting your continued lines.

Using Section Markers

InDesign offers another marker called the section marker that lets you insert specific text into your document and update it by just changing the marker text.

The section marker is defined as part of a section start (see Chapter 4), and it's meant to be used in folios to put in the section name or chapter name. But you can use it anywhere you want — and for anything you want, not just for section or chapter labels.

To define a section marker (there can be only one per section, of course), open the Pages panel (Window⇨Pages, or ⌘+F10 or Ctrl+F10) and choose Numbering & Section Options from the panel's flyout menu. In the resulting dialog box, type a text string in the Section Marker field. Then click OK.

To use the marker, have the text insertion point active in whatever text frame you want to insert it, and then choose Type⇨Insert Special Character⇨ Markers⇨Section Marker. That's it!

Using Text Variables

The section marker was clearly the inspiration for the new text-variable feature. Why stop at section markers? With InDesign CS3's new text variables, you can define an unlimited number of text variables that InDesign will happily update across your documents whenever you change them or your layout does.

Creating text variables

To create a text variable, choose Type⇨Text Variables⇨Define. You'll get the Text Variables dialog box shown in Figure 22-1. It lists existing text variables — including the seven ones predefined in InDesign: Chapter Number, Creation Date, File Name, Last Page Number, Modification Date, Output Date, and Running Header. Any of them that you create will be added to this list.

The source of the number used in the Chapter Number text variable is something you define as part of a book. For each document in a book, you can specify its chapter number using the Document Numbering Options dialog box accessed from the book panel's flyout menu. Chapter 23 explains books and how to set the chapter number.

To create a new text variable, click New. You'll get the New Text Variable dialog box shown in Figure 22-2. Give the variable a name in the Name field, and choose the type of variable you want from the Type pop-up menu. Your choices are the seven predefined types plus Custom Text, which lets you put in any text of your choosing. (This means you can create more than one variable for, say, File Name or Modification Date. You might do this because you want them formatted differently in different usage scenarios.)

The options for formatting the chosen type of variable varies based on the type of variable it is. Three options are available for more than one type of text variable:

- **Text Before and Text After:** These two fields — available for all Type pop-up menu options except Custom Text — let you add any text you want before or after the variable. For example, you might enter the word *Chapter* in the Text Before field for a Chapter Number variable. Note that both fields have an unnamed pop-up menu to their right from which you can select a variety of common symbols and spaces.

- **Style:** This pop-up menu lets you select the style to apply in the Chapter Number, Running Header (Character Style), and Running Header (Paragraph Style) text variables.

✔ **Date Format:** This field and its associated pop-up menu lets you choose the desired date and time formats for the Creation Date, Modification Date, and Output Date text variables. Examples include *MM/dd/yy* to get a date like 05/08/62 and *MMMM d, yyyy* top get a date like August 15, 1962. Don't worry about memorizing codes — just pick the desired options from the pop-up menu instead.

Several other variables have unique options:

✔ **Custom Text:** This has the fewest options. Just enter the desired text, including choosing special characters such as spaces and dashes from the unnamed pop-up menu to the right of the Text field. That's the only field to adjust for this text variable.

✔ **Last Page Number:** In addition to the Text Before, Text After, and Style formatting controls, this type includes one unique control: the Scope pop-up menu. Here, you choose between Section and Document to tell InDesign what you mean by last page number: the section's last page or the document's.

✔ **File Name:** In addition to Text Before and Text After formatting controls, this type has two unique check boxes — Include Entire Folder Path and Include File Extension — to tell InDesign exactly how much of the filename to include. If both are unchecked, InDesign will include just the core file-name, such as `Jun 07 TOC`. Checking the Include Entire Folder Path will add the file location before the core filename, such as `MacintoshHD: Projects:Jun 07 TOC` or `C:\Projects\Jun 07 TOC`. Checking the Include File Extension will append the filename extension, such as `June 07 TOC.indd`.

✔ **Running Header:** The formatting options for these two types are the most complex, as shown in Figure 22-2. The two Running Header menu options have two options not available to other Type pop-up menu options:

• **Use:** This determines which text to use: First on Page uses the first text on the page that has the specific style applied, while Last on Page uses the last text on the page that has the specific style applied.

• **Options:** Here, you can control whether the punctuation of the source text is retained or not in the running header (check Delete End Punctuation to remove it) and whether the running header overrides the text of the source text's capitalization (check Change Case and then choose the appropriate capitalization option: Upper Case, Lower Case, Title Case, or Sentence Case).

Title case means that the first letter of each word is capitalized, while Sentence Case means that only the first letter of the first word in each sentence is capitalized.

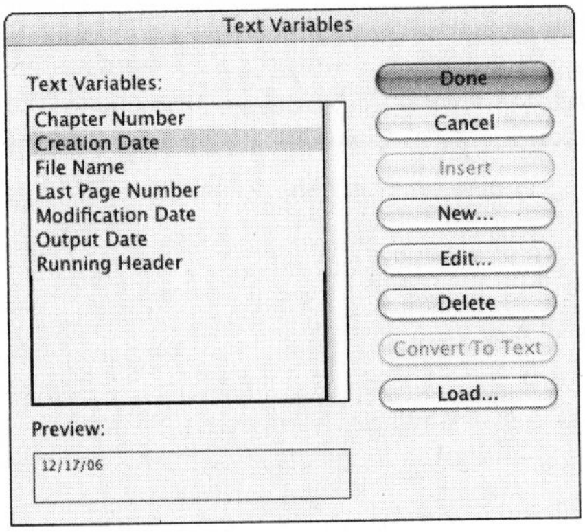

Figure 22-1:
The Text
Variables
dialog box.

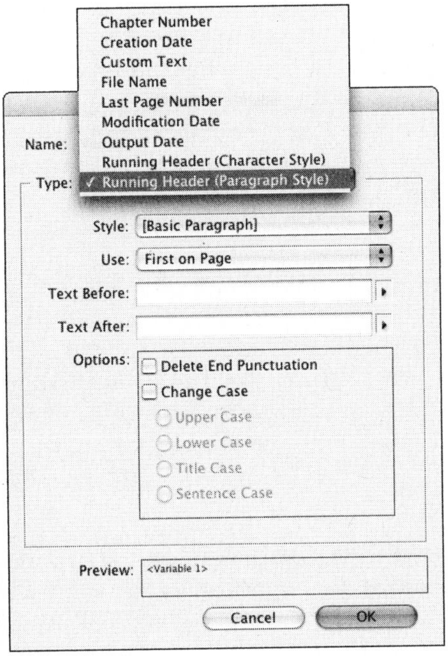

Figure 22-2:
The New
Text
Variable
dialog box.

Editing and managing text variables

Editing text variables is very much like creating them: Just select the variable
to change and click Edit in the Text Variables dialog box. You'll get the
Edit Text Variable dialog box, which is identical except for its name to the
New Text Variable dialog box covered in the previous section.

You can also import text variables from other documents by clicking Load in the Text Variables dialog box, and then choosing the document to import the variables from. After choosing a document, you'll get the Load Text Variables dialog box, where you can select which variables are imported and handle name conflicts.

To get rid of a text variable, select it from the list in the Text Variables dialog box and click Delete.

To convert a text variable in your document to the actual text, highlight it and either choose Type➪Text Variables➪Convert Variable to Text or, if you happen to be in the Text Variables dialog box, click Convert to Text.

Inserting text variables

Inserting text variables in your document uses the same essential process as inserting a special character such as a section market, except you use the Text Variables menu option: Choose Type➪Text Variables➪Insert Variable, and then choose the desired variable from the submenu. If you happen to be in the Text Variables dialog box, click Insert.

Using Hyperlinks

Both Web pages and PDF files can include hyperlinks, the clickable hot spots that direct a browser to open a new file or page. It's a whole new way to deliver related contents through an active cross-reference. And InDesign lets you add hyperlinks to your documents, so if they are exported to the PDF or Web formats, those links are clickable.

InDesign uses its Hyperlinks panel (Window➪Interactive➪Hyperlinks) to add, edit, and delete hyperlinks. In a sense, a hyperlink is a character attribute — it's applied to selected text. Figure 22-3 shows the Hyperlinks panel and its flyout menu.

Creating hyperlinks

Although the process is straightforward, InDesign's terminology can make it a bit confusing on how to start. You first create a hyperlink destination — the place a hyperlinks goes to, or its *target* — by choosing New Hyperlink Destination from the Hyperlinks panel's flyout menu. Figure 22-4 shows the dialog box. You give the destination a name in the Name field and then choose from one of the three options in the Type menu:

✔ **Page.** This option lets you specify a specific page in a selected document. If you select this option, InDesign provides a Page field in which you specify the page number to open in the selected document, as well as the Zoom Setting pop-up menu, which lets you select how the page is displayed. (Options are Fixed, meaning at the default size in Adobe Reader; Fit View; Fit in Window; Fit Width; Fit Height; Fit Visible; and Inherit Zoom, which uses the current zoom setting in Adobe Reader.)

✔ **Text Anchor.** This option lets you specify a specific piece of text in the selected document. This would be the selected text.

✔ **URL.** This is a Web page address (the official name is Uniform Resource Locator), as shown in the New Hyperlink Destination dialog box in Figure 22-4. If you select this option, InDesign displays the URL field in which you type the Web address.

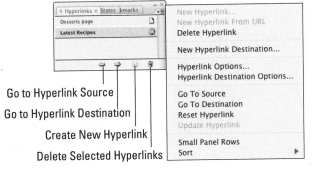

Figure 22-3:
The
Hyperlinks
panel and
its flyout
menu.

With the destinations defined, you can now create the hyperlinks to them (the hyperlink *sources*).

To create a hyperlink to another PDF file, you can't use the New Hyperlink Destination method. You must use the New Hyperlink method described next.

To create a hyperlink source:

1. **Select the text or frame you want to be a hyperlink's source, and then choose New Hyperlink from the Hyperlinks panel's flyout menu.**

   That opens the New Hyperlink dialog box, as shown in Figure 22-5.

2. **Type a name for the hyperlink source.**

   This lets you apply the same link to more than one location in your document — sort of a character style for hyperlinks. If the name already exists, an error message appears when you click OK — there's no way to know ahead of time if the name has already been used in the document.

Links to other documents

The process for linking to other documents depends on whether those documents are on the Web or on a CD or internal server.

If you want to create a hyperlink to another document, such as on a CD or server, you must do so in the New Hyperlink Destination dialog box, using the Page option. You cannot first create a destination hyperlink. Also, unintuitively, you must browse for the actual InDesign file to which you want to link. But the link will be to the PDF version of that file, which means you must be sure to create the PDF of that other document and use the same filename, except for the filename extension. For example, if you link to `filename.indd`, the link will actually be to

`filename.pdf`. This approach requires that you have all the target files in InDesign format — you cannot link to a specific PDF file created in another program or by someone whose source files you don't have access to.

By contrast, Web links can link to any object available on a Web server, including PDFs, so you would simply use a hyperlink to a Web address, such as `http://www.zangogroup.com/filename.pdf`, in the New Hyperlink dialog box. Note that such Web links cannot be made to a specific page inside a PDF file, as InDesign allows when making links from one document to another as described in the previous paragraph.

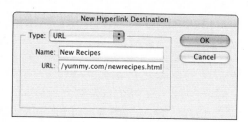

Figure 22-4:
The New Hyperlink Destination dialog box's three variants are (from top to bottom) URL, Page, and Text Anchor.

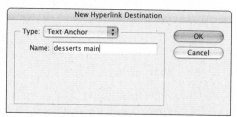

3. **If the hyperlink is to another InDesign document, you can select that document by choosing Browse from the Document pop-up menu.**

4. **Use the Type pop-up menu to determine what you're hyperlinking to.**

   You have the same three options as in the New Hyperlink Destination dialog box's Type menu — Page, Text Anchor, and URL — as well as All Types, which, if chosen, displays previously defined hyperlinks in the document.

5. **Use the Name pop-up menu to select a previously defined hyperlink destination (target) or an anchor.**

   You can also create a hyperlink to an Unnamed destination by leaving the Name pop-up menu set to [None]. But I advise against the [None] method because that hyperlink destination won't appear in the menu for future hyperlink sources, making it hard to modify later.

6. **In the Appearance section, you can control how the hyperlink appears on-screen:**

   • Use the Type pop-up menu to choose Invisible Rectangle or Visible Rectangle. The Invisible Rectangle option gives no visual indication that the text contains a hyperlink, except that the mouse pointer becomes a hand icon when the reader maneuvers through the document. (You would typically pick this option when you've used blue underline as a character attribute for the hyperlink text to mirror the standard Web way of indicating a hyperlink.) The Visible Rectangle option puts a box around the text using the four settings below (they are grayed out if Invisible Rectangle is selected).

   • The Highlight pop-up menu lets you choose how the source text or frame is highlighted: None, Invert (reserve the foreground and background colors), Outline (places a line around the source), and Inset (places a line around the source, but inside any frame stroke; for text, it's the same as Outline).

   • The Color pop-up menu displays Web-safe colors, as well as any colors you defined in the document.

   • The Width pop-up menu lets you choose the thickness of the line used in the Outline and Inset options from the Highlight pop-up menu. The choices are Thin, Medium, and Thick.

   • You can choose the type of line in the Style pop-up menu: Solid or Dashed.

If your text includes a valid hyperlink, such as `www.InDesignCentral.com`, you can select it and create a URL hyperlink automatically by choosing New Hyperlink from URL in the Hyperlinks panel's flyout menu.

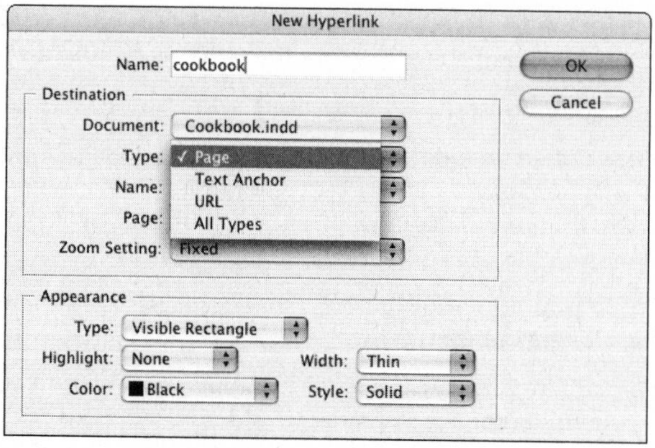

Figure 22-5:
The New
Hyperlink
dialog box.

After your hyperlink sources are defined, you can easily apply them by selecting text and clicking an existing hyperlink source from the Hyperlinks panel. You can also jump to the source or destination by selecting the desired hyperlink in the Hyperlinks panel and choosing either Go to Source or Go to Destination from the flyout menu, or click the Go to Hyperlink Source or Go to Hyperlink Destination iconic buttons at the bottom of the panel. These make a handy way to verify the links are correct.

Modifying and deleting hyperlinks

It's also easy to modify hyperlinks: Choose Hyperlink Options from the Hyperlinks panel's flyout menu to open the Hyperlink Options dialog box, which has the same options as the New Hyperlink dialog box, shown in Figure 22-5, to modify the source. Similarly, to modify hyperlink destinations, choose Hyperlink Destination Options from the palette menu to open the Hyperlink Destination Options dialog box, and then select the target from the Name pop-up menu. The Hyperlink Destination Options dialog box's options are the same as the New Hyperlink Destination dialog box shown in Figure 22-5.

You can change the source text or frame by selecting it, and then clicking the hyperlink name in the Hyperlinks panel, and finally choosing Reset Hyperlink from the panel's flyout menu. To change the target for a hyperlink to an InDesign document, choose Update Hyperlink from the flyout menu (press and hold Option or Alt to select a file that is not open).

To delete a hyperlink target, choose it in the Hyperlink Destination Options dialog box, and then click Delete. (Click Delete All to delete all targets defined in the document.)

To delete a hypertext source, select it in the Hyperlinks panel and then choose Delete Hyperlink from the flyout menu or click the Delete Selected Hyperlinks iconic button at the bottom of the panel.

When you export your InDesign files to PDF files (choose File⇨Export, or press ⌘+E or Ctrl+E, and choose Adobe PDF from the Format pop-up menu), be sure to select the Hyperlinks option in the Include section of the General pane in the Export PDF dialog box. If you export to the XHTML format to create a Web page from your InDesign document (File⇨Cross-Media Export⇨ XHTML/Dreamweaver), the hyperlinks are included automatically. (And note that you don't need to use Adobe's Dreamweaver Web editing software to work on these exported Web pages; any HTML editor or HTML-capable text editor will do.)

Chapter 23

Publishing Books

• •

• •

Not only is InDesign useful for short documents like ads and newsletters, but it also can comfortably handle longer, multi-chapter documents such as books and manuals. The most common and easiest way to build longer documents, especially those created by more than one author or contributor, is to create multiple InDesign documents and then assemble them into a larger book.

InDesign's book feature lets you

✔ See who is working on each chapter and when.

✔ Update styles and swatches across documents for consistency.

✔ Update page numbers across multiple documents.

✔ Create a unified table of contents and a unified index for multiple documents, using the techniques covered in Chapter 21.

✔ Easily print or create a PDF file from all the chapters of a book.

Book Basics

In InDesign, a *book* is a specific type of file that you create to track chapters or multiple documents that make up the book. Using InDesign's book panels, you can add, open and edit, rearrange, and print chapters of the book. The book palette is nice for workgroups because multiple users can open the same book and access different chapters; it also works well if you are a single user working on a multi-chapter book.

Creating a new book

To create a new book, choose File⇨New⇨Book. The New Book dialog box lets you specify a location for the book and give it a name. Click Save to create and open the book.

Opening and closing a book

Open an existing book by using the File⇨Open command (⌘+O or Ctrl+O). Each book will appear in its own panel. (If several books are open, the panels will be contained in a free-floating panel group.) When viewing folder and disk contents via the Mac's Finder or Windows's Explorer, you can also double-click a book's icon or filename to open it.

To close a book's panel, and any book documents that are in it, simply click its close box.

Adding chapters to books

A new book panel is empty — you need to add chapter documents to fill it up. To do this, click the Add Document iconic button — the + icon on the bottom-right of the book's panel (see Figure 23-1) — or use the Add Document option in the book panel's flyout menu. Use the Add Chapter dialog box to locate and select the first chapter you want to add. Click the Add button to make this the first chapter in the book. Repeat this process to add to the book all the chapters you have ready (you can also add more later).

Chapters are listed in the book panel in the order in which you add them. You may want to rearrange them to match the actual order of the book project — especially if you are numbering the book automatically from start to finish, since InDesign will number them based on their order in the book panel. To rearrange the relative position of chapters, just click and drag chapter names up or down within the panel to put them in the desired order.

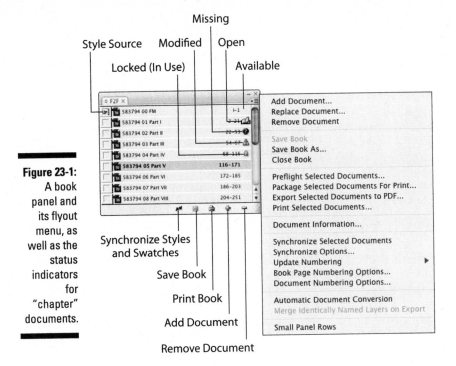

Missing

Style Source   Modified   Open

Locked (In Use)   Available

Add Document...
Replace Document...
Remove Document

Save Book
Save Book As...
Close Book

Preflight Selected Documents...
Package Selected Documents For Print...
Export Selected Documents to PDF...
Print Selected Documents...

Document Information...

Synchronize Selected Documents
Synchronize Options...
Update Numbering
Book Page Numbering Options...
Document Numbering Options...

Automatic Document Conversion
Merge Identically Named Layers on Export

Small Panel Rows

Synchronize Styles
and Swatches

Save Book

Print Book

Add Document

Remove Document

Figure 23-1:
A book
panel and
its flyout
menu, as
well as the
status
indicators
for
"chapter"
documents.

Working on Chapters

To work on a chapter in a book, first open the book and then double-click the
chapter name in the book's panel. The chapter opens in InDesign just like any
other InDesign document. For a chapter to be opened, it must be marked as
Available, as explained in the next section. When you finish editing a chapter,
save and close it as usual.

Replace an existing chapter with another document by selecting the chapter
in the book panel and choosing Replace Document from the flyout menu.
Navigate to a new document, select it, and click the Open button. InDesign
will replace the selected chapter with the new document.

Delete chapters from a book by choosing Remove Document from the flyout
menu or by clicking the Remove Document iconic button (the – icon) at the
bottom of the panel.

InDesign offers three other menu options in the flyout menu that come in
handy for managing a book: You can save books by choosing Save Book, save
to a new name by choosing Save Book As, and close the book by choosing
Close Book (any changes to the book are not saved, although a warning box
gives you the chance to save any unsaved changes).

Finding out about chapter status

When you use the book panel in a workgroup, it provides helpful status reports about each chapter. (Figure 23-1 shows the icons used to indicate a chapter's status.) The statuses are

- ✔ **Available:** The chapter can be opened, edited, or printed. Only one user at a time can open a chapter.

- ✔ **Open:** You have the chapter open and can edit it or print it. Nobody else can open the chapter at this time.

- ✔ **In Use:** Another user has the chapter open. In this case, you cannot edit or open the chapter.

- ✔ **Modified:** The chapter has been changed since the last time you opened the book panel. Simply click the chapter name to update it.

- ✔ **Missing:** The chapter's file has been moved since it was added to the book. Double-click the chapter name to open the Find File dialog box and locate it.

The Document Information menu option in the book panel's flyout menu provides useful information. When you select a chapter and choose this option, you can see the file's modification date, location, and page range, and you can replace the chapter with a different document.

Taking advantage of style sources

The first chapter you add to the book is, by default, the style source. You can tell which chapter is the style source by the icon to the left of the chapter name. In most cases, you want the styles, swatches, and so on to remain the same from chapter to chapter. The style source in an InDesign book defines the styles and swatches that are common to all the chapters in the book.

If you decide to make a different chapter the style source, all you need to do is (in the book panel) click in the column to the left of that chapter's filename. This moves the icon indicating the style source to that chapter. But note that indicating a style source is not the end of the story; to ensure formatting consistency, you will need to synchronize all the book's chapters to that source, as explained in the next section.

Synchronizing formatting

When you use the Synchronize feature, InDesign makes sure that the paragraph styles, character styles, table styles, cell styles, object styles, trap presets, TOC styles, master pages, and color swatches in each chapter in the book match those in the style source. This enforces consistency, but also means you have to make sure you choose the correct chapter as the standard, because its settings will override the other chapters' settings.

The book panel includes a Synchronize iconic button, as well as a Synchronize Selected Documents or Synchronize Book menu item in the flyout menu. Before you synchronize, make sure that you're happy with the styles, master pages, and other settings you've established in the style source and then follow these steps to synchronize:

1. **Be sure that all chapters are available for editing.**

2. **Choose the style source by clicking the box to the left of the source chapter so that the style-source icon appears.**

3. **Choose Synchronize Options from the book panel's flyout menu, which opens a dialog box.**

   Make sure that every type of item you want to synchronize — Object Styles, TOC Style, Character Styles, Paragraph Styles, Table Styles, Cell Styles, Master Pages, Numbered Lists, Text Variables, Trap Presets, and Swatches — is checked.

   (InDesign CS3 adds the ability to synchronize master pages across book chapters, as well as the new table styles, cell styles, numbered lists, and text variables.)

4. **Select the chapters you want to synchronize and either click the Synchronize button or choose Synchronize Selected Documents from the flyout menu.**

   If no chapters are selected, InDesign assumes you want to synchronize *all* chapters; the menu option Synchronize Book will appear in the flyout menu rather than Synchronize Selected Documents in that case.

5. **Compare the styles (character, paragraph, object, table, cell, and TOC), swatches (color, tint, and gradient), text variables, numbered lists, master pages, and trap presets, in the style source to those in each chapter.**

   If anything is different, the information in each chapter will be updated to match the style source. If someone changed the typeface in a style sheet in a chapter, it will revert to the typeface specified in the style source. If anything is missing from a chapter — for example, if you just added a swatch to the style source but not to other chapters — that information is added to each chapter. If a chapter uses its own style or swatch not defined in the source style, that unique style or swatch is *not* changed or removed — these local additions are retained.

By using the synchronize feature, you give each chapter the same basic set of styles and swatches as the style source, although you can still add more of these specifications to individual chapters. Keep in mind that synchronizing doesn't repair the formatting fiascos that can happen when multiple users work on the same book. Be sure everyone who needs to know the standards for the design has access, ahead of time, to that information.

Printing Chapters and Books

Using the book panel, you can print any chapters with the status of Available or Open. Here's how:

1. **To print the entire book, make sure no chapters are selected.**

   To print a contiguous range of chapters, Shift+click the first and last chapters that you want to print. To print noncontiguous chapters, ⌘+click or Ctrl+click the chapters to select them.

2. **Click the Print Book iconic button or choose Print Book or Print Selected Documents in the book panel's flyout menu (the option will depend on whether chapters are selected in the book panel).**

   The standard InDesign Print dialog box opens. Note that the option to choose all pages or a range of pages is grayed out — you must print all chapters in the selected chapters.

3. **Make any adjustments in the Print dialog box.**

4. **Click Print to print the chapters.**

You can also output a book to PDF by using the Export Book to PDF or Export Selected Documents to PDF menu items in the flyout menu. These menu items work like their equivalent Print versions.

Working with Sections in Chapters

Section-based page numbering is fairly common in book-length documents because it lets you, for example, restart page numbering in each new section, such as 4.1, 4.2, and so on. Creating a section start is also the only way to start a document on a left-facing page. InDesign gives you two choices for numbering book pages: You can let the book panel number pages consecutively from one chapter to the next, or you can add sections of page numbers, which carry through the book until you start a new section.

Numbering pages consecutively

If your book chapters don't have sections, use consecutive page numbering, in which the first page number of a chapter follows the last page number of the previous chapter (for example, one chapter ends on page 224, and the next chapter starts on page 225).

Consecutive page numbering is applied by default in InDesign. If for some reason a document resets its numbering, go to that document, open the Section dialog box (choose Numbering & Section Options in the Pages panel's flyout menu), and select Automatic Page Numbering.

Consecutive page numbering works as follows:

- Whenever you add a chapter that contains no sections, or that has section numbering set to Automatic Page Numbering, InDesign numbers pages consecutively throughout the book.

- As you add and delete pages from chapters, InDesign updates all the page numbers in the chapters that follow.

- You can force InDesign to renumber all the pages by choosing Repaginate from the book panel's flyout menu — this is handy if you changed section options in some chapters and want the book to see those changes.

Numbering pages with sections

When chapters you add to books already contain sections of page numbers (implemented through the Section dialog box, which you access via the Numbering & Section Options menu option in the Pages panel's flyout menu), section page numbering overrides the book's consecutive page numbering. The section page numbering carries through chapters of the book until InDesign encounters a new section start. So if one chapter ends on page *iv,* the next chapter starts on page *v* unless you start a new section for that chapter.

For more in-depth information about section numbering, see Chapter 4.

Setting chapter numbers

You can also see and modify any chapter's page numbering settings by selecting the chapter in the book panel, then choosing Document Numbering Options from the flyout menu. Figure 23-2 shows the dialog box. The top half of the dialog box is the same as the Pages panel's Section dialog box, whereas the bottom half — the Document Chapter Numbering area — lets you control the chapter numbering style and the chapter number itself.

The Document Chapter Numbering controls in the Document Numbering Options dialog box are new to InDesign CS3. You can force a chapter to have a specific number by selecting the Chapter Number option, have the chapter use the same chapter number as the previous document (such as when you break a chapter into two documents), and have InDesign automatically number the current document by incrementing from the previous document's chapter number.

The chapter number defined here — whether manually overridden or automatically adjusted — is what is used by the Chapter Number text variable, explained in Chapter 22.

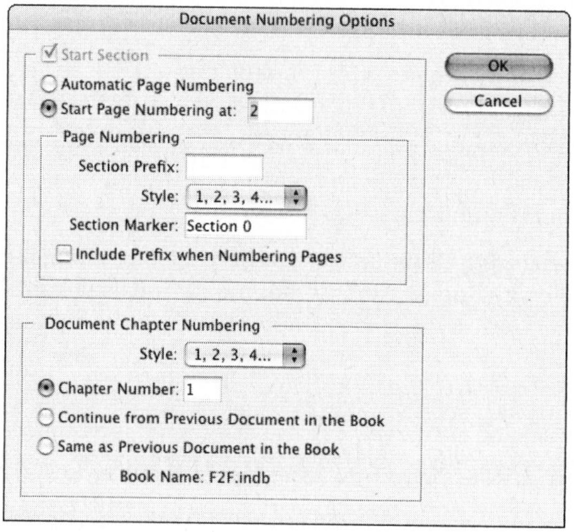

Figure 23-2:
The
Document
Numbering
Options
dialog box.

Part VII
Printing and Output Essentials

The 5th Wave   By Rich Tennant

"I've used several spreadsheet programs, but this is the best one for designing quilt patterns."

In this part . . .

Finally, your layout is done. It's beautiful, it's well-written, and you're eager to share it with your readers. This part shows you how to take the final step to print, create a PDF version of your layout, or even export to the Web's HTML format so you can distribute it to the world at large. InDesign gives you a lot of control over output, so you can optimize the results based on what you are printing it to, such as ensuring color fidelity and the best possible image resolution. Then you can start the whole creation, refinement, and output process over again with your next layout!

Chapter 24

Setting Up for Output

- -

- -

Y ou've finished your document and you want to share it with the whole world, or at least your audience. So you reach for your mouse and choose File⇨Print or quickly press ⌘+P or Ctrl+P so you can print.

Stop. Cancel. If this is your first print job with InDesign, you need to make sure that you've properly set up your printer to get the results you need. The process for doing so varies based on your operating system, and you can find instructions at the author's Web site at www.InDesignCentral.com.

You also should do a visual proof of your layout before you print. It's amazing what you don't notice when you're focused on specific elements as you lay out a page. Change your view setting so the entire page or spread fits in the window (choose View⇨Fit Page in Window or View⇨Fit Spread in Window, as desired) and then review your pages.

That visual check is a critical step before printing, but you should also use InDesign's tool to examine your document and, if you are printing in booklet form, you should use InDesign's tool to arrange pages in proper printing order.

Checking Your Document before Printing

InDesign has a preprinting checkup capability called preflighting. The *pre-flighting* capability examines your document for any issues of concern and gives you a report on what might need to be fixed.

Giving InDesign a preflighting target

Before you run the Preflight tool, you may want to set up your printer output so the tool accurately checks your document's setup in anticipation of, for example, whether you plan to output color separations or spot colors. To do this, choose File⇨Print Presets⇨Define to open the Print Preset dialog box, and then click New. The New Print Preset dialog box appears, giving you the same options as the Print dialog box (covered in Chapter 25). Click OK when you are finished with your preset, then click OK again to close the Print Presets dialog box and return to your layout. (You can also save settings in the Print dialog box by clicking Save Preset before printing.)

But don't confuse InDesign's print setup with the operating system's printer setup. InDesign's Print dialog box contains a button called Printer (on the Mac) or Setup (in Windows) that lets you change print settings for all applications — it's essentially a shortcut to the operating-system controls described earlier in this section. You should change these operating-system settings only for output controls that InDesign's Print dialog box does not provide.

You may wonder why you need a preflighting capability to check for things such as missing fonts and images: After all, InDesign lists any missing fonts and graphics when you open a document. The answer is that sometimes fonts and graphics files are moved *after* you open a file, in which case you won't get the alerts from InDesign. This is more likely to happen if you work with files and fonts on a network drive, rather than with local fonts and graphics. Preflighting also checks for other problematic issues, such as the use of RGB files and TrueType fonts.

If you're working with the InDesign book feature (see Chapter 23), you can preflight the book's chapters from an open book's panel by using the Preflight Book option in its flyout menu. (If one or more documents in the book are selected in the panel, the menu option changes to Preflight Selected Documents.) The options are the same as for preflighting individual documents.

Using InDesign's preflighting capability is easy: Choose File⇨Preflight or press Shift+Option+⌘+F or Ctrl+Alt+Shift+F. In a few seconds, a dialog box appears that shows the status of your document. Here's what the six panes in the Preflight dialog box do:

✔ **The Summary pane** (shown in Figure 24-1) shows you a summary of alerts. If your document has layers, you can select or deselect the Show Data for Hidden Document Layers option. If selected, layers that won't print are analyzed for font, image, and other issues. Select this option only if the person receiving your document plans on printing hidden layers. For example, in a French-and-English document, you may have hidden the French layer for proofing but still want it checked because the service bureau is instructed to print the document twice — once with the English layer on and the French layer off, and once with the English layer off and the French layer on.

✔ **The Fonts pane** (shown in Figure 24-2) shows the type of each font (Type 1 PostScript, OpenType, or TrueType) so you can spot any TrueType fonts before they go to your service bureau. (TrueType fonts usually don't print easily on imagesetters, so use a program like FontLab FontStudio or TransType to translate them to PostScript instead.) It will also show if any fonts are missing from your system. You can search for missing fonts, as well as replaced unwanted TrueType fonts, by clicking Find Font.

✔ **The Links and Images pane** shows whether any graphics files are missing or if the original image has been modified since you placed it in your layout. You can click Update to correct any such bad links one at a time, or Repair All to have InDesign prompt you in turn for each missing or modified file. The pane also shows whether a color profile is embedded in your graphics in case files that should have them don't or in case a file that should not have an embedded profile does. (See Chapter 25 for all the goods on color profiles.) It also alerts you if you use RGB images. Although such images will print and color-separate, InDesign provides the warning because it's usually better to convert RGB images to CMYK in an image editor or illustration program so you can control the final appearance, rather than rely on InDesign or the output device to do the translation.

✔ **The Colors and Inks pane** shows the color of the inks that will be used in the output. (If you are printing color separations, these correspond to the color plates that will eventually be used to print the document on a printing press.) You can't modify anything here — it's simply for informational purposes — but it's a handy way to ensure that you aren't accidentally using a spot color that will print to a separate color plate when you meant to print it as a process color using the standard CMYK plates.

✔ **The Print Settings pane** shows how the document is configured to print in the Print dialog box. This is why it's key to configure the output settings, as described earlier, before preflighting your document.

✔ **The External Plug-ins pane** shows any plug-in programs that are required in order to output the file. Amazingly, some third-party plug-ins make changes to the InDesign document that require the same plug-in to be installed at each computer that opens the file. This dialog box alerts you if you have such a dependency.

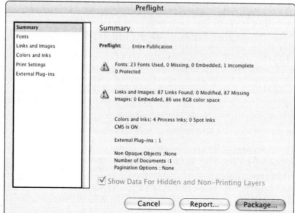

Figure 24-1:
The
Summary
pane of the
Preflight
dialog box.

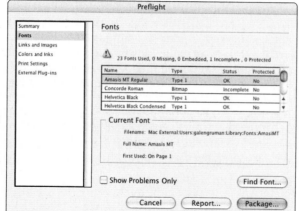

Figure 24-2:
The Fonts
pane of the
Preflight
dialog box.

You can limit the status list in most panes to display only problems by selecting the Show Problems Only option.

By clicking Report, you can generate a text file containing the information from the Preflight dialog box's panes, which you can give to your service bureau to check its settings and files against.

You can also click Package to gather all related fonts and files into one folder for delivery to a service bureau or other outside printing agency. Click Cancel to exit the Preflight dialog box and go back to your document.

Setting Up Booklets

One of the trickiest types of documents to print is a folded booklet: You can't simply print the pages in sequence and have them end up on the right location on the final sheets of paper — when you fold them, you'll find the page order is rearranged due to the folding, especially in two-sided documents.

The tried-and-true approach is to use a booklet template that essentially provides a map of where pages should be so that when they are printed and folded, they end up in the right place — and then arrange your pages in that order via the Pages panel. Figure 24-3 shows the natural order (1-8) that you typically think a booklet has, as well as the actual page order (8,1; 2,7; 6,3; and 4,5) in which it must be printed to appear as a sequence of 1 through 8.

There is an easier way: The Print Booklet dialog box (File⇨Print Booklet). Here, you arrange your pages in the Pages panel in sequential order (1-8, in this case) and let the InDesign software figure out how to rearrange them for printing. Much easier! Figure 24-4 shows the Print Booklet dialog box's Setup pane.

The Print Booklet dialog box (and File menu option) replaces the InBooklet SE dialog box (and File menu option) from previous versions of InDesign. The capabilities are practically identical, although the user interface has changed. (The only real functional difference is that InBooklet SE let you specify precisely what crop marks and related options to show, whereas Print Booklet relies on InDesign's Print dialog box to do so.) InBooklet SE was a trial version of the more capable InBooklet plug-in, but the company that made this plug-in was bought by Adobe's archrival Quark, which promptly ended plug-in support for InDesign. Adobe thus created its own Print Booklet feature to plug the gap.

Figure 24-3:
Left: the logical order of pages for a folded booklet. Right: the order pages must be moved to so they print in the right sequence to be folded.

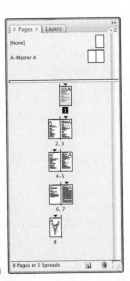
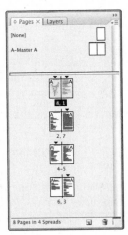

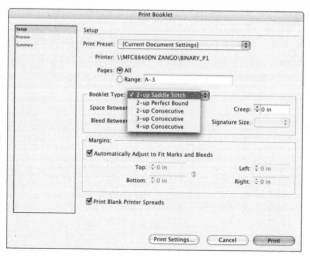

Here are the key controls:

✔ **Booklet Type:** This pop-up menu is the key control. Here, you choose the type of booklet, which tells InDesign how to arrange the pages when printing so they are in the right sequence after folding. Your options are

- **2-up Saddle Stitch:** a folded sheet that contains two pages on each side, with the staples in the centerfold, between the pages. This is used in newsletters, smaller magazines, and many office documents.

- **2-up Perfect Bound:** a folded sheet that contains two pages on each side, where the pages are stacked and folded, then cut and held together with a glued backing or spine-based binding. This is typically used in books, larger magazines, and catalogs (because the square binding holds more pages than saddle-stitching does).

- **2-up Consecutive:** a sheet that contains two pages on one side, with each page then cut and bound. This is essentially normal printing except that it uses a two-page sheet to print two pages at a time rather than a separate sheet for each page.

- **3-up Consecutive:** like 2-up Consecutive, except there are three pages on a sheet.

- **4-up Consecutive:** like 2-up Consecutive, except there are four pages on a sheet.

✔ **Space Between Pages** (not available for 2-up Saddle Stitch) and **Bleed Between Pages** (available for 2-up Perfect Bound only): These options let you adjust the relative spacing among pages and objects, typically to provide additional white space around the folds.

✔ **Creep** (not available for the Consecutive options): This option shifts pages' contents away from the spine in increasing amounts as pages fall from the center of the booklet to the outside of the booklet. Because outside pages have to fold over many inside pages, their content can end up obscured in the inside margins because their gutter is eaten up by folding over those other pages. The Creep option corrects this problem.

✔ **Signature Size** (available only for 2-up Perfect Bound): This option specifies how many pages are printed on each side of a sheet: 4, 8, 16, or 32.

✔ **Automatically Adjust to Fit Marks and Bleeds:** This option ensures that crop marks, bleeds, and other content that appears outside the page boundary are properly handled for the chosen booklet type. If not checked, you can manually adjust these settings using the Top, Bottom, Left, and Right fields.

When using these features, consult with your professional printer or service bureau for the appropriate settings. If you are printing the documents yourself, do a test run, then fold, cut, and/or staple the sample document to make sure it works as expected before printing out lots of copies. The Preview pane, shown in Figure 24-5, shows the results of your choices, but doing a dry run is always the safest option.

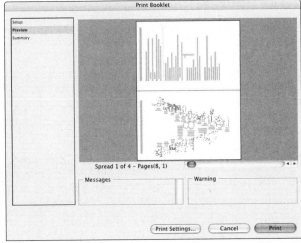

Figure 24-5:
The Preview pane of the Print Booklet dialog box.

When you're happy with your settings, choose Print to get the standard Print dialog box (covered in Chapter 25). You can also choose Print Settings to set up printer-specific controls (also covered in Chapter 25).

Chapter 25

Printing and Other Output Techniques

*P*rinting is more complex than just choosing File➪Print. At least, it can be, depending on what you're printing and on what printing device you're using. For example, printing a full-color brochure involves more settings and steps than printing a proof copy to your laser printer or inkjet printer. So as you go through this chapter, keep in mind that many steps aren't relevant every time you print — but understanding the basics of printing ensures that you follow the right steps for each type of project. When you know the steps for printing one document, the process for printing every other document is very easy.

Calibrating Color

If you're producing color documents for printing on a printing press, you may want to use InDesign's built-in color calibration tools. In a sense, you have to, because InDesign's color calibration is always on. But color calibration is something you don't do in a vacuum — you have to do it in your graphics programs as well, so that every piece of software that handles your graphics is working from the same color assumptions.

If you use Adobe Creative Suite 3, you can use a consistent color management system (CMS) in all of the print-oriented CS3 programs, ensuring consistent color. For scanned images, digital camera photos, and the like, you can also tell InDesign the source device so InDesign knows the color assumptions that the device makes and can use that information to adjust the colors during printing accordingly.

Ensuring consistent color

You can set the CMS settings in InDesign by choosing Edit➪Color Settings (there is no keyboard shortcut unless you assign one yourself, as explained in Chapter 3) to get the dialog box shown in Figure 25-1.

Many of Adobe's Creative Suite 3 applications have the same dialog box, although sometimes you access it in different ways:

- **Bridge CS3:** Choose Edit➪Creative Suite Color Settings, or press Shift+⌘+K or Ctrl+Shift+K. This sets the defaults for all CS3 applications, although you can modify individual applications as noted below. Note that if individual applications' color settings differ from the CS3-wide settings, you will see a note to that effect at the top of the affected applications' Color Settings dialog boxes.

- **Acrobat Professional 8:** Choose Acrobat➪Preferences or press ⌘+K on the Mac, or choose Edit➪Preferences or press Ctrl+K in Windows. Then go to the Color Management pane. Note that this pane's appearance differs from the appearance of the Color Settings dialog boxes in the other Creative Suite 3 applications.

- **GoLive 9:** Choose Edit➪Color Settings. (No keyboard shortcut is available.)

- **Illustrator CS3:** Choose Edit➪Color Settings, or press Shift+⌘+K or Ctrl+Shift+K.

- **Photoshop CS3:** Choose Edit➪Color Settings, or press Shift+⌘+K or Ctrl+Shift+K.

Note that there are no CMS controls for the following CS3 applications: Adobe Device Manager, Dreamweaver, and Flash Professional.

When you place a bitmapped image into InDesign, the CMS applies the default settings defined in the Color Settings dialog box (choose Edit➪ Color Settings). If the document has no embedded color profile, a dialog box appears with a list of color profiles, as well as options to apply the default you've set up in InDesign or to apply no profile. (If you choose not to apply a profile, the color won't be adjusted during printing.)

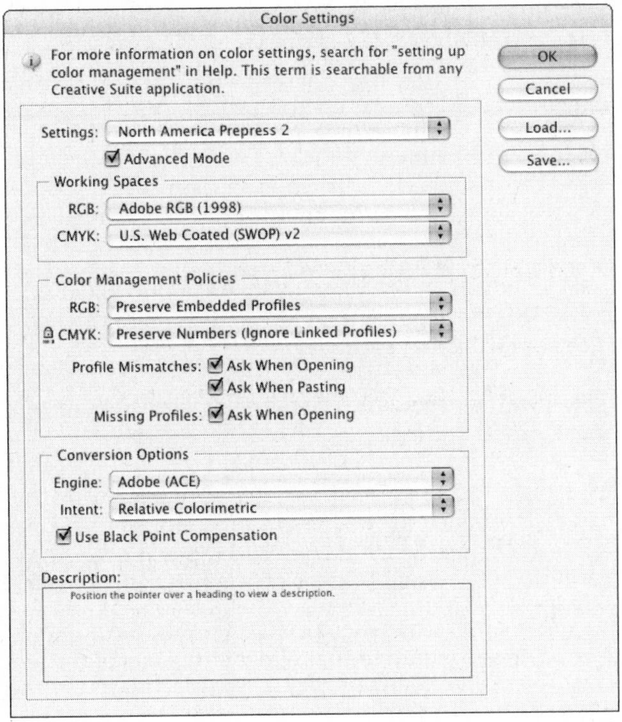

Figure 25-1:
The Color
Settings
dialog box
lets you set
application
color
defaults.

Whether or not there are embedded profiles for the document, you can change the color settings for specific images as follows:

- As you import each file, select Show Import Options in the Place dialog box (choose File⇔Place or press ⌘+D or Ctrl+D) when you place a graphic into InDesign. In the resulting Image Import Options dialog box, go to the Color pane and select the appropriate profile from the Profile menu.

- Any time after you place an image, select it and choose Object⇔Image Color Settings to apply a different profile. (You can also choose Graphics⇔ Image Color Settings from the contextual menu that appears when you Control+click or right-click a graphic in InDesign.)

Saving color management preferences

You can save and use color management settings in other documents. The process is simple: Click Save in the Color Settings dialog box to save the current dialog box's settings to a file. If you want to use the saved color-settings information in another document, open that document and click Load in the Color Settings dialog box, and then browse for and select the color settings file. That's it! This is a handy way to ensure consistency in a workgroup.

Changing document color settings

If you put together a document with specific color settings, but then decide you want to apply a new profile across your pictures or replace a specific profile globally in your document, you can

- ✔ Choose Edit⇨Assign Profiles to replace the color management settings globally.
- ✔ Choose Edit⇨Convert to Profile to change the document's color workspace. It also lets you change the CMS engine, rendering intent, and black-point compensation settings.

Be sure to consult with a production manager or service bureau manager if you change these expert settings.

Note that there's real overlap in these two dialog boxes. Using the Assign Profiles dialog box to replace the document profile does the same job as the Convert to Profile dialog box when it comes to replacing the profiles. The only difference is that the Assign Profiles dialog box can also remove profiles from the document.

Calibrating output

When you're ready to output your document to a printer or other device, set the profile and rendering intent for that destination device in the Color Management pane of the Print dialog box (choose File⇨Print or press ⌘+P or Ctrl+P), which has an Options section with the Color Handling and Printer Profile pop-up menus. Here you select the appropriate option for your output device. (If you don't know, ask an expert.)

Choosing Print Options

When your document is ready to print, go to the Print dialog box (choose File⇨Print or press ⌘+P or Ctrl+P). The Print dialog box has eight panes as well as several options common to all the panes. (I cover just the essential ones here.) Change any options and click Print, and InDesign sends your document to the printer. Figure 25-2 shows the dialog box.

If you're working with the InDesign book feature (see Chapter 23), you can print the book's chapters from an open book's panel by using the Print Book option in its flyout menu. (If one or more documents in the book are selected in the panel, the menu option changes to Print Selected Documents.) The setup options are the same as for printing individual documents.

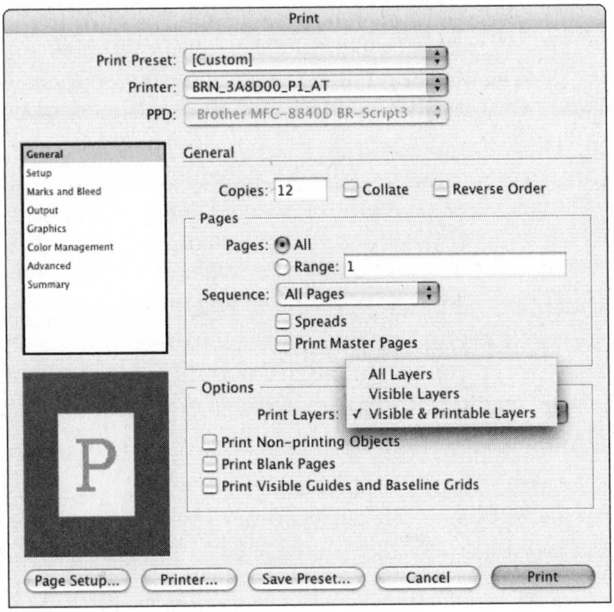

Figure 25-2:
The default view for the Print dialog box.

Common options

The common options available in the dialog box, no matter what pane is selected, are as follows:

✔ **Print Preset pop-up menu:** This pop-up menu lets you choose a previously defined set of printer settings, which makes it easy to switch between, say, a proofing printer and a final output device.

✔ **Printer pop-up menu:** This pop-up menu lets you select the printer to use.

✔ **PPD pop-up menu:** This pop-up menu lets you select PostScript Printer Descriptions, which are files that contain configuration and feature information specific to a brand and model of printer. You usually install these into your operating system by using software that comes from your printer manufacturer. If InDesign finds no compatible PPDs, it uses generic options. If InDesign finds just one compatible PPD, it uses that automatically; otherwise, it lets you select a PPD.

✔ **Save Preset button:** Clicking this button saves any settings that you change in the Print dialog box and lets you choose a name for those saved settings for reuse. If you change the dialog box's settings but don't save these changes as a print preset, InDesign changes the name of the current settings in the Print Preset pop-up menu to [Custom] to remind you the settings are changed and unsaved.

You can also create print presets by choosing File⇨Print Presets⇨Define, or edit an existing preset by choosing File⇨Print Presets⇨*Preset Name*. When you click New or Edit in the resulting dialog box, a dialog box identical to the Print dialog box appears, except that the Print button becomes the OK button.

✔ **Setup button (Windows); Page Setup and Printer buttons (Mac):** These buttons give you access to printer-specific controls. You use these dialog boxes to specify options such as printing to file, paper sources, and printer resolution. Note that if you add a printer, you may need to quit InDesign and restart it for it to see the new printer.

✔ **Cancel button:** Clicking this button closes the Print dialog box without printing. Use this if you've clicked Save Preset but don't want to print, as well when you have any reason not to print.

✔ **Print button:** Clicking this button prints the document based on the current settings.

✔ **Page preview subpane:** This subpane at lower left shows the current settings graphically. The page is indicated by the blue rectangle, and the direction of the large *P* indicates the printing orientation; in Figure 25-2, shown previously, the *P* is unrotated. The figure's subpane shows that the paper itself is the same size as the page (the page is shown in white, and if the paper were larger than the page, you'd see a light gray area around the page indicating the excess paper). This preview changes as you adjust settings in the dialog box.

The General pane

The General pane contains the basic settings for your print job. Most are self-explanatory, but note the following:

✔ When specifying a range of pages in the Pages Range option, you can type nonconsecutive ranges, such as **1–4, 7, 10–13, 15, 18, 20**. If you want to print from a specific page to the end of the document, just type the hyphen after the initial page number, such as **4–**. InDesign figures out what the last page is. Similarly, to start from the first page and end on a specified page, just start with the hyphen, as in **–11**. InDesign lets you type absolute page numbers in the Range field. For example, typing **+6–+12** would print the document's 6th through 12th pages, no matter what their page numbers are.

✔ Selecting the Spreads option prints facing pages on the same sheet of paper, such as putting two letter-size pages on one 11-x-17-inch sheet. This is handy when showing clients proposed designs, but make sure you have a printer that can handle a large paper size or that you scale the output down to fit (through the Setup pane, which I cover in the following section).

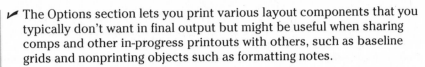

✔ The Options section lets you print various layout components that you typically don't want in final output but might be useful when sharing comps and other in-progress printouts with others, such as baseline grids and nonprinting objects such as formatting notes.

✔ A new control in the Options section is the Print Layers pop-up menu, which gives you additional control over how layers are marked as non-printing print. It used to be that if you marked a layer as nonprinting, you would have to leave the Print dialog box to open the Layers panel to make it printable. Now, you can skip that step and override layers' nonprinting status using this pop-up menu. The default option, Visible & Printable Layers, honors your layers' printing status. Visible Layers prints all visible layers, including those marked as nonprinting. All Layers prints both visible and hidden layers, including those marked as nonprinting. (See Chapter 5 for more on layers.)

The Setup pane

The Setup pane is where you tell InDesign how to work with the paper (or other media, such as film negatives) to which you're printing. The options are straightforward, so I just highlight a few notes and tips:

✔ **Custom paper size:** Choosing some printer models will in turn let you choose a Custom option in the Paper Size pop-up menu, in which case you type the dimensions in the Width and Height fields, as well as position the output through the Offset and Gap fields. These latter two options are usually used when printing to a roll, such as in an imagesetter using photo paper (called *RC paper,* a resin-coated paper that keeps details extremely sharp), so you can make sure there is space between the left edge of the roll and the page boundary (the offset), as well as between pages (the gap). Most printers can't print right to the edge, thus the Offset setting. You also want a gap between pages for crop and registration marks, as well as to have room to physically cut the pages.

✔ **Transverse option:** Don't use the Transverse option, which rotates the output 90 degrees, unless your service bureau or production department tells you to. Otherwise, you might have your pages cut off on the final negatives.

✔ **Tile options:** Use the Tile options to print oversized documents. InDesign breaks the document into separate pages — called *tiles* — that you later can assemble together. To enable tiling, select the Tile check box, and then choose the appropriate option from the adjoining pop-up menu:

- **Manual:** This lets you specify the tiles yourself. To specify a tile, you change the origin point on the document ruler, and the new origin point becomes the upper-left corner of the current tile. (To change the origin point, just drag the upper-left corner of the rulers to a new position in your document.) To print multiple tiles this way, you need to adjust the origin point and print, adjust the origin point to the next location and print, and so on, until you're done.

- **Auto:** This lets InDesign figure out where to divide the pages into tiles. You can change the default amount of overlap between tiles of 1.5 inches by using the Overlap field. The overlap lets you easily align tiles by having enough overlap for you to see where each should be placed relative to the others.

- **Auto Justified:** This is similar to Auto except that it makes each tile the same size, adjusting the overlap if needed to do that. (The Auto option, by contrast, simply starts at the origin point and then does as much of the page as will fit in the tile, which means the last tile may be a different width than the others.) You can see the difference between the two by watching how the page preview window at left changes as you select each option.

The Marks and Bleed pane

The Bleed and Slug area of the Marks and Bleed pane controls how materials print past the page boundary. A bleed is used when you want a picture, color, or text to go right to the edge of the paper. Because there is slight variation on positioning when you print because the paper moves mechanically through rollers and might move slightly during transit, publishers have any to-the-edge materials actually print beyond the edge, so there are never any gaps. It's essentially a safety margin. A normal bleed margin would be 0p9 (⅛ inch), although you can make it larger if you want.

A *slug* is an area beyond the bleed area in which you want printer's marks to appear. The reader never sees this, but the workers at the commercial printer do, and it helps them make sure they have the right pages, colors, and so on. Like the bleed, the slug area is trimmed off when the pages are bound into a magazine, newspaper, or whatever. (The word *slug* is an old newspaper term for this identifying information, based on the lead slug once used for this purpose on old printing presses.) The purpose of the slug is to ensure there is enough room for all the printer's marks to appear between the bleed area and the edges of the page. Otherwise, InDesign will do the best it can.

It's best to define your bleed and slug areas in your document itself when you create the document in the New Document dialog box (choose File⇨New⇨ Document or press ⌘+N or Ctrl+N), as covered in Chapter 3. You can also use the Document Setup dialog box (choose File⇨Document Setup or press Option+⌘+P or Ctrl+Alt+P). The two dialog boxes have the same options; if they don't show the Bleed and Slug section, click More Options to see it.

But if you didn't define your bleeds previously, you can do so in the Print dialog box's Marks and Bleed pane. You can also override those New Document or Document Setup document settings here. To use the document settings, select the Use Document Bleed Settings option. Otherwise, type in a bleed area by using the Top, Bottom, Left, and Right fields. If you want the four fields to be the same, click the broken-chain iconic button to the right of the Top field; it becomes a solid chain, indicating that all four fields will have the same value if any is modified. Any bleed area is indicated in red in the preview pane at the bottom left.

If you want to set the slug area, select the Include Slug Area option. InDesign then reserves any slug area defined in the New Document or Document Setup dialog box. You can't set up the slug area in the Print dialog box.

The Output pane

The next pane is the Output pane, which controls the processing of colors and inks on imagesetters, platesetters, and commercial printing equipment. For proof printing, such as to a laser printer or an inkjet printer, the only option that you need to worry about is on the Color pop-up menu, which controls whether the colors print as color or as grayscale.

The options in the Output pane are for experts and should be specified in coordination with your service bureau and commercial printer — these options can really mess up your printing if set incorrectly.

One area that you should set is in the Ink Manager dialog box. Accessed by clicking Ink Manager, the Ink Manager dialog box, shown in Figure 25-3, gives you finer controls over how color negatives output. If any colors should have been converted to process color but weren't, you have three choices:

✔ **Click the spot color iconic button.** You can override the spot color in the Ink Manager dialog box by clicking this button (a circle icon) to the left of the color's name. That converts it to a process color. (Clicking the process color button, a four-color box icon, converts a color back to a spot color.) This is the way to go for a quick fix.

✔ **Make the spot color a process color instead.** Do this by closing the Ink Manager and Print dialog boxes, and editing the color that was incorrectly set as a spot color in the Swatches panel (choose Window⇨ Swatches or press F5) as I cover in Chapter 7. This ensures that the color is permanently changed to a process color for future print jobs.

✔ **Convert all spot colors to CMYK process equivalents.** Do this by selecting the All Spots to Process option. This is the easiest method to make sure you don't accidentally print spot-color plates for a CMYK-only document.

The other Ink Manager options are for experts and should be changed only in consultation with your service bureau, production department, and/or commercial printer.

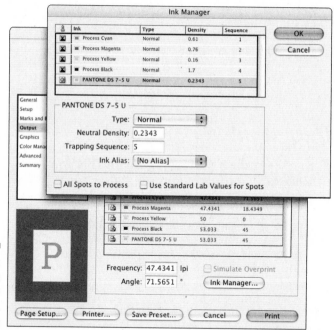

Figure 25-3:
The Ink Manager dialog box.

The Graphics pane

By using the Graphics pane, you control how graphics are printed and how fonts are downloaded. The options here are meant for professional printing, such as to imagesetters, in situations where you're working with a service bureau or in-house printing department. This is also an expert area, so change these settings only after consulting with an experienced pro.

The Color Management pane

The Color Management pane is where you manage color output (apply color calibration). Most options should be changed only in consultation with your service bureau or production department.

One option you should be able to change on your own is Printer Profile. Use this pop-up menu to select the device to which the document will ultimately be printed. This is by default the same as the profile selected in the Edit Color Settings dialog box, which I cover earlier in this chapter, in the section "Calibrating Color."

The Advanced pane

The options in the Advanced pane let you control graphics file substitutions in an Open Prepress Interface (OPI) workflow and also set transparency flattening, which controls how transparent and semitransparent objects are handled during output. Again, these are expert options you should change only in consultation with your service bureau or production department.

The Summary pane

The final Print dialog box pane is the Summary pane. It simply lists your settings all in one place for easy review. The only option — Save Summary — saves the settings to a file so you can include it with your files when delivering them to a service bureau or for distribution to other staff members so they know the preferred settings.

Creating a Document Package

Have you ever given a page-layout document to a service bureau only to be called several hours later because some of the files necessary to output your document are missing? If so, you'll love the Package feature in InDesign.

This command, which you access by choosing File⇨Package or pressing Option+Shift+⌘+P or Ctrl+Alt+Shift+P, copies into a folder all the font, color-output, and graphics files necessary to output your document. It also generates a report that contains all the information about your document that a service bureau is ever likely to need, including the document's fonts, dimensions, and trapping information. You can also create an instructions file that has your contact information and any particulars you want to say about the document.

When you run the Package command, InDesign preflights your document automatically and gives you the option of viewing any problems it encounters. If you elect to view that information, the Preflight dialog box appears. You can continue to package your document from that dialog box by clicking Package after you assure yourself that none of the problems will affect the document's output. If it finds no problems during the automatic preflighting, InDesign will not display the Preflight dialog box.

Before you can actually package the document, InDesign asks you to save the current document, and then fill in the Printing Instructions form. You can change the default filename from Instructions.txt to something more suitable, such as the name of your print job. Often, you'll leave the printing instructions blank — use the form only if you have *special* instructions.

If you *don't* want to create an instructions form, don't click Cancel — that cancels the entire package operation. Just click Continue, leaving the form blank. Similarly, you must click Save at the request to save the document; clicking Cancel stops the package operation as well.

The next step is to create the package folder. You do this in the dialog box that follows the Printing Instructions form, which on the Mac is called Create Package Folder and in Windows is called Package Publication. Figure 25-4 shows the Mac version, which except for the name at the top is the same as the Windows version.

Figure 25-4:
The Create Package Folder dialog box for Mac is called the Package Publication dialog box in Windows.

In the dialog box, you can select what is copied: the fonts, color-output profiles, and *linked graphics* (graphics pasted into an InDesign document rather than imported are automatically included). You can also tell InDesign to update the graphics links for those that were modified or moved; if this Update Graphic Links in Package option isn't selected, any missing or modified graphics files won't be copied with the document.

You can tell InDesign to include fonts and links from hidden layers (which you would do only if you want the service bureau to print those hidden layers or if you were giving the document's files to a colleague to do further work).

You also can specify whether the document should use only the hyphenation exceptions defined within it. This often makes sense because it ensures that the printer's hyphenation dictionary — which may differ from yours — doesn't cause text to flow differently.

Finally, you can choose to view the report after the package is created — on the Mac, InDesign launches TextEdit and displays the report file, and on Windows it launches Notepad and displays the report file.

Click Save (on the Mac) or Package (in Windows) when everything is ready to go. Your document is placed in the folder you specify, as is the instructions file (the report). Inside that folder, InDesign will also create a folder called Fonts that includes the fonts, a folder called Links that has the graphics files, and a folder called Output Profiles that has the color output profiles.

I strongly recommend using the Package feature. It ensures that your service bureau has all the necessary files and information to output your document correctly.

Exporting PDF Files

Sometimes you want to create a PDF file for distribution on the Web, on a CD, on a corporate intranet, or even by e-mail. PDF creation is a really easy task in InDesign. First choose File⇨Export or press ⌘+E or Ctrl+E. The Export dialog box appears, which, like any standard Save dialog box, lets you name the file and determine what drive and folder the file is to be saved in. The key control in the Export dialog box is the Formats pop-up menu, where you choose the format (in this case, Adobe PDF). Then click Save.

If you're working with the InDesign book feature (see Chapter 23), you can export the book's chapters to PDF files from an open book's panel by using the Export Book to PDF option in its flyout menu. (If one or more documents in the book are selected in the panel, the menu option changes to Export Selected Documents to PDF.) The setup options are the same as for exporting individual documents.

After you select Adobe PDF in the Export dialog box's Formats pop-up menu and give the file a name and location in the File Name and Save in areas, click Save to get the Export Adobe PDF dialog box shown in Figure 25-5. The dialog box has six panes; the General pane is displayed when you open the dialog box. There are several options that are accessible from all six panes.

If you know how to use Acrobat Professional, you know how to set up your PDF export. If not, it's best to consult with a local expert because PDF export options are as complex and job-specific as the print options I cover earlier.

Common options

There are some basic options available in all the panes that you should feel comfortable setting on your own:

- ✔ **Adobe PDF Preset pop-up menu:** This pop-up menu lets you select from both predefined sets of PDF-export settings (similar to the printer presets covered earlier in this chapter), as well as any presets you or someone else may have created.

- ✔ **Compatibility pop-up menu:** This pop-up menu lets you choose which PDF file version to save the file as. Your options are Acrobat 4 (PDF 1.3), Acrobat 5 (PDF 1.4), Acrobat 6 (PDF 1.5), Acrobat 7 (PDF 1.6), and Acrobat 8 (PDF 1.7). Choosing Acrobat 4 (PDF 1.3) is the best option for documents that you want to distribute on CD or over the Web because it ensures the broadest number of people will be able to view the file. But it also limits the ability to use some features, particularly those that protect the document from unauthorized usage such as copying its contents. Choose a later version only if you're certain that your intended recipients use that version of Acrobat or Acrobat Reader. For example, if your company has standardized on Acrobat 6 and the document will be used only internally, picking the Acrobat 6 (PDF 1.5) option makes sense. Likewise, if you're sending the PDF file to a service bureau, use the version of Acrobat that the service bureau uses because later versions of Acrobat support more features, especially for commercial printing. (PDF formats 1.5 and later, for example, support native transparency.)

- ✔ **Save Preset button:** Click this to save any settings made in the Export Adobe PDF dialog box as a new preset. (You can also define new PDF presets by choosing File⇨PDF Export Presets⇨Define.)

- ✔ **Export button:** Click this to create the PDF file based on the settings that you selected in the various panes.

Using Distiller job options

InDesign also lets you import settings from Acrobat Distiller job-options files, which are similar to InDesign's PDF presets but are created in the Adobe Acrobat Professional software. You can load such job-option files by clicking Load in the Adobe PDF Presets dialog box (choose File⇨PDF Export Presets⇨Define).

You can use the Adobe PDF Presets dialog box to create and edit the job-option files for sharing with Acrobat Distiller (part of Acrobat Professional) and other Creative Suite users; just click Save when you're done. When creating or editing these PDF presets, you get the same options that I describe elsewhere in this section for the Export Adobe PDF dialog box.

The General pane

Use the General pane, shown in Figure 25-5, to determine what is exported. The Pages option gives you the same flexibility as the Print dialog box's Pages option, which I cover in the earlier section "Choosing Print Options." Similarly, the Spread option works like the same-name option in the Print dialog box.

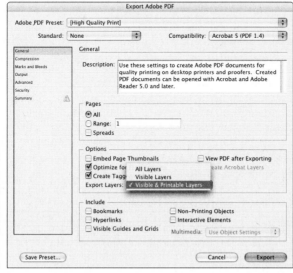

Figure 25-5: The General pane of the Export Adobe PDF dialog box.

In the Options section, you can select the following options:

- ✔ **Embed Page Thumbnails:** Select this option if you're creating a PDF file to be viewed on-screen. Thumbnails help people to more easily navigate your document in the Adobe Reader program. However, if you're sending the PDF files to a service bureau or commercial printer for printing, you don't need to generate the thumbnails.

- ✔ **Optimize for Fast Web View:** Always select this option — this minimizes file size without compromising the output.

- ✔ **Create Tagged PDF:** Select this option to embed XML tag information into the PDF file. This is useful for XML-based workflows and Adobe eBooks. If you don't know what XML or eBooks are, you don't need to select this option.

- ✔ **View PDF after Exporting:** Select this option if you want to see the results of the PDF export as soon as the export is complete. Typically, however, you shouldn't select this option because you likely will have other things you want to do before launching Adobe Reader (or the full Acrobat program, if you own it) to proof your files.

- ✔ **Create Acrobat Layers:** If you selected Acrobat 6 (PDF 1.5) or later in the Compatibility pop-up menu, you can select this option, which outputs any InDesign layers to separate layers in Acrobat. (Acrobat 6 was the first version of Acrobat to support layers.) If you choose a different Compatibility option, Create Acrobat Layers is grayed out.

- ✔ **Export Layers:** This new pop-up menu gives you additional control over how layers marked as nonprinting are exported to the PDF file. It used to be that if you marked a layer as nonprinting, you would have to leave the Export Adobe PDF dialog box to open the Layers panel to make it exportable. Now, you can skip that step and override layers' nonprinting status using this pop-up menu. The default option, Visible & Printable Layers, honors your layers' printing status. Visible Layers exports all visible layers, including those marked as nonprinting. All Layers exports both visible and hidden layers, including those marked as nonprinting. (See Chapter 5 for more on layers.)

In the Include section, you set what elements of the document are included in the PDF file. You can select the following options:

- ✔ **Bookmarks:** This takes InDesign table-of-contents (TOC) information and preserves it as bookmarks in the exported PDF file.

- ✔ **Hyperlinks:** This preserves any hyperlinks added in InDesign. Otherwise, the hyperlinks are converted to standard text in the PDF file. (Chapter 22 explains how to create hyperlinks in InDesign.)

✔ **Visible Guides and Grids:** This includes the on-screen guides and grids in the output version — an option you'd use only when creating PDF files meant to be used as designer examples, not for readers or for prepress.

✔ **Non-Printing Objects:** This includes any objects marked as Nonprinting through the Attributes pane (choose Window➪Attributes).

✔ **Interactive Elements:** This preserves interactive objects such as buttons rather than convert them to static graphics.

✔ **Multimedia:** This pop-up menu lets you control how embedded sound and video are handled. This option is available only if you choose Acrobat 6 (PDF 1.5) or later in the Compatibility pop-up menu. The options are Use Object Settings, Link All, or Embed All. In InDesign, you can embed a sound or movie file, or link to one. This option lets you override the individual settings and make all such objects embedded or linked.

The Compression pane

All the options in this pane compress your document's graphics. For documents you're intending to print professionally, make sure that for the Color, Grayscale, and Monochrome image types, the No Sampling Change option is selected, and that Compression is set to None. You don't want to do anything that affects the resolution or quality of your bitmap images if you're outputting to a high-resolution device.

But it's fine to select the Crop Image Data to Frames option because this discards portions of pictures not visible on-screen, reducing file size and reducing processing time during output. (Imagesetters and other devices usually have to process the entire image, even if only part of it is actually printed.)

You can also select the Compress Text and Line Art option. It compresses vector graphics (both imported and those created in InDesign) as well as text, but does so without affecting output quality.

For the rest, stick with the defaults based on the preset you chose, or check with your production department.

Marks and Bleed pane

The Marks and Bleed pane in the Export Adobe PDF dialog box works just like the Marks and Bleed pane in the Print dialog box, which I cover earlier in this chapter.

The Output pane

The Output pane has two sections — Color and PDF/X — where you control color calibration. Adjust these only if you're creating a PDF file meant to be used by a service bureau to print the final document on paper or to create plates for commercial printing. Ask the people at your service bureau what settings they prefer for this pane's options.

The Advanced pane

The Advanced pane in the Export Adobe PDF dialog box has the same options as the Advanced pane in the Print dialog box, which I cover earlier in this chapter. Like the Output pane, these options are relevant only if you're generating a PDF file that your service bureau or commercial printer will use to create the final printed output from.

Security pane

The Security pane, shown in Figure 25-6, has no relevance to documents intended to be output at a service bureau or commercial printer, so make sure the Require a Password to Open the Document and the Use a Password to Restrict Printing, Editing, and Other Tasks options are not selected in that case.

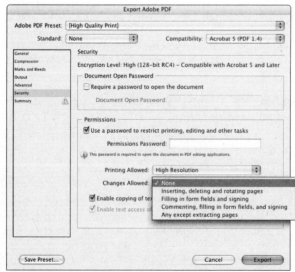

Figure 25-6:
The Security
pane of the
Export
Adobe PDF
dialog box.

These settings are useful if you're publishing the document electronically because they control who can access the document and what they can do with the document once it's open. Here's how these settings work:

- ✔ **Encryption Level:** This section's options depend on the option set in the Compatibility pop-up menu; Acrobat 5 (PDF 1.4) and higher use High (128-Bit RC4) encryption, while earlier versions use 40-bit RC4.

- ✔ **Document Open Password:** In this section of the Security pane, you can require a password to open the exported PDF file by selecting this option and typing a password in the associated text field. If you don't type a password here, you're forced to type one in a dialog box that appears later. To access protected content, recipients must use the Security pane in Acrobat (choose File⇨Document Properties or press ⌘+D or Ctrl+D).

- ✔ **Permissions:** Here, you determine what restrictions to place on the PDF file. Note that the options will vary based on what version of the PDF format you selected in the General pane.

  - • **Use a Password to Restrict Printing, Editing, and Other Tasks:** You can restrict recipients' actions by selecting this option and then specifying permissible actions by using the Printing Allowed and Changes Allowed pop-up menus, as well as selecting from among the options that follow (the number of options displayed varies based on the preset chosen). You can also require a password to allow editing of the file in another application. Your management options include the following:

  - • **Printing Allowed:** You can select None, Low-Resolution (150 dpi), or High Resolution. You would disable printing to ensure that the material can be read only on-screen.

  - • **Changes Allowed:** You can select None; Inserting, Deleting and Rotating Pages; Filling in Form Fields and Signing; Commenting, Filling in Form Fields, and Signing; or Any Except Extracting Pages. (*Signing* means using digital signatures to verify sender and recipient identities.)

  - • **Enable Copying of Text, Images, and Other Content:** If it's okay for recipients to use the PDF file's objects, select this option.

  - • **Enable Text Access of Screen Reader Devices for the Visually Impaired:** If you want the file to be accessible to visually impaired recipients who use text-reader applications, select this option. This option is available only if you are exporting to Acrobat 5 (PDF 1.4) or later.

  - • **Enable Plaintext Metadata:** For documents with *metadata* — authoring information associated with XML documents and Web pages — you can make that metadata visible to Web-based search engines and similar applications by selecting this option. This option is available only if you are exporting to Acrobat 6 (PDF 1.5) or later.

Settings for on-screen usage

If your output is destined for use on a monitor — such as from CD, on the Web, or in a corporate intranet — use these settings when exporting to PDF files:

✔ In the General pane, select the Optimize for Fast Web View option. Also, check Spreads if your facing pages are designed as one visual unit.

✔ In the Compression pane, change the two Image Quality pop-up menus to Low. Also, choose any of the Downsampling or Subsampling menu options in all three image types' sections. The pixels-per-inch (ppi) value should be either 72 (if you intend people just to view the images on-screen) or 300 or 600 (if you expect people to print the documents to a local inkjet or laser printer). Pick the ppi value that best matches most users' printers' capabilities. For the Compression pop-up menus, choose Automatic (JPEG) for the color and grayscale bitmaps, and CCITT Group 4 (the standard method for fax compression) for black-and-white bitmaps. Set Quality to Maximum for color and grayscale bitmaps. Finally, select the Compress Text and Line Art option.

✔ In the Marks and Bleeds pane, make sure no printer's marks are selected.

✔ In the Security pane, select the security features (Document Open Password and Permissions) and the options for which you want to add security. Uncheck the Enable Copying of Text and Graphics option to prevent readers from copying and pasting your content, and select None from the Printing Allowed pop-up menu to prevent printing. The Changes Allowed pop-up menu options control whether readers can add extra pages, add comments to the file, fill in forms, delete pages, or rotate pages. Typically, you'd choose either Filling in Form Fields and Signing (so readers could complete forms) or Commenting, Filling in Forms, and Signing (so readers can complete forms and add their own comments) — both options keep the user from accessing the underlying content of your PDF files.

The Summary pane

The final Export Adobe PDF dialog box pane is the Summary pane, which simply lists your settings all in one place for easy review. The only option — Save Summary — saves the settings to a file so you can include it with your files when delivering them to a service bureau, or for distribution to other staff members so they know the preferred settings.

Exporting to the Web

InDesign CS3 now lets you export your layouts to the XHTML format that Web editors such as Adobe's Dreamweaver and GoLive can open for further work. (Note that you'll usually want to do further work in a Web editor both to take advantage of Web-specific formatting options and to rework the layout to better fit the horizontal "page" size of a Web browser.) With InDesign CS3's newfound ability to export to the XHTML format, not just create an XML version specific to Adobe's GoLive Web editor, as in previous versions, you can more easily create Web pages based on print documents.

XHTML is a version of the well-known Hypertext Markup Language (HTML) format that adds more consistent structure to make it easier to present pages consistently across Web editors and browsers. You probably didn't even know that your Web editor was creating XHTML-formatted Web pages when you saved your pages, but any Web editor worth its salt has been doing that for a few years now.

To export a layout to XHTML format, simply choose File⇨Cross-Media Export⇨XHTML/Dreamweaver. (And despite the name, your files are not limited to use by Adobe's Dreamweaver software.) If you want to export just specific items on a page, select them with one of the selection tools before choosing this menu option.

You'll get the Save As dialog box, where you choose the disk and folder to store the exported Web page, as well as the page's filename. After you click Save, you'll get the XHTML Export Options dialog box, shown in Figure 25-7, in which you specify how InDesign converts the layout to the Web format. Unless you're Web-savvy, ask your Web master what settings to use:

- ✔ In the General pane, you choose whether to export the currently selected objects or the entire document, as well as how to handle bulleted and numbered lists. The default mappings — Map to Unordered Lists for bullets and Map to Ordered Lists for numbers — work for most sites. But you can also have InDesign convert either or both such lists into plain text rather than using the Web's list functions.

- ✔ In the Images pane, you choose how your images are converted to the Web's GIF and JPEG formats, selecting options such as image quality and color palette.

- ✔ In the Advanced pane, you set how text formatting is converted to the Web's version of styles, called *cascading style sheets*, or *CSS*. It's preferable to choose External CSS as the export option, since that choice has the Web pages use a single style file that all Web pages can refer to, ensuring consistency (much like InDesign's styles offer). Note that InDesign does not create a CSS file for you; you or your Web designer must create it in a Web editing program. Also in this pane, you can specify an external JavaScript file to link to — again, something your Web designer or programmer will have created separately.

Click Export when done with your settings.

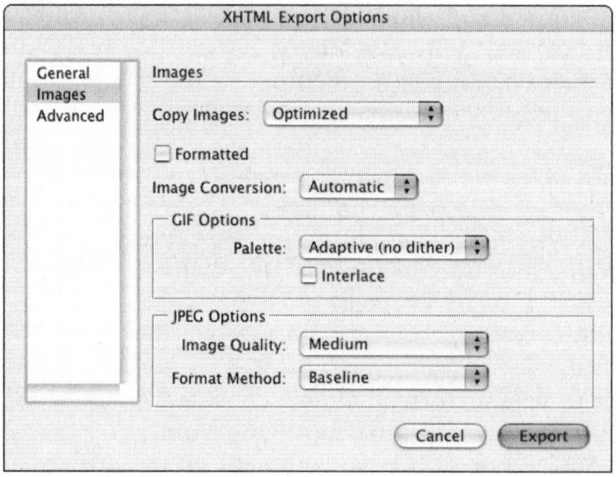

Figure 25-7:
The Images
pane of the
XHTML
Export
Options
dialog box.

XHTML Export Options

General	Images
Images	
Advanced	

Copy Images: Optimized

☐ Formatted

Image Conversion: Automatic

GIF Options
Palette: Adaptive (no dither)
☐ Interlace

JPEG Options
Image Quality: Medium
Format Method: Baseline

Cancel   Export

The export process is simple, so it's easy to forget that converting print layouts to the Web's format is rarely a "point and shoot" activity. Expect your Web designer to do major work on those exported pages in his or her Web editing program, to optimize them for the Web environment. That's no reflection on you or InDesign, just the reality of working in different media.

Part VIII
The Part of Tens

The 5th Wave   By Rich Tennant

"Look-what if we just increase the size of the charts?"

In this part . . .

This part of the book was what inspired David Letterman's Top 10 lists. Well, it could have! Forget about slogging through the details. Here, you get the quick hits on everything from the coolest new features, the best resources to augment your InDesign IQ, and what you need to keep at the top of your mind if you're switching from QuarkXPress or PageMaker. Think of it as popcorn from a book!

Chapter 26

Top Ten New Features in InDesign CS3

A
dmit it — you came here before looking at the rest of the book. I can't blame you — we all love to know what's new. Well, InDesign CS3 has a lot of new stuff. Much of it falls into the category of nice little touches that make something that much easier to use. But there are also a bunch of "hey, let's see what the users can do with this" kind of new thing just to keep everyone's brain sharp. You'll have your favorite new features, of course, but because I'm writing the book, I get to tell you mine!

Interface Changes

If there's one thing I hate, it's a program that changes its user interface on every version, just for the sake of change. That just makes me relearn what I was already good at, without making me more productive. I wasn't exactly thrilled when I heard Adobe was changing the Creative Suite interface again.

Collapsing panels

But one interface change has wormed its way into my heart: the collapsing panels. (Set them by enabling the Auto-Collapse Icon Panels in the Interface pane of the Preferences dialog box; choose InDesign⇨Preferences⇨Interface or press ⌘+K on the Mac, or choose Edit⇨Preferences⇨Interface or press Ctrl+K in Windows.)

The various panels at the side of the monitor remain easy to access with a click of their names, and when you select a different panel, the last one you worked on just slides back to the side of the monitor. As Figure 26-1 shows, that saves clutter and does some work for me. Neat!

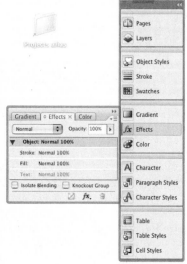

Figure 26-1:
Collapsed panels let you work with just one at a time, without taking all your screen real estate.

Page previews

InDesign CS3 now shows a preview image of your pages in the Pages panel. That makes it easy to figure out what page you want to go to, thanks to the visual reminder of what's on each page. Plus this new feature works inside a panel you're using a lot anyhow, so it's not taking up more screen space, like the Navigator panel does (the previous way to get this visual aid).

You can control whether these page previews display by choosing Panel Options from the panel's flyout menu. In the Panel Options dialog box, select the desired icon size and make sure Show Thumbnails is checked. You can also set separate view settings for master pages.

Faster tool switching

InDesign CS3 introduces a quick new way to switch between the Selection tool and the Direct Selection tool: Just double-click an object.

Working with Layout Elements

Object manipulation is at the heart of what a layout program does, so it's no surprise there are some very cool additions in this area of InDesign.

Master-page import

This may seem like a "Doh! Why didn't they think of that already?!" feature — and it is. But it's still wonderful to have: The ability to import master pages. Before, you had to create a new master page in your document, and then copy the elements from another document using old-fashioned copy-and-paste. That's a lot of work!

A nice touch is that if any of the imported master pages have the same name as your current document's master pages (such as the default name A-Master), a dialog box appears, giving you the choice of replacing the current master pages with the imported ones that use the same name or of renaming the imported master pages, so you keep what you have and add the imported ones. InDesign does the renaming for you. Likewise, InDesign will also alert you if the imported master pages use different dimensions than the current document's pages.

Object-level search

A really painstaking task in any layout is going through it to fix formatting to frames, lines, or other objects once the design standards have changed. Previous versions of InDesign delivered one way to ease that burden — the object styles feature described in Chapter 10 — but even if you use these styles, you will still have local formatting applied to at least some objects that can be a real pain to change throughout a layout.

That's where the Object pane of the Find/Replace dialog box comes in. It lets you replace attributes throughout your document, no matter what they are applied to, using the familiar approach of search and replace. (Figure 26-2 shows that pane.) This is another of those "Well, that seems obvious" features that for some reason never was obvious in the 20-plus-year history of desktop publishing software.

Reusable saved search queries

Bonus points for the new ability to save your searches — of objects, text, or special characters — so you can reuse them over and over!

Figure 26-2:
Search and
replace now
handles
object
attributes.
That'll ease
your
workload!

Lighting effects

No, you're not using Photoshop. It really is InDesign CS3 that lets you apply rich controls over transparency and lighting, so you can now create effects such as embossing and beveled edges *and* control the intensity and direction of shadows and light. As part of these enhancements, you'll find a significantly revised interface for transparency and related controls, not the least of which is the renaming of the Transparency pane to the Effects panel.

And not only are there a bunch of new lighting effects — inner shadow, outer glow, inner glow, bevel and emboss, satin, directional feather, and gradient feather — that you can apply individually or in combination, but InDesign now also lets you apply these lighting effects to your choice of an object's frame, fill, or contents. You could get carried away and create altered-state kinds of layouts, but I know you can control yourself. Figure 26-3 shows some examples.

Multiple file placement

You can now select multiple files — text and/or graphics — by Shift+clicking a range or ⌘+clicking or Ctrl+clicking multiple files one by one in the Place dialog box. Just click once for each file imported, or Shift+⌘+click or

Ctrl+Shift+click to have InDesign place all files on the page in separate frames. The loaded-text icon or loaded-graphics icon will show the number of files to be placed — as well as a mini preview of each file so you know what you're placing at each step!

Plus, you can move through these icons using the left- and right-arrow keys, so you can place these files in any order you want, not just in the order you selected them originally.

Figure 26-3: Examples of InDesign's many new lighting effects. Who needs Photoshop?

Text Controls

The other heart of publishing is text: the typographic and other manipulations of words on the page that make them more than mere words on a page. InDesign has long been super-powerful on the typographic front, so it's cool that new capabilities in the text arena appear in other aspects of text handling — just to keep us from thinking that typography is all there is when it comes to text!

Text variables

With InDesign CS3's new text variables, you can define an unlimited number of text variables that InDesign will happily update across your documents whenever you change them or your layout does. This capability may seem prosaic, boring even. But it's just the opposite.

Don't be surprised to find yourself having InDesign automatically update your page folios with chapter and section information, ensuring that the publication dates for the hundreds of reports you have to manage are always correct, and even that the issue date is correct across all your magazine's pages. That's the power of variable text!

Style groups

To help you find the desired style in documents that have dozens of them, InDesign now lets you create style groups, which create a folder in the various styles panels' style list that you can open and close as desired. I realize that this appeals to the "I love to organize" set — not the majority of free-thinking designers whose style lists are littered with duplicate styles with inconsistent names that meant something last week but not today. I'm not that organized — I've never used a day planner, for example, and my filing system is really a Post-its-and-piles system — but I hate searching for things I use a lot. So style groups seem really cool to me, a way to put the styles I use a lot in one place where I might actually find them! Give them a whirl.

Chapter 27

Top Ten (Or So) Resources for InDesign Users

. . . .

In This Chapter

▶ Discovering useful Web sites

▶ Using Adobe Web resources

▶ Finding books to read

. . . .

*W*hen you're ready to expand your horizons beyond what I can squeeze into the pages of this book, check out this chapter. No matter what type of information you're looking for, you can find it here among this handy list of InDesign resources.

Web Sites

Web sites are a great on-going resource because they let you keep up with news, techniques, and product versions. Here are four sites that belong in your bookmarks.

InDesignCentral

`www.indesigncentral.com`

To help you keep up with the dynamic field of publishing, I've created an independent Web site that helps InDesign users stay current on tools and techniques. InDesignCentral provides the following resources:

✔ **Tools:** Links to plug-ins, scripts, utilities, and Adobe downloads.

✔ **Tips:** My favorite tips, as well as reader tips.

✔ **Resources:** Print publishing links, Web publishing links, Mac OS X links, and Windows links.

✔ ***Adobe InDesign Bible* series and *QuarkXPress to InDesign: Face to Face*:** Excerpts from the books, including updates from after the books' releases and color versions of the screen images from the chapters that cover color.

Figure 27-1 shows the site's home page.

Figure 27-1:
Visit
InDesign-
Central for
useful tips
and tricks.

The Adobe Web site

www.adobe.com

The friendly people at Adobe, who gave the world InDesign, recognize the value in providing useful information for users of their software solutions. The Adobe Web site offers InDesign tips and tricks, guides, interactive tutorials, and lists of user groups. It's worth your while to visit the site now and then to see what's new. Be sure to check out the InDesign community area for pro tips and help from users just like you. Figure 27-2 shows an InDesign-related page from the Adobe site.

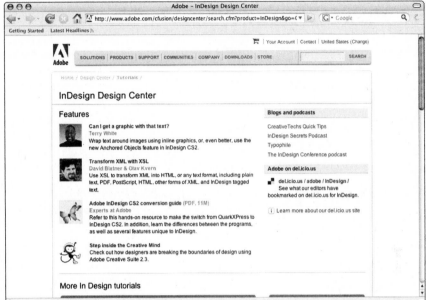

Figure 27-2:
At the Adobe Web site, you can find useful information on InDesign, such as the tips page shown here.

InDesign User Group

www.indesignusergroup.com

Seeking to help InDesign users share skills and tips, Adobe is supporting local user groups in many cities. Here's your chance to extend your InDesign knowledge and enlarge your personal network of graphics and layout experts.

You can also find links to several how-to guides from Adobe.

Creativepro

www.creativepro.com

Looking for the latest product and industry news? Go to Creativepro.com, an online magazine that also functions as a resource and reviews center.

Magazine Resources

The Web has revolutionized content delivery, but a good old-fashioned magazine is hard to beat for the richness of its information and the ability to take advantage of its knowledge almost anywhere you happen to be.

InDesign Magazine

```
http://www.indesignmag.com
```

This PDF-delivered bimonthly magazine takes the expertise of a whole bunch of InDesign power users and puts it into one place, giving you a regular flow of great ideas, tips, and tricks. While it's not as convenient as a print magazine, the PDF format does have the advantage of being easy to store and keep with you wherever your computer happens to be.

Layers magazine

```
www.layersmagazine.com
```

A great resource for tips and tricks specific to the Adobe universe of products is *Layers* magazine, which produces six glossy issues each year, chock-full of tips and how-to advice.

Macworld magazine

```
www.macworld.com
```

Macworld magazine remains a spectacular resource for publishers of all skill levels, providing graphics guidance as well as general news and advice about the Mac platform that most designers use.

Recommended Books

Wiley Publishing, Inc., the publisher of this book, also offers a wide range of books to help layout artists and publication designers exploit publishing tools to the fullest. The following four books could be of great use to you to expand your InDesign knowledge and related areas of expertise:

✔ *Adobe InDesign CS3 Bible,* by Galen Gruman, gives you extensive insight and tips on using the newest versions of InDesign in professional publishing environments.

✔ *QuarkXPress to InDesign: Face to Face,* also by Galen Gruman, shows you how to make the move from QuarkXPress to InDesign. You'll be running at full speed in no time, leveraging your knowledge of QuarkXPress and translating it into InDesign's approach.

✔ *Adobe Creative Suite 3 Bible,* by Ted Padova, Kelly L. Murdock, and Wendy Halderman, provides an all-in-one resource for users of Adobe's cornerstone tools (Photoshop, Illustrator, Acrobat Professional, and InDesign).

✔ *Digital Photography: Top 100 Simplified Tips & Tricks,* by Gregory Georges, provides clear, illustrated instructions for 100 tasks that reveal cool secrets, teach time-saving tricks, and explain great tips to make you a better digital photographer. To help you understand the implications of digital photography on the production process, *Total Digital Photography: The Shoot to Print Workflow Handbook,* by Serge Timacheff and David Karlins, offers complete, end-to-end workflow advice from shoot to print in a full-color presentation.

Chapter 28

Top Ten Must-Knows for QuarkXPress Refugees

In This Chapter

▶ Transferring QuarkXPress files to InDesign

▶ Understanding what works differently

You've jumped on the InDesign bandwagon after seeing everything it can do. Your problem is that a lot of QuarkXPress is still stuck in your brain. This chapter helps you make the mental switch so that you can become a native InDesigner.

Also, consider picking up a copy of *QuarkXPress to InDesign: Face to Face,* by Galen Gruman (Wiley Publishing, Inc.), which shows you side by side how to do in InDesign what you know how to do in QuarkXPress.

Opening Those Old QuarkXPress Files

InDesign opens QuarkXPress and QuarkXPress Passport files — but only in versions 3.3, 4.0, and 4.1. If InDesign sees any problems when opening these files, it gives you an alert so you know what to fix in the converted file. After the file opens, it is untitled, so you need to give it a new name.

Paying Attention to Selection Tool Differences

If you're a QuarkXPress veteran, the toughest thing about switching to InDesign is the set of tools. InDesign's Selection tool only lets you move and resize objects, and the Direct Selection tool lets you reshape objects and work with graphics. In InDesign, you use the Type tool to work with text, but you can't move or resize text frames while you're using it.

Using Keyboard Shortcuts for Tools

Because InDesign requires a lot more switching among tools than QuarkXPress, your mouse hand can tire very quickly. To avoid that, embrace InDesign's single-letter shortcuts for selecting tools.

Table 28-1 shows the shortcut translations for common activities.

Table 28-1	Keyboard Shortcuts Translated from QuarkXPress to InDesign	
Action	*QuarkXPress Shortcut*	*InDesign Equivalent*
Preferences	Option+Shift+⌘+Y or Ctrl+Alt+Shift+Y	⌘+K or Ctrl+K
Get Text/Picture	⌘+E or Ctrl+E	⌘+D or Ctrl+D for Place
Paragraph formats	⌘+Shift+F or Ctrl+Shift+F	Option+⌘+T or Ctrl+Alt+T
Character formats	⌘+Shift+D or Ctrl+Shift+D	⌘+T or Ctrl+T
Style Sheets palette	F11	⌘+F11 or Ctrl+F11 (Character Styles panel), Shift+⌘+F11 or Ctrl+Shift+F11 (Paragraph Styles panel)
Spelling (word)	⌘+L or Ctrl+W	⌘+I or Ctrl+I
Modify dialog box	⌘+M or Ctrl+M	No equivalent
Duplicate	⌘+D or Ctrl+D	Option+Shift+⌘+D or Ctrl+Alt+Shift+D
Step and Repeat	Option+⌘+D or Ctrl+Alt+D	Shift+⌘+V or Ctrl+Shift+V
Lock/Unlock	F6	⌘+L or Ctrl+L (lock), Option+⌘+L or Ctrl+Alt+L (unlock)
Ungroup	⌘+U or Ctrl+U	Shift+⌘+G or Ctrl+Shift+G
Send to Back	Shift+F5	Shift+⌘+[or Ctrl+Shift+[
Send Backward	Option+Shift+F5 or Ctrl+Shift+F5	⌘+[or Ctrl+[
Bring to Front	F5	Shift+⌘+] or Ctrl+Shift+]
Bring Forward	Option+F5 or Ctrl+F5	⌘+] or Ctrl+]

Thinking Panels, Not Dialog Boxes

Keep in mind that many InDesign menu commands simply display a panel (which may already be open) rather than showing a dialog box. Get used to deciphering icons or using Tool Tips on the panels because InDesign doesn't have as many dialog boxes containing named fields as you're used to in QuarkXPress. Also, InDesign implements contextual menus on a broader scale than QuarkXPress, so you can Control+click or right-click objects, rulers, and more to make changes quickly.

Using Familiar Measurements

InDesign uses all of the QuarkXPress measurement abbreviations, as well as its own. For example, InDesign accepts QuarkXPress's use of " to indicate inches, as well as InDesign's own standard of `in` and `inch`.

Knowing Differences in Documents

By and large, documents in InDesign and QuarkXPress are the same. You have master pages, layers, and pages. You can also set bleeds for objects that go beyond the page boundary. The biggest difference is that InDesign's master text frame lets you automatically flow text from page to page, whereas the QuarkXPress equivalent (an automatic text box) places an empty text box on each page for you to use as you see fit.

Working with Objects, Not Items

In QuarkXPress, you're used to distinct items such as text boxes, picture boxes, lines, and maybe text paths. In InDesign, you have more flexible objects such as paths and frames that can contain graphics or text.

Approaching Text from a New Perspective

In many cases, InDesign works with text very differently than QuarkXPress, even though the fundamental capabilities are the same in both programs. Veteran QuarkXPress users will be frustrated initially with InDesign's more-laborious approach to text flow and formatting, but will eventually appreciate some of InDesign's more powerful capabilities such as stroke formatting and nested styles.

Starting with the Direct Selection Tool for Graphics

Importing and manipulating graphics in InDesign is very similar to QuarkXPress. As long as you remember to use the Direct Selection tool to select a graphic rather than its frame, you and the InDesign graphics features will get along fine.

Paying Close Attention When Printing

InDesign and QuarkXPress offer many of the same output capabilities, such as print styles (called *print presets* in InDesign), PDF export, color calibration, and color separation support. But there are some notable differences beyond the different organization of their Print dialog boxes. For example, InDesign doesn't have any options to change image contrast or line-screen element for grayscale and black-and-white images, as QuarkXPress does. You need to apply such effects in an image editor.

Chapter 29

Top Ten Must-Knows for PageMaker Orphans

In This Chapter

▶ Transferring PageMaker files to InDesign

▶ Comparing how the two programs work

Y ou've finally thrown in the towel. After all, it's been eight years since the last release of PageMaker, and both Windows and Mac OS X have made PageMaker a real anachronism on your computer. So you're making the switch. Yet you have a lot of PageMaker still in your brain. This chapter helps you shift your mental gears so that you can become an InDesign user.

Fortunately, Adobe has retained a lot of PageMaker's approach in InDesign, so you can mainly focus on what's new rather than what's different. The basic methods for working with frames, lines, and pages are the same in both programs. What you get with InDesign is more control, with improved tools for drawing, formatting text, and manipulating objects.

Open Those Old PageMaker Files

InDesign opens PageMaker files saved in versions 6.0, 6.5, and 7.0. If InDesign sees any problems, it gives you an alert so you know what to fix in the converted file. After the file opens, it is untitled. You need to give the file a new name so that you don't accidentally overwrite that original PageMaker file.

You Now Have Three Selection Tools

The basic selection, object-creation, and navigation tools in InDesign are similar to those in PageMaker, but InDesign has *three* selection tools:

- Use the **Selection tool** to move or resize objects.

- Use the **Direct Selection tool** to reshape objects, change the end points of lines, and work with objects in groups. The Direct Selection tool also works like PageMaker's Crop tool, letting you move graphics within a frame.

- Use the **Position tool** to do what you were used to doing with PageMaker's Crop tool. It duplicates some of the Selection tool's functionality and some of the Direct Selection tool's functionality, so you might want to throw away this PageMaker crutch and just use the two native InDesign tools.

Switching Your Shortcuts

InDesign uses many different keyboard shortcuts than PageMaker did, so be aware of the differences. Table 29-1 highlights the main differences.

Table 29-1	Keyboard Shortcuts Translated from PageMaker to InDesign	
PageMaker Shortcut	*Result*	*InDesign Equivalent*
⌘+B or Ctrl+B	Styles pane	⌘+F11 or Ctrl+F11 (Character Styles panel), Shift+⌘+F11 or Ctrl+Shift+F11 (Paragraph Styles panel)
⌘+I or Ctrl+I	Indents/tabs dialog box	Shift+⌘+T or Ctrl+Shift+T
⌘+E or Ctrl+E	Edit in Story Editor	⌘+Y or Ctrl+Y
⌘+L	Spell-check	⌘+I or Ctrl+I
⌘+' (apostrophe) or Ctrl+' (apostrophe)	Control palette	Option+⌘+6 or Ctrl+Alt+6
⌘+J or Ctrl+J	Colors pane	F5 (Swatches panel)
⌘+8 or Ctrl+8	Layers pane	F7
Option+⌘+8 or Ctrl+Alt+8	Master Pages pane	⌘+F12 or Ctrl+F12 (Pages panel)

PageMaker Shortcut	Result	InDesign Equivalent
⌘+U or Ctrl+U	Fill and Stroke dialog box	⌘+F10 or Ctrl+F10 (Stroke panel)
Shift+⌘+E	Align dialog box	Shift+F7 (Align panel)
Option+⌘+E	Text Wrap dialog box	Option+⌘+W or Ctrl+Alt+W

Setting Aside Time to Set Preferences

You have so many preferences options in InDesign that you may wonder whether you'll ever leave the Preferences dialog box after you start setting them! Fortunately, you can set preferences at any time, so go ahead and start working with InDesign as it comes out of the box and then update preferences as specific needs arise.

Working with Objects, Not Elements

As with other aspects of InDesign, when you work with objects, you gain more than you lose. The types of objects (called *elements* in PageMaker) are similar — text frames, graphics frames, and lines — but InDesign offers more variations of them and more controls over their formatting.

Don't Worry Much about Text Differences

InDesign gives you more control over text formatting, such as the ability to stroke and fill characters in InDesign. Note that there are no type-style buttons — InDesign requires you to choose the appropriate version of a typeface rather than apply bold and italic to the general typeface. Other type styles are listed in the Character panel's flyout menu.

Don't Worry Much about Graphics, Either

InDesign and PageMaker are very much alike when it comes to importing and manipulating graphics. InDesign lets you click and drag graphics files into a layout in addition to using the Place command (choose File⇨Place or press ⌘+D or Ctrl+D), as well as create clipping paths and automatically scale graphics or frames for you.

A Different Way to Change Pages

The one feature you'll miss about PageMaker is those neat little page icons in the lower-left corner of the document window. In shorter documents especially, the icons provided a quick, easy method for jumping to pages. Get used to using the Page Number text field and arrows at the bottom of the document window or the buttons at the bottom of the Pages panel instead.

And to make the transition a little easier, note that you can use the Page Number pop-up menu (at the bottom left of the document window, next to the Page Number field) to get a pop-up list of pages, which is very similar to the PageMaker page icons row.

Creating Colors Is Different

Most of your work with colors happens through the Swatches panel (choose Window⇨Swatches or press F5) — not through the Colors panel, as PageMaker users might think. To share colors among documents, click and drag a colored object into another document window.

Using the Command Bar

In addition to adding the Position tool, which acts like PageMaker's Crop tool, InDesign offers the Command Bar panel (called the PageMaker toolbar in previous versions) that provides 30 iconic buttons (see Figure 29-1) to allow quick access to various operations. You open and close this toolbar by choosing Window⇨Object & Layout⇨Command Bar.

Figure 29-1:
The
Command
Bar panel.

Index

• C •

• *G* •

• *T* •

175
High-Impact
Resumes

175
HIGH-IMPACT
RESUMES

Richard H. Beatty

John Wiley & Sons, Inc.
New York • Chichester • Brisbane • Toronto • Singapore

Copyright © 1996 by Richard H. Beatty
Published by John Wiley & Sons, Inc.

This publication is designed to provide accurate and authoritative
information in regard to the subject matter covered. It is sold
with the understanding that the publisher is not engaged in
rendering legal, accounting, or other professional services. If
legal advice or other expert assistance is required, the services
of a competent professional person should be sought.

Library of Congress Cataloging-in-Publication Data:

Beatty, Richard H., 1939–
    175 high-impact resumes / Richard H. Beatty
      p.   cm.
    Includes bibliographical references.
    ISBN 0-471-12398-6 (pbk. : alk. paper)
    1. Resumes (Employment)   I. Title.
  HF5383.B324   1996
  808'.06665—dc20   95-50578

Printed in the United States of America
10 9 8 7 6 5 4 3 2 1

To my competent, motivated, and ever efficient
Office Manager, Michele Brown, who played a major role in
helping me to pull this project together.

Preface

This book gets quickly to the heart of the target—what is important to preparing a "high-impact" resume—one that will command the attention of prospective employers and stack the employment deck in your favor. There is much you can do to improve the overall effectiveness and impact of your employment resume, and the benefits of such improvement to your job-hunting campaign are countless!

This book is divided into three chapters. The first of these chapters provides a complete blueprint and step-by-step instructions for preparing a "high-impact" resume, including a sample resume that can be used to model your own resume.

To facilitate learning, the key elements of the model resume are numbered on the face of the resume sample itself. As the chapter proceeds, each of these components is then systematically described in detail, so there is a clear understanding of its design, content, and overall importance to resume effectiveness.

By following this step-by-step process and using the model resume and chapter instructions, the reader should be able to easily prepare a highly effective resume.

Chapter 2 contains 125 high-impact resumes. They represent the resumes of experienced persons who, in many cases, have several years of work experience. They are "actual" resumes that have been hand-picked from more than 25,000 resumes received by the author's company during the past five years. As such, they represent a broad cross-section of resume samples, and were chosen for inclusion in this book on the basis of their overall strength and impact. Although these are authentic resumes, minor alterations have been made in the interests of protecting the privacy and confidentiality of the candidates.

In Chapter 3, you will find 50 high-impact resumes of recent college graduates who have little if any professional work experience. Many are seeking their first full-time, entry-level professional job in their chosen field. As with the resumes of experienced personnel in Chapter 2, these college resumes are actual resumes that have been carefully selected and have been somewhat altered to protect the identity and confidentiality of the individual.

The collection of resumes contained in this book is intended to stimulate your thinking on how to improve the effectiveness and impact of your resume. By reviewing what others have done to create good resumes, you will come across some helpful ideas and techniques that will serve to increase the overall impact and forcefulness of your own resume document.

To facilitate the use of Chapters 2 and 3, you will want to refer to the Contents. You will discover that like resumes (i.e., resumes of persons working in the same fields or occupational areas) have been grouped together throughout the book. This will help you to identify those resume samples that most closely correspond to your areas of occupational interest and personal need.

It is believed that by following the step-by-step resume instructions in Chapter 1, and then using the resume samples contained in the subsequent chapters to further upgrade and strengthen your initial resume draft, you will end up creating a highly effective resume that will serve you well throughout your entire job-hunting campaign.

I wish you great success in your pursuit of a meaningful and satisfying career, and I hope that, through this book, I might somehow help you to achieve what you are capable of becoming. Best wishes for career success!

RICHARD H. BEATTY

West Chester, Pennsylvania
January 1996

Contents

1

The High-Impact Resume

Having a hard-hitting, high-impact resume can do wonders for the effectiveness of your job search. The validity of this statement becomes particularly evident when you examine the variety of ways this document is used by employers in deciding which employment candidate to hire. Let's take a moment to consider various uses and their clear and very real impact on the employer's hiring decision.

• Communications Document

Your resume is first and foremost a communications document. Its purpose is to communicate clearly and succinctly to employers your work-related skills and abilities. If your resume communicates effectively, employers will be able to easily understand and assess your qualifications for current openings. If your resume is poorly organized and sloppily written, communications will be impeded and the employers will likely move on to the next resume on the pile, never giving yours a second thought.

• Marketing Document

Your resume is also a marketing document that can persuade employers of your value for the type of work for which you are applying. Your resume must do a solid job of convincing employers of your "unique value" when compared to the many other employment candidates with whom you must compete. Failure to quickly and effectively establish this value will relegate your resume to the reject pile. If you get a reply at all, it's likely to be the infamous "no" letter.

• Interview Road Map

Frequently, a resume serves as a kind of interview road map. As such, it can have significant impact on interview results.

How many times have you participated in or observed the interview process where the interviewer uses the resume as the basis for guiding the interview discussion? In doing so, the interviewer generally goes through the resume line by line, asking appropriate probing questions along the way.

A poorly organized and badly written resume can create confusion and waste valuable interview time while the employer seeks clarification. Additionally, if poorly prepared, your resume may also guide the interviewer down some side roads and back alleys that you may not wish to traverse (i.e., focusing discussions on your shortcomings and failures).

Conversely, if well written and thoughtfully organized, your resume is likely to keep the interviewer on the main highway and focused on your strengths and successes. The choice is yours. Either way, your resume is bound to have significant impact on the outcome of your interviews.

• Post-Interview Comparison Document

Following the interview process, when the interview team meets to make a decision among candidates, your resume may be used as the basis for comparing you with other candidates. If the comparison is to be favorable, your resume must be well designed, causing your qualifications to make you stand out from the others. A thoughtful, well-constructed resume can go a long way toward moving the hiring decision in your favor. A poor resume, on the other hand, almost guarantees that you will not make the cut.

As you can see, your employment resume is in many ways the focal point or keystone of your job-hunting process. Taking the time and effort to prepare a thoughtful, well-organized resume is sure to have major payoff for your job search efforts.

THE HIGH-IMPACT RESUME

What is a high-impact resume? What does it look like? What are the important elements that contribute to its effectiveness? How do you prepare such a resume? These are the key questions that will be answered in this chapter.

Two primary factors contribute to resume effectiveness: *format* and *content*. Both are critical to resume performance, and they must be carefully balanced to construct a high-impact resume. Neither can be sacrificed in favor of the other if you are to create a resume document that will have maximum impact.

The format is the "physical layout" of the information on the resume. It is the way the information is "displayed" on the sheet of paper. To be effective, the resume format must be simple, neat, well organized, and visually pleasing. It must offer little reader resistance and should, in fact, greatly enhance "readability" of the document. To be effective, design your resume for quick reading and easy identification of your key qualifications for the position in question.

The format used in the sample resume (pp. 3 to 4) is a good example of a neat, clean, and uncluttered layout. You can see how easy it is to read this document quickly and to extract the key qualifications and accomplishments with

KEITH W. WARREN
① ➤ 102 Ocean View Road
Seattle, WA 19075
(206) 722-0643

OBJECTIVE: Operations or general management position at the division or corporate level where
② ➤ strong manufacturing background and leadership skills will be fully utilized.

RELEVANT   Proven manager with strong manufacturing performance and demonstrated leadership
SKILLS: ability. Excellent "people skills" combined with solid technical knowledge. Well
③ ➤ versed in modern management concepts and approaches including: self-directed work
teams, re-engineering, TQM, MRP, JIT, etc.

EMPLOYMENT HISTORY:

1994 to Present   **GENERAL PAPER COMPANY, INC.**   Chicago, IL
④ ➤ *A leading international Fortune 100 consumer and commercial paper products company*
with annual sales of $6.5 billion.

Group Plant Manager (1996 to Present)
⑤ ➤ Report to Vice President of Operations with P&L accountability for 4 manufacturing
plants ($800 MM budget, 3,500 employees, staff of 8).

- Met or exceeded all volume, cost and quality objectives -- 3 years running.
⑥ ➤ • Directed cost reduction efforts resulting in 20% cost reduction ($16 MM savings).
- Initiated self-directed work teams, improving employee morale and productivity.
- Re-engineered manufacturing operations, reducing headcount 12% ($19 MM).
- Built/started up 800 TPD pulp mill on time and under budget ($5 MM savings).

Plant Manager - Greenville, NC (1994 - 1996)
Reported to Group Plant Manager with P&L responsibility for 1200 TPD pulp mill
($300 MM budget, 1,300 employees, staff of 6).

- Turned mill around from $3 MM loss in 1994 to $15 MM profit in 1996.
- Re-engineered operations, reducing headcount 20% ($12 MM savings).
- Directed team that reduced raw material costs by 15% ($6 MM savings).
- Implemented self-directed work teams, eiiminating all first line supervisors.
- Led TQM effort, reducing customer quality complaints by 90% in 2 years.

1986 to 1994   **WILSON PAPER COMPANY**   New York, NY
A $1.5 billion manufacturer of coated and specialty papers sold to the printing and
publishing industry.

Operations Manager - Green Bay, WI (1992 - 1994)
Reported to Plant Manager of 500 TPD paper coating and converting mill. Functional
responsibility for manufacturing, engineering and maintenance. Managed staff of 5
managers, 40 salaried professionals and 300 hourly employees ($45 MM budget).

- Reduced headcount 10% with simultaneous 20% increase in productivity.
- Led successful start up of $40 MM coating operation -- completed 3 months early and $1.5 MM under budget.
- Trained entire operation (345 employees) in SPC/TQM, resulting in first year 80% quality improvement ($5 MM annual savings).

Department Manager - Coating (1990 - 1992)
Reported to Operations Manager with accountability for running 120 employee fine paper coating operation ($18 MM budget).

- Saved $2.5 MM annually through implementation of raw materials JIT program.
- Redesigned mix room, reducing labor costs 20% ($1 MM annual savings).
- Improved employee morale/productivity through increased participation in department decision-making.

Senior Process Engineer - Coating (1987 - 1990)
Reported to Department Manager - Coating. Provided engineering support to department through design, installation and start up of new coating equipment ($3 MM annual capital budget). Also provided engineering trouble-shooting support on major coating problems. Managed 2 Process Engineers.

Process Engineer - Coating (1986 - 1987)

Associate Process Engineer - Coating (1986)

EDUCATION: B.S., Mechanical Engineering
                      Bucknell University, 1986
                      Cum Laude
                      Tau Beta Psi

PROFESSIONAL: Professional Engineer, State of Michigan, 1988
                      President, TAPPI (Green Bay Chapter), 1991
                      Vice President, TAPPI (Green Bay Chapter), 1989 & 1988
                      Member, ASME, 1985 to Present

                      2 U.S. Patents

little or no effort. Notice also how the use of tools such as white space, bold type, underlining, capitalization, italics, and bullets creates good visual separation of the material presented, greatly enhancing the ease with which this resume can be read.

Resume content, on the other hand, refers to the actual information presented in the resume (i.e., employers, dates of employment, positions held, key responsibilities, major accomplishments, and the like). Good format enhances resume "readability," while it is resume content that actually "makes the sale"! To understand what content is important and how it should be presented in the resume, you must ask yourself the following two questions:

- What is it that the employer needs to know about me and my qualifications in order to make a good employment decision?
- What is the logical order or sequence in which to present this information to facilitate the employer's decision?

Good answers to both of these questions are essential to creating an effective employment resume that will motivate the employer to pursue your employment candidacy. The following instructions for preparing a high-impact resume will provide meaningful answers to these important questions.

PREPARING YOUR RESUME

The balance of this chapter is dedicated to providing you with step-by-step instructions for preparing a high-impact resume. To facilitate this process, I have included a sample high-impact resume (see pp. 3 to 4), and have numbered each of the key resume components for your easy reference. To assist you in the preparation of your resume, I will systematically present each of the numbered resume components in the order in which they appear on the resume document with a thorough explanation of each. If you follow this approach carefully, by the time we reach the end of the chapter, you should have what it takes to prepare a highly professional resume that will serve you well throughout your job-hunting campaign.

① Resume Heading

As can be seen on the sample resume, the resume heading (see item #1) is comprised of three pieces of information. . . your name, address, and telephone number. Where appropriate, you may also want to include your office number, fax number, and/or e-mail address.

As shown, the heading is normally presented in bold type using one type size larger than the balance of the resume text. In the sample resume, I have used 14 point type for the heading, with the balance of the resume text displayed in 12 point type. Note the use of all capital letters, which serves to set the candidate's name apart from the rest of the resume heading.

The resume heading is typically separated from the next major resume component (Objective) by three lines of white space. (See sample resume.)

② Objective

Candidates who fail to include a well-defined job search objective on their resume are placing themselves at a great competitive disadvantage. In such cases, since the employer is now uncertain of the type of position sought, it will require that the employer call the candidate for clarification on this point. Most won't bother!

In this day of downsized organizations, spartan staffs, and crushing workloads, most employers lack the time, resources, and desire to make frivolous phone calls of this type. This is particularly true at this time when there are a plethora of well-qualified candidates on the market from which to choose (most of which already have clearly-stated job objectives on their resumes). Don't place yourself at a competitive disadvantage by excluding this important information from your resume!

When writing your objective statement, be sure not to use too narrow an objective. Doing so may cause the employer to screen you out from positions in which you may have an interest. On the other hand, don't be too vague either. An objective statement that is too broad or too vague will make it unclear as to the type of position you are seeking. This would again require the employer to call you for clarification, an unnecessary step that most will be unwilling to take!

As you can see from our model resume, a well-constructed objective statement normally includes two basic elements: job level and functional area(s). In our sample resume, job level is defined by Keith as "management position at the division or corporate level." Functional areas are defined by Keith as "operation or general management." In combination, these convey a clear understanding of Keith's objective to the employer and, as stated, are not unusually narrow or restrictive in scope.

③ Relevant Skills

The inclusion of a "relevant skills" area on the employment resume is a fairly recent phenomenon that has exploded in both usage and popularity in recent years. Today, an estimated 95% of all resumes include this component. Although uniformly used by the great majority of job seekers, there seems to be little uniformity in the title used for this section of the resume. Other titles include the following:

- Summary
- Executive Summary
- Key Qualifications
- Qualifications Summary
- Key Skills

- Skills Summary
- Highlights
- Qualifications Highlights
- Skills Highlights

Whatever the title used, this section has one primary purpose: to motivate the employer to read the rest of the resume. The relevant skills section provides a brief three- or four-line summary highlighting what the candidate considers to be his or her most salient skills and qualifications for the position sought (i.e., the job search objective).

④ Company Name and Description

In preparing the "Employment History" section of your resume, note that "company" employment dates are positioned at the left-hand margin of the resume. Dates during which a given position was held with that employer (i.e., "job" dates), by contrast, are placed in parenthesis to the immediate right of the title of the position. This approach provides good visual separation between "employment" dates and "job" dates, and avoids the general confusion that so frequently results when the employment candidate positions both dates at the same margin. (Note, for example, how easy it is to distinguish between company employment dates and job dates in the sample resume. There can be no confusion here!)

Additionally, by placing company dates at the left margin next to the name of the employer, you provide better visual "compartmentization" of the resume, enhancing ease of employer readership. Doing this causes company names to visually stand out from job titles, which are then presented as a logical subset under the company name at which these jobs were performed.

Also enhancing such visual separation is the fact that company names are presented in bold type and underlined with *all* letters of the name set in capitals. Additionally, location of the company's corporate headquarters is positioned at the right margin in line with the company's name.

Job titles (see sample resume ⑤), on the other hand, are set in bold type and make use of both capital and lower case letters. This again serves to visually separate company names from job titles and enhances overall resume "readability."

As ④ illustrates, company name is followed by a brief description of the company. This normally includes such information as organization size, products manufactured (or services provided), and annual sales volume. Notice how this company description is set in italics, further reinforcing the visual separation between employer information and job information.

It is important to provide this information to prospective employers. They want to know what size and type company you worked for so that they can make some reasonable deductions about your probable fit with their own organization. An employer who is a widget manufacturer, for example, is going to want to know whether you have had any exposure to the manufacture of widgets. If this information is not provided, the employer may well pass on your resume in favor of another candidate who has had experience in that employer's industry and/or product line.

Don't just automatically assume that the new prospective employer is going to be familiar with the companies for whom you have worked. This may not be the case, and by failing to present this information in the resume you may well be placing yourself at a competitive disadvantage when compared to those who have furnished this information to the employer. There is a natural tendency for employers to prefer candidates who are familiar with their industry and product lines. This cuts down on training time and in most cases ensures that the candidate will "hit the ground running" rather than requiring an extensive industry and product orientation period.

⑤ Job Description

The next section of the resume presents both the job title of the position held as well as a brief description of that position (see ⑤ on the sample resume). There are five key elements to include when constructing this portion of your resume. These are as follows:

1. Job Title
2. Job Dates (i.e., dates employed in that position)
3. Reporting Relationship (i.e., title of the person to whom you reported)
4. Size and Scope of Position Held (described in quantitative terms)
5. Functional Responsibility (specific functions for which you were accountable for performing or managing)

Job titles, as illustrated on the sample resume, are set in bold print, are underlined, and make use of both capital and lower case letters. This helps to clearly distinguish them from employer names and visually separates and subordinates this information from information describing the employer. This is fitting treatment, since descriptions of positions held are really a kind of information "subset" and offer further information about the kind of work performed for that employer.

A final word about job titles: If the job title of the position you held does not effectively communicate the nature of the work performed, and there is a generic job title that better communicates this information to the outside world, by all means use the generic title. Since a key purpose of the resume document is to effectively communicate your qualifications to others in a way that they will be clearly understood, don't handicap yourself by using the actual job title. This is especially true today since many organizations have created unusual job titles that have internal meaning but have little or no meaning to the outside world.

For example, if your job title is "Technology Enabler," but you really are a Research Project Engineer, by all means use the title "Research Project Engineer." No one on the outside will understand the meaning of "Technology Enabler," but most will have a pretty clear understanding of the term Research Project Engineer. Likewise, if your internal job title is Director of Technology Enabling, but you really are serving in the capacity of Director of Research & Development, by all means use the title Director of Research & Development on your resume.

Unlike the employment application, you have a certain amount of "poetic license" and flexibility in the resume that is not provided in the formal employment application. Since a key purpose of the resume is to clearly convey a good understanding of your qualifications, use of generic rather than actual titles can often make the job easier and help you to accomplish your goal. Be sure not to "guild the lily" however by calling yourself a vice president when your actual position level was that of a director or manager. This will not set well with the prospective employer since it is a clear attempt at misrepresenting your credentials.

In the case of the employment application, it is strongly recommended that you use "exact" job titles rather than the generic ones used in the resume. Since this is a formal, legal document, you will want to make sure that all information presented is accurate and precise. You should not assume that you have the same latitude that you have with the resume, where there is far greater flexibility.

If the job was located at a site other than the corporate headquarters, you may want to make this fact evident by showing the location of the position immediately to the right of the job title. Notice how this is accomplished on the sample resume.

Job dates (i.e., dates during which you were employed in a given job) are best positioned immediately to the right of the job title and are enclosed in parenthesis. As discussed earlier this serves to make the distinction between job date and employer dates very clear, and will eliminate any possibility of confusion. To list both of these dates in the same margin of the resume can often confuse the prospective employer and, if the resume is being read quickly (which is usually the case during its initial scan by the employer) the reader may misinterpret the dates as dates of employment with *different* employers suggesting that you lack employment stability. So, be sure to distinguish between these two dates by positioning employment dates with a given employer at the left margin of the resume (as shown in the sample resume), with job dates positioned in parenthesis to the immediate right of the job title.

Following the job title and dates, you will need to provide a brief description of the position held. Employers need to know how closely the positions you have held resemble the position they have to offer. Such information as reporting relationship, job size and scope, and functional responsibilities are essential to the employer's ability to make such an assessment. Take a moment or two to study the brief job description shown at ⑤ on the sample resume.

Start the job description by describing your reporting relationship. Starting this statement with the words "report to" or "reported to" and then following this with your boss' title makes this a simple task.

Next, provide a brief description of your key functional responsibilities—the key things you are responsible for doing. If you are a manager, cite here the various business functions for which you are accountable. For example, "Functional responsibility includes, business planning, corporate finance, money and banking, and international finance." On the other hand, if you are an entry level clerk, describe the key functions you are accountable for performing. For example, "Functionally responsible for mail delivery, filing of correspondence, assistance in filing monthly financial reports, arranging executive travel schedules, and meeting set up and coordination."

Prospective employers need to have a clear understanding of your functional job responsibilities to determine if you have performed the same or similar work to the position they are offering. This will infer to employers that you have the requisite skills and abilities essential to successful performance of the position which they must fill.

When describing the positions you have held on your resume, it is also important to provide a quantitative description of your work. This serves to give the prospective employer a clearer understanding of the size, scope, and complexity of the job you were performing. The employer is looking for clear signs that you have successfully handled positions of similar scope and complexity to the open position, thus giving the employer a "warm feeling" about your ability to handle the position in question.

Besides describing the breadth of your functional responsibility, which we previously discussed, one of the best ways to clearly convey the scope and complexity of the positions held is to include "quantitative" descriptions of the work you have preferred. If you are a manager, indicating the size of your staff, budget size, sales volume, and the like will clearly serve to get this critical information across. If, on the other hand, you are an administrative assistant, your quantitative description could include the number of bosses served, the volume of correspondence typed, the volume of records processed, and the like. Such quantitative descriptions will serve to effectively communicate the size, complexity, and demands of your job, providing the prospective employer with important information for assessing your match with the current opening.

In the sample resume, you can see how effectively quantitative descriptions are used to get across the size, scope, and complexity of each of the positions held by Keith Warren. Note how succinctly and concisely this information is presented. There are no wasted words, and yet the employer should be able to come away with a very clear understanding of the important elements: reporting relationship, functional responsibilities, and size and scope of the position. This is all important information that the employer needs to make a reasonable decision about your qualifications and fit with the current position.

⑥ Key Accomplishments

Of all the elements of the resume, this section of the resume document is perhaps the most important to "making the sale." In years past, it was sufficient for the resume to provide the prospective employer with a simple job description showing functional responsibilities and scope of your position. This is no longer the case!

In the current work environment, where many organizations have undergone considerable downsizing and managers are under great pressure to accomplish far more with considerably fewer resources, managers feel a strong urgency to be sure that they are hiring hard-working, productive employees. For the most part, they need to hire persons who require little or no hand-holding, who are well-motivated, and who will produce a high volume of work with excellent quality.

As a result, employers are paying far more attention to the Key Accomplishments section of the resume. They want to know, "What is it that you have done? What significant contributions have you made to current or past employers for whom you have worked?" A record of continuous accomplishments and significant results in each position held will prove very convincing to the employer that you have what it takes to be successful in the position they have to offer. Perhaps no other single component of the resume will do more to affect your job-hunting success than the key accomplishments section. It is important, therefore, that you put considerable thought and effort into developing this section of the resume.

To do this, I suggest that you list each of the positions you have held on a separate sheet of paper. Below each job title, list a minimum of three to five major accomplishments or improvements that you brought about while in each position. Copies of old performance evaluations and salary reviews may prove particularly helpful in identifying these key results.

If you get stuck in performing this exercise, here is something that has proven helpful to many who have experienced difficulty in remembering past accomplishments. Think about the condition of the job when you first entered it. What were the key problems that existed? What did you do to resolve these issues? What were the results of your efforts? It is important in each case to identify three to five major improvements for each of the positions you have held. Once identified, reorder these accomplishments with regard to the type of position you are seeking. List the most important accomplishment first, the second most important accomplishment second, and so on. This should then be the same order in which these accomplishment statements are presented on the resume document.

When writing each of these accomplishment statements, start with a verb. This will force you to be concise. Note how this is done on the sample resume. Follow the verb with the thing or area you acted on, then follow this with a "quantitative" end result. Taking time now to study a few of these accomplishment statements on the sample resume will serve to quickly get the point across.

The use of quantitative results conveys to the resume reader the degree of improvement you brought. For example, simply stating that you "increased sales" has little meaning. Stating, however, that you "increased sales 50% in the first year" gives a much stronger message that is likely to grab the employer's attention. Where possible, then, express your key accomplishments in quantitative terms that serve to highlight the extent or degree of improvement. This is a key part of making sure that your resume will be high-impact, and that it will maximize your chances for employment.

Should you have difficulty recalling exact percentages or numbers, it is okay to use the words "approximately" or "about" as long as you know that you are in the ballpark. So, for example, you could state "annual savings approximately $1 MM," rather than simply indicating that there were savings (without citing the magnitude).

Note in reviewing the sample resume that each major accomplishment has been preceded by a bullet serving to highlight it. Additionally each key accomplishment section of the resume has been separated from its corresponding job description by two lines of white space. This causes the key accomplishments to stand out from the balance of the resume text, drawing the reader's attention to them.

If these accomplishment statements have been thoughtfully prepared, you will likely realize the benefits of this preparation during the course of the employment interview. Since the employer frequently uses the resume as a kind of interview road map when conducting the employment interview, and since the special highlighting used in the resume will tend to draw focus to your key accomplishments, there is a good likelihood that much of the employment interview will be focused on these accomplishments. Thus, much of the interview will tend to examine these accomplishments in greater detail, allowing you the opportunity to showcase your key strengths and capabilities.

If done particularly well, this section of the resume will do much of the selling for you. If thoughtfully prepared, showing three to five significant accomplishments for each of the positions you have held, the resume will show a solid history of hard work and accomplishment, suggesting to the interviewer that you are well-motivated, hard-working, dedicated, and productive. These are key attributes that most employers will find highly desirable.

⑦ Earlier Positions

It is not necessary to provide much detail on positions held early in your career. Your recent job experience is usually far more germane to your current job search objective than positions held earlier in your career. In fact, most earlier positions (see ⑦ on sample resume) should simply show job title and dates, with no job description or key accomplishments cited. In this way, you will conserve resume space, allowing you to devote far more space to current positions and qualifications rather than using valuable space to describe early positions that will probably have little bearing on the outcome of your employment candidacy.

If age is a potential barrier to your employment candidacy, you may want to consider dropping some of these early positions off the resume entirely. This action can be justified to the prospective employer, should you be queried as to why this was done, on the basis that there was limited space on the resume and you felt it more important to cite current qualifications than to devote valuable resume space to earlier career positions which have little or no bearing on the level or type of position you are seeking.

If the employer demands further explanation or suggests that you have violated some ethical standard, tell the employer that you were also concerned about the potential for age discrimination and wished not to be judged unfairly. Such explanation is likely to cause the issue to evaporate quickly!

To further disguise your age, simply leave graduation dates off your resume when presenting your educational credentials.

⑧ Education

As illustrated on the sample resume, the Education section lists the degree and major on the first line, followed by the name of the school and date of graduation on the second line. The third and fourth lines, where appropriate, are devoted to listing academic honors. Education is normally positioned after Employment History for an experienced candidate. However, it is usually listed right after the Relevant Skills section of the resume, for relatively recent graduates who have little or no professional experience. Such positioning would be most appropriate, since the recent graduate's education is likely to be the most important qualification that they have to offer.

If you have advanced degrees, list the highest level degree attained as the first entry. This is then followed by listing the next highest degree followed by the undergraduate degree.

⑨ Professional

Listing of your professional qualifications comes next. As shown on the sample resume, this normally includes professional certifications received, offices and memberships held in professional and trade association, and other appropriate items lending testimony to your qualifications as a professional in your field.

This section of the resume can also be used to cite patents held, publications written, speeches and lectures presented, special recognitions and awards received, or other evidence of your professional skills and competencies. Don't overdo this section, however, and stick to those items that have some reasonably significant bearing on your qualifications for the position sought.

Miscellaneous

The modern resume presents only job-relevant information. Topics that are not relevant to your ability to perform the targeted job should be excluded from the resume entirely. For this reason, most resumes today purposely exclude nonrelevant topics such as hobbies and extracurricular activities. Also excluded is all personal information such as age, height, weight, health, and marital status. None of these topics have much if anything to do with your ability to perform the job, and are therefore best left off the resume.

Writing Tricks and Techniques

Careful review of the sample resume will show that certain writing tricks and techniques were employed to make this resume a brief, concise, and relatively forceful document. Note how these techniques were used in the resume sample and employ them when writing your own resume. You should find the following writing tricks and techniques particularly beneficial in improving the overall quality and impact of your resume.

- Use of articles (e.g., a, an, and, the) are unnecessary and should, for the most part, be eliminated from the resume. They usually add no meaning or clarity to the resume.

- Eliminate the use of personal pronouns (e.g., I, me, you, they, them, us). Such pronouns are unnecessary in a resume and tend to distract from its impact and forcefulness.

- Avoid complete sentences when writing an effective resume. Highly descriptive clauses and phrases can communicate quite forcefully.

- Be concise. Eliminate all unnecessary words from the resume that do not enhance its meaning or impact. To do this, carefully read each word of the finalized resume, and ask yourself the following question, "If I eliminate this word, will I change the meaning or impact of this statement?" If removal of the word does not change the meaning or impact of the statement, then remove it! It serves no particular purpose!

- Begin most resume sentences or statements with a *verb*. Doing so will almost automatically force you to be brief and concise. Try it! Review the sample resume in this chapter and observe the high percentage of statements contained in the resume that begin with a verb. Most of them!!

By now you should have a clear understanding of what is important in preparing a high-impact resume, one that will be viewed favorably by the employer and provide you with the competitive advantage that you will need to come up on the winning side of the employment equation. Perhaps no other element of your job search is more important than your resume. So make the most of this opportunity to prepare a good one!

2

Sample Resumes—
For Experienced Persons

This chapter contains a total of 125 carefully-chosen resume samples covering 30 different occupational areas. These are *actual resumes* that have been carefully selected and hand-picked from a large group of well over 25,000 resumes received by my firm over the past five years. As such, they represent a broad cross-section of resume samples and were chosen for inclusion in this book on the basis of their overall strength and impact.

Although these are actual resumes, they have been altered to protect the identity of their author. These alterations include names, addresses, phone numbers, names of employers, dates of employment, and so on. This was done to protect the privacy and confidentiality of each employment candidate. Other than these superficial changes, however, these resumes are authentic. The format and basic content of each resume remain as originally submitted.

Although the format and content of the high-impact resume contained in Chapter 1 of this book are *strongly recommended* as a model for tailoring your own resume, looking at actual samples of other strong resumes should serve to stimulate your thinking on how to further strengthen resume document.

To facilitate use of this section of the book, I suggest that you see the Contents contained on page ix. You will discover that these resume samples have been grouped into similar categories by occupational area and page numbers have been provided. Thus, all sample accounting resumes are grouped together in one section of the book, marketing in another, technical in another, and so on. Use of this Contents should prove helpful to you in locating those resume samples that most closely correspond to your own occupational area and employment objective.

Kenneth V. Martin

18 Empire Road
Everett, Washington 82165
505 - 953-0872

Fourteen years P&L and Balance Sheet responsibility as Division President, domestically and internationally, in manufacturing environments.

Strong record of achievement in re-engineering companies while building sales, market share, people and profit, and adding significant value in marketing, operations and finance functions. Personal strength in business development and team building.

BUSINESS HISTORY:	**AIR-FLO CORPORATION**	**1983 - Present**

A leading manufacturer of fans serving the commercial, industrial, retail, and institutional markets with facilities in the United States, Canada and Mexico with revenues of $300 million.

President - Residential Division, Seattle, WA   1995 - Present

Asked by Board of Directors to turnaround break-even business of $65 million consisting of three brands: Breezy, Air-Lite and Wind Pro. These were sold through retail, wholesale and specialty channels. Responsible for P&L and balance sheet, two manufacturing facilities (USA, Mexico), sales, marketing, finance, engineering, HR and 450 employees.

Reviewed and reduced product lines, re-engineered operations for profitability, and relocated one facility to improve costs and customer service.

Results:
- Reduced manufacturing overhead by $3.5 million.
- Improved customer service from 10 days to 72 hours with 98% line item fill.
- Planned and implemented a real-time warehouse management system.
- Planned and executed a complete facility relocation.
- Overall ... positioned the business to grow over the next five years ahead of projected market growth.

Vice President, Marketing, Chicago, IL   1993 - 1995

Recruited by President to manage sales and marketing of $300 million multi-brand organization.

KENNETH V. MARTIN   *PAGE 2*

Results:
- Developed strategic sales plan.
- Grew sales by 15% in falling new commercial construction market.

President - Lighting & Controls, Cleveland, OH   1989 - 1993

Full P&L and balance sheet responsibility for a $15 million manufacturing operation of lighting and controls for the commercial and industrial markets. Functional responsibility for sales, marketing, finance, engineering, HR, and operations with 120 employees.

Results:
- Grew market share from 4 percent to 19 percent.
- Increased profits from break-even to 16 percent.
- Planned and executed the consolidation of two companies into one viable operation.

Sales Manager - Lighting & Controls, Cleveland, OH   1983 - 1989

Results:
- Grew sales an average of 15 percent per year.
- Developed territorial sales and distribution capabilities.

EDUCATION: B.A., Business (Marketing)   1983
University of Vermont

Center for Creative Leadership   1992

SAMUEL R. PETERSON

300 East 7th Street
Lansdale, PA 19332

office: (215) 699-3231
home: (215) 412-1346
fax: (215) 699-3232

CHIEF EXECUTIVE/OPERATING OFFICER

Seasoned and effective CEO/COO general manager. Strong track record managing turnarounds, new ventures and high growth business. Good crisis manager. High energy, aggressive. Results-focused team leader. Effective organization builder. Solid leadership, strategy and analytical skills.

EXPERIENCE

PRESIDENT/CEO   **1996-Present**
CRITICAL CARE PARTNERS, INC.
Philadelphia, Pennsylvania

CCP integrates proprietary electronic technology and outcomes management systems with specialized nursing and pharmacy expertise to reduce cost of care and to improve clinical and quality-of-life outcomes. The company has created and set the standard for a new, $2 billion potential niche market. Company valuation increased from $3 million to $15 million during the period.

- Created and implemented the company's vision and business strategy.

- Ramped annualized revenues from $500,000 to $2.5 million in three years (500%); turned around beta site operating income from -30% to +25%; exceeded corporate net income plan.

- Managed Medicare reimbursement to obtain coverage, establish policy, increase reimbursement rates. Increased Medicare patient margins from 18% to over 45%.

- Raised $8 million in operating capital through stock sale.

- Conceived and directed development of a patient data base and management/acuity systems to prospectively manage patient outcomes. Positioned CCP to capitalize on managed care opportunities with risk management and at-risk strategies.

- Installed and upgraded organization and infrastructure; expanded from 50 employees at three sites to 125 employees at eight sites.

- Conceived and directed a national clinical study (and local studies) with leading health care centers and thought-leaders which defined the clinical and cost value of the company's patient care.

PARTNER   **1991-1996**
THE BEDFORD PARTNERS
Boston, Massachusetts

A consulting firm for CEOs, COOs, sales/marketing executives and investors. Client firms included both start-up and established health care companies and home care providers. Assignments dealt with strategic and operational issues involving high growth, turnaround or corporate change.

- New business, new product, acquisition programs. Opportunity and risk assessment, due diligence, strategy development, business plan, marketing/organization plans. Implementation.

- Weak/failing business situations. Problem analysis, options assessment, strategy development. Assisted implementation of corrective actions.

- Interim management. Temporary senior manager to run the business, put new programs and organizations into place, deliver results until permanent executive is installed.

- Organization development. Programs to strengthen the effectiveness of senior management, sales, marketing and customer service organizations.

EXECUTIVE VICE PRESIDENT, MARKETING   1988-1991
UNITED MEDICAL TECHNOLOGIES, INC.
New York, New York

Directed worldwide sales, marketing and business development for this $500 million company with core businesses in electronic imaging and medical instrumentation technologies.

- Achieved 35% sales increase, improved margin and marketing productivity despite unfavorable international currency movements, and severe product quality, development and regulatory problems.

- Built an aggressive sales/marketing team for U.S. and international markets through management style, reorganization, personnel changes, management systems and personal development.

VICE PRESIDENT/GENERAL MANAGER   1986-1988
TECH-PUMP, INC.
Wilmington, Delaware

Led this $25 million entrepreneurial manufacturer of artificial heart pumps through a period of transition and high growth, following acquisition and consolidation by a multinational and the departure of the founder.

- Increased sales and pre-tax profits 25% and 20% respectively; inventory turns up 18%; receivables (DSO) down 5%.

- Installed organization and systems infrastructure to manage the size and rapid growth of the business, the new competitive and regulatory pressure, and the needs of the multinational parent company: recruited CFO, VP Operations and finance, engineering, manufacturing and marketing Directors; installed Standard Cost, Inventory Control, Forecasting/MRP, Labor Standards, MBO and Information systems.

DIRECTOR OF MARKETING   1979-1986
BERNSTEIN & ROWE, INC.
Philadelphia, Pennsylvania

Reporting to the president of this start-up venture, set up marketing and distribution, developed all marketing and product plans, managed the development and launch of the first products, established policies. Captured 15% market share with $9 million sales.

Prior assignments with B&R included International Marketing Manager, New Product Development Program Manager, Sales Representative.

EDUCATION

MBA (Marketing), 1979, New York University
BME (Mechanical Engineering), 1977, University of Maryland
Pi Tau Sigma Engineering Honorary Society
Various AMA courses and management seminars

CHARLENE P. BOWEN
18 Ocean Drive East
Grove Beach, CA 60922

Home: (414) 620-4121
Fax: (414) 820-0101

SUMMARY

Proven record in executive management (P&L), operations management, program management, engineering and marketing. Demonstrated ability to develop and manage multiple projects in a fast paced environment. Extensive hands-on experience in virtually every area from business development to final production and delivery. Strong executive presence coupled with excellent presentation skills. Entrepreneurial spirit, team motivator with keen sense of urgency.

WORK HISTORY

FASTENER TECHNOLOGY, INC., San Diego, CA   **1996 - Present**

Executive Vice President/General Manager Operations

Responsible for the turnaround of non-performing divisions of this $180 million company that manufactures and sells specialty fasteners to the aircraft and aerospace industries. Answer to the President of the Structures Group.

- Restored one $60 million division to profitability within three (3) months that had been losing over $4 million per year and currently managing a second $40 million division that will become profitable by January 1 by replacing key management, right-sizing and instituting strict cost controls.

- Restored customer confidence by settling outstanding warranty claims and implementing corrective action to improve overall product quality and eliminate warranty returns.

AERO CONTROL SYSTEMS, INC., Los Angeles, CA   **1991 - 1996**

President and Chief Executive Officer

Full P&L responsibility for this $30 million 300 employee company that designs and manufactures aircraft instrumentation and control systems. AERO Control Systems was a major turnaround situation.

- Implemented company-wide cost reduction/right-sizing.

- Rebuilt customer confidence by reducing delinquencies by 75%.

- Upgraded skills via training and selective hiring. Completely rebuilt the Quality Staff.

- Updated manufacturing concepts and systems.

- Fostered open communications by practicing management by walking around.

Charlene P. Bowen

AIR ENGINEERING CORPORATION, Los Angeles, CA **1986 - 1991**

Vice President, Operations

Operating Officer for this $5 million company that overhauls and repairs gas turbine engines and provides maintenance services to military and commercial aircraft. Answered to the President & CEO.

- Accomplished a major improvement in customer satisfaction by significantly reducing engine overhaul turn time from well over 100 days to under 30 days.

- Maintained divisional profit levels while reducing overhaul and repair prices which further improved customer satisfaction.

- Expanded market share in a shrinking market by more than 25% in less than three years.

- Negotiated exclusive agreement for an indicated production of turboshaft engine used by leading U.S. commercial helicopter manufacturer.

PRATT & WHITNEY AIRCRAFT, East Hartford, CT **1980 - 1986**

Program Manager (1984 - 1986)

Department Manager (1982 - 1984)

Project Engineer (1980 - 1982)

EDUCATION

Massachusetts Institute of Technology, MSME 1980

Massachusetts Institute of Technology, BSME 1978

CYNTHIA A. PETERSON

322 Sunset Court
Hillsdale, GA 40651
Home: 404-495-6351 • Office: 404-422-6161

PROFILE:

Results-driven executive with strong background in general management, sales, marketing and distribution. Strong experience in consumer products and electronics. Trained in markets at Procter & Gamble. People-oriented leader who builds strong corporate culture. Decisive strategic operator driving revenues and managing rapid growth.

EXPERIENCE:

ATLANTA CELLULAR COMMUNICATIONS   1996 to Present

President & General Manager
One of the largest cellular phone operating companies in the United States. Responsible for all company operations, including customer service, sales and marketing, engineering, regulatory and legal affairs.

- Grew revenue, subscribers, and profits from $30M to $120M in six years. Excellent gross margins.
- Built enlightened corporate culture during rapid growth (from 50 to 800 employees). Reduced turnover from 30% to 10%; improved customer satisfaction from 72% to 94%.
- Positioned company against larger, better-known competitor as the quality provider.
- Ramped-up operations (from 75 to over 250 cell sites) and managed one transition to digital transmission.
- Despite record profits, successfully lobbied Georgia legislature and public utilities commission thwarting additional regulation.

R.C.A. CORPORATION   1987 to 1996

Vice President & General Manager, Television Products (1991 - 1996)
Managed United States operations for all television products (including direct television).

- Increased profitability of T.V. Division by 12%.
- Increased revenue 25%.
- Introduced new direct T.V. line.
- Launched large screen projection T.V. product line.

Director, Marketing (1989 - 1991)
Responsible for developing and implementing product line marketing strategy for all television products.

CYNTHIA A. PETERSON   Page 2

- Planned and launched R.C.A. *Thin Line* television business.
- Developed new market channels through enlarged dealer network.
- Initiated first R.C.A. partnerships with Sears, Circuit City, Silo, Wards and Home Depot.

Director, National Accounts (1987 - 1989)
Responsible for R.C.A. Consumer Product sales to national accounts.

- Developed national accounts program, increasing sales from $62MM to $175MM.
- Obtained/increased distribution for R.C.A. products at Wal-Mart, K-Mart, Sears, Wards, Circuit City, Silo, Target, Best Products and Service Merchandise.

PROCTER & GAMBLE COMPANY   1981 to 1987

Regional Sales Manager   (1983 - 1987)

District Sales Manager   (1982 - 1983)

Marketing Representative   (1981 - 1982)

Sales Representative   (1981)

EDUCATION:

M.B.A., Boston University, 1981
B.A., Business Administration, University of New Hampshire, 1979

COMMUNITY INVOLVEMENT:

- Director, Atlanta Federal Bank
- Executive Director, United Fund Drive (Greater Atlanta)
- Member, Georgia Council of Female Executives

PETER J. KOVACH

19 Connelsville Road
Middletown, NY 39521

(315) 721-4132 (Business)
(315) 426-3152   (Home)

SUMMARY:

Over twenty years of progressive experience in general management and marketing within consumer products industry, with a track record of achieving results in highly competitive product categories. Consistently increased market share and profit through strategic focus, team orientation and solid execution.

EXPERIENCE:

GENERAL FOODS CORPORATION, White Plains, NY   **1985-Present**

Vice President and General Manager, Specialty Businesses   1995-Present
Full P&L responsibility for a $415MM business unit which includes recent acquisition of Antonio's Pizza business. Direct nine manufacturing locations with total organization of 1,200.

- Led acquisition team and managed integration including development of organizational structure and staffing plans and site consolidations. Reduced costs by $7MM.
- Exceeded monthly sales/volume goals by 5% since acquisition.
- Increased operating income for frozen pizza line by 12%.

Vice President of Marketing and Sales, Frozen Foods   1993-1995
Directed marketing and sales functions for this $1.9 billion frozen foods business which resulted from the consolidation of Frozen Vegetables and Frozen Dinners Divisions. Portfolio included brands such as Green Giant, Birds Eye, Swanson and Fresh Taste distributed through retail channels. Managed marketing staff of 80 and field sales force of 350 with advertising/promotion budget of $60MM and trade promotion program budget of $300MM.

- Initiated five-year strategic development effort and directed implementation achieving:
  - Volume gain of 5MM cases and share gains on all major brands within 12 months.
  - Product improvement on Green Giant brands which increased volume 15% since introduction.
  - Introduced large size products which have generated $75MM+ in sales with 75% ACV distribution.
- Introduced recycled packaging to meet environmental needs. Test markets currently 50% ahead of volume goals with 100% ACV distribution.
- Increased frozen vegetable volume 2.1MM cases (10%) despite entry of new major competitor.
- Identified/corrected major product packaging problem. Volume increased as a result, reversing 7% decline in prior nine months.

Vice President and General Manager - Hot Beverages Group   1990-1993
Vice President of Marketing and Sales - Hot Beverages Group   1986-1990
Vice President of Marketing - Hot Beverages Group   1985-1986

Assumed increasing marketing and sales responsibility leading to general management assignment with full P&L responsibility for this $375MM business. Managed marketing staff of 40 people, sales department of 75 and three manufacturing locations with 630 hourly employees.

PETER J. KOVACH   PAGE 2

- Strategically refocused business on growth opportunities and restaffed/upgraded marketing and sales organization Grew volume $146MM to $375MM in sales, while growing profits from 4% to 12.5% with an ROA that exceeded 25%. Specific achievements included:

  - Identified need for and introduced three new products which now account for $60MM in sales.
  - Revitalized Sweet Java brand resulting in sales increase of over $45MM through design upgrades, strengthened copy and EDLP approach to list price.
  - Introduced licensed characters on Cha Cha Coffee which now account for more than $35MM in sales. Led negotiations with licensor and developed creative executions.
  - Identified pre-measurement concept/opportunity and developed it into a national business with sales of $12MM and potential of $40MM.
  - Created and implemented profit-based sales incentive plan.

BEARHURST FOODS COMPANY, Pittsburgh, PA   **1979-1985**

<u>Director of Marketing</u>   1984-1985
Responsible for all brand management activities for this $500MM company. Brands included Bearhurst Pears, Bearhurst Peaches and Bearhurst Frozens. Managed 25 employees with A&P budget of $125MM.

- Led development and introduction of Bearhurst's new advertising campaign, which is still on air. Exceeded category norms and improved awareness by five percentage points.
- Developed Olympic sponsorship program and related incentive program which increased sales 7%.
- Introduced Bearhurst Mixed Vegetables as a national brand. Grew cases by 1MM units.

<u>Director - Canning Business</u>   1982-1984
Led multi-functional business team of six managers in development and commercialization of a new canning process with capital budget of $100MM.

- Led Midwest roll-out of "Bearhurst's Best". Achieved 7% share.
- Recommended and obtained approval for application of process for replacement alternatives which developed into $25MM business. Business now earns 20%+ ROA.

<u>Brand Management</u>   1979-1982
Progressive marketing assignments within the Frozen Products group, from Assistant Product Manager to Group Product Manager within four years. Managed Bearhurst Coffee's freeze-dried conversion which provided quality performance and enabled brand to break 10% share level for the first time, and to eventually reach its current number two position in the marketplace.

THE PROCTER & GAMBLE COMPANY, Cincinnati, OH   **1978-1979**

<u>Brand Assistant</u>, Folgers Coffee
Managed two national promotion events and introduced packaging change.

MILITARY: U.S. Army, 1969 - 1971

EDUCATION: M.B.A., Marketing, Penn State University, 1978
                     B.A., Business, Penn State University, 1976

WALTER H. CREIGHTON

121 Piney Way
Dayton, Ohio 64113
(316) 432-1476

OBJECTIVE:

To join an organization in an executive capacity where I can apply my leadership and management skills toward improving the firm's growth and long term viability as a successful business concern.

EXPERIENCE:

Harlowe Corporation   **(1992 to Present)**

Vice President and General Manager
Management of all divisional resources toward accomplishment of the division's long and short term goals. Responsibilities include direction of all Product Management/Marketing, Customer Service, Engineering, Production, Quality assurance, Material Control, and Human Resource functions toward company goals.

Specific Accomplishments:
• personally cultivated business relationships with several major domestic and international OEM clients.
• Doubled overall manufacturing labor efficiency during four year period.
• Increased sales per employee by 125% during five year period.
• Sales growth of tooling products of 250% during five year period.
• Established Systems Division with average annual sales growth of 45% during six year period.
• Improved response time on customer shipments from 21 days on average of 0.6 days for tooling products.
• Earned Excellence Award for achievement of 97.5%+ inventory accuracy with less than 1% financial error.
• Installation of AMAPS MRPII system for material planning and control.
• Reduction of "out of box" product quality problems by 76% during four year period.
• Improved product reliability on mainline products by two to seven fold.
• Earned numerous Preferred Supplier Awards from customer for superior quality (0 PPM defects) and delivery.
• Initiated program to obtain regulatory agency approvals for primary products to improve sales in international markets.
• Transformed manufacturing environment via capital investment program to upgrade machining equipment and develop in-house capabilities for critical processes.
• Preparations for ISO 9000 audit in early 1998.

WALTER H. CREIGHTON, Page Two

Electro Graphics, Inc.   **(1980 to 1992)**

Director, Research and Engineering   (1989-1992)
Responsible for R&D and product development of new printing, duplicating, copying and record processing products, and full complement of ancillary products.

Manager, Manufacturing Engineering   (1986-1989)

Manager, Advanced Manufacturing and Producibility Engineering   (1985-1986)

Manager, Manufacturing Engineering - Assembly Operations   (1982-1985)

Manufacturing Engineer   (1981-1982)

Quality Assurance Engineer   (1980-1981)

EDUCATION:

Ohio State University
B.S., Major - Operation Management, Minor - Marketing, 1978
M.B.A., Major - Operations Management, 1980

Loyala University, currently enrolled toward M.A. in Organizational Development

Illinois State Scholarship Recipient, 1970

WILSON T. JONES
130 Rampart Way
Atlanta, Georgia 40114

Home: 404-693-5197   Office: 404-796-2110

OBJECTIVE

Executive position offering P&L responsibility for division/group of large company. Alternative would be significant operating responsibility with smaller company where equity is included.

SUMMARY OF QUALIFICATIONS

Proven track record in diverse businesses, domestic and international, across all major business functions, most recently as division president. Company experience includes manufacturing, engineering, sales and distribution of industrial boilers and utilities. Annual sales ranged from $4.5 million to $125 million in recent years.

EXPERIENCE

GEORGIA POWER & UTILITY INC., Atlanta, GA   1995 - Present
President and CEO

$125 million power and utility manufacturing and engineering firm. Hired by new owners to streamline operations and improve profitability.

- Increased profitability and cash flow throughout management transition period.
- Directed the consolidation of three manufacturing facilities into single location.
- Planned and managed the consolidation/relocation of 45,000 SKU inventory valued in excess of $20 million.
- Streamlined distribution sales network.
- Initiated actions to begin ISO 9000 quality certification.
- Established and managed newly reorganized corporation to acquire additional products/companies to complement existing products.
- Evaluated foreign companies for possible acquisition.

COMBUSTION BOILERS, INC., Decatur, GA   1990 - 1995
President - Industrial Division

Managed $95 million plus (sales) industrial boiler business with 6 facilities and 11,000 employees. Autonomous division with complete P&L responsibility.

- Directed company growth from $20 million to over $95 million in sales, restoring profitability.

WILSON T. JONES   PAGE TWO

- Led sales and marketing efforts with major domestic and international customers and distributors.
- Negotiated domestic and international distribution and license agreements with Asian and European companies.
- Directed the administrative and marketing activities that led to the sale of the business to Georgia Power & Utility in 1995.
- Initiated Total Quality Management.
- Renegotiated and directed $32 million military power boiler (U.S. Navy) program.
- Converted ships' boiler manufacturing facility, equipment, and staff to industrial boiler production.
- Consolidated four boiler divisions into one, reducing overhead by $2.9 million.
- Saved over $5 million by closing two of three manufacturing divisions.
- Instituted team building, empowerment, and employee training, improving productivity, reducing cost and decreasing turnover.
- Managed non-union and union facilities.

COMBUSTION METALS, Norcross, GA   **1988 - 1990**
President - Annual sales $8.5 - $12 million.
Precision metal formed boiler plating components.

WINSLOW ENGINEERING, Reston, CA   **1982 - 1988**
VP-Controller - Annual sales $4.5 - $12 million.
Engineering and start-up industrial boilers and utilities for the pulp and paper industry.

COMBUSTION ENGINEERING, Albany, NY   **1978 - 1982**
Accounting Manager
Cost Accountant

EDUCATION

BS, Accounting/Business, S.U.N.Y., 1978

ANTHONY HOPKINS, CPA
18 Memorial Drive
LaGrange, IL 95072
(206) 694-0125 (H) • (206) 972-3030 (0)

OBJECTIVE: Senior level position in Financial Management.

PROFESSIONAL EXPERIENCE:

1986 to   **CORSON GROUP, LTD.** - London, England
Present   *A $1.5 billion diversified holding company based in the U.K.*

Nordwick Chemical Specialties
A Division of Corson Group (LaGrange, IL)
NCS is a $90 million producer of specialty chemicals for the pulp and paper industry, manufacturing in three U.S. facilities.
Vice President of Finance & Administration (1995 - Present)
Responsible for accounting, data processing, and personnel with four managers reporting to me and a staff of 19.
- Improved the financial forecasting procedures allowing us to issue accurate and timely forecast of sales and profits to local and corporate management.
- Promoted the data processing department's effectiveness by improving its timeliness, accuracy and responsiveness to its internal customers.
- Transformed NCS's budgeting process by establishing a program that included functional managers in the budgets' preparation and focused them on their role in achieving budgeted results.
- Controlled annual audit costs allowing no increase in fees for the third year in a row.
- Identified cost saving opportunities decreasing losses at a troubled manufacturing facility by $500,000 per year.
- Developed alternatives to dispose of two years accumulation of excess inventory.
- Participated in development of incentive compensation programs for personnel in sales, marketing, purchasing, manufacturing and distribution which were paid from cost savings and sales increases.
- Key person on project to identify a data processing system that would incorporate all NCS businesses.
- Coordinated a division-wide review of suppliers with goal of consolidating purchasing of $100 million of raw materials.

Nordwick Graphics
A Division of Corson Group (Grand Rapids, MI)
Nordwick Graphics is a $40 million producer of graphic arts supplies produced in three domestic plants and sold through a world-wide distribution system.
Director of Accounting (1990 - 1995)
Responsible for accounting, data processing, personnel and purchasing departments. Supervised four managers and a staff of 13.
- Oversaw operations of two subsidiary companies, including the development of budgets, operations reviews and capital project reviews.
- Participated in negotiations for establishment of joint venture with Australian company including preparation of operating forecasts and capital requirements.

ANTHONY HOPKINS, CPA   Page 2

Director of Accounting (continued)

- Prepared worldwide sales forecasts for $40 million graphic arts supplier coordinating with U.K., European and Australian sales companies.
- Performed due diligence for acquisitions identifying significant systems needs and rationalization opportunities.
- Established inventory controls that reduced inventory shrinkage from 6% to 1%.
- Developed data processing systems for production control, sales cost control and perpetual inventory tracking.
- Developed PC-based financial reporting templates to produce monthly financial reports and forecasts.
- Reduced accounts receivable days outstanding from 85 days to 45 days of sales.

Nordwick Papers
A Division of Corson Group (Green Bay, WI)
Nordwick Papers is a $15 million specialty coater of papers and films.
Vice President Finance & Administration (1986 - 1990)
Responsible for accounting, data processing, and personnel with a staff of five.
- Maintained relationships with lending bank enabling company to maximize its borrowing potential.
- Established new subsidiaries, setting up accounting, personnel and information systems.
- Directed conversion of data processing system to Corson Group's system without disrupting operations.

1980 to 1986	**"BIG SIX" PUBLIC ACCOUNTING** *Audit Department Manager* Managed audit and tax engagements for real estate, manufacturing, retail, and hospitality clients of Coopers & Lybrand.
1978 to 1980	**UNITED STATES ARMY**

EDUCATION:

1982	**CPA** - Michigan
1978	**Michigan State University** - East Lansing, Michigan MS Accounting
1976	**Michigan State University** - East Lansing, Michigan BS Accounting

PROFESSIONAL AFFILIATIONS:

- American Institute of Certified Public Accountants
- Michigan Society of Certified Public Accountants

LINDA D. BRIDGES
12 Washington Circle
West Chester, PA 19445
Phone: (610) 696-1234

OBJECTIVE

Challenging administrative position within professional environment providing opportunity for growth and career advancement.

PROFESSIONAL EXPERIENCE

AGRI-TECH CORPORATION (West Chester, PA)   **1996 - Present**
Leading agricultural biotechnology company focused on development and marketing of premium, fresh and processed, branded fruits and vegetables developed through advanced biotechnological breeding, genetic engineering and other technologies.

Administrative Assistant
Report to Vice President of Business Development providing full range of administrative support services to staff of nine managers, professionals and scientists in the marketing, sales and product development functions.

- Provide domestic and international corporate travel arrangements through local travel agency
- Set up both national and international meetings
- Type and distribute all correspondence utilizing WordPerfect for Windows
- Prepare presentations utilizing Harvard Graphics for Windows
- Compile database of business card files utilizing Alpha4 for DOS
- Work with Product Development group to provide product samples to interested parties
- Handle and sort incoming mail, responding to routine correspondence when appropriate
- Screen and field incoming phone calls for the Business Development department
- Organize and maintain Business Development files on a current basis

DATA SYSTEMS, INC. (Malvern, PA)   **1994 - 1996**
Major data services company providing electronic record keeping and analytical services to the automobile insurance industry and regulatory agencies.

Accounting Associate
Reported to Supervisor of Non-Sufficient Funds (NSF) within NJ-JUA (high risk automobile insurance) account.

- Researched and processed automobile insurance NSF checks using mainframe computer system
- Tested and maintained new policy procedures utilizing dBase software on personal computer
- Assisted customer service personnel in analyzing insured and producer related problems

Linda D. Bridges   Page 2

<u>DAVIDSON TEMPS</u> (Springfield, PA)   1993 - 1994

<u>Clerical Assistant</u>
Assigned to Accounting Department at Data Systems, Inc. to perform research assistance, data entry, billing and filing. Assignment resulted in full-time employment.

<u>THE BOOK FACTORY</u> (King of Prussia, PA)   1990 - 1995

<u>Bookseller</u>
Worked part-time while employed full-time and while attending school.

EDUCATION

Delaware County Community College (Newtown Square, PA)
Associates Degree, Business Administration, 1994

Henderson Senior High School (West Chester, PA)
Diploma, Business and Secretarial Studies, 1990

SKILLS

Proficient in:
- WordPerfect (DOS and Windows)
- Microsoft Office (Word 6.0, Excel, Power Point 4.0)
- Harvard Graphics (DOS and Windows)
- Microsoft Windows 3.1
- Microsoft DOS 6.2
- Alpha4

Familiar with:
- Lotus 1-2-3
- Microsoft Word for Windows
- VideoShow/Picture It

HONORS & AWARDS

- National Honor Society
- Future Business Leaders of America, Secretary
- Professional Secretaries International Scholarship
- Berkeley School Award for Outstanding Achievement in Business Education
- Katherine Gibbs Junior Leadership Award
- Porter Insurance Company Scholarship

MICHELE MARIE FLEMING

321 New Holland Drive
Philadelphia, PA 19384
(215) 374-2158

SUMMARY

Seasoned Administrative Assistant with over ten years experience providing full range of administrative and secretarial support services to senior level executives and their staffs. Experience in finance, accounting, manufacturing and human resources. Known as a volume producer who readily adapts to rapidly changing priorities. Strong interpersonal and leadership skills.

ACCOMPLISHMENTS

Manufacturing:

- Served five years as Administrative Assistant to Vice President-Operations for Fortune 100 consumer goods manufacturer (12 plants; 7,000 employees).
- Provided full range of administrative and secretarial support services to staff of six senior managers, handling demanding workload and consistently meeting tough deadlines.
- Created, prepared, typed and distributed wide range of standard and custom manufacturing reports for distribution to senior management (including President and Board Chairman).
- Maintained highly confidential files involving salary administration, performance evaluation ratings, organizational changes and the like.
- Trained Manufacturing secretarial staff in use of the new TelStar Fast Track Manufacturing Reporting System; oversaw successful implementation of same.
- Composed sensitive letters, drafted speeches and oversaw preparation of multimedia presentations for key senior management meetings.
- Received special merit awards for outstanding performance (two years).

Human Resources:

- Served two years as Administrative Assistant to Division Vice President Human Resources - Commercial Products (three plants; 3,800 employees; staff of 12).
- Employment Assistant to Director of Corporate Staffing for three years.
- Updated, maintained and oversaw accuracy of over 3,800 personnel records (over 20,000 annual transactions).
- Screened over 6,000 applications and employment resumes annually, handling all correspondence and composing special letters where required.
- Researched and initiated purchase of Resumax, a resume scanning and tracking system resulting in $35,000 annual savings in resume handling costs.

Michele M. Fleming

Accounting:

- Processed over $250 million in accounts payable annually with high degree of accuracy.
- Processed salaried payroll for Corporate Staff ($45 million; 800 employees).

WORK HISTORY

1993 to Present	General Products Corporation (Corporate Offices)	
	Administrative Assistant to VP - Operations	(1996 - Pres.)
	Administrative Assistant to VP - Human Resources	(1993 - 1996)
1990 - 1993	American Capital Equipment Corporation (Corporate Offices)	
	Employment Assistant to Director of Staffing	
1984 - 1990	Wilson Corporation (Consumer Division)	
	Senior Accounts Payable Clerk	(1988 - 1990)
	Accounts Payable Clerk	(1986 - 1988)
	Payroll Clerk	(1984 - 1986)

EDUCATION

Millersville University (Millersville, PA) 1984
Associates Degree, Accounting

Winston High School (New Holland, PA) 1982
Diploma, Business Major

COMPUTER SKILLS

WordPerfect 5.2   Excel
Microsoft Works 3.0   Lotus 1-2-3
Resumax   Harvard Graphics

ROSE MARIE LEWIS

505 Rolling Road
Willistown, GA 79455
(715) 775-9028

CAREER SUMMARY

Friendly, outgoing receptionist/administrator with twelve years' experience in a variety of office and business settings.

PROFESSIONAL EXPERIENCE

PLANT TECHNOLOGY CORPORATION (Atlanta, GA)　　　　　**1996 - Present**
Leading agricultural biotechnology company which applies a full spectrum of technologies to develop, commercialize and market premium branded fruits and vegetables.

Corporate Receptionist

- Answer, screen and route incoming phone calls for the company, its subsidiaries and joint ventures, (approximately 200-300 calls per day).
- Sort and distribute mail for all departments, joint ventures and subsidiaries.
- Assemble and update company information packets.
- Manage mass mailings from 200 to 2,000 pieces.
- Handle routine responses to information requests from investors and customers.
- Handle and distribute incoming fax correspondence as well as send outgoing documents.
- Maintain schedule for use of conference rooms.
- Provide administrative back-up and support for various executive assistants as needed.
- Supervise relief receptionist.
- Maintain office and conference room supply inventories.
- Responsible for outgoing mail: domestic, foreign, Federal Express, etc.

WAVERLY EDUCATION ASSOCIATION (Waverly, NJ)　　　　　**1995 - 1996**

Office Manager

- Responsible for a variety of administrative and secretarial duties.

OVERLAND ENGINEERING SURVEY COMPANY (Decatur, GA)　　　　　**1990 - 1995**

Secretary, Reporting to Principles

- Responsible for secretarial and administrative functions for four directors, five managers and other support staff.

Page 2   Rose Marie Lewis

RETAIL SQUARE (Medford, NJ)   **1989 - 1990**

Administrative Director, Reporting to Vice President & General Manager

· Supervised mall maintenance and other personnel.
· Handled secretarial and administrative functions for mall Vice President.

JOHNSON BROTHERS ICE FOLLIES (Atlanta, GA)   **1980 - 1989**

Professional Figure Skater

· Began as chorus member and understudy and advanced to various featured character roles.

Figure Skating Teacher

· Worked at various skating rinks and schools in the greater Philadelphia area.

OFFICE SKILLS

· Merlin phone system
· Federal Express Powership Computer System
· Pitney Bowes postage meters
· Word Processing and data entry

EDUCATION

Haverford Junior College, 1978 - 1980

SANDRA W. SMITH

1225 Running Brook Road
Wilmington, DE 18336
Res: (302) 388-6333

OBJECTIVE

Full charge bookkeeper with growth-oriented company offering opportunity for career advancement and professional development.

EDUCATION

Peirce Junior College (Philadelphia, PA)
Associates Degree, Administrative Accounting, 1987

Marple Newtown Senior High School (Newtown Square, PA)
Diploma, Accounting & Business Major, 1985
Received Service Award, 1985

PROFESSIONAL EXPERIENCE

WALDEN HEATING AIR CONDITIONING, INC. (Media, PA)   **1995 - Present**
$14 million HVAC contractor serving residential and industrial clients throughout Pennsylvania, New Jersey and Delaware.

Full Charge Bookkeeper (1997 - Present)
Report to President/Owner with responsibility for performing all accounting functions through preparation of monthly financial systems (one Write Plus, Version 2). Accountable for quarterly payroll tax returns, W-2's, 1099's, accounts receivable, accounts payable, collections and daily cash management. Oversee day-to-day office functions including benefits administration, customer service, order entry and equipment delivery.

Key Accomplishments:

·   Reformatted financial statements using "Percentage of Completion" method
·   Converted to in-house payroll, eliminating external payroll service ($8,000 annual savings)
·   Set up and maintained new purchase order/inventory control system
·   Set up and maintained new job costing system (using Lotus 1-2-3 spreadsheets)
·   Automated financial forecasting and budgeting functions
·   Managed company in President's absence.

Senior Bookkeeper (1995 - 1997)

Sandra W. Smith

ROBERT GORDON ASSOCIATES, INC. (Springfield, PA)   **1993 - 1995**
A $5 million systems consulting firm with specialization in the design and installation of manufacturing cost control systems in the pharmaceutical industry.

Full Charge Bookkeeper
Reported to President/Owner with responsibility for all accounting functions through preparation of monthly financial statements. Prepared quarterly payroll tax returns, W-2's, 1099's and daily cash management reports.

Key Accomplishments:

- Installed and implemented new manufacturing/accounting software (i.e., Basic Four Manufacturing) using an MAI UNIX computer system.
- Assisted in preparation of computer system proposals and ordering equipment
- Provided customer support on software questions

NATIONAL REFRIGERATOR CORPORATION (Cherry Hill, NJ)   **1991 - 1993**
A $120 million manufacturer of industrial and commercial refrigeration equipment with distribution and installation of equipment in the Northeastern United States.

Controller's Assistant
Reported to Controller with responsibility for all accounts receivable functions including bank deposits. Handled credit/collections (350 accounts) and filled in for accounts payable/payroll personnel as needed.

METALLURGICAL PRODUCTS COMPANY (Exton, PA)   **1989 - 1991**

Bookkeeper
Reported to President of this $2 million metallurgical testing laboratory. Performed all accounting functions through trial balance.

KEYSTONE SHIPPING COMPANY (Philadelphia, PA)   **1986 - 1989**

Accounting Clerk
Reported to Accounting Manager of this $150 million shipping company. Processed and approved expense reports for all domestic and overseas shipping crews (850 employees) and wire transfer of funds for same. Performed bank reconciliations for domestic and international accounts.

COMPUTER SKILLS

Software: One Write Plus (Version 2), Job Track/Job Costing, Lotus 1-2-3, Basic Four Manufacturing, WordPerfect
Hardware: MAI UNIX, Laser 486 Personal Computer, Various printers and peripherals

Wayne C. Dickinson

1201 Skyview Terrace
Phoenix, Arizona 89042
(602) 694-8201 (Home) • (602) 741-9305 (Office)
(602) 741-9304 (Fax)

SUMMARY OF QUALIFICATIONS:

Corporate real estate and facilities director with significant experience in rapidly changing business environments. Creative and accomplished. Exceptional ability to lead others in the development and execution of visions, strategies and systems to meet individual needs and corporate objectives. Experience includes new-construction planning and development; remodelling and expansion project management, real estate leasing, acquisition and disposition; and facilities management

CAREER EXPERIENCE:

Bartlett Company, Inc., Phoenix, Arizona (1992 - Present)
An $800 million manufacturer of high-end leisure furniture.

Director, Corporate Real Estate and Facilities (1996 - Present)

- Created the corporate real estate function, including development and implementation of cohesive strategies and policies for real estate and facilities management.

- Oversaw a domestic real estate portfolio of 1.89 million square feet, including planning, design and construction, leasing, acquisition and disposition; facilities operations and records management.

- Managed a staff of 96 and operating budget of $9 million. Directed capital projects up to $85 million.

- Initiated an integrated facilities management system for Arizona and California (plant and headquarters) operations.

- Led cross-company team to develop and implement corporate environmental goals and objectives.

- Achieved over $4 million in quality cost savings for corporate real estate and facilities operations in a three-year period.

Director, Properties Development (1992 - 1996)

- Led the greenfield planning, development, design and construction of $85 million, 500,000-square-foot, 218-acre headquarters campus.

- Pulled together the architectural team. Orchestrated realization of a coherent vision to meet the cultural expectations and practical needs of disparate groups; improved communication and productivity.

- Completed two-year project on budget and ahead of schedule.

- Led remodelling and consolidation of corporate administrative function for 115,000-square-foot facility in Phoenix, AZ (involving the relocation of over 200 employees).

- Directed expansion of computer room facilities in Phoenix, AZ facility (involving side-by-side construction work).

Borg-Warner Corporation, Chicago, Illinois (1983 - 1992)
A $2.4 billion equipment manufacturer and business services company.

Venture Manager, Technology Center (1989 - 1992)

- Led the planning, design and construction of a $27 million, 250,000-square-foot R&D technology center in Chicago, IL. Completed project on schedule and under budget.

- Initiated planning study to identify space requirements in response to growth.

- Conducted site selection process; negotiated unique, highly complex land-lease agreement to indemnify company from prior environmental contamination on site.

Manager, Facility Planning (1987 - 1989)

Created and implemented a facility planning function for the company in response to business and strategic changes.

Initiated a multi-functional planning strategy that successfully integrated individual facility needs with overall company strategies.

Established office standards program; administered space allocations.

Hazardous Materials Coordinator (1983 - 1987)

Developed and administered the Hazardous Material Control Program, initiating improved procedures and training.

EDUCATION:

Bachelor of Science - Biology and Chemistry (1983)
University of Wisconsin, Madison, WI

Numerous Seminars: IDRC World Congresses
Corporate Facilities Planning: American Management Association
Improving Management Skills: University of Chicago
UNIX and APICS studies

JANET BUYERS

10 Lakeview Court   Residence (713) 277-5550
Harrisonville, VA 08648   Office (713) 977-0770

SUMMARY

Senior level executive with extensive experience reducing costs, enhancing and consolidating services, managing crises and reducing headcount.

PROFESSIONAL EXPERIENCE

MANAGEMENT CONSULTING SERVICES, Reston, VA   **1998-Present**
Vice President, Sales and Operations

Sell and implement expansive business management services to Fortune 500 companies (including sale of largest corporate account in company's history). Represent rapidly growing provider of corporate outsourcing services with an established annual growth rate of 20-30% (growth projected to exceed 1000% by the year 2000). Full service outsourcing and consultative services include: space planning, facilities management, mail distribution, purchasing, reception/secretarial, central files management, forms/graphics printing and copy centers.

BALLENTINE & WHITNEY, New York, NY   **1996-1998**
Director of Facilities & Building Services

Managed staff of 75 and $30 million budget addressing the reorganization, automation and development of services impacting facilities and space planning, meetings and conference planning, cafeteria and catering services, purchasing, central files, mail room and security. Created more professional, cohesive groups and significantly reduced expenses.

- Directed largest corporate New York City move since 1976. Strategic consolidation of space and elimination of redundant and nonessential services reduced annual occupancy costs by $10 million and operational costs by $1.5 million.

- Created and implemented (previously non-existent) budget planning and tracking process across all divisions, thereby enabling accountability, stringent savings and uniform procedures.

- Introduced and implemented CAD (computer aided design) system that handled all B&W New York space (500,000 sq. ft.) and provided vital information on all physical space, furniture inventory, voice and data locations as well as personnel locations. Comprehensive database enabled the automation of in-house relocations and reconfiguration with an annual savings exceeding $1.4 million.

JANET BUYERS

FAMILY LIFE INSURANCE COMPANY, Princeton, NJ   **1989-1996**
Vice President - Corporate Administrative Services (1992-1996)

Managed service areas including building operations, cafeteria, purchasing, duplicating services, forms and graphics, micrographics, transportation, mail, records management, corporate condominiums and space planning. Provided consulting services to agency lease administration for 49 agencies nationwide.

- "Building of the Year" award recipient in 1995 after setting up separate corporation to run operations internally (42 acres, 635,000 sq. ft.). Eliminated all outside management fees and commissions, significantly improved services and reduced operation costs by $1.50 per sq.ft. within nine months.

- Successfully managed execution of complex disaster recovery plan following weekend fire and flood (May 1995). All impacted areas and (70) employees were fully operational by 6:00 AM Monday morning (within 48 hours of mishap).

- Managed contracted insurance agreements and related files, thereby enabling the recapture of $1 million dollars in fire/flood damages.

District Administrative Manager (1989-1992)
Reorganized services negatively impacting corporate profitability.

- Implemented cost center budgets for all service areas. Managed to operate below budget ($2 million annual savings) while enhancing overall quality of services. Simultaneously managed two of the largest moves in company's history.

WAGNER ELECTRONICS, Camden, NJ   **1987-1989**
District Administrative Manager

- Ran operations and leasing administration for nine facilities with a budget of $8 million.

- Managed seven facility moves in 11 months. Oversaw major telecommunication installation resulting in a 25% reduction in company costs and an actual capital budget attainment within 1%.

EDUCATION

B.A., Management, Lehigh University, 1987
Certified RPA (Real Property Manager)
Executive Development Program

PROFESSIONAL AFFILIATIONS

Adjunct Professor of Real Estate - Columbia University
Building Owners and Managers Association International
Facility Management Association
Female Executives
Notary Public
Executive Women of New Jersey

CALVIN T. JONES
12 Mission Hill Road
Beverly Hills, CA 80261
(915) 746-9147

Overview

Financial manager with experience in business analysis, mergers and acquisitions, budgeting, P&L responsibility, SEC reporting, treasury operations, credit, general accounting. Over 16 years of accomplishment in the entertainment, computer equipment and consumer products industries. Strong administrative, technical and organizational skills and special expertise with departmental restructuring and development. Skilled in MIS applications, personal computers, cash management, cost and general accounting systems. MBA.

Professional Experience

WERNER PRODUCTIONS, INC., Los Angeles, CA   **1996 - Present**

Director of Finance
Direct all financial accounting and reporting, treasury and cash management, human resources and employee benefits, risk management and insurance and MIS activities for this $180 million production company through a staff of five controllers as well as human resources and data processing professionals.

- Restructured corporate and division financial departments to handle growing needs of business by improving management reporting and improving communications with operating departments.

- Initiated cash management and capital spending and budgeting policies resulting in tighter control of company assets and greater concentration of resources in those areas where needed most.

- Negotiated and arranged for $26 million of new financing to be used for acquisition of new company and purchase of state-of-the-art video and graphics equipment.

- Consolidated data processing centers, reduced use of outside consultants, negotiated new software purchase agreements and hardware maintenance contracts and reallocated system resources resulting in savings of $1/2 million annually.

- Saved company $1/4 million annually by reviewing operations of one of the commercial post production divisions and recommending negotiation of new utility allocations, consolidation of billing and operations areas and elimination of a messenger service contract.

FINANCIAL FORUM, INC., Los Angeles, CA   **1994 - 1996**

Management/Financial Consultant
Consulting firm specializing in expanding the capabilities and productivity of corporate financial and accounting departments, providing computer information system studies and implementation including orientation of personnel and managing financial assets using conservative investment philosophy.

- Developed client proposals specifying phase-by-phase process to maximize utilization of present system or to acquire advanced hardware and software, implement installation and initial operation of new system including orientation of personnel.

- Worked with client organizations to restructure accounting and finance functions in anticipation of changing future needs resulting in greater productivity while reducing overall personnel costs.

- Provided investment management services for $4 million portfolio achieving return on assets of 30 and 42 percent during 1995 and 1996 respectively while maintaining the fund's objective of capital preservation.

Calvin T. Jones

KENWOOD SYSTEMS, INC., Pasadena, CA   1990 - 1994

<u>Corporate Controller</u>
Controlled all financial and MIS activities for this $210 million multinational manufacturer of computer peripherals by designing and implementing the Company's manufacturing, sales and financial systems, developing cash management procedures, directing risk management, treasury operations, management reporting, budgets, credit and collections and contract administration.

- Established worldwide MIS function and directed upgrade of computer equipment by purchasing two AS400 systems and integrated software resulting in worldwide savings of $1.5 million annually.

- Restructured US and Japanese financial organizations resulting in more timely and improved management reporting.

- Initiated worldwide cash management and capital spending approval policies resulting in tighter control of company assets and greater concentration of resources in those areas where needed most.

- Developed and implemented credit approval and collection procedures resulting in collection of $900,000 of past due accounts and continued payment of current accounts in accordance with terms.

- Reduced costs of worldwide insurance program by 15% while significantly improving coverage in all areas and establishing a corporate risk management program.

THE MORTON COMPANY, Los Angeles, CA   1988 - 1990

<u>Manager of Corporate Accounting</u>
Directed all accounting and reporting activities through a staff of 30 management, professional and clerical personnel. Responsible for financial systems and procedures, general accounting, accounts payable, cost and inventory accounting.

- Initiated monthly financial closings, both domestically and internationally, providing management with timely and accurate reporting.

- Automated accounting systems and streamlined work methods resulting in more efficient use of personnel and resources. Installed McCormack & Dodge General Ledger and Accounts Payable Systems.

- Recommended freight management system resulting in $250,000 annual savings.

- Implemented, as part of a team, a Data 3 MRPII inventory control system in a System 28 environment resulting in a 25% reduction in raw material inventories and an annual savings of $400,000 in carrying costs.

DARMIN MANUFACTURING, INC., San Diego, CA   1981 - 1988

<u>Manager of Worldwide Accounting</u>	1986 - 1988
<u>Supervisor of General Accounting</u>	1985 - 1986
<u>Senior Inventory Accountant</u>	1984 - 1985
<u>Inventory Accountant</u>	1981 - 1984

Education

UNIVERSITY OF SOUTHERN CALIFORNIA, Los Angeles, CA
<u>Graduate School of Business</u>. MBA Degree in Accounting   1981
<u>College of Arts & Science</u>. BA Degree in Economics and Political Science   1979

SANDRA R. SHANE
12 TIMBER TRAIL
CLEVELAND HEIGHTS, OHIO 16421

Home: (306) 995-6271
Business: (306) 831-0101

OBJECTIVE: Top Financial Management position in the manufacturing sector.

STRENGTHS:

Business Judgement	People Development	Analytical Capability
Interpersonal Skills	International Experience	Diverse Background

EXPERIENCE:

1994 - Present

FEDERAL CHEMICALS, INC.
Division Controller
Specialty Chemicals, Cleveland, OH

Senior Financial Executive of a diversified, $500 million, international specialty chemicals business. Major businesses are located in United Kingdom, Belgium, France, Canada, and the U.S. Major accomplishments:

- Improved financial performance by divesting low return businesses and downsizing the overhead structure. Improved return on capital and return on sales by 20% and 25% respectively.
- Realigned the financial function to eliminate non value added services and strengthen the organization. Reduced total expenses and personnel by 33%.
- 1995 Chairman - Financial Improvement Awards Program. Developed corporate program to recognize and reward sustained outstanding individual performance.
- Led effort to reduce investment base and improve cash flow performance.

1990 - 1994

Director Finance
Measurement and Control Instrumentation, Pittsburgh, PA

Equivalent CFO position for a $130 million division. Major businesses are located in the U.S., Canada, United Kingdom, France, Belgium, Netherlands, and Singapore. Extensive international travel and personnel contact. Major accomplishments were:

- Provided leadership to improve the financial performance from a $8 million net loss to a $13 million net profit.
- Successfully completed the acquisition of Blane Instrument Co.
- Directed the establishment of improved internal controls throughout Europe.
- Reduced fixed manufacturing costs by $2.5 million per year by consolidating two manufacturing locations into one.

1989 - 1990

GENERAL MACHINERY CORPORATION
Division Controller
Pump Division, Bloomfield, NJ

Sandra R. Shane

Directed the Financial / M.I.S. functions of a diverse, international division of General Machinery. Division consisted of three autonomous operating units located in the U.S., Canada, Mexico, and United Kingdom. Total sales - $60 million; net income $4.2 million. Number of employees - 700.

- Provided financial leadership and guidance to five business unit comptrollers.
- Restructured an operating unit to return the business to profitability.
- Directed the development of strategic plans, operating plans, and monthly forecasts.

1988 - 1989

ROSS MIDLAND CORPORATION
Vice President - Finance
Materials Handling Division, Midland, MI

Directed the financial function of Marketing and Distribution company with sales in excess of $300 million. Major accomplishments were:

- Negotiated with two major German companies to establish a joint venture.
- Designed and developed a financial organization to support the requirements of this newly formed company.

1986 - 1988

Controller
Mobile Plant, Mobile, AL

Responsible for the financial function of an $70 million, 600-employee manufacturing facility. Directly supervised 12 employees. Major accomplishments were:

- Established controls which reduced inventory loss from $3 million to $30,000 over a two year period. Total inventory was $30 million.

1984 - 1986

Corporate Manager of Investment Analysis
Midland, MI

Controlled a $95 million capital budget. Presented capital plans and investment proposals to the Executive Committee of the Board of Directors. Developed new corporate policy and procedure manual for Investment Analysis. Introduced the policy through seminars presented in the U.S., Germany, France, Belgium, Brazil, and Australia.

1984

Senior Financial Analyst
Midland, MI

1983

Financial Analyst
Midland, MI

EDUCATION: 1983   **DREXEL UNIVERSITY**
Philadelphia, PA   M.B.A. - Finance

1981   **UNIVERSITY OF DELAWARE**
Newark, DE   B.A. - Accounting

WILMA A. DIXON

106 Briar Lane, Columbia, MD 19742
(315) 694-3126

CAREER SUMMARY

Senior financial manager with strategic responsibility for domestic and international financial, operational, and EDP functions, most recently Group Controller with a large multinational consumer products firm. Superior leadership, organizational, and writing skills.

BUSINESS EXPERIENCE & ACCOMPLISHMENTS

JOSEPH E. SEAGRAM & SONS, Baltimore, Maryland
A distiller and marketer of fine blended whiskey with annual sales of $2.5 billion. Operated as the worldwide center for marketing production and financial strategy related to Seagram Whiskeys.

Group Controller   1996-Present
Joined the company as Controller for USA distributor with subsequent elevations in responsibility over both domestic and international operations. Senior level financial manager, directing all finance, planning, and accounting functions. Responsible for business analysis and interpretation of trends, management reporting, cash and working capital management, financial services, and automated systems.

- Liquidated USA distribution company and managed financial aspects of major restructuring while maintaining normal operations with a 50% reduction in staff.

- Composed a strategic plan recommending consolidation of two major distributors to take advantage of natural synergies, implemented by top management.

- Created an integrated management reporting system that cut 3 days out of the monthly cycle and eliminated 10-12 hours of overtime per month.

- Created financial operations for new worldwide strategic business unit that included the establishment of a new domestic company to import into the USA, the development of work procedures, restaffing, and the installation of internal controls.

Controller - Seagram's Seven Crown Group   1993-1996

- Created and implemented international financial services and cash management, eliminating capital requirements of $5.8 million, reducing inventory from 95 turn days to 55 days, and decreasing US$ exposure from $20 million to $18 million.

- Installed a foreign exchange management system, including risk quantification of $35 million, translation versus transaction budgeting, and the means to track gains and losses from contracts. Saved $120,000 in the first four months and $3.6 million in the first fiscal year.

- Developed and implemented financial controls and increased productivity through automation. This included a complete overhaul and integration of general ledger systems that reduced turnaround times by 4-5 days and eliminated 10-20 manhours per week plus a budgeting and forecasting system with an accuracy rate of better than 99%.

- Established controls over South American operations with the introduction of a direct liaise, the computerization of manual financial systems, and the development of procedures and timetables that raised the compliance rate for international consolidations to 100%.

- Successfully negotiated and documented trading arrangements, including an alternative cost transfer scheme with Scottish unit that resulted in perpetual savings of $750,000 annually.

SCOTT PAPER COMPANY, Philadelphia, Pennsylvania
A leading international consumer products company with annual sales of $5.2 billion.

Assistant Plant Controller - Chester Plant   1990-1993
Responsible for month-end financial reporting, accounting services, and analysis. Assisted with annual budgets and various special projects.

- Developed and implemented procedures to account for the assimilation of 5-15 new hires and capital purchases of nearly $500,000 million per week.

- Eliminated emergency overtime and improved reporting compliance to 100%.

- Co-managed the installation of new mainframe financial reporting software, including planning the installation, testing the results, assisting with de-bugging and training staff.

GEORGIA PACIFIC, Atlanta, Georgia
A major Fortune 100 pulp and paper company with annual sales of $6.3 billion.

Financial Analyst   1987-1990
Performed all phases of manufacturing accounting, including financial planning, general accounting and cost accounting.

- Acted as exclusive financial advisor for a wholly-owned subsidiary with annual sales of $4.5 million, including general accounting, cost accounting and physical inventories.

- Developed comprehensive physical inventory procedures, training up to 1,600 people per year, calculating inventory adjustments up to $150,000 and defending results with internal and external auditors.

Associate Financial Analyst   1985-1987

- Developed computerized budgeting system for twelve cost centers that eliminated 5-10 man days per cycle.

- Conducted training program for other staff members in the use of LOTUS 1-2-3.

EDUCATION

M.B.A. North Carolina State University. Honors Graduate (GPA: 3.6), 1985.
B.S.   North Carolina State University. Honors Graduate (GPA: 3.9), Phi Beta Kappa, 1983.

CRAIG P. MADISON, CPA
814 Fulton Drive
Framingham, MA 10247
(603) 421-1427 Home
(603) 399-1846 Office

OBJECTIVE: Financial Management or Controller

SUMMARY: Financial professional with 14 years of progressively responsible management positions within the Financial Services industry.   Developed strong proficiencies in leadership and organization as well as special skills in:

- Accounting and Financial Analysis
- Budgeting and Planning
- Staff Selection & Development

- Project Management
- Internal Controls
- Mainframe and PC Systems

EXPERIENCE: <u>BANK OF BOSTON, Boston, MA</u>   1996 - Present

Controller - People's Bank of Boston
People's Bank is the legal entity for Bank of Boston's domestic consumer lending business ($1.3 billion in assets).   Controller is responsible for all accounting, internal & external reporting, budgeting & planning, financial controls and cash management.

- Direct the Bank's regulatory and other external reporting (FDIC/Federal Reserve, rating agencies, audited financial statements).   Coordinate annual FDIC and State of Massachusetts examinations.

- Prepare the annual budget and quarterly financial forecasts.

- Developed an Internal Controls program and procedures manual.

- Revised product profitability reports and implemented comprehensive ratio/trend analysis to improve the level of management reporting.

- Developed work measurement standards for the Bank's operational departments via PC modeling to improve work flows, control costs and evaluate performance.

- Implemented many financial system enhancements including a new general ledger/accounts payable system, mainframe financial reporting database and PC based applications for planning and analysis.

Craig P. Madison, CPA

FEDERAL BANK & TRUST CORPORATION, Boston, MA 1990 - 1996

Vice President, Finance - Federal Bank & Mortgage Corporation
Directed all finance activities for Federal's start-up mortgage banking subsidiary. Responsible for the accounting & financial reporting, planning, treasury and human resource functions.

- Prepared the annual Business Plan and Operating Budget. Also developed the five-year long range strategic plan.

- Designed and implemented a monthly management report package.

- Converted a microcomputer General Ledger/Accounts Payable system to a mainframe based accounting system.

- Obtained funding to meet daily loan requirements and administered the cash management function.

- Presented the financial results at monthly Board of Directors' meetings.

- Selected, managed and developed a staff of 15 employees.

FIRST BANK OF BOSTON, Boston, MA 1985 - 1990

Accounting Officer
Supervised professional accounting staff of seven. Diversified accounting and financial reporting responsibilities included preparation of financial statements for 10 domestic companies, review and consolidation of financial statements for foreign subsidiaries, budget analysis, management, tax and regulatory reports.

EDUCATION: Boston University
Master of Business Administration, Major: Finance (1985)

Boston University
Bachelor of Science, Major: Accounting (1983)

AFFILIATIONS: American Institute of Certified Public Accountants
Massachusetts Society of Certified Public Accountants
Boston University, Business & Economics Alumni Association

LINDA C. STEINER, CPA
20 Greenhill Road
Pittsburgh, PA 18211
Residence: 717/644-3526
Office: 717/273-8700

SUMMARY

Senior Executive with over 17 years in-depth experience in finance, treasury, accounting, strategic planning, acquisitions, divestitures and investor relations. Enthusiastic and hard-working executive with the objective of improving operating performance, profitability and business growth, by providing quality financial/administrative/operational direction.

References would substantiate fast track progress including:

- Results oriented team builder
- Strategic planner and implementor
- Effective communicator
- Proficient M&A strategist
- Proactive developer of internal controls and reporting systems
- Integrity in the financial and investment community
- Strong analytical skills

PROFESSIONAL EXPERIENCE

MACHINE TECHNOLOGY CORPORATION   **1995 to Present**

A publicly-held international company. World leader in the development and manufacture of technologically advanced production machinery. Revenues in excess of $380 million.

As <u>Vice President - Finance & Treasurer</u>, developed financial resources for restructuring the company back to its core business. Directed worldwide staff of 34 accounting, finance and MIS employees. Reported directly to the Chairman and President.

- Developed and implemented marketing plan to divest five non-core companies. Targeted 200 potential buyers resulting in the sale of three companies in separate transactions in 18 months. The $78 million received exceeded original estimates by over 10%.

- Negotiated $75 million of bank revolving credit facilities with more favorable terms. Commitment fees were reduced 50%.

- Directed improvement program in internal control systems and procedures, substantially reduced the risk of significant error. Improved the accuracy consistency and quality of financial information for staff and line management's use.

- Instituted a comprehensive profit improvement program to reduce indirect expense in anticipation of cyclical decline in sales. Annualized fixed overhead expenses were reduced from $54M to $42M in 24 months.

Linda C. Steiner, CPA   Page 2

WESTON CORPORATION   **1985 to 1995**

A publicly-held manufacturing company producing hardware and industrial fasteners. The company has revenues of approximately $115 million and 800 employees.

Vice President - Finance and Treasurer	**1993 - 1995**
Corporate Controller	**1989 - 1993**
Controller	**1985 - 1989**

Provided financial direction as the company grew from $25M to $115M in revenues. Growth resulted from strategic turnaround acquisitions. Recruited from KPMG to effect turnaround of a troubled business. Directed divisional businesses with a hands-on operational style. Worldwide staff of 55 accounting, credit, treasury, tax and MIS employees. Reported directly to the President and CEO.

- Performed substantial due diligence procedures on all acquisition candidates. Completed multiple international acquisitions increasing revenues by $65 million.

- Assessed and verified manufacturing cost information to assure profitability on government contracts and new product development.

- Designed and installed new manufacturing/accounting/reporting systems. Converted all acquired companies to centralized MIS system.

- Developed and managed third-party vendor finance programs to enhance sales by providing low interest leases to customers. Interest rates were 2-4% below small business borrowing rates.

KPMG PEAT MARWICK   **1981 to 1985**

KPMG Peat Marwick is a "Big 6" public accounting firm providing audit, tax and management consulting services worldwide. Rapidly progressed to management position in six years.

Senior Audit Manager	**1984 - 1985**
Audit Manager	**1983 - 1984**
Auditor	**1981 - 1983**

Specialized in audits of commercial manufacturing and financial institution firms. Produced consistently superior results in all assignments.

EDUCATION

BBA -- University of Michigan -- 1981

NEIL J. GLAVIN, CPA

55 Orange Blossom Drive
Kansas City, MO 07648

Home: (815) 778-4296
Office: (815) 709-5027
(800) 599-8300

SUMMARY

A results oriented, Senior Financial Executive with extensive experience in consumer packaged goods and OTC pharmaceutical industries, both domestic and international. Outstanding record of leadership and achievement in both line and staff positions.

Demonstrated accomplishment in:

- Asset/Liability Management
- Budgeting/Forecasting
- Controllership
- Financial Analysis
- Internal Audit

- Strategic Planning
- Acquisition Reviews
- Joint Ventures
- Organizational Structuring & Restructuring
- Management Information Systems

EXPERIENCE

PHARMACO LTD.   1992 - Present

INTERNATIONAL DIVISION - Consumer Health Group
Vice President, Finance   *1997 - Present*

Directed finance and IS activities for this fast growing $700 million in revenues division which covered the world excluding the U.S. and Western europe.

- Directed financial team which negotiated the establishment of a joint venture in Central & Eastern Europe which resulted in a $6.5 million reimbursement of start-up costs.

- Led a multi-disciplined team which developed a plan to generate hard currency foreign exchange for our joint venture in China by exporting raw materials. In addition to generating the needed FX, reduced raw material cost to our plants by 20-35% on the exported materials.

- Streamlined and automated worldwide financial reporting systems which resulted in faster, consistent, actionable results reporting.

PHARMACO HEALTH - USA
Vice President, Finance   *1994 - 1997*

From 1987 to 1992, this $300 million marketing and sales division absorbed a smaller division, took responsibility for manufacturing (three plants) and assumed responsibility for Mexico. By 1992 revenues had grown to $425 million.

NEIL J. GLAVIN, CPA   Page 2

- Led a multi-disciplined task force which recommended and then implemented a new integrated software system. This AS 400 based system which replaced a mainframe system resulted in annual software licensing and hardware operating savings of $1.8 million.

- Redesigned business processes to create a "one stop shopping" customer service department which improved customer service with a 15% decrease in headcount in the departments affected.

- Reorganized the finance department at division headquarters to participate in cross functional brand teams. This resulted in increased productivity, better communication and more efficient processes.

- Part of a three man team which managed the Division in the absence of a President for most of 1991. Overachieved budget by 109% of sales and 104% of operating profit.

- After the recall of a potentially contaminated product, compiled a list of all losses and obtained settlement from the vendor's insurance company. Received reimbursement for all out-of-pocket expenses and negotiated an additional settlement of approximately $6 million for lost business by using data obtained from the sales and market research departments.

PHARMACO LTD.
Corporate Audit Manager   *1993 - 1994*
Audit Supervisor   *1992 - 1993*

- Responsible for scheduling, staffing and coordinating audit at all domestic locations. Reported to the Corporate Audit Director. Managed eight professionals.

COHEN & GORMAN PRODUCTS, INC.
Controller, Consumer Products Division   *1990 - 1992*

- Conducted an audit of payments to food brokers which uncovered several instances of defalcations. The company recovered approximately $430,000 in misappropriated funds and replaced six brokers.

- Implemented annual reviews of product costs with marketing, manufacturing and finance personnel which resulted in annual cost of goods savings of approximately $1 million.

Controller Personal Products Division   *1987 - 1990*

- Developed a computerized tracking system for cooperative advertising payments which resulted in a 20% decrease in customer deductions and virtually eliminated over payments.

EDUCATION

Kansas State University	MBA - Taxation	1987
Kansas State University	BA - Accounting	1985
MD Certified Public Accountant		1989

D A V I D   C.   B E R N H A R D

Home Address: 201 Rutherford Way, Devon, PA 19341   Home: (610) 424-9058   Work: (610) 399-3200

Work Experience:

1991 - Present   **Pacific Chemical Company, Inc.**

International Financial Coordinator, Corporate Headquarters, Wilmington, DE (1996 - Present)
Direct interface between company's corporate headquarters and the European/Asian International
locations to ensure timely and accurate financial results and business performance data.
- Consolidation of eight companies with 1998 revenues of $750M and gross profits of $96.5M.
- Forecast and evaluate currency exposure of international operations and hedging contracts.
- Direct corporate funding process to provide working and investment capital to region.
- Annual budget preparation and monthly comparison reports and forecasts.
- Coordinate all updated policies and business procedures in accordance with US GAAP and
  company policy.

Sales/Marketing Services Supervisor, Specialty Chemical Division, El Paso, TX (1992 - 1996)
Direct and manage staff of three handling marketing operations, international and domestic
distribution, establishing production and inventory levels for manufacturing. Prepare and monitor
operating and capital budgets and handle financial analysis for specialty chemical business servicing
crude oil pipelines.

- Establish and maintain $4M equipment administration program tracking equipment location and
  costs, saving workload requirements by 20%.
- Perform economic lease/purchase evaluations of contract proposals.
- Negotiate $3M annual sales and service contracts with vendors and equipment leasing firms.
- Presented sales/marketing proposals to prospective pipeline companies.
- Implement and manage new order entry system to accommodate $80M annual sales volume.

Senior Inventory Coordinator/Analyst, Specialty Chemical Division, El Paso, TX (1991 - 1992)
Monitor $3M of inventory consisting of over 250 products, generate monthly inventory level, location
and bad-order reports, special studies and analysis as required.

- Volume planning and coordination.
- Set up/directed physical inventories for 21 domestic chemical stocking locations.
- Design, implement and manage reporting system for senior management identifying all bad-order
  domestic products.
- Eliminate unreconciled inventories backlogged for over two years, completed project
  independently in less than one year. Nominated and received distinguished company award.

1986 - 1991   **General Petroleum Corporation**

Assistant Group Controller, General Refineries, Green Bay, WI (1987 - 1991)
Consolidate and report financial results for two refineries. Direct and monitor capital and operating
budgets. Act as corporate liaison between refineries and parent company.

- Assist in design and implementation of new financial reporting and cost accounting systems.
- Develop and maintain cash management and forecasting program to maximize use of company
  funds.
- Successfully handled division divestitures when business units were sold to private investor
  groups.

Cost Accountant (1986 - 1987)
Product costing of over 200 division products and quarterly development of plant fixed overhead
costs.

1983 - 1986   **Fidelity Bank of Iowa**

Loan Analyst and Assistant Cashier, Dubuque, IA

Education: **B.A., Accounting**, Central University of Iowa, December, 1983
Symphony, Lotus, dBase, WordPerfect, Freelance, Windows, AS400

JEFFREY L. SINGER

152 Harding Place
Sacramento, CA 94586

Office: (415) 557-0500
Home: (415) 631-2241
Fax: (415) 266-9601

SUMMARY

Nineteen years financial management experience in a variety of businesses, ranging from equipment manufacturing to financial services, with one of the worlds largest diversified companies. Strategic thinker with excellent analytical and communication skills and strong international and M&A experience.

PROFESSIONAL EXPERIENCE

UNIVERSAL PRODUCTS COMPANY   **1983 - Present**
Unistar Container Division
Glendale, CA
World's largest lessor of bulk liquid container systems.

<u>Vice President and Chief Financial Officer</u>   1998 - Present

- Managed the day-to-day financial operations of this $350 million business during a period in which assets grew from $500 million to $1.9 billion.

- Valued, negotiated and closed (as part of a four-person team) the $600+ million acquisition of Unistar's largest competitor, leading to the doubling of Unistar's assets and $22 million in increased earnings in the first year.

- Negotiated two cross-border leveraged leases, lowering financing costs on $100 million of new equipment to rates below comparable U.S. Treasuries and saving $750,000 in annual carrying costs.

- Established pricing guidelines and assisted Marketing in developing new or varied products to fuel continued profitable growth, resulting in over $350 million in new financing business closed in 1992.

Universal Capital Commercial Real Estate Financing   **1995 - 1998**
Newport Beach, CA
Provider of mortgage financing on existing commercial properties located in the U.S., Canada and Europe and construction financing on U.S. residential development projects.

<u>Manager - Financial Planning and Analysis</u>

- Managed the financial, information systems and service center operations of a business whose assets grew from $1.3 billion to over $3.0 billion in three years.

- Developed comprehensive financial analysis and planning models which enabled the business to better understand and manage its growing earnings.

- Negotiated bridge financing facilities which permitted transactions to be closed according to customers' needs while preserving Universal Capital's ability to manage its debt-equity ratios and maintain its AAA rating.

JEFFREY L. SINGER   PAGE 2

- Created the financial infrastructure needed to support the business' international expansion, including the establishment of servicing support and routines to manage funding, tax, accounting and foreign exchange risk.

Universal Pump Business   **1992 - 1995**
Smithville, NJ
Manufacturer of residential and industrial pumps and metering devices.

Manager - Business Analysis

- Directed the financial planning and analysis of this $120 million business and coordinated efforts which resulted in a 43% improvement in return on sales and a 12% reduction in real base costs in three years.

- Participated on a task force which overhauled the businesses' hourly wage system, making it simpler, more flexible and more competitive and reducing projected labor costs 30% in four years.

- Reviewed a high-profile new product program and recommended that it be abandoned as too expensive and too difficult to manufacture within established specifications and cost. The program was terminated and the $20 million in program funds was redeployed.

Universal Silicones   **1983 - 1992**
Reading, PA

Finance Manager   1988 - 1992
Specialist - Business Analysis   1983 - 1988

EDUCATION

Universal's Manager Development Course - 1990

Universal's Financial Management Program - 1987

B.S. in Information Technology and Honors Graduate, Albright College, Reading, PA - 1983

Numerous technical and leadership development courses and seminars

ORVILLE D. KINCANNON

126 Hillcrest Circle
Bristol, Connecticut 64153

Home: (203) 623-1067
Office: (203) 244-6400

CAREER SUMMARY

Senior Financial Manager with 15 years of diverse assignments with Everseal Incorporated. Experience includes financial planning, forecasting, manufacturing cost control, capital justification, marketing and product line support and acquisition analysis.

PROFESSIONAL EXPERIENCE

EVERSEAL CORPORATION   **1987 - Present**

Manager, Systems Integration - *Home Products Division* (1998-Present)
Managed projects and coordination of IS services for high-impact financial applications. Ensured implementation objectives were realized by IS and financial systems users.

- Developed specifications for a $1.4 million automated claims processing system saving $500,000 annually.
- Reengineered customer order fulfillment and claims cycle. Identified 30% cycle time reduction and $11 million cash flow opportunity.
- Justified major enhancements in payable and receivable systems; reduced staffing 15% saving $85,000 annually.
- Participated in vendor analysis and contract negotiations.

Manager, Financial Planning and Analysis - Corporate (1997-1998)
Coordinated planning process for all divisions. Assessed integrity of divisional plans and forecasts. Identified areas of earnings vulnerability and recommended contingency actions. Recommended capital requests to CFO and CEO.

- Developed manufacturing strategy for seasonal products reducing variances $4 million annually and eliminating payments to subcontractors.
- Identified warehousing consolidation opportunity saving $650,000 annually.
- Recommended termination of divisional computer service contracts and full utilization of internal mainframe systems savings $250,000 annually.

Manager, Financial Planning and Analysis - *Home Products Division* (1994-1997)
Directed development of financial projections and budgets for a $900 million consumer products division. Prepared annual profit, competitive action and five year strategic business plans. Managed capital justification and acquisition analysis processes.

- Implemented systems to monitor actual versus planned product costs identifying variances for inflation and productivity.
- Justified capital projects exceeding $50 million annually and over 50 new products.

ORVILLE D. KINCANNON   **Page Two**

- Implemented analysis and valuation techniques for seven acquisition targets valued at $500 million.
- Led evaluation and assimilation of $15 million Mexican acquisition.

Manager, Manufacturing Accounting (1992-1994)
Managed inventory and expenses for six manufacturing and distribution locations. Operations included over 200 presses and $150 million in annual overhead expenditures.

- Reduced variances by $2 million per year.
- Established controls monitoring $15 million of inventories consigned to subcontractors.
- Reduced annual physical inventory losses by $500,000.

Senior Manufacturing Accounting (1991-1992)
Approved inventory and cost of sales closing entries. Prepared budgets and reconciled inventories. Reported product line profitability and return on investment.

Financial Analyst (1989-1991)
Prepared operating budgets and annual profit plans. Reported capital spending to corporate management. Completed tax and audit schedules.

Corporate Auditor (1987-1989)
Conducted compliance audits and tests of operational controls. Investigated divisional performance issues related to manufacturing scrap, variances and inventory controls.

DELANEY & COMPANY - Hillsboro, OH   **1986**
Accountant

NATIONAL INDEMNITY - Columbus, OH   **1984 - 1986**
Manager Policy Services/Business Process Analyst

EDUCATION

M.B.A. - 1994
University of Connecticut

B.B.A. - 1984
Utah State University

CONFIDENTIAL RESUME

Matthew H. Clarke

909 Hemlock Lane
Newport Beach, CA 18521

Home: (414) 848-5237
Office: (414) 250-9700
E-Mail: abcde@fgh.edu

SUMMARY: An accomplished strategic planning and business analysis manager with experience in the telecommunications, aerospace, utility and health equipment industries. Substantial achievements in strategic business planning, business process re-engineering, marketing, new business development and competitive intelligence.

PROFESSIONAL EXPERIENCE:

1995-
Present

Director of Strategic Planning
Streamline Communications, Inc. (SCI), Los Angeles, CA
A 100 year-old west coast telecommunications holding company with interests in local telephone service, publishing, long distance and network services, equipment and telemarketing.

- Architect of SCI's first strategic plan in 1990 which helped transform the company into a market-based, customer-oriented, entrepreneurial organization. Results: Since 1990, revenues have increased by 100%, net income by 150%, and achieved 15% ROI objective two years ahead of Plan.

- Extensive "hands-on" involvement working with SCI's Strategic Business Units in helping develop and implement strategic plans consistent with and flowing into SCI's corporate objectives and strategies. Pursued balance between top-down strategic direction and bottom-up implementation.

- Successfully managed a "turnaround task force" to improve profitability of SCI's business systems unit from 1993's net loss of $820K to current rate of plus $240K.

- Oversaw development of new business venture plan transforming MIS department into a telecommunications billing and operations support software/services provider for external telecommunications customers and internal SCI customers.

- Instrumental in forming SCI's new Communications Services Unit to bundle long distance, private line, data and telecommunications equipment as a "one-stop" source which has increased both market share and revenue and earnings growth.

- Coordinated development of SCI's plans to enter Cable Television, Distance Learning and Internet Access businesses; led to Cable TV acquisition and enhancement of local loop broad band capability.

1990-
1995

Director of Planning Coordination
EAE Electronics, LTD, Flight Simulation Division, Fire Hills, CA

- Developed strategic planning process that successfully transformed management focus to being market-driven.

- Coordinated development of Australian subsidiary marketing plan - increased market share in mid-East, southwest Asian markets.

- Managed Division's market research & acquisition analysis activity; supported development of Training Services Division.

- Prepared Division's strategic plan presentations to Board of Directors.

1987-
1990
Manager of Market Planning
EnviroSafe Corporation, Binghampton, NY
Manufacturer of air pollution control systems for the automotive industry.

- Developed marketing information and competitive intelligence systems which assisted increase in market share.

- Supervised two major market research projects involving new, high-tech removal systems.

1985-
1987
Senior Planning Analyst
Howland Corporation, Manchester, NY
Manufacturer of hospital and medical equipment/process control systems.

- Conducted market/finance analysis in support of acquisition activities.

- Developed operating strategies and growth plans for specialty chemicals and analytical instruments divisions.

1980-
1985
Product Planning Analyst/Marketing Specialist
Commercial Boiler Systems, Inc., Groveport, OH
Manufacturer of boiler cleaning systems and nuclear control rod drives for the electric utility industry.

- Internal consultant for business ventures; developed & marketed new products.

1977-
1980
Military Service: Electronic Countermeasures Specialist
U.S. Army Security Agency

EDUCATION: B.S., 1977, University of Scranton, Scranton, PA. Top third of class.
Post graduate studies and seminars in: Strategic Planning, Acquisitions and Finance.

REFERENCES: Available on request.

NATHANIEL J. SIMPSON

6218 Colonial Drive
Wilmington, DE 18725
(302) 344-6110 Work
(302) 922-2403 Home

SUMMARY

Extensive experience managing domestic and international manufacturing and logistics operations. Broad range of business responsibilities including purchasing, inventory management, production planning, manufacturing systems and operations analysis.

PROFESSIONAL EXPERIENCE

QUENCH BEVERAGES, Wilmington, DE   **1989-Present**
A $5 billion operating unit of Amalgamated Bottlers and the world's fourth largest soft drink manufacturing and bottling company. Brands marketed include: Orange Slice, Tropical Cola and Canadian Springs sold in over 120 countries.

Director, Operations Analysis, Wilmington, DE   1996-Present
Connecticut Beverages Technical

Report to the Senior Vice President of Technology. Responsible for developing strategic programs to improve operating costs and organizational efficiency.

- Conducted an analysis of corporate R&D functions and recommended changes that will reduce product development cycle time and technical cost.

- Performed an analysis of U.S. and European manufacturing cost structures. Implementation of recommended changes will reduce product costs by approximately 20%. Also assessed the potential impact of NAFTA on North American manufacturing operations.

Director, Concentrate Manufacturing Operations, Wilmington, DE   1991-1996
Quench Beverages, Concentrate Manufacturing

Responsible for soft drink concentrate manufacturing and materials management operations in U.S., Canada, and Mexico. Also accountable for manufacturing quality, technical support, and information systems for facilities in Ireland, Spain, Ecuador, Brazil and Asia. Reported to Vice President of Concentrate Manufacturing. Staff of 68.

- Responsible for managing five major post acquisition manufacturing consolidations resulting in annual savings of $22 million.

- Negotiated raw material supply contracts producing cost reduction of $5 million.

- Developed manufacturing sourcing strategies and cost improvement programs for operations in Europe, North America, South America and Asia.

NATHANIEL J. SIMPSON   Page 2

- Formulated a global manufacturing system strategy for manufacturing facilities in U.S., Ireland, Spain and Canada. Successfully installed Business Planning and Control operating systems utilizing IBM AS400 hardware at each facility.

- Designed and implemented a global manufacturing quality program. Initiative enhanced product quality and reduced product write-offs by 45%

- Led team responsible for a Philippines manufacturing feasibility study encompassing financial analysis, legal/tax revision, plant design and site selection.

Director, Inventory Planning, Wilmington, DE   1989-1991
Reported to Director of Materials Management with staff of eight. Directed production planning and inventory management functions for multiple site manufacturing and distribution network for a $550 million business unit whose core business consisted of cocktail mixers and non-alcoholic sparkling wines.

DEVONSHIRE FARMS SPECIALTY GROCERY PRODUCTS   **1981-1989**
Boston, MA

Director, Production Planning & Inventory Control
Major brands include Red Hot Steak Sauce, Bull's Eye Mustard and Poncho Villo Mexican food products. Managed departments engaged in production planning for four food manufacturing facilities Responsibilities also included inventory management and warehouse replenishment for a network of 18 distribution centers. Reported to Director of Physical Distribution, with staff of four.

- Member of team that implemented order processing, inventory management, sales forecasting and DRP systems. Inventory savings of $6 million and customer order lead time reduction of 45% were achieved.

- Provided logistics support for numerous new product introductions while maintaining customer service levels at +99%.

EDISON ELECTRIC CORPORATION   **1979-1981**
Philadelphia, PA

- Graduate Student Training and Placement Program.

- Engineering assignments on team responsible for designing a new major appliance manufacturing facility.

- Materials Management responsibility for industrial Battery Charger facility and Mexican sub-assembly operation.

EDUCATION

M.B.A., 1987, Management Information Systems
Tufts University - Medford, MA

B.S., 1979, Mechanical Engineering
Tri-State University - Angola, IN

Richard F. Kean
122 Old Mill Trail
Portland, OR 71912

OFF: 207-954-4370   HOME: 207-953-6601

Marketing and Sales Executive with extensive experience and a progressive track record within the pulp and paper industry. Strong technical and organizations orientation and an ability to work closely with manufacturing to optimize the fit of mill capabilities to customer needs while maximizing profitability.

PROFESSIONAL EXPERIENCE

GORDON PAPER COMPANY, Portland, OR   **1981 - 1998**

Manager, Product Development and Strategic Planning   1996 - 1998
Pulp and Coated Paper Group
Primary responsibilities are to guide pulp and coated paper divisions in developing a new five year strategic plan, coordinate product development activity focusing on recycled paper, and participate in dumping case brought against European producers.

- Developed a full line of recycled coated paper grades to support new de-inking plants in three mills.
- Managed Gordon Paper's efforts and appeared as industry expert in European dumping case. Imports dropped 35% in 1996, 14% more in 1997.
- Directed work of mills and marketing groups for new five-year plan for 400,000 ton, $300MM business. Organized and wrote plan and board presentation.

Division Manager, Coated Papers Division   1991 - 1996
Responsible for marketing, sales and field technical services for the $200MM Coated Paper Division, the company's largest fine paper product line.

- Increased sales by 40% to support new 120,000 ton machine in Mississippi; this $212MM project was initiated by marketing to meet product mix and peak growth requirements of specialty market in 1993.
- Enriched the mix at high-cost Idaho mill with entry into wood-free coated market for $30MM in new sales. Doubled sales to smaller, regional merchants at $35/ton higher profit than that for larger brokers. Reduced spot sales as a result.
- Added three man field technical staff and reduced customer claim settlement time by 64%, costs by 29%. Saved $8MM in 1994 by stockpiling in first quarter slump and selling off inventory in fall market upturn.

Manager, Marketing and Sales, Coated Papers Division   1985 - 1991

- Added seven new positions to serve new sales volume and service needs. Increased sales 40% to fill new lightweight coated machine started in Washington in 1986.
- Reversed plan to shut down California mill in 1988 by adding new products that fit the machines better than prior mix. With 45% of sales in 1987, mill had 55% of profits.
- Repaired merchant relations with 18-month image campaign that turned 22,000 tons in 1985 into 190,000 tons by 1987. Ran full during 1986-1988 industry slump.

RICHARD F. KEAN   Page Two

Product Manager, Printing and Label Papers, Uncoated White Group   1981 - 1985

- Developed new catalog papers line with service guarantees for small customers. Expanded sales five-fold to 55,000 tons in two and a half years.
- Promoted higher profit offset sheet sales to 80% of mix versus industry average of 50% while growing uncoated printings from 115,000 to 245,000 tons in four years.
- Improved label profitability 25% by maximizing merchant sheet business, heavyweights, and direct sales to specialty converters.

SIMPSON INTERNATIONAL   **1977 - 1981**

Product Manager, New Products

- Reorganized product development activities to eliminate poorly researched products and focus on those with market potential. Coordinated expansion at Oregon mill and development of new in-line calendering process.
- Developed new business proposal for $25MM plant to make non-structural building panels from recycled fiber.
- Led marketing team of joint venture with major petrochemical company in development of synthetic pulp for papermaking. Directed all field studies.

GATWICK & COMPANY, INC.   **1972 - 1977**

New Product Engineer

- Did cold-call prospecting, market research, technical coordination, and field trials for release papers, solvent coating base, microspheres papers, other technical and specialty papers. Responsible for sales of solvent holdout and release papers.

Project Chemist   1970 - 1972

- Performed process improvement on paper machines, product development on uncoated specialties. Reduced form bond field rejects 70% with improved winding methods. Cut steam use on two largest machines by 16% to save $95,000/year.

EDUCATION

B.S. Pulp and Paper Engineering, University of Maine, Orono, ME (1970)

KAREN L. WHEATING
1408A Tower Place
Chicago, IL 61823
(312) 492-1807

SUMMARY OF QUALIFICATIONS

Operations Management. . . International Logistics. . . Strategic Planning

Management level professional with 12 years of continued career progression and key accomplishments. Diverse background including operations, international logistics and strategic planning responsibilities. Seeking key position with growth-oriented organization.

EXPERIENCE

AMERICAN CONSUMER PRODUCTS, INC.   **1983 - Present**

International Planning Manager, Chicago, IL (1995-Present)
Responsible for overall logistics direction, analysis and leadership to ACP's worldwide affiliates, licensees and direct customers of household chemicals and cleaning products, representing sales in excess of $2.1 billion in 32 countries.

- Managed all logistics activities for the most ambitious product roll-out in the history of the company, introducing new soup products into 32 countries in six months. Activities included coordinating production on two continents, developing distribution channels and assuring supply of strategic raw materials.

- Saved $1.7 million in transportation costs, by developing more efficient methods of loading and distribution.

- Created a database saving over $2.7 million in raw material costs, by identifying global raw material price differences in local markets.

North American Planning Manager, Chicago, IL (1993-1995)
Responsible for the initiation, management and coordination of production, materials, inventory and customer service for a $1.5 billion business unit with over 1,000 SKU's and 12 production sites. Also responsible for timing and location of additional capacity, allocation of production and transfer requirements.

- Reduced customer service failures 83%, best results in the history of the business unit.

- Developed a plan improving the introduction date of major new product by ten months, providing an additional $35 million in revenue.

- Improved inventory turns 15%.

KAREN L. WHEATING   **Page Two**

Mill Planner - ACP Plant, Raleigh, NC (1991-1993)
Responsible for inventory management, customer service and production scheduling of ACP's largest facility.   Supervised the production planning and customer service staff.   Facility shipments were in excess of $500 million.

- Analyzed and implemented 20% downsizing of operation resulting in $15 million savings.

- Improved inventory turns 65% to 51 turns per year.

- Used linear programming techniques to reduce waste, saving an additional $2.1 million.

Operations Manager - ACP Plant, Norcross, GA (1987-1991)
Managed department for a key raw material used in the manufacture of window cleaner. Responsible for cost, quality, customer service and the safety of 36 operators within the department.

- Successfully reduced quality defects 75% to less than 200 parts per million.

- Implemented a new inventory replenishment technique saving the company $650,000.

- Reduced waste, saving the company $500,000 per year.

- Reduced accidents 32% through implementation of safe work practices.

Planning Analyst - Chemicals Division, Chicago, IL (1985-1987)

Area Planner - Cleaner Division, Chicago, IL (1983-1985)

EDUCATION

M.B.A.,	Duke University, Durham, North Carolina	1983
B.S.,	Industrial Management, Georgia Tech., Atlanta, Georgia	1981

GREGORY D. HOCKSTETTER
46 Amethyst Drive
San Francisco, California 18465
Home: (651) 671-8669
Office: (651) 466-2018

SUMMARY

A financial executive with solid domestic and international experience, having performed the full breadth of the CFO function as Controller at a $1 billion corporate headquarters, Treasurer and Controller at a $2.6 billion corporate headquarters, Controller at a $1 billion manufacturing division and as CPA with a "Big Six" firm.

PROFESSIONAL HISTORY

FULLER COMPANY, San Francisco, CA   **1994-1998**

A subsidiary of Simpson Paper Company engaged in the production and sale of pulp and wood products along with the management of timberlands in North America. Over 30% of company's $2 billion in sales are export sales, primarily to Asian and European markets.

Corporate Controller - Fuller Company   *12/94-10/98*

- Directed annual and quarterly SEC reporting for Fuller Company, a NYSE listed master limited partnership, as well as reporting related to a $500 million shelf registration, $220 million 7.5% notes and a medium-term note program.

- Coordinated the preparation of operating plans/budgets along with presentations to senior management.

- Evaluated options, performed analysis, prepared presentations, and reviewed contracts related to an acquisition of $500 million of timberlands in Australia.

- Managed accounting, consolidations, external and internal reporting, financial planning and forecasting, risk management and capital planning/expenditure functions.

PORTER STEEL WORKS, Allentown, PA   **1982-1994**

A steel producer with annual sales of $3.4 billion, is engaged in the manufacture and sale of flat-rolled steel products along with the mining and pelletizing of iron ore and the mining of coal.

Vice President - Porter Steel Works   *12/93-11/94*
Treasurer   *08/90-12/93*

- Established a treasury function at Porter Steel Works when SMP Corporation, a Japanese steel maker, purchased 50% of PSW from Werner Corporation. Established and maintained banking relationships with domestic and foreign banks and obtained credit without guarantees from either parent.

- Negotiated and established approximately $790 million of innovative credit facilities, including $250 million revolving credit agreement and $85 million related letter of credit commitments; $405 million of project financing including construction and permanent financing with vendor and equity sources; $14 million variable rate pollution control issue and various other facilities including lease lines.

- Directed treasury operations, credit, accounts receivable, tax, and risk management.

GREGORY D. HOCKSTETTER   PAGE 2

Controller - Porter Steel Works   09/89-08/90

- Directed accounting functions, consolidation, internal and SEC reporting, as well as cost analysis and forecasting.

Assistant Controller - Whitcore Steel Group (the predecessor of Porter Steel Works)   11/88-09/89

- Coordinated the development of accounting systems to establish the steel group as a separate company and the development of accounting systems to centralize the management of cash disbursements, accounts receivable, salary payroll and market analysis.

- Represented management in the negotiations and sale of a major division.

- Managed accounting functions, cost analysis and forecasting.

Central States Division, Cleveland, OH (Porter Steel Works' largest division and a fully integrated steel mill with sales of $1.5 billion.)

Vice President and Controller - Central States Division   01/87-11/88
Assistant Controller   08/86-01/87

- Defined markets and strategic direction, including the rationalization of facilities to minimize costs and serve markets.

- Directed divisional accounting, budgetary planning, market analysis, cost analysis, methods studies (including industrial engineers), the development and implementation of standards, and management information services.

Manager of Cost and Methods - Central States Division   12/83-08/86

- Utilized standard cost system to improve productivity and costs. Implemented market profitability analysis.

General Supervisor of Accounting - Central States Division   11/82-12/83

- Improved productivity of department and the credibility of data output used in budgeting, planning and market analysis through procedural and system changes.

ALEXANDER & COMPANY, Detroit, MI   **1975-1982**

Certified Public Accountant

- Managed both tax and audit engagements in a broad variety of enterprises. Experience was obtained in manufacturing, service industries, retailing, banking, investment holding, franchise negotiations, and joint ventures.

EDUCATION & PROFESSIONAL CERTIFICATION

Wayne State University, B.A. in Accounting, 1975

CPA - State of Michigan. Certificate No. 077145

Member, AICPA

MARTIN D. CARTER

2354 East 121st Street
Clearfield, Illinois 66209

Home: 815-861-1333
Office: 815-541-7521
FAX: 815-541-0921

CAREER OBJECTIVE:

Senior management position with a growth oriented, customer focused organization requiring strong leadership, business planning, problem solving and innovative administration skills.

BACKGROUND SUMMARY:

Twenty years of progressive responsibility in the domestic/international environments of the pharmaceutical, consumer products and medical device industries with a strong success record in: cost reduction, reorganization, process redesign, performance management and strategic development.

PROFESSIONAL EXPERIENCE AND ACCOMPLISHMENTS:

MEDCO PHARMACEUTICALS - Springfield, Illinois   **1991 to Present**

Accounting Services Director, Corporate (1997 to Present)
Responsibilities include management of five departments and a support staff of over 30 associates including payroll, accounts payable, accounts receivable, travel/expense administration and benefit accounting. Significant achievements include:

- Reduced voucher payments outstanding over 30% and increased on-time payments by 20% through procurement process redesigns.
- Lowered service expenses by 35% with increased transaction productivity and efficiency through greater utilization of technology and process changes.
- Consolidated benefits accounting with compensation and benefits resulting in reduced service costs, faster claims processing, reporting and communications between trustee, record keeper and corporate.

Prescription Products Division Controller (1991 to 1997)
Responsibilities grew initially from a Sales and Marketing Controllership role to full financial and customer service support for the largest revenue division of the company with $3.4 billion in sales. As key financial representative on the Division President's staff, achieved significant growth and business success in several broad areas:

- Developed performance measurement and incentive plan objectives which successfully launched four new products in six months and grew earnings 25% for three consecutive years.
- Created a strategic intent and long-range business plan as our vision for the balance of the decade.
- Implemented a Customer Information Center which centralized incoming calls, reduced the number of incoming phone lines, reduced the number of dropped calls/busy signals from 60% to 18% and provided call response benchmark statistics.
- Established a managed care/Medicaid rebate claims processing group in response to OBRA legislation

Martin D. Carter

ACUVISION, INC. - Wheeling, West Virginia   **1989 to 1991**

International Division Controller
Newly created position provided unique organization, planning and reporting challenges for fast growing $60 mm dollar division. Key accomplishments include:

- Developed and implemented PC-based financial planning and forecasting system.
- Expanded responsibility for customer service and export orders processing. Process and reorganization efforts reduced lost and duplicate shipments, provided improved order confirmations and improved order status reporting.
- Lowered 120 days receivables by 45% through aggressive collection efforts.

BRISTOL MEYERS - Nashville, Tennessee   **1984 to 1989**

International Consumer Products Division
Manager, Financial Planning/Treasury Operations   (1987 - 1989)
Manager, Consolidations and Financial Reporting   (1985 - 1987)
Manager, General Accounting, Dexter, Inc.   (1984 - 1985)
Established financial accounting, reporting and planning functions for the relocated Dexter Corporation and the newly-created International Consumer Products Division. Key accomplishments include:

- Relocated a $100 mm corporate office through planning, organizing and managing the relocation process for accounts payable, cash receipts/disbursements, fixed assets, retail store accounting and inventory management. Hired and trained a staff of 20 in support of five ledgers, 58 retail stores, three manufacturing sites and one distribution center.
- Merged and reorganized five business units under one $300 mm worldwide division. Developed consolidation and operating requirements (internal/external), determined resource needs, hired, trained and developed a six person support staff and established financial reporting credibility.
- Initiated and developed uniform legal entity and proforma planning and financial reporting for 26 foreign subsidiaries utilizing an IBM System 38, M&D ledger software and integrated telecommunications technology. Reduced closing cycle 25% while expanding reporting capabilities to include product, SBU and geographic income, balance sheet and cash flow statements.

PENNECO AUTOMOTIVE, BECKER MFG. DIVISION - Wilmington, Delaware   **1982 to 1984**

Senior Financial Analyst
Responsible for capital and financial planning, international reporting and consolidation and capital appropriation preparation and analysis.

BRISTOL MEYERS - Edison, New Jersey   **1980 to 1982**

International Pharmaceutical Division
Consolidations Supervisor
Designed and implemented an automated proforma reporting system that reduced labor time 58%, increased reporting frequency, and expanded reporting capabilities to include product and geographic information. Preparation time was reduced from three weeks to one.

EDUCATION:

Graduate Work: New York University, Finance and Business Management
Undergraduate: State University of New York - B.A., Business/Economics, 1980
Continuing: Sales & Marketing Management Program, Illinois State University

CAROL W. MADISON
1421 Oliver Drive
Cherry Hill, NJ 19605

Residence: (609) 395-6170
Business: (205) 721-4833

DIRECTOR OF CREDIT AND COLLECTIONS, a highly-experienced credit professional possessing strong analytical and communication skills, and comprehensive bankruptcy experience for Fortune 500 companies. Managed all aspects of credit policy, including establishment of terms of sale and accounts receivable management in competitive markets.

UNIVERSAL CHEMICALS, INC., Philadelphia, PA   **1996 - Present**

An $800 million manufacturer of polymer specialties and chemical intermediates for the industrial market.

Director, Credit and Collections
Exercise total management responsibility for corporate credit and collections activities, inclusive of policy making; accounts receivable; consolidation and administration of U.S. and Canadian subsidiaries and divisions. Direct management and support staff of 30.
- Manage monthly accounts receivable portfolio of $50 million.
- Developed and introduced financial analysis program for evaluation and establishment of credit lines, facilitating control and reducing risk exposure.
- Initiated Vendor Credit Review Program as means of protecting long range interests.
- Played major role in integration and consolidation of multiple acquisitions into corporate operation.
- Responsible for all U.S. and Canadian credit/collections activities and resolution of deductions.
- Represent corporate interests in bankruptcy cases.

WARNER MANUFACTURING COMPANY, Newark, NJ   **1995 - 1996**

Manufacturers of consumer housewares with annual sales of $600 million.

Consultant
Served as independent consultant at the request of Chase Bank, lender at time of bankruptcy filing.
- Evaluated integrity of accounts receivable.
- Established collections programs and procedures effectively increasing collections over 100% first month and 300% second month.
- Created account reconciliation teams enabling timely identification of problems impacting cash flow.
- Reviewed merchandise return procedures and presented recommendations for improving controls.
- Initiated credit/risk evaluation analysis to identify and approve shipments to credit worthy customers.
- Functioned as finance liaison to sales and customers.

NATIONAL STEEL CORPORATION, Pittsburgh, PA   **1990 - 1995**

A $2.3 billion manufacturer of sheet metal and lighting fixtures.

Director, Credit and Collections (1993 - 1995)
Responsible for all policy aspects of credit, collections, accounts receivable, cash application, claims functions and co-op administration for U.S. operations. Supervised five managers and 32 clerical employees. Responsible for the subsidiary Canadian Credit Manager.

CAROL W. MADISON   Page Two

- Integrated sheet metal products division into the U.S. lighting division resulting in $90,000 annual savings and Dun & Bradstreet contract reduction of $25,000.
- Consolidated co-op administration function in-house with annual savings of $50,000.
- Key member of task force which established a full line distribution center, improving efficiencies and significantly reducing freight cost to customers.
- Consolidated cash application function under the credit department, resulting in quicker application of payments and identification of deductions.
- Applied analytical and negotiations skills in major bankruptcies and/or work-out situations to maximize returns on bad debt receivables and incremental sales.
- Established separate credit operation for Letters of Credit for export business which led to a more expeditious method of credit approval and timely shipments.

Credit Manager, U.S. (1990 - 1993)
Responsible for the extension of credit and collection of receivables for the U.S. division.
- Responsible for staffing and training of division credit personnel in all credit, collections and bankruptcy procedures, producing uniformity in problem-solving.
- Developed a collection program resulting in quicker conversion of accounts receivable for improved cash flow.
- Reorganized the U.S. credit operation resulting in total account responsibility for each Regional Credit Manager and subordinates, facilitating customer and sales relationships.

SMITH CORONA CORPORATION, Courtland, NY   **1983 - 1990**

Manufacturers of office machines and business equipment with revenues of $500 million.

Director, Credit and Collections/Credit Manager
Directed general policy-making and control of corporate credit, collections and accounts receivable departments ensuring profitable growth and sales development. Developed a proactive team approach with marketing and sales functions relating to customer/credit base. Analyzed, advised and projected financial soundness of daily business activity relating to legal, purchasing and marketing departments.
- Developed a progressive and effective collection program which increased cash flow.
- Established independent credit/collection department which facilitated company expansion into video and PC software market.
- Redesigned procedures and systems that efficiently processed orders via "credit by exception".
- Implemented the inclusion of personal computer system which streamlined procedures in credit, claims and collections departments.
- Managed all procedures to ensure timely retirement of investments in accounts receivable.

PRIOR POSITIONS   **1979 - 1983**

Credit Administrator, A.O. Smith Corporation   (1980 - 1983)
Marketing Cost Analyst, Rockwell International Corporation   (1979 - 1980)

EDUCATION

B.A., Accounting, University of Rhode Island, 1979

PROFESSIONAL AFFILIATIONS

Regional Board of Directors, National Association of Credit Management

WILLIAM A. DETRICK

23 Sutton Road
Columbia, MD 21606
(301) 421-1305 (H) or (301) 796-8140 (O)
Fax (301) 947-1501

Fifteen plus years as accessible senior-level human resources generalist in diverse large and small corporate cultures... Proven leader, communicator, problem-solver and strategic/tactical planner... Line and staff experience with domestic and international companies... Start-up, continuous improvement, rightsizing, turnaround and union-free achievements... Staffing, training and development, team building and reengineering innovator... Compensation, benefits and personnel practices designer... Due diligence, sale of company, and business shutdown facilitator... Information services and manufacturing background... PC fluent.

SELECTED CAREER ACCOMPLISHMENTS

VICE PRESIDENT - HUMAN RESOURCES   **Maxwell Company**   1995 - Present

Selected as Human Resources Executive by Vulcan Consulting, an interim management company for this $70 million manufacturer of pumps and controls. Charged with fostering and leading Human Resource initiatives designed to maintain attractiveness of business during asset sale/due diligence process.

*   Delivered high-quality due diligence results for parent, division, and three buyer companies. Restored and enhanced workplace accord and middle management cohesiveness.

*   Optimized retention, productivity and motivation in domestic and offshore facilities through effective use of stay-bonuses, employee recognition and severance plans.

*   Served as liaison between company, parent and three buyer companies. Orchestrated equipment dispersal and records dispersal and destruction.

*   Implemented leadership and project management training to support a reengineering initiative that projected a 50-75% reduction in process time and costs.

*   Met ongoing compensation, benefits and employee relations needs. Administered salary continuance, COBRA and outplacement resources for multiple locations.

DIRECTOR OF HUMAN RESOURCES   **Rancor, Inc.**   1993 - 1995

Turned around functional operation for a seven site, 1300 employee equipment manufacturer with annual revenues of $600 million. Managed 17 employees.

*   Implemented workforce downsizing and realignment of supervision, saving $1.5 million/annum, without disruption in the retained workforce.

*   Introduced exempt performance planning and appraisal practices that resulted in significantly higher satisfaction levels among employees.

William A. Detrick   Page Two

* Resolved impending $11 million FAS-106 liability problem and saved $575,000 per year with minimal effect on corporate reputation and employees by modifying health coverages and administrative procedures.

* Spearheaded leadership, team building and facilitation training rated as "best ever" by participants and their managers.

VICE PRESIDENT - HUMAN RESOURCES   **Leisure Craft, Inc.**   1987 - 1993

Led department start-up. Teamed with peers to develop and advance a business and people sensitive Human Resource agenda for world class manufacturer of quality leisure furniture. Notably influenced, as officer and executive committee member, the strategic and tactical planning for this $450 million per year business. Key participant in operational decision-making for all functional disciplines.

* Led "start-up" of Human Resource function and designed and instituted "first ever" comprehensive corporate policies, practices and benefits programs. Managed team of eight employees responsible for Human Resources, Community Relations and Employee Services.

* Effectively integrated cultural diversity and forged six years of union-free workplace harmony through supervisor and management development, employee relations and communications programs and rigorous employee involvement.

* Led community relations initiatives which earned an "employer of choice" reputation and positioned the company as a recognized corporate citizen.

* Designed and implemented "first ever" flexible compensation programs, including pay-for-skills, perfect attendance, work-at-home and temporary employment that achieved turnover and absenteeism levels below 1.7% and 1.3% respectively.

* Developed and instituted health care cost control measures that held premiums and increases well below national averages.

* Designed and implemented successful full-featured compensation and benefit plans, exempt/non-exempt performance and salary review programs, wage and salary incentive plans, and executive compensation and retirement plans.

VARIOUS POSITIONS   **General Motors Corp.**   1977 - 1987

Performed increasingly responsible functions. Began as hourly technician and ultimately served as Manufacturing Supervisor and Plant Level Human Resources Manager.

EDUCATION

B.A., Business Management, University of Virginia, 1977
(GPA: 3.42)

Donald E. Patterson
12 Lakeview Drive
Shaker Heights, OH 16950

Home: (216) 596-8021   Office: (216) 799-8181

Human Resource Executive with 19 years experience with quality *Fortune* 500 companies.
Experience leading productivity teams resulting in an annual $5 million cost reduction including:

* closing excess capacity locations ($1 million)	* reducing health cost by 15% ($450,000)
* redesigning compensation packages ($1 million)	* consolidating acquisitions ($1 million)
* negotiating new labor with United Steel Workers	* reducing overtime ($500,000)

Track record of analyzing total business needs and implementing plans that satisfy employees needs
while improving the competitiveness of the business.

EXPERIENCE:

1996 - Present **LINCOLN STEEL CORP.,** Cleveland, OH
Vice President of Human Resources
Reporting to the President, responsible for organization, staffing, compensation
and benefits, communications, total quality leadership, labor relations, training and
development, safety and legal compliance for seven locations with $300 million in
sales.

- Managed negotiations of two contracts with the USWA resulting in controlled
  cost, greater flexibility, and use of teams and "Temporaries".
- Developed new executive and salaried incentive plans including stock options
  and SERP's with annual savings of more than $1 million.
- Coordinated the organization's first restructuring resulting in $1.5 million
  annual savings.
- Initiated development in leadership, strategic planning and performance
  management.
- Defeated a Salaried Union organizing attempt.
- Established new rating and job structure policies.

1993 - 1996 **BAXTER COMMERCIAL PRODUCTS, INC.,** Toledo, OH
Vice President of Human Resources
Reported to the President with classic HR responsibilities including union
avoidance for six domestic and three European locations with sales of $600
million.

- Participated in leading a culture change of continuous value improvement to
  enhance quality and competitiveness while reducing cost.
- Managed the integration of two acquisitions (one domestic; one European).
- Participated in downsizing two locations with high regard for associates.

Donald E. Patterson - Page 2

- Reorganized Product Development, International Sales & Marketing and Advanced Manufacturing resulting in 30% greater new product output and customer focus.
- Assisted in establishing self-directed work teams with higher quality and lower costs.
- Defeated two organizing attempts by labor unions early in my tenure.
- Participated in the design and implementation of new health insurance coverage.
- Increased effectiveness of the HR function with automated systems while reducing costs.
- Conducted annual Human Resources Reviews to identify the needed skills to implement Strategic Plan and allow for succession.

1979 - 1993   **DRESSER INDUSTRIES,** Corporate Offices, Dallas, TX
Director of Human Resources - Industrial Equipment   (1990-1993)
Division had five locations with over 1,500 employees.

- Led the Division into strategic planning, goal setting, and performance management.
- Planned the consolidation of two facilities resulting in $400,000 savings.
- Negotiated a one-year extension to contract while resolving a termination settlement with United Auto Workers in Detroit.
- Designed and implemented flexible benefit plan.
- Introduced employee involvement at two locations (Cleveland and Philadelphia) changing from strike situations to cost reduction of hundreds of thousands.
- Negotiated a first-time contract with United Auto Workers in Atlanta as the result of an earlier election; employees later decertified the UAW.

Employee Relations Manager - Commercial Products, Chicago, IL   (1987-1990)
Total classic employee relations function for two non-union plants.

- Developed uniform policies while reducing staff by 35% through the introduction of systems. Trained my successor.
- Enhanced work environment with the introduction of employee involvement saving hundreds of thousands of dollars annually.
- Member of Dresser's corporate-wide team for cost management and HR computerization. Delivered the specifications for the system.

Personnel Manager - Conveyor Equipment, Atlanta, GA   (1983-1987)

- Conducted foreman training. Provided a method of discipline that resulted in over 100 justifiable terminations in a workforce of 2000.
- Negotiated a team concept with AWA, reducing scrap by 50%.

Finance and Accounting Intern - Conveyor Equipment, Atlanta, GA (1979-1983)

EDUCATION: **Michigan State University** - MS in Organizational Development, 1979.
Penn State University - Bachelors in Business Administration with honors, 1977.

VERONICA C. HILL
121 Stadium Road
Vernon Hills, Illinois 60601
Home 708/791-8952
Work 708/277-7091

OBJECTIVE: **Senior Human Resources Management** position requiring a generalist with an MS degree and experience in all human resource management functions emphasizing compensation, management development, recruiting, organization development, employee relations and minority affairs in diverse domestic and international environments.

EXPERIENCE:

Aug. 1996-Present **COMMONWEALTH INSURANCE**, Lincolnshire, IL

Director - Human Resources, Securities Department, Plainfield, IL
Report to Chief Investment Officer. Responsible for all human resources activities for 410 employees in the Investments Group. Promoted from Corporate position as **Director - Staffing & Recruiting** (managed 32 employees involved in local and college recruiting, in-house temporary program, community employment and outplacement center).

- Designed and implemented a non-qualified voluntary investment plan which provided employees with the opportunity to defer bonuses on a pre-tax basis for three to 21 years.

- Designed and obtained management commitment for a banded compensation structure which combined 13 salary grades into five bands.

- Successfully managed numerous employee layoffs, including some sensitive situations, avoiding grievances and potential costly litigation.

- Implemented changes resulting in productivity and/or cost savings. Utilized desk-top publishing to reduce advertising costs, decentralized campus recruiting expenses to reduce corporate overhead, increased use of in-house temporary (clerical & professional) employment organization to 98% of temporaries employed, utilized use of national career fairs and minority organizations to reduce recruiting costs, canceled a costly and inefficient community recruiting/training program.

- Designed a national college recruiting strategy based on needs of business and major field offices incorporating a University Executive concept. Developed strategies for each school and created a national advertising strategy to reduce costs and better target student populations. Developed partnership with Commonwealth Foundation to support funding which corresponded to recruiting needs.

- Developed a concentrated campus minority recruiting strategy which increased minority hires by 18% in the first year and resulted in recognition by *Afro-American* and *Hispanic Collegian Quarterly* of Commonwealth as a top 100 company employer.

1987 - 1996 **UNIVERSAL ELECTRIC COMPANY**, Cambridge, MA

(1994 - 1996) **Consultant - Recruiting Issues,** University Recruiting Development Dept.
Responsible for developing corporate minority and MBA recruiting strategies and recommending actions. Implemented strategies across company's businesses.

VERONICA C. HILL   Page Two

- Conceived minority strategy and developed partnership with Universal Electric Foundation including scholarship funding of over $1 million. Implemented program by involving Universal University Executive business recruiting teams with historically black schools which resulted in recognition of Universal as a significant player by national minority organizations.

- Re-targeted MBA hiring strategy from corporate business level. New focus coupled with comprehensive communication program increased commitment and hires.

(1993 - 1994)   **Manager - Human Resources**, Universal Trading Company
Reported to President of this $3 billion international business with over 500 employees worldwide. promoted from position as **Manager - Organization Development & Staffing**.

- Redesigned organization structure to accommodate changing business requirements including reducing census 50% and consolidating product groups. Actions contributed to one year business reversal from $3 million loss to break-even.

- Analyzed industry pay standards and designed bonus program tied to business goals to place company in more competitive compensation position. Improved new hire acceptance rate 50% and halted loss of key personnel.

- Sourced and hired international and specialty talent in widely diversified commodity and technical fields. Beat all hiring time standards and minimized recruiting costs.

- Led management team in creating and implementing succession plan including employee career development activities which improved retention and speeded staff process.

(1987 - 1993)   **Human Resources Representative**, Universal Corporate Consulting
Responsible for managing the full scope of HR activities for 300 employees in this technical consulting organization. Earlier, as **Coordinator/Specialist - Relations Programs** oversaw and executed numerous HR programs.

- Restructured secretarial staff into pooled system. Reduced overtime 80%, turnover 50% and absenteeism 60% while maximizing productivity.

- Developed Affirmative Action Plan conforming to government regulations, met or exceeded hiring/promotion goals and passed federal audit.

EDUCATION: **MS - Human Resources Management**, Danbury University, Danbury, CT- 1987
BS - Business Administration, Hampshire University, Fairfield, CT - 1985

HONORS: YWCA Achievement Award for Professional Women - 1992
Universal Electric's Key Recognition Award - 1988

PERSONAL: INROADS of Chicago, Board of Directors
Member, National Human Resource Society

Victoria A. Anderson
5006 Third Avenue, Apt. 134
New York, NY 12282
(202) 650-8414

OBJECTIVE

Human Resources Director or Vice President responsible for total HR support of a company or division with 20,000 or more employees. Consider smaller start-up or fast growth.

SUMMARY

Strong background in Human Resources management gained through experience in two Fortune 100 corporations, primarily in direct Customer Service businesses. Experience includes overall HR responsibility for a major corporate business including planning, developing and implementing all HR related programs. Supported five different businesses. Responsible for providing HR support to over 24,000 employees in 30 countries. Strategically directed strong build-ups, severe downturns and organizational restructuring. Experienced in domestic and international. Strengths include:

- Ability to integrate HR into the business
- Providing HR strategic direction
- Team leader and facilitator
- Effective communicator at all levels

- Successful at stabilizing crises and uncertainties
- Innovative problem solving prevention
- Understanding of operations (factory & field)
- Reengineering and aligning business to need

EXPERIENCE

LORAL CORPORATION, New York, NY   **1995 - Present**

Director of Human Resources
Manage total Human Resources Operations for Loral Corporation including the strategic planning, developing and implementing all HR related programs supporting over 24,000 employees in 30 countries. Responsible for worldwide operations, domestic and international.

- Active member of the management team which restructured three companies into one company unit.
  - Led the restructuring of three HR organizations, in three companies, into one new HR organization
  - Directed the design, development and implementation of the reduction-in-force package and process.
  - Facilitated reengineering and consolidating of HR processes for speed, quality and consistency.

- Integrated HR with business objectives and aligned HR initiatives to directly impact these objectives.
  - Established HR initiatives, specific projects, project teams and action plans to achieve initiatives.
  - Active on management team to design individual incentives and scorecards focused to achieve business goals.
  - Implemented a management communication plan with all employees focused on achieving specific results.

Victoria A. Anderson page two

BASF CORPORATION, Parsippany, NJ   1984 - 1995

Human Resources Director, Coatings and Colorants Division   *1991 - 1995*
Manage total Human Resources for a major corporate business including planning, developing and implementing all HR related programs. Responsible for compensation and benefits, employee relations, employee development, employment health & medical and safety supporting up to 3500 employees. Experienced in domestic and international.

- Integrated Human Resources with the business objectives.
  - Developed and implemented programs which improved the ratio of sales per payroll.
  - Business achieved #1 position in the company for highest employee attitude ever.
  - Established Safety Awareness and Prevention programs reducing lost work days 70% in three years.
  - Instituted Total Quality Management and Communication programs at all levels.

- Pro-actively resolved problems through effective listening, negotiating and preventive measures.
  - Avoided a Union Campaign/Union Attempt by involving employees to set up improvement programs.
  - Resolved all unfair labor charges in company's favor and successfully completed three OFCCP audits.
  - Reengineered processes to reduce cycle time and improve products and service.
  - Restructured HR Corporate Policy to be more competitive while retaining employee sensitivity.
  - Recognized for gaining the trust and confidence of all employees by serving them as customers.

- Provided HR strategic direction to continue profitability through both growth and downsizing cycles.
  - Directed employee involvement, continuous improvement and customer focus.
  - Continually upgraded employee skills and contributions through retraining and restructuring.
  - Instituted Self-Evaluation and Career Reviews to manage people resources and avoid lay-offs.
  - Strategically managed development of Self-Directed Work Teams requiring 30% fewer employees.

- Established a reputation for excellent comprehension of operations, both factory and field.
  - Experienced in domestic and international field operations.
  - Strengthened communications between field and factory by establishing annual field meetings.

Human Resources Director, Consumer Products Division   *1989 - 1991*
Managed total Human Resources including employment, compensation and benefits, employee relations, development, health & medical, and safety for an operation of 2600 employees.

Group Compensation Manager, Fibers Division   *1987 - 1989*
Responsible for Compensation and related activities including establishing competitive salary structure for a Division of Corporate with 7500 employees. Coordinated all compensation related activities up through Division President and served on compensation and benefits committees to determine corporate policy.

Employment/Training Manager, Fibers Division   *1986 - 1987*
Human Resources Representative, Fibers Division   *1984 - 1986*

EDUCATION

M.B.A., Management, New York University   1984
B.S., Industrial Management, New York University   1982

BRENDA A. JACKSON

41 Willow Avenue   (516) 837-0147 (H)
Adia, MI 75019   (516) 936-0800 (O)

SUMMARY

Results-oriented Human Resources Manager with 12 years of progressive experience in high technology and consumer products industries. Primary areas of expertise include **Employee Relations, Staffing, EEO and Compensation & Benefits**. Three years of experience assisting an Application Team in successfully pursuing and winning the *Malcolm Baldrige National Quality Award*.

EXPERIENCE

AMWAY CORPORATION, Adia, MI   **1995-Present**
The largest direct sales organization in the consumer products industry. Fortune 500 Company with customers in 23 countries and annual retail sales in excess of $2.5 billion.

Human Resources Manager, Distribution Group
Responsible for establishing, implementing, directing, planning and coordinating all Human Resources activities required to support five Regional Distribution Centers located in New York, Chicago, Los Angeles, Dallas, Atlanta and Boston. Serve as consultant and business partner to management team to facilitate ongoing development of proactive employee relations programs.

- Developed and implemented a decentralization strategy which significantly improved HR services within each of the six regions.

- Negotiated a 20% reduction in the hourly mark-up for temporary personnel provided by contract labor agencies.

- Established cost-effective staffing procedures which resulted in a 60% reduction in the cost-per-hire for exempt professionals.

- Achieved a $100,000 annual reduction in Workers Compensation payments through effective safety programs and aggressive case management.

LOCKHEED CORPORATION, Dallas, TX   **1985-1995**
A global, high-technology manufacturing and engineering company with 70,000 employees and annual revenues in excess of $10 billion.

Regional Human Resources Manager, Missiles & Space Company   1993-1995
Responsible for leading, organizing, and developing the Human Resources Team to provide a comprehensive array of support and services for 6000+ employees at multiple sites throughout the United States.

- Implemented a new staffing process that significantly reduced cost and cycle-time while improving the company's overall image on college campuses.

BRENDA A. JACKSON   **PAGE TWO**

- Successfully initiated the policy framework, communication and implementation strategy to establish the company's second smoke-free work site.

- Directed and implemented a new performance development process which resulted in increased employee empowerment and a more effective, team-oriented culture.

- Served as a member of the Malcolm Baldrige National Quality Award application writing and support team for the Human Resources Utilization Section.

Employee Relations Manager, Aeronautical Systems Company   1989-1993
Responsible for leading and coaching the Employee Relations function to provide value-added support and services for 2000+ management, engineering and manufacturing employees.

- Member of the Human Resources team responsible for developing and implementing a new reduction-in-force policy that guided the company in successfully downsizing several operating units.

- Established a systematic tracking mechanism which provided real-time EEO status reporting capabilities prior to commencing reduction-in-force actions.

- Chaired a Creative Action Team that designed, developed and distributed a *Career Development Guide* to facilitate professional development and career planning for over 2000 employees.

Personnel/Compensation/Staffing Administrator, Missile & Space Company   1986-1989
Responsible for providing generalist and specialist support for the Manufacturing, Engineering and Quality Assurance divisions within the Missile & Space Company.

- Managed an aggressive College Recruiting Program which hired and relocated over 300 college students annually from the best engineering universities throughout the U.S.

- Established computer systems capabilities which resulted in more effective decision-making with regard to Compensation, EEO and Affirmative Action.

- Designed, developed and delivered a series of training programs to improve employee performance during periods of explosive business growth.

Assembly Supervisor, Missiles & Space Company   1985-1986
Supervised 30 employees in the assembly of missile components.

EDUCATION

M.S.,	Industrial Relations, Cornell University, Ithica, NY	1985
B.B.A.,	Personnel Administration, Michigan State University, East Lansing, MI	1980

AUDREY S. WALKER
22 Butternut Lane
Morristown, NJ 08057
(609) 641-1934

EXPERIENCE

BETA TECHNOLOGY, INC.   **1990 to Present**
Publicly held agricultural biotechnology company with four subsidiaries and two major operating joint ventures.

Senior Human Resources Administrator (1997 - present)
Report to Vice President, Human Resources and Administration of this leading biotechnology company. Responsibilities include managing flexible compensation, the self-insured health plan and other personnel functions.

Major Accomplishments:

- Manage administration of four company 401(k) plans.
- Effectively administered COBRA compliance for former employees affected by the company downsizings.
- Reduced (by 80%) turnaround time from claim to payment of the flexible spending account reimbursement.
- Managed the Summer Intern Program which employed an average of 35 students per year.
- Designed, implemented and managed Human Resources Information System, to track and report employee information for management decision making.

Human Resources Representative (1995 - 1997)
Reported to the Director, Human Resources and Administration. Responsibilities included administration of all company benefits.

Major Accomplishments:

- Established company medical department through subcontracting with private physician which resulted in reduction of workers' compensation lost-time.
- Designed and administered an employee survey, the response to which resulted in changes to the benefits plans to better serve the needs of the employees.
- Designed and implemented new employee orientation procedures which resulted in smoother integration of new hires into the organization.

Administrative Services Supervisor (1994 - 1995)
Reported to the Director, Human Resources and Facilities. Responsibilities included supervising receptionist and office assistant and providing administrative support to the office.

Major Accomplishments:

- Planned and coordinated the Annual Shareholder's and Scientific Advisory Board Meetings.

Audrey S. Walker   Page 2

- Reduced the cost of shareholder communication program by careful list validation, eliminating unnecessary mailings.

Office Manager (1990 - 1994)
Reported to Executive Vice President. Responsibilities included general administrative and executive secretarial assignments.

Major Accomplishments:

- Trained and supervised co-op students.
- Designed and implemented various office information reports.

SAVORY SOUP COMPANY   1986 to 1990

Secretary to Director of Research
Typed scientific manuscripts, bibliographies, reports and correspondence. Prepared slides for presentations.

SHADY ACRES NURSING & CONVALESCENT HOME   1984 to 1986

Secretary to the Director of Nursing
Recorded minutes, tabulated time cards, prepared monthly nursing coverage schedule. Updated employee records.

EDUCATION

Camden County College (Dean's List)
Associates Degree, Business Management Technology (1995 - Present)

Penn State University (Fall, 1993)
Certificate in Professional Human Resources

COMPUTER SKILLS

WordPerfect, Lotus, Freelance, Harvard Graphics,
By Design Graphics, First Resource (Human Resource Database)

PROFESSIONAL AFFILIATIONS

Society for Human Resources Management
Tri-State Human Resource Management Association

WILLA B. PARKER
806 Skinner Drive
Norwalk, Connecticut 91317
(202) 613-1475 Home
(202) 712-3141 Office

EXPERIENCE

AMERICAN INTERNATIONAL BANK, New York, NY   **1996 - Present**
Senior Vice President/Director of Worldwide Compensation and Benefits
Principal accountabilities include the strategic design, development and implementation of all direct and indirect compensation programs to include executive compensation, variable pay programs, base pay plans, welfare and qualified and non-qualified retirement plans for all domestic and international locations (20 countries, 70,000 employees and 18,000 retirees). Examples of recent achievements:

- Orchestrated one of the largest compensation and benefit mergers in the financial services industry.
- Designed, developed and implemented one of the first all-employee financial planning programs.
- Managed the company benefit costs at 0% growth over the last three years and down for 1997.
- Introduced a service-based compensation consulting unit to service line business units.
- Developed and implemented flexible benefits program and introduced Managed Care Health Program for all domestic employees.
- Reduced FAS 106 (retiree welfare costs) liability by over $40 million annually, one of few companies to successfully impact past retirees.
- Revised executive compensation program with focus on increased share ownership.
- Decreased growth in fixed personnel expense through increased use of variable pay plans for non-executive population.
- Developed and implemented successful compensation and benefit template for integrating over 18 acquisitions.
- Reengineered HR support areas and initiated outsourcing of all non-value oriented activities; i.e., benefit/pension administration, due diligence, compensation, etc.

ITT CORPORATION, New York, NY   **1994 - 1996**
Director of Worldwide Compensation
Principal accountabilities included the design, implementation and administration of all executive compensation to include long-term restricted stock, phantom stock and stock option programs, short-term management and sales incentive programs, deferred compensation, Board of Director compensation, salary management policies and programs, equity of job evaluations in operating divisions, development of total remuneration strategies for domestic and international locations (95 countries and 110,000 employees) and tactical implementation. Examples of achievements:

- Developed long-term incentive plan with performance based restricted stock.
- Developed extensive compensation communications program to facilitate change and increase executive awareness.
- Converted NQSO/SARs to broker/dealer NQSOs, thus saving $85 million in P&L costs.
- Designed and implemented performance-based long-term deferred cash and phantom stock plans for foreign subsidiaries.
- Developed alternative reward programs to allow management greater flexibility in retaining high performers.
- Introduced new expatriate compensation program to maximize equity and transferability across all operating companies.
- Developed total remuneration measurement strategy to determine overall compensation and benefit competitive posture.

WILLA B. PARKER   PAGE TWO
(510) 938-4163

THE HAY GROUP, New York, NY   1990 - 1994
Practice Director for the Northeast
Responsibilities included analyzing client business conditions in order to develop effective compensation and
benefit strategies, executive compensation programs (i.e., short/long-term cash incentive vehicles, stock based
incentive plans, competitive base pay programs, deferred compensation plans); salary management programs, job
evaluation systems, compensation audits and surveys. Performed business development activities such as
conducting seminars, delivering speeches and designing special topical surveys.

LITTON INDUSTRIES, INC., Beverly Hills, CA   1986 - 1990
Director of Compensation & Benefits
For domestic and international activities (50,000 employees). Responsibilities included designing and
implementing management incentive programs, multi-location base pay programs, maintained corporate-wide job
evaluation system (Hay), recommended and administered expatriate and foreign national compensation policies
and procedures. Recommended, implemented and administered all health and welfare benefit programs including
profit sharing, medical, life insurance, etc. Examples of achievements:

- Reduced welfare benefit costs by $3 million by revising benefit funding arrangements.
- Revised expatriate compensation programs to maximize tax effectiveness.
- Recommended termination and recapture of $50 million in excess pension assets.

McKESSON CORPORATION, San Francisco, CA   1982 - 1986
Manager, Compensation and Benefits
For domestic and international activities. Responsibilities included designing and implementing executive and
middle management incentive programs, multi-location base pay programs, innovative sales incentive plans,
automated salary planning and budget modeling, corporate-wide job evaluation programs, performance
management systems and recommended and administered expatriate compensation policies and procedures.
Designed, implemented and administered all health and welfare benefit programs including 401(k) plan, self-
administered, self-funded medical programs. Examples of achievements:

- Established and implemented sales incentive plans to maximize asset utilization, deployment and margins.
- Revised short-term management incentive plan to better link company and individual performance.
- Developed and implemented corporate-wide computerized job evaluation program.
- Instituted expatriate/TCN compensation program.
- Revised health plans to increase cost effectiveness.
- Designed and implemented 401(k) plan.

LONE STAR GAS COMPANY, Dallas, TX   1979 - 1982
Manager of Administration
Duties involved wage and salary administration, recruitment policy, development, safety, communications,
supervision of support services.

EDUCATION

B.S., Management, U.C.L.A., 1979

PROFESSIONAL ACTIVITIES

Frequent speaker at national conferences for ACA, Conference Board, AMA, etc.
Published several articles on mergers and acquisitions, benefits, etc.
Certified Compensation Professional

SUSAN A. RICCO

12 Sharon Circle
West Chester, PA 19382

Home: (610) 696-4066
Work: (610) 565-3141

OBJECTIVE: Challenging Benefits and/or Compensation position with a progressive company where broad management skills and knowledge can be fully utilized.

PROFESSIONAL EXPERIENCE:

1972
to
Present

SCOTT PAPER COMPANY, Corporate Headquarters (Philadelphia, PA)
World's largest manufacturer and marketer of sanitary tissue products with annual sales of approximately $4 billion and 20,000 employees worldwide.

Manager of Qualified Plans (1994 - Present)
Report to Manager of Compensation & Retirement. Primary responsibility for Hourly and Salaried Investment Plans (10,000 participants) and Salaried Retirement Plan (10,500 participants). Design, communicate and, through the use of outside suppliers, direct the administration of these Plans. Manage external relationship for Executive Tax Planning and Preparation Service. Executive contact for compensation and benefits information.

Significant Accomplishments:

- Serve on Project Team to design, implement and communicate new Defined Contribution Retirement Plan for salaried employees (2,500 participants). Project to be completed June, 1995.
- Provided benefits technical support for five divestitures involving 4,800 employees.
- Serve on Project Team to change recordkeeper and voice response system for Hourly and Salaried Investment Plans. Project to be completed June, 1995.

Manager of Job Evaluation & Comparative Analysis (1993 - 1994)
Reported to Manager of Total Pay. Responsibility for managing Corporate Job Evaluation System and completing various compensation surveys used to determine salary line and ranges. Provided compensation and benefits information for input to the annual proxy statement. Managed external relationship for Executive Individual Financial Planning. Executive contact for compensation and benefits information.

Significant Accomplishments:

- Served on Project Team to develop and implement simplified Base Pay Structure ("broadbanding").
- Implemented ten job ladders for non-exempt employees in Philadelphia.

Manager of Compensation & Benefits Services (1990 - 1993)
Reported to Director of Benefits and supervised two employees. Directed the process of delivering timely and accurate information to Corporate Headquarters, Field Sales, Expatriate and Third Country National active and retiree groups across the spectrum of employee benefits (Group Insurance, Investment Plans and Retirement Plans). Managed Long Term Disability, Total and Permanent Disability and Death claims processing and counseling. Expanded and maintained interactive benefits communication system. On a corporate-wide basis, provided financial planning capability development through seminars and interactive benefits communication system. Responsible for Human Resources Policy formulation, updating and approval.

Significant Accomplishments:

- Developed and implemented Services Group concept.
- Provided benefits technical support for three acquisitions, two divestitures and one plant closure.
- Coordinated financial planning and outplacement assistance for significant work force reduction program.

Manager of Thrift Plans & Financial Planning Assistance (1982 - 1990)
Reported to Director of Benefits and supervised two employees. Managed Hourly and Salaried Investment Plans and Employee Stock Ownership Plan administration and communication. Managed interactive benefits communication system. Managed corporate-wide personal and pre-retirement financial counseling (executive and group) programs.

Significant Accomplishments:

- Implemented hourly and salaried 401(k) programs.
- Implemented company-wide Employee Stock Ownership Plan (ESOP) for all salaried and hourly employees.
- Developed quarterly Investment Plan Newsletter.
- Developed and implemented interactive benefits communication system.
- Developed and implemented Executive Individual and Group Personal and Pre-Retirement Planning Programs.

IR Operations & Administration Project Assistant (1979 - 1982)
Reported to Director of Human Resources - Operations & Administration. Responsible for job evaluation for all plant sites and various administrative projects.

Various Administrative Positions within Human Resources (1972 - 1979)

PC SKILLS: Multi-Mate, Microsoft Windows 3.1, Microsoft Word 6.0, Microsoft Excel 5.0

MILDRED A. CARTER

210 Seashell Lane
Orlando, FL 93293

Office: (413) 652-4176
Home: (413) 255-7621
Fax: (413) 560-4141

OBJECTIVE

Senior level human resources development position responsible for organization development, executive management development, and training.

EXPERIENCE

1995 - Present

PRIME CONSULTANTS, INC. - Orlando, FL
A management consulting and training firm whose client organizations are typically in the manufacturing and high tech industries. A leader in attracting Florida State Employment Training funding for clients.

As **Senior Consultant**, I am responsible for conducting organization-wide assessments and designing complete training and education curricula for all clients; as well as designing, developing, customizing and conducting training in cultural change, empowerment, leadership and management development, quality communications and other OD implementations. Perform executive assessments, provide coaching, and help develop individualized development strategies and plans. I also operate as a freelance training and development consultant.

- Designed, developed, and conducted new executive and senior manager transitions which increased their assimilation effectiveness by 300%.

- Trained and facilitated over one hundred self-directed work teams resulting in 25% to 75% productivity gains.

- Designed and customized results oriented leadership development programs for top teams.

1991 - 1995

NATIONAL IMAGING SYSTEMS, INC. - Atlanta, GA
One of the fastest growing medical imaging companies in the world, with $130 million annual sales, 650 employees throughout the U.S.

As **Manager, Management and Organization Development**, I was responsible for internal OD/Management consulting, reengineering studies, corporate-wide executive/management education, training and development, and succession planning. Assisted the CEO and other Executive Team members in determining their development needs, personalized development plans, university executive programs, and coordinated supporting resources.

- Planned and facilitated Business Reengineering studies which trimmed inventory $1.5 million, cut G&A expenses 20%, and restructured Sales and Service from four regions to three.

MILDRED A. CARTER   **Page Two**

- Designed and installed company's first corporate executive and management succession planning system in a six month period; half the time allotted.

- Designed and orchestrated first Leadership and Effective Management Course for high potential middle and senior level managers; 55% below the planned budget.

1986 - 1991   **GENERAL ELECTRIC SPACE SYSTEMS - Valley Forge, PA**
Aerospace company with $40 billion annual sales and 42,000 employees.

As **Senior Organization Development Consultant**, my primary responsibilities involved designing executive development programs, coaching senior managers on their succession plans, team building, executive off-site conferences, quality improvement methods, and internal management consulting.

- Redesigned the two-year Executive Development Program to focus primarily on key business strategies and improvement of executive leadership and management practices.

- Improved response to customer's Request for Quotation by 300% and improved delivery time on military spares by 35%.

- Facilitated continuous improvement projects totalling more than $50 million in savings.

- Improved succession planning effectiveness resulting in an 80% selection rate.

EDUCATION   1986 - MBA   Business Management
                              Michigan State University, East Lansing, MI
                 1984 - BS   Business Management
                              Cleveland State University, Cleveland, OH

Organization Effectiveness Consultant Course - Monterey, CA, 1991
Advanced Organization Effectiveness Program - Monterey, CA, 1988

Qualified trainer for these international programs:

- "The Right Way to Manage," Conway Quality, Inc.
- "Seven Habits of Highly Effective People," Covey & Associates
- "Situational Leadership," Blanchard Training, Inc.
- "Managing for Productivity," ODI, Inc.

Jean A. Wagner	**902 Somers Road**
(908) 792-8133	**Princeton, New Jersey 80903**

CORPORATE RELATIONS

Highly influential team builder with several successful years
in management and governmental affairs.
Effective communicator at all levels.

- Regulatory Compliance
- Team Supervision
- Corporate Training
- Public Speaking
- Collateral Material

- Marketing Management
- Video Production
- Communications
- Corporate Liaison
- Business Development

Selected Career Highlights

Manager, Legislative and Government Affairs
Johnson & Johnson, New Brunswick, NJ   1995 - Present
Protect the interests of one of the nation's leading pharmaceutical, healthcare and consumer products companies, a NYSE listed corporation with over $12 billion in annual sales.

- Interact with legislators, trade associations, and lobbyists to represent the company's position on various issues.
- Prepare written statements and formal reports to communicate significant legislative developments to management, nationwide.
- Represent the corporation at legislative conferences and industry group meetings throughout the U.S.
- Assist the Investor Relations Department in preparation of innovative presentation shown to 30 securities analysts.
- Coordinated successful nationwide campaign involving more than 100 legislators to pass federal legislation favorable to the industry.
- Led task force of mid-level managers which provided expert knowledge on federal legislation affecting pharmaceutical operations.
- Authored compliance manual and presented training seminars to more than 100 managers and vice presidents.

Product Manager
Johnson & Johnson, McNeil Pharmaceuticals, Springhouse, PA   1991 - 1995
Created and marketed a consulting service designed to assist pharmacists with inventory and pricing.

- Traveled nationwide to promote consulting services with pharmacists and company sales force as well as to represent the company at trade shows.
- Managed and operated consulting activities for three analysts and conducted numerous training sessions.

Jean A. Wagner   **Page Two**

- Designed and developed marketing brochures, promotional items, various advertisements and training videos.
- Prepared, planned and managed yearly operational budget of $1 million and wrote business plan for start-up venture.
- Coordinated and presented continuing education program entitled, *Inventory and Pricing Strategies*, to more than 300 participants.
- Increased gross profits for participating pharmacies by implementing new training programs and consulting services.

Pharmacist

C.V.S., Chester County, PA   1987 - 1991

Assisted in managing operations and staff of retail chain store pharmacies. Compounded and priced an average of 300 prescriptions per day.

- Interacted with other health professionals regarding patient care as well as informed and instructed patients regarding product information and drug therapy.
- Participated with team of pharmacists to generate $1.9 million per year in prescription sales and managed drug inventory of nearly $150,000.

Pharmacist

Cut Rite Drugs, West Chester, PA   1985 - 1987

Personal Profile

SETS PRIORITIES LOGICALLY... WELL ORGANIZED
ESTABLISHED CLEAR LINES OF COMMUNICATION... GRASPS TECHNICAL MATTERS QUICKLY
PAYS ATTENTION TO DETAIL... SETS GOALS/ESTABLISHES CONTROL/FOLLOWS THROUGH
EFFECTIVE NEGOTIATOR IN SOPHISTICATED ENVIRONMENTS

Education & Software

M.B.A., cum laude, Rutgers University, 1993
B.S. in Pharmacy, magna cum laude, University of Pennsylvania, 1985

PC / Windows
WordPerfect / Excel / Lotus / Harvard Graphics / WinFax
Lexis / Nexis / WestLaw

AVAILABLE FOR TRAVEL AND RELOCATION

Keith Curry
928 Waterbury Avenue
Chicago, Illinois 19487
Home: (302) 747-9381

EXECUTIVE SUMMARY

Public relations executive with proven ability in strategic planning, project management and mass communications. Strong background in translating corporate messages into appropriate communications media: publications, films, exhibits, entertainment and special events. Productive manager of community and media relations. Experienced in reporting for major news media and in directing the public relations function in non-profit, private and public companies.

Special expertise in:
- Entertainment production
- Written and visual communications
- Creative special events and exhibits

PROFESSIONAL EXPERIENCE AND ACCOMPLISHMENTS

TROPI-COLA COMPANIES, INC. - Chicago, Illinois   **1993-Present**
Director of Corporate Communications

Directed public relations for nation's fifth largest soft drink company with staff of one communications specialist and two editors. Responsibilities included planning, budgeting, publications, media relations, special events, entertainment production, major exhibit management, and public relations activities to enhance the company's image with its publics.

- Directed development of a strategy to boost the company's support among Hispanics, generating strong national media coverage and on-going ties to Hispanic leaders.

- Recommended, booked and produced local and national entertainment acts including Natalie Cole, Reba McEntire, Kenny Loggins and many others, all of which received standing ovations, creating a favorable impact on customer relations.

- Created and published a 100-page award-winning book, "Tropi-Cola Recipes" which has been reviewed favorably in newspapers across the country and ordered by more than 80,000 consumers.

- Directed the creation and operation of two major image-enhancing Tropi-Cola industry exhibits, effectively managing the million-dollar annual budget.

- Created and managed production on budget of a 15-minute film to introduce the corporation and industry to prospective employees and other audiences.

KEITH CURRY   Page Two

THE SUNSHINE COMPANY - Cleveland, Ohio   **1992-1993**
Director of Corporate Communications

Directed public relations function for Sunshine while closing the company's public affairs
function in Detroit and moving it to the Cleveland headquarters.

BROADCAST AGE - Cleveland, Ohio   **1989-1992**
Cleveland Bureau Chief

Managed news coverage of advertising and marketing activities in the Midwest for major
marketing weekly.

THE CLEVELAND PLAIN DEALER - Cleveland, Ohio   **1986-1989**
Business Writer

U.S. NAVY   **1982-1986**
Following graduation from Officer Candidate School, served aboard *USS FRIGATE*
as Administrative Assistant to the Executive Officer, and as Public Information Officer.

EDUCATION

B.A., Accounting, Penn State University (1982)
M.B.A., Communications, Cleveland State University (1992)

PROFESSIONAL AND COMMUNITY AFFILIATIONS

Member, Public Relations Society of America
Member, National Meeting Professionals

ARTHUR J. RYAN
349 Cardinal Lane
Tulsa, Oklahoma 74801
(405) 884-1401

SUMMARY

Entrepreneurial leader with diversified experience in the development, implementation and operation of projects, services and businesses. Visionary with proven ability to inspire individuals to work toward common goals and accomplish desired results. Demonstrated strength in quickly understanding and handling complex technical and operational issues. Strong customer focus. Easily adapts to foreign cultures and business practices.

PROFESSIONAL EXPERIENCE/ACCOMPLISHMENTS

BAHR PRODUCTS COMPANY - Tulsa, Oklahoma   **1991 - Present**
Division of Bahr AB - Munich, Germany
Director, Administration   1996 - Present

Directed a 24-person technical team ($2.5 million budget) responsible for telecommunications, multi-platform computers, voice and data networks and administration services.

- Created a central data network and desktop support team providing expanded services while reducing labor requirements by 33%.

- Reengineered the IS work practices, cross-training associates to provide personal and professional growth opportunities while ensuring maximum support capabilities.

- Established key headquarters relationships and gained corporate buy-in to drive technology standards, policies and new system applications.

- Reduced cycle times of business processes by developing concept, marketing benefits and implementing LAN and WAN based information sharing applications.

Director, Customer Affairs and Distribution   1991 - 1996

Directed a 60-85 person work unit at four sites ($5 million budget) responsible for Customer Services, Distribution, Credit Management and Accounts Receivable.

- Negotiated agreement between two adversarial divisions on unified sales policies, terms and conditions necessary for common sales and distribution infrastructure.

- Within nine months, implemented reengineered multi-site national operations supporting more than $100 million in revenue for the consolidated consumer products division.

- Improved customer service levels from 85% to 98%, accounts receivable current from 90% to 95% and transportation cost from 3% to 2% of sales.

Arthur J. Ryan
Page 2

DORSETT LABORATORIES - Tulsa, Oklahoma   **1989 - 1991**
Division of Bahr AB - Munich, Germany
Manager, Planning   1990 - 1991

Developed new business opportunities. Established business planning concepts and guidelines, directed annual planning process and monitored company performance vs. plan.

*   Led a six-person Sales Operations Task Force to identify customer needs, recommend marketplace opportunities and develop restructuring plans for a 125-person organization.

*   Evaluated the market rationale, financial implications and business risk of various acquisitions and licensing opportunities ranging in size up to $100 million.

Planning/Financial Analyst   1989- 1990

*   Managed the business planning process and provided financial analysis for marketing and sales plans ($70 million revenue) and capital projects ($5-$8 million annually).

BAHR S.A.   **1986 - 1989**
Division of Bahr AB - Munich, Germany
Manager, Pharmaceutical Technology

*   Acquired cultural sensitivity and language skills to effectively motivate, negotiate and manage diverse people and operations.

*   Accelerated new product introductions by implementing a structural planning process between Marketing, Research and Registration at national and international headquarters.

*   In three years, saved the company over $500,000 by improving management practices and departmental work processes for production operations.

EDUCATION

M.B.A., Oklahoma State University at Tulsa, 1986
B.S. in Pharmacy, Oklahoma State University, Stillwater, OK 1984

DAVID W. KRAMER
144 Blue Rock Drive
St. Louis, MO 45725
(904) 655-1347

Summary of Experience

Over twenty years of diversified information systems experience in hi-tech manufacturing and consulting, with 16 years in the management and control of all information systems functions. In-depth knowledge of process re-engineering, large-scale implementation projects, and the economics and use of standardized hardware and software strategies. Extensive financial and manufacturing background.

1996 to Present

Renior Corporation, St. Louis, MO
$4+ billion worldwide corporation producing automotive and electronic equipment.

Corporate Director Information Systems. Reporting to the Chief Financial Officer. Responsible for applications of computer technologies for the U.S. corporation, including business data processing, CIM/CAD/CAM, product R&D, telecommunications, office automation and advanced computer applications. Staff of 200 with a budget of $37 million.

- Reduced information systems budget to 1% of sales, while supporting a compound sales growth of 10%

- Replaced mainframe computers with cost-effective minicomputers, and eliminated or outsourced remaining legacy systems, saving $1 million annually.

- Implemented common financial systems in six divisions and two joint ventures, saving 1800 accounting staff days per year.

- Received "Quality Systems Achievement" award, 1996.

- Designed and implemented an international communications network that doubled the traffic capacity for all data, image and voice traffic between North America, Europe and Asia while reducing costs by 10%

- Selected and installed standardized manufacturing software/hardware systems and centralized systems support, which eliminated 42 systems positions.

- Controlled engineering systems budgets and structured corporate-wide project approvals and capital investment procedures.

- Implemented customer/supplier EDI, reducing inventories by $21 million.

1994 to 1996

Executive Information, Inc., Chicago, IL
A privately-held $40 million computer services company.

Director, Management Information Systems. Complete responsibility for MIS functions and product marketing coordination for an international computer service bureau and software company. Directed micro and mainframe software product development, technical support, laser printing services, and information center activities. Supervised staff of 82 with a budget of $26 million.

- Used creative financing techniques to upgrade hardware/software systems that reduced budget by $300,000 while sustaining processing volume increases of 40% per year.

- Established executive MIS product steering committee.

DAVID W. KRAMER   Page 2

- Introduced laser business graphics, stand-alone PC software and training centers as new viable product lines which added $6 million in sales within two years.

- Developed company business and marketing plans used for successful IBM Value-Added Remarketeering (VAR) proposal.

- Reduced annual MIS employee turnover from 18% to 2%.

1991 to 1994   **Barnes & Roche, Inc.,** Autumn Insurance and Publishing Companies, Chicago, IL
Specialized publishing/insurance division of a multi-billion dollar conglomerate.

Manager of Information Services. Responsible for financial and publishing systems development, technical support functions, corporate computer center, word processing center and telecommunications.

- Developed a long-range business plan and established computer strategy for a sister insurance division working with its CEO.

- Initiated the use of PC's to solve specific financial and administrative applications, which were not feasible on the mainframe computer.

- Consolidated four word processing centers into one corporate department, reduced staff, expanded output by 40%, saved $160,000 per year. Project received recognition in national publication.

- Selected and implemented new accounting system which reduced accounting staff by 30% and compressed monthly closing cycles by five working days.

1990 to 1991   **United Trust Bank Corporation,** Dalton, IL
One of the largest commercial bank holding companies in the midwest.

Coordinator of Standards and Controls. Directed the efforts of the bank's project managers to create standards and procedures to guide the professional staff of 280 applications analysts and programmers. Also served as staff consultant for on-line and database software systems.

- Designed and implemented a project methodology for feasibility studies, system designs, software development, implementations and audit reviews, which eliminated the need for outside consulting contract worth $1 million per year.

- Established project reporting procedures that measured project status for executive and Board of Directors presentations.

1988 to 1990   **Concord Electric Corporation,** Dayton Products Division, Dayton, OH
$65 million division manufacturing computerized telephone switch equipment.

Manager of Information Systems. Responsible for all data processing department activities. Served as member of executive staff. Coordinated MIS functional goals and objectives as they related to the short-term and long-term business plan.

- Directed the conversion of manufacturing system from an IBM mainframe to a Hewlett-Packard minicomputer, which increased services and reduced EDP budget by 10%.

- Implemented an on-line shop floor control system to collect time/attendance, shop order tracking, job cost and payroll information that reduced payroll errors by 95% and increased production information accuracy by 90%.

- Developed inventory analysis program that reduced inventory by 8% and eventually increased inventory turns 300%.

DAVID W. KRAMER   Page 3

- Established project family groupings that significantly improved accuracy of the quarterly master production schedule, which delayed the need for a new plant for three years.

- Represented divisional manufacturing and information systems functions in a multi-million dollar software development project.

1982 to 1988 **U.S. Air Force**, **Wright Patterson Air Force Base, Dayton, OH**

Senior Staff Analyst. As a civilian, served as the senior advisor for all data processing aspects for the division. Responsible for providing technical guidance to middle and upper management regarding computer utilization, specifications and "develop or buy" policies for computer hardware and software systems.

- Managed the design and implementation of an on-line production and work-in-process information system serving the reporting and planning needs of upper management and staff of 600+ professional engineers.

- Supervised a group of 40 programmers/analysts that implemented an IBM information retrieval system which included the conversion of 1.5 million document database in less than six months.

- Designed an on-line image and graphics system to analyze, store and retrieve imagery from real-time satellite telemetry.

1976 to 1982 **Mt. Clair Community College**, **Mt. Clair, NJ**

Professor of Data Processing. Part-time, taught advanced level computer courses, including Manufacturing Systems, Business Applications, Information Management theory, Real Time Systems and data Processing Management.

1972 to 1976 **Meadville Technology Laboratories**, **Princeton, NJ**
A high-tech consulting company specializing in government/industrial research.

Senior Client Consultant/Analyst. Responsible for P&L of client projects, system design and analysis contract negotiations, project estimation and management from governmental and industrial projects.

- Programmed computer software to plot maps of the lunar landing sites for the Apollo Lunar Expedition.

- Designed, programmed and managed various large governmental projects for the Department of Defense and Federal Bureau of Investigation.

- Provided technical support for the project to automate the Library of Congress.

SUMMARY OF TECHNICAL EXPERIENCE:

HARDWARE: IBM (Mainframe & AS 400), NAS and AMDAHL, DEC-IBM minicomputers, Hewlett-Packard and personal computers.

SOFTWARE: COBOL, FORTRAN, RPG, Assembler and BASIC.

APPLICATIONS: Manufacturing, Finance/Accounting/Treasury, Distributed Processing, Data Base Systems, Local and Wide Area Networks.

EDUCATION:

M.B.A., Wharton School, University of Pennsylvania, 1988
M.S., Mathematics, Drexel University, 1975
B.S., Computer Science, Penn State University, 1972

WILMA E. SWANSON
48 Warminster Road
Lancaster, PA 17473
(717) 577-4436 (Home)
(717) 651-1749 (Office)

SUMMARY

Experienced, progressive and innovative Information Systems professional with 26 years of broad-based management experience in application design and development, strategic planning, budgeting, client support services and large scale operations management. Proven leadership strengths in personnel development, team building, portfolio management, vendor negotiations, technology innovations and client relations and support. Strong interpersonal skills, results-oriented and dedicated to cost effective business solutions and customer satisfaction.

PROFESSIONAL EXPERIENCE

HIGGINS TOBACCO COMPANY - Lancaster, PA   **1993 to Present**

Director, Information Resources
Executive in charge of company-wide personal computing, office systems, mainframe end-user computing, engineering service, information resource administration, disaster recovery planning, data access security systems availability, business forms design and management and operations facilities planning. Directed the operations of the data centers, telecommunications and software execution. Budgetary responsibility of $7 million and a staff of 12.

- Participated as a member of a steering committee that identified cost savings opportunities and recommended the consolidation of data centers and staff realizing $500,000 in personnel savings and $150,000 in hardware savings.

- Implemented Total Quality Management for the operations staff and supported the creation of self-directed work groups resulting in improved organizational effectiveness and productivity by reducing overtime and absenteeism.

- Directed the development of microcomputer hardware and office systems software standards for an installed base of 400 with annual purchases in excess of $3 million.

- Established an in-house training facility providing technical career development and office systems software training realizing $2.8 million cost avoidance the first year of operation.

- Assembled a task force to investigate client server local area network computing resulting in the identification of direction, development of standards, selection of hardware, operating software and communication protocol thereby creating a controlled environment for growth and development.

- Led a team that developed an Executive Information system which reported on key business critical success factors and competitive activities.

WILMA E. SWANSON   Page 2

HARVEST BRANDS, INC. - Clearfield, OH   **1990-1993**

Director, Information Resources
Directed the design, development and implementation of major business systems with budgetary responsibility of $4 million and a staff of 30 to 45.

- Directed and coordinated the implementation of common financial systems for all merged and purchased entities under HBI including common ledger, accounts payable, accounts receivable, asset and payroll systems.

- Implemented a company-wide consumer relations system which introduced the first 800 number service, automated personal consumer responses and integrated reporting customer issues to sales, manufacturing and quality control.

- Led a team that developed a microcomputer-based database/reporting system assuring availability of complete and accurate critical information to senior executives for business calls to key customers.

TABOR CANDY COMPANY - Chicago, IL   **1984-1990**

Group Manager, Information Resources
Managed the activities of the staff engaged in the design and implementation of large scale financial, payroll and personnel systems. Budgetary responsibility of $3 million, staff of 14.

- Managed the development and implementation of a four-year Information Systems strategic plan with successful implementation of new on-line financial and payroll/personnel systems.

BOYER CORPORATION - White Plains, NY   **1981-1984**

Project Manager

- Implemented the consumer products group national sales reporting system.

- Introduced new technologies for program developed and report production.

DREYFUS CORPORATION - New York, NY   **1980-1981**

Programmer/Analyst

EDUCATION

B.B.A., Marketing, Bucknell University, Lewisberg, PA, 1980

JOSEPH A. McDERMOTT

709 West Capitol Boulevard
Bridgeport, CT 84103
(201) 648-3966
Fax: (201) 648-3968

CAREER SUMMARY

General Counsel for medium and large corporations. Manage legal departments and counsel senior management on mergers and acquisitions, environmental problems and other difficult and controversial issues. Anticipate problems and develop practical solutions with bottom-line sensitivity.

PROFESSIONAL EXPERIENCE

WALTERS CORPORATION, Bridgeport, CT   **1997 - Present**

$6 billion natural resources company, producing 25% of the U.S. brass supply as well as major quantities of gold and silver.

Vice President, General Counsel, Secretary and Member of Board of Directors

Member of senior management group; responsible for all legal affairs; managed a ten person law department.

- Negotiated and oversaw drafting of engineering and construction contracts for $450 million smelter construction project, saving considerable outside counsel fees.

- Negotiated $800 million acquisition of Fargo, Inc., a mining, oil and gas and heavy metals company.

- Crafted a program for cleanup of ninety years' mining waste while avoiding "Superfund" designation, saving tens of millions of dollars in oversight costs.

IDEAL ENTERPRISES, INC., Cleveland, OH   **1994 - 1997**

A $275 million manufacturer of building products, including windows, doors, siding and accessories. An LBO company formed in June 1994; previously a wholly-owned subsidiary of Carthage Steel Corporation.

Vice President and General Counsel

- Positioned LBO company for sale by divesting subsidiaries not related to core businesses, thereby maximizing return on LBO investment.

- Negotiated the successful sale of company to Lexington, Inc.

- Precluded EPA interference with sale of company by anticipating clean-up requirements, thereby avoiding potential years' delay of sale and several million dollars' oversight expenses.

CARTHAGE STEEL CORPORATION, Pittsburgh, PA   **1987 - 1994**

Counsel

Responsible for legal affairs of Carthage's Diversified Group, including five subsidiaries. Directed internal investigations.

- Supervised antitrust, securities, product liability, toxic tort, real estate and trademark litigation.

- Conducted Carthage Steel Corporation's legal compliance program at 12 major plant locations.

GALLAGHER & GALLAGHER, New York, NY   **1980 - 1987**

Associate, Litigation/antitrust group.   (1985 - 1987)

Law Clerk, part time, while attending law school.   (1980 - 1985)

EDUCATION/MILITARY

Columbia University School of Law, J.D., 1980
Activities: Class President
Honors: Top 1/4; Member, Law Journal

Colgate University, A.B. English Literature, 1975
Honors: Pennington Scholar
           New York State Regents Scholarship

Captain, U.S. Army, Intelligence Corps (1975-80).

BAR ADMISSIONS/PROFESSIONAL ACTIVITIES

- Licensed in Connecticut, New York, Pennsylvania and Ohio.
- Member, Ethics Advisory Opinion Committee, Legislative Affairs Committee (Connecticut Bar Association).

SANDRA B. SLOAN

302-A Seventh Avenue
Dayton, Ohio 64136
Office (613) 822-9462 ♦ Home (613) 844-2110

SUMMARY

Senior Manager with division of Fortune 500 corporation with consistent record of success in increasingly responsible positions. Educated and experienced in materials management, purchasing, production control and integrated business systems.

EXPERIENCE:

1983 - Present

EAGLE-PICHER INDUSTRIES, INC., Plastics Division, Dayton, OH
A division of a Fortune 500 NYSE corporation with annual sales of $190 million.

Materials Manager, **(1994 - Present)**
Responsible for directing the Division's production and inventory control functions, includes: purchasing, order entry, order engineering, materials planning, production scheduling, warehouse and shipping and receiving. Also responsible for facility and machine maintenance.

- Reduced inventories significantly during a time of expansion.

- Increased service levels while reducing inventory.

- Increased revenue from freight rebates by $80,000 annually.

- Reduced raw materials 45% by implementing supplier stocking program and better scheduling techniques.

- Project leader for the implementation of a new integrated business systems software.

- Implemented preventative maintenance program for production machinery.

Purchasing Manager, **(1990 - 1994)**
Responsible for directing the Division's purchasing function, including the procurement of materials, services and capital equipment for $190 million division, by working directly with managerial and supervisory personnel in four plants including one international plant location.

- Implemented Division purchasing practices and procedures.

- Significantly reduced and maintained highly competitive raw material costs.

- Instrumental in implementing computer software for purchasing.

- Developed method and wrote PC software to aid in inventory usage and vendor analysis.

- Implemented vendor qualifications program.

Production Analyst, **(1987 - 1990)**
Special projects manager reporting to the Vice President and General Manager, working to analyze procedures and develop manufacturing strategies.

- Developed techniques for manufacturing small quantities of specialty polymer coatings.

- Developed system, wrote software, and installed hardware for EDI link with major remote sales office.

- As safety manager, helped create a safer manufacturing environment by working with chemical suppliers and personnel to eliminate possible hazardous products and conditions.

Account Specialist, **(1983 - 1987)**
Responsible for managing a major account with over $2 MM in sales.

- Improved margins 100% during the first six months.

- Opened additional business, increasing volume by 20%.

- Helped develop new manufacturing technique to customize product.

EDUCATION: B.A., Business Management, Ohio State University, 1983

Certified by the National Association of Purchasing Management (C.P.M.)

Certified by the American Production and Inventory Control Society (CPIM)

Juran Quality Control

Trained facilitator for high performance work teams

ROGER F. GORMLEY
183 Hazelhurst Drive
Macon, Georgia 44922
404/756-2867

SENIOR LEVEL EXECUTIVE with twenty-five years of line/staff/internal consulting experience in customer service, order fulfillment, logistics and product service. Strong decision-making, team-building, process reengineering, TQM, trouble shooting and cost avoidance skill set. Harvard MBA.

EXPERIENCE:

1995 - Present   **GENERAL TELEPHONE OF GEORGIA,** Macon, GA
General Manager, Supply & Transportation
- Re-engineered purchasing/logistics functions, resulting in 66% reduction in work staff while accommodating 80% growth in work.
- Reduced staff budget from $18.4 million annually to $13.1 million.
- Reduced inventory levels from $17 million to $5.9 million.
- Reduced cycle time from 24 days on uniform/office supplies to two days.
- Re-engineered ordering/fulfillment process from paper to touch-tone electronic entry.
- Set and achieved goal of employee development to benchmark 5% training level.

1991 - 1995   **MIDWEST TELECOM,** Deerfield, IL
Staff Director, Logistics and Standards
- Created and directed a team which saved $25 million on $850 million annual purchases.
- Negotiated purchase agreements, saving 48% on switching equipment costs of $285 million and 28% on cable costs of $30 million.
- Served as in-house consultant to senior management on purchasing, distribution, inventory control and incentive compensation in preparation for centralization and corporate restructuring.
- Prepared recommendations and advised on inventory levels, materials standards.
- Provided comparative analysis for eight operating units.

1983 - 1988   **GENERAL TELEPHONE OF CONNECTICUT,** Norwalk, CT
Northern Region Director, Customer Service
- Provided supervisory and administrative direction, to area encompassing two-thirds of Connecticut's 1.2 million customers, producing 60% of company's Connecticut revenue.
- Directly supervised management staff, reporting to an operation vice president.
- Successfully converted Connecticut from 13 district headquarters to two regional territories reducing operating costs by 50% and increasing operating performance and productivity.
- Represented management at union negotiations and personnel evaluations. Personally evaluated every job in conversion to Hay System.

EDUCATION: **1991 -   HARVARD BUSINESS SCHOOL,** Cambridge, MA
Masters of Business Administration
1983 -   GEORGIA TECH, Atlanta, GA
Bachelor of General Studies Degree

CREDENTIALS:
- Licensed Pilot
- Member, National Association of Purchasing Managers
- Member, American Management Association
- Certified Purchasing Manager

MICHAEL D. BURCH

25399 Harwood Avenue
Adrian, MI 80401

Home: (635) 625-6564   Office: (635) 592-1707, Ext. 435

OPERATIONS EXECUTIVE

Pro-active executive offering a strong background in production planning, purchasing, warehousing, distribution, inventory management, order processing, systems design, transportation, and customer service. Excellent people management skills, coupled with the ability to communicate effectively, enhancing the management of a large group of professionals.

KENILWORTH PET FOOD CO., Adrian, MI   1996 - Present
Director of Logistics
Direct all aspects of production planning, purchasing, warehousing/distribution, inventory control, customer service and transportation for Kenilworth's Grocery Products Division.

- Reduced division-wide inventory carrying costs by 25% or $10MM through implementation of cycle-time compression program. Program encompassed all functional areas within product supply chain.

- Improved overall customer service to wholesale and retail accounts by 10% through institution of CRP/ECR programs. Escalation in O-T-D and product fill-rate performance directly supported domestic and international sales in excess of $600MM.

- Fostered partnerships with suppliers and created formal Vendor Certification Program. Subject program yielded vast improvements in component and raw material quality and cost.

- Reduced base line operating budget by $4.8MM through implementation of accelerated cost reduction program. Program entailed utilization of "ABC" accounting techniques and served as pre-requisite to division's re-engineering of manufacturing/logistics processes.

- Directed all business logistics components of Kenilworth's $20MM pet food launch into the Asian marketplace.

SHERWOOD PHARMACEUTICALS, INC., Des Moines, IA   1988 - 1996
Manager of Logistics

Directly managed multiple site logistics operation for Sherwood's Pharmaceutical Manufacturing Division. Areas of responsibility included material warehousing, distribution, inventory management, order processing, transportation and customer service functions.

- Responsible for operating budget of $9MM, staff of 10 managers and 175 direct/indirect employees. Managed a 300,000 square foot conventional warehouse, a 35,000 unit automated Hi-Rise facility, and all sub-contract distribution centers.

Michael D. Burch

- Instrumental in development and implementation of MRP II technologies and strategies. Integrated modules such as MCS, PCS and DRP in support of Sherwood's "Just in Time" production concept. Created and implemented the Inventory Control Department.

- Spearheaded development and implementation of TQM and SPC programs, which eliminated $2MM in cost of non-conformance.

THE CENTENNIAL CORPORATION, Kingston, RI   1986 - 1988
Distribution Consultant

- Corporate distribution systems consultant serving Centennial's major subsidiaries and minority-owned affiliates. Direct responsibility for corporate distribution planning and customized application use.

- Project Manager, Corporate-Record Information and Storage Systems Development. Directed all facets of project analysis, functional specifications development and systems implementation for nationwide record/claim data management program.

CITIZEN CORPORATION, Paramus, NJ   1983 - 1986
Manufacturing/Distribution Facility
Plant Manager

- Full line responsibility for management of flagship plant servicing Citizen's largest Forms Management customer base. Managed staff of three departmental managers and operations personnel consisting of 40 non-exempt/exempt employees.

- Directed all facets of facility including plant budgeting, production inventory control and maintenance of multi-plant management information systems program.

- Coordinated all physical plant set-up, in charge of interviewing, hiring and training of selected personnel. Implemented all systems and procedures for the newest operational facility in Citizen's Business Forms Division.

EDUCATION

B.S., Psychology, Farley College - 1983
Winton, Connecticut
Executive Development Program - 1986
University of Pittsburgh

HOWARD A. HOLCOMBE
109 Stevens Drive
Bartonville, OK 55927
Res: 713-229-7963
Bus: 713-212-9200

PROFILE: International Business, Sales and Marketing Manager with more than 15 years in the Sporting Goods Industry, now seeking a new Senior Management challenge and opportunity. Areas of expertise include:

- Strategic Planning
- Operations Management
- Distribution/Logistics

- International Sales & Marketing
- Licensing/Sourcing
- Product Development

PROFESSIONAL EXPERIENCE:

ROYAL SPORTS GROUP, INC., Oklahoma City, OK   **1984 to Present**
A division of Pendelton Sport Systems

Helped manage the International business and marketing growth of this $300 million leader in the Sporting Goods industry to a position where 50% of total revenues came from international sales to 90 countries. Matrix-managed staff of 32 employees, directed purchases of $80 million of goods worldwide, and managed expense budgets up to $500,000.

Director - Global Logistical Systems (1995-Present)

- Developed, implemented and managed the company's global logistical systems and operational procedures.
- Provided effective and efficient control in planning and maintenance of the company's inventory.
- Reduced inventories by 38% ($26 million) in 1996 and consequently reduced credit lines and interest expense.
- Implemented systems and procedures that reduced Asian sourcing lead times by 20%.

Director - International Strategic Planning/Special Projects (1994-1995)

- Managed the company's International Department.
- Worked with the International Field Managers to finalize 1995 business plans inclusive of sales forecasts, budgets, pricing and objectives.
- 1995 Business Plan was achieved and record billings and profit level were reached.
- Participated in the development of strategic plans that addressed future growth, and customer, consumer and corporate needs.
- Identified significant opportunities for improvement within the company then analyzed and developed solutions.
- Decentralized order processing, distribution, forecasting and inventory planning into three business units (U.S., U.K., Asia) to be more responsive to local market needs.
- Fine-tuned and helped link forecasting, inventory requirements planning and sourcing systems between offices in five different countries.

Marketing Manager (1993-1994)

- Negotiated licensing agreement with the Warner Brothers and managed the marketing of Royal Sports' products.
- Developed *Jock Master* brand, product and collections exposure through television product placement, tie-in promotions and in-store merchandising programs.
- Managed new business development which provided $3.5 million of incremental sales from 1,000 U.S. storefronts and distributors in 20 countries.
- Implemented in-store merchandising program that received "1993 Best of Industry Award" from National Retail Merchandising Association.

International Sales Operations Manager (1989-1993)

- Developed, coordinated and implemented international marketing plans, forecasts, inventory control programs, procedures, policies, budget and administrative programs.
- Developed, managed and expanded international customer relationships. Travelled to 30 countries to work with customers.
- Achieved 392% sales growth in four years.
- International sales grew to account for 50% of total company sales. Grew distribution to more than 90 countries.

Project Manager (1986-1989)

- Directed and managed the product development, sourcing and marketing of racquet strings, sport bags, soft goods, machines and accessories.
- Achieved 113% sales growth in three years.
- *Jock Master* string product line profit margin increased by 20% and the category grew to the #3 position in the U.S.

Technical Manager - Stringer Education & Services (1984-1986)

- Responsible for developing a comprehensive grass roots stripping & technical education program for dealers and distributors.
- Provided *Jock Master* sponsored players with stringing and equipment services at major tennis tournaments.
- *Jock Master* rackets became the #2 choice of tournament professionals during this period providing the company with a major marketing advantage.

TENNIS PROFESSIONAL   **1980 to 1984**
Taught and developed beginner through world-class players at Lakeland Heights Tennis Club, Lakeland Heights, NJ. Managed club's pro shop.

EDUCATION: Baker University, Columbus, Ohio
B.S., Business Administration/Marketing, 1980

BARBARA P. THORNTON

(414) 936-8214

816 GREEN MEADOW ROAD

GLENDALE, CA 60812

Experienced in all phases of Material Management, Purchasing, Production Planning, Master Scheduling, Production Control, Inventory Management and Distribution.

EXPERIENCE

GLENDALE MANUFACTURING COMPANY, GLENDALE, CA   1995 to Present
DIRECTOR OF PURCHASING

Responsible for the Purchasing, Inventory and Material Planning for this $110 million industry leader of consumer houseware goods. Report directly to the owners of the company and direct the activities of three professional vendor/schedulers and one inventory manager in the areas of material procurement, inventory levels and on-time performance. Knowledgeable in MRP, SPC and TQM techniques.

- Instituted "state-of-the-art" Partnership Purchasing Programs on key commodities which saved in excess of $2.3 million over a two-year period.

- Developed and expanded off-shore sourcing realizing a net savings of over $750,000.

- Instrumental in the start-up of a new injection molding department. Initiated planning parameters, production scheduling techniques and inventory levels which achieved internal production of over 90% of plastic requirements in less than one year.

- Reduced inventory levels over $500,000 while supporting a 20% increase in sales and the start-up of a new injection molding department through improved ordering techniques and vendor stocking programs.

BURBANK TECHNOLOGY, INC., BURBANK, CA   1991 to 1995
MANAGER OF CORPORATE PURCHASING AND MATERIALS

Responsible for the Purchasing, Inventory, Shipping/Receiving and Traffic functions of this $80 million world-class electromechanical producer. Directed the activities of four professional buyers and six vendor schedulers in the areas of material procurement, scheduling and capital expenditures with budgetary responsibility in excess of $32 million. Negotiated all freight carrier contracts for a multi-plant distribution environment with a freight budget responsibility of over $5 million.

- Instituted "Partnership Purchasing Program" and "Vendor Analysis Program" resulting in a 15% average reduction in pricing and a 20% improvement in supplier delivery performance. Bottom line savings over $800,000.

- Reduced inventory levels over 30%, or $4.5 million, through improved vendor delivery Performance and implementation of supplier stocking programs.

BARBARA P. THORNTON   Page 2

- Reduced company L-T-L (Less Than Truckload) carrier base and renegotiated freight contracts resulting in increased freight discounts and savings in excess of $500,000.

- Sourced, negotiated, certified and implemented outside fabricators and subcontracting services for company's major product line resulting in over $1 million in cost savings and cost avoidances.

WILSON-MARTIN COMPANY, LOS ANGELES, CA   1985 to 1991
MANAGER OR PURCHASING AND DISTRIBUTION SERVICES

Responsible for the Purchasing, Traffic, Warehousing, Shipping and Receiving functions for the Wilson-Martin consumer products division with sales of $50 million.

- Through aggressive negotiations, maintained a favorable purchasing price variance which yielded a divisional savings of approximately $500,000.

- Reduced expense spending 20% for a $500,000 savings through improved computerized order/vendor visibility and control.

- Instituted vendor performance measurements for raw materials suppliers, improving vendor delivery performance to 95% on time and successfully meeting MRP (Material Requirement Planning) objectives.

- Implemented a Traffic Program that saved over $330,000 in freight charges by maximizing freight discounts on combined inbound/outbound poundage.

MANAGER OF PRODUCTION PLANNING AND INVENTORY CONTROL

Responsible for the Production Planning, Production Control, Customer Service, Shipping and Receiving and Inventory (Raw Material, Work-In-Progress, Finish Stock) for the commercial products division. At the apex of our manufacturing cycle, directed the activities of 24 salaried and 42 wage employees in the areas listed above.

EARLIER EXPERIENCE   1977 to 1985

Held progressive managerial positions in production planning and inventory control at Johnson & Johnson (New Brunswick, NJ).

EDUCATION

Rutgers University, New Brunswick, NJ
Bachelor of Science in Industrial Management, 1977

Member of American Production and inventory Control Society (APICS)
Member of the National Association of Purchasing Management (NAPM)

LAWRENCE G. UTER, Jr.
42 Clover Lane
Adia, MI 32714

Office: (214) 668-2001   Home: (214) 944-3151

SUMMARY

Accomplished professional with more than fifteen years experience. Areas of concentration include purchasing, management and production. Specific skills are in negotiation and contract management, use of databases for sourcing and analysis, budget preparation, materials management, cost control and facilities management. Recognized by both management and peers for integrity, dependability and flexibility in meeting objectives.

PROFESSIONAL EXPERIENCE

AMWAY CORPORATION, Adia, MI   **1996 - Present**

Commodities Buyer
Manage staff of three, responsible for purchasing more than $20,000,000 annual volume of catalogs, promotional items, sales aids and collateral materials.

- Developed and implemented strategy to use internal versus external production resources for product catalogs resulting in annual savings of more than $1 million.
- Provided expertise in establishing first formal company-wide purchasing department and developed operating guidelines.
- Utilized Manufacturing Resource Planning (MRP-II) and Just-in-Time (JIT) techniques which reduced complaints, missed deliveries and inventory.
- Analyzed purchasing practices and implemented consolidation and streamlining process resulting in first year savings of $500,000 and continued cost reductions.

ASSOCIATION OF PURCHASING PROFESSIONALS, Washington, DC   1994 - 1996

Administrator
Responsible for day-to-day operations for 300-member organization with annual budget of $1.5 million.

- Re-established operations which included securing office facilities, reorganizing files and renewing membership interest.
- Developed long-term fiscal and strategic plans and managed association operations at the direction of ten-member board.
- Developed monthly meeting programs for membership addressing business, technical and social interests.
- Arranged quarterly business seminar programs made available to members and industry in general.
- Sourced, selected, negotiated and promoted extensive seminar program for bi-annual trade show.

LAWRENCE G. UTER, Jr.   PAGE TWO

PA DEPARTMENT OF AGRICULTURE, Harrisburg, PA   1989 - 1994

General Services Director
Supervised and directed 17-person department which included photography, printing, mailroom, warehouse, creative design and facilities management.

- Eliminated wasteful purchasing practices by consolidating purchases which saved $100,000 the first year.
- Restructured warehouse personnel which reduced unemployment expenses and overall salaries while increasing productivity.
- Utilized expertise to modify design and production of printed support materials which provided more efficient and less costly manufacturing.

UTER PRESS, Harrisburg, PA   1986 - 1989

Owner
Operated small commercial printing company with full fiscal and production responsibilities. Provided printing for military bases, Commonwealth of Pennsylvania and dozens of small businesses in the Harrisburg area. Gross annual sales averaged $125,000

U.S. NAVAL PRINTING OFFICE, Atlanta, GA   1982 - 1986

Printing Specialist
Sourced, competitively bid, awarded and administered printing contracts for governmental printing needs in the southeastern United States.

- Sourced and managed a variety of printing requirements valued at more than $1,000,000 annually.
- Developed detail specifications used to solicit bids for printed materials.
- Gained expertise during three-year printing management program which resulted in promotion to GS-11 Printing Specialist.

EDUCATION

A.A.S., Printing Technology, 1982
New York Institute of Printing Technology, Rochester, NY

Additional Courses:

Frontline Leadership Program
MRP-II Seminar

AFFILIATIONS

Member, Florida Institute of Technical Printing

MICHAEL H. SANDSTROM
26 High Valley Road
Laguna Beach, CA 80793
414-972-1844

SUMMARY

Manufacturing/operations manager with 16 years experience and accomplishments as a cost reduction manager and innovative leader. Rapid growth in Fortune 500 environments of technology leaders. Strong P&L track record with functional management experience in all disciplines of manufacturing operations. Hands-on expertise in both job shop (batch) and continuous flow manufacturing environments. High energy, results-oriented manager with excellent leadership and interpersonal skills. Emphasizes quality and company success through communication, employee involvement and participation. Knowledgeable and practical business strategist with direct experience in the following areas:

- Full P&L, Budgeting
- Profit Improvement
- Company Restructuring
- Total Quality Management
- World Class Manufacturing

- Cost Reduction
- Productivity Enhancement
- Asset Management
- Materials & Inventory Management
- Strategic Planning

EXPERIENCE

TECHTRONICS, INC., Irvine, CA   **1995-Present**
Leading manufacturer and supplier of printed circuit boards with sales of $95 million annually.

Director, Manufacturing Operations
P&L responsibility for a business unit engaged in the manufacture of printed circuit boards. Functional responsibilities include manufacturing, quality, manufacturing engineering, product engineering, materials, and maintenance. In addition to functional responsibilities, position requires strategic planning, leading, and organizing of the operational activities of the unit.

- Increased manufacturing efficiency 20% by implementing a training program which used employee input and involvement.
- Improved yield 28% by restructuring the production operation process.
- Increased unit production 35% through tooling, fixturing, mechanization and automation.
- Implemented team concept by creating functional and cross-functional teams.
- Restructured production environment from high volume/low mix to low volume/high mix.

CYBER TECH, INC., Huntsville, AL   **1993-1995**
Contract manufacturer engaged in manufacturing and supplying printed circuit boards to the Original Equipment Manufacturer marketplace. Site sales of $40 million per year.

MICHAEL H. SANDSTROM   Page 2

Vice President and Plant Manager
Full P&L responsibility for 325-employee manufacturing facility engaged in printed circuit board and computer assembly. Direct reports included quality, manufacturing, materials, manufacturing engineering, test engineering, programs management, and plant cost accounting. Frequent and strong interface with a large, diverse and complex customer base. Operated in a multiple plant environment. Critical success factors were timely communication, coordination of programs, and support of activities with other manufacturing locations.

- Turned around a three-year negative profitability trend within nine months by restructuring production and eliminating unprofitable customers.
- Reduced overhead and manufacturing variances by 40% through work in process reduction, value analysis of tasks, duties, and responsibilities and staff reduction.
- Implemented continuous flow manufacturing through a rigid scheduling process.

COMPU-PRO, INC., San Diego, CA   **1987-1993**
Manufacturer and distributor of modems with annual sales of $250 million.

Vice President, Manufacturing
Responsible for all manufacturing activities including production, quality, mechanical engineering, manufacturing engineering and materials management. Key success factors were insuring competitive product cost, meeting exact quality standards, and maintaining optimum inventory levels.

- Implemented a TQM program which reduced defects per unit from 4 to .05.
- Reduced annual costs of consumable materials by 5% by purchasing direct from OEMS, hiring professional buyers, and upgrading expertise in procurement group.
- Established a Corporate Procurement function for purchasing capital equipment and non-consumables. Resulted in savings of 20+% annually.
- Implemented Surface Mount Technology in the manufacturing operations.
- Met World Class Manufacturing performance standards.

AMP INCORPORATED, Oxnard, CA   **1981-1987**
A world leader in the manufacture and supply of electronics with annual sales of $3 billion.

Production Manager
Site manager of $80 million sales volume facility with 900 employees. Responsible for production, engineering, quality, production control, maintenance and employee relations.

- Implemented Quality Circles.
- Reduced equipment downtime by implementing an area maintenance program.

EDUCATION

M.B.A., Finance, University of Southern California, 1981
B.S., Industrial Engineering, U.C.L.A., 1979

SUSAN A. BAKER

1214 Blue Ridge Road   Office (615) 374-9564
Greenville, NC 21015   Home (615) 374-6012

SUMMARY

Accomplished Operations Manager with extensive experience in Manufacturing, Quality Control, Engineering and Maintenance. Progressive leader with strong team-building skills, focused on quality, productivity and results. Capable of improving profit margin through automation, development of human resources, and continuous process improvement programs. Solid budget development and financial management skills.

Hands on/Take Charge   Strong Communication Skills   Innovative/Progressive

SELECTED HIGHLIGHTS

* Successful, on time start-up of new plant. Hired and trained employees, implemented and directed all major operations. Increased annual production rates by 15% in second and third year of operation.

* Expanded plant bringing in new equipment and automated processes resulting in $1.4M annual cost savings.

* Turned around problem relationship with manufacturing, quality and sales, increased market acceptance of product, cut customer complaints in half in two years.

* Reduced plant downtime and product cost by implementing Continuous Process Improvement programs for plant equipment and processes.

* Implemented "Total Productive Maintenance" program reducing required maintenance personnel by 70% and improving employee ownership and productivity.

EMPLOYMENT HISTORY

WEXLER MANUFACTURING, INC., Greenville, North Carolina   1994 - Present
As **Manufacturing Manager** direct two levels of supervision for a manufacturing and maintenance operation of furniture manufacturing company with sales of $30 million.

* Responsible for the start-up of all plant operations. This was accomplished on schedule and under budget. Turned a projected eighteen month loss into a profit after six months of operations.

* Continuously improved the overall plant productivity. Quality and process losses average typically about 1%. Routinely have groups working together to solve both technical and personnel problems.

* Developed and directed the implementation of production scheduling and reporting procedures. Prepared yearly expense and capital budgets.

EMPLOYMENT HISTORY (continued)
Susan A. Baker
page two

- Involved in the implementation of a totally integrated computer network system for handling MRP, inventory, and the general ledger.

- Responsible for corporate safety and environmental compliance responsibility. Directed response to extensive OSHA inspection resulting in no fines or penalties.

- Directed implementation of computerized maintenance work order, spare parts inventory management, and downtime reporting systems, reducing downtime and increasing productivity.

CONTAINER CORPORATION OF AMERICA   1985 - 1994

CCA PLANT, Ashville, North Carolina (1991 - 1994)
As **Quality Control Manager** of container manufacturing and distribution facility with annual sales in excess of $40 million, directed department of inspectors responsible for quality assurance and product acceptance.

- Lowest complaint settlement costs of all CCA manufacturing plants.

- Worked directly with customers and sales people to develop comprehensive quality action plan which addressed market weakness and recaptured lost business.

CCA TECHNOLOGY CENTER, Chicago, Illinois (1987 - 1991)
As **Development Engineer**, developed and implemented new manufacturing process for 18 Folding Carton manufacturing plants.

- Assisted in the automation of manufacturing operations through equipment selection and system design.

- Completed over a dozen equipment development projects from design through plant installation. Received two United States Patents.

CCA PLANT, Renton, Washington (1985 - 1987)
As **Process Engineer** had sole responsibility for all projects and process engineering functions.

- Construction and start-up of a $5 million plant expansion.

- Successfully, handled all dealings with Government Environmental agencies.

EDUCATION

1985 M.S., Chemical Engineering, University of Washington

1983 B.S., Chemistry, University of Washington

WARREN R. NEWMAN
1529 Vista Way
Grand Rapids, MI 33701
work (813) 335-9117
home (813) 331-4477

SUMMARY

Over sixteen years of broad-based manufacturing experience rising to the position of plant manager with a "world class" Fortune 200 company. Previous assignments included managerial positions in engineering, capital planning, purchasing, finance and systems.

PROFESSIONAL EXPERIENCE

Cummins Engine Company, Specialty Motor Division, Grand Rapids, MI   1995 to Present
Plant Manager

Total operational and financial responsibility for a $60 million, 750-person, non-union, fractional hp, vertically integrated motor plant producing 4800 motors/day.

- Doubled inventory turnover from 12 to 24 by creating cellular manufacturing, focused factories and set-up reduction.
- Orchestrated the ramp-up of production components for an 80% output increase to a highly successful Mexican assembly facility.
- Directed strategic program to transfer production among four plants to improve profitability and create a market focused operation.
- Increased pump motor sales 20% through improvements in cost, quality and customer service.
- Improved productivity 7% through improvements in fabrication and flow.
- Developed plans for ISO 9000 implementation.
- Implemented $2.5 to $3 million in cost improvements annually.
- Guided the creation of empowered hourly/salary teams to improve product quality in a TQM environment.

Goulds Pumps, Inc., Syracuse, NY   1993 to 1995
Plant Manager

A $70 million annual sales operation with 475 employees involved in machining and assembly associated with the manufacture of pump systems.

- Achieved record quarterly production 15% over previous record.
- Improved production control and MRP systems.
- Installed new production methods cutting cost 20%.
- Reorganized staff improving teamwork and plant performance.
- Reduced inventories 15% in less than eight months.
- Transformed quality mind set from detection to prevention.
- Developed comprehensive strategic plan for new owners.

Packaging Machinery Corporation, Columbus, OH   1980 to 1993
Manager Manufacturing Engineering (1991 - 1993)

Responsible for $8 million budget and activities of 150 people for $800 million producer of packaging machinery.

WARREN R. NEWMAN   page 2

- Developed master plans reorganizing multiple facilities.
- Launched new product introduction, on time and 30% under budget.
- Coordinated activities of seven JIT hourly/salary teams.
- Identified and implemented set-up reductions of 10-80%.
- Installed eight manufacturing cells reducing space by 30%.
- Initiated comprehensive preventative maintenance system.

Information Systems Manager (1989 - 1991)
Headed seven-person department responsible for development, operations and maintenance of information systems in an IBM-4341 DOS/VS environment.

- Implemented a shop order system saving $1.1 million.
- Headed development of long range master systems plan.
- Developed programs to highlight and analyze inventory problems.
- Conducted division-wide information systems training sessions.
- Led systems efforts to consolidate multi-plant purchasing functions.

Manager of Purchasing (1987 - 1989)
Managed 11-person purchasing department responsible for all scheduling and procurement of $150 million of production, sub-contract and support materials for a fabrication/assembly operation.

- Consistently achieved over $1 million in favorable price variances.
- Reduced inventory 20% through JIT purchasing and consignment.
- Negotiated multi-year contracts realizing 5-50% cost reductions.
- Implemented automated purchase order system tied to plant MRP.
- Assumed Materials Manager's responsibilities for nine month period.

Manager of Financial Planning and Analysis (1985 - 1987)
Supervised four individuals in the planning, analysis and forecasting of a $400 million division operating as an independent profit center.

- Developed annual and five year plans with senior management.
- Prepared monthly forecasts for division P&L and cash flow.
- Assumed Controller's responsibility for four month period.

Project Manager   (1983 - 1985)
Manufacturing Engineer   (1980 - 1983)

EDUCATION

B.S. Electrical Engineering (with Honors), 1980
Bucknell University, Lewisburg, PA
Elected to Tau Beta Pi

ORGANIZATION SERVICE

Member, Institute of Electrical Engineers

GEORGIA A. ANDERSON

92 Greenview Circle   (816) 794-0782
Richmond, VA 86032

OBJECTIVE

A challenging position which provides the opportunity for utilization of my manufacturing, financial and managerial skills.

SUMMARY OF QUALIFICATIONS

- Demonstrated ability to effectively manage start-up/turnaround situations
- Consistent record of achieving and surpassing desired results and creating new methods and procedures
- Proven record of people development

CAREER HISTORY AND SELECTED ACCOMPLISHMENTS

MAXWELL PACKAGING, INC., Richmond, VA (1995-Present)
Operations Manager
Responsible for the management of three manufacturing facilities and a warehouse/distribution center totaling 480,000 square feet and 850 employees involved in the manufacturing, packaging and distribution of flexible packaging in a multi-shift environment. Annual sales of $50 million, with direct expense budget responsibility of $10 million and capital budget averaging $1 million.
- Instituted standards and methods resulting in an increase in production efficiency of 17%.
- Installed a safety pro-ram that reduced lost work days by 78% with corresponding effect on workers compensation insurance rates.
- Created annual and preventive maintenance programs for both manufacturing equipment and facilities which resulted in greatly reduced downtime saving $175,000 per year.
- Improved inventory controls and reduced physical inventory to book variance by $117,000, or to .003%.
- Revamped quality inspection program resulting in significant reduction in rework expense.
- Started cost improvement program with savings of $121,000.
- Prepared new product costing estimates.

UNIVERSAL INVESTMENT CORPORATION, Ashville, NC (1991-1995)
Senior Vice President and Chief Financial Officer
President - U.I. Securities, Inc. (Subsidiary)
President - Southland Packaging, Inc. (Subsidiary)
Responsibilities included structuring, obtaining and negotiating project financing, corporate finance, coordinating and supervising direct participation program securities sales, cash management. budget preparation, regulatory compliance, asset management, acquisition and divestitures and overall management of flexible packaging company.
- Instituted cash management and investment programs.
- Structured $40 million in project financing in the health care, airport, housing and public/private sectors.
- Restructured $15 million in debt in response to the Tax Reform Act of 1991.
- Broadened relationships with investment bankers, lenders and broker/dealers.
- Reorganized plant management and practices to cause return to profitability.

BIRMINGHAM NATIONAL BANK, Birmingham, AL (1987-1991)
Vice President and Manager - Financial Institutions Division
Responsible for the overall management of the division which served the Bank's relationship with firms in the financial industries with a loan portfolio of $100 million, deposits of $50 million and fee income to $4.1 million. Voting member of Regional Loan Committee and member of Strategic Planning Task Force.
- Refocused Division to a corporate finance/investment banking direction.
- Developed and instituted comprehensive marketing plan.

GEORGIA A. ANDERSON   Page 2

- Established both near and long-term goals and objectives and restaffed the Division to provide the requisite base of experience.
- Created syndication/networking capabilities.
- Provided product capability to all bank customers in structured/specialized credits.
- Directed policy creation on off-balance sheet credit products, funds management exposure, and specialized credit products.
- Improved bottom line profitability $900,000.

JORDAN MANUFACTURING COMPANY, Atlanta, GA (1983-1987)
<u>Director of Operations - Jordan Finance Company (1985-1987)</u>
Responsible for the formation of the captive finance subsidiary, all finance programs, documentation, credit and collection procedures.

- Defined the initial scope of business and developed initial organizational structure and inter-company agreements.
- Created new finance and lease programs, implemented marketing support systems and instituted policies and procedures for proper management control.
- Successfully resolved several preexisting accounts saving the company over $1 million in bad debt exposures.
- Provided focused financing support of product sales.

<u>Manager - International Credit and Finance (1983-1985)</u>
Responsibilities included making credit decisions on all export shipments from Jordan-U.S. locations, arranging export financing for customer purchases from all Jordan worldwide locations, working closely with the Assistant Treasurer in the area of bank relationships, foreign subsidiary financing, capitalization requirements and cash management.

- Created in-house distributor and end user finance programs.
- Developed outside sources of financing.
- Negotiated attractive import financing from the German Government resulting in a $1.5 million savings.
- Effected refinancing of foreign subsidiary debt at significantly lower rates.
- Participated in a major foreign divestiture.
- Traveled to and transacted business throughout Europe, Middle East and Central and South America.

AUGUSTA NATIONAL BANK, Augusta, GA (1979-1983)
<u>Cash Management Representative (1982-1983)</u>
Responsibilities included designing collection and disbursement systems for major customers of the Bank.

<u>Administrative Assistant - Commercial Division (1981)</u>
<u>Credit Analyst (1980-1981)</u>
<u>Management Training Program (1979)</u>

EDUCATION

UNIVERSITY OF NORTH CAROLINA
   M.B.A., Finance (1979)
   B.S., Accounting (1977)

SECURITIES LICENSES

General Securities Representative (Series 7)
Uniform State Securities Registration (Series 63)
General Securities Principal (Series 24)

MICHAEL S. LAWTON
12 Baylor Drive
Arlington, Texas 90135
(205) 667-2103 (Res.)
(205) 937-4120 (Bus.)

OBJECTIVE: A management position in production/operations with a company that will utilize my experience and skills to meet business objectives and support my commitment to customer service, employee development and continuous improvement.

SUMMARY: Experienced, results-oriented manager with progressive and increasing responsibility in Production Management, Operations, Quality Control and Human Resources.

EXPERIENCE:

JOHNSON & JOHNSON, New Brunswick, NJ
A $12.4 billion pharmaceutical, health care and consumer products company.

Production Manager, Dallas, TX   **1995 - Present**
Reporting to the Director of Operations, directing five Department Managers and 290 employees in all aspects of manufacturing and packaging for divisional sales of approximately $300 million.

- Managed site's profit improvement program which resulted in yearly savings of over $1 million for six consecutive years.

- Implemented the establishment of production line teams that resulted in numerous operational improvements including the elimination of line Group Leaders with associated savings of $250,000.

- Successfully coordinated the validation and production start-up of approximately 25 products transferred to Dallas from a sister plant that was closed.

- Worked closely with R&D and Marketing to successfully launch a major new product line with estimated annual sales of $40 million.

- Implemented single minute exchange of dies (SMED) program which reduced line equipment changeover time by as much as 60%. This resulted in increased available capacity eliminating the need for capital expenditures.

- Assisted with the education/implementation of Safety Training Observation Program (STOP) at Dallas for supervision.

- Developed and implemented a right-first-time program for Production. This quality improvement effort (quality at the source) reduced inventory and improved customer service levels.

Production Manager, Fort Washington, PA   **1993 to 1995**
Reporting to the Plant Manager, directing two Department Managers and approximately 100 employees in all aspects of manufacturing and packaging for divisional sales of approximately $60 million.

- Coordinated the installation of a fully computerized integrated powder manufacturing system resulting in annual savings of approximately $220,000.

- Managed cost reduction program which generated annual savings of approximately $300,000.

- Implemented monthly operation meetings to enhance employee-employer relations, improve communications and provide for employee feedback and ideas.

Employee Relations Manager, Dallas, TX   **1991 to 1993**
Reporting to the Plant Manager, this position was responsible for all human resource issues and policies for the Dallas facility of approximately 500 employees.

- Developed and maintained programs to prevent third party intervention in the management of the operations.

- Developed and implemented a participative problem solving program which resulted in the formation of nine operating teams whose mission was to both identify and solve daily production problems in their respective departments. On average, this program had annualized savings of $20,000 and promoted employee involvement.

- Streamlined compensation program to provide for better equity between job levels.

Other positions and promotions leading to management responsibilities:

Supervisor of Aerosol Filling
Quality Control Manager
Assistant Supervisor, Aerosol Filling

EDUCATION:

Texas A&M University - BA in Biology, Minor in Chemistry, 1985

RODNEY S. DeLONG
1425 Darion Circle
Portland, OR 31592

(206) 357-9321 Office
(206) 425-1362 Home

OBJECTIVE

Operations/Manufacturing Management leading to Business Management

QUALIFICATIONS

A proven leader with a record of successes in industrial manufacturing. Direct management of manufacturing facilities in the chemical and food industries. Successfully introduced high performance work systems concepts within the manufacturing function of the business. In current role, plan and manage a four plant operation spanning the continent with total annual sales of $190 million employing 530 people: $35 million new plant start-up, repositioning of an aging technology through the transfer of European technology, and turnaround of the company's only unionized facility. A proven motivator and developer of people.

PROFESSIONAL EXPERIENCE

WALTON CHEMICAL COMPANY   **1990 to Present**
Portland, Oregon
<u>Director of Manufacturing, Specialty Chemicals</u>   (1996 - Present)
Manage the manufacturing operation of the largest business in the company. Key thrust for the business is to maintain low cost position in the industry through continuous upgrade of technology and introduction of team-based work systems. Three primary accountabilities in this role are optimizing the performance of the producing sites, creating an integrated manufacturing strategy that improves the relative competitive position of the business, and coordinating the transfer of technologies and systems among the plant operations in North America and Europe.

Accomplishments and Results

* Developed a cohesive strategy and operational plans for four manufacturing facilities, resulting in a 100% profit gain in two years.

* In a facility operating at a loss, exceeded ROA targets in two years, reduced waste by 40%, increased saleable output by 35%, reduced personnel by 40%, and significantly improved profitability.

* Implemented an innovative management and labor relations strategy in a key facility that initiated a collaborative rather than adversarial relationship and reduced grievances by more than 90%. Production was increased by 25% in one year; value added cost reduced by 30%.

* Served as key member on the Business Leadership Team with Walton North America, developing vision, mission, objectives, and strategy. Served as the key resource in creating both company and business direction.

Resume of: Rodney S. DeLong - Continued   Page Two

* Served as the company champion for the Total Quality Management planning and implementation process. Within the first year the structure, plans, and resources were in place to create the change necessary to reach the stated objectives. This initiative included the implementation of ISO 9002 and Total Productive Maintenance at each manufacturing site.

* Created and led a Global Manufacturing Network for the purpose of information sharing, technology transfer, and identifying common initiatives to manage for the global business.

* Co-managed the development of $60 million capital improvement program, with a particular emphasis on facility relocation, capacity expansion, and corporate campus planning.

Manager of Site Operations - Seattle Plant	(1995 - 1996)
Plant Manager - Seattle Plant	(1992 - 1995)
Plant Manager - Portland Plant	(1990 - 1992)

THE FRITO LAY COMPANY   **1986 to 1990**
Allen Park, Michigan

Assistant Manager	(1988 - 1990)
Plant Engineer	(1987 - 1988)
Plant Industrial Engineer	(1986 - 1987)

EDUCATION

UNIVERSITY OF CHICAGO - M.B.A., General Management & Finance Major (1986)

OREGON STATE UNIVERSITY - B.S., Mechanical Engineering (1984)

KENT W. GIVENS
15 Golden Road
Long Beach, CA 21755
(414) 496-8500

PROFILE: Excellent background in Distribution/Transportation Operations and Engineering, with recent experience in the Manufacturing environment.

EXPERIENCE:

1989 - Present   **EVON COSMETICS, INC.**   LOS ANGELES, CA

(1997 - Present)   *DIRECTOR, MANUFACTURING OPERATIONS*
Responsible for all operational aspects of this formerly subcontracted $6 million thermoforming discipline with documented in-house savings exceeding $600,000 annually. Developed and monitored long and short-term critical path production schedules for over 125 major marketing programs. Responsibilities also included attainment of hourly labor performance against budgeted standards as well as the direct control of all Thermoforming Department financial expenditures.

Major Accomplishments:
- Increased labor productivity by 15%.
- Effected a positive component usage variance in excess of $100M against budget.
- Increased safety performance by 37%.

(1995 - 1997)   *ASSISTANT DIRECTOR, RAW MATERIALS MANAGEMENT*
With an annual budget of nearly $8 million, was responsible for the physical movement of all inbound manufacturing components and raw materials to our Los Angeles, Huntington Beach and San Diego sites. This included both domestic and international suppliers.

Major Accomplishments:
- Conducted the first ever rate negotiation sessions for Freight In operations, which resulted in a 20% reduction in expenditures as a percent to Cost of Goods.
- Established vendor LTL consolidation programs for each of the three Evon sites which resulted in substantial cost savings with no adverse effects upon service.

(1995)   *ASSISTANT DIRECTOR, EVON COLOGNE GROUP*
Was instrumental in the start-up of this uniquely new $200 million operation established in San Diego, CA.

Major Accomplishments:
- Designed the physical layout of the shipping dock, hired and trained the clerical and hourly staff, and directly supervised the day-to-day shipping and transportation operations during its infancy stages.
- Wrote all procedural manuals related to our functional disciplines.
- Developed tonnage and service statistical reports enabling efficient administrative controls and analysis of operational performance.

(1994)

ASSISTANT DIRECTOR, DISTRIBUTION
With yearly expenditures exceeding $9 million, was responsible for all aspects of transportation of finished goods to retail customers and between company facilities, both via common carrier and the Evon corporate fleet.

Major Accomplishments.,
- Through motor carrier rate negotiations, LTL and small shipment consolidations, as well as improved shipping dock labor methods, effected annual cost reductions of $1.8 million.

(1989 - 1994)

MANAGER, DISTRIBUTION ENGINEERING
Prepared, in detail, the annual divisional $7 million plus labor budget. Provided cost versus savings analyses on all operations improvement projects and determined the associated facility capacity and manpower requirements. Planned and developed proposals for capital expenditures related to facilities upgrade and new equipment purchases amounting to approximately $2 million annually.

Major Accomplishments:
- Developed and implemented work performance standards within the Evon Distribution Division, which resulted in yearly $750,000 labor cost savings.
- Provided long-term cost savings to justify a $4 million Distribution automation project.

1986 - 1989   **A. T. KEARNEY, INC.**   NEW YORK, NY

ASSOCIATE
Representing one of the largest management consulting firms in the world, duties included extensive travel to client locations performing audits and detailed studies of transportation and distribution operations. Responsible for data gathering, analysis, recommendations development, and final written report preparation.

EDUCATION: **RUTGERS UNIVERSITY,** New Brunswick, New Jersey
- M.B.A., 1986
- B.A. Degree, Business Administration, 1984

DARRELL L. MARSHALL
133 Howard Court
Clearview, IL 34521
(615) 564-9372

OBJECTIVE: To obtain a challenging senior-level manufacturing position.

EXPERIENCE:

1986 - Present   **AVON PRODUCTS COMPANY**   CHICAGO, IL

1994 - Present   *SENIOR PRODUCTION MANAGER, CONTAINER DECORATING DIVISION*
Responsible for total profit/loss, scheduling, purchasing of all production and maintenance supplies, maintenance, acceptable quality of finished components, job completion, safety, GMPS, and utilization of labor.

Major Accomplishments:
- Reversed a divisional loss of $750,000 in 1994 to a profit of $1.2 million in 1996.
- Designed and implemented a scrap program that provided an annual savings of $500,000 and brought job completion to 100%.
- Developed and set up cost savings program which realized annual cost savings of $250,000.

1993 - 1994   *PRODUCTION MANAGER, PROMOTIONAL DIVISION*
Responsible for on-time production of finished work, efficient utilization of labor, acceptable quality of final product, job completion, safety, GMP compliance, and receiving and stores.

Major Accomplishments:
- Designed and implemented $.5 million in cost savings programs.
- Produced all promotions on time, despite being handicapped by late component deliveries and moving our operation twice.
- Had positive labor variance of approximately 20,000 hours.

1990 - 1993   *SENIOR PRODUCTION SUPERVISOR, PROMOTIONAL DIVISION*
Responsible for efficient utilization of labor, setting up and clearing of production lines, acceptability of finished products, safety, GMPS, and receiving and stores.

Major Accomplishments:
- Despite a 50% increase in volume, late component deliveries, and a large, new work force, produced all promotions on time and achieved a positive variance of 10,000 hours.

1986 - 1990   *PRODUCTION SUPERVISOR, PROMOTIONAL DIVISION*
Responsible for running production lines, efficient utilization of labor, acceptability of finished product, and safety.

1980 - 1986   **MAXWELL PAPER COMPANY**   HOWELL, IL

1986   *PRODUCTION AND INVENTORY CONTROL COORDINATOR*

1985 - 1986   *BRANCH MANAGER*

1985   *MANUFACTURING SUPERVISOR*

1983 - 1985   *PRODUCTION FOREMAN*

1980 - 1983   *MACHINE TENDER*

EDUCATION: **UNIVERSITY OF CHICAGO,** BS - Business Management, 1980

RICHARD M. MARTIN
14 Pickering Way
Cleveland Heights, OH 25421

Home: (306) 871-4120   Office: (306) 544-9001

OPERATIONS EXECUTIVE

Proven operations executive with successful results in the management of all functions in manufacturing and plant operations, including P&L responsibility. Particular strengths in cost control, systems, business strategic planning, problem-solving and introduction of new technologies and changes for operational improvement. Resourceful leader with excellent communication and interpersonal skills.

POWER TECHNOLOGIES, INC. - Cleveland, OH   1995 - present
This company designs and manufactures steam turbines and pumps for the industrial and petrochemical markets. The company required significant upgrades of productivity, equipment and processes to improve its competitive position in the marketplace.

Manager - Manufacturing Operations
Responsible for machining, assembly, test, purchasing, material control, manufacturing engineering, plant engineering and environmental compliance for a $150 million plus sales plant. Managed an organization of 425 individuals, 375 of which were union production and maintenance employees. Responsible for a $42 million expense budget.

- Achieved the highest sales in over ten years and reduced backlogs by 30% through organizational restructuring and attention to details,

- Reduced inventories $3 million by setting objectives and measuring against the objectives.

- Improved productivity 8% and reduced costs 10% by implementing multidiscipline task forces to address inefficiencies.

- Put in place a joint procurement program with international divisions, which reduced material costs by $2.4 million annually.

- Implemented state-of-the-art computer numerical control five-axis machining and robotic welding, resulting in product quality improvements.

- Converted an adversarial labor relationship to one of mutual trust through participative management.

WARNER PUMP COMPANY - Huron, OH   1984 - 1995

Manager - Manufacturing Operations - Sandusky, OH (1991 - 1995)
This plant manufactures custom pump systems for the industrial and defense markets. Mature facility that required major upgrades of productivity, systems, equipment and processes to assure survival in a very competitive marketplace. Responsible for machining, assembly, test, materials, production control, quality assurance, manufacturing engineering and maintenance for a $70 million sales plant with a $21 million expense budget Managed an organization of 320 individuals, 270 were union production, maintenance and clerical employees. Promoted from Production Manager to Manager - Manufacturing Operations.

- Reduced cycle times by 20% by implementing eight manufacturing cells.

- Improved costs and reduced budgets 10% through instituting cost control and accountability.

RICHARD M. MARTIN

Manager - Manufacturing Operations (Continued)

- Improved productivity 20% by methods improvements, control of direct labor and attention to quality.

- Reduced vendor base 30% and set up fifteen alliances with key suppliers. This resulted in significant lead time reductions and improvements in vendor quality.

- Improved on-time shipment 28% by implementing a disciplined production system.

- Reduced inventories over 45% through attention to control and reduction of cycle times.

- Negotiated three labor contracts that achieved greater flexibility of workforce utilization.

Plant Manager - Toledo, OH (1989 - 1991)
This plant manufactured and overhauled specialty pumps for the industrial, petrochemical and utility markets. Profit and loss responsibility for die plant. Responsible for marketing, engineering, manufacturing, finance and human resources functions.

- Strengthened the marketing and engineering functions by recruiting highly qualified personnel.

- Improved productivity 10% by implementing an operator involvement program.

- Improved income 26% by cost reduction and cycle time improvement.

- Reduced inventories 36% through attention to control and reduction of cycle times.

- Improved on-time shipments from 60% to 98% with the implementation of new PC-based production systems.

- Achieved an orderly close down of the facility and transferred products to other plants.

Manager - Technical Services (1984 - 1989)
Implemented an integrated facility and equipment plan involving six plants, reduced quality costs by 50% on four product lines and transferred product lines between plants.

GENERAL ELECTRIC COMPANY - Fairfield, CT   1974 - 1984
Selected for the General Electric Manufacturing Management Program, which involved rotating six month assignments as Production Control Specialist, Buyer, Q. C. Process Specialist, Value Engineer and Foreman. After program graduation, held a series of increasing responsible positions at various plant locations as Manufacturing Engineer, Manager - Production Control, Manager - Advanced Manufacturing and Process Engineering, Manager Manufacturing Engineering and Manager - Mechanical Design Engineering.

EDUCATION

B. S., Electrical Engineering - 1974
Michigan Technological University
Houghton, Michigan

OTHER ACTIVITIES

General Electric Manufacturing Management Program Graduate

JAMES H. FARWELL

309 Peabody Lane
Columbia, MD 16412

Home: 401-766-9059
Office: 401-885-1400

SUMMARY OF EXPERIENCE

Considerable experience in a manufacturing/operational environment, servicing the consumer hardware, industrial and sporting goods industries. Personally responsible for domestic and off-shore manufacturing facilities and processes ranging from $70 million to $200 million. Achieved significant accomplishments within extremely competitive markets via the use of strong leadership skills, creative problem solving methods, new product development and enhanced employee capabilities through self-directed work teams.

PROFESSIONAL EXPERIENCE

DIRECTOR OF CHAIN OPERATIONS   1991 - 1999
Troy-Bilt Tools, Baltimore, MD
Troy-Bilt is a manufacturer of welded and weldless chain and chain accessories servicing the consumer hardware, industrial, automotive, marine and forestry markets.

- Total responsibility for P&L of this $185,000,000 company which includes four manufacturing facilities, eight distribution centers and 1200 employees.

- Initiated and implemented the following major projects: ISO 9000, OPC/SPC, Bar coded shop floor control system, vendor certification program and the introduction of self-directed work teams.

- Personally responsible for the development of off-shore manufacturing relations offering extreme flexibility in the manufacturing of labor intensive products.

- Established a unique consignment program for the procurement of all major raw materials.

- Relocated a 200,000 sq. ft. southeastern chain facility into the Baltimore plant within a nine month time period with no disruption in production of service.

- Realized internal cost reduction programs yielding in excess of $1,000,000 annually for the past six years.

- Responsible for a 40% reduction of inventories and 35% reduction of salaried staff within my employment history at Troy-Bilt while reducing period costs from 18+% to 9.1%.

- Received two patents for new product.

- Was responsible for new three-tier, two-level wage structure and "management by council" concept to support empowered team philosophy.

VICE PRESIDENT, OPERATIONS   1987 - 1991
Troy-Bilt/Hanover Chain, Richmond, VA
Hanover Chain was a manufacture of fastner hardware for the industrial, consumer hardware and saddlery markets, acquired by Troy-Bilt.

- Manufacturing and marketing responsibilities for this $7,000,000 per year organization.

- Responsible for the design and manufacture of complete new zinc die cast snap and pulley line.

- Responsible for the establishment of Far East manufacturers for labor intensive processes.

134

JAMES H. FARWELL   **Page Two**

- Strongly positioned family-owned company for acquisition by larger corporation via:

    - Leader in marketplace
    - Low inventories
    - Efficient manufacturing processes
    - Good profitability
    - Sound manufacturing facility and staff

VICE PRESIDENT, MANUFACTURING   1984 - 1987
OmniPower Pump, Inc., Richmond, VA

- Responsible for manufacturing facility and new product design for this producer of residential and commercial pumps.

- Responsible for an award-winning submergible pump utilizing a zinc die cast design which eliminated 70% of required machine operations.

- Introduction of in-line manufacturing concept reducing product costs by 20 + %.

DIRECTOR OF MANUFACTURING   1980 - 1984
Coleman Arms Corporation, Reston, VA
Manufacturer of Pellet and BB Guns. Hired as a product designer and promoted three times to Director of Manufacturing.

- Directly responsible for the design and development of new products which ultimately grew the company from $1 million to $16 million.

- Received four patents for new product designs all of which were mass produced and sold to the sporting goods industry.

- Wrote and implemented a Total Quality Control procedures manual.

- Implemented a computerized materials planning system for all phases of manufacturing and procurement.

- Was instrumental in the planning and construction phases of new 100,000 sq. ft. manufacturing facility.

- Was responsible for the design and implementation of an in-line process for the fabrication of CO_2 powered products.

- Ultimately responsible for the total manufacturing facilities and processes which included three plants and 230 employees.

    - Decreased inventories by 30%
    - Decreased period costs by 25%
    - Increased EBT to a level of 28%

EDUCATION

VIRGINIA POLYTECHNICAL INSTITUTE, Bachelor of Science, Mechanical Engineering, 1980

SPECIALIZED TRAINING

TROY-BILT INDUSTRIES, Finance for Non-Financial Managers, 1988
DIMENSIONS INTERNATIONAL, Strategies for Employee Empowerment, 1993

CLIFFORD H. ROONEY
34 CAPTAIN'S ROW
FREEPORT, NJ 07728
(609) 499-6443

OBJECTIVE: Production Supervisor position within a growing organization.

SUMMARY: People-oriented supervisor who believes the ability to change and adapt to new technology is necessary in today's competitive marketplace. I am confident that my knowledge, ability and adaptability will be an asset to any organization.

EXPERIENCE:

1975 - 1998   **LOREAL INC.**   WINSTON, NJ

1992 - 1998   PRODUCTION SUPERVISOR
Supervised 80-100 employees in a high-speed filling, packaging and production process. Responsible for running eight different units, as well as training new supervisors and machinists.
Major Accomplishments:
- Instituted a response team of operators and mechanics who responded to line-stoppages, decreasing downtime between repairs by more than 20%.
- Instituted preventive maintenance program that decreased stoppages by 30% over a two year period.
- Responded to OSHA safety requirements with 92% efficiency for the production floor.

1990 - 1992   QUALITY CONTROL SUPERVISOR
Responsibilities included insuring that the final product at the packaging plant met the assigned specifications. Inspected all aspects of the high-speed packaging process, including line speeds, video jets, coders, cappers, box assemblers, pressure fillers, shrink wrappers and labelers. Promoted to the position of Production Supervisor.
Major Accomplishments:
- Instituted a program using electrical weight checking to insure proper fill height specifications within the aerosol filling units.
- Although this position was offered to me on a temporary basis while I was a union employee, my accomplishments warranted an opportunity to advance to Production Supervisor.

1981 - 1990   GRADE A MACHINIST
Responsible for line changeovers, which included the adjustments and changes of machine parts for valvers, actuators, MRM fillers, Goldberger labelers, crimpers and automatic ferrel coders. Responsibilities also included 85% up-time on all running, filling and packaging machinery on the production floor.
Major Accomplishments:
- Instituted training program for new machinists within the company, using procedure guidelines developed by area directors under the advice of department personnel.
- Directed the use of safety gear on all filling lines within hazardous areas: protective glasses, robes and gloves. This reduced lost time accidents by 35% in one year.
- Trained area personnel on the use of hazardous propane and butane gasses used as a propellant in the filling of colognes and perfumes.

EDUCATION: **BRECKENRIDGE SR. HIGH SCHOOL**, Breckenridge, New Jersey; Graduated 1981

JERRY L. MADISON
841 Lumber Lane
Kings Cove, ME 87955
(410) 377-6438 Home
(410) 495-1700 Office

OBJECTIVE:

Senior operations management position at a major operating facility for a growing pulp and paper or related company, where broad management skills in operations can be fully utilized.

EXPERIENCE:

1998
to
Present

AMERICAN PULP & PAPER CORPORATION

Director, Pulping Operations - Portland Mill
Report to Vice President & Resident Manager of this 1,200 TPD bleached kraft pulp mill. Direct staff of six department managers, 36 professionals and 157 hourly personnel ($240 million operating budget). Functional responsibility for pulp manufacturing, utilities and environmental protection.

Key Accomplishments:

- Directed successful start-up of $200 million power and recovery capital project with less than 24 hours lost mill production (American's largest capital project ever).

- Increased pulp production by 155 TPD in single year through improved utilization of existing capacity.

- Reduced pulp manufacturing costs by over $24 per ton (8%) with resultant annual savings of $12.7 million.

- Directed start-up of state-of-the-art lime mud dryer and kiln (first of its kind in North America).

- Achieved $5 million additional annual cost savings in steam generation through optimization of fuel mix.

- Reorganized pulp and utilities department for better focus on multiple priorities.

1995
to
1998

KRANSTON MANUFACTURING

Manager, Pulp Manufacturing - Kelsey, ME Mill
Reported to Production Manager, Pulp, Power & Wood of this 550 TPD bleached kraft pulp mill. Managed staff of eight supervisors and 75 hourly employees ($73 million operating budget). Functional responsibility for all pulp manufacturing.

Key Accomplishments:

- Key member of team responsible for planning, process design and equipment selection for $275 million pulp mill modernization and expansion project.

- Increased existing pulp mill production by 27 TPD, despite planned mill obsolescence.

- Achieved $1.8 million annual cost savings in pulp manufacturing costs.

1983
to
1995

PORT CHARLOTTE PAPER COMPANY

Assistant Technical Director - Port Charlotte Kraft Mill (1993 - 1995)
Reported to Technical Director of this 1,500 TPD brown and bleached kraft pulp and paper mill. Managed staff of eight technical professionals and 20 nonexempt support personnel with functional responsibility for process engineering, pulp and paper quality control, testing laboratory and environmental compliance.

Key Accomplishments:

- Developed mill-wide process database and information system.

- Key member of bleach plant implementation core group ($50 million bleach plant capital project).

Pulping Area Supervisor	(1992 - 1993)
Technical Assistant to Paper Mill Superintendent	(1991 - 1992)
Pulp Mill Tour Supervisor	(1988 - 1991)
Technical Assistant to Pulp Mill Superintendent	(1986 - 1988)
Process Engineering Assistant	(1983 - 1986)

EDUCATION:

M.B.A., University of Maine, 1995
GPA: 3.4/4.0
B.S., Pulp & Paper Science, Washington State University, 1983
GPA: 3.2/4.0

MILITARY:

United States Navy, 1974 - 1980
Petty Officer, 2nd Class
Interior Communications Technician
Honorable Discharge - September, 1980

BARTON R. JOHNSON
543 Stoneybrooke Lane
Atlanta, GA 50079
404-529-9329

CAREER SUMMARY

Experienced general manager with significant P&L operations responsibility. Demonstrated ability in building and managing teams which improve profit performance, generating results in all facets of the operation. Contribute equally well in growth and turnaround environments, domestically and internationally.

BUSINESS EXPERIENCE

JOHNSON SCIENCE INC. A Wilson Laboratories Subsidiary   **1996 to Present**
Vice President Operations

Responsible for operational profitability, plant management and engineering in five plants throughout North America for this $32 million contract analytical chemistry subsidiary. Direct environmental efforts, customer service and support and material handling. Manage an $18 million operating budget.

- Co-developed a critical joint venture company with another contract laboratory, generating $4 million in sales annually from a key $150 million customer.

- Negotiated the acquisition of a competitor whose combined sales will nearly double the East Coast business and position the organization for greater market penetration.

- Successfully directed the design and construction of a leading-edge, 75,000 square foot, $5 million custom analytical laboratory facility, on time and within budget. Additional profits from incremental sales and elimination of shipping costs will exceed $475,000 annually.

AMERICAN LABORATORIES, INC.   **1992 to 1996**
Vice President/General Manager

Total P&L general management responsibility for two distinct businesses generating sales of $20 million annually. Directed sales and marketing, manufacturing, R&D, finance, procurement, and manufacturing representative organizations.

- Turned around the business and reduced scrap an average of 25% for three major customers by developing and launching a sophisticated scanning device for Amatron, an $8 million division manufacturing printing industry control devices.

- Increased national account revenues $1.5 million annually for Microdyne, a custom sterilization division. Effectively accelerated the construction of a mega sterilization chamber, 25% larger than industry standard.

- Accelerated the availability of $950,000 in revenue generation by successfully bringing a plant (60,000 square feet) on-line early while managing all operations of three other sterilization facilities.

BANISTER, INC.   **1990 to 1992**
Vice President Operations

Managed the profitability and provided the strategic general management direction to worldwide production, corporate manufacturing engineering, distribution, purchasing, and business planning. Directed four manufacturing plants in the United States and Ireland with a worldwide staff of 100. Developed and managed the performance of $65 million operating budget and $10 million capital budget.

- Protected a $50 million product line and saved $1 million annually through innovative sourcing, negotiation of vendor contracts, and contingency plans.

- Saved $500,000 in material costs annually by managing the launch of MRP II, including executive education, consultant selection, and company-wide implementation strategy.

- Eliminated $800,000 annually in material spoilage by upgrading operational performance through "best demonstrated manufacturing practices" and comprehensive training.

- Averted increased operating costs of at least $500,000 in key pilot plant with 90 employees by successfully turning aside an aggressive union organizing campaign.

DEXTER, INC.   **1980 to 1990**
Vice President Manufacturing   1984 - 1990
Director of Manufacturing   1980 - 1984

Directed production activity, domestically and internationally, in seven plants in the United States, Puerto Rico, Dominican Republic and Singapore. Managed manufacturing, materials management, engineering, human resources, finance, and distribution. Developed and managed a budget of $300 million and directed 5,000 employees.

- Contributed $15 million in added profits annually by reducing standard costs 5% for five consecutive years. Gains were achieved through manufacturing efficiencies and off-shore sourcing of materials and production of finished goods.

- Eliminated $3 million in operational costs by strategizing and closing a major Kansas manufacturing facility which improved system-wide plant utilization and product closing.

- Provided the strategic manufacturing and business direction for the successful start-up launch, and ongoing operation of highly profitable production plants in Singapore the Dominican Republic, and a key joint venture in Shanghai, China. Shipped 200 million units annually within five years.

PREVIOUS BUSINESS EXPERIENCE

As **Director of Manufacturing Engineering** at Victor, Inc. (1975 - 1980), was responsible for operational planning and analysis, engineering process controls, contract packaging, vendor negotiations and production. Installed inventory investment controls for seven divisions, reducing on-hand inventories $70 million while optimizing manufacturing coverage.

While at Durall Laboratories, Inc., held increasingly responsible technical management and manufacturing management positions from 1972 - 1975.

EDUCATION

M.B.A.   Industrial Management, 1972
            New York University
            New York, NY

B.A.   Economics, Boston University, 1970
            Boston, MA

KAREN R. SCHEINER
32 Bunting Drive
Grand Rapids, MI 82526
(615) 746-8422

Results-oriented manager with extensive experience in high pressure, time sensitive businesses and proven record of success in on time delivery of products/services. Innovator in logistics and scheduling for large, complex, 24-hour a day operation. Decision maker/leader with labor union, reengineering/restructuring, OSHA, and employee development background. Team builder/player able to prioritize and supervise employees. Excellent communication and training skills.

FEDERAL EXPRESS CORPORATION   **1987 to Present**

REGIONAL MANAGER   1995-Present
Manage entire operation (ten centers) with over 600 employees including hiring, inventory, and training for large division of this overnight delivery company.

* Oversee daily operations of ten-center division with **50,000 customers** handling over **200,000 packages per day** and annual budget exceeding $32 million.

* Restructured service operation to reduce management and supervisory personnel, saving company **$250,000 per year**.

* Initiated changes in facility and handling procedures, reducing damage to packages and saving company **$500,000 per year**.

* Developed relationships with staff resulting in contract approval with teamsters union by vote of over 80% and simultaneously cut staff by 20%.

* Managed training program which resulted in promotion of seven managers from supervisory staff.

* Retrained safety department and other staff in ongoing documentation of controls and procedures, gaining favorable audit from OSHA on an ongoing basis.

* Implemented company-wide computer delivery system one month ahead of schedule and became first in district to do so.

* Implemented new training program for operations managers to provide for resolution of customer problems.

TRAINING MANAGER   1994-1995
A special assignment including intensive three month session as training instructor for newly promoted supervisors.

* Trained supervisory personnel from all 52 states on controlling budget and costs.

* Scheduled other instructors and reported directly to Corporate Training Director.

Karen P. Scheiner   **Page Two**

SORT MANAGER   1993-1994
Coordinated all phases of operational start-up for Scan Sort program in Grand Rapids, MI.

*   Planned and implemented **start-up** Scan Sort program which handled over 28,000 packages per day from its inception.

*   Developed training program and wrote training manual for hourly and management personnel, insuring safety and a high level of customer satisfaction.

*   Scheduled hourly staff, planned all volume and cost control.

SCANNING COORDINATOR   1991-1993
Acted as region coordinator to control implementation of package scanning procedure throughout all of Michigan, Illinois, Ohio and West Virginia.

*   Implemented new high tech scanning procedure in 165 facilities in two months (ahead of schedule), training/directing 12 people who facilitated implementation process.

*   Implemented three cost saving plans to be used in districts that recouped $195,000 in excess labor costs annually.

*   Completed project under budget for travel and associated costs.

OTHER POSITIONS

Center Manager, Supervisor, and Driver.   1987-1991

EDUCATION/SEMINARS

B.A., Business Administration, University of Toledo, Toledo, OH, 1991

Employee Relations Workshop

Labor Relations Workshop

Time Study Seminar

JAMES R. SANDERS
33 Watson Way
Columbus, Ohio 60331

Home: (613) 695-0822   Office: (613) 492-1307

SENIOR LEVEL OPERATIONS EXECUTIVE SUMMARY

Innovative operations executive with a strong background in logistics and customer service processes. A leader with profit and growth motivation who creates a spirited team and is experienced in distribution network, optimization, information systems design, customer consulting and efficient consumer response initiatives.

PROFESSIONAL EXPERIENCE

TRANSPORT TECHNOLOGY, INC., Columbus, Ohio   **1997 - Present**
Leading outsourcing company in logistics and distribution with sales of $300 million.

Director of Distribution
Manage Distribution, Customer Service and Transportation for four major Household and Personal Products Manufacturers. Sales targeted to Grocery, Hardware and Mass Merchandiser accounts. Responsibilities include management of carrier, warehouse and customer service personnel, manufacturing and marketing support, customer process integration, systems design and associate development for personal growth and in support of teamwork. Responsible for $120 million operating budget.

COLGATE-PALMOLIVE COMPANY, New York, New York   **1990 - 1997**

Distribution Network Operations Manager;
Transportation Manager; National Planning Manager
Managed National Distribution Network for the Corporation ($7 billion sales). Responsibilities included site selection, carrier selection and measurement, construction, hiring and training, system design, network inventory management, customer consulting and operating budget of $300 million.

- Designed and constructed ten distribution centers including all negotiations of leases and purchases and hiring of entire operations staff.
- Designed distribution computer system resulting in significant savings and customer service improvements.
- Implemented RF terminal/scanner paperless warehouse operating system resulting in savings of $6 million.
- Designed and implemented cycle count and inventory control system resulting in zero inventory loss in six years.

James R. Sanders   Page Two

- Motivated, through total employee involvement, distribution teams to virtual zero defect quality levels in shipping accuracy, inventory accuracy, accident prevention and attendance.
- Introduced customer consulting programs for key accounts.
- Designed and implemented a Supplier Quality Program for the Transportation Network resulting in benchmark performance levels in cost and service.
- Developed operating company measurement and reporting systems resulting in order fill rate improvements of 95%, out-of-service transportation cost reductions of $3 million and inventory turn improvements of 6-9 weeks.

LEVER BROTHERS COMPANY, New York, New York   **1979 - 1990**

Sales and Distribution Service Manager; Transportation Manager; Manufacturing Supervisor; Distribution Manager
Managed customer service operations servicing one-half of the United States.

- Coordinated the design and implementation of ORACLE order entry system resulting in consolidated customer service, transportation and distribution.
- Implemented customer deduction system reducing claims from 1,000 to 200 in on-hand open files.
- Negotiated Teamster contracts resulting in job combinations from 22 job groups to three.

EDUCATION

B.A., Business Management
Rutgers University, 1979

CLAYTON B. SMITH

32 Hemlock Lane
Manheim, PA 18214
(610) 852-2406

SUMMARY:

Shirt sleeves manager with a record of consistent success in meeting profit objectives and in using quality management techniques. Focused experience in operations management, TQM, supply management, ISO 9001 and process improvement. Effective leader who creates a results-oriented team environment.

WORK EXPERIENCE: York International Corporation, Lancaster, PA

Director, Quality Systems (1996-Present)
- Reduced, by 25%, nonconformances in the contract review and design control areas through the use of process mapping and benchmarking.
- Led a company of 1000 employees through the ISO 9001 process and received registration. The undertaking was a major project and required proven project management skills.
- Trained personnel in the use of TQM, facilitated team building and benchmarking initiatives.

Director, Supply Management (1993-1996)
- Developed suppliers and negotiated terms for $120M (annual) purchase of material.
- Reduced the number of approved suppliers from 2800 to 700.
- Managed a supplier quality control group and instituted a supplier certification program that resulted in an increase in on-time delivery from 82% to 93% and a decrease in defects by 22%.

Plant Manager - multiple plants, Assembly & Distribution (1987-1993)
- Increased gross margin 55% by consolidating operations and cutting overtime from 22% to 7% while directing a $6M, 120-employee plant. Responsible for profit and loss, engineering, machining, purchasing, inventory control, building facilities and union negotiations.
- Boosted turns ratio from 2 to 3.5 on $1.5M inventory by cycle counting.

Project Manager, Air Conditioner Parts Operations (1982-1987)
- Expanded sales from $1.5M to $4M by increasing direct customer contact and developing several supplier partnering agreements. Reduced cycle time of proposal and contract administration functions by introducing electronic documentation.

Prior to 1982
- Test engineering, R&D, mechanical and electrical design.

EDUCATION: B.S. - Mechanical Engineering, Lehigh University

JENNIFER A. LARSON
41 CANTOR LANE
CAMBRIDGE, MA 04931
(617) 942-1380

An Operations professional with a demonstrated record of achievement in manufacturing management, material control, and quality. Results oriented with experience in planning and implementing production strategies and control projects that contribute to the bottom line. Team player, solid interpersonal skills, strong commitment.

OBJECTIVE: Executive manufacturing position with plant operations responsibility.

PROFESSIONAL EXPERIENCE:

1983 - Present   **AMERICAN HARDWARE COMPANY**
Fasteners Division, Boston, MA

International manufacturer of hardware supplies with sales of $700 million. Certified ISO 9001.

(1995 - Present)   DIVISION MANAGER, TOTAL QUALITY

Responsible for implementation and management of divisional strategy based on a system of prevention and continuous improvement utilizing employee involvement. Crosby concepts form the foundation of the process. Scope includes corporate, sales, R&D, as well as seven International and U.S. based manufacturing facilities. Certified Crosby instructor, trained ISO 9000 internal auditor.

- Planned and completed education of 6000 employees in the concepts of continuous improvement.
- Established requirements in concert with internal and external customers, vendors and supporting business units to eliminate non-conformance and improve business processes.
- Savings of $14MM achieved by identifying and reducing non-conformance.
- Achieved reduction of divisional finished goods reject rate by 60%.
- Implemented cross functional corrective action and customer/supplier interface teams.
- Provided guidance and support to other divisions and international subsidiaries.

(1993 - 1995)   PLANT MANAGER, FASTENERS

Managed all administrative and manufacturing activities for this multi-functional, multi-facility operation of 740 employees.

Jennifer A. Larson
Page 2

Responsibilities included new product and equipment pilot trials, technology transfer, validation and new product launch interfacing with divisional groups of R&D, Advanced Engineering and Q.A. which reside at plant site. Responsibilities included manufacturing, quality control, materials management, safety and environment, human resources and engineering.

- Achieved annual cost reductions in excess of $1.5 million.
- Implemented cellular manufacturing reducing lead time by 16% while improving productivity 10% within a four-month period.
- Held indirect operating cost budgets to a 4% increase over a four year time frame offsetting inflation and minimizing cost impact during a period of 20% growth in volume.
- Improved quality, reducing lot rejection by 66%.
- Implemented TQM and chaired the Quality Improvement Team utilizing the Crosby approach.
- Led five successful contract negotiations within an aggressive union environment.
- Managed global and multi-plant task groups to determine global production strategies and plant loading. Task group decisions estimated to save $4 million annually.
- Participated in implementation of MRP and SFC. Trained in SPC. Responsible for compliance to FDA, OSHA, DEP and EPA regulations.
- Recognized as "Global Plant Manager of the Year" in 1994 (the first and only recipient).

(1989 - 1993)   PLANT MANAGER, HAND TOOLS

Managed all hand tools production, shop floor scheduling, manufacturing, engineering, and safety for a 620 employee operation.

(1987 - 1989)   OPERATIONS MANAGER

Responsible for all hand tools production and related components encompassing 550 employees.

(1985 - 1987)   PRODUCTION MANAGER

Responsible for all hand tools assembly and packaging with operations consisting of 200 employees and an $8M budget.

(1983 - 1985)   PRODUCTION SUPERVISOR

EDUCATION: - Bachelor of Science-Mechanical Engineering
University of Massachusetts, 1993

- Attended Boston University M.B.A. Program, 1991-1993

PROFESSIONAL AFFILIATIONS:

- Health Industry Manufacturing Association (H.I.M.A.)
- American Society for Quality Control (A.S.Q.C.)

KAREN A. SLOAN

8 Old Saw Road • Columbia, Maryland 06135
Office: (301) 291-8281 • Home: (301) 442-8963

SUMMARY:

Technical Director having extensive quality, scientific and operations management experience with a continuous record of increased responsibility and demonstrated excellence in the pharmaceutical/chemical industry. Broad quality perspective, results oriented and technically current. Key strengths:

- Leader/manager of people, change, organizational units and projects from inception through completion to meet customer, quality and business expectations.
- Problem solver/innovator with the ability to comprehend and interpret the complex inter-relationships among customers, quality, regulations, processes, operations and technologies.
- Inventive scientists who delivers novel, cost-effective methodologies, equipment and facilities.

PROFESSIONAL EXPERIENCE:

SHERMAN LABORATORIES, INCORPORATED - Baltimore, MD   1995 - Present
Director of Quality Control
Direct the Quality Control Department and six Lab Groups.

- Led operation into compliance with FDA expectations by restructuring the operations, implementing interlocked tracking logs, upgrading training, taking charge of the methods function, and upgrading the staff.
- Designed, equipped and staffed three new lab buildings, with a budget of $4MM, to meet ISO 25 standards.
- Directed the development and validation of equipment, tests, methods and procedures in support of meeting CGMPs and GALPs.
- Defined the standard operating procedures for methods development and validation to address FDA concerns as well as to assist the R&D Department with their programs.

BIOTECH LABORATORIES, INCORPORATED - Columbia, MD   1988 - 1995
Director Laboratory Quality Assurance (1990-1995)
Led the Laboratory QA function.

- Developed and implemented systems for lab operations, staffing and auditing including the design of labs (2). Budget $3MM.
- Developed, implemented and managed systems for: sample tracking, raw materials, in process label control, CGMP compliance, stability testing and LIMS ($1MM) as well as methods development and validation.

Manager of Quality Control Laboratory (1988-1990)
Directed the Bulk Chemical QC Laboratory.

- Brought laboratory up to FDA standards by structuring and adding defined procedures, and organizing the laboratory.

KAREN A. SLOAN

BASF WYANDOTTE (NOW BASF AMERICA) - Fairfield, NJ   **1980 - 1988**
Senior Research Chemist (1984-1988)
Supervised a biocides residue/impurities lab and assisted in formulations development.
- Created a novel HPLC method for key impurities.
- Improved the formulation for two existing products.
- Led a computer selection project for the parent company.

Research Chemist (1980-1984)

EDUCATION:

PENN STATE UNIVERSITY - State College, PA   **1978 to 1980**
Postdoc

UNIVERSITY OF PENNSYLVANIA - Philadelphia, PA   **1978**
Ph.D., Analytical Chemistry

M.S., Inorganic Chemistry   **1976**

URSINUS COLLEGE - Collegeville, PA   **1974**
B.A., Chemistry

Additional Training:
Technical courses on software auditing, various facets of pharmaceutical industry, QA for Labs (Statistics, QC Charting, SPC and Lab QA), Perkin-Elmer LIMS/CLAS System, Lab Automation and QC; In-House Xerox Course on Personnel Supervision; Home-Study Course on Management.

PROFESSIONAL AFFILIATIONS:

American Society for Quality Control, American Chemical Society, AOAC International

BRENT B. BOWERS

. . . .

18 Country Club Lane   West Orange, New Jersey 08796   (908) 642-8246
Office: (212) 470-9300

PROFILE

An accomplished professional with fifteen plus years of solid "hands on" background and "practical" experience, encompassing all aspects of package design and development. Well versed in a wide variety of packaging concepts and componentry with superior knowledge relating to primary and secondary manufacturing processes. Equally versed in a variety of project management techniques, with proven ability to effectively define, plan and implement and administrate all project related activity of substance. A pragmatic self-starter who can easily grasp corporate objectives and can respond to same in a most favorable and consistent manner.

PROFESSIONAL EXPERIENCE

AVON PRODUCTS, INC. - New York, New York (1995 - Present)
A $3.6 billion manufacturer of and direct marketer of cosmetic products.

Manager - Technical Package Development

Focus: Provide technical direction for <u>conceptual</u> development of new packages (Skin Moisturizers). Define, plan, implement and manage all aspects of <u>technical</u> development from concept approval to first production, including initial performance and compatibility testing.

Selected Accomplishments:
- *Developed 18+ new packages (1996) supporting Skin Moisturizer sales in excess of $190 million.*
- *Reduced conceptual and final package development time frames 25% via Concurrent Activity Planning and timely follow-up.*
- *Reduced manufacturing costs $500,000 (1996) via aggressive value analysis, planning and implementation of viable projects.*

OPERATIONS CONSULTING GROUP, INC. - Princeton, New Jersey (1993 - 1995)
An innovative, multi faceted group, structured to provide technical assessment, direction and administrative support to all major markets.

President of Operations
Focus: Provide technical direction for the conceptual design and development of new packaging, including cost effective redesign of existing. Assist clients in evaluating/improving facilities, planning project objectives, developing time frames and cost structure favorable to marketing strategies. Manage contracted projects from conception to first production.

Selected Accomplishments:
- *Participated in the evaluation of a Fortune 500 manufacturing facility. Increased production efficiencies 40%.*
- *Improved condition, integrity and efficiency of first generation production tooling (hair shampoo package) 30%.*
- *Directed the design, construction and qualification of second generation tooling, improving efficiencies an additional 20%.*

JOHNSON & JOHNSON CONSUMER PRODUCTS, INC. - Skillman, New Jersey (1990 - 1993)
A $5.1 billion manufacturer of cosmetics and consumer products.

Senior Tool Engineer
Focus: Provide technical direction for the design and development of general packaging and product delivery systems. Manage approved tooling projects obtaining desired part quality, performance and manufacturing efficiencies. Manage corporate asset base (custom tooling) maintaining condition, integrity and production capability throughout planned life.

BRENT B. BOWERS

. . . .

Selected Accomplishments:
- *Analyzed tooling capacity of core product line. Developed/incorporated a comprehensive tool maintenance program, extending tooling life 50%.*
- *Developed/implemented a capital project reporting system. Eliminated unauthorized spending. Improved development time frames 20%.*
- *Evaluated supplier resources. Integrated selected activities with internal resource activities, reducing internal labor 15%.*

MARTINSON COMPANY, INC. - Philadelphia, Pennsylvania (1985 - 1990)
A $500MM manufacturer of children's toys.

Project Manager - Specialty Tooling
Focus: Provide technical direction in the design and development of cost effective packaging and/or assembled activity products. Define, plan, implement and manage approved tooling projects in support of design objectives. Manage corporate asset base via timely assessment and direction for repair, refurbishment and/or replacement as needed to meet business needs.

Selected Accomplishments:
- *Proposed aggressive Vertical Integration Plans. Utilized $750,000 funding and reduced manufacturing costs $800,000 first year. Coordinated project team focus and efforts second year and collectively reduced manufacturing costs an additional $1,200,000.*
- *Proposed and implemented value added revisions to a failing product line, resulting in product resurrection and $200,000 additional sales (patent awarded). Initiated development of a sister product and increased sales an additional $150,000.*
- *Evaluated competitor product infringement. Developed alternate design recovering lost annual sales in excess of $200,000 (patent awarded).*
- *Developed off-shore tooling support centers in Portugal, England and Switzerland. Reduced annual tooling investment 30%.*
- *Developed and incorporated a Specialty Tooling Data Base for accurate tracking of 300+ custom tools. Data Base instrumental in developing annual budgets and curtailing unnecessary spending on obsolete product lines.*

CONTINENTAL PRECISION CORP., INC. - South Plainfield, New Jersey (1980 - 1985)
A respected leader in the design and construction of custom injection mold tooling used in plastic part fabrication.

Senior Mold Engineer
Focus: Assist client base in the design and development of complex plastic componentry. Recommend revisions where possible for most cost effective molding, decorating and assembly. Design custom tooling, coordinating efforts of engineering and contracted support services. Manage all aspects of construction, qualification testing and revision where needed to meet part design and/or tool performance objectives.

Selected Accomplishments:
- *Participated in the design and development of a proprietary product line, contributing to corporate exposure, growth and profitability. Later, proposed/assisted in development of custom assembly equipment reducing manufacturing costs 20%.*
- *Developed a unique mechanical device to facilitate "in mold" closing of a complex fitment, reducing assembly costs 15%.*
- *Developed various in-house engineering standards, formats and procedures reducing mold development time frames 15%.*

EDUCATION

B.S., Packaging Engineering
Michigan State University, 1980

DAVID M. DeSANTIS   203 Dakota Drive, Morrisonville, NJ 07748

Office: (212) 861-4874   Home: (609) 761-6083

Senior packaging/purchasing executive with extensive experience in developing and launching new products for the fragrance and cosmetic industry. Broad technical expertise in saleable and promotional packaging, point-of-purchase displays, manufacturing processes and supplier capabilities. Direct complex projects and coordinate effectively with marketing, design, sales, and operations. Develop strategic partnerships with global supplier base. Strong track record in managing staff & budgets.

PROFESSIONAL EXPERIENCE

DESIGNER COSMETICS CO., Division of Cosmair Company, New York, NY   **1993-Present**

Senior Director of Package Development
Oversaw and implemented all new brand introductions, seasonal promotional programs, and point-of-purchase displays. Led the development process from the brainstorming stage through final production. Worked closely with marketing/creative departments to determine the feasibility of all projects. Also provided project leadership and tracking for the operations teams.

- Directed the team that launched four of the most successful fragrances in the U.S. (*Ecstacy, Ecstacy for Men, Enrapture, Enrapture for Men*). Opened the Asian market to *Loving and Loving for Men*, which paved the way for the full roll-out of all other brands.

- Technical advisor to Chairman of the Board, his staff, and other recognized designers during the early design stages. This accelerated the process and enhanced the final package quality.

- Converted all saleable SKU's to a universal package design that is environmentally and legally acceptable worldwide. The universal package:
  - reduced corporate inventory by 30%
  - provided major administrative efficiencies in most departments

- Managed, within budget, the $3.6MM capital account for tools, dies, molds, prep and separations for all brands. Controlled the packaging general ledger expenses of $1MM.

- Initiated computerization that reduced development time and improved the accuracy of cost estimates and BOM's. Introduced electronically transmitted art work to graphic suppliers.

REVCO COSMETICS CO., New York, NY   **1991-1993**

Group Director, Group I Cosmetics
Developed, specified and coordinated the production of packages for 250 projects in Revco's core cosmetic business. Associated closely with new product marketing to develop patented products such as a nail enamel pen, three-in-one eye shadow palette and nail gel.

- Built and motivated a packaging team of five that controlled multiple new product launches and provided promotional support for those programs.

DAVID M. DeSANTIS   **Page Two**

- Engineered the redesign of the eye and face compact line to an open cell presentation which greatly improved the product merchantability.

THE GLAMOUR GROUP, New York, NY   **1986-1991**

Package Development Manager, 1988-1991
Controlled prestige fragrance and cosmetic development for designer brands (Caress, Embraceable, Pour Homme and Béaute). Introduced new product launches, seasonal promotions, point-of-purchase displays, and brand maintenance.

Purchasing Manager, 1987-1988
Managed supplier selection, purchase and delivery of all primary packaging ($14MM) with a team of four.

- Negotiated annual contracts for major commodities (glass, pumps). Monitored performance against contracts on an ongoing basis.

Senior Purchasing Agent, 1986-1987
Responsible for the purchase and delivery of folding cartons and custom injection molding.

NATIONAL CHEMICAL, Pinkerton, NJ   **1981-1986**

Buyer of Packaging Components and Chemicals

- Purchased primary and secondary components and controlled subcontract filling/assembly for Sophia and Gatsby divisions.

- Bought 12 raw materials that were purchased under a corporate contract for use in all domestic factories.

AJAX CHEMICAL CO., Middlebrooke, NJ   1979-1981

Sales Representative

- Serviced major existing accounts and cold-called to develop new business for resins.

- Completed 12-month marketing/sales trainee program in nine months.

EDUCATION

B.S., Business Administration, University of Vermont   1979

DOUGLAS J. WARREN
806 Patriot Lane
New Hope, PA 19682
(215) 692-8306

PROFILE: Results-oriented mechanical engineer with over seven years experience in project management, process engineering and project engineering with a technology leader. Accomplished project manager with ability to clearly define project goals and effectively use resources to achieve them.

PROFESSIONAL EXPERIENCE:

POLY TECHNOLOGY, INC., Princeton, NJ (1990 - Present)

Project Manager, Fibers Division (1995 - Present)

- Selected to serve as project manager for Johnson & Johnson. Work with J&J's Advanced Product Engineers on all aspects of launching a new category of surgical sutures including suture design, material selection, prototype design, failure mode analysis, field trial and production start-up.
- Managed development of new technology to streamline manufacturing process. Directed research efforts of Fiber Products Division to develop a super absorbent polymer structure. Worked with customers to refine the process. Applied for a patent on the streamlined process.

Project Engineer, Fibers Division (1992 - 1995)

- Championed the effort to prevent loss of $3.2 million/year Kimberly Clark account due to severe product defects. Directed the efforts of KC's material development and manufacturing teams and designers to redesign the materials and manufacturing process. Verified improvements through field tests.
- Collaborated on the development of a patented fluid absorption test.

Process Engineer, Laminated Products Division (1990 - 1992)

- Led a team of 12 manufacturing associates in the start-up of a new fabric lamination production line. Determined process condition for 12 products. Standardized operating procedures to ensure products met specifications. Resulted in $12 million annual sales.
- Designed and conducted a statistical experiment to study the effect of four process variables on polymer lamination. Identified key variable which had the most impact. Significantly reduced time and cost to isolate this variable.

EDUCATION: **Bachelor of Science in Materials Science, 1990**
University of Pennsylvania, Philadelphia, PA

PROFESSIONAL TRAINING: Introduction to Designed Experiments and Data Analysis (1990)
Strategy of Experimentation (1990)
Theory of Manufacturing Constraints (1992)
Leadership Effectiveness Training (1992)
Critical Problem Solving (1993)
Critical Problem Solving (1994)
Effective Communicating (1996)

WALTER C. CUMMINS
12 Mission Hill Drive
Palos Verdes, CA 89522
(414) 875-9281

SUMMARY

Senior Process Engineering Manager with over 15 years experience in chemical plant design and start-up in the chemical and pharmaceutical industries. Proven strengths in engineering and business management encompassing planning, staffing, scheduling and executing the conversion of product and processes into profitable ventures. Demonstrated expertise in chemical plant design and start-up, process flow diagrams - piping and instrument diagrams, polypropylenes, air laid equipment, precision cast parts, materials, tooling and machining, design layout and modification of castings, manufacturing process control, gas desulfurization, gas turbines.

EXPERIENCE

UNIVERSAL MEDICAL PRODUCTS INC., Los Angeles, CA   **1996-PRESENT**
<u>Manager, Process Engineering</u>

Responsible for maintaining existing operations, quality of inventory maintenance and warehousing. As part of the Research and Development function, led the design group in the development of concepts into products and manufacturing processes. Report to Senior Director, Research & Development for this $580MM manufacturer of surgical dressings.

- Improved prototype process for manufacturing of surgical dressings using existing equipment resulting in a five-fold increase in production.
- Improved equipment uptime to 95%.
- Supervised staff of 38 people, including plant maintenance operations, warehousing and engineering. Personally hired 60% of personnel.
- As Project Manger for a $60 million absorbent dressing manufacturing operation, developed and installed integrated processes capable of producing 10 million cases per year.
- Managed various aspects of development and construction of $30 million advanced Research & Development Facility.
- Improved reject rate from 15% to 2%.
- Led contract negotiations with engineering consultants.

PRATT & WHITNEY, East Hartford, CT   **1989-1996**
<u>Mechanical Design Engineer</u>

Responsible for evaluating aircraft gas turbine engine hardware for fit and function relative to engine performance. Reported to Director of Engineering.

WALTER C. CUMMINS   **PAGE TWO**

- Performed analysis of discrepant jet engine parts and identified anomalies in design and/or manufacturing process.
- Coordinated the redesign or modification of parts.
- Evaluated tooling for high volume production of large and small castings to ensure machinability and proper function/fit in products.
- Evaluated and approved all casting layouts provided by vendors, and served as the sole approving authority for all casting tools used at Pratt & Whitney.
- Performed extensive interface with vendors and coordinated corrective action for defective casting and machining operations.
- Audited mechanical design of jet engines.

ARCO CHEMICAL COMPANY, Newtown Square, PA   **1985-1989**
<u>Project/Process Engineer</u>

Responsible for the design and installation of new equipment for a polypropylene extrusion manufacturing facility. Evaluated and modified existing equipment which resulted in significant cost reduction. Trained extrusion line operators. Responsible for two high volume polypropylene film extrusion lines.

EPA SYSTEMS ENGINEERING, INC., Philadelphia, PA   **1983-1985**
<u>Project/Process Engineer</u>

Responsible for the design and development of a pilot flue gas desulfurization system including the design of PFD's and P&IDS. Accomplishments included the planning, coordination and startup of a pilot unit. Developed test program for the unit and provided training and supervision of the client company's plant personnel during the start-up phase. Also prepared the operating manual for the unit.

EDUCATION

B.S., Chemical Engineering, Drexel University, Philadelphia, PA, 1983

DOUGLAS A. FULLER, P.E.

6 Mountain Top Road
Stamford, CT 06132

Bus: (203) 521-1725
Res: (203) 369-6116

OBJECTIVE: Vice President or Director of Engineering position

EDUCATION: **M.B.A.**
New York University, New York, NY (1989)

B.S. - Mechanical Engineering
Bucknell University, Lewisberg, PA (1983)

SUMMARY: Fourteen years diverse engineering experience mostly with customer division of $6 billion multinational consumer products corporation.

- Managed and provided strategic leadership for various Engineering organizations;
- Developed and implemented leading edge Computer Integrated Manufacturing (CM) systems;
- Designed, fabricated and developed proprietary, state-of-the-art high speed automated machinery;
- Developed and implemented strategic vision for engineering;
- Championed implementation of innovative technology;
- Demonstrated superior skills in managing technical people and projects;
- Design to Market champion with extensive project work and coordination.

ATTRIBUTES: Highly professional, organized and demanding management style. Strong leadership and conflict management skills. Proven technical and design competency. Broad-based, accomplished computer knowledge and skills. Outstanding track record for meeting goals and objectives through teamwork. Sound businessman. High energy. Results oriented. Decisive. Committed. Interface with all levels of management. Good listener and communicator. People oriented. Entrepreneurial, takes chances.

PROFESSIONAL EXPERIENCE:

COLGATE PALMOLIVE, New York, NY   **1983-Present**

1996 to Present   **DIRECTOR OF ENGINEERING**
Responsible for all technical operations in support of eight manufacturing locations for this $6 million consumer products manufacturer. Recruited, developed and managed 150 person technical staff. Accountable for $200 million capital and $60 million operational budget. Established organizational objectives and initiatives in line with corporate goals and strategies. Responsible for discovery and assessment of new product and process acquisitions. Evaluate technical capability and processability including level of automation through due diligence process. Managed facilities, energy programs, pollution prevention and environmental compliance efforts. Selected accomplishments include:

- Planned, developed and implemented strategic engineering, re-organization;
- Core team member for major new product launch. Exceeded all program goals.
- Established world-wide communication and team-building programs;
- Attained tenfold increase in knife life utilizing design of experiments, metallurgical and advanced FEA structural analysis;

Douglas A. Fuller, P.E.   Page 2

- Reduced top consumer complaint quality problem by 40%;
- Reviewed and approved four pending product acquisitions;
- Consolidated three manufacturing operations to one location with no disruption to customer service.

1993-1996 **PROGRAM MANAGER,** *Computer Integrated Manufacturing (CIM)*
Researched, designed and implemented integrated manufacturing software solutions in concert with company's World Class initiatives. Managed team of six direct reports and 30 outside consultants. The $25 million project scope included hardware and software selection, vendor and subcontractor negotiations and project management and coordination. Selected accomplishments:

- Installed leading edge shop floor process control and material tracking system employing 90+ work stations, multiple file servers and LAN's in two manufacturing plants;
- Reduced downtime outages by 25% through accurate data capture and reporting;
- Achieved targeted cost savings via waste containment and obsolete parts reduction;
- Spearheaded academic/industry liaisons with MIT, CMU, Duke, RPI and Bellcore;
- Partnered with Microsoft (beta test site) while establishing advanced working knowledge of leading edge PC LAN technology and networking;
- Installed 20 seat file server-based networked CAD system using AutoCAD.

1989-1993 **PLANT ENGINEERING GROUP MANAGER**
Responsible for plant equipment performance, secondary development and maintenance plant-wide. Managed staff of 12 engineers and 85 craftsmen. Coordinated new product introductions. Implemented major operating cost reduction programs. Selected accomplishments include:

- Aggressively recruited and upgraded personnel to increase department capability. Redesigned job responsibilities and implemented measurable performance objectives;
- Managed $2 million department budget. Reduced administrative spending by 10% each year while initiating aggressive operating cost cutting programs saving over $100,000 annually;
- Established intensive PM program and repair part testing program reducing plant downtime;
- Attacked plant fire safety issues (fire rate reduction of 30%). Received Colgate Palmolive Achievement Award recognizing my department's machine safety guarding effort corporate-wide.

1987-1989 **SENIOR DESIGN ENGINEER**
Advanced rapidly from *Associate Engineer* position. Performed conceptual design of new products and processes. Managed and supervised the design, detailing and fabrication of $10 million machine design program. Exceeded overall program requirements. Installed machinery at multiple international locations. Developed and implemented various process and productivity enhancements.

1983-1987 **DESIGN ENGINEER**

OTHER: **Professional Engineer,** NY License 37291, 1989
Colgate Palmolive Achievement Award Winner, 1991, 1993, 1995
Member of the National Society of Professional Engineers

MITCHELL COVENTREE
421 Basking Ridge Road
Whitehall, PA 15238
(412) 336-6376

SUMMARY

Twenty-five years of professional experience as an engineer and manager. Management and technical achievements in process and plant floor engineering; project management; sensors; measurement systems and methods; product and equipment development and engineering; and environmental technology. Significant experience in metals, chemicals, energy, and plastics industries. Results oriented with strengths in leadership, organization, and interpersonal skills; and the ability to drive implementation of manufacturing technology improvements.

PROFESSIONAL EXPERIENCE

KEYSTONE BRASS & ALUMINUM COMPANY, Allentown, PA　　　　　1996 to Present

Section Head, Measurement Technology

- Identified customer needs, managed programs, and provided leadership for the development and implementation of solutions involving: sensors, measurement systems, non-destructive evaluation (NDE) methods and instrumentation -- for plants throughout Keystone.

- Directed work of a diverse mix of technologists: material, electrical, mechanical, and chemical engineers; physicists; and consultants -- to the resolution of historically difficult industry-wide problems and implementation of the technology in Keystone plants (e.g., automated ultrasonic plate inspection, in mill plate temperature measurement, non-contact sheet flatness measurement).

- Commercialized instrument products/technology; some marketed and sold worldwide.

PACIFIC OIL AND GAS, Dallas, TX　　　　　　　　　　　　1987 to 1996

Senior Engineering Associate, Process Engineering　　　　　1994 - 1996
Program Director, Process Engineering　　　　　　　　　1990 - 1994
Senior Research Engineer, Process Development　　　　　　1987 - 1990

- Saved over $3MM annually with developed natural gas processing technology. Provided engineering and tech support to field sites processing natural gas and refinery fuel gas.

- Conceived and championed through approval, a $18MM program designed to ready Pacific Oil and its venture partner, Houston Oil, for the commercialization of oil shale conversion and to develop the design data for a commercial plant.

- Built and managed a multi-company team for the resulting program, including the logistics and relationships between Houston Oil, Pacific Oil and representatives of Euro-oil of France, the licensee of the technology. The results-oriented team peaked at well over 100 people and successfully executed the above program.

- Served as Project Manager for the design and construction of the $8MM grass roots processing facility. It was the first-of-its-kind and was completed on time and within budget.

MITCHELL COVENTREE....   page two

PACIFIC OIL (cont'd)

- Designed and installed an integrated process control and data management system with feedback from many instruments and sensors, monitoring process and stream conditions, quantities, and compositions.

- Developed chemical products and processes; e.g., indene and vinyl toluene.

- Reduced catalyst consumption by developing a process that was implemented in refineries for removing impurities of oxygenated compounds from HF alkylation feedstock.

FOSTER NATIONAL LABORATORIES, Oklahoma, City, OK   1984 to 1987

Research Engineer

- Reduced SO_2 sorbent requirement in fluidized bed combustion (FBC) coal boilers by at least 60% with developed high temperature sorbent regeneration process. Received Foster Recognition Award in 1986.

- Developed several instruments for FBC coal boilers.

ROCHESTER INSTITUTE OF TECHNOLOGY, Rochester, NY   1982 to 1984

Instructor and Consultant

- Consulted on air pollution control and taught undergraduate engineering mathematics.

FORD MOTOR COMPANY, AUTO BODY DIVISION, Deerborne, MI   1980 to 1982

Engineer

- Provided engineering design, testing, and technical support for injection molding, extrusion, and other fabrication processes for plastic components. Conceived and developed new application of molded glass-filled polyolefin mechanical body components which was commercialized by Ford Motors.

EDUCATION

Ph.D., Chemical Engineering, Michigan Technological University - Houghton, MI - 1980
B.S., Chemical Engineering, Michigan State University, East Lansing, MI - 1976

HONORS & AWARDS

- Honorary Engineering Member of Tau Omega Pi, 1971.
- Outstanding Employee Contributions Award, Pacific Oil, 1989 and 1994.
- Honorary Scientific Member of Sigma Pi, 1995.
- Keynote Speaker, 1996 International Engineering Association Conference, Berlin, Germany.
- 4 Patents, 17 Publications.

CHRISTOPHER J. BACH, P.E.
24 Blue Ridge Road
Nashville, TN 42755
(810) 642-9351

OBJECTIVE:

Management position utilizing extensive experience in manufacturing, engineering and project management.

CAREER SUMMARY:

Fourteen years of progressively responsible positions in Engineering and Operations Management with expertise in design, start-up, project management, system optimization, productivity improvement, organizational design/development, manufacturing, inventory control and distribution.

BUSINESS EXPERIENCE:

COLGATE-PALMOLIVE COMPANY, Nashville, TN   1989 to Present

Technical Services Manager (1995 - Present)
- Responsible for Site Engineering, Maintenance, Quality Control and Sanitation.
- Developed and implemented programs to improve QC Department effectiveness and response time.
- Utilized team-based methodology to upgrade site OSHA and GMP compliance.
- Delivered significant cost reductions ($1M) through electric rate savings and packaging line automation.
- Utilized TOM principles to improve utility department efficiencies and emergency preparedness.
- Managed site SARA Title III programs.
- Developed and executed water and sewer contracts with the local municipality.

Group Engineering Manager (1994 - 1995)
- Multiple plant responsibility.
- Reduced natural gas costs by 35%.
- Developed and installed automated material handling system which reduced costs by $400K annually.
- Developed a team-based manufacturing organization.
- Implemented programs which reduced equipment downtime by 30%.
- Developed and installed equipment Vision Systems and automation which reduced costs by $200K annually.
- Automated the plant's finished goods inventory control system (4m cubic foot warehouse).

CHRISTOPHER J. BACH, P.E.   Page 2

Plant Engineering Manager (1991 - 1994)
- Managed department of 35 professional and 60 hourly employees.
- Developed and implemented manufacturing line improvements which increased output by 37%.
- Converted manufacturing equipment to PLC controls.
- Sourced equipment from Korea and Japan to reduce costs and improve deliveries.
- Responsible for $30M capital budget.

Engineering Supervisor (1989 - 1991)
- Managed department of five professional and 75 hourly employees.
- Responsible for $4M annual fixed budget and $8M capital budget.
- Managed major facility expansion.
- Implemented automated work order and maintenance management system.

CARR INDUSTRIES, Memphis, TN   1988 to 1989

Operations Manager
- Multiple plant responsibility.
- Managed all aspects of window and door manufacturing, warehousing and distribution operation.
- Developed and implemented a bonus program based on team performance.
- Improved customer service and product quality using TQM principles.
- Reduced manufacturing cost per unit by 10%.

INTERNATIONAL PAPER COMPANY, Purchase, NY   1983 to 1988

Project Manager   (1987 - 1988)

Field Engineer   (1985 - 1987)

Systems Engineer   (1983 - 1985)

PROFESSIONAL CERTIFICATE:

Registered Professional Engineer, State of Tennessee.

EDUCATION:

Master of Business Administration, S.U.N.Y.   1983

Master of Science, Mechanical Engineering and Metallurgy   1982
Cornell University

Bachelor of Science, Mechanical Engineering, Cornell University   1980

Rhonda V. Ferguson, Ph.D., D.A.B.T., R.A.C.

1042 Willow Street
Elgin Park, IL 90821
(716) 246-8015 (residence)
(716) 547-2013 (office)
(716) 547-2014 (fax)

QUALIFICATIONS SUMMARY

Extensive experience evaluating the safety of drugs including biologics and a major fat substitute; training/ experience writing INDs, NDAs, PLAs, ELAs and food additive petitions; received regulatory concessions from FDA for approval of new drugs and a fat substitute where test requirements were in a state of flux; obtained funding and managed multi-million dollar safety/toxicity test programs; achieved time/cost savings via competitive bidding and strategic placement of study "packages". Board certified in toxicology and regulatory affairs. Based on this training and experience, a position managing drug safety and/or regulatory affairs at a small- to medium-sized biopharmaceutical/pharmaceutical company would be a good fit.

PROFESSIONAL HISTORY

[1994-present] **Abbott Laboratories, Abbott Park, IL**

Director, Preclinical and Clinical EPG Safety Test Program

- Direct the design and conduct of all IND/NDA type preclinical and clinical safety studies to obtain worldwide approval for a low- to no-calorie fat substitute. Responsible for the toxicologic/histopathologic interpretation of data. Manage 12 professionals/five clinical consultants who supported safety studies.

- Successfully influenced FDA and Canada's HPB regulatory approval policy for novel foods/macro additives through private meetings as well as industry activities: publications, FDA/industry sponsored workshops to review/resolve technical issues. Obtained project compliance with GLPs, GCPs, and GMPs.

- Obtained multi-million dollar funding for the safety test program of a new fat substitute working with the executive management of Abbott Laboratories and, most recently, a major chemical company.

- Negotiated and managed a total of over $20 million in contracts at seven outside research facilities. Through competitive bidding and strategic placement of preclinical and clinical safety studies, saved over $3 million and 1-3 years off a 4-6 year program.

[1992-94] **Toxico, Inc., Atlanta, GA**

Toxicology Consultant/Expert Witness

- Successfully resolved technical issues in Products' Liability, Workmen's Compensation, and DUI cases.

[1990-92] **Merck Research Laboratories, Drug Safety Evaluation Department, West Point, PA**

Group Leader - Toxicology

- Served on interdisciplinary project teams for the development and safety evaluation of numerous pharmaceuticals and biologics.

- Set up the in-house GLP-compliant toxicology laboratory for dog, rabbit, mouse and rat studies.

- Managed eight professionals as Group Leader in General Toxicology.

- Directed the planning, scheduling and conduct of in-house and most contract lab drug safety studies.

Rhonda V. Ferguson, Ph.D., D.A.B.T., R.A.C.
Page 2

- Authored numerous preclinical summaries for INDs submitted to FDA in support of new drugs while at Merck Reviewed INDs and NDAs prior to their filing. Negotiated safety test programs for various drug candidates with FDA's CDER.

- Reviewed safety data on new drugs for several potential acquisitions.

- Designed and reviewed protocols and data from clinical studies with particular drug safety issues.

[1984-90] **Duke University, School of Pharmacy, Durham, NC**

Assistant Professor of Pharmacology & Toxicology - Tenure granted

- Established and administered this graduate toxicology program which maximally had an enrollment of 25 students. Chairman or co-chairman of doctoral committees for nine graduate students.

- Managed five technicians in a NIDA research program on narcotic drug toxicity related to metabolism.

- While at Duke, Toxicology Consultant/Expert Witness in FDA Food Adulteration, Products' Liability, and Medical Mal practice cases.

[1982-83] **Richter Laboratories, Ann Arbor, MI**

Staff Toxicologist and Study Director

- Managed three technicians in conduct of various toxicity/safety studies.

EDUCATION and TRAINING

[1982-84] **NIH Post Doctoral Trainee in Toxicology** - Schools of Medicine, Public Health and Pharmacy, University of Michigan, Ann Arbor, MI.

[1982] **Ph.D. in Toxicology** - NIH Predoctoral Trainee, University of California, Department of Pharmacology & Toxicology, School of Medicine, San Francisco, DA

[1976] **B.S. in Biochemistry** - Department of Biochemistry, University of Pennsylvania, Philadelphia, PA East Lansing, MI

PROFESSIONAL CERTIFICATION

[1995] **Regulatory Affairs Certification [R.A.C.]** - Certified by the Regulatory Affairs Certification Board for biologics, drugs and medical devices.
[1990] **Diplomate, American Board of Toxicology [D.A.B.T.]** - Recertified in 1990 and 1995.
[1985-present] **Expert in Toxicology** - Recognized by various State and Federal Courts.

MEMBERSHIPS in PROFESSIONAL ORGANIZATIONS

- Society of Toxicology
- American College of Toxicology
- International Society of Regulatory Toxicology and Pharmacology
- International Society of Ecotoxicology and Environmental Safety

THOMAS R. GRANT, Ph.D.

3016 Hidden Valley Drive
Chesterfield, CT 70131

(203) 922-2284 Home
(212) 449-1300 Office

SUMMARY

Manager with over 17 years experience in plant start-up, product development, process development and business development. A troubleshooter with broad range of contributions spanning process technology, new business development, marketing, and strategic planning. B.S., M.S. and Ph.D. degrees in Chemical Engineering from University of Wisconsin.

EXPERIENCE

WITCO CORPORATION, New York, New York   **1996 - Present**

A $1.5 billion chemicals and petroleum refining company.

Manager, **Development**

- Responsible for process design, process development, and manufacturing assistance at R&D center.

- Manage 42 professionals. Member of the new business development strategy team.

THIOKOL CORPORATION, Ogden, Utah   **1980 - 1996**

Diversified manufacturer of chemicals and propellent systems for the aerospace and defense industries. Annual sales $1.3 billion.

Manager, **Aerospace & Defense Products**   1994 - 1996

- Assumed P&L responsibility for a $200 million/year business segment with a pre-tax profit of $25 million.

Manager, **Business Development**   1991 - 1994

- Responsible for R&D, manufacturing and marketing new products with a focus on aerospace and defense applications.

- Managed a proposed joint venture to manufacture and market rocket propellent with a minimum of $40 million annually.

- Responsible for a $20 million government contract to develop a liquid gun propellant. Full deployment could result in a new $200 million/year business for Thiokol by end of decade. First orders obtained in 1994 and 1995 exceeded $6 million.

- Headed a joint development program for a leading new candidate for advanced bomb fill as part of the Department of Defense's mandate for insensitive munitions. Sales exceeded $2 million through 1994; could grow to $100+ million annually by 2005.

THOMAS R. GRANT, Ph.D.   Page Two

Manager, **New Product Development**   1987 - 1991

- Transferred to the Technology Center, which was established to focus on new strategic businesses in specialty chemicals. Successfully managed the following programs:
  - Test marketing of residential water treatment systems.
  - Test marketing of revolutionary new electronic coating.
  - Commercialization of an automatic chemical feed system for the electronics industry.

Manager, **Process Technology**   1985 - 1987

- Organized and staffed a new department and led a development effort in a newly-acquired polymers additive business. Directed a $2 million R&D budget. Constructed a multi-million dollar semi-works unit to commercialize new products. Successfully commercialized four new specialty chemicals increasing sales by 25% annually.

- As Technology Representative on a long-range planning task force, identified potential new thrust areas for Thiokol. As a direct result, in 1986, Thiokol acquired Thompson Chemical Corporation, an electronic chemicals company.

Senior Group Leader   1983 - 1985

Project Leader   1980 - 1983

EDUCATION

University of Wisconsin, Madison, Wisconsin
 Ph.D. in Chemical Engineering   1980
 M.S. in Chemical Engineering   1978
 B.S. in Chemical Engineering   1976

LINDA P. WATKINS, Ph.D.

1401 Collegiate Way   (908) 655-0987   Princeton, NJ 80932

SUMMARY

A research chemist with international experience in process development and synthetic chemistry. Specific research activities include development and scale-up of crop protection and specialty chemicals from lab to pilot plant. Special expertise in analytical methods such as IR, UV, NMR, GC and HPLC. Strong ability in conducting technical analysis, project management and problem solving.

PROFESSIONAL EXPERIENCE

AGRI-CHEM, INC., Newark, NJ   **1995 - Present**
A chemical company involved with the manufacture of agricultural and specialty chemicals. Annual sales are $95M.

Research Associate, Process Development
- Synthesized and developed specialty chemicals and processes
- Developed oxidation process for a herbicide intermediate with potential production of several million pounds per year.
- Improved a process in a photoinitiator resulting in potential savings of $44 million per year.
- Generated customer lab samples for evaluation.

ICI AMERICAS, INC., Wilmington, DE   **1989 - 1995**
Agricultural Chemicals Division
A leading specialty chemicals company involved with the development and manufacture of agricultural chemicals and intermediates. Annual sales are $4 billion.

Research Scientist, Process Development
- Managed, coordinated, scheduled and executed laboratory and pilot plant experiments. Economical evaluation of competitive and in-house technologies.
- Coordinated and executed process development of five step process for a herbicide with potential sales of $60M annually.
- Reduced toxic impurities in major chemical to less than 1 ppm during production resulting in a $2.1M savings.
- Developed a co-catalyst system resulting in a potential savings of $2 million per year.
- Developed stripping process for key intermediate resulting in potential reduction of cycle time by 25% at 98% efficiency.
- Implemented toll manufacture of major crop protection chemical with annual sales of $7M.
- Managed Crop Protection Process Development Group supervising 18 scientists, engineers and technicians. Activities involved more than 35 projects having an annual budget of $3.4M.

LINDA P. WATKINS, Ph.D.   Page Two

SCOTT PAPER COMPANY, Philadelphia, PA   **1980 - 1989**
A $5 billion manufacturer of consumer and commercial paper products.

<u>Senior Research Scientist</u>, Corporate Research and Development (1983-1989)
- Carried out laboratory and pilot plant experiments.
- Performed development research on TMP pulping process.

<u>Research Scientist</u>, Corporate Research and Development (1980-1982)

EDUCATION

University of Delaware, Ph.D., Organic Chemistry, 1980
University of Delaware, M.S., Organic Chemistry, 1978
Penn State University, B.S., Organic Chemistry, 1976

ASSOCIATIONS

Member, American Chemical Society since 1980

PATENTS

8 U.S. Patents (3 pending)

MARLENE DAWKINS, Ph.D.
803 Sunset Circle
Ocean Beach, CA 82113
(414) 271-3526 (Home)
(414) 725-0883 (Office)

PROFESSIONAL SUMMARY

Results-oriented technical professional with experience solving both research and development problems. Experience organizing, managing and implementing technical projects. Can successfully function in a supervisory capacity, as an individual contributor or in a team environment.

PROFESSIONAL EXPERIENCE

1990 to
Present

GENERAL POLYMERS, INC. - San Diego, CA
R&D Associate   (1993 to Present)
Senior R&D Chemist   (1990 to 1993)
Consult and collaborate with project scientists on task teams. Collect, analyze and interpret technical data. Develop new analytical methods and supervise laboratory technicians in areas of X-Ray Photoelectron Spectroscopy (XPS), X-Ray Diffraction, Electron Microscopy and Particle Characterization.
- Managed and supervised Slippery Surfaces Evaluation Task Force. Developed polyurethane coating with 30% less surface friction.
- Conceived, designed and developed a data logger to monitor polyurethane coated surfaces on conveyor system slide. Technology enabled business group to increase slide durability and reduce manufacturing costs by 20%.
- Co-conceived and co-developed a new PVC resin that could be spray-painted on to metal surfaces to increase surface slip.
- Co-conceived and co-developed a new coating for pigment filler for PVC resin. The coated filler reduced manufacturing costs of PVC siding 20%.
- Conceived and developed a new quality control procedure for manufacturing polyurethane foam which reduced analysis time and cost by 35%.

1986 to
1990

JOHNSON MATTHEY - Malvern, PA
R&D Chemist
Analyzed and interpreted technical data obtained from test reactors to evaluate performance of developmental and competitor's catalysts. Synthesized and developed experimental catalysts. Technical consultant to plant personnel. Designed and built a fixed bed reactor system for catalyst evaluation.
- Developed test reactions (slurry phase and fixed bed) and analytical methods, GC and LC (gas and liquid chromatography) for catalyst analysis.
- Supervised the work performed by two technicians in areas of GC and LC.
- Identified key variables in production of new proprietary catalysts in bench-top experiments and modified manufacturing process.
- Supervised the technology transfer of modified manufacturing process into the manufacturing plant increasing production by 150%.

Marlene Dawkins, Ph.D.
Resume - Page 2

1984 to   **UNIVERSITY OF MICHIGAN** - Ann Arbor, MI
1986   Research Fellow, Center For Advanced Polymer Research
           Collected, analyzed and interpreted technical data obtained on experimental
           polymers using surface science (XPS). Supervised and directed graduate students
           and had research budget responsibility.
           - Synthesized and characterized properties and performance characteristics of
             experimental polymeric materials using test reactors, chemisorption and XPS.
           - Designed and supervised construction of portions of the Center's Polymer
             Analysis Laboratory.
           - Consulted for Dow Chemical in polymer testing and evaluation.
           - Consulted for Chevron and Mobil Oil in polymer research, testing and data
             analysis.

EDUCATION

1984   University of Pennsylvania, Philadelphia, PA
               Ph.D., Physical Chemistry

1980   University of Pennsylvania, Philadelphia, PA
               M.S., Physical Chemistry

1979   University of Delaware, Newark, DE
               B.S., Chemistry

PROFESSIONAL SOCIETIES

- Member, American Vacuum Society, American Physical Society, American Chemical
  Society, Society for Applied Spectroscopy, Eastern Electron Spectroscopy Society.

PATENTS AND PUBLICATIONS

- Eight U.S. patents.

- Eleven publications in professional journals, books and trade papers.

ALBERT J. HARDING, Jr.
819 Plymouth Avenue
Fairfield, MI 36553
(207) 552-9566

Objective: Senior Chemical Engineer or Consultant

Professional Profile

Seasoned senior engineer with record of solving tough technical and environmental problems for Dow Chemical Company. Effective communicator across cultural, organizational and skill-level lines. Diverse and successful research and development background with particular expertise in:

- Lab-to-plant scale-ups
- Flowsheets, simulations, statistics
- Economic evaluations
- Polymerizations, separations, mixing
- Plant start-ups
- Physical and chemical analytical methods
- Experimental (Taguchi) designs
- Electronic searching for information

Professional Experience

Dow Chemical Company, Inc., Midland, MI   **1966 to Present**

Intellectual Properties and Regulatory Affairs, Consultant   (1995-Present)
- Communicated effectively with Koreans to interpret and influence modification of importation laws without exposing proprietary product information
- Solved information-flow problem delaying product shipment by up to three weeks
- Established product composition database and computer program to determine composition of regulated substances
- Prepared Material Safety Data Sheets (MSDS) for over 3,000 polymer products, using electronic searching to find latest toxicological and regulatory information
- Searched electronically for patent and research prior-art for use by Legal and Research
- Compiled five years of import data on over 1200 products for Canadian and Philippine inventories

Polymer, Engineering Research, through Research Associate   (1989-1995)
- Led team in completing two lab-to-plant transfers of major product lines more than ten percent ahead of schedule and twenty percent under budget; included planning and scheduling, assembling design basic data, interfacing with design and construction, training operators and leading both start-ups
- Initiated independent research in mixing, waste incineration, polymer stability, films and foams; each study met the goal of significantly improving product and process performance or lowering operating cost
- Designed and conducted experiments and computer simulations to identify crucial chemical principles or four process development teams -- two fluoroelastomers, one polyester and one polyether-ketone product line, make all supporting economic evaluations and serve as interface for analytical and process instrumentation

Plant Technical, Manufacturing and Planning, through Senior Engineer   (1979-1989)
- Developed a sophisticated purification procedure to recover and sell a by-product from acrylonitrile plant that launched a very profitable new Dow product within two years of my arrival at the site
- Solved start-up problem in two weeks that had delayed new line of TiO_2 flame reactor for months by applying self-authored computer program and statistical process control analyses
- Rotational assignments at four sites with monomers, TiO_2, polymers, textile fibers and elastomers
- Supervised operators of semiworks and commercial continuous and batch processes in day-to-day operations, plant tests and cost control

Education

MS, Chemical Engineering, University of Pennsylvania, 1979
BS, Chemical Engineering, Old Dominion University, 1975

MICHAEL SWIFT

965 Ashland Avenue
Portland, Oregon 45385

Residence: (206) 772-3662
Messages: (206) 433-7950

CAREER OBJECTIVE

Innovative research/customer oriented problem solving targeting composite/materials concepts and solutions involving project conception, time line development, personnel and equipment allocation.

BACKGROUND SUMMARY

Extensive and diversified technical/customer interaction experience in the application of composites to the consumer and aerospace industries. Particularly effective in developing and implementing novel ideas solving unmet materials requirements. History of success implementing technical accomplishments from laboratory experimentation to production scale. Experienced in cost analysis and process/materials comparisons. Excellent technical, written, verbal, and interpersonal communication skills.

CAREER HISTORY

RICHFIELD CHEMICAL COMPANY, Portland, Oregon   1986-Present

Project Leader - Special Projects   1994-Present

- Served as international technology liaison transferring $20MM of intellectual property to foreign companies. Specified equipment, suppliers, tolling sources, markets and cost analysis.

- Conceptualized and commercialized high density foam composite. First year sales of $1MM with an ROI of greater than 40%.

- Played an instrumental role in the development process of thin film, spirial wound membranes for specific gas/liquid phase reactions with a potential market of 1000MM pounds.

- Served on technical team responsible for integrating pulp and staple derivatives of a novel aramid-like fiber into the competitive markets of printed wiring boards, abrasive applications, fire retardant uses and wet processing aids.

Senior Research Engineer   1989-1994

- Served as technical expert in non-woven wet process development/troubleshooting and scale-up of composite materials for specific customer applications.

- Interacted with numerous aerospace companies for commercialization of structurally reinforcing composite foams for radar absorbing applications having a potential market value of $10MM/year.

- Designed, set up and specified equipment for a Resin Transfer Molding (RTM) laboratory. Supervised and trained five people on theory, principles and operation of equipment. Studied in-mold flow characteristics of resin/pre-form geometry.

- Developed magnetic composite materials for frequency dependent electromagnetic response. Established program for manufacture of basic materials and fabrication of functional products.

MICHAEL SWIFT

CAREER HISTORY (Continued)

Research Engineer   1986-1989

- Optimized fiber reinforced composite materials for fast compression molding. Studied blank size distribution and placement, in-mold flow studies, thermal stability and optimization of physical properties in relation to geometric shape.

- Designed, set up and specified equipment for a Reaction Injection Molding (RIM) laboratory. Supervised and trained six people on theory, principles and operation of equipment.

EDUCATION

MS	Polymer Chemistry and Materials Science	Ohio State University, Columbus, OH	1986
BS	Chemical Engineering	Ohio State University, Columbus, OH	1982

ASSOCIATIONS/RECOGNITIONS

Society for the Advancement of Materials and Process Engineering
Special Recognition Award for Excellence in Research

PATENTS/PUBLICATIONS

Holder of 25 U.S. Patents.
Wrote 20 internal technical papers for Richfield Chemical Company.

HOWARD W. ROTHSTEIN, Ph.D.
317 Langston Court
Collins, IL 71542
216-444-2404 (H)
216-717-4039 (O)

OBJECTIVE: A senior management position in the Research and Development area of a pharmaceutical, related health care or chemical company.

SUMMARY: A pharmaceutical executive with extensive experience in the identification and management of Research and Development Programs. Management and scientific experience includes:

- Developed and implemented new and ongoing discovery research programs.
- Transferred technology of candidate drugs to kilolab and pilot plant scale.
- Reviewed and submitted CMC documents to INDs and NDAs.
- Developed regulatory strategy for Candidate Drugs.
- Effectively managed $3.7 million chemistry department budget to support $5 million research and development effort.
- Lectured extensively on original research and topics in medicinal chemistry.
- Served as Adjunct Professor of Bio-Chemical Engineering at the University of Chicago, College of Pharmacy.

PROFESSIONAL: PROMEDICO, INC., PHARMACEUTICAL PRODUCTS DIVISION
EXPERIENCE: Bakersfield, IL (1990 - Present)

Director of Chemistry
Report to Vice President, Research and Preclinical Development with responsibility for discovery chemistry and chemical development projects, including four direct reports and a staff of 32, 17 of whom are Ph.D.'s. Approximately one-third of the staff was recruited during the last four years. Together with the Director of Pharmacology, organized and managed discovery teams, reviewed progress with senior management and consultants and recommended initiating of clinical trials on discovery compounds.

- Established programs to maintain and increase professionalism: dual ladder career path, seminar programs, scientific meeting presentations.
- Served as permanent member of Preclinical Research and Development Management Team, Patent Strategy Committee and Research Council.
- Led the Inhalation Anesthetic Discovery Team that synthesized novel structure classes of new chemical entities that are in advanced preclinical testing.
- Organized a receptor-based approach to antiemetics that led to a recommendation for clinical testing of a promising compound.
- Managed an intravenous Anesthetic Program that led to clinical trials of five Candidate Drugs.
- Worked with Licensing and Acquisition group to evaluate potential in-license drug candidates.

- Discovered a novel neuromuscular blocking agent that began clinical trials.
- Hired ten Ph.D. and M.S./B.S. chemists for discovery and development.
- Developed synthesis for new chemical entities that were scaled up to kilolab and pilot plant.

PHARMCO LABORATORIES, Waukegan, IL (1980 - 1990)

Assistant Director of Regulatory Affairs (1988 - 1990)
Reported to Senior Director of Regulatory Affairs, with responsibility for developing regulatory strategy for development projects. Reviewed and submitted documents to INDs an NDAs. Attended FDA Advisory Committee meetings.

Section Head, Central Nervous System Research (1980 - 1988)
Started as a laboratory scientist synthesizing new chemical entities in the gastrointestinal, cardiovascular and central nervous system disease areas. Led a section of 12 chemists (mostly Ph.D.'s) in discovering analgesic and anti-ischemic compounds. With biology section head, developed and implemented research plans.

- Personally conceived and synthesized three Candidate Drugs that entered clinical trials.
- Organized and chaired a symposium on New Initiatives in Central Nervous System Research

EDUCATION: **Ph.D. - Biochemistry**, Michigan State University (1979)
M.S. - Medicinal Chemistry, Michigan State University (1977)
B.S. - Pharmacy, University of Illinois (1975)

Postdoctorals
Drexel University - Peale Sabbatical Program (1983)
Georgetown University, NIH Fellow (1979 - 1980)

Ongoing professional development courses

PATENTS: Awarded 24 US Patents

PUBLICATIONS: Published 12 articles in refereed journals

MEMBERSHIPS: American Society of Chemical Engineering
American Association for the Advancement of Science
New York Academy of Sciences
American Pharmaceutical Association

CERTIFICATIONS: Registered Pharmacist

Vincent A. Giordano

23 Basking Ridge
West Huntley, Michigan 12492

Tel. 619-555-7157

Summary

An accomplished Engineering and R&D Manager with over ten years of management experience in product and advanced technology development. Broad experience planning, organizing and guiding programs in ceramic materials and process R&D for high technology applications. Technical expert in the field of glass and advanced ceramic technology.

Experience

1997-present

Consultant, Independence Glass & Ceramic Corporation
Operate an independent engineering consultancy in the field of advanced glass and ceramic technology. Clients are primarily in high technology and materials based industries.

1989-1997

Manager Materials Development, Corning Glass, Inc.
Held a variety of increasingly responsible technical, staff and management positions. Developed a broad base of skills leading engineering and R&D work on novel glasses, ceramics, and processes for state-of-the-art applications in electronics. Applications have spanned a diverse array of technologies including flat panel computer data displays, magnetic data storage, microelectronics packaging, fiber optics and precision specialty materials. Accomplishments include:

- Pioneered an innovative materials system that led to the commercialization of a new flat panel data display product which generated $100 million per year new business revenue.

- Established and staffed a state-of-the-art laboratory facility for the development of sophisticated glasses, glass-ceramics, metals, composites and thin/thick film materials.

- Developed materials and processes meeting performance, reliability, and cost objectives which were key to attainment of business strategies.

- Managed a one million dollar operating budget.

- Supervised an advanced degree R&D staff of 12 people.

- Transferred and commercialized technology from R&D to manufacturing which enhanced competitiveness and productivity.

- Established and administered industrial and university R&D contracts.

- Fostered collaboration, teamwork and innovation that led to numerous inventions and technical breakthroughs.

Vincent A. Giordano

1986-1989   *Project Engineer*, Brockway Glass Co., Brockway, Ohio
Member of the engineering staff at a corporate RD&E center. Initiated and conducted projects in glass science and manufacturing technology for cathode-ray tubes, scientific apparatus and electronic devices.

Education   B.S., Chemical Engineering, Princeton University, Princeton, NJ, 1986

Patents & Awards
- Holder of four U.S. patents
- Recipient of Corning Glass'"Outstanding Innovation Award" for U.S. patent 5,932,070 that enhanced the performance and manufacturability of plasma flat panel data displays.

Professional
- Registered Professional Engineer, New York and Ohio
- Member, American Society of Chemical Engineers
- Member, Materials Research Society

Eileen B. Marks
12 Border Avenue
Bellvue, WA 80617
Home: 206 897-5191

SUMMARY:

Senior executive/general manager with extensive experience in marketing/sales and profit and loss responsibility and graduate of Harvard Business School.

EXPERIENCE:

Martin Equipment Company, Inc. (1996 - Present)

Vice President - Direct the sales and marketing of three divisions which total $118 million with 18 direct sales people and four manufacturing representative organizations. Assist the President with strategic planning. Product lines include automated manufacturing equipment, precision machining, precision stamping and contract manufacturing. Markets served are mainframe computers, telecommunications, semiconductors, medical instrumentation automotive and disk drives.

- Grew sales to OEM market $5 million in one year and quoted over $60 million in potential new business over five years.
- Member Corporate Quality Council - implemented "Sigma Program" throughout the company to improve quality three orders of magnitude in three years.
- With $750,000 in capital, justified a rapid prototyping facility that delivers over 70% ROI per year.
- Justified capital investments with ROCE of 25% or greater, e.g. CAD/CAM, Wire EDM, Machining Centers, etc. Over $2 million invested in 24 month period.
- Chairman Corporate Rewards and Recognition Committee.

General Instrument Corporation (1992 - 1996)

Business Manager - Supervised direct staff of six with total organization of 20 including product managers, application engineering, pricing and program management functions. Product responsibility included broad-band network products, high-speed cable assemblies, RF connectors, "Thin-Net" LAN tap.

- Charged with responsibility for $150+ million of bookings; a 50% increase over the previous year at 20% gross margin.
- Improved sales from $100 million to $145 million for a 45% increase. Chairman of the acquisition committee which developed a strategy for RF connectors. Implemented forecasting by part number which improved lead times from 12 weeks to three weeks on high volume components.
- Served on several committees including premise network, electronic distribution, competitive analysis.

<u>Director of Business Planning</u> - Supervised staff of two product managers and an application engineer.

- Implemented cable assembly strategic plan which focused on high-speed assemblies in the computer, instrumentation, medical and automatic test equipment markets.

Universal Engineering, Inc. (1989 - 1992)

<u>Director of Marketing</u> - Supervised staff of five with a total marketing organization of 25 people including product managers, industry marketing, customer service and order entry. Products included commercial connectors, ribbon connectors, cable assemblies and cable. Markets served were telecommunications, industrial, computer and peripherals and commercial and military.

- Charged with sales of $50 million; a 20% increase over previous year, at a 28% gross margin.
- Introduced nine new products in 1990 that produced $4 million sales first year with a $12 million potential in five years.
- Implemented distributor policies to improve part number turnover and increase gross margin.
- Increased exports and imports 80% ($6MM) and 40% ($6MM) respectively.
- Negotiated private label agreements with Asian suppliers to address $500 million market not served.
- Developed strategies for commercial products for investment of $2 million which would generate sales of $15 million at 40% gross margin.
- Coordinated marketing for commercial products worldwide; including Europe, South America, Far East, Japan and United States.

Ameritech, Inc. (1985 - 1989)

<u>Product Manager</u>   (1987 - 1989)
<u>Marketing Manager</u>   (1985 - 1987)

Responsible for the computer and electronic interconnect products for board-to-board, wire-to-board and wire-to-wire applications which included investment justification, managing the programs through engineering, pricing, manufacturing and sales organizations.

- With a capital investment of $1.9 million, developed seven new products that generated sales at a rate of $12 million annually with ROI of more than 50%.
- Directed the development of 16 new products that have $30 million potential in sales producing a divisional growth rate of 25% annually with ROI of 80% - 100%.
- Developed 18 additional products, incorporating robotic insertion, surface mounting and automated discrete wire cable assembly systems.

EDUCATION:

M.B.A., Harvard Business School, 1985
B.S.,   Electrical Engineering, Rochester Institute of Technology, 1983

Barbara A. Krug

14 Sommerville Road
Ocean Grove, CA 80621

(615) 820-9419

PROFESSIONAL SUMMARY

Innovative marketing and product development/management professional with strong communication, negotiation, and decision making capabilities. Extensive technical background provides the ability to perform successfully in a variety of technical disciplines.

EXPERIENCE

Product/Marketing Manager, Euclid Corporation   *(1996 - Present)*

- Established product development process to streamline development cycle, reduce costs, and effectively use resources.
  - Reduced development cycle from one year to three months.
- Successfully penetrated new markets through development and launch of two service offerings;
  - Consulting Services resulted in $500,000 in revenue bookings in first six months.
  - Speech Writing Services resulted in over $250,000 in revenue bookings during first year.
- Cultivated partnerships with industry vendors to increase services sales and perform joint product development.
- Coordinated R&D Budgeting process for new product development.
  - Analyzed budget to assure proper allocation of funds.
  - Tracked development process versus expenditure of funds.
- Created effective marketing programs which resulted in a 50% increase in commercial services business.
- Conducted market research to determine feasibility of offerings using internal and external resources.
- Designed and developed marketing materials for service business offerings including;
  - Trade show exhibits, Video and audio tapes, Product brochures and data sheets.
- Developed and conducted sales training courses for services sales consultants.

Account Representative, Compaq Computer Corporation   *(1993 - 1996)*

- Identified strategic marketing opportunities through relationship management of senior executive staff of CoreStates Financial Services.
- Maintained direct responsibility for developing and implementing Compaq work station marketing strategy for CoreStates nationwide. Efforts resulted in 10% increase in market share over two years.
- Directed five month consulting study to analyze the feasibility of imaging technology use within CoreStates' Financial Services business unit.

Barbara A. Krug   *page 2*

EXPERIENCE (cont'd)

- Effectively coordinated resources and activities with nationwide IBM marketing teams to provide solutions across all CoreStates business units.
- Negotiated special contracts for volume bids with internal Compaq headquarters management.
- Consistently achieved 100% of quota.
- Received *Branch Managers Award for Excellence in Line of Business* for contributions to marketing effort.

Senior Technical Buyer, Compaq Research Center   *(1990 - 1993)*

- Responsible for evaluation and purchase of optical and laser systems for research community, including specification, analysis, negotiation, and installation planning.
- Negotiated and reviewed purchase contracts, service contracts, and software license agreements.
- Functioned as liaison between research community and external vendors and organizations.
- Successfully developed pc-based database of vendor information to streamline buying process.
- Scheduled and hosted technical talks and seminars for research community members.
- Represented Compaq at various technical shows and exhibits.

Technical Buyer, Compaq Research Center   *(1987 - 1990)*

EDUCATION

Bachelor of Science - Physics, 1987
Cornell University

ADDITIONAL SKILLS

PC Environments: DOS, MacIntosh
Applications: Excel, Word, Lotus 1-2-3, Persuasion, Harvard Graphics, Paradox, DBase IV

WINSTON W. SPOONER

20 Billings Road
Manhassett, NY 18242

Res: 212 246-8957
Bus: 212 846-9212

OBJECTIVE: Managerial position in Marketing Consumer Products or Services.

SUMMARY: Broad consumer marketing experience with major corporations, the last four years with Lever Brothers. Demonstrated ability to develop and implement advertising and promotional strategies, increasing share and ROI (return on investment). Strong written and verbal communication skills, with ability to interface effectively at all levels. Computer literate and aggressive user of spreadsheet, word processing and graphic software packages, including Lotus/Excel, Harvard Graphics, Power Point, Word for Windows and ProWrite.

WORK EXPERIENCE:

1995-Present **LEVER BROTHERS COMPANY, New York, NY**

Marketing Manager - Military Sales
Recruited to assume line marketing responsibility for developing and implementing plans and programs for worldwide military retail sales of $40 million annually of Lever Brothers consumer products. Frequent interface with sales and marketing management in three divisions in development of sales/expense forecasts as well as implementation of strategic and tactical marketing and promotional plans.

- Reduced marketing expenses 25% and maintained sales volume in the face of a 20% contraction in the military market.

- Developed and implemented an integrated marketing approach that built established brand to a record 52% share.

- Streamlined development and delivery of sales and marketing communications and support materials on accelerated schedules at reduced costs.

- Introduced special pack promotions to highly resistant military market generating incremental volume through increased display support.

- Designed and initiated "government required" forms utilizing shared computer technology, allowing sales to customize presentations for headquarter accounts.

- Increased productivity of critical manager's meetings by restructuring the format into logical, easily digested segments.

Winston W. Spooner   Page 2

1983-1995   **FLORSHEIM SHOE COMPANY, Chicago, IL**

Retail Brand Director (1993-1995)
Established marketing objectives and strategies, integrating all advertising, point-of-sale, and promotional plans and programs for 200 + retail outlets accounting for $150 million in annual sales. Frequent interface with advertising agencies, vendors and field sales force. Supervised three-person brand team.

- Initiated and implemented consumer targeted radio station in-store, enhancing the audio environment, allowing for promotional messages, and generating revenue by selling air time to vendors.

- Developed retail color coding system that simplified shopping, visually reinforced store positioning and energized the environment through effective use of point-of-sale strategy.

Advertising Manager (1990-1993)
Developed creative and media placement strategies in support of grand openings, promotions, image advertising and ongoing campaigns. Acted as communication liaison among management, agencies and sales. Supervised TV and print media production.

- Initiated first co-op advertising effort that generated $500,000 + in media exposure at a cost of $100,000.

- Increased advertising effectiveness by adapting TV advertising to point-of-sale through creation of video programs nationwide.

Merchandise Distribution Manager (1987-1990)
Frequent interface with Sales, Buying, and Manufacturing with responsibility for establishing sales forecasts and assignment of inventory to 200 retail outlets. Also trained associate merchandise managers, and provided in depth sales analysis for buyers.

Associate Merchandise Manager   (1985-1987)
Management Training Program/Store Manager   (1983-1985)

COMPANY SPONSORED TRAINING:

- Kellogg Graduate School of Management: "Consumer Marketing Strategies"
- American Management Associates: "Management in a Team Environment"
- David Bootnick Associates: "Improving Communication Effectiveness"
- Karras Associates: "Effective Negotiating"

EDUCATION:

CITY COLLEGE OF NEW YORK, New York, NY
B.S., Business Management, 1983

CAROL W. DAVIS

42 Pine Woods Road
Danbury, Connecticut 80622

Business: (212) 493-0700
Residence: (716) 872-9142

CAREER SUMMARY

Senior executive with over 18 years of progressively responsible experience in new Products Marketing and Marketing Research at leading U.S. food companies including Wexler Foods, Quaker Bakeries and Nabisco. Outstanding record of developing award-winning new products as well as building and leading effective organizations. Results-oriented, strong team player and creative problem solver.

BUSINESS EXPERIENCE

WEXLER FOODS, New York, New York   **1991 to Present**
A $1.2 billion manufacturer of frozen and convenience foods and a subsidiary of Federated Foods, Inc. Federated Foods is a $7 billion international food business with operations in 40 countries.

Vice President Marketing, Convenience Foods   **(1995-Present)**
Responsible for directing a major corporate initiative to enter the convenience foods market through internal development. Direct all aspects of new product development and marketing, including concept generation, product formulation, naming, packaging, positioning, advertising, marketing research, marketing plan development and capital planning.

- Generated new product revenues of over $45 million in 1996 with the successful national launch of Fast Favorites, Quick Delights and Microwave Fantasy lines.
- Named one of the Top 100 Marketers in the country by *Advertising Age* magazine (June, 1997)
- Introduced ten major new products and drove revenues of Wexler Foods from $800,000 in 1995 to over $1.2 billion by 1998. Brands launched over this period included:

    - Micro-Magic - Generated annual sales approaching $110 million, became the #1 selling brand for Wexler and was named an AMA Edison Award winner as one of the Top 10 New Products of 1996. Also won award for outstanding package graphics.
    - Short Order Chef - Generated first year sales of $95 million, won the AMA's Edison Gold Award as one of the Best New Products of 1997, and received a Silver Level Award for excellence in advertising.
    - Five-Minute Favorites - Was developed in less than one year and achieved sales of $50 million, exceeding plan by 10% in first year.

- Wexler Foods named New Products Marketer of the Year by both the American Marketing Association and *Food Business* magazine in 1997.

Director, Marketing Research   **(1991-1995)**
Responsible for the leadership and overall direction of the Marketing Research Department. Thoroughly knowledgeable in a full range of research techniques including all types of custom research, syndicated data sources, decision-support systems and forecasting and volumetric modeling.

- Successfully "turned around" the Marketing Research function by upgrading and training the staff, introducing improved research methods and techniques and re-established credibility with brand marketing and senior management.

Carol W. Davis   Page Two

- Directed the development of an internal new products forecasting model which was significantly more accurate than simulated test market services.
- Served as strategic advisor to the President's Staff on such issues as changing consumer lifestyles and overall market trends.

QUAKER BAKERIES, Philadelphia, Pennsylvania   **1987 to 1991**

Manager of Marketing Research Department
Responsible for marketing research support on all retail and food service product line including new and established brands.

- Significantly enhanced brand management analysis and planning capabilities by developing a state-of-the-art computer-based marketing decision support system.
- Significantly improved forecast accuracy through development of a model-based forecasting system.
- Reviewed and helped develop long range plans and annual operating plans.

NABISCO INTERNATIONAL, INC., New York, New York   **1983 to 1987**

Research Manager   **(1985-1987)**
Research Supervisor   **(1983-1985)**
Performed a broad range of marketing research studies on assigned brands including concept and product testing, advertising, packaging and name testing, A&U's and test marketing. Recipient of Chairman's Award for business analyses and econometric modeling on Krunch-Berry cereal which led to development of marketing plan resulting in record sales and profits.

THE MARKET PARTNERSHIP, New York, New York   **1979 to 1983**

Senior Analyst
Progressed from Analyst to Senior Analyst with responsibility for three of the company's largest clients: Nabisco Foods, General Foods and Scott Paper Company. Responsible for the design, analysis and presentation of consumer research findings to client management

EDUCATION

M.B.A.   Harvard Business School, 1979
               Graduated third in class of 105. Full tuition scholastic scholarship

B.A.   University of Pennsylvania, Psychology Major, 1977
               Graduated tenth in class of 1200

PROFESSIONAL ASSOCIATIONS

American Marketing Association
Association of National Advertisers

WILBUR B. MARSHALL
8 Lewis Road
Wilmington, DE 19898
Voice/Fax (302) 644-3492

Summary:

General Management/Marketing executive with 13 years domestic and international chemical industry experience.

Specific expertise: Sales, Marketing and Marketing Research, Strategic Planning, Acquisitions, Joint Ventures, and Business Strategy development and implementation.

Professional Experience:

HERCULES, INC., Wilmington, DE   **(1998 to Present)**
($5.2 BILLION CHEMICALS MANUFACTURER)

Vice President Marketing & Sales-Paper Chemicals Division, Wilmington, DE

Worldwide P&L responsibility for marketing and sales of paper chemical lines manufactured in four countries with sales in 60 foreign countries, sold through direct sales forces in major markets and distributors/agents in other countries. Promoting sale of starch-based chemical system (SBCS) manufactured at new plant is top priority project. (Sales: $15 million, Operating Budget: $1.5 million; Staff: 20)

- Initiating empowerment culture in stifled environment.
- In first year achieved 25% Sales and Volume growth in SBCS 10% overall products.
- Evaluating strategic product line additions, with possibility of significantly changing entire character of division through growth and acquisitions.

WALDO CHEMICALS, INC., Pittsburgh, PA   **(1996 to 1998)**
($60 MILLION, INTERNATIONAL SPECIALTY POLYMER COATING MANUFACTURER)

Vice President, International Specialty Group
President, South America
Member, Board of Directors, Europe

Established new business unit to support manufacturing, marketing and sales of specialty finishes in South America. (Operating Budget: $3 million; Staff: 35)

- Achieved $3.1 million in annual sales and cumulative profit of $1.2 million in three years.
- Established two wholly-owned operations in France and Germany.
- Converted JV in Spain to 100% owned subsidiary.
- Formed JV in Netherlands, adding $3 million in sales revenues in second year.

NORTON CHEMICALS, INC., New York, NY   **(1984 to 1996)**
($6.3 BILLION WORLDWIDE MANUFACTURER OF COMMODITY AND SPECIALTY CHEMICALS)

Director of Marketing & Sales, *Coatings Division*   (1994 - 1996)

Profit and Loss responsibility for worldwide marketing and sales of paper coating product lines. (Sales: $30 million; Operating Budget $2.5 million; Staff: 60)

WILBUR B. MARSHALL - P 2

- Improved sales efficiency and customer coverage by 30%.
- Resolved three complex claims saving $500,000.
- Negotiated new two-year contract, increasing sales 15%.
- Rewrote agent/distributor contracts reducing company's liability exposure by $1.3 million.

Manager, Strategic Planning, *Pulping Chemicals Division* (1992 - 1994)

Determined internal consistency of strategic plans for two pulping chemicals divisions and submitted recommendation to senior corporate management; reviewed joint venture projects and made further recommendations for international acquisitions. (Staff: four)

- Analyzed over 150 companies and recommended ten international acquisition candidates.
- Developed and presented additional value criteria to acquisition specifications for European investment bankers, resulting in identification of three candidates.

Region Sales Manager, Southeast Region (1990 - 1992)

Turned around sales and profits for 30 industrial chemical products (Sales: $15 million; Operating Budget: $2.0 million; Profit: $1.7 million; Staff: three)

- Achieved 20% growth in sales and profits.
- Concluded sales of $3 million to three new business areas.

Product Sales Manager - Paper Chemicals Division (1987 - 1990)

Responsible for marketing, sales and overall business operations for this $60 million product line as it moved from order control to active selling mode. (Budget: $500,000; Staff: three)

- Developed and implemented strategic marketing plan for Europe and contributed to global strategic plan.

Sales Representative, Southwest Region (1984 - 1987)

Accountable for $5 million sales for 30 industrial chemical products serving eight industries in Texas, Arizona, California and Nevada.

- Increased sales and profits 15% per year in recessionary period.
- Negotiated exclusive contract resulting in annual sales of $400,000.
- Launched three new products resulting in $750,000 additional revenue.

Education: B.S., Chemistry, University of Delaware, 1984

SANDRA R. BERNARD

15 Pheasant Run
West Chester, PA 19382

Residence: (610) 431-2544
Office: (610) 631-8989

OBJECTIVE

A senior level sales and marketing position requiring demonstrated skills in leadership, planning and communication which result in increased profitability.

Qualified by 16 years of experience in positions of increasing responsibility for the profitable marketing of products within the consumer products industry. Background includes consistent record of achievement in the following areas:

- Sales & Marketing Management
- National Account Management
- Advertising
- P&L Management
- Sales Promotion
- Product Development
- Market Research
- Strategic Planning

PROFESSIONAL EXPERIENCE

PFIZER INC., CONSUMER GROUP   **1995 - Present**

Direct all marketing functions including consumer advertising and promotion, marketing services, account marketing programs, and special product development for Pfizer's top 75 accounts (sales volume - $940MM). Manage budget of $6.3MM and staff of 36.

Vice President Sales & Marketing

Accomplishments:
- Directed effort to expand and reorganize Account Marketing department. Increased staff from 18 to 36 members. Reassigned accounts by dollar volume and geographically.
- Produced an additional $25MM in sales from account specific product development. Expanded this service to cover Pfizer's top ten accounts.
- Developed national promotional strategy to compete with competing shaving products companies. Promotions produced $4.8MM in increased profit.

THE GILLETTE COMPANY   **1981 - 1995**

Fourteen years of results-oriented experience within this $1.9 billion manufacturer of consumer shaving products. Experience includes directing all sales and marketing functions for assigned accounts (or region) covering all consumer trade classes (mass merchant, food, drug, deep discount, catalogue, specialty, etc.)

Senior Sales Manager, National Accounts   *1994 - 1995*
Created and executed marketing and sales programs for WalMart Corporation. Coordinated activities and provided direction for 150 sales representatives with regards to WalMart. WalMart sales volume - $300MM.

Accomplishments:
- Produced 20% increase at WalMart versus previous year.
- Introduced first promotional pack featuring free audio cassette with purchase.
- Directed and managed the inventory of all WalMart products at their 105 distribution centers.
- Secured distribution for triple track razor at WalMart.

District Sales Manager   *1992 - 1994*

Managed, motivated, and directed 14 sales representatives in the Boston, Massachusetts district. Was held accountable for quota achievement, P&L management, promotion, advertising activity, and forecasting as well as career development of team members.

    Accomplishments:
- Number one ranked district (nationally).
- Number two ranked district (nationally).
- Three marketing representatives were promoted to managerial positions.

Major Account Manager   *1991 - 1992*

Created and executed marketing and sales programs for the following national accounts: Rite Aid, CVS, Acme and Super Fresh.

    Accomplishments:
- Received Performance Excellence Award signifying Number One Sales Manager in nation.
- Achieved 30% increase in sales at assigned accounts.

Special Markets Manager   *1991*

Managed and directed eight (8) food brokers accountable for all Supermarket business located in the Northeast region.

    Accomplishments:
- 100% quota achievement in all product categories.
- Secured new distribution for the Flex Trac razor at Shop Rite (only supermarket chain to carry this product).

Marketing Representative   *1986 - 1991*

Met and exceeded sales quotas at assigned accounts through the planning and execution of account specific marketing programs and promotions.

    Accomplishments:
- 1991 - Excellence Award winner signifying the nation's number one marketing representative.
- 1990 - 100% quota achievement in all product categories.
- 1989 - 100% quota achievement in all product categories.
- 1988 - Ranked number two marketing representative nationally.

RJR NABISCO COMPANY   **1981 - 1986**
Account Manager   *1983 - 1986*
Account Supervisor   *1982 - 1983*
Account Representative   *1981 - 1982*

EDUCATION

VILLANOVA UNIVERSITY, Villanova, PA
    B.S., Marketing   1981

    Continued professional development includes participation in programs in the areas of leadership, coaching, presentation, interviewing, and writing skills.

DONALD J. BORKERT

31 Rock Creek Lane, McAllister, TX 39415   Office 715/497-5151 • Home 715/697-4331

CAREER SUMMARY

Seasoned sales and marketing professional with extensive experience in the areas of:

- Pricing
- Product line P&L
- Competitive analysis
- Forecasting
- Sales force management
- Market research

- Strategic planning
- Distribution channel design
- Contract negotiation
- New product commercialization
- Competitive acquisitions
- Customer service

Results-oriented, self-motivated team contributor with a proven ability to lead efforts in the areas of account acquisition, competitive strategies, market segmentation and profitability improvement.

BUSINESS EXPERIENCE AND ACCOMPLISHMENTS

Electro-Laminates, Inc., Houston, TX   **1985 to Present**
A $100 million global business providing specialty engineered laminates to the electronics industry.

Marketing Manager (1996 - Present)
Report to the Director of Sales and Marketing with key responsibilities in national and international coverage of end use OEM accounts, applications development and new product launch. Directly supervised a staff of six marketing and technical professionals.

- Led a successful customer-linked commercialization effort from which a new product category was launched, capturing more than $2 million in sales in the first year.
- Established product application teams within the industry supply chain, achieving cost containment and cycle time reduction at all levels.
- Facilitated an alliance with a major OEM, resulting in exclusivity for product qualification testing in a computer application. Successful testing will lead to more than $10 million in new product sales annually.
- Formulated programs, working with sales teams and regional managers, to initiate and introduce new products and productivity options to customers and distributors.

Sales Manager (1993 - 1996)
Responsible on a national basis for all sales activities, pricing policies, sales contracts, competitive analysis, forecasting, customer and technical service associated with a $40 million network of 11 distributors at 22 locations. Reported to the Director of Sales and Marketing.

- Analyzed markets and prepared accurate sales forecasts with distributors' senior management.
- Implemented a mix-driven, volume-based incentive rebate plan increasing sales by 30% in 1995.
- Prospected, recruited and secured long-term arrangements with new distributors resulting in revenue increases exceeding $9 million.
- Planned and initiated distributor training programs.
- Established requirements for distributor certification to comply with MIL-SPEC and other institutional approval ratings.
- Promoted and applied Total Quality Leadership techniques to streamline distributor policies and reduce overall bureaucracy, with regard to claims, special pricing requests and transportation.

DONALD J. BORKERT   Page Two

District Sales Manager (1991 - 1993)
Reported to the National Sales Manager, responsible for $25 million in sales throughout the Northeastern U.S. and Mexico via an organization of three directly reporting salespersons, four distributors and two manufacturer's representatives.

- Exceeded regional sales quotas by 10% in 1991 and 15% in 1992 while maintaining a 5% price premium over competition.
- Re-established Mexican sales base, growing sales from $2 to $6 million.
- Mobilized cross-functional teams to capture new accounts.

Market Research Manager (1989 - 1991)
Responsible for establishing and maintaining product line pricing to meet corporate profitability goals on a national basis. Also responsible for conducting research for competitive and strategic purposes. Reported to the Director of Marketing. Directly supervised four employees.

- Implemented pricing mix strategies enabling price increases exceeding 3%, resulting in profit gains of $4.2 million.
- Managed and negotiated all pricing and contracts for $60 million SBU on a national basis.
- Successfully prepared and justified appropriations requests for capital expenditures in excess of $4 million.
- Led competitive analysis efforts in all segments of market in order to develop and implement appropriate business response.

Product Manager (1988 - 1989)
Reported to the Marketing Manager, responsible for management of three basic product lines. Primary focus included: P&L, market share, forecasting and product line rationalization.

- Organized product rationalization effort in the aftermath of a business acquisition.
- Assisted in the commercialization of new products.
- Focused efforts on the assimilation of the acquired business into the existing one.

Contracts Manager   (1987 - 1988)
Sales Associate   (1985 - 1987)

EDUCATION AND PROFESSIONAL TRAINING

B.S. Business Administration - Texas A&M, 1985
Graduated Magna Cum Laude - Major: Marketing

- Company-Sponsored Professional Training -

Management Development Conference • Total Quality Leadership Training
Strategic Pricing Seminar • Value Selling Workshop
Total Quality • Middle Management Training • Leadership Training Workshop

BRUCE T. HARTZ
25 Croft Lane
Devon, PA 19087

Work: (215) 422-6571
Home: (215) 431-2135

SUMMARY: Senior Marketing executive with strong leadership skills and a proven track record of profitably growing both large national brands and smaller niche products. Strengths include strategy development, consumer marketing and team building. Successful career includes marketing, business development, strategy and finance assignments.

PROFESSIONAL EXPERIENCE:

NATIONAL HOME PRODUCTS COMPANY, Philadelphia, PA   **1996 - Present**

Category Director - Cleaning Products Unit
Report to Vice President of Marketing with overall responsibility for three major brands: WONDER CLEAN, AMAZE AND GLORY SHINE. Received additional responsibility in 1997 for WIZZARD Glass Cleaner, the company's largest brand. Manage existing base business, new product development and Marketing organization's total quality roll-out. Supervise staff of nine.

- Led Floor Wax business turnaround through aggressive in-store promotion focus and product improvement. Additionally developed and launched one new product into test market. Grew volume and increased profits 30%.
- Initiated AMAZE new products program and launched AMAZE PLUS premium product to regain category leadership. Increased share and profits 20% and 12%, respectively.
- Developed and implemented GLORY SHINE EDLP sales strategy which has significantly exceeded payback requirements.
- Revised WIZZARD Strategic Plan to address emerging competitive issues and new product opportunities. Managed advertising development process which delivered superior copy.

BEATRICE FOODS, Chicago, IL   **1983 - 1996**

Brand Manager - Spread Fast Peanut Butter (1994 - 1996)
P&L responsibility for Beatrice's largest brand representing $500MM in sales. Duties included managing a $60MM advertising and promotion budget and staff of four.

- Established successful long-term category/brand volume growth strategy.
- Developed record testing advertising designed to reposition the brand and extend product usage.
- Implemented aggressive short-term sales and consumer programs to stabilize share.
- Led development of innovative market level event sponsorships designed to address local consumer and trade opportunities.
- Led development of several value-added spreadable products for test market.

Brand Manager - Red Hot Barbecue Sauce (1992 - 1994)
Managed P&L for this $30MM brand, including a $6MM advertising and promotion budget and one Associate Brand Manager.

- Successfully defended brand against a major new competitive entry and achieved best volume growth (25%) of any Beatrice brand.
- Developed three new television ads designed for use in regional/seasonal copy strategy.
- Designed and implemented a local marketing program to enhance national consumer events, including USTA and professional horse show sponsorships.
- Developed several new Meat Sauce products for test market and successfully introduced Bull's-Eye Hot-N-Spicy nationally.

Brand Manager (1990 - 1992)
Managed P&L for this $80MM business (ice cream) and supervised one Assistant Brand Manager.

- Repositioned Beatrice Ice Cream as "fantasy" dessert and increased sales 10%.
- Increased distribution during key periods through special packaging and targeted trade/sales incentives.
- Aggressively managed and increased Toppings profits through developing low cost copacking relationships and short-term sales incentives.
- Recommended and implemented Beatrice's Pineapple Ice Cream market withdrawal.

Manager of Business Development - Grocery Products Group (1988 - 1990)
Reported to the Vice President of Marketing & Strategy with responsibility for developing a growth plan, including acquisition, for the Frozen Foods Group.

- Developed five category-specific growth strategies and prioritized internal and external development activities.
- Established Frozen Foods Group Acquisition Plan and coordinated the strategic planning process.
- Purchased Porter Foods retail brands for $100MM in 1989.
- Led several acquisition studies and coordinated both internal analysis and outside consulting/investment banking teams.

Senior Analyst - Marketing Strategy (1987 - 1988)

- Assessed financial and strategic implications relating to the uncoupling of Wilson Company and Beatrice Foods.
- Provided Chairman and Chief Executive Officer with operating group performance analysis.

PREVIOUS POSITIONS (1983 - 1987)

Held a series of increasingly responsible assignments in Finance and Strategy which included an 18-month field assignment working on cost and capital planning at a major manufacturing facility; a traditional financial planning and reporting assignment in an operating division; and financial/strategic planning for a divested business unit.

EDUCATION:

- MBA, **Wharton Business School**, 1983
- BBA, Finance, **University of Pennsylvania**, 1981

ACHIEVEMENTS:

- Received President's Award (1995)
- Received Beatrice Frozen Foods Leadership Award (1993)
- Received Beatrice's Creativity Award (1991)

BERNARD W. REGAN

3588 Connestoga Road, S.E.
Blissfield, Michigan 49585

Home: (606) 234-2887
Office: (606) 454-4397

BACKGROUND SUMMARY

Fifteen years proven experience in international marketing and business development. Experience in country, regional and global business units. Demonstrated ability to improve sales and profits. Assertive, motivated results oriented. Innovative problem solver with ability to implement. Trilingual - Spanish and German.

WORK EXPERIENCE

NU-QUEST ENTERPRISES - Detroit, Michigan   **1995 to Present**
A worldwide, $7 billion+ manufacturer and marketer of consumer products.

Manager, International Marketing - Primarily responsible to develop and market the soap and shampoo product lines in all international markets. Manage a staff of six professionals to ensure that appropriate strategies and product launch goals are developed and implemented. Hire, train and conduct performance evaluations.

Accomplishments:

- Provided necessary management that has increased current divisional sales to more than $300 million annually
- Personally developed the soap line and broadened the scope of soap and shampoo business.
- Introduced new shampoo line into Japan that generated an increase of over $20 million in business.
- Successfully introduced new scented soap line into Europe.

GERBER PRODUCTS, INC. - Philadelphia, Pennsylvania   **1990 to 1995**
A $50 million+ manufacturer and distributor of infant goods.

International Marketing and Sales Manager - Hired with specific objective to establish an international presence for Gerber Products infant goods business.

Accomplishments:

- Established markets in Canada, U.K., Germany and Spain, resulting in a four-fold increase in sales.
- Negotiated and developed distributor contracts and established international pricing policies.
- Initiated trade/consumer advertising campaign in the U.K., resulting in 1500 new sales outlets and establishing a foothold with major retailers such as Beall's and J.C. Penney's.
- Initiated and implemented bilingual packaging program for Canada which allowed the company's entry in that market.

PHOTO MART CORPORATION - Baltimore, Maryland   **1983 to 1990**
A worldwide manufacturer and distributor of consumer/industrial photographic and imaging products.

Bernard W. Regan   PAGE 2

Marketing Manager - Worldwide Export Operations (1989-1990) - Promoted to direct worldwide export sales and marketing programs for all consumer photographic and video products. Developed marketing plans, strategies, budgets, pricing strategies, sales promotion campaigns and advertising program for export markets.

Accomplishments:

- Directed marketing programs for worldwide offices in Hong Kong, Paris, London and Florida.
- Redesigned Wide Lens camera system to reduce cost per unit picture.
- Successfully entered export market with profitable new video products.
- Shifted advertising strategy from national media to more localized advertising and sales promotions. Increased sales while reducing advertising budget by $500,000.

Regional Marketing Manager (1985-1989) - Originated and implemented sales and marketing strategies in Columbia, Ecuador, Panama and Venezuela to increase market share. Responsible for developing sales programs, distributor relations/contracts and advertising campaigns.

Accomplishments:

- Conceived, planned and implemented new street photography program in Latin America, increasing market share by 35%.
- Redirected industrial marketing programs which doubled hardware and film sales.
- Negotiated, administered and monitored distribution contracts to ensure exclusivity of product sales.
- Significantly increased amateur camera sales through creative sales promotions and advertising campaigns.

Resident Marketing Director - Germany (1983-1985) - Hired, trained and directed a staff of seven professionals, all German nationals. Increased sales by $1.2 million.

WARRING DRUG INC. - New York, New York   **1980 to 1983**
Warring Drug is a worldwide $2.0 billion diverse manufacturer of ethical, OTC and household products.

Various Assignments in New York, Mexico and Columbia - Joined the company in the Marketing/Product Management area and was assigned to various marketing functions (i.e., marketing research, product management for new products) and overall orientation to subsidiary operations in Mexico and Columbia. In 1978, reorganized regional sales territory in Columbia, which was completed without a reduction in sales. Promoted to National Sales Manager for Columbia.

JOHNSON & JOHNSON - New Brunswick, New Jersey   **1978 to 1980**
Worldwide manufacturer of ethical pharmaceutical products.

Medical Sales Representative - Awarded Regional Salesman of the Year in 1975, ranking second in the nation in overall sales.

EDUCATION

American University, Washington, DC
Master in International Management, 1978

Lehigh University, Bethlehem, PA, B.A., Economics, 1976

EZRA N. WICKERSHAM

14 Darlington Drive
Newark, DE 19898

Home: (302) 597-8325
Office: (302) 694-8381

SUMMARY

International sales, marketing and business development executive serving Fortune 250 chemical companies. Specific responsibilities in large account management, staff recruitment and motivation, new product introduction, pricing and profitability. Demonstrated successes in European and Asian cultures in joint venture companies.

PROFESSIONAL EXPERIENCE

ICI AMERICAS   1996 - Present

Director, New Business Development (Commercial Development)

- Created, staffed and led Commercial Development group.

- Developed market focus Mission, Goals and Strategy for the CD group.

- During initial four years, generated project opportunities providing $400 million in revenue. Provided three year return on $95 million of investment.

- Presented a plan for the global manufacturing synergy for new key intermediates.

- Utilized $7 million R&D budget for new product development and pilot plant operations.

- Administered $2.8 million operating budget.

- Managed total project including sales and marketing, contract negotiations and investment proposal preparation for a new specialty intermediate product ($8.5 million revenue, high margin).

- Supervised development of lube additive replacement for a major component of engine oils for both automotive and industrial users. Negotiated a contract with a major oil company to supply their total requirements on a take or pay basis.

- Delivered market opportunity for new herbicide intermediate family of products ($200-300 million annually, $55 million investment). Single source position for 10 million pounds with newly developed account.

- Directed the plan preparation for market entry into remediation chemistry ($60 million revenue $29 million investment).

DOW CHEMICAL COMPANY   1980 - 1996

Manager, Marketing Development   1992 - 1996

- Established a group of new pesticide intermediate products from zero base to $30 million sales in two years.

EZRA N. WICKERSHAM
Page Two

- Developed applications for existing products for specialty uses resulting in $50 million of additional sales.

- Structured marketing and sales function, as a director of this $25 million joint venture company with Honshu Chemicals (Japanese company) and served as Corporate Secretary/Treasurer (officer) of the joint venture.

- Negotiated contracts for this joint venture company to include; JV agreement, plant services contract, land lease agreement, technology licensing contract, utilities agreements.

Marketing Manager - Organics   **1990 - 1992**

- Developed and executed global marketing plan and strategies for $180 million specialty herbicide intermediate business. This activity included joint venturing with companies in Italy and the U.K. plus worldwide pricing responsibility.

- Negotiated supply contracts with key executives at major customer overseas locations.

- Improved profitability in a declining price market by lowering manufacturing costs 20 percent.

- Designed and implemented a "special accounts" program yielding $8 million additional revenue during decline in the agricultural chemicals business.

International Marketing Manager   **1989 - 1990**

- Completed market development for $62 million joint venture intermediates plant in Mexico.

- Increased Mexican market share in inorganic chemicals business from 20% to 45% in 24 months, without reducing prices and with domestic competition.

- Developed European sales opportunities from U.K. joint venture for Dow herbicide intermediates businesses.

- Discovered and developed $18 million of new organic and inorganic product business in Australia.

Account Manager   **1986 - 1989**

R&D, Technical Service Purchasing   **1980 - 1986**

EDUCATION

B.S., Chemistry, University of Delaware, 1980
Finance and Accounting Courses, University of Delaware, 1993

CAROL A. BORMAN
70 Willow Drive
Freeport, Pennsylvania 15404

707/434-0653 (Residence)   707/922-6565 (Business)

SUMMARY

Fourteen years' experience in consumer packaged goods marketing and sales, with an emphasis on business strategy and new product initiatives. Functional experience includes business planning and profit delivery, television, print and radio advertising development; promotion concepts and execution; brand repositioning; new products exploration/launches and personnel recruiting and development.

EMPLOYMENT HISTORY

1987 to Pres., **BARLOW FOODS, INC.**, Scranton, Pennsylvania

1996 - Pres.   *General Manager - New Business Ventures*

Responsible for new product strategy and execution; trade marketing start-up and personnel development of eight marketing professionals and three support staff. Responsibility for $40MM in sales and $8MM in marketing spending; $400MM G&A. Report to Vice President - Retail Marketing Division.

- Restarted new products function for retail marketing, led venture teams on new products/acquisition efforts (including Mexican food category); launched Gravy Master line.
- Repositioned Far East brand noodles with business and product strategy improvements.
- Successfully developed the trade marketing function.

1994 - 1996   *General Manager - Vinegar, Sauces and Gravies*

Responsible for Vinegar, Steak Sauce, Barbecue Sauce, Specialty Sauces, and Gravy business planning, strategy and execution and personnel development of six marketing professionals and four support staff. Responsibility for $300MM in sales and $80MM in marketing spending; $2MM G&A. Reported to Vice President - Consumer Products Division.

- Improved departmental profitability by +16%; formed a "sauces" business unit.
- Initiated new media usage with co-op radio on Gravy during peak season; drive leadership share.
- Repositioned Barlow Vinegar as "the good food vinegar"; initiated Barlow Cleaning Vinegar Spray as a new product idea.

1993 - 1994   *General Manager - Ketchup and Sauces*

Responsible for Ketchup, Steak Sauce and Specialty Sauces business planning, strategy and execution and personnel development of seven marketing professionals and three support staff. Responsibility for $250MM in sales and $75MM in marketing spending; $500MM G&A. Reported to Vice President - Consumer Products Division.

- Initiated and developed proposal to launch new recyclable, unbreakable, clear Ketchup bottle.

Carol A. Borman   **Page 2**

- Initiated and coordinated NFL event sponsorship; representing Barlow in a "60 Minutes" interview with Harry Reasoner and an "NBC Nightly News" segment on the NFL.
- Repositioned steak sauce as an "adult ketchup" to build new usage; improved household penetration by +3.5%; increased volume +10%.

1992 - 1993   *Group Product Manager - Ketchup*

Responsible for Ketchup business planning, strategy and execution; administration of $65MM in marketing spending and personnel development of three marketing professionals and one secretary. Reported to Vice President - Consumer Products Division.

- Developed, tested and nationally expanded a new award-winning advertising campaign targeted to teens. Helped reverse category consumption and share declines.
- Coordinated the addition of a consumer-friendly handle to the 32 oz. plastic container.

1990 - 1992   *Product Manager - Baby Food Products*

Responsible for assessing the potential, planning and executing the national launch of Barlow's baby food product line. Reported to General manager - Marketing.

- Planned and participated in the national sales meeting; took the show "on the road" for broker visits; helped sell-in on various account calls; introduced shelf management to Sales.
- Developed the consumer 800 line and coordinated the first medical marketing program at Barlow.
- Achieved 99% ACV nationally (only one holdout account) and sold 2.9MM cases year one.

1987 - 1990   *Associate Product Manager - New Products, Baby Food*

1984 to 1987, **UNITED BRANDS, INC.**, Cincinnati, Ohio

1985 - 1987   *Brand Assistant - Cake Mixes*
1984 - 1985   *Sales Representative - Case Food Division*

EDUCATION

M.B.A., Marketing Concentration, University of Michigan, (1984)
B.S., Marketing, Ohio State University (1982)

RELATED INFORMATION

- Total Quality Management Training, Crosby and Juran.
- Recognized in various publications (e.g., *Fortune, Business Week, Executive Report, USA Today, Savvy Woman, Executive Female*) as a "person to watch".

MARK B. GRUDEN
1401 Sycamore Lane
Bellingham, Washington 80220
(505) 796-4132

PROFESSIONAL SUMMARY

Management Professional with significant experience building and leading high-volume, high-profit sales, marketing and product management teams. Combines sales, marketing and technical expertise with an excellent knowledge of industrial markets and products to gain a competitive advantage and win major market share. Successful in driving forward innovative product development programs into new and expanding business markets. Expertise includes:

- Strategic Business Planning
- Budgeting/Product Pricing
- Market Research/Analysis
- Advertising/Marketing Programs

- Sales Management
- Manufacturing Support
- Sales Training/Incentive Programs
- Acquisition Investigation

PROFESSIONAL EXPERIENCE

WAYERHAEUSER COMPANY   1986-Present
A worldwide leader in the forest products industry ($9 billion sales).

Product Manager-Plywood & Lumber   1995-Present
Broad-ranging authority for developing strategic business plans, innovative product offerings, training field sales teams, developing product pricing and distribution channels, launching nationwide advertising/marketing campaigns, investigating acquisition alternatives, generating a TQM program and implementing all phases of the business plan. Led the entire new business product development cycle from initial concept and management approval through full-scale roll-out.

- Increased sales 45% and profits 20% within two years.
- Spearheaded the development of a nation-wide network of over 30 distributors during a two-year period which accounted for over 50% of product sales.
- Developed and introduced eight new products and systems in 1996. Five year sales are projected to exceed $95 million with a solid 18% gross profit margin.
- Initiated a new job title, job description and incentive program for specialty products sales representatives which helped fuel aggressive growth.

Product Manager-Lumber   1992-1995
Promoted from field sales management to key position leading product management activities for core product line (annual sales of $700 million and gross profits of $105 million). Focused efforts on extending leadership position in a highly competitive industry. Responsible for developing new products, implementing creative sales incentive plans and leading high-profile marketing communication programs. Reported to Vice President, Marketing.

- Developed award-winning product which generated $1.2 million in revenues within first two years.
- Received several prestigious "best read advertisement" awards from various trade publications.
- Generated $600,000 gross profit in 1994 by implementing an innovative sales incentive program.

Regional Sales Manager   **1990-1992**

Directed all sales and business development activities for Southeast Region ($250 million sales). Recruited and led a team of 12 sales representatives calling on contractors, residential builders and other channels in the building materials market. Established sales plans and objectives, identified target accounts and niche markets for focused development efforts, and managed sales/product training.

- Received the 1991 Sales Management Award for outstanding performance.
- Successfully penetrated Home Depot during account's entry into market.
- Achieved significant 15% sales improvement during a period with flat market opportunity by capitalizing upon specific markets with demonstrated growth potential.
- Trained and sponsored a sales representative who received the 1992 President's Club Award.

Sales Representative   **1986-1990**

Sold/marketed the complete line of company products throughout the Orlando, Florida market. Sold to both design professionals (for specification) and dealers/contractors (for material).

- Sales volume was largest in the region at more than $100 million with results earning several special recognition awards.

EDUCATION

Bachelor of Science - Civil Engineering, 1986
GEORGIA TECH, Atlanta, Georgia

STERLING B. DAVIES
12 Fuller Circle
West Chester, PA 19382

Residence: 610/431-2424   Office: 610/826-4005

QUALIFICATION SUMMARY

Client-oriented executive with over 18 years of senior management responsibilities in product management, client and technical training, and technical support for two computer companies. Consistently recognized for exceptional organizational and planning abilities, balanced with excellent interpersonal and people-development skills, with staffs of up to 100 people and annual budgets to $5 million. A strong record of proactive problem-solving, program innovation and high achievement of financial performance goals.

EXPERIENCE PROFILE

SHARED MEDICAL SYSTEMS, INC. (Malvern, PA)   **1987 - Present**
A $180 million company which develops, markets, and services automated systems for the health care industry in the United States and Canada.

Director, Product Management (1995 - Present)
Responsible for planning and implementing product strategies to complement national marketing strategies for the health care industry. Researched, defined and managed the development process for computer-based products and services marketed to the U.S. health care channel.

- Developed executive relationships within health care companies, leading to joint product planning agreements and shared investments in software development; resulting products had shorter development cycle and were produced at lower cost.

- Planned and implemented expansion of primary product initial line from MacIntosh to IBM-based systems, thus realizing significantly wider market penetration.

- Defined and acquired "super processor" product to penetrate health care conglomerate account not previously serviced by SMS. First year sales netted in excess of $4.2 million.

- Chaired divisional time-to-market improvement team which exceeded first-year objectives in product introduction processes by 20 percentage points.

- Raised staff morale and accountability through new communication programs, training assignments and formalized position descriptions; also converted department managers to MBO-based evaluation program. Earned rating in top 5% of Division for personal managerial effectiveness.

Director, Client Training Services (1993 - 1995)
Responsible for developing and delivering full-line product training for clients and technical support personnel through classroom programs and on-site seminars. Provided telephone "help desk" support across all product lines for U.S. clients and SMS field staff.

- Significantly improved group profitability and productivity by consolidating staffs and facilities while raising department rating to "exceeds expectations" level on annual client satisfaction survey.

- Consistently exceeded services revenue and student activity objectives while lowering costs; final year accomplishments included 130% of training revenue objective, 112% of service billing objective and 10% under budget.

- Defined and initiated a client training service for HMO's as an incremental revenue source to SMS. First year revenues were 128% of plan.

Director, Educational and Consulting Services **(1990 - 1993)**
Responsible for developing and delivering all product training and documentation services for clients and SMS technical support personnel. Planned and managed product certification and field-release processes for the SMS Service organization.

- Defined, staffed and implemented a systems consulting group to provide product optimization services to clients, and a new revenue stream for SMS; this has since become a major internal profit center with multimillion dollar annual sales.

- Initiated contractual training services for health care companies to absorb excess staff capacity and generate incremental revenue; independently acquired and fulfilled contracts worth more than $500,000 in first year.

- Organized and staffed the first centralized documentation services function within the company; established standards, formats and processes which significantly improved quality and product image, reduced costs and earned national awards for the materials.

Director, Product Training & Support **(1987 - 1990)**
Responsible for providing all product training for clients and for SMS technical support personnel, plus all sales training for systems sales representatives. Defined and established all educational policies and procedures for internal and external representation.

- Proposed, planned and successfully managed transition of client training services from a cost-center to a profit center operation; annual revenue level exceeded $500,000 within three years.

- Designed and implemented centralized inquiry and enrollment system to streamline administrative processes; saw immediate payback in reduced costs and increased class attendance.

- Restructured Sales Training organization to streamline programs, reduce costs and focus industry-specific sales knowledge; resulted in improved sales-call success ratio and employee retention.

- Initiated standardized sales techniques training and first interviewing skills training for field sales organization.

UNIVERSAL SYSTEMS, INC. (Boston, MA)   **1979 - 1987**
An international organization which develops, manufactures, and markets computers, peripherals and communications systems and services to worldwide markets.

Manager, Client Educational Services **(1983 - 1987)**
Responsible for managing a staff of computer education specialists providing technical instruction for client and corporate personnel involved in the programming, operations, and installation activities of USI products and systems; responsibilities evolved from local line manager to functional direction for eight geographic centers.

Instructor, Marketing Educational Services **(1979 - 1983)**
Responsible for conducting computer systems classes for client and USI personnel; course content ranged from logic fundamentals to file design to languages and executive seminars.

EDUCATION

Drexel University, Bachelor of Science, Computer Science, 1979

RUSSELL W. GRANT

OBJECTIVE: Senior level Corporate Advertising position in a consumer products corporation or a major division, depending upon size of company and job content.

SUMMARY: Over thirty-six years of hands-on experience directing the planning, budgeting, media, production and control of Noxel's advertising.

EXPERIENCE:

1987 - Pres. **NOXEL, INC.** NEW YORK, NY

1995 - Pres. VICE PRESIDENT, ADVERTISING SERVICES
1992 - 1995 DIRECTOR, ADVERTISING SERVICES
Responsible for development, management and control of 42 brand advertising budgets totalling more than $70 million. Supervision of outside agencies and in-house agency planning and executing of print and broadcast media. Managed Noxel's in-house advertising agency. Responsible for the administration of the entire Advertising Department.

Major Accomplishments:

- Achieved significant prime positioning of company's advertising in major magazines and on network television.
- Produced all the *Charlene* fragrance and hair care commercials from the brands' introduction in 1992 until 1997. *Charlene* was world's #1 selling fragrance and country's #2 selling hair care product during that period.
- Conceived and implemented the first and only tie-in promotions with the Miss America Pageant beginning in 1994.
- Successfully negotiated more than 20 major super models/actresses/actors exclusive contracts. Worked with them and supervised the production of the advertising in which they appeared.
- Supervised a 16-person in-house advertising agency handling over half of company's annual media and production expenditures.
- Negotiated a significant reduction in agency compensation, saving $2 million a year.
- Managed and controlled all expenditures without ever exceeding a budget/forecast.

1990 - 1992 MANAGER, ADVERTISING ADMINISTRATION

Major Accomplishments:

- Coordinated media and creative presentations between agencies and marketing/sales personnel.
- Managed the entire advertising budget on a quarterly/annual basis, reporting regularly to senior management.
- Conceived and set up Noxel's in-house advertising agency in order to be more efficient and more responsive to specific brands.

RUSSELL W. GRANT   **PAGE TWO**

1987 - 1990   TELEVISION COORDINATOR

Major Accomplishments:

- Supervised the production of eight live television commercials a week on two different networks.
- Unified the television production work of five different advertising agencies under one direction, bringing order and cost control.

1980 - 1987   **GRANT ADVERTISING**   NEW YORK, NY

1983 - 1987   TELEVISION PRODUCER
Produced live commercials for beer, ice cream, luggage and health care products.

1980 - 1983   ASSISTANT TELEVISION PRODUCER
Arranged studio facilities and assisted in casting talent for television and radio commercials.

EDUCATION: **RUTGERS UNIVERSITY**
Bachelor of Business Administration, 1980

CONTACT: 2920 Merrick Drive   (516) 774-1951
Pittsfield, NY 10661

BARBARA A. ALTHOUSE

1201 Sunset Circle
Berkeley Heights, CA 89731
(810) 694-3020

SUMMARY

A results-oriented sales professional with experience in medical equipment and chemical product sales. Performance areas include sales and marketing, relationship management and staff training and development. Proven ability to select, develop and promote motivated employees within an organization. Consistent outstanding record of exceeding personal and corporate sales objectives. Awarded company's top sales award six times.

PROFESSIONAL EXPERIENCE

SMITHKLINE BEECHAM, Philadelphia, PA   **1984 - Present**
(A multi-division international pharmaceutical and chemicals company with sales of $5 billion.)

Regional Accounts Manager - West Coast   (1996-Present)
Responsibilities include all major accounts in Arizona, California, Washington and Oregon. Directed sales efforts for four different product areas - imaging systems, nuclear medicine, anesthesiology and catheterization - for selected institutions.

- Managed a business area and 12 regional sales specialists. Area had combined sales of $55MM.
- Liaison with national accounts buying groups, regional purchasing networks and hospital affiliated networks.
- Achieved top volume sales nationally out of 12 regions.

Regional Sales Manager - Imaging Systems   (1991-1996)
Responsible for imaging systems operations in the mid-west region, which had sales in excess of $25M. Geographic area included Wisconsin, Illinois, Michigan, Indiana and Ohio.

- Managed 14-person sales force whose responsibilities included both direct sales and sales through distributors.
- Grew the region assigned by approximately 150% over a five-year period. Sales grew from $10MM to $25MM.

Regional Manager - Imaging Systems   (1987-1991)
Managed the south-central region which consisted of Texas, Oklahoma, Arkansas and Louisiana. There were nine sales representatives servicing this area in 1987.

- Sold imaging systems products including cardiac catheterization equipment, chest x-ray units and ultra sound devices.

BARBARA A. ALTHOUSE   **Page Two**

Sales Trainer - Corporate Marketing   (1985-1987)
- Responsibilities involved training new sales people in all product groups sold by SmithKline Beecham.

Sales Representative - Imaging Systems   (1984-1985)
- Sold imaging systems to hospitals and clinics.

CHEMCO, INC.   **1982 - 1984**
(Manufacturer of biological reagents.)

Sales Representative

- Sold chemical reagents and chemicals to hospitals, independent labs and clinics. One of the top three producers out of the 35-person sales force in the country.

EDUCATION

B.S., Biology, Clemson University, 1982

COMPUTER SKILLS

- Microsoft Word
- WordPerfect
- Lotus Notes and E-Mail
- First Choice
- Microsoft Power Point
- Microsoft Access and Excel

NANCY R. TURNER

32 Windmill Road • Charlotte, NC 40334 • Telephone (701) 927-3433

PROFILE: Results-oriented General Manager with strong sales and marketing background. Demonstrated ability to build winning organization, establish trade relations with key customers and grow brands into market leaders. Recognized innovator with strong analytical and strategic planning skills.

PROFESSIONAL EXPERIENCE: THE BALDWIN COMPANY, Charlotte, NC (1995-Present)

Vice President, Sales & Marketing

Revived flagging $325MM franchise. Within six months, built strong sales and marketing ream, developed and implemented new advertising campaign, revitalized brand sales, and reorganized for market driven focus.

- Launched new product line, increasing retail sales 40% over test market.
- Directed and motivated 220-man, DSD sales force and distributor network.
- Improved media efficiencies 35% over previous year.
- Achieved $500MM annual savings on market research suppliers.
- Reduced days of supply and set program to eliminate short-dated inventory.

Direct Reports: VP Sales, Marketing Directors, Marketing Services, Public Relations, Shops and General Manager Canada/Mexico/Latin America.

WILSON LABORATORIES, Atlanta, GA (1979-1995)
Consumer Products Division

Vice President, General Manager (1992-1995)

Responsible for long-range strategic plan and short term operating results of $150MM consumer health products division.

- Increased division sales 15% over prior year.
- Increased division operating profit 19% over prior year.
- Successfully defended against competitive threat.

Direct Reports: VP Marketing, VP Sales, Market Research, Business Development, Training, Medical, Regulatory and Clinical Development.

Vice President, Marketing (1990-1992)

Responsible for strategic direction of all brands and new product development.

- Continued sales and market share growth on all key brands.
- Implemented new products program, including an Rx to OTC switch.

Direct Reports: Products Group Directors and Media Director.

NANCY R. TURNER

Product Group Director (1988-1990)

Responsible for all nutritional and OTC products.

- Launched Slim-Cal, achieving the second leading brand position in category.

Direct Reports: Product Managers and Assistant Product Managers.

Senior Product Manger (1987-1988)

Responsible for Slim-Cal, Vitatabs and Fibertabs.

- Turned around declining Vitatabs franchise into second leading brand in category.

Product Manager (1985-1987)

Responsible for Slim-Cal.

- Turned around declining Slim-Cal franchise into #1 brand in category.

National Sales Merchandising Manager (1984-1985)

Responsible for trade class specific programs.

District Sales Manager (1983-1984)
Coordinator, Sales Training (1981-1983)
Territory Sales Manager, Pharmaceutical Division (1979-1981)

EDUCATION:	**UNIVERSITY OF DELAWARE** B.S., Biology, 1979
EXECUTIVE EDUCATION:	**COLUMBIA UNIVERSITY** General Management (1979) Marketing Management (1986)
	DUKE UNIVERSITY General Management (1993)
	DARTMOUTH COLLEGE Marketing Management (1984)

JULIA B. STERLING
804 Brookthorpe Blvd.
Ocean Grove, CA 08135
(416) 694-3080, Fax (416) 872-2135

Results-oriented sales professional with proven record of success in route sales and account management. High energy, innovative, and self-directed marketer/salesperson with experience in large and small corporate environments. Seeking position in which I can use marketing, sales, and management skills to help a company grow.

SELECTED ACCOMPLISHMENTS

SALESPERSON/CUSTOMER LIAISON   1995-Present
Frito-Lay, Inc.

A $4 billion snack food corporation, largest such corporation in the world, employing approximately 50,000.

* Generated **over $350,000 per year** in sales by managing customer relationships and increasing shelf space and promotional efforts.

* Planned daily inventory, sales estimates, store displays, and relationship management for multiple store client base in fast-paced supermarket environment.

* Consistently **exceeded prior year sales** by 10% and sales projections by 3-4%.

* Received several **awards** for maintaining highest percentage above prior year in specialized promotions and overall sales performance.

* Trained prospective sales staff in techniques of sales and account management.

* Served as troubleshooter for accounts where problems developed, **saving division $175,000** in two years.

SALES/MARKETING REPRESENTATIVE   1993-1995
San Francisco Bottling Company

Soft drink bottling/distribution company employing approximately 200 in San Francisco area and serving large and small store customer base.

* Opened 24 new accounts within **first six months** increasing revenues by over $31,000 per year.

* Re-established/strengthened customer relationships and improved customer service increasing sales **in excess of 10%** over prior year for an average sized account.

Julia B. Sterling   Page Two

* Managed relationships with customers to **maximize growth** and product visibility.

* Developed **new marketing/sales strategies**, increasing shelf space and promoting product lines using a variety of techniques.

* **Attained or exceeded goals** in each period, significantly increasing overall sales over prior year.

MANAGEMENT TRAINEE/MACHINE PLACEMENT SALESMAN   1989-1993
Pepsi Bottling Company of San Diego

Division of second largest soft drink manufacturing company in the world with sales in excess of $7 billion.

* Placed 750 vending machines in previously untapped market sites, resulting in increased revenues of **$3.1 million per year.**

* Scouted territory, made cold calls, and followed up leads in new construction and office buildings.

* **Negotiated new contracts** for sale and lease of machines as well as ongoing service agreements.

* Planned for inventory use, possible sales, and revenues in preparation for calls in buildings where tenants were changing.

EDUCATION

San Diego State University, 1989
B.A., Marketing

FRITZ A. LUDWIG

1201 Lazy Lane   Home: (404) 492-6105
Stone Mountain, GA 40615   Office: (404) 493-8333

BACKGROUND SUMMARY

A creative, goal oriented Sales Manager with broad experience in the consumer products packaged goods industry. Successful in the analysis and planning needs for strategically developed business building programs. A history of progressively increasing responsibility for effectively managing personnel, operations and sales performance.

PROFESSIONAL EXPERIENCE

WAGNER FROZEN FOODS, Orlando, FL   **1992 - Present**
A $500 million frozen foods processor and marketing company.

Managing Director - Eastern Region (1994 - Present)

- Manage $230 million sales, marketing and customer support operation extending from Virginia through New England and New York State. Responsible for all business activities including P&L, systems support, financial reporting, logistics and personnel development.

- Developed regional strategies involving product mix, promotional spending and merchandising activities that exceeded profit objective by 4%. Region is the most profitable in the company ($132 million).

- Redesigned regional workforce into multi-functional core and dedicated customer teams in order to efficiently meet customer systems, research and product supply needs while designing and implementing profitable volume building promotional opportunities.

- Directed category management planning processes with our customers. Typical result was the implementation of a revolutionary "Store within a Store" program, strategically designed to attract retailer's targeted consumers of frozen meals. Increased weekly sales by 23%.

- Developed and delivered in-house software application training program in order to improve the effectiveness of a division wide roll-out of computers.

- Implemented cost containment measures to achieve savings of $1 million from a fiscal 1995 operating budget of $7.7 million. Identified further cost savings opportunities to produce a 1996 operating budget 11% lower than the 1996 actual spending (-$720,000).

<u>**Manager - Sales Development Group**</u> (1992 - 1994)

- Developed product variations targeted at wholesale membership club business. Involved in packaging design, pricing and business forecasting.

- Devised alternate promotional program on items to generate merchandising support through convenience store channels of distribution.

FORT HOWARD PAPER COMPANY, Green Bay, WI   **1987 - 1992**
A $1.5 billion manufacturer of consumer paper products.

<u>**Divisional Sales Manager**</u>

- Managed sales operation in seven state area including personal accounts and a three person sales team. Exceeded assigned sales quota every year.

- Secured new customers through cold calling, business analysis and demonstration of products and support benefits. New customer examples include Schnuek's Markets, St. Louis; Venture Stores, St. Louis; Dillons Supermarkets, Springfield, MO; Malone & Hyde, all divisions; and Wetterau, all divisions.

- Grew business base of existing customers through the development of strategically targeted line extensions.

SCOTT PAPER COMPANY, Philadelphia, PA   **1985 - 1987**
<u>**District Sales Manager**</u>

PROCTER & GAMBLE DISTRIBUTING COMPANY, Cincinnati, OH   **1983 - 1985**
<u>**Unit Manager - Coffee Division**</u>

EDUCATION

B.S., Economics, University of Cincinnati, 1983

INTERESTS

Athletics, Flying, Computers
Habitat for Humanity
Little League Coach
Sunday School Teacher

WILLIAM C. CAREY

102 Sutton Drive • Deerfield, MI 62150
(816) 924-0135

SUMMARY:

Fast track achiever in sales/sales management with 16 years experience in medical testing services and equipment. Extensive, in-depth expertise in medical technology and research including degree credentials and registration as Medical Technologist (ASCP). Proven leadership, organizational and communication skills with ability to sell both services as well as products.

PROFESSIONAL EXPERIENCE:

BAXTER HEALTH CARE CORPORATION - Deerfield, IL   **1996 to Present**
National Accounts Manager, Testing
Responsible for the consultative sale of clinical laboratory and substance abuse testing. Prepare proposals and presentations, bids and contracts. Present laboratory services to corporate medical personnel and other groups and individuals using various video materials.
Results:
- Focused on Fortune 1000 corporations as well as small and medium size private and public companies requiring NIDA and Forensic Drug Testing as well as clinical testing.
- Developed Michigan/Illinois area into a $1.6 million territory in two years for Industrial/Corporate Testing.

CARTER INSTRUMENTS - Indianapolis, IN   **1994 to 1996**
Territory Manager
Responsible for training of distributor representatives, as well as for direct sales of blood analyzer product line. Participated in distributor sales meetings, conventions and functions involving end-user relationships.
Results:
- Developed 12-state territory achieving 185% of quota in first six months.
- Established close working relationship with sales and management personnel of Medical Scientific, Inc.
- Successful in identifying key independent laboratory distributors in 12-state territory and negotiated contracts to sell new analyzer system to end-users.

CHEM-METRICS CORPORATION - Richmond, VA   **1992 to 1994**
Capital Equipment Representative
Sales specialist for the direct sales of chemistry analyzers in the southeast territory. Arranged and guided client tours and instrument demonstrations at corporate headquarters. Prepared presentations, competitive cost analyses and proposals for groups and individuals.
Results:
- Successfully introduced K-1, K-2 and R-4 Chemistry Analyzers.

WILLIAM C. CAREY

WELL-TEST, INC. - Atlanta, GA   1987 to 1992
District Sales Manager, 1990-1992
$8 million sales district. Responsible for all forecasted sales and management of district sales organization. Sold program for wellness testing at large corporations.
Results:
- Reorganized sales force with 35% new hires in one year.
- Implemented new training program focusing on account management, goal setting, feedback systems and educational meetings.
- Sales force achieved or exceeded quota each quarter.

Sales Representative, 1987-1990
Responsible for selling clinical laboratory testing to physicians, hospitals and researchers.
Results:
- Doubled Georgia territory sales volume in 18 months.
- Sales Representative of the Year, 1988.
- Ranked in "Top 10" sales performers and promoted to Sales Manager.

KLINE LABORATORIES - Greenville, NC   1982 to 1987
Medical Lab Technologist

EDUCATION:

GEORGIA INSTITUTE OF TECHNOLOGY - Atlanta, GA
B.S. Medical Technology (Honors), 1982

PROFESSIONAL MEMBERSHIPS:

American Society of Clinical Pathologists

KEITH F. FRANKLIN

1205 Warner Avenue
Allentown, PA 18266
(215) 425-6161 (H) or (215) 340-9010 (O)

Problem solving, top-performing, results oriented sales/marketing leader with ten plus years of comprehensive sales management, sales/marketing and operations experience...Spearheaded significant sales and profit growth, built strong teams, motivated employees, and initiated cost effectiveness programs...Hands-on manager with proven operations, P&L, start-up, business development and customer service achievements.

SELECTED CAREER ACCOMPLISHMENTS

SENIOR SALES MANAGER   **Service Concepts, Inc.**   **1992 - Present**

* Exercised complete sales, operational and P&L responsibility for a start-up service company.

* Increased sales from $0 to $1.5 million/annum, trained sales teams and cultivated partnerships.

* Opened key national accounts, led entry into new markets, built sales/marketing team, instituted strong customer service program and organized operational team.

* Instituted productivity improvement and cost reduction programs, subcontracted services and built working relationships with financial institutions, fleet leasing and insurance companies.

* Developed/implemented strategic and tactical business and sales/marketing plans.

REGIONAL SALES MANAGER   **Redmond Consulting Group**   **1983 - 1992**

* Built sales tenfold from $150,000 to $1.5 million/annum.

* Developed customer service/sales support teams and marketing infrastructure to support a $20 million business.

* Instituted business plans, established functional responsibility, directed supervisory team and managed three department heads with 40-50 employees and a sales team of seven.

* Developed/implemented flexible rate/pricing schedule and fostered cost effectiveness programs that saved more than 25%.

* Regional sales team ranked #1 or #2 based on highest percent of sales growth from 1987 to 1991.

SALES MANAGER   **Consolidated Insurance Co.**   **1981 - 1983**

* Built Life/Health Insurance sales force that increased sales revenues 40% in first year.

Other employment: Department Manager (Montgomery Ward), District Manager (Golden Petroleum)

EDUCATION

B.A., Business, Penn State University, 1980

WALTER F. THOMPSON
12 Logan Street
Fort Worth, Tx 09244
(209) 375-0928 Home
(209) 365-9031 Office

SUMMARY

A results-oriented professional sales and account manager with a proven track record managing national accounts in the plastic resin and plastic film industries for a major Fortune 100 chemical company and a regional plastic converting company. Key successes in penetration, issues/service management and developing new business and increasing market share.

PROFESSIONAL EXPERIENCE

POLY-PAC CORPORATION - Dallas, Texas   **1996-Present**

General Sales Manager - Films Division
Responsible for the marketing plan, sales implementation and consumer base for the films division of a newly-organized polyethylene plastics operation.

- Directed all management efforts to establish the creation of a new polyethylene film division including resin selection, quality control parameters and equipment utilization.

- Grew the film customer base from 0-31 customers taking them from development status to commercial status in the first year of operation ($6 million sales).

- Generated new business opportunities in the second year which increased business by 150%.

E.I. DuPONT COMPANY, Wilmington, Delaware   **1979-1996**

Account Manager - Philadelphia, PA   1991-1996
Responsible for $40 million polystyrene and polyethylene film territory managing the business issues and relationship with the largest distributor ($12 million) of polystyrene film sold into the envelope window market and increased direct sales of specialty polymer film products in the Northeast region.

- Exceeded sales plan in 1992, 1993 and 1994 by 8-10% per year.

- Initiated and managed a Quality Task Force utilizing the Continuous Improvement Process to improve product quality - reducing returns from 2.8% to .3% with annual savings of $250,000.

- Instituted and chaired an innovative "make and hold" program to overcome lengthy lead time problems generating 100% supply positions at three major olefin film customers and an additional $400,000 in sales revenue per year.

- Reduced collection time of past due receivables saving over $500,000 annually.

Walter F. Thompson   Page 2

Account Manager - Detroit, MI   1987-1991
Responsible for $35 million sales territory, managing the largest DuPont polyethylene account in the disposable film market and increasing sales volumes of resins at major extrusion and molding accounts.

- Negotiated and signed a three-year, $40 million contract at the largest disposable film account under extreme competitive pressures producing 20% additional sales volume and limiting competitor participation.

- Initiated relationship; focused on technology fit; and closed sale to a new injection molding customer leading to $25 million sales in four years.

- Sold a specialty food packaging account generating $3 million of new business in the first year.

- Exceeded sales plan in 1987, 1988, 1989 and 1990, earning sales achievement and cash awards.

Senior Sales Specialist - Philadelphia, PA   1980-1987
Responsible for polyolefin, polystyrene, and engineered resin sales to new and developmental accounts in the Ohio, Pennsylvania and New York areas and New England States.

- Generated $1 million per year in new business from a new specialty blow molding account.

- Managed a new product introduction at a specialty roto molding account yielding $3.2 million of new business over three years.

- Grew territory sales volume 120% in six years.

Sales Representative - Philadelphia, PA   1979-1981

EDUCATION

Bucknell University (1979)
Bachelor of Business Administration

PROFESSIONAL AFFILIATIONS

Member S.P.I. (Society of Plastic Industries)
Member S.P.E. (Society of Plastics Engineers)
Committee Member EMAA (Envelope Manufacturers Association of America)

WAYNE L. LUTHER
22 Ridge Road
Fullerton, California 08622
(416) 692-4102

SUMMARY

Accomplished sales executive with 12 years of experience in managing, selling and marketing with food service companies in a high profile role directing the sales success of an organization. Previous background includes both operational and sales management in the Food Service Industry.

PROFESSIONAL EXPERIENCE

1996 to Present   SPECIALTY FOODS, INC., Los Angeles, California
A $120 million international manufacturer of specialty foods and food ingredients.

Vice President - Chains
Developed and led the first national account sales effort for the company. Report to the Senior Vice President, Marketing & Sales. Responsible for $2.1 million sales budget which contributed 20% gross profit for the company, selling specialty foods and seasonings.

- Instituted sales and marketing program directed towards national account business which successfully sold 15 major national restaurant chain accounts within the first two years.
- Grew the department's sales from start-up to $1.4 million in four years, contributing $350,000 in company profits.
- Trained and directed the chain account efforts of the 53 Regional Sales Managers. In the first two years, company added 12 new regional chains increasing annual sales by $750,000.
- Developed national account marketing and promotional programs which stimulated the addition of seven national account purchasing contracts. These contracts added $500,000 in sales annually at a gross profit of $125,000.

1994 to 1996   WALDEN FOOD PRODUCTS CO., Atlanta, Georgia
$90 million manufacturer and distributor of gravies, sauces and food seasonings.

Vice President, Sales & Marketing
Responsible for sales budget of $90 million dollars, $14 million in profits; managed staff of six Regional Sales Managers and three R&D scientists. Reported to the President.

- Directed team which developed 20 new products to be sold to food companies. These new items achieved $2 million in sales within first two years.

- Increased sales volume by 20% the <u>first</u> year through a revamped outside sales force. This $18 million increase exceeded the first year sales budget and returned $2.7 million in profit.
- Successfully led the first focused national account sales effort, selling $4 million to six national accounts. This generated $600,000 gross profit.

1986 to 1994   PILLSBURY FOOD SERVICE COMPANY, Minneapolis, Minnesota
A $200 million subsidiary of the $4.5 billion Pillsbury Company which manufacturers and sells ready-to-eat convenience foods to the food service industry.

Director of Chain Sales   1990-1994
Managed eight Regional Account Executives; three Marketing Professionals; four Research and Development Scientists. Reported to Vice President of Sales & Marketing. Sold wide range of ready-to-eat cereals and convenience foods (i.e., waffles, sauces, gravies, food bases, etc.) to large national restaurant and food chains.

- Reorganized and restructured the national account department to be "account targeted". Increased sales from $30 million to $65 million in three years.
- Developed first multi-functional business team (Sales, Marketing and Research & Development) devoted exclusively to the growth of National Account sales. This change allowed National Account sales to grow by $25 million in three years.

Regional Sales Manager - West   1989-1990

District Sales Manager   1987-1989

Sales Representative   1986-1987

EDUCATION & AFFILIATIONS

B.A. - Business Management, University of Wisconsin, 1986

Completed numerous IFMA workshops and seminars on management, selling (Development & Managing Brokers; Developing a National Account Department); segment sales courses. How to sell different sales segments such as: mid-size chains; growth chains; contract feeders; specialty chains; Cash N' Carry.

SALES AWARDS

- Regional Sales Manager of the Year, 1989, 1990
- District Sales Manager of the Year, 1988
- Sales Rookie of the Year, 1986

TYLER W. BRADLEY

814 Bay View Drive
Portland, ME 02166
(605) 433-9172

OBJECTIVE

Senior management position requiring international sales and marketing expertise.

SUMMARY

Fifteen plus years of increasing responsibility in sales, marketing and general management.

- Extensive multi-national experience
- Strong leader and team builder
- Strong technical background
- Expertise in licensing joint ventures and start-up operations

EXPERIENCE

VACU-PUMP, INC., Portland, ME   1995 - Present
$65M U.S. manufacturer of industrial pumps for the rubber, petrochemical and plastics industries with manufacturing operations in the U.S. and Germany and sales offices worldwide.

Director, International Sales
Report to Vice President - Sales & Marketing. Responsible for managing and growing business for the Corporation in the Pacific Rim (Latin and South America, the Far East/Asia-Pacific).

- Established and managed international sales management and coordination department at corporate headquarters.
- Restructured international field sales organization for Far East and Latin America. Reorganized and relocated Vacu-Pump Asia from Hong Kong to Singapore. Staffed and managed Vacu-Pump Asia, a sales/marketing company for the Far East and Asia.
- Increased new equipment sales from $6M in 1995 to $20M in 1992.
- Restructured/managed sales representative network for the Americas and Asia Pacific. Personally led breakthrough in Far East by winning contracts in petrochemical, plastics and rubber sectors. Negotiated major contracts in China, Taiwan, Korea, Thailand and Mexico.
- Concluded license arrangement with Westinghouse joint venture for pump repair and overhaul in Singapore.

INDEPENDENT CONSULTANT   1993 - 1995
Awarded contracts in defense, aerospace and industrial markets sectors in U.S. and Europe.

TYLER W. BRADLEY   Page Two

WARNER CONTROL SYSTEMS, Boston, MA & Berlin, Germany   1990 - 1993
Division of Warner Technology, a $500M U.S. manufacturer of computer control systems for the industrial, defense and aerospace markets with manufacturing operations in the U.S., U.K., Germany, France and Japan.

Director, International Sales, Warner Control Systems and General Manager, WCS AB
Reported to President. Responsible for managing and growing business worldwide.

- Restructured international organization. Created, staffed and managed WCS, a sales/ marketing company for Europe, Africa and Middle East. Achieved 78% sales growth to $32M between 1990-1993. P&L responsibility for WCS.
- Personally led breakthrough of in-tech product line by wining contracts with aircraft OEM's in Italy, India and France. Negotiated five major aerospace contracts.
- Established/managed sales network for Pacific, the Americas and the Far East.
- Restructured European organization in 1992 to be consistent with new management's philosophy.

POWER DYNAMICS, INC., Boston, MA   1985 - 1990
U.S. manufacturer of industrial gas turbine power and compression systems for the oil/gas, petrochemical and industrial markets.

Director of Engineering Services

- Recruited to develop and manage all technical functions in major expansion of company activities in Europe. Reported to Vice President and Managing Director.
- Established/staffed technical group engineering, project management and procurement.
- Won/completed two major turnkey projects ($40M) in Sweden, Germany and the U.K.

STONE & WEBSTER ENGINEERING, Boston, MA   1982 - 1985

Project Manager

EDUCATION

BSME, University of Massachusetts, 1982

LANGUAGES

Fluent French and German; Knowledge of others.

DONNA T. SCHULTZ
12 Duckling Road
Cortland, NY 12906

Home: (315) 286-4407   Office: (315) 386-9162

SUMMARY

Experienced sales professional with 16+ years of proven performance selling to industrial distributors.

- Hiring & Training
- End-user Penetration
- Evaluating, Local Markets

- New Product Introductions
- Local/National Marketing Programs & Promotions
- Competitive Analysis & Sales Strategies

PROFESSIONAL EXPERIENCE

CORTLAND PAINT & CHEMICAL COMPANY   **1980 - Present**
Industrial chemical and paint manufacturer with annual sales of $135 million.

Director of Industrial Sales (1994-Present)
Sell complete line of industrial paints (both aerosol and bulk), electronic coatings and specialty products with sales of $85 million. Manage national sales manager, three national account managers, three regional managers and 25 manufacturer's reps. Products sold through 900 industrial, contractor and specialty distributors.

- Increased sales 15% in 1996 and exceeded all budgeted goals on top and bottom line, as well as reducing selling expense. Increased sales 10% in 1995.
- Combined the selling of Easy Way and Spread Right from two rep forces to one allowing greater opportunity for distributor to consolidate product lines.
- Negotiated exclusive membership with large independent contractor marketing group, increasing sales from $500,000 to $1.6 million.
- Negotiated exclusive agreement with West Coast Distributors overcoming competition from RustOleum. Projected 20% sales increase with members and growth of business from $750,000 to $5+ million over a two year period.
- Developed special incentive structure for manufacturers reps by combining financial and sales recognition award, which increased enthusiasm, motivation and fostered a 20% sales growth for 75% of reps.

Manager of Sales & Marketing (1990-1994)
Managed sales and marketing functions worldwide.

- Introduced first international sales meeting with classroom breakout sessions for training and developed forum for the exchange of information between sales force and top management.
- Introduced new line of mold inhibitive paint called Clear Flow. Sales grew to $2 million in three years.

DONNA T. SCHULTZ   *Page Two*

- Introduced new rust inhibitive chemical intermediate achieving sales of $4 million in first year.
- Launched new line of environmentally safe mold release intermediates that grew business to $3.2 million over a three year period.
- Marketed and negotiated exclusive rights for sale of a paint mixing system. Sales grew to $2 million at 30% gross profit in first year.

National Sales Manager (1986-1990)
Grew sales through industrial distributors using three regional managers working, closely with manufacturer's reps. Worked closely with marketing to assist in relabeling, cross reference charts, fine-tuning sales/policies and timely promotions on key products.

- Increased sales 32% in 1989 and all regional managers and national sales manager won the President's Circle Excellence award.

Regional Sales Manager (1985-1986)
Managed $3 million in sales and $3.1 million in regional manufacturing sales.

- Established network of 12 master distributors resulting in increased sales of 35% annually since 1986.

Regional Sales Manager (1983-1985)
Managed $1.2 million, one direct sales rep, and ten manufacturing reps covering three territories.

- Received award for largest dollar gain in 1984.

Inside Sales (1980-1983)
Worked closely with manufacturing, technical and outside sales as well as assisting industrial distributors.

EDUCATION & TRAINING

B.A., Marketing, S.U.N.Y. - 1979

HOWARD F. KAUFMAN
1240 Valley Stream Road
Detroit, Michigan 82142
(313) 695-0871

OBJECTIVE: A position in Product/Brand Management or Marketing

SUMMARY: Six years Marketing and Sales experience in the consumer product industry. Expertise in marketing research, competitive and trend analysis, merchandising strategies, category management and new product launches. A track record of growing market share and sales volumes with focus on the most profitable items.

EMPLOYMENT HISTORY:

National Foods, Inc.
Sales Accountant Representative, Brewmaster Coffee Division   1995 to Present
Manage accounts generating $30 million in annual sales. Responsible for increasing distribution points, sales volume and profit margins. Manage $250,000 merchandising budget. Supervise two field assistants.

- Grew market share 38% in the first three quarters of new product roll-out. Directed a market research program that resulted in the highest district rate of growth.

- Doubled annual growth rate of Brewmaster flavored coffees by introducing special packaging and shipper programs. Improved product loyalty and recognition.

- Increased category sales 20% and product turns 20% for a major retail chain.

- Focused merchandising dollars and marketing campaigns on the most profitable brands. Resulted in 20% sales increase of products with a 30% or higher profit margin.

- Introduced eight new items in one year through effective business planning and strong customer relations. Held the highest rate of new item introduction in the district.

- Provided quarterly volume estimates for production planning. Consistently proven accurate within 3-5%

Field Merchandiser   1992 to 1995
Developed and sold account programs and designed shelf layouts for 75 stores in the Cleveland territory. $1 million annual sales.

- Ranked #1 in the district due to superior display sales and in-store merchandising. Led to job promotion.

Howard F. Kaufman   Page 2

American Home Food Products, Inc.
Field Merchandiser   1989 to 1992
Introduced and sold consumer packaged goods in the Chicago market. Coordinated sales promotions, analyzed competitive products and promotional materials.

EDUCATION:

M.S. - Organizational Management (GPA 3.79), 1989
Penn State University
Masters Thesis - Total Quality Management

B.S. - Business Administration/Marketing, 1987
Penn State University

PROFESSIONAL DEVELOPMENT PROGRAMS:

Negotiation Skills
Trade Promotions
New Product Launch
Product Development
Estimating
Cultural Diversity
Management Training

MARIAN F. CLARKE
144 Devon Road
Valley Forge, PA 19832
(610) 447-9283 Residence
(610) 386-4927 Business

PROFESSIONAL SUMMARY

Sales and Marketing Executive with strong leadership skills and track record of proven results. Twelve years of broad, in-depth experience in management, P&L, restructuring, team building, employee development and succession planning. Consistently exceed profitability, productivity and sales objectives.

PROFESSIONAL HISTORY

KAUFMAN TECHNOLOGY, INC., Valley Forge, PA   **1990 to Present**
A leader in the field of services and instrumentation for the biotechnology and medical markets.

Regional Director   **1996 to Present**
Responsible for all aspects of sales, service, local marketing, administration, office management and employee development. Accountable for $32 million in revenue and 75 employees. Full P&L responsibility.

- Highest sales growth in 1997/1998.

- Overall profitability/employee highest in corporation.

- Reorganized entire division into multi-functional work-teams, dramatically improving customer service quality and response time, and empowering employees to "take risks".

- Developed and implemented key programs in marketing and sales management resulting in increased business at targeted accounts. Key account business increase by 25%.

- Implemented targeted selection interviewing process.

National Sales Manager   **1993 to 1996**
Laboratory Automation Software Systems Division of Kaufman. Accountable for sales force, tactical marketing programs, promotional and advertising programs.

- Profit increase of 65%.

- Improved market share 10%.

- Headed task force responsible for 25% reduction in product development time.

- Promoted to Regional Director in 1996.

Continued...

MARIAN F. CLARKE   Page two

PROFESSIONAL HISTORY

KAUFMAN TECHNOLOGY, INC. (Continued)

District Sales Manager   **1992 to 1993**
Accountable for staff of 13 sales and support personnel and $6 million in revenue. Promoted to National Sales Manager of Kaufman subsidiary in 1993.

Sales Representative   **1990 to 1992**
Responsible for key accounts in New York area. Doubled territory revenue in 18 months. Promoted to District Sales Manager in 1992.

ORTHO DIAGNOSTICS   **1987 to 1990**
Medical supplies division of Johnson & Johnson, Inc.

Sales Representative
Consistently recognized in "Top Ten" of company. National "Sales Representative of the Month" three times.

EDUCATION

UNIVERSITY OF PENNSYLVANIA
Bachelor of Science - Biology, Chemistry - 1987

DREXEL UNIVERSITY
M.B.A. in process - 1995 to Present

REFERENCES

Furnished Upon Request

MICHAEL B. MacPHERSON
8211 Hastings Drive
Somerset, PA 19380
(610) 431-4055 (H)
(610) 431-0021 (O)

SUMMARY

Sales professional with the ability to communicate well with clients who are primarily sophisticated, well-educated and wealthy entrepreneurs, CEOs, doctors, lawyers and other executives, as well as those from other professions who are purchasing "big ticket" items.

WORK EXPERIENCE

Regional Sales Manager, Dream House, Inc., Philadelphia, PA   **1990 - Present**
Responsible for sales of pre-engineered, single family contemporary homes to a wide variety of affluent customers throughout Pennsylvania, New Jersey, Delaware and Maryland.

- Sold over 300 individually designed pre-manufactured homes for years on a 100% commission basis.

- Established trust, confidence and rapport with individuals and couples who were about to spend an average of $500,000 on a new single-family home -- their dream house.

- Marketing and sales strategies I developed in New Jersey were so successful over a five year period that my territory was split. I trained the new sales staff.

- First to market and advertise Dream House in major home shows throughout Pennsylvania and New Jersey which increased regional business by 25% annually. Emphasis on home shown was then duplicated in all other regions of the country at the insistence of the corporate marketing department.

- Designed custom contemporary single family homes as a modification of the standard architecture. this "Masters in Architecture through Experience" was achieved on my own (no-corporate training) by hard work and self-study.

Owner - Residential Painting and Home Repair Business, Scranton, Pennsylvania   **1987 - 1990**

Director - Scranton Youth Program, Scranton, Pennsylvania   **1985 - 1987**
Responsible for creation, organization and implementation of all youth commission programs. Responsible also for writing funding proposals to state and federal government agencies. Interviewing, employment of staff, community relations and solicitation of funding was part of the job.

EDUCATION

B.A.   Sociology, 1983, Plymouth University, Laconia, New Hampshire
M.Ed. Psychological Services, 1985, Westminster College, Westminster, Massachusetts

OTHER ACTIVITIES

State of New Jersey, Racquetball Champion, Singles, 1995
East Loveland Township Recreation Commission, Planning Committee

CATHERINE B. SIMON
5121 Paxon Chase
Malvern, PA 19433

Home: (215) 955-0978   Office: (215) 934-7040

OBJECTIVE

A position in healthcare field sales that allows me to take advantage of a successful career in Customer Service

PROFESSIONAL EXPERIENCE

CENTURY HEALTHCARE, Blue Bell, PA   **1991 - Present**
Scientific Products Division

Customer Support Supervisor   1996 - Present
Report to Area Customer Service Manager with responsibility for coordinating activities of seven Customer Support Representatives handling $4.9 million in capital equipment purchases, $7 million in sales contracts, $7 million of Century's Quality Assurance Program (QAP), and $10 million in vendor rebates.

- Responsible for selection and training of all department members.
- Developed a protocol that increased customer phone service levels by 30% within twelve months.
- Ongoing program implemented to reduce QAP inventory write-offs.
- Decreased department operational overhead by 14% within six months.
- Direct multi-functional interface with Sales, Sales Management, Area Vice President, Marketing, Finance, customers and Manufacturing.
- Instrumental in assisting with the consolidation of the New Jersey and Pennsylvania regions.

Capital Equipment Coordinator   1995 - 1996
Pioneered new position within Scientific Products Division. Responsible for all capital leases and purchases in the northeastern region totaling $5 million annually.

- Implemented new lease control system. This approach was adopted by Scientific Products nationwide.
- Developed program to consistently implement price increases of all lease agreements. This was also adopted by Scientific Products nationwide.
- Coordinated equipment shipment and installation with both field sales and customers.
- Trained sales force throughout northeast region on capital equipment leasing procedures.

Customer Service Representative   1991 - 1995
Coordinated activities for key accounts in greater Philadelphia area involving 80,000 products.

- Directly handled orders and special pricing for accounts generating annual revenue of $12 million dollars.

CATHERINE B. SIMON   **Page 2**

- Direct responsibility for Abbott Laboratories, the largest reference lab in the northeast.
- Voted Employee of the Quarter for Eastern Regional Office.

DIAGNOSTICS LABORATORIES, INC., Wayne, PA   **1989 - 1991**

Customer Service Representative
Managed 200 accounts for manufacturer/distributor of medical instruments and supplies.

- Duties expanded to include 40 home dialysis patients by monitoring inventory of supplies.
- Additional responsibility added to include inventory management for Wilmington, DE distribution center.
- Participated in the training of new employees.

DUNHILL-BUSH, INC., Falls Church, VA   **1988 - 1989**

Product Controller/Expeditor
Developed work order schedules for parts and materials for manufacturer of Heating, Cooling and Refrigeration units. Expedited raw materials and forecasted completion date of finished goods to sales. Served as a liaison between management and production.

EDUCATION

Bachelor of Business Administration - 1988
ANDREW JACKSON UNIVERSITY, HARRISONBURG, VIRGINIA

BARBARA F. FLEGAL
Tower Place, Apt. 141-C
1015 Champion Drive
San Francisco, CA
(207) 246-1945 (Res.)
(207) 336-4210 (Bus.)

PROFILE:

Customer Service and Sales Manager with 14 years of varied experience with a major financial institution. Particular expertise in:

- Centralized customer service/staffing/phone volume management
- Training employees and monitoring results
- Quality control development and implementation
- Complaint management tracking and follow-up implementation
- Strategic business planning, budgeting and expense control
- Inbound Telemarketing/Sales

**PROFESSIONAL
EXPERIENCE:**

COMMERCE BANK, San Francisco, CA (1997-Present)

Assistant Vice President, Loan/Telemarketing Services
Manage staff of 16, personnel budget of $415,000. Direct phone volume tracking, full and part-time hiring, product and office equipment training, sales goal tracking, evaluation and incentive planning, and multiple telemarketing project implementation.

Selected Accomplishments:

- Successfully managed Loan/Telemarketing Unit that produced $65 million in booked credit outstandings through 1997. This produced $1.5 million in margin income to the bank.

- Created and trained a team of senior sales consultants to test telemarketing of a high-end specialized bank product to existing clientele. As a result of this test, the bank's multi-product customer base increased 20% when overall telemarketing was completed by branch personnel.

- Designed and implemented a monthly evaluation for all sales consultants which produced individual improvement prior to annual review and increased unit productivity.

FIRST CALIFORNIA BANK, San Francisco, CA (1985-1997)
Assistant Vice President, Centralized Customer Service (1991-1997)

Managed staff of 15, personnel budget of $350,000. Directed personnel hiring, customer service and sales skills training, bank product training, complaint management, development of quality control standards, and staffing in conjunction with phone/time management.

Barbara F. Flegal
Page Two

Selected Accomplishments:

• Utilized innovative hiring practices to create a quality team of customer service consultants to respond to the needs of both internal and external customers. As a result, this team consistently out-performed competitors in areas of customer service and sales, as measured by an independent Customer Service Shopper's Study.

• Expedited new employee training by creating a "mentoring" program and developing a self-taught training manual. These techniques increased trainee confidence and enabled them to assume customer service responsibilities faster.

• Successfully developed and implemented career pathing within unit. This innovation coupled with creative staffing led to a turnover percentage of under 2%, well below the customer service industry average. Overtime expense was also eliminated.

• Created quality control standards to enhance service provided to internal and external customers. This reduced errors in work forwarded to other units.

• Created a management process to follow up on customer complaints. The utilization of this process enhanced the customers' image of First California Bank.

• Successfully controlled expenses within planned budget allocations throughout the history of the unit.

Assistant Vice President, Banking Officer, Teller (1985-1991)
Various staff sizes and asset, liability and personnel budgets. Directed teller operations, training of tellers and platform personnel, audit controls, customer servicing, budget control, new business planning, staffing, and marketing and sales objectives throughout the retail branch system.

EDUCATION: California State University, San Francisco, CA
B.A., Accounting, 1984

American Institute of Banking
Principles of Banking, Commercial Law, Marketing and other courses

PROFESSIONAL   Power and Influence   Performance Appraisal Development
DEVELOPMENT   Effective Business Writing   Coaching and Counseling
COURSES: Interviewing Skills   Interpersonal Relationships
                      Sales Management   Customer Service Management

ALAN J. DOUGHERTY
380 NW 14th Street
Norwalk, CT 74355
(203) 668-7201

SUMMARY

Professional with 20 years of management experience in bringing state-of-the-art high tech products to national and international markets. Broad experience in program/project management, marketing, merchandising, development engineering, manufacturing, financial analysis and operations management. Exceptional communication, interpersonal and leadership skills. Excellent background in staffing professional teams, OEM, trade shows, foreign negotiations, semi-conductor process/manufacturing, equipment and tool design.

PROFESSIONAL EXPERIENCE

AMERICO COMPUTER CORPORATION, Norwalk, CT   1978-Present

OEM PROGRAM MANAGER/SENIOR PLANNER   1997-Present
Developed OEM executive accounts; negotiated comprehensive technical requirements and developed non-Americo logo solutions. Negotiated OEM contracts; provided lines of delivery to meet supply/demand, manufacturing and delivery. Developed a working team to assure customer quality and satisfaction.

- Planned and implemented the infrastructure for new OEM business opportunity within PC company which generated sales revenue of over $150M/per year.
- Established generic OEM contract that became corporate standard.
- Provided turnkey implementation for customer quality satisfaction while maintaining profit margins.
- Planned and implemented team building training sessions that formed a cohesive unit from teams located at four different geographic locations.
- Bid Manager for large airline account that resulted in millions of dollars of revenue.

PROGRAM MANAGER   1994-1997
Developed and implemented strategic direction that provided technical, marketing and merchandising assistance to all vendors developing Anstar hardware for PC systems. Managed over 25 trade shows worldwide and special events activities, planning, staffing, show venues, demonstrations, logistics and PR after show activities (Asia, Pacific Rim, South Pacific, Europe and Russia).

- Demonstrated to the industry that Anstar Architecture was a viable PC platform which generated a 10% increase in sales.
- Received Excellence Award.
- Planned, developed and implemented the infrastructure to technically support over 500 hardware developers of personal computer adapters/cards.

SENIOR ENGINEERING MANAGER   1992-1994
Managed project office team of professional engineers who provided design criteria to Americo-related products utilizing the PC as a development base. Also designed customized solutions to meet special bid requests for quotations from different industries.

- Developed and implemented requirements and specifications for innovative PC hardware technology.
- Negotiated multiple industry solutions and generated sales revenues in the multiple of millions of dollars.

- Implemented controls and processes which resulted in reducing turnaround time and increasing productivity.
- Managed R/3 development engineering project office for Model 3A; 3B; 3C; and 3D. Released from development engineering to manufacturing all systems within schedule and cost objectives.

LASER PRINTER DIVISION (LPD)
PRINTER MANAGER   1989-1992
Managed a $150M Personal Computer Printer Program with a team of 15. Responsible for worldwide profits, tactical/strategic planning, development engineering, quality and customer satisfaction.

- Directed technology development and financial requirements for PC printers, negotiated with vendors worldwide to establish the first vendor printer for PC usage within Americo.
- Succeeded in establishing LPD into a profitable PC printer business.
- Received Division Excellence Award.

VENDOR TECHNOLOGY   1986-1989
Directed worldwide off-shore development and procurement activities of products for early PC hardware development which incudes power supplies, motherboards, keyboards, displays and printers.

- Negotiated and contracted various products that established a savings of both dollars and resources in developing early PC hardware.
- Implemented the first vendor purchased products for internal PC hardware.

POWER-MISER DEVELOPMENT   1985-1986
Development Engineer responsible for mechanical design and implementation of power supplies.

SEMI-CONDUCTOR PROCESSING
EQUIPMENT DEVELOPMENT   1980-1985
Development/Manufacturing/Process/Equipment Engineer for semi-conductor devices.

- Co-founder of Americo Corporation's Contamination Control Committee which established clean room standards.
- Received Contamination Control Award.

Prior to 1980
Design Engineer/Quality Engineer

- Mechanical design engineer for upper atmosphere sounding devices (Government Contract).
- Mechanical design engineer for oceanographic calibration facilities and installation (U.S. Navy contracts).

EDUCATION

Columbia University, New York City, NY
Graduate Studies in Business and Finance

New York University, New York City, NY
B.S., Mechanical Design

KEVIN L. CARTER
80 Beasley Circle
Columbia, Maryland 90322
(202) 875-9052

EXPERIENCE

1996-Present   VICE PRESIDENT OF DEVELOPMENT - Martin Development Co.   Baltimore, MD
Responsible for: Management of 21-person Residential Development Department; work out of company's residential portfolio; entire development process through design, construction, marketing, sales and property management.

- Resurrected a $60 million, 650-unit golf course community.
- Settled a failed $12 million defaulted bond issue in Federal Court.

1992-1996   DEVELOPMENT MANAGER - Rancore Properties, Inc.   Washington, DC
Responsible for: All multi-family development, marketing, leasing, property management and asset management; all financial and feasibility analyses; selection of development team. Design sequence and liaison with construction management.

- Developed one of the finest institutional grade, 20-story apartment buildings in the DC area.
- Consistently leased above market rents for the residential and office component.

1990-1992   DIRECTOR OF DESIGN & CONSTRUCTION - Manheim Contractors   Baltimore, MD
Responsible for: Implementation of new project, site selection and master plan, pricing; contract control in selection of design team and general contractor; managing product design; project construction; leasing and property management support.

- Saved $18 per square foot during development of company's typical office product.
- Reduced the development schedule on each project by six months.

1986-1990   VICE PRESIDENT OF DEVELOPMENT - Bay Front Development   Essex, MD
Responsible for: Entire development process for $30 million of residential property; project viability, land acquisition, design, construction and permanent financing, marketing, sales and supervision of construction management.

- Obtained over $22 million in acquisition and construction financing in 18 months.
- Founded a real estate company, mortgage company, and construction division to maximize internal profits.

1982-1986   PROJECT MANAGER - Faulkner Construction Company   Baltimore, MD
PROJECT MANAGER - Essex Construction, Inc.
Responsible for: Construction of multiple retail projects from bid through completion; subcontractor and purchase contracts; cost control; liaison with developer, tenant, architect, and engineer; scheduling document submittal/approval.

- Simultaneously managed seven separate projects in three different states on-time and under budget.

EDUCATION

1982   B.S., Civil Engineering, North Carolina State University

DAVID W. LITTLE

911 Concord Way
Houston, TX 74136
(205) 951-4370

Results-oriented entrepreneurial leader with extensive experience in full service commercial real estate development and management. Certified Public Accountant/ CFO with successful track record in transaction structuring, acquisition, financing, asset management, investment maximization and rasing equity. Significant expertise as a growth strategist through the use of intensive management, building renovation/ expansion, financial structuring and opportunistic acquisition.

SELECTED ACCOMPLISHMENTS

Executive Vice President/CFO   **1990-Present**
Houston Ventures Management, Inc.

Founding principal of $215 million full-service real estate company providing property acquisition, management, leasing, asset management and management consulting services. Portfolio includes office buildings, shopping centers, apartments and industrial facilities.

* Structured real estate investment trust (REIT) including negotiation with investment bankers, overseeing audits on over 20 partnerships, and preparation of prospectus.

* Supervised management of 26 properties owned by Houston Ventures Management, resulting in annual revenues of over $24 million and attaining an occupancy rate of 94%.

* Renovated, repositioned and developed 20 properties.

* Created and developed accounting department, planning/implementing new systems and procedures as company grew.

* Developed and built seven projects, overseeing site acquisition, preparing bid packages, processing and verifying financial transaction during construction.

* Secured all financing for company and over 30 related partnerships, originating, negotiating and closing over $300 million in real estate debt.

* Negotiated and structured an innovative three year fixed premium on insurance policy, saving over $150,000 per year.

David W. Little   Page Two

Senior Vice President/Chief Financial Officer   1986-1990
Walden Partners, Inc.

Real estate acquisition and development company specializing in office buildings.

* Structured real estate syndications involving assets of $50 million, preparing prospectus for investors and closing transactions.

* Directed investments for personal trust funds consistently achieving a high level of return.

* Evaluated needs of accounting department and installed computerized account system, negotiating with vendors and providing for training for accounting staff.

Senior Accountant   1983-1986
Accountant   1982-1983
Price Waterhouse

A Big Six public accounting and management consulting firm.

* Implemented new inventory system for major retail client.

* Directed audit for firm's largest publicly held regional client.

EDUCATION/CERTIFICATION

University of Texas, 1982
Bachelor of Science in Business and Accounting

Certified Public Accountant

PROFESSIONAL AFFILIATIONS

American Institute of CPA's
Texas Institute of CPA's
International Council of Shopping Centers

VICTORIA A. STYER
12 Bay Vista Road
Berkeley, CA 90714
(206) 696-4071 (Res.)

SUMMARY: Take-charge sales management executive with 11 years of management and marketing experience in the full service brokerage, banking and public sectors. Successfully parlayed leadership/interpersonal skills into proven record of accomplishment. Particular areas of expertise include:

- Recruiting, training and developing sales teams that consistently exceed production objectives.

- Designing and creating strategically positioned branch office delivery systems.

- Improving customer service by managing development and deployment of innovative relationship-building strategies.

PROFESSIONAL EXPERIENCE: SAN FRANCISCO NATIONAL BANK, San Francisco, CA (1993-Present)

Vice President - Securities Marketing

Manage 18-member sales team responsible for the active distribution of a diversified investment product menu to clients and prospective customers throughout California. Sales credits increased 130% from $3.1M to $7.1M.

Selected Accomplishments:

- Motivated sales staff members to increase average individual sales performance by 200% from $120,000 in 1994 to $360,000 in 1995.

- Developed and delivered an extensive in-depth internal sales training program, which resulted in the complete acquisition of product knowledge and selling strategies for all new hires.

- Successfully implemented a marketing plan for the introduction of SFNB's California Tax Exempt Income Fund, which, since inception in 1993, has grown to over $60 million.

- Delivered frequent presentations to consumer bank employees to heighten awareness of products and services capabilities. Resulted in significant sales increases.

- Successfully diversified product menu by adding Brokerage Services and Collateralized Mortgage Obligations.

- Significantly expanded sales strategies and reduced dependence upon Tax Free Municipal Bonds as primary revenue source by more than 30% in four years.

Victoria A. Styer
Page Two

- Modified internal operating systems/procedures to improve cost effectiveness; enhanced distribution and customer response times.

- Worked with Office of Comptroller of the Currency and National Association of Securities Dealers to define impacts for federally mandated compliance requirements; directed company-wide implementation of new standards.

S.F.N.B. BROKERS, INC., San Francisco, CA (1989-1993)
Vice President - Sales Manager

Directly managed complete development of an eight-brokerage office system. Oversaw all phases which included: construction, outfitting, staffing, budgeting, and development/execution of each respective marketing plan.

SHEARSON LEHMAN/AMERICAN EXPRESS, San Francisco, CA (1986-1989)
Financial Consultant

Provided continuous Financial Management and Portfolio Analysis for a large retail and institutional customer base. Established customer's goals and objectives, then made appropriate product and service recommendations.

EDUCATION: B.A., Finance & Accounting, Oregon State University, 1986

Numerous financial services industry related conferences, seminars and workshops.

LICENSES: Series 7, National Association of Securities Dealers, General Securities Series 63, Uniform Securities State Law
Series 24, National Association of Securities Dealers, Principal
Series 53, Municipal Securities Rulemaking Board, Principal

JOAN A. SWANSON

1401 Lake Drive
Alexandria, VA 82751
(210) 642-9105

Results-oriented, entrepreneurial leader with proven record of success in start-up, turnaround and growth of profit centers. Skilled relationship builder/manager with extensive experience in rapid and sustained growth of fast paced, high pressure businesses. Major strengths include strategic planning/implementation, team building and development new market segments.

WORK EXPERIENCE

BRANCH MANAGER   1996-Present
American Financial Services, Washington, DC

Start-up manager for East Coast office of American Financial Services, one of the largest credit services in the U.S. with annual sales in excess of $400 million.

- Built east coast operation, hiring and training staff of 35 and producing annual sales **in excess of $90 million** within three years.

- Increased market share of First National Bank business from **5% to 50%**, or $2.0 million per month.

- Created innovative competition among collectors, leading first team to exceed Bank of Boston quota by **$30,000 in first month** of assignments.

- Developed and implemented call accounting software, causing **revenue increase of $150,000**.

- Developed office budget and achieved 10% profit by third quarter of operation.

ASSISTANT BRANCH MANAGER   1995-1996
Federated Credit, Inc., Philadelphia, PA

Promoted to help lead turnaround situation for branch office of large, privately-held collection firm with 10 branches and 260 employees.

- Increased branch revenue by **$150,000 per month in 60 days**, making profit for office for first time in six months.

- Recruited and trained personnel, increasing office staff by **50% in 60 days** and turning around morale to pave the way for increased business.

- Set up new system and developed guidelines for monitoring inventories on a daily basis, **increasing productivity** and speeding up collections.

Joan A. Swanson   **Page Two**

- Closed **over 48,000 files** which had been inactive to decrease backlog and focus office on most profitable business. Total review was accomplished within 20 days.

- Developed system to insure contract compliance, **increasing compliance rate to 99%** with CoreStates USA, leading to significantly higher collection rates and an increase in business.

NATIONAL OPERATIONS MANAGER/EASTERN REGION   1990-1995
Federated Credit, Inc., New York, NY

Primary responsibility included ensuring compliance with company policy by all branch offices in Eastern United States.

- Wrote/implemented weekly inventory tracking system which was reported to top management resulting in hiring of 30 new personnel and increase in **profitability to over 10%.**

- Streamlined monthly review process for senior management, decreasing report of essential information from **200 to 10 pages** and highlighting situations in which special attention was needed.

- Wrote new company training program and set up pilot training sessions which resulted in **25% increase** of average size of payment per collector.

EDUCATION

B.A., Accounting   1980
University of Rhode Island

VICTOR E. KENT
10 Winding Way
Cherry Hill, NJ 08432

(609) 642-1573 *(Home)*   (609) 852-1357 *(Office)*

SUMMARY QUALIFICATIONS

Senior financial services line manager with profit and loss responsibility. Significant results include sales increases, motivational speaking, profitability increases, cost containment, merger/acquisition search and completion and portfolio management. Wharton Business School MBA with Big Six experience.

PROFESSIONAL EXPERIENCE

AMERICAN NATIONAL BANK   **1995 - Present**

American National Bank acquired Farmer's Savings & Loan, (see below) at which time I was selected by the CEO to direct the group of banks. The acquisition represented 15% of the resulting company. Seven months later, I undertook three additional acquisitions, adding six banking facilities.

VICE PRESIDENT - REGIONAL SALES MANAGER

- Acquisition returned to profitability through operations in first year. Today, has the highest internal ROA of all regions.

- Changed operations to sell asset products through the individual banks.

- Consolidated three banking facilities, improving customer service and product delivery, and eliminated a production facility.

- Achieved product sales exceeding the historical sales records of the prior company with 50% of the personnel (150/300).

- Reduced personnel, eliminating duplicate functions and expanding the use of banking facilities.

- Performed individual and group sales training and instituted a value added sales program.

FARMER'S SAVINGS & LOAN ASSOCIATION   **1991 - 1995**

Recruited to this $400 million mutual savings and loan association. Attractive due to opportunity to succeed the CEO in a few years.

SENIOR VICE PRESIDENT - CHIEF FINANCIAL OFFICER

- Led capital acquisition search, resulting in four viable candidates and a definitive agreement in six months.

- Managed $100 million investment portfolio. Eliminated external manager and restructured portfolio, achieving yield targets and small trading gains.

- Implemented profitability and cost accounting system. PC-based, internally designed, fully allocated cost and revenue driven system.

- Prepared strategic plan. Identified cost reductions, revenue increases and capital concerns (pre-regulatory change).

VICTOR E. KENT
Page Two

AMERICAN NATIONAL BANK   1990 - 1991
Successor to First Savings of Georgia.

SENIOR VICE PRESIDENT - DATA PROCESSING

- Agreed to remain with successor to complete two primary objectives:

  - Determined data processing direction. Dissolved one major in-house data center and converted three separate companies to a single servicer. Company with servicer today.
  - Negotiated the sale/dissolution of a Florida joint venture. Recreated the financial records and rebuilt the data base. Locations were Orlando and Tampa, Florida.

FIRST SAVINGS OF GEORGIA   1989 - 1990

CHIEF FINANCIAL OFFICER

- Recruited as Vice President and Controller; made Chief Financial Officer within seven months.

- Negotiated sale of $2.1 billion stock savings bank to successor noted above in 1990. Sale precipitated by dissident shareholder actions. Return to shareholders exceeded 400%.

PRICE WATERHOUSE   1982 - 1989

SENIOR MANAGER - AUDIT

Audit clients included $3.6 billion multinational commercial finance company, $2.3 billion consumer finance company, commercial banks, other consumer finance, diversified holding company and foundry operations. Financial statements issued included annual reports, Forms 10 and various registrations under the 1933 and 1934 acts with respect to acquisitions and security issuances. Instructor for national and regional training and computer audit specialist.

PROFESSIONAL

CPA, State of New Jersey, 1982
Director, Pioneer Mortgage Service Company, 1989 - 1990
Director, PAR Leasing Corporation, 1989 - 1990

EDUCATION

MBA, Wharton Business School, 1982
BA, Penn State University, 1980

PHILLIP P. JESTER
12 Sea Spray Circle
Laguna Beach, CA 90725
Home: (414) 776-9041
Work: (414) 256-8400

Sixteen years managerial experience in retailing, marketing and operations. Responsibilities include: negotiation and acquisition of retail sites; divestiture of under-performing sites and management of service station chains. Five years experience as an officer and vice president serving on the Executive Committee which manages a company with $89 million in petroleum product sales and related services.

WORK STYLE

Entrepreneurial manager with a results-oriented philosophy. Team player with strong leadership abilities.

BUSINESS EXPERIENCE

1994 - Present   COASTAL PETROLEUM, INC., Los Angeles, CA
Vice President
Responsible for the overall management of 35 retail stations and eight franchised parts outlets with revenues of $80 million and 295 personnel. Executive Committee member involved in the management of the Company.

- Negotiated and acquired 29 retail sites in three states during a two-year period. Developed and implemented all operating policies and procedures.
- Improved profitability of the division through significant reductions in expenses and effective marketing strategies.
- Administered an $8 millon acquisition and capital expenditure budget. Created and implemented customer service and store level training programs.
- Reorganized division and introduced new positions and concepts to promote empowerment and reduce overhead.
- Improved sales and volumes by 80%.
- Increased the Division's cash flow by $60 million.

1985 - 1994   TEXACO, INC., White Plains, NY
Marketing Advisor (1992 - 1994)
Led the task force which developed an Automotive Parts Franchise Program for service station dealers.

- Conducted market and consumer research to assess industry direction.
- Developed standards for dealer enrollment.
- Determined training programs, nationwide warranty offer, program compliance <u>mechanism</u> and franchise fee structure.
- Recommended necessary organizational structure.

Phillip P. Jester   Page 2

District Manager (1989 - 1992)

Managed and operated 30 company-owned retail service stations with total annual sales of $95 million and a personnel complement of 230 employees. Duties included: evaluating and recommending investment decisions, setting retail prices, developing promotions and programs to stimulate sales, motivate employees, control expenses and improve customer service and store image.

- Significantly improved retail profitability through staff reductions, improved vendor contracts and other operational efficiencies.
- Developed major safety and employee motivation and recognition events.

Store Supervisor (1988 - 1989)

Managed seven Automotive Parts and Accessories Centers with annual sales of $18 million and 110 employees. Duties included monitoring accounting controls and procedures, administering personnel practices and developing programs and promotions for improving operating practices and employee productivity.

Marketing Analyst (1985 - 1988)

Evaluated and automated field and staff functions to improve productivity. Directed the design of a management information system for the West Coast marketing region.

EDUCATION

Boston University
M.B.A., 1985
Major: Management

University of Massachusetts
B.S., 1980
Major: Marketing

JUDITH D. BRIDGES
4035 Second Avenue, 106-B
New York, New York, 12109

Residence: (212) 648-9421   Office: (212) 641-8200

SUMMARY

Entrepreneurial success in retail merchandising, including design and product development, planning, marketing, implementation of programs and management. Exceptional problem solving, team building, communication, analytical, strategic planning and negotiation skills. Unique ability to bring people together for accomplishment of common goals and successfully exercise creativity in both merchandising and product development.

PROFESSIONAL EXPERIENCE

NORDSTROM, INC,   **1981 - Present**
Nordstrom East, New York, NY (1995 - Present)

Divisional Merchandise Manager
Responsible for planning, development, advertising and profitability of the Women's Sportswear and Cosmetics areas, which include: Clothing, Leather Goods, Handbags, Gloves, Perfumes and Cosmetics. Directly responsible for the 21 stores of Nordstrom East with volume in excess of $35 million.

- Expanded Liz Claiborne sportswear business from $2 million to $5.3 million while maintaining gross margin in excess of 50%.
- Refixtured the entire division with new fixtures from Liz Claiborne at no cost to the company, a savings of over $150,000.
- Created excitement and enthusiasm and increased sales by negotiating promotional appearances of several well-known celebrities.
- Promoted one buyer to store merchandise manager.

Nordstrom East, Falls Church, VA (1992 - 1995)

Merchandise Consultant
Responsible for the planning, development, sales promotion and profitability of Women's Sportswear. Supervised two buyers while simultaneously maintaining direct buying responsibilities for small leather goods. Directly responsible for annual volume in excess of $10 million.

- Expanded Liz Claiborne sportswear business from $500,000 to $1.5 million with no margin deterioration.
- Promoted three assistants to Group Sales Manager positions within one year and promoted one buyer to a senior-level buying position in Women's Accessories.

JUDITH D. BRIDGES   PAGE TWO

Buyer (1985 - 1992)
Managed the planning, development, acquisition, presentation, sales promotion and profitability for the Women's Shoe Department for Nordstrom's ten stores in the Northeast. Annual volume in excess of $4 million.

- Increased volume by over 250% while also maintaining a 250% increase in profits, making the department an important profit center at Nordstrom.
- Developed all private label programs covering five product labels in four major categories.
- Represented Nordstrom on a continuing basis in the Far East and Europe as a key member of their Product Development Team.
- Planned and implemented departments in four new Nordstrom stores and the complete renovation at 15 others.

Prior Buying and Management Experience

Nordstrom Northeast, Danbury, CT (1981 - 1985)
Progressed through Nordstrom's Training Program and held positions of: Junior Assistant Buyer - Women's Clothing; Sales Manager - Sporting Goods and Toys; Senior Assistant Buyer - Women's Robes and Loungewear, and Group Sales Manager - Women's Sportswear & Cosmetics.

EDUCATION

Bachelor of Science - Marketing, 1981
New York University

WILLIAM R. BASS
MOSCOW, RUSSIA - 212-636-9301 (U.S. MESSAGE SERVICE)

OBJECTIVE

A high-impact financial position requiring creative and innovative approaches to strategy development, problem solving, and achievement of business and financial goals.

CAREER SUMMARY

Advanced very rapidly to partner after only eight years with an international "Big 6" accounting firm, continuously operating on the leading edge of new practice areas and business trends, as exemplified by Russian assignment. Tax and business advisor with 16 years of heavy transaction-related consulting to rapidly growing businesses, from venture capital financed technology start-ups to large multinationals. Strong finance, accounting, and legal knowledge on many transactional issues has been a key contributor to success. Leader of national efficiency/ technology initiatives related to corporate tax return compliance practice.

BUSINESS EXPERIENCE

DELOITTE & TOUCHE   **1982 - Present**

PARMER, Tax Division - Moscow, Russia (1995 - Present)

Assumed responsibility for neglected, demoralized, and under-resourced tax practice comprised of eight professionals, six of which had less than six months tenure, and after seven recent terminations/departures, including predecessor.

- Achieved dramatic improvement in division profitability to $650,000 for FYE December, 1997 (after $150,000 loss for year of arrival). Profit level is fully costed, and after all partner distributions and expatriate allowances and costs. This was one of the higher profit levels in the worldwide tax practice on a per partner basis for the year.

- Built team, net of two more terminations, to 18 professionals by fall 1996, through internal and external recruitment.

- Dramatically improved client service capability, quality, and responsiveness and instituted intensive training program and recruitment effort.

- Quickly developed high degree of personal technical competence in Russian tax, accounting, legal, and business matters.

- Served over 100 clients from all over the world, including several Fortune 500 companies investigating expansion opportunities in Russia.

Repatriating February, 1998 to Dallas, TX to assume engagement tax partner responsibility similar to previous position in Chicago.

WILLIAM R. BASS....... Page Two

PARTNER - Chicago, Illinois (1990-1995)

Engagement tax partner on a variety of primary manufacturing clients providing comprehensive corporate, partnership, individual executive, and employee compensation tax consulting and compliance services, and representation in tax controversies before tax authorities. Clients served included major automobile manufacturers.

- Merger and acquisition coordinator for Midwest Region and member of firm-wide Mergers and Acquisitions Tax Specialty Team.

- Technical specialist in all aspects of LBO'S, tax-free mergers, divestitures, takeovers, bankruptcies, restructuring, golden parachutes, joint ventures, leasing, consolidated returns, and other transaction and capital structure related matters.

- Regular instructor at internal D&T training courses and partner/manager workshops on M&A.

- Sparked early roll-out of national efficiency program to introduce advanced software and reengineered methodologies to corporate compliance practice. Supervised final beta test sign-off by practice offices on internally developed corporate tax software.

- Participated on task force responsible for defining requirements for next generation corporate tax software and for developing the case and strategy for starting a new specialty line aimed at reengineering management practices, especially data management, in large corporate tax departments.

MANAGER - St. Louis, Missouri (1986 - 1990)

Joined Deloitte & Touche in 1982, advancing through several junior-level positions until making Partner in 1990.

EDUCATION

MBA, WHARTON BUSINESS SCHOOL, UNIVERSITY OF PENNSYLVANIA   **1982**
Finance concentration.

BA, ACCOUNTING, BUCKNELL UNIVERSITY   **1980**
- Graduated summa cum laude.
- Awarded Phi Beta Kappa.
- Passed C.P.A. examination upon graduation.

DARLENE A. HANSEN
1501 Clifton Circle
Norwalk, CT 80970
(203) 696-4082

EXPERIENCE:

ALEXANDER CONSULTING, New York, NY   **1995 to Present**

Lead Associate, Operations Management Group
Direct consulting engagements for various Fortune 100 companies in business strategy, business process re-engineering, strategic sourcing, manufacturing/operations strategy, distribution and logistics, strategy and product innovation/technology development.

- Led business re-engineering efforts in several diversified manufacturing, utilities and oil transport companies to streamline their manufacturing, distribution and customer service delivery processes resulting in $100 - $400 million in cost savings over 3-5 year periods.
- Rationalized order fulfillment strategy for a global pharmaceutical client resulting in 40% ($30 million) reduction in overall distribution costs in North America.
- Assisted a global energy and automation client in developing channel strategy and customer service improvement resulting in fewer product lines and 30% reduction in finished goods inventory.
- Assisted several key clients in developing and implementing Strategic Sourcing capabilities which led to $40 to $100 million in cost savings.
- Assisted a leading news and entertainment network in developing long-term technology strategy for global expansion.
- Assisted a building materials client with post-bankruptcy profit improvement strategy. Reduced corporate overhead by 50%, streamlined sales forces and manufacturing operations, resulting in $30 million annual cost reduction.
- Participated in due diligence effort which led to a billion dollar acquisition by a venture capital firm.

BASF CORPORATION, Parsippany, NJ   **1988 to 1995**

Manager, Business Analysis & Strategy Development
Reporting to the CFO, initiated and formulated annual strategic plan, product line P&L analysis, economic studies of major acquisition and capital investment and special projects in cost reduction, market expansion and new product development.

- Achieved strategic cost reduction of $6-10 million through shutdown of a major production facility, product redesign/positioning and usage of alternative raw materials in existing products.
- Counseled top management on strategic issues in product line profitability, competitive pricing and cost saving opportunities.

DARLENE A. HANSEN   Page 2

Manufacturing Manager
Reporting to Senior VP of Operations, formulated and implemented productivity
improvement strategies through (1) in-depth analysis of manufacturing productivity in 13
operating locations, (2) upgrading of manufacturing technology and (3) improving product
quality through increased employee involvement (EI), and statistical process control
(SPC). Position required hands-on factory floor involvement, supervision of multi-plant
activities and large program/project management.

COOPERS & LYBRAND, New York, NY   **1987 to 1988**

Staff Consultant
Managed project teams in developing innovative concepts and systems using state-of-the-
art technologies to improve mail coding, sorting and distribution of US Postal Service.

WESTINGHOUSE ELECTRIC CORPORATION, Pittsburgh, PA   **1984 to 1987**

Project Engineer/Design Engineer
Conducted engineering design works and testing, contract negotiations, vendor selection
and qualifications and project management for mass transit systems in New York City,
Washington, DC and San Francisco.

EDUCATION:

THE WHARTON SCHOOL, University of Pennsylvania, Philadelphia, PA

Master of Business Administration   **1990**
Major: Finance and Operations. Minor: Strategic Planning. Tutored undergraduate
students and worked on research projects on distribution and market research with
Wharton faculty to support family.

MASSACHUSETTS INSTITUTE OF TECHNOLOGY, Cambridge, MA

Master of Science in Mechanical Engineering   **1984**
Specialized in Automation, robotics and human factor studies. Member of Graduate
Student Council.

Bachelor of Science in Mechanical Engineering   **1982**
Specialized in combustion engineering and control theory. Minor: Economics. Member
of national honor societies - Tau Beta Pi and Pi Tau Sigma. Completed degree in 3 years
and was in the top 1% of class.

CAROLYN A. BARLOW
309 Brighton Street
Alexandria, VA 18392
(704) 875-9135

Results-oriented, self-motivated leader with proven record of success in direct marketing and tele-communications. Recognized manager/team builder and strategic planner with significant P&L responsibility. Extensive experience formulating and implementing policy for fund raising offices serving multiple, diverse client base.

AREAS OF EXPERTISE

Team Building   *Fund Raising*
Strategic Planning   *Personnel Development*
Relationship Management   *Cost Control*
Marketing/Telemarketing   *Innovative Product Development*

SELECTED ACCOMPLISHMENTS

Manchester Consulting Group, Inc.   **1992 to Present**

A political management consulting firm providing business services for non-profit, grassroots environmental and consumer organizations. Services include political consulting, fund raising, list management and development, market research, public education, layout, design, and printing.

DIRECTOR   1996 to Present

- Turned around declining consulting operation with diminishing client base, restructuring operations and implementing plans for potential client growth to make office profitable.

- Cut expenses 15% in $500,000/annum office, reducing payroll from 40% to 303% of revenues and increasing productivity an average of 25% per canvasser.

- Organized/maintained ongoing relationships with entire client base which included weekly client briefings, special liaison relationships, and development of innovative programs for membership management.

- Built and supervised teams in 20 person staff which carried out fund raising and delivery of services to clients, significantly raising morale and increasing employee retention rate.

- Organized/implemented special membership development projects including targeted legislative action alerts, newsletters, and other campaign support.

- Researched/recommended and negotiated deal for state-of-the-art automated call management system which keeps records up to date and helps direct all list management and fund raising efforts for multiple client base.

- Recruited, trained, and developed potential staff leadership. Responsible for growth and promotion of two of MCG's highest rated supervisors.

Carolyn A. Barlow   Page Two

Manchester Consulting Group, Inc. (cont'd)

Promoted within 18 months from Fund Raiser.

MANAGER OF FUND RAISING   1993-1996

- Led office to growth of over $800,000 in two years.

- Designed/implemented program of list management and growth for company, achieving $9.50 return per name in market where average is $3.00 per name.

- Trained/supervised staff of 18 canvassers in telemarketing skills, motivating fastest growing office in company to reach highest profits ever.

- Researched and implemented Tele-Direct CAT and EISI Call Management System serving entire client base.

- Created cold calling and direct mail campaign for Friends of the Philadelphia Zoo, resulting in growth from 1,500 to over 9,000 pledged annual contributors in 18 months.

FUND RAISER   1992 - 1993

- Received award for outstanding fund raising results in 1992.

- Developed membership for Crime Victims Association, increasing their overall size by 40% and their revenues by over $1.2MM in one year.

- Planned/conducted numerous public education events and legislative action alerts on behalf of clients in seven states.

- Served as liaison between client and Manchester Consulting, preparing updates on political and legislative activities and other relevant information.

- Traveled extensively to client locations as troubleshooter, fund raiser, and trainer. Built staff in three client-based offices.

EDUCATION

M.B.A., Marketing   1992
Oklahoma State University

Bachelor of Science, Marketing   1990
Oklahoma State University

CONWELL LEINBACH
1533 Gristmill Drive
Scranton, PA 17344

610-933-8131

EDUCATION

M.B.A., Penn State University (1976)

B.S., Business Administration, Cornell University (1974)

EXPERIENCE

UNIVERSITY OF SCRANTON - Scranton, PA   (1994 to Present)

CHAIRMAN - DEPARTMENT OF BUSINESS ADMINISTRATION. Responsible for curriculum development, faculty evaluation, community relations and budget supervision. Taught upper level undergraduate/graduate management and marketing courses including: Strategic Management, International Marketing, Human Resources Management, Marketing Management, Production Management, Sales Management, Labor Relations, Marketing Research, International Business and Advertising.

- Developed M.B.A. degree program.
- Provided consulting and implemented specialized training programs to assist local businesses.
- Revised undergraduate business program.
- Recruited faculty.

WELDON INDUSTRIES - Utica, NY   (1992 to 1994)

PRESIDENT of a $20 million manufacturer of industrial equipment. Full profit and loss responsibility for all phases of corporate operation, including: marketing/sales, engineering, accounting and manufacturing. Formulated corporate policy and instituted strategic planning. Installed three-year and annual business plans with budget. Introduced Management-By-Objectives program. Implemented a new product development plan. Initiated sales training. Developed Zero Defects program. Eighty-six person, two plant organization. Staff directly supervised: Vice-President of Marketing/Sales, Vice-President of Manufacturing, Controller and Director of Engineering as well as Legal Counsel and Advertising Agency.

- Introduced the first sales and labor forecasting system.
- Designed a marketing program for manufacturers' representatives, which increased sales 15%.
- Initiated control programs resulting in 10% reduction in inventory levels.
- Developed completely new product.

ROME MANUFACTURING, INC. - Rome, NY   (1988 to 1992)

PRESIDENT of an $8 million manufacturer of capital equipment. Directly responsible for corporation, including manufacturing, sales/marketing, finance, engineering, and accounting. Instituted long-range planning. Developed annual and five-year business plan and budget. Formulated policies and objectives. Designed detailed action plans for all elements of the business. Developed corporate organizational structure. Created a management development program to meet projected needs. Directed the evaluation of acquisitions. Total number of personnel under direction, approximately 125. Directly reporting: Director of Sales/Marketing, Director of Manufacturing, Director of Finance, Director of Engineering, Legal Counsel and outside Auditors. Also various consultants.

CONWELL LEINBACH   (2)   RESUME

- Doubled sales first year by developing international markets.
- Completed major profit turnaround of company in first year.
- Developed new, fully integrated marketing programs resulting in a 50% increase n market share.
- Reduced labor cost by 23%.

FIRE TOOLS, INC. - Binghampton, NY   (1985 to 1988)

VICE-PRESIDENT AND GENERAL MANAGER of a $4 million manufacturer of fireplace tools and accessory products. Responsible for corporate operation including sales/marketing, production and finance. Developed annual business plan and budget. Established and maintained a system of controls of a financial and operational nature that assumed timely management information of performance versus plan. Oversaw the activities of 120 employees. Direct reports: Sales Manager, Manufacturing Manager, Controller, Auditors and Legal Counsel as well as Engineering, Design and Training Consultants.

- Increased sales by 17%.
- Introduced brand differentiation which increased customer loyalty.
- Defeated unionization attempt by Steel Workers.
- Installed new system of warehousing and inventory control which reduced shipping time 30%.

HAWTHORNE LABORATORIES, INC. - Albany, NY   (1980 to 1985)

DIRECTOR OF MARKETING for a $6 million manufacturer of specialty chemicals. Responsible for management of the total marketing effort and the formulation of marketing plans. Directed all marketing activities to achieve profit objectives. Developed marketable product lines. This responsibility encompassed the full range of marketing strategy and tactical execution, including such areas as pricing, selection of market segments for special emphasis and specifying the necessary product characteristics. Supervised three Product Managers, Advertising Manager, Sales Training Manager, Marketing Assistant and Staff.

- Increased overall sales by 78% and profits by 137%.
- Assisted in major profit turnaround of company in first year.
- Developed and introduced three complete product lines resulting in increased volume and profitability.
- Developed a three-dimensional direct mail program which was a key factor in increased sales.

DOW CHEMICAL COMPANY - Midland, MI   (1976 to 1980)

SENIOR MARKET ANALYST (1979 - 1980)
SALES REPRESENTATIVE (1976 - 1979)

3

Sample Resumes—For Recent College Graduates

In this chapter, you will find 50 carefully-selected sample high-impact resumes of recent college graduates. In contrast with the resumes provided in Chapter 2, the resumes contained in this chapter represent individuals who have little or no professional-level experience. Most, in fact, are seeking their first full-time, professional position in their chosen career field.

Although these are actual resumes of employment candidates, they have been altered in the same ways as the previous resumes, to conceal the identity of the authors.

Careful review of these resume samples will provide some excellent ideas for preparing an effective entry-level resume for use in your first professional job-hunting campaign.

To locate those sample resumes that most closely correspond to your own job-hunting objectives, you may want to refer to the Contents (see page x). In reviewing the Contents, you will note that the resume samples contained in this chapter have been conveniently grouped into 13 occupational categories, allowing easy identification of those resumes most related to your own career interests and objectives.

Karen W. Clarke

Present Address	**Permanent Address**
42 E. Windsor Dorm #11	12 New Pond Road
East Lansing, MI 13745	Kent, Ohio 91314
(512) 446-9952	(713) 925-6317

OBJECTIVE

To obtain a permanent position with a company that utilizes my previous work experience, interpersonal skills, and leadership ability.

EDUCATION

Michigan State University: East Lansing, MI
B.S. in Accounting, May 1997
Cumulative GPA: 3.38/4.0; Major GPA: 3.33/4.0; Dean's List (2)

WORK EXPERIENCE

Automotive Rentals Inc.   Willingboro, OH
Accounting Clerk (GL, AP)   Summers '94 & '95
- handled petty cash box which contained $1000.
- managed four accounts and set up billing of lessees, researched problem accounts and made adjusting entries.
- performed reconciliations of general ledger accounts.
- oversaw daily inventory and input control.
- rehired repeatedly for summers and holidays.

Friendly Restaurant   Kent, OH
Waitress   6/90-12/92
- performed responsibilities of cashier and hostess when needed.
- trained new employees.
- received Employee of the Week.

ACTIVITIES

Phi Gamma Nu Professional Business Fraternity
- served as Pledge Class Treasurer.
- involved with Financial Affairs and Philanthropy committees.
- raised funds: Michigan State Dance Marathon (largest student philanthropy in U.S.)

Student Advisor - College of Business Administration
- helped incoming students with transition to college.

Red Cross Club & Special Olympics Club
- volunteered 10-15 hours per semesters

COMPUTER SKILLS

Systems: IBM, Tandy, MacIntosh
Packages: Lotus 1-2-3, Excel, Professional Write, Dbase III+, Pascal, Minitab, MacWrite II

BARBARA A. BINGHAM

School Address
Room 106, Wagner Hall
University of Wisconsin
Madison, WI 93702
(904)775-0837

Permanent Address
32 Winding Lane
Clinton, WI 23826
(904) 533-3449

OBJECTIVE

To obtain an entry level position in a business firm which will utilize my educational background and allow development of my abilities to their fullest potential.

EDUCATION

1994-present

University of Wisconsin, Madison, WI
Accounting Major, Dean's List 2nd, 3rd and 4th semesters, present grade point average 3.58/4.0, will graduate May 1998.

1990-1994

Clinton High School, graduated in the top 10% of the class from the Excel Program which included advanced classes in Science, Math and English.

EXPERIENCE

August 1995
to July 1996

Accounting Clerk, USA Video, Inc., Clinton, WI
Responsibilities include: handling of multiple company payroll, processing of accounts payable, assisting the Controller in monthly closing activities, updating selected general ledger accounts, handling cash receipts, filing, phones, preparing bank reconciliations and analysis reports.

March 1995
to Aug. 1995

Office Clerk, Advanced Medical Associates, Warring, WI
Responsibilities include: preparation and follow up of Medicare Reviews, processing orders for medical supplies and equipment, preparing invoices for insurance companies and customers, preparation of billing and inventory books on a monthly basis, coordinating letters to insurance companies and customers, filing, phones.

September 1994
to March 1995

Assistant to Bookkeeper/Cashier, Smythe Pharmacy, Fort Smith, WI
Responsibilities include: preparation of charges for pick up, handling of register, verification of incoming inventory, stocking of shelves, filing, phones.

August 1992
to Dec. 1994

Cashier, Lee's Gallery, Clinton, WI
Responsibilities include: handling of register, assisting manager in all aspects of store opening and closing, verification of inventory, making of bank deposits, assisting in floor moves, phones.

ACHIEVEMENTS

Awarded Wayne Scholar
Member of Golden Key National Honor Society

REFERENCES

Available upon request

KIMBERLY A. BARTON

Permanent Address
14 Willow Drive
Winchester, VA 28465
(804) 572-8712

Local Address
206 Jackson Hall
University of Virginia
Charlottesville, VA 28578
(804) 664-1572

OBJECTIVE: To obtain an entry level position in Accounting.

EDUCATION: Bachelor of Science in Accounting, May 1997
University of Virginia
GPA: 3.37/4.00   Major GPA: 3.26/4.00

Relevant Courses:

Financial Accounting I, II	Corporate Finance
Managerial Accounting	Business Law
Federal Income Taxation	Int'l Business Operations

HONORS:
Golden Key National Honor Society
Phi Eta Sigma Freshman Honor Society
Dean's List - 2 semesters

WORK EXPERIENCE:

Clerk - UVA Athletic Department   6/95 - 8/95
- organized and developed football tickets
- Receptionist for athletic director

Secretary - Winchester High School   5/94 - 8/94
- developed and implemented the scheduling, billing and grading
  procedures for the computer
- responsible for efficient functioning of the office

Secretary - Wainscott & Neilson Law Firm   5/93 - 8/93
- prepared legal documents
- filed employee wages, documents and research

ACTIVITIES:
The College of Business Administration
- Overall Steering Committee Advising Program
- Student Advisor
Order of Omega
Gamma Phi Beta Sorority
- Panhellenic Delegate
- Assistant Membership Chairman
Panhellenic Council - Assistant Rush Coordinator
IFC/Panhellenic Dance Marathon Morale Team - 2 years
IFC/Panhellenic Spring Week Skits Committee
Beta Alpha Psi Accounting Honors Fraternity
Business Student Council

REFERENCES: Available upon request.

DEBORAH C. BASS

HOME ADDRESS:
28 Rosetree Terrace
Little Rock, AR 20343
(236) 775-0926

SCHOOL ADDRESS:
University of Maryland 2D-377
College Park, MD 19302
(301) 335-9479

OBJECTIVE: To obtain a position in the accounting department of a large corporation and progress within the organization

EDUCATION: The University of Maryland, College Park, MD
- Candidate for Bachelor of Science, Accounting - May 1998
- Cumulative GPA 3.36, Accounting GPA 3.2

RELEVANT COURSES:

Intermediate Acctg I & II	Financial Acctg	Business Writing
Managerial Acctg I & II	Corporate Finance	Business Logistics
Federal Income Taxation	Computer Science	Business Law
Quantitative Business Analysis	Micro & Macro Economics	MIS

PROFESSIONAL EXPERIENCE:

Accounting Clerk, Chase Bank of Maryland (2/94 - Present)
- Daily maintenance of the general ledger system.
- Reconcile branch settlement to currency and coin account.
- Balance official checks.
- Prepare accounts payable checks to be remitted on a weekly basis.
- Prepare ATM, Loan, CD, and Investment monthly reports.

Cashier, Britches Great Outdoors (5/93 - 9/95)
- Managed problems and complaints for customer sales and returns.
- Trained new cashiers.
- Performed opening and closing procedures.

ORGANIZATIONS: Beta Alpha Psi, Honorary National Accounting Fraternity

Vice President Finance, Kappa Kappa Alpha Sorority
- Prepare yearly budget
- Control disbursements of a $40,000 account

Purchase Fund Chairman Kappa Kappa Alpha Sorority
- Responsible for a $5,000 account.

Financial Committee, University of Maryland Dance Marathon
- Billed and collected $745,000 in donations

Homecoming Committees, The University of Maryland
- King and Queen, 1996
- Student Relations, 1995

ACHIEVEMENTS: Dean's List - The University of Maryland, Spring, 1996
Chase Bank of Maryland Scholarship

TECHNICAL SKILLS: Experience with Lotus 123, dBase, Microsoft Word and PASCAL

ANN R. WILSON

Local Address:
235 Wayne Hall
Ohio State University
Columbus, Ohio 38575
(206) 375-9847

Permanent Address:
122 Winston Avenue
Barrings, Virginia 90875
(715) 624-2355

Objective:
To gain a challenging entry level accounting position with a company in corporate accounting.

Education:
OHIO STATE UNIVERSITY, Columbus, Ohio
B.S. in Accounting. Degree expected: December, 1997
Overall GPA: 3.56/4.0; Major GPA: 3.43/4.0

Work Experience:
INTERNATIONAL BUSINESS MACHINES CORP., Tarrytown, NY
Accounting Intern, January 1996 - July 1996
- Facilitated recording of charges between IBM US & IBM UK
- Communicated with UK to improve billing process
- Acquired knowledge of intercompany accounting
- Developed professional and communication skills
- Trained incoming interns

WILLIAM D. BEEL, CPA, Barrings, VA
Secretary, February 1995 - August 1995
- Organized office and daily schedule
- Typed financial reports
- Scheduled appointments
- Completed tax forms and reports

PRICE BLASTER SUPERMARKETS, Barrings, VA
Office Clerk, February 1993 - August 1995
- Accounted for the cash and checks from front end to the office
- Deposited large sums of cash and checks
- Satisfied customer needs
- Worked in video department

Campus Activities:
- Beta Alpha Psi - National Accounting Fraternity 1995 - present
- Golden Key National Honor Society 1995 - present
- Dean's List - 1994, 1995, 1996
- Society of Business Interns 1996 - present
  - Secretary 1997
  - South Campus Committee Chairperson - 1997
- Resident Assistant Candidate - 1997

Interests:
- Physical Fitness, Traveling, Reading

William A. Fuller

Present Address:
320 Yale Avenue.
Apartment 22-B
Carlisle, PA 18502

Home Address:
814 Sharon Circle.
West Chester, PA 19382
(610) 697-8264

OBJECTIVE: To apply my knowledge and experience to a public accounting position.

EDUCATION: **DICKENSON UNIVERSITY**
Carlisle, PA
B.S. in Accounting, May 1998
Overall GPA: 3.47
Related Course Work:
- Advanced Financial Accounting
- Advanced Business Law
- Business Policy Management

RELATED WORK
EXPERIENCE: REED ENGINEERING. INC., Reading, PA   May 1996 - Present
Assistant Accountant and Financial Analyst
- Assisted in day-to-day payroll activities
- Responsible for daily production output analysis reports
- Prepared monthly operations reports
- Assisted in random financial report preparation
- Actively participated in long-term corporate goal research project

OTHER WORK
EXPERIENCE: DICKENSON UNIVERSITY, Carlisle, PA   Feb. 1997 - Present
Tutor
- Tutored students in accounting, computer science, and psychology

SERVICEMASTER, West Chester, PA   May 1993 - Sept.1995
Floor Specialist Custodian
- Professional carpet cleaning, floor refinishing and buffing
- Basic custodial responsibilities

ACME MARKETS, West Chester, PA   June - Sept.1992
Stockperson
- Assisted customers in various capacities
- Stocked shelves

SELF EMPLOYED ($100+/wk)   1990 - Present
Extensive work in areas of:
- Lawn care, snow removal, driveway sealing

ACTIVITIES: Beta Alpha Psi, National Accounting Fraternity
Accounting Club
Dickenson University Marching Band
Various Intramural Sports - softball, basketball, volleyball
Varsity Crew Team

SHARON P. PARKER

Home Address:	125 Ridge Rd. Hartford, CT 16922 (203) 665-9875	School Address:	110 Pear Street, B-4 Storrs, CT 17847 (203) 822-5164

OBJECTIVE: To be able to utilize my leadership and interpersonal skills in a full time position within the field of Business Logistics.

EDUCATION: **THE UNIVERSITY OF CONNECTICUT**, Storrs, CT
B.S. Degree in Business Logistics expected May 1998
Cumulative GPA: 3.69/4.0; Major GPA: 4.0/4.0

COMPUTER EXPERIENCE:

Microsoft Word	MacWrite	Lotus 1-2-3	Minitab
dBase III+	Turbo Pascal	BASIC	

WORK EXPERIENCE:

The Hartford Group, Inc. (ARA Food Services), Hartford, CT — May 96 - Aug. 96
Assistant Chef
* Planned and prepared daily menus and elaborate catering trays.
* Responsible for inventory, ordering of all supplies, and logging of bills.
* Successfully implemented new inventory system to limit stock and prevent stockouts.

Tuckerville Inn, Tuckerville, CT — May 95 - Jan. 96
Waitress
* Efficiently and skillfully served food and beverage to customers.
* Responsible for correctly billing and collecting payment from patrons.
* Trained new employees after only two days of employment.

The Doll Shop, Sturbridge, CT — May 90 - Aug. 90
Painter/Craftsman
* Prepared and assembled wooden, collector's item dolls for painting.
* Skillfully painted and stained detailed dolls which carry my signature.
* In charge of training new painters.

Taylor, Briggs & Stratton Law Office, Bristol, CT — June 92 - Nov. 92
Filing Clerk
* Filed, obtained, and destroyed outdated case files.
* Responsible for updating filing system, client relations, and all mailings.

HONORS:
Marsha Lewis Memorial Scholarship
Council of Logistics Management's College Bowl Challenge, 2nd place, Captain
Golden Key National Honor Society
Phi Eta Sigma National Honorary Fraternity
Dean's List (4 out of 5 semesters)

ACTIVITIES:
ALPHA KAPPA PSI Professional Business Fraternity
- President
- Treasurer
- Pledge Selection and Dance Marathon Committees
- Chapter Delegate, National Convention
President, Residence Hall Floor
University of Connecticut Marketing Association
- Company Seminar and Career Night Committees
Logistics Association
Freshman Orientation Leader
Intramural Volleyball, Basketball (Champions), Softball, Coed Football

SANDRA E. FLEMING

College Address:
10 Holyoke Avenue, Apt. 5
Amherst, MA 19774
(603) 650-4970

Home Address:
118 Green Valley Drive
Pittsfield, MA 15668
(214) 6224-1466

OBJECTIVE A full-time position in Business Logistics with special interests including but not limited to purchasing, warehousing, and traffic management.

EDUCATION

The University of Massachusetts, Amherst, MA
Bachelor of Science in Business Logistics expected in January 1997.
Current GPA: 3.9
Relevant coursework:

Business Logistics Management
Purchasing & Materials Management
Warehousing & Physical Distribution

Transportation
Traffic Management
Highway Engineering

Temple University, Philadelphia, PA
College of Business Administration

EXPERIENCE

Project Support Services Expeditor: General Electric Company   6/95 - 1/96
Responsibilities: liaison between suppliers and end users; handling details of purchase orders; expediting orders; establishing relationships and maintaining regular contact with suppliers; troubleshooting for engineering; customer service; purchasing; supplier visit; attended supplier trade show; project team meetings; trained successor.
Special Projects: developing execution plans for field coordination teams on major construction projects; developing orientation manual; producing organizational charts, overheads, and flow charts on Freelance software; presentation to supervisor and department managers; autofaxing purchase orders to suppliers.

Salesperson: Victoria's Secret, Christmas 1994
Receptionist: Greenfield Technologies, Summer 1994
Waitress: Franco's Italian Cuisine Summer 1993
Clerical Assistant: Temple University, 9/92 - 4/93

HONORS AND ACTIVITIES

Teaching Assistant for Business Logistics Management
Transportation Research
U. Mass. Logistics Association Chairman: Interaction Committee
U. Mass. Marketing Association
U. Mass. Concert Choir
DuPont Scholarship in Business Logistics - 1994
Traffic Club of Pittsfield Scholarship - 1995, 1996
The Honor Society of Phi Kappa Phi
Golden Key National Honor Society
Dean's List: All semesters

HOBBIES Aerobics, reading, fishing, weight lifting, waterskiing, and singing

DOUGLAS R. BURKHARDT

School Address:
62 Weldon Ave., Apt C4
Syracuse, NY 15669
(315) 974-8135

Permanent Address:
12 Ridge Rd.
Utica, NY 12464
(315) 775-0822

OBJECTIVE: To obtain a permanent position related to the field of Business Logistics.

EDUCATION: B.S. in Business Logistics, May 1998
Syracuse University   GPA 3.51

HONORS: Dean's List 3 of 5 semesters
Golden Key National Honors Society

WORK EXPERIENCE:

Housing and Food Services   9/96-present
Syracuse University
- Worked as a cook, busboy, and dishperson
- Handled materials and equipment as well as customers

Career Development and Placement Services   8/95-5/96
Syracuse University
- Answered student and recruiter questions about CDPS
- Stocked shelves, kept library presentable
- Performed some secretarial duties

Landscaping and Contract Work   Summers 93,94,95,96
- Worked as a laborer
- Collected fees and discussed bids with clients
- Supervised other employees

Reardon Architecture   Winter/Spring Break 95, 96
- Worked as a packer
- Assembled, packaged, and wrapped finished product for shipment

OTHER EXPERIENCE:

Utica Parks and Recreation
Joseph Klaus Bricklayer
Intramural Volleyball Official

ACTIVITIES:

Syracuse University Volleyball Club
-   Vice President, member USVBA, USVBA official, Team Representative
Syracuse University Business Logistics Association
-   Active Member
Intramural Sports
St. John's Church
-   Active leader of activities

ANTHONY P. SPANARO

CURRENT ADDRESS: PERMANENT ADDRESS:
22 Rosedale Ave., Apt. #213   206 Summit Drive
Ann Arbor, MI 13479   Pittsburgh, PA 18069
(316) 844-5769   (717) 396-6877

EDUCATION: The University of Michigan, Ann Arbor, MI

B.S. in Economics (May 1998)
Major GPA: 4.00/4.00; Cumulative GPA: 3.90/4.00

Ridgeview High School, Beaver, PA
Graduated June 1994; Cumulative GPA: 3.93/4.00
Gifted/High Potential Classes

AFFILIATIONS/ACTIVITIES:

Economics Association	1997
Beta Gamma Sigma	
- Honor Society for Collegiate Schools of Business	1997
The Honor Society of Phi Kappa Phi	1997
Golden Key National Honor Society	1996-Present
Phi Eta Sigma Honor Society	1995-Present
Intramurals: Basketball, Football	1994-Present
High School National Honor Society	1992-1994
Who's Who Among American High School Students	1991-1992
Varsity Basketball Team	1991-1994
- All-Star Conference - Senior Year	
Varsity Golf Team	1990-1994
- All-Star Conference - Senior Year	

WORK EXPERIENCE:

Falls Township   May-August 1996
825 Verdon Road, Bealy, PA
Laborer - involved in operations concerning township maintenance

Green Lawn and Landscape, Inc.   Summers 1994, 1995
206 Overpass Road, Beaver, PA
Landscaper - performed general landscaping duties

Lanstown Car Wash   March-May 1994
22 Oregon Road, Kiley, PA
Car Wash Attendant - supervised operations in owner's absence

Self-Employed Lawn Service   Summer 1992

- REFERENCES AVAILABLE UPON REQUEST -

SAMUEL D. DENNER

Temporary Address
52 E. College Ave.
Los Angeles, CA 84937
(714) 972-8136

Permanent Address
262 Bay View Drive
Berkeley Heights, CA 38475
(714) 644-8725

OBJECTIVE: To obtain a full-time position in the field of securities analysis and financial management.

EDUCATION: THE UNIVERSITY OF SOUTHERN CALIFORNIA, Los Angeles, CA

B.S. in Economics (May 1997)
College of Business Administration
Cumulative G.P.A.: 2.89/4.00

Relevant Coursework:
- Industrial Organization
- Money and Banking
- Intermediate Microeconomic Analysis
- Intermediate Macroeconomic Analysis
- International Economics
- Public Finance
- Corporate Finance
- Financial Accounting
- Managerial Accounting
- Lotus 1-2-3, dBase III+, Minitab, PASCAL

WORK EXPERIENCE:

Clareton Township, Clareton, CA
Clean Community Supervisor   5/95-8/95 & 5/94-8/94
- managed community volunteer groups in roadside clean-ups
- approved refuse for recycling
- conducted searches for future clean-up sites

Clareton Township, Clareton, CA
Road Department Employee   6/92 - 8/92
- repaired township roadways
- assisted in overall maintenance of township grounds and facilities

ACTIVITIES:

UCLA Economics Association
UCLA Financial Management Club
UCLA Intramural Basketball and Softball

JOAN A. SANDERS

CURRENT ADDRESS
32 E. Maple Ave., Apt. A-6
Raleigh, NC 24958
(919) 824-9763

PERMANENT ADDRESS
305 Mountain Terrace
Charlotte, NC 14729
(704) 564-4948

OBJECTIVE
To obtain an entry level position in marketing research. Special area of interest is international markets.

EDUCATION
North Carolina State University, Raleigh, NC
Will receive a Bachelor of Science degree December 1996
    Major: Economics and International Business
    Minor: German

HONORS
- Golden Key National Honor Society
- Delta Phi Alpha German Honor Society
- Dean's List (4 semesters)
- G.P.A. of 3.47/4.0

RELATED COURSES

International Economics (3 Cr.)	Introductory Marketing (3 Cr.)
Adv. International Economics (3 Cr.	Global Marketing (6 Cr.)
International Business Policies (3 Cr.)	

STUDENT ACTIVITIES
- Studied abroad in Cologne, Germany (Spring 1995)
- Secretary of the International Business Association
  - Managed all correspondence and records and performed other duties assigned by the IBA
- German tutor on campus (Spring 1994)
- Little Sister at Delta Upsilon Fraternity

EXPERIENCE

Meridith Dining Commons   Fall 1994, Fall 1995, Spring 1996
Performed various food preparation, dishroom, and customer services.

Kingston Temporary Services   Summer 1995
Performed various secretarial duties

Wilton Publishing Company   Summers 1993, 1994
Worked with computers in processing returned books.

REFERENCES
Available upon request

PETER W. JENKINS

Permanent Address:
18 Windy Hill Dr.
Wernersville, PA 19635
(610) 692-2837

Temporary Address:
40 W. College Ave., Apt. C-5
State College, PA 16801
(814) 861-7340

EDUCATION:

The Pennsylvania State University, University Park, PA
Bachelor of Science in Finance, December 1997
Overall G.P.A.: 3.25/4.0

Relevant
Coursework

Managerial Accounting
Financial Accounting
Intermediate Financial Accounting
Speech Communications

Corporate finance
Financial Management
Commercial Bank Management
Effective Business Writing

WORK EXPERIENCE:

IBM   6/96-1/97
Pre-Professional Tax Analyst   Southbury, CT

- Filed monthly sales tax returns
- Audited monthly exception reports
- Interpreted tax laws for branch offices
- Determined tax exempt status of customers
- Daily work required extensive knowledge of Lotus 1-2-3

Smith Barney   12/95-5/96
Sales Associate   State College, PA

- Initiated marketing strategy for new fund, LINC
- Developed skills in prospecting and presenting
- Managed spreadsheet data base on Lotus 1-2-3

Kmart   8/93-1/96
Stock Clerk/Salesperson   Reading, PA

- Worked 30-40 hours a week while full time student
- Coordinated inventory flow
- Assisted customers

ACTIVITIES & INTERESTS:

Boy Scouts, Earned Eagle Scout Award (1993)
- Held numerous leadership positions
- Organized and coordinated over 200 man hours for renovation of campsite
  at Allegheny Portage R.R. National Historic Site
Economics Association of Penn State
Peer Tutor (Calculus and Quantitative Business Analysis)
Intramural Softball and Football

REFERENCES:

Available Upon Request

WILLIAM C. DUCKWORTH

Home Address:
92 Wellington Drive
Malvern, PA 19315
(610) 648-3634

Campus Address:
4365 Locust Street, 9-D
Philadelphia, PA 19803
(215) 447-9837

EDUCATION: The University of Pennsylvania, GPA: 3.1/4.0
B.S. Degree in Finance, December 1998

Relevant Coursework:
Corporate Finance
Financial Management
Investment Valuation
Money and Banking

Introductory Financial Accounting
Introductory Managerial Accounting
Intermediate Financial Accounting
Intermediate Macroeconomics

Current: Intermediate Financial Accounting II, Capital Budgeting, Speculative Markets

WORK EXPERIENCE:
IBM, Albany, NY
Fixed Asset Accounting
June 1997-December 1997

- Cooperative assignment where I was responsible for insuring that proper controls existed to track and maintain all capital fixed assets
- Major duties included RAID (Rental Asset Inventory & Depreciation) RNB/BNR reconciliation, performed tool audits/tracking, System/Table Access Security, and provided financial approval for expense purchase requisitions

Winton Hill Apartments, Wayne, PA
Lifeguard
January 1993-August 1996

- Responsible for the safety and well being of swimmers
- Enhanced my decision-making skills and improved judgement skills
- Pool maintenance

Chester County YMCA, West Chester, PA
Camp Swim Instructor/Lifeguard
Summer 1993-Summer 1996

- Taught Red Cross approved swimming techniques to campers
- Presented water safety instruction to advanced swimmers

ACTIVITIES & INTERESTS:
- Vice President and Treasurer of Bistro House (1995 & 1996)
- Brother of Delta Chi Alpha, Professional Business Fraternity
- Member of The Financial Management Association National Honor Society
- Society of Business Interns
- Proficient user of Lotus and PASCAL
- Certified in CPR
- Certified in Advanced Lifesaving and Water Safety
- Intramural Athletics

REFERENCES: Available upon request

HAROLD C. KREIDER

School Address
2 Common Avenue
Orono, ME 13285
712-437-9784

Home Address
12 Stoney Creek Rd.
Wilbraham, MA 16374
603-743-5667

OBJECTIVE Challenging position in finance, accounting, or management.

EDUCATION The University of Maine, Orono, ME 1994-1998
B.S. In Finance; Cum GPA: 3.2

RELEVANT COURSEWORK

Corporation Finance
Investment Valuation
Financial Management of
  the Business Experience
Commercial Bank Management
Speculative Markets
Financial Markets
Money and Banking
Monetary Theory and Policy
Managerial Accounting
Financial Accounting

Business Computer Applications
  Lotus 1-2-3, Basic, Pascal
Business Policy Formulation/Control
Basic Managerial Concepts
Real Estate Fundamentals
Risk and Insurance
Property and Casualty Insurance
Industrial Organization
Principles of Marketing
Public Speaking
Business Writing

RELATED EMPLOYMENT

WATERMAN AND COMPANY, Springfield, MA 1995-1996
Provided staff support for a family-owned CPA firm which maintains a large number of small business and individual accounts. Handled account updating, organization of data for quarterly returns, bank reconciliations, time/billing, and all related computer entries. Worked F/T, Summer of 1995, and P/T during college breaks as needed.

HERDER'S CUTLERY, Springfield, MA 1994-Present
Given sole responsibility for business operations during assigned shift with a specialty shop (Springfield Mall). Gained extensive experience in direct sales, opening/closing, daily reporting, and making deposits. Worked up to 35 hours/week during the summers and holiday vacations.

STUDENT LEADERSHIP

Chi Delta Alpha Fraternity 1994-1998
- *Treasurer* - Manage house budget of $45-50K/semester. Served on Executive Board; worked with Alumni Board Treasurer.
- *Ticket/Admissions Chairman* - In charge of ticket sales and admissions for a major cancer fund-raiser (13,000+ participants).
- *Athletic Chairman:* - Recruited, screened, selected, organized, and scheduled teams for 10 sports. Finished with Top 5 ranking.

Undergraduate Student Government, Department of Control 1996

Interfraternity Council, Department of Control 1997

HIGH SCHOOL BACKGROUND Graduated with 3.6 GPA, College Preparatory; National Honor Society; Student Government (Delegate); Varsity Tennis Team (Captain).

REFERENCES Available upon request.

DAVID R. BRAXTON

Temporary Address
21 East Campus Blvd.
Tucson, AZ 29486
Phone: (602) 449-8076

Permanent Address
12 Green Way
Austin, TX 57950
Phone: (415) 699-0473

EDUCATION

The University of Arizona, Tucson, AZ
B.S. in Finance (May 1998)
Overall G.P.A. 3.31/4.00

RELEVANT COURSEWORK

Corporation Finance
Microeconomic Analysis
Money & Banking

Intro to Financial Accounting
Macroeconomic Analysis
Intro to Managerial Accounting

CURRENT

Investment Valuation
Strategic Management

Financial Management of Business
Intermediate Macroeconomic Analysis

WORK EXPERIENCE

National Bank of Texas, Austin, TX
Teller   May 1996 - August 1996
- managed a cash drawer containing up to $10,000
- coordinated electronic fund transfers
- conducted random audits of both mine and fellow employee's vaults
- updated customer records on a daily basis

Le Grange Discount Warehouse, Denton, TX
Cashier/Delivery Person   May 1995-August 1995
- operated cash register
- monitored inventory and processed merchandise orders
- delivered orders of flowers and trays

Green Valley Pharmacy, Austin, TX
Cashier/Rx Clerk   January 1994 - December 1994
- monitored inventory and processed merchandise orders
- updated computer data base containing customer files
- cross referenced customer records in order to avoid dangerous combinations of drugs
- processed and recorded prescription orders

Little Caesars Pizza, Austin, TX
Cashier/Cook   November 1992 - December 1993
- operated cash register prepared food
- earned 5 star employee status

ACTIVITIES

Campus: 1995 Dance Marathon Security Team member, 1996-97; Interfraternity Council Board of Control Housechecker, 1997; Greek Mixer Physical Plant SubChair, Summer 1997; Give Your Share Volunteer.

Fraternity: Member, Delta Chi, Fall 1995; House Manager, Spring 1996; Assistant Pledge Master, Fall 1996; Pledge Master, 1995 & 1996; Spring Week Co-Chairperson; Intramural Softball.

REFERENCES

Furnished upon request

MARTIN W. BAKER

LOCAL ADDRESS:
42 East Benton Avenue, C-4
East Lansing, MI 12847
(512) 664-9848

HOME ADDRESS:
12 Sunny Court
New Hope, PA 19250
(215) 996-4137

EDUCATION:

THE MICHIGAN STATE UNIVERSITY, East Lansing, MI
B.S. in Finance, December 1997
GPA: 3.41/4.00
Dean's List four semesters
Business Logistics Minor
Accounting: Two Financial and Two Cost Accounting Courses

**WORK
EXPERIENCE:**

IBM, Tarrytown, NY
Pre-Professional Accountant, January 1996 - June 1996
- Used computers (Lotus) to do accounting transactions.
- Dealt with many facets of fixed assets.
- Gave formal presentations to upper management.

Sesame Place Theme Park, Langhorne, PA
Area Supervisor, January 1994 - September 1994
- Supervised staff of over 150 employees.
- Ordered food on a daily basis.
- Called repairmen and suppliers when needed.

Supervisor, January 1993 - December 1993
- Enforced company policies.
- Calculated daily sales.

Line employee, May 1991 - December 1992
- Operated cash registers.
- Prepared food and sold it to customers.

**CAMPUS
ACTIVITIES:**

Financial Management Association, 1995 - 1997
- Actively participated in functions and meetings.

Economics Association, 1995 - 1996
- Attended functions outside of school and went to seminars.

Intramural Tennis, 1993 - 1997
- Played singes and doubles.

REFERENCES:

Available upon request

MARY ANN WERNER

Permanent Address
18 Bellview Drive
Princeton, NJ 03485
(609) 554-9840

Temporary Address
22 College Avenue, 8-C
Newark, DE
(302) 443-9847

Education

The University of Delaware
Major: Business Management; **Minor: Spanish**
B.S., December 1996
Overall GPA: 3.3/4.0 Major GPA: 3.6/4.0

Experience

E. I. DuPont de Nemours & Co., Inc. - Wilmington, DE
Financial Analyst Intern - 1995
- Assisted in the reconciliation of 9 DuPont Merck Pharmaceutical Co. expense ledgers
- Researched DuPont/Merck costs and decided whether covered in the service contracts
- Created a procedures manual on the service contract reconciliation process
- Trained personnel on computer systems and the service contract reconciliation
- Researched expenses for DuPont account owners as a member of a "hotline"
- Made presentations to management on status of projects and related accomplishments

Princeton Federal Savings Bank - Princeton, NJ
Accounts Payable Clerk/ Receptionist - Summer 1994
- Assisted various Vice Presidents at Corporate Headquarters
- Posted transactions into accounts payable ledgers
- Typed, examined and verified payments
- Operated communication network

Teller - Summer 1993
- Responsible for up to $35,000+ daily
- Opened various accounts including money market and certificate of deposit accounts
- Sold and redeemed U.S. Savings Bonds
- Transacted money on an on-line computer system and proved cash daily

Community Federal Bank - Princeton Junction, NJ
Teller - 1992
- Handled large sums of money from the Federal Depository
- Transacted and verified cash daily
- Performed data entry on an off-line computer system
- Maintained good customer relations

**Honors &
Activities**

Dean's List (2 Semesters)
DuPont achievement Award
Management Club
Blood Drive Volunteer
Singer/Performer

References

Available Upon Request

CAROLYN A. BEATTY

Current Address
1805 Venango Ave., Apt. #6
Philadelphia, PA 19847
(215) 596-9683

Permanent Address
23 Kring Rd.
Johnstown, PA 16335
(716) 434-3794

OBJECTIVE: To obtain a position in a management training department.

EDUCATION: **Temple University**, Philadelphia, PA,
B.S. in **Management**--expected in May 1998
Emphasis in Industrial Organization Psychology
Major GPA 3.05/4.0

WORK
EXPERIENCE:

The College of Business   8/96-Present
Computer Lab Supervisor
Work an average 20-24 hrs/week maintaining IBM, Hewlett Packard, and Macintosh hardware, training students and faculty in the general use of computer hardware and software, and monitoring and troubleshooting several local area networks.

QVC Home Shopping Network   Summers 1996, 1995
Jewelry Rebuyer Assistant
Entered orders into inventory system and maintained current order data. Reorganized and updated information in the filing system. Learned Paradox database program.

Returns and Surplus Assistant/Department Assistant
Requisitioned merchandise for sale and distributed returns and surpluses to outlet stores. Took the initiative to learn computerized inventory system to accurately pinpoint location and quantity of merchandise on order and to significantly reduce the time to requisition goods and distribute returns and surplus. Developed a department procedures manual and used it to train permanent employees.

Genuardi's Supermarkets, Inc.   11/91-8/94
Customer Service Cashier
Assisted with customer service. Maintained balanced cash control. Helped train new cashiers and assisted them in solving customer complaints.

OTHER
EXPERIENCE:

The Temple Collegian, Philadelphia, PA   1/95-12/96
Office Representative
Trained new office representatives and solved customer complaints. Designed over--the-counter advertising. Required 7 hrs per week.

COMPUTER
KNOWLEDGE: DOS; Microsoft Word (IBM & Mac); Word for Windows; PC-Write; Harvard Graphics; Mac Paint; Mac Draw; Lotus; dBase III +; Paradox; Minitab; Ready, Set, Go; and Pascal.

ACTIVITIES: **Alpha Kappa Psi, Professional Business Fraternity:**
- Chairperson for Public Relations & Bylaws Committees, Pledge Selection Committee.

Penn State Marketing Association

ALLEN D. MARKS

PRESENT ADDRESS
73 West College Avenue
Miami, FL 24839
(912) 477-0958

PERMANENT ADDRESS
12 Regina Road
Atlanta, GA 28475
(415) 844-9857

EDUCATION

University of Miami, Miami, FL
B.S. Business Management, August 1997
G.P A. (3.14/4.0)

EXPERIENCE

University of Miami   1996-Present
Proctor, Basic Management Concepts Course:
Distributed, collected and sorted exams and answer sheets.
Responsible for insuring an acceptable testing environment.
- Gained leadership and communication skills.

The Borough of Wayneville   1996-1997
Road Crew and Parks Crew, Department of Public Works:
Prepared daily fuel, work and time schedule reports.
- Gained communication skills and demonstrated responsibility.

Max's Burgers and Fries   1995-1997
Cook, Customer Service:
Responsible for analyzing and ordering inventory.
- Gained communication and leadership skills.

The Discount Mart   1993-1994
Deli Attendant, Customer Service:
Responsible for handling cash receipts at end of the business day.
- Gained communication skills and demonstrated responsibility.

Wendy's   1992-1993
Cook, Customer Service:
- Gained communication skills and demonstrated responsibility

HONORS/
ACTIVITIES

Dean's List - One Semester
Active Member of The Miami University Marketing Association
- Fund Raising Committee
- Company Seminars Committee
Varsity Baseball,1993 - 1995

COMPUTER
SKILLS

Lotus 1-2-3, WordPerfect, dBase III +, MiniTab, MacWrite,
PASCAL

REFERENCES PROVIDED UPON REQUEST

JOHN D. FOSTER

Current Address:
34 West Long Ave., Apt. 34
Austin, TX 28496
(825) 795-0463

Permanent Address:
8 Rose Terrace
Birmingham, AL 18375
(215) 742-5662

OBJECTIVE

To obtain an internationally focused position which utilizes my knowledge of Management and International Business.

EDUCATION

B.S. in Management/International Business, December 1996
Minor in Labor Studies
The University of Texas
Overall GPA: 3.3/4.0; Major GPA: 3.8/4.0

WORK EXPERIENCE

Intern - United Parcel Service, Birmingham, AL   1994-1995
-- Processed shareowner stock repurchases
-- Updated on-line stock management system
-- Researched and prepared special projects
-- Prepared routine reports on Lotus program

Carpenter - Calter Builders, Teaboro, AL   1993
-- Designed and built interior/exterior fixtures
-- Solicited customers
-- Purchased and delivered materials
-- Met precise deadlines

Machine Operator - Martin Technologies, Birmingham, AL 1992
-- Manufactured aircraft parts for U.S. government contracts
-- Produced extremely detailed components
-- Granted low security status

HONORS

Attended University of Melbourne, Australia   Spring 1995
Accepted into highly competitive International Business major
Dean's List (3 semesters)
Sigma Iota Epsilon National Honorary Management Fraternity

ACTIVITIES

Alpha Kappa Psi Professional Business Fraternity
   -- Business Fraternity Council Representative
   -- Social Committee Chairman
Vice President, International Business Association
Total Alcohol Awareness Program Director (TAAP)
Teaching Assistant for Introductory Business Course (BA 103A)
Student Blood Coordinator for Red Cross Club

SKILLS

Basic German
Lotus 1-2-3, Aldus Freehand, Harvard Graphics, WordPerfect, Wordstar, Microsoft, dBASE III+

JANET L. FRANKLIN

Current Address:
22 Clinton Street, Apt. 2-A
Boulder, CO 23859
(614) 948-4928

Permanent Address:
14 Fuller Drive
Glendale, CA 19058
(714) 246-9574

OBJECTIVE   A position as a Computer Programmer or a Systems Analyst.

EDUCATION   University of Colorado
B.S. Degree in Business Administration, May 1998
Major in Management Information Systems
Cumulative G.P.A. 3.39

Relevant Courses:

Information Processing Systems	Cobol
Accounting Information Systems	Business Writing
Managerial Accounting	Speech Communications
Financial Accounting	Risk and Insurance

EXPERIENCE   UNIVERSITY OF COLORADO   January 1996-Present
Lab Attendant - Center for Academic Computing

Duties include maintaining computer hardware and assisting users on
Macintosh, IBM PS/2, IBM AS/400, and IBM VWCMS with various
software packages.

COLMAR TEMPORARY SERVICES   May 1996-August 1996
Administrative and Clerical Worker
Assignments included USX Cyclone Fence and GMAC.
Duties included quoting proposal bids, preparing purchase
order forms, and office administrative duties.

FRESHWAY DRY CLEANERS   May 1995-August 1996
Customer Service Worker
Duties included serving customers in a computer automated
environment.

BUNS OF CINNAMON   April 1993-January 1995
Crew Leader
Duties included supervising crew and managing the daily operations of
the bakery.

HONORS   Scholarship of the Metals & Mining Industry
College of Business Administration Scholarship
Golden Key Honor Society
Alpha Lambda Delta Honor Society
Dean's List

REFERENCES   Furnished upon request.

KAREN W. GLEASON

Temporary Address
11 S. College Ave., Apt. #5
State College, PA 16801
Phone: (814) 663-1987

Permanent Address
4 Orchard Drive
Blue Bell, PA 19836
Phone: (215) 645-4472

EDUCATION:
The Pennsylvania State University, University Park, PA
B.S. in Management Information Systems (May 1998)
Minor: Legal Aspects of Business
Overall G.P.A.:   3.47/4.00
G.P.A. in major: 4.00/4.00

RELEVANT COURSEWORK:
Introduction to Management
  Information Systems
Business Program
  Applications: LOTUS, DOS
Introduction to Management

Managerial Accounting
Quantitative Methods
Macroeconomics
Legal Environment
  of Business

CURRENT COURSEWORK:
Accounting Information Systems
Business Information
  Processing Systems

Corporate Finance
Introduction to Operations
  Management

WORK EXPERIENCE:
Sterling Drug, Inc., Malvern, PA
Packaging Operator   June 1996-August 1996
• ensured accuracy of incoming materials
• performed quality inspections on finished products
• developed strong interpersonal skills

Hershey Park, Hershey, PA
Cashier/Salesclerk   June 1995-August 1995
• recorded and processed customer sales
• managed customer relations
• developed use of supervisory skills
• performed daily inventory analysis

ACTIVITIES/ HONORS:
Sigma Iota Epsilon (Management Honor Society)--President ('97-'98)
Residence Halls Advisory Board of Penn State--Secretary (1996)
Phi Mu Delta Little Sister--Fund Raising Chairman (1996)
Information Systems Association -- Membership Committee ('96-'97)
Phi Eta Sigma -- Distinguished Freshman Honor Society
Hershey Park -- Outstanding Employee Award

REFERENCES:
Available Upon Request

COLLIN D. PETERS

Home Address
22 Kimberly Lane
West Chester, PA 19382
Phone: (610) 431-3236

School Address
216 Roberts Hall
Bucknell University
Lewisburg, PA 19847
(717) 458-9563

OBJECTIVE: To obtain a position with a dynamic company that will utilize both my computer skills and business background.

EDUCATION: **Management Information Systems Major**
Bucknell University
Graduation: December 1997
GPA: 3.66/4.00

RELEVANT COURSEWORK: Honors: Macro Economics, Corporate Finance, Strategic Management, Marketing Principles, Accounting Ethics

MIS: Accounting Information Systems, Decision Support & Expert Systems, Business Information Procedures, Systems Analysis Design

Computer Languages: dBase III+, R:Base, Lotus 1-2-3, Cobol, Hpaccess

HONORS & ACTIVITIES: University Scholars Program
Golden Key National Honor Society
Alpha Delta Lambda National Honor Society

WORK EXPERIENCE: **Wharton Electronics**   5/96 - 12/96
Accounting and Information Systems Co-op

- As we changed from a functional to a Business Unit organization, I worked with others developing reports to determine each product's profit margin. This project provided management with an essential tool to change the way they do business.

- My supervisor at Wharton, completed evaluation of my work for Bucknell. He gave me an "A" for the credits I received, and stated that he would go to "extraordinary lengths" to hire me again. A copy of this evaluation is available upon request.

I enjoy traveling and am willing to relocate

Thomas J. Collins

Present Address
25 East River Ave., Apt. #8-G
Urbana, IL 24839
(217) 822-8573

Permanent Address
216 Winslow Drive
Springfield, OH 24368
(416) 448-9475

EDUCATION

University of Illinois, Urbana, IL
MAJOR: Management Information Systems
DEGREE: B.S., 1997
GPA: 3.68 (4.0 in major)

HONORS/ACTIVITIES

-   Deans List (University of Illinois)
-   Golden Key National Honor Society
-   University Scholars Program
-   Phi Sigma Pi National Honor Fraternity
-   Information Systems Association
-   University of Illinois Men's Bowling Team
-   National Honor Society (high school)
-   Who's Who Among American High Schools

WORK EXPERIENCE

Summer 1996
 and
Summer 1995

WAYLAND INDUSTRIES, Springfield, OH
(full-time) Swimming pool water analysis and technical/
operational support; chemical manufacturing and blending.

1/92 - 8/96

COLLEGE BOWL, Urbana, IL
(part-time and full-time) Pinsetter
-   maintenance and mechanical repair; bowling lessons; customer service
    and counter help.

COMPUTER SKILLS/ABILITIES

Computer Language and Software Experience
-   COBOL
-   Turbo Pascal
-   Lotus 1-2-3
-   WordPerfect
-   IBM DOS
-   Harvard Graphics

Computer System Experience
-   IBM PCs
-   IBM 3090 VM/CMS
-   IBM AS/400

REFERENCES

Upon request

RICHARD A. BARLOW

School Address
24 East Morrin Avenue, Box 650
College Park, MD 13275
(301) 832-9847

Permanent Address
25 Duncan Road
Columbia, MD 13725
(301) 652-9038

OBJECTIVE: To obtain an entry level position that will enable me to utilize and further develop my analytical and interpersonal skills.

EDUCATION: University of Maryland   August 1993 - Present
Candidate for Bachelor of Science in Marketing   December 1997
Minor in Economics

WORK EXPERIENCE:

Reno's Auto Parts Inc., College Park, MD   August 1996 - Present
Sales Representative
- Prospected potential customers.
- Performed financial and collection responsibilities for clientele.
- Conducted new product demonstrations resulting in increased sales.

Fisher Auto Parts Inc., Arbutus, MD   May 1996 - August 1996
Assistant Store Manager
- Performed all management functions in a store with monthly volume of $30,000 including sales, market targeting, order processing, accounts receivable, handling of returned merchandise and payroll.

Fisher Auto Parts Inc., College Park, MD   August 1995 - May 1996
Delivery Person
- Responsible for the efficient delivery of parts to local service establishments.
- Emphasis in opening and closing procedures, receiving and inventory maintenance.

HONORS & ACTIVITIES:

Dean's List, Fall 1996
University of Maryland Marketing Association Member
Phi Kappa Sigma National Fraternity
- House Manager: Spring 1995 and Fall 1995
- Executive Board Committee
- Centennial Celebration Planning Committee
- Intramural Sports
Special Olympics Volunteer

REFERENCES: Available upon request.

JOHN P. TOWSON

CAMPUS ADDRESS (until 5/8/97)
58 University Drive Apt. 1-B
Tallahassee, FL 18374
(912) 642-8937

HOME ADDRESS
206 Shady Road
Jacksonville, FL 18344
(912) 355-9827

OBJECTIVE   To obtain an entry-level position in marketing; special interests in retailing, customer service and public relations.

EDUCATION   **FLORIDA STATE UNIVERSITY**
Bachelor of Science in Marketing, expected December 1997
3.41/4.0 overall GPA; 3.44 in major

INTERNSHIP   <u>**EXHIBIT REPRESENTATIVE**</u>   June 1996-January 1997
Walt Disney World/General Motors, Orlando, FL
*   Represented General Motors and Walt Disney World
*   Greeted and assisted guests at World of Motion
*   Coordinated Technical Information Reports
*   Conducted surveys and developed training program revisions
*   Researched information and attained knowledge of car industry
*   Monitored and maintained show quality

EMPLOYMENT   <u>**ASSISTANT TO THE MANAGER**</u>   Summers 1993-1995
Franklin Martin Inc., Jacksonville, FL
*   Handled computer applications and conducted inventory checks
*   Filled customer orders and prepared shipments
*   Restocked shelves and mixed paint

ACTIVITIES   *   **AMERICAN MARKETING ASSOCIATION**
*   **FLORIDA STATE MARKETING ASSOCIATION**
Marketing Services and Advertising Committees
Achieved Award for Outstanding Membership
*   **FLORIDA STATE TRACK CLUB**
Budget Director, Spring 1994
*   **STUDENTS AGAINST DRIVING DRUNK**

HONORS   *   **DEAN'S HONOR LIST**
Spring 1994; Spring 1995
*   **GOLDEN KEY NATIONAL HONOR SOCIETY**
*   **PHI ETA SIGMA NATIONAL HONOR SOCIETY**
*   **MARY WALKER MEMORIAL SCHOLARSHIP**

REFERENCES   Available upon request.

TERRANCE T. CROCKETT

Temporary Address
36 East Falls Avenue
Madison, WI 12948
(914) 653-0948

Permanent Address
1426 Old Forge Road
Minneapolis, MN 97837
(214) 637-9824

OBJECTIVE: To obtain an entry level position with a dynamic company that will allow me to utilize my education, interpersonal skills and work experience.

EDUCATION: University of Wisconsin
Bachelor of Science in Marketing, Anticipated December 1997
Emphasis: Sales and Sales Management
GPA: Major 3.61/4.00; Cumulative 3.20/4.00
Dean's List - Fall 1995, Spring 1996

WORK EXPERIENCE:

Smith Barney   1/97 - Present
- Client account analysis and evaluation
- Developed direct mail marketing plan
- Stock research and evaluation
- Managed $100,000 paper portfolio

Self-Employed Painter   1990 - Present
- Owner-operator, placed bids and negotiated contracts
- Recruited and hired employees each summer
- Monitored project progress to ensure highest quality job completion
- Followed up with customers to ensure satisfaction

Field House Attendant   9/94 - 10/95
University of Wisconsin Indoor Sports Complex
- Responsible for monitoring activities and locking up field house

ACTIVITIES:

Division of Undergraduate Studies Advisory Board
- Serve on a committee to improve the interaction of the University of Wisconsin administration with the undergraduate community
- Student-to- Student Subcommittee, greeted and conferred with incoming Division of Undergraduate Studies students

Chi Alpha Sigma
- House Manager
- Social Chair
- House Cook

University of Wisconsin Student Recruitment Task Force
- Represented University of Wisconsin to home area high schools in order to attract qualified individuals to the University.

REFERENCES: Available upon request

RONALD K. SWEENEY

300 Bartram Circle
New Brunswick, NJ 08816
(908) 876-9273

OBJECTIVE:	To use my marketing and advertising skills in a position involving public relations and promotions.

EDUCATION:

Rutgers University, New Brunswick, NJ
B.S. in **MARKETING** -- expected in May 1998
Emphases: promotions, international marketing
Major GPA 3.05/4.0

The Center for European Studies, Maastricht, The Netherlands
University of Limburg -- 8/97-12/97
<u>Relevant Courses</u>:
Economics of European Integration
The European Political and Legal Environment
Management in an International Environment
Multinational Marketing Strategy
German

WORK EXPERIENCE:

<u>The New Collegian</u>, New Brunswick, NJ

1/97-5/97

Marketing Specialist
- Re-designed and updated look of marketing report
- Formulated questions for telephone survey
- Assisted Marketing Manager in on-going activities

1/96-12/96

Advertising Sales Representative
- Generated sales exceeding $29,000 from 6/96 - 12/96
- Serviced and maintained 12-25 local accounts daily
- Created advertisements on graphics computer system
- Managed all contracts, payments, and billing for clients
- Developed interpersonal and time-management skills

INTERESTS & ACTIVITIES:
- <u>The New Collegian</u>, Merit Scholarship Recipient
- Public Relations Co-Chairperson, Alpha Kappa Psi Professional Business Fraternity
- Rutgers University Marketing Association
- Orientation Leader, Fall 1995
- French and German languages
- International travel, music, ballroom dance

JUNE S. GEAR

Local Address

31 East Vail Avenue
Morgantown, West Virginia 13284
(314) 557-9426

Permanent Address

280 Commonwealth Drive
Camp Hill, PA 16374
(717) 325-8972

OBJECTIVE: To obtain an entry level position in the field of marketing that utilizes my sales, leadership, and business background.

EDUCATION: West Virginia State University, Morgantown, West Virginia
BS Degree in **Marketing** with an emphasis in Psychology, May 1998
Cumulative GPA: 3.36; Major GPA: 3.43

RELATED COURSEWORK:

Introduction to Marketing	Introduction to Financial Accounting
Introduction to Management	Buying Behavior
Introduction to Managerial Accounting	Introduction to Psychology
Marketing Research	Computer Science
Corporate Finance	Sales Management
International Business	Business Logistics

EXPERIENCE:

WEST VIRGINIA STATE MARKETING ASSOCIATION
Director of Fundraising   4/97-4/98
- Responsible for overseeing and motivating committee members
- In charge of organizing and creating new fundraising activities to help support WVSMA

FRANKLIN FASHIONS, Camp Hill, PA
Assistant Manager and Salesperson   6/95-1/97
- Gained experience in the retail industry by participating in sales, payroll, and supervision of employees
- Assisted in merchandising and helped coordinate advertising campaigns and sales promotions

THE SPORTS CORNER, Harrisburg, PA
Salesperson   8/93-8/94
- Assisted in merchandising and maintaining inventory control
- Sharpened interpersonal skills through various sales transactions
- Responsible for opening and closing transactions each day

THE LIMITED, Camp Hill, PA
Sales Associate   6/93-1/94
- Top salesperson for five consecutive weeks
- Winner of store-wide sales contest for highest cumulative sales
- Assisted in training new employees
- Prepared eye-catching displays

ACTIVITIES:

Dean's List
West Virginia State Marketing Association
Orientation Leader for Incoming Freshmen
Morale Committee - IFC Dance Marathon
Business Student Council
Football Recruiting Hostess
Staff Member - Regatta Philanthropy
Dorm Complex Representative

VIRGINIA A. WILLIAMSON

Present Address
19 Warren Circle
Houston, TX 23958
(614) 957-9847

Permanent Address
22 Old Post Road
Oklahoma City, OK 37458
(517) 994-7493

OBJECTIVE: A position involved with planning and implementing marketing strategy for a company.

EDUCATION: **The University of Houston**
B.S. in Marketing, December 1992
GPA 3.48/4.00
Dean's List past four semesters.

RELATED EXPERIENCE:

Development Intern   January-August 1996
Houston Symphony Association, Houston, TX
- Created and implemented a volunteer incentive and evaluation program.
- Reviewed/approved daily and weekly Telefund reports.
- Conducted yearly prospect research; updated database.
- Distributed donor benefits; helped plan events.

Sales Associate   Summers 1994, 1995
Turbon's Inc., Broken Arrow, OK
- Assisted customers locate and select merchandise by serving as a personal consultant.
- Displayed merchandise; controlled inventory.
- Named a Top Sales Associate for May 1994.

Accounts Receivable Assistant   Summer 1994
Calton Environmental, Inc., Oklahoma City, OK
- Researched delinquent accounts to determine cause of nonpayment.
- Facilitated payment by serving as an information link between company and client.

Telemarketer   November 1993-March 1994
Person-to-Person Marketing, Inc., Houston, Texas
- Conducted direct marketing calls to selected customers, persuading them to renew their magazine subscriptions.

ACTIVITIES: **Alpha Kappa Psi Professional Business Fraternity**   1995-present
- Executive Committee: planned activities, oversaw three committees, conducted ceremonies.
- Fundraising Chairman: achieved $2,000 fundraising goal.
- Alumni Communications, Pledge Selection Committees.

University of Houston Marching Band   1994-present
- Also participated in Basketball Pep Band and Concert Band.

Warren H. Bransford

School: 12 East Lancaster Avenue, Apt #2C, Wayne, PA 19872   (610) 751-9124
Home: 5105 Ocean Drive, Ocean City, NJ 19315   (609) 554-8931

EDUCATION   Villanova University
                  B.S. in Operations Management, December 1997
                  Minor in Business Logistics

ACHIEVEMENTS Overall Grade Point Average: 3.4
                  Golden Key National Honor Society member

EXPERIENCE   McNeil Consumer Products Co., Fort Washington, PA
                  (A Johnson & Johnson subsidiary; producer of the Tylenol® family of products)

1/97-7/97   Planning Coordinator, Fort Washington Planning Department
                  • Planned material requirements for over 150 components and finished goods
                    using AMAPS and communicating with manufacturing floor
                  • Managed on-line information database (FOCUS) for Fort Washington Planning
                  • Assisted in reducing company back orders by $0.4M within one month through
                    careful attention to material management and customer service issues
                  • Initiated implementation of Finite Capacity Scheduling System software
                  • Developed comprehensive manual for Tactical Purchasing functions

6/95-1/96   Tactical Buyer, Chemical Purchasing Department
                  • Placed $1M in purchase orders daily using Cullinet system
                  • Reduced delivery non-conformances by 80% through effective communication
                    and correspondence with over 70 external chemical suppliers
                  • Introduced EDI order placement by coordinating with suppliers
                  • Trained new Buyer in Chemical Department
                  • Developed comprehensive manual for Tactical Purchasing functions

                  Villanova University, Villanova, PA
8/94-5/95   Student Security Assistant; night watchman
8/94-5/95   Research Lab Assistant

                  The Villanova Collegian, Inc., Villanova, PA
5/94-1/95   Office Representative

COMPUTER   IBM PC (including Windows), Macintosh and mainframe environments.
SKILLS   Languages: Basic, Focus, Fortran-77, Pascal, Siman
                  Business Systems: AMAPS (MRP), Cullinet (Purchasing), FOCUS
                  Applications: AutoCad, dBase, Lotus, Minitab, STORM, various word
                                      processing packages.

ACTIVITIES   Delta Sigma Pi, Professional Business Fraternity
                  Society of Business Interns, founding member
                  American Production & Inventory Control Society, student member
                  Villanova University Ski Team
                  Villanova University Racquetball Club

KENNETH E. DENTON

SCHOOL ADDRESS
28 Quarry Road
Scranton, PA 17570
(717) 647-9837

PERMANENT ADDRESS
39 East 7th Street
Clarke Summit, PA 18450
(717) 445-9872

OBJECTIVE: Obtain an operations management position in a production facility.

EDUCATION:

University of Scranton, December 1997
- B.S. in Operations Management
- **Financed 95% of education**
- Dean's List (Spring 1996)
- Overall GPA 3.2/4.0
- Major GPA 3.4/4.0

Relevant Coursework
- Facilities Management
- Operations Planning and Control
- Materials Management
- Quality Assurance
- Computer Science
- Effective Speech
- Business Writing
- Business Logistics

In-company Research Project with Kalstadt Mills
- Redesigned a warehouse and worked on warehouse efficiency
- Worked on transportation of goods to the distribution center
- Incorporated a FIFO inventory system in the distribution center
- Worked with ABC classification in a warehouse

WORK EXPERIENCE:

Porter Corporation, Mahoopany, PA
Inventory Auditor   Summers 1991-1996
- Redesigned and inventoried auto parts room
- Placed orders and expedited for government contracts
- Received and checked orders

Pennsylvania Liquor Control Board, Scranton, PA
Liquor Store Clerk   Winters 1992-1996
- Maintained inventory for Store #1366
- Received shipments and stocked shelves
- Assisted customers in finding products
- Performed cashier and check-out duties

ACTIVITIES:

Delta Epsilon Phi Fraternity
Executive Board Member   Spring 1994-1997
- Rush chairman: responsible for building membership
- Secretary, responsible for corresponding with headquarters
- Alumni Liaison, responsible for corresponding with the alumni
- Kustos, Advisor to the executive board committee

REFERENCES: Available Upon Request

MARSHA D. REARDON

75 Cedar Street
Allentown, PA 18018
(215) 847-3857

EDUCATION

Lehigh University
B.S., Operations Management with Honors, May 1998
Minor: Business Logistics
G.P.A.: 3.73/4.00; Major: 3.81
Honors Thesis: Total Quality Management

RELEVANT COURSES

Operations Management	Quantitative Business Analysis I & II Honors
Quality Assurance Honors	Management Honors
Simulation	Advanced Calculus I and II

CURRENT

Intro to Business Logistics	Facilities Management
Transport Systems	Business Logistics Management
Traffic Management	Operations Planning and Control
Materials Management	Management Information Systems

PROFESSIONAL EXPERIENCE

Credit Office/Sales Associate   6/93-1/96
Orr's of Bethlehem, Bethlehem, PA
- Assisted customers and registered sales
- Checked and placed stock
- Took inventory
- Counted, balanced, and deposited store monies
- Monitored outgoing and incoming calls
- Handled credit payments and questions

Data-Entry   Summer 1995
Fulier Company, Bethlehem, PA
- Updated files using the company's mainframe
- Entered data into Lotus spreadsheets
- Did small-scale data collection and compilation projects

Temporary Clerical   Summer & Winter 1996
United Parcel Service, Lehigh Valley, PA
- Made collection calls on delinquent accounts
- Researched customer problems
- Prepared bills
- Balanced books
- Opened mail and prepared payments for processing

COMPUTER SKILLS

Hardware: IBM PC, Macintosh, Lehigh University Mainframe
Software: Lotus 1-2-3, dBase III+, Siman IV, Minitab, Q&A, Pascal, MacWrite, WordPerfect

HONORS & ACTIVITIES

Dean's List, University Scholars Program, Golden Key National Honor Society, Woman's Chorus, Keynotes, University Choir

MILDRED E. MASTERS

Current Address
45 Upper Terrace #5-A
Ithica, NY 19801
(315) 644-9829

Permanent Address
63 Pine Tree Avenue
Thornton, PA 19336
(610) 346-5542

OBJECTIVE: To obtain an entry level position in Management Science/Operations Research or Management Information Systems.

EDUCATION: Cornell University
Bachelor of Science in Quantitative Business Analysis
Minor in Business Law
Graduation August 1997
Cumulative GPA: 3.22/4.00; Major GPA: 3.61/4.00

RELEVANT COURSES:

Forecasting	Linear Programming
Simulation	Operations Management
Statistical Methods	Business Writing and Public Speech

COMPUTER SKILLS: In both Mainframe and PC environments: SIMAN, SAS, Q&A, FORTRAN, LINDO, Lotus 1-2-3, Minitab, deBase III+, MEMO, DOS, Excel, Paradox, Turbo Pascal and various word processors.

RELATED EXPERIENCE:

CORNELL UNIVERSITY, Ithica, NY
School of Hotel Management, Spring 1997
- Forecasted future statistics for a local restaurant from actual data
- Used Box Jenkins methods as well as Exponential Smoothing

MBNA AMERICA, Newark, DE
Cornell Extern Program, 1/5/97 -1/10/97
- Received hands-on experience in customer contact areas
- Learned various aspects of the student segment of MBNA's portfolio
- Developed ideas for Cornell account acquisition, retention and control

AIR PRODUCTS AND CHEMICALS, Allentown, PA
MIS/Telecommunications Intern, Summer 1996
- Developed statistical reports using SAS
- Maintained and created databases using Q&A
- Trained coworkers in specific database usage for billing purposes
- Updated form programs previously created in MEMO

OTHER WORK: **KEYSTONE INVESTMENT CORPORATION,** Holidays
GRANT VOGEL COMPANY, Summer 1995
MILLER'S DEPARTMENT STORE, Summer 1994
BLOCKBUSTER VIDEO, 8/92 - 4/93

HONORS/ ACTIVITIES:

Early college admission	Alpha Chi Delta
Dean's List 7th semester	Certified SCUBA diver
Management Science Club	Modeling

References available upon request

Barbara G. Clemson

School Address:
22 College View, Apt 4-G
Boulder, CO 13482
(914) 665-9786

Home Address:
20 Sea Mist Lane
Newport Beach, CA 13968
(714) 227-9082

Objective

An entry level position as a management consultant or systems analyst

Education

UNIVERSITY OF COLORADO
B.S. in Quantitative Business Analysis, expected May 1998
Major GPA - 3.36   Overall GPA - 3.36   Dean's List - 2 semesters

Related Courses: Statistical Methods for Business Decisions, Simulation of Management Systems, Advanced Business Statistics, Management Information Systems, Computer Programming with Business Applications, Data Processing, Calculus, Linear Algebra

Work Experience

Mathematics Aide, DEPARTMENT OF THE NAVY   Summer 1996
- Wrote up program specifications
- Worked on a special project team
- Tested data and debugged COBOL programs

Service Representative, BLOCKBUSTER VIDEO   Summers 1995, 1996
- Served customer needs
- Controlled cash transactions

Sales Representative, Receptionist, BONNER MARKETING   Summer 1995
- Performed door-to-door sales
- Filed order forms as they were received
- Explained job responsibilities to prospective employees

Crew Trainer, Crew Chief, MCDONALD'S   June 1992-August 1994
- Managed daily receipts and grill area
- Trained new employees and opened the store in the morning

Honors and Activities

- Delta Delta Gamma sorority (elected to pledge chairperson 1995-1996)
- Alpha Lambda Delta national honorary fraternity (inducted 1995)
- Business Student Council (programming committee, resume book committee)
- Management Science Club
- Inducted into *The Dean's List* (1995)

ANDREA C. LANDON

Permanent Address
12 Briarbush Rd.
Grand Rapids, MI 23460
Telephone: (601) 938-4866

Temporary Address
20-C East Hall, Un. of Michigan
Ann Arbor, MI 34958
Telephone: (615) 849-4857

OBJECTIVE: To obtain an entry level position that utilizes my statistical and analytical educational background.

EDUCATION: BS in Quantitative Business Analysis
Legal Environment of Business Minor
University of Michigan
Expected graduation May 1998

Major GPA 3.26/4.0; Cumulative 3.06/4.0

Relevant Courses
Quantitative Business Analysis
Elementary Business Statistics
Statistical Programming Packages

Survey and Sampling
Business and Society

SKILLS: Computer: Basic, Cobol, Pascal, dBase III+, Lotus, WordPerfect, SAS, Minitab, SPSS, Fortran, Siman

Foreign Language Four years Spanish; One semester German

EXPERIENCE: Peer Tutor, University of Michigan Writing Center   1997-1998
- Tutored during drop-in hours
- Advised individuals on various written works

Terminal Operator, Wilstar Corporation   Summer 1996
- Made decisions based on issuing credit reports
- Solved customer problems and responded to inquiries

Collector, First Bank of Grand Rapids   Summer 1995
- Handled 30, 60-day delinquent credit card accounts
- Answered limited customer service inquiries

ACTIVITIES &
HONORS: President, Phi Chi Theta Professional Business Fraternity   1997-1998
- Oversaw all fraternity activities
- Presided over the Executive Council

Founding Sister, Kappa Delta Chi Sorority   Fall 1996
- Pride Leader: Group leader acting as liaison to Executive Council
- Gift Mart Chairman: Ordered Kappa Delta Chi items through national organization
- Risk Management Committee

Business Student Council

Spring Week Special Events and Activities Overall Committee
- Scheduled acts for performances on campus
- Organized and oversaw contests and competitions

Dean's List 3rd Semester

VICTOR A. KING

Local Address:
50 West College Avenue #5
Amherst, MA 28475
(603) 576-9970

Permanent Address:
5 North Woods Road
Birnhardt, MA 38476
(603) 550-9847

EDUCATION

THE UNIVERSITY OF MASSACHUSETTS
B.S. in Quantitative Business Analysis; Emphasis in Operations Management
G.P.A. in major: 3.48/4.00;   G.P.A overall: 3.05/4.00
Graduation: December 1997

SIGNIFICANT COURSEWORK
MATERIALS MANAGEMENT In-company project
- analyzed inventory control consequences of a paper machine for the Brown Company

FACILITIES MANAGEMENT Case study
- analyzed facility location, facility layout and capacity planning problems using past history of companies

SIMULATION OF MANAGEMENT STUDIES Individual project
- designed computer program to simulate present sorting production line at U.S. Post Office in Amherst, then altered program to represent future technological innovations and evaluated the expected effects

COMPUTER SKILLS
- SIMAN Simulation Programming
- LINDO Linear Programming
- STORM Software Package
- PASCAL
- Lotus/Symphony
- Minitab
- Microsoft Word
- WordPerfect

WORK EXPERIENCE

Operations Management
RESEARCH ASSISTANT TO PROFESSOR ROBERT JOHNSON   August 1995 - May 1996
- acquired and outlined research material on Computer Aided Design and Quality in Manufacturing
- evaluated books from student's perspective to aid in Professor Johnson's textbook writing
- graded homework and quizzes for computer simulation class

Research Support Center
LIBRARY AIDE   August 1996 - Present
- helped patrons use business indexes and reference guides

The Bakery
SALES ASSISTANT   July 1995 - Present
- handled money and communicated with the public when selling bakery products

ACTIVITIES
- Orientation Leader for Freshmen
- Intramural Sports Chairperson
- Red Cross Volunteer
- Dormitory Social Historian

WARREN L. BRITES

Current Address:
18 S. Apple Street, Apt. 5
Houghton, MI 13857
(735) 784-9067

Permanent Address:
22 Acorn Lane
Iron Mountain, MI 17465
(635) 775-0985

OBJECTIVE: To utilize my knowledge and skills in Finance, Economics, and Real Estate in a Financial Management position.

EDUCATION: MICHIGAN TECHNOLOGICAL UNIVERSITY
Houghton, MI
Bachelor of Science, December 1997
Major: Real Estate with an emphasis in Finance
Minor: Economics

RELEVANT COURSES:

Investment Valuation
Financial Management
Strategic Management
Management Concepts
Valuation of Real Property
Real Estate Finance and Investment

Speculative Markets
Corporation Finance
Money and Banking
Capital Budgeting
Business Law

EXPERIENCE: PACE MEMBERSHIP WAREHOUSE   1995-Present
- Chosen to represent Pace at different stores and sell memberships
- Helped coordinate the customer service department at the new store
- Handled returns and complaints; issued new membership cards
- Ordered inventory; arranged displays

MAKRO MEMBERSHIP WAREHOUSE   1992-1995
- Provided customer service; handled complaints; took returns; issued "Makro passports"; cashiered
- Took inventory and made sales at the jewelry counter
- Helped transfer stores from Makro to Pace

ACTIVITIES: Finance Club
Real Estate Club
1996 Intramural Softball Champions
Intramural Racquetball

REFERENCES: Available upon request.

DONALD T. TRAUB

617 Mayor Street
Bloomington, IN 13749

Telephone: (319) 774-9806

OBJECTIVE: To obtain an entry-level position in the Real Estate and/or Finance field.

EDUCATION: Indiana University
B.S. Candidate College of Business Administration,
Real Estate Major, Degree Expected December 1997.

Relevant Courses:

Real Estate	Urban Geography	Management	Finance
Economics	Business Law	Marketing	QBA
Computers	B Log	MIS	Int'l Bus.

MILITARY: <u>Disbursing Clerk</u>, United States Navy   5/92-5/94
- Traveled extensively in Bahrain, United Arab Emirates, Saudi Arabia and Oman.
- Provided customer service for personnel concerning disbursing questions, processed numerous pay accounts for payrolls and special payrolls, assisted in processing monthly financial returns.

<u>Disbursing Clerk</u>, United States Navy   11/95-4/96
- Activated under Operation Desert Shield/Storm

WORK EXPERIENCE: <u>Assistant Rental Consultant</u>, Hoosier Real Estate Group   1/97-pres.
- Worked in Apartment Store Office under Property Mgr., assisted in showing of apartment buildings, approval of prospective tenants and processing of leases; searched for new tenants and performed various other duties.

<u>Carpenter</u>, Briggs Construction   Summer 94-96
- Constructed homes according to blueprint, remodeled homes and commercial properties and became familiar with structural defects.

ACTIVITIES: Real Estate Club, Indiana University
International Association of Corporate Real Estate Executives
Habitat Program Volunteer, Indianapolis Area
Racquetball Club, Indiana University

ORVILLE C. DICKERMAN

SCHOOL ADDRESS
45 E. College Avenue
Manhattan, KS 23958
(214) 774-8507

PERMANENT ADDRESS
10 Dogwood Drive
St. Louis, MO 23475
(413) 970-8724

PROFESSIONAL OBJECTIVE:

To contribute in a professional environment where my strong communication skills, coupled with a sincere desire to learn, may make duties productive and enjoyable for myself and my employer.

EDUCATION:

Kansas State University
Bachelor of Science in Real Estate
Anticipated Graduation: May, 1998
Cumulative Grade Average: 3.07

RELATED COURSEWORK:

Accounting	Calculus	Quantitative Business Analysis
Economics	Finance	Business Logistics
Management	Real Estate	International Business
Marketing	Business Law	Computer Programming

COMPUTER SKILLS:

BASIC, Pascal, Lotus 1-2-3, DBase III +, Minitab, MacWrite, MacDraw, and Word Perfect

ACTIVITIES:

Sophomore Business Enterprise Teaching Assistant
Appointed Junior Business Enterprise Teaching Assistant
Member Kansas State Real Estate Club
Member 1991 Kansas State Boxing Club
Captain of various Intramural sports teams
Member of Kansas State University 1994-95 National Club Championship Ice Hockey Team

RELEVANT WORK EXPERIENCE:

1994 - Present	Self Employed (T-shirt distribution business)
Summer 1995-96	Workman & Kohler, P.C., St. Louis, MO (Administrative duties in a corporate law firm)
Summer 1996	Raydan Services, St. Louis, MO (Developed radio advertising)

REFERENCES: Furnished upon request

Brian F. Longsong

30 Keane Dr., Apt. 10
Ann Arbor, MI 13452
(415) 697-0909

EDUCATION

University of Michigan, Masters in Business Administration, emphasis in marketing, finance, and land development, expected August 1998

US Military Academy, West Point, Bachelor of Science, Engineering, May 1989

EXPERIENCE

Construction Superintendent, Cornwell Development Company -- Responsible for all facets of construction including scheduling, coordinating, and supervising the work of all subcontractors; and approving monthly fund distributions. Took over as superintendent of a 92-unit, $10M condominium complex after 3 months as an assistant superintendent. Successfully completed the project and turned the units over to individual owners. Completed a 198-unit, $22M, apartment complex in 38 weeks (from ground breaking to completion). The project was under budget, two weeks ahead of schedule, and a high-quality product. (May '94 to Nov. '96)

Facility Engineer, US Army Corps of Engineers, Captain -- Responsible for developing long-range construction programs; reviewing plans and specifications for all new construction, and the allocation, utilization, and maintenance of over 2.4M square feet of existing facilities. Developed and gained approval for a construction program involving over $50M worth of new construction; planned a successful reorganization of commercial and residential facilities to accommodate the needs of a newly formed unit consisting of 1,000 soldiers. (March '92 to May '94)

Support Platoon Leader, US Army, 8th Engineer Bn. -- Supervisor of 40 soldiers, responsible for the utilization and maintenance of over $35M worth of heavy engineer equipment and mobile bridging. Heavy weapons training officer responsible for running integrated multi-weapon live firing exercises. (May '91 to March '92)

Company Executive Officer, US Army, 2nd Engineer Bn. (Korea) -- Responsible for the maintenance, training, mess, and supply operations of a 160-man combat engineer company deployed along the DMZ in the Republic of Korea. Developed and implemented a maintenance program which led to a 9% increase in on-line operating time and won a Maintenance Excellence Award. (Nov. '90 to May '91)

Platoon Leader, US Army, 2nd Engineer Bn. (Korea) -- Responsible for maintaining the combat readiness of a platoon of 35 construction and demolition specialists in the Republic of Korea. Unit explosives officer responsible for training and safety on live explosive ranges and missions. (Dec. '89 to Nov. '90)

HONORS AND ACTIVITIES

- Teaching Assistant, Finance Department, University of Michigan, -- I teach a finance problem-solving lab to undergraduate Junior level business majors.
- Licensed Professional Engineer (Virginia - Mechanical)
- Distinguished graduate, US Army Engineer School

GRADUATION   August 1998

Lawrence H. Spillmore

LOCAL ADDRESS
4503 Tram Creek Rd., #4
Los Angeles, CA 18239
(714) 284-9506

PERMANENT ADDRESS
31 Price Street
Austin, TX 75791
(903) 839-8475

EDUCATION

University of Southern California, Masters in Business Administration, emphasis in telecommunications management, expected December 1997; current GPA 4.0.

University of Southern California, Bachelor of Science in Electrical Engineering, May 1996; overall GPA 3.25.

EXPERIENCE

Associate Electrical Engineer, AMP Packaging Systems (APS), Round Rock, TX -- programming in turbo basic and turbo C; Printed Circuit Board (PCB) Electrical Analyses; R&D in microwave Triple and microstrip transmission lines; PCB testing (Summer '91, Spring and Fall '94 -- total one year, full-time, as part of the cooperative engineering program).

Associate Telecommunications Engineer, Comtech Consulting Engineers, Inc., Los Angeles, CA -- cost allocation program development for double-ring fiber-optic network in Los Angeles, CA; database development and management for "Fiesta California" telecommunications project in Huntington Beach, CA; engineering support (July '95 to July '96, part-time).

HONORS AND ACTIVITIES

UCLA: member of the Freshmen Honor Society ('92), National Honor Society ('92), International Honor Society ('93), Golden Key Honor Society ('93); on the Electrical Engineering Honor Roll for Spring '92, Dean's List ('91-'92).

UCLA: member of the MBA/MS association, active participant in the "Europe Club" student organization.

OTHER POTENTIALLY APPLICABLE INFORMATION

- Passed the Engineer-In-Training Examination (EIT).
- Will graduate at age 22.
- Tri-lingual (French, Hebrew, and English) / Cross-cultural background.
- Familiar with many spreadsheet, word processing, database, and programming software for both the MAC and PC (DOS, Lotus 123, Excel, Quattro Pro, DBase3, MS Word, WordPerfect, MacWrite, Sprint, PSPICE, MathCad, Turbo Basic, Turbo C, Pascal, Fortran).

GRADUATION   December 1997.

David J. Potter

LOCAL ADDRESS
33 Prospect Ave. #2-H
Bryan, TX 77803
(409) 822-6453

PERMANENT ADDRESS
Windy Knoll Road
Aberdeen, TX 69123
(214) 238-4958

EDUCATION

Texas A&M University, Masters in Business Administration, emphasis in Business Analysis/MIS, expected May 1998; current GPA 3.50

Texas A&M University, Bachelor of Science in Aerospace Engineering, August 1994; Overall GPA 2.9

EXPERIENCE

Engineer, General Dynamics, Fort Worth, TX, F-16 Stress Analysis Airframe --
Determined structural integrity of F-16 fighter; proposed a repair for the test aircraft; approved design modifications for future airplanes; communicated structural requirements to the design group; automated production of stress reports using the CAD/CAM graphics system (August 1994 to January 1996)

Co-op Engineer, General Dynamics, Fort Worth, TX, CAD/CAM Engineering --
Coordinated specifications between departments in development of a data base; organized and presented quarterly status report to the planning office (August 1992 to January 1992)

Co-op Engineer, General Dynamics, Fort Worth, TX, Propulsion Analysis --
Acted as liaison between General Dynamics and the engine manufacturer; produced and submitted engine performance data to airplane customers; coordinated progress of engine modifications to U.S. Air Force (January 1992 to May 1992)

HONORS AND ACTIVITIES

MBA/MS Association
Texas A&M Corps of Cadets, August 1989 to May 1993
Distinguished Student 1990

COMPUTER SKILLS

MS DOS: Lotus 123, dBase, Harvard Graphics, Wordperfect, MS Word
MACINTOSH: Excel, MS Word, MacWrite
LANGUAGES: Fortran, C, BASIC

GRADUATION   May 1998

Douglas F. Sanders

LOCAL ADDRESS
223 E. 42nd Street
New York, NY 17226
(212) 426-9046

PERMANENT ADDRESS
22 Ridge Way
Plano, TX 76435
(419) 339-7849

EDUCATION

New York University, Masters in Business Administration: emphasis in management information systems, degree expected May 1998; current GPA 4.0 (as of March 1997).

Cornell University, Bachelor of Science in Aerospace Engineering: focus in control systems and astrodynamics; degree received May 1987; Magna Cum Laude; GPA 3.83.

EXPERIENCE

Manager, Titan 11 Guidance Analysis & Software Validation Group, Martin Marietta Corporation, Denver, CO -- Supervised the software engineering group, whose charter was to validate computer programs which guide unmanned rockets carrying various satellites into space. Composed detailed work plans, schedules, and developed labor estimates for new contracts. Managed the department's cost accounts in accordance with Cost/Schedule Control Systems criteria. Achieved a 20% cost reduction for analyses which were conducted to support the launch of a defense satellite mission. Interfaced with customer representatives from the United States Air Force, other contractor firms, and internal departments regarding the design, development, and flight readiness of the guidance software. (November 1990 to August 1996).

Engineer 11, Advanced Projects Flight Controls Group, Northrop Aircraft Division, Hawthorne, CA -- Responsible for development of software for advanced aircraft simulations. Tasks included flight control algorithm design, analysis, testing, and mathematical modelling of various aircraft systems. Communicated with government and company test pilots in the simulators, obtaining evaluations of the flying qualities of fighter aircraft. (June 1987 to October 1990).

HONORS AND ACTIVITIES

Received three commendations for exemplary job performance at Martin Marietta. Member of Phi Kappa Phi, Sigma Gamma Tau, and Tau Beta Pi honor societies. Member of American Institute of Aeronautics & Astronautics; served as committee chairman at Cornell University Student Chapter 1986-87. Plano High School Valedictorian 1983. Elected National Honor Society President 1982-83. Named in Who's Who Among American High School Students, National Register of Commended Scholars, and Society of Distinguished American High School Students 1983.

COMPUTER SKILLS

Mainframe: CDC Network Operating System, UNIX Workstations, IBM TSO.
Macintosh: Microsoft Word, Excel, MacDraw, CricketGraph, NCSA Telnet, SmartForm Assistant, Microphone II, SoftPC.
PC DOS: Lotus 123, WordPerfect, dBase III Plus.

GRADUATION May 1998.

Michael P. Lanxton

LOCAL ADDRESS
42 Bendex Road #2-A
College Station, TX 77840
(409) 972-8223

PERMANENT ADDRESS
20 Dove Way
Fort Smith, AK 23842
(513) 665-0982

EDUCATION

Texas A&M University, Masters of Business Administration, Expected degree date: August, 1997. Graduate School Specialty Electives: Total Quality Process, Engineering Economics and TQM, Polymer Engineering Computer Aided Design and Engineering.

Texas A&M University, B.S. Mechanical Engineering, GPA: 3.3, Degree date: August 11, 1995.

EXPERIENCE

Graduate Assistant; Texas A&M University, Technology Licensing Office, College Station, TX. Research Assistant: Interface with University inventors; conduct patent and literature searches, application and market research, and pursue industries which could benefit from the technology (Fall 1996 - present).

Camp Counselor; Kanakuk Kamps, Branson, MO. Christian Athletic Camp; top rated in America; Cabin Counselor for 13 and 16 yr. age kids; Instructor for tennis, volleyball, wind surfing and soccer; led Bible studies and counseled kids (Summer 1996).

Co-op Engineer; General Dynamics, Fort Worth, TX. Liaison Engineer: Resolved manufacturing and engineering problems, coordinated between production and design engineers, completed required design, drafting and document changes (Fall 1994).

Co-op Engineer; General Dynamics, Fort Worth, TX. Assistant Design Engineer: Worked on advanced test project. Involved mechanical design, CAD/CAM, composites technology, aircraft structures and coordination between project groups (Spring 1994).

Co-op Engineer; General Dynamics, Fort Worth, TX. Engineering Assistant: Delivered electronic hardware and documentation to and coordinated with people throughout plant. Performed mechanical design on CAD/CAM for manufacturing problems (Summer 1993).

Summer Intern; Southwest Research Institute, Emissions Control Department, San Antonio, TX. Engineering Assistant: Assisted in experimental and literature research, prepared figures and data for technical papers, computed engineering calculations (Summer 1992).

HONORS AND ACTIVITIES

TAMU - Distinguished Student Award - Spring '91, '92; M.E. Dept. Scholarship '91, '92; Tau Beta Pi, Engineering Honor Society; Pi Tau Sigma, Mechanical Engineering Honor Society; Memorial Student Center Council - Operations Committee '91; Opera and Performing Arts Society '92-'93; Campus Crusade for Christ; ASME; MBA Association; TAMU Intramural Sports; Tennis singles and doubles, Flag Football, Soccer, Softball and Basketball.

GRADUATION   August 1997

Sandra R. Pillam
216 Salt Grass Terrace, Apt. 5-D
Gainesville, FL 18237
(219) 477-9242

EDUCATION

University of Florida, Masters of Science in Human Resources Management, expected December 1997; current GPA 3.81

Auburn University, Bachelor of Arts in Management, May 1992; Overall GPA 3.2. Major GPA 3.9

EXPERIENCE

Human Resources Assistant, Sun Oil Company, Oklahoma City Refinery, Oklahoma City, OK; Professional Summer internship -- Assisting labor relations staff in preparation for December 1997, contract negotiations; preparing summations of labor arbitration cases; assisting staff with various needs related to employees at the Oklahoma City Refinery (Summer 1997).

Graduate Assistant, Department of Management, Graduate School for Business, University of Florida, Gainesville, FL -- Assisting several faculty in the Department of Management with research and class preparation for graduate and undergraduate level courses in management (Fall 1995 - present); Interviewing 76 undergraduate applicants for the College of Business administration's "CBA Fellows" Program (Fall 1996); Working with faculty from the Departments of Management, Urban Planning, Family Medicine, and Statistics on a project funded by the National Institutes of Health, investigating the effects of health facility design on patients' compliance with treatment and on staff's absenteeism/turnover behavior -- leading a four-person research team, coordinating data collection and entry, budgeting/expense management of a $150,000 research grant (Fall 1995 to Summer 1996).

Senior Banking Representative, Teller Supervisor, Consumer Lender, National Bank of Georgia, Atlanta, GA -- Supervising six tellers at a branch office, including quarterly performance appraisals and annual salary reviews, developing programs to enhance teamwork, with a special emphasis on group efforts to improve customer service; Consumer Lending authority level two of five: authority to independently lend up to $15,000 secured and $5,000 unsecured per customer; responsible for 25% of monthly sales for the branch (January 1993 to August 1995).

HONORS AND ACTIVITIES

President, Graduate Women's Business Network, Un. of Florida, 1996-97
Member, Society for Human Resource Management, Un. of Florida and National
Member, MBA/MS Association, University of Florida, 1995-present
Catcher, MBA/MS Co-Rec Softball team, "The Masters," Spring 1997
Member, American Institute of Banking, Atlanta, GA, 1993-95

GRADUATION   December 1997

Regina A. Washington

LOCAL ADDRESS
40 Cortney Street, Apt. D-2
East Lansing, MI 23958
(615) 342-9837

PERMANENT ADDRESS
12 Plumtree Circle
Media, PA 19485
(610) 366-9382

EDUCATION

Michigan State University, Master of Science in Management with a concentration in Human Resource Management Candidate, May 1998.

Bucknell University, Bachelor of Science, Major: Psychology, May 1995.

Bucknell University Studies Abroad Program, Cortona, Italy. Marble sculpting and drawing, June-August 1994.

EXPERIENCE

Graduate Assistant, Department of Management, Michigan State University (September 1996 to present) -- assist two professors, including the Department Head of Management, in research.

Intern, The Hay Group, Philadelphia, PA, HR management consulting firm (Spring 1995-Summer 1995) -- organization of job satisfaction surveys and result, compiling self-help packets for feedback, marketing research (Christmas 1996) -- co-wrote report on HR strategies for Workforce 2000.

Assistant in Operations, GraphTech, Inc., Malvern, PA (Spring 1994, Fall 1994) -- graphic design, training documentation development, software testing, electronic forms design (Christmas 1992, Fall 1993) -- receptionist.

Tutor, Bucknell University (Fall 1992, Spring 1993) -- tutored students in software use, computer hardware installation, troubleshooting.

HONORS AND ACTIVITIES

Graduate Women's Business Network, Treasurer
MBA/MS Association Member
Dean's Honor List, Honor List
Allison Meyers Scholarship, 4 years
USSR Friendship Force Exchange
Catalyst Committee Chair
Intramural Association, board member,
Artwork selected for 25th Annual Mostra, Cortona, Italy

COMPUTER SKILLS

PC DOS: Lotus 123, dBase, WordPerfect, MSWord, Wordstar
MACINTOSH: PageMaker, Microsoft Word, MacWrite, MacDraw

GRADUATION   May 1998

Laura A. Kelleter

LOCAL ADDRESS
P.O. Box 14
East Lansing, MI 13948
(415) 437-9473

PERMANENT ADDRESS
18 Tyler Lane
Green Bay, WI 13958
(615) 433-9374

EDUCATION

Michigan State University, Master of Science in Human Resource Management, expected May 1998; current GPA 3.75

Penn State University, Bachelor of Arts in English and Spanish, May 1996; Graduated with Honors -- completed 36 hours of Honors Courses; GPA 3.4

EXPERIENCE

Summer Intern, Human Resources, Johnson & Johnson, New Brunswick, NJ-- Worked on Equal Employment Opportunity and Team Effectiveness projects (Summer 1997).

Graduate Assistant, Department of Management, Michigan State University -- Compiled a mailing list of Human Resource Executives to be used in a department research project; reviewed textbook galleys; assisted in grading tests (September 1996 to present).

Summer Intern, Human Resources, Dow Chemical Company, Midland, MI -- Developed and moderated a New Employee Orientation Program; identified issues and impacts of the current disability reporting process and made recommendations to improve the process; coordinated tours, activities, and weekly lunch speakers for summer interns (May 1996 to August 1996)

Tour Guide and Desk Worker, Visitor Center, Michigan State University -- Scheduled visitor appointments; showed prospective students around campus (September 1994 - May 1996)

Summer Intern, Human Resources, Scott Paper Company, Philadelphia, PA -- Coordinated the summer intern program including tours and activities and compiled a manual for the coordination of this program; developed supervisor guidelines outlining pre-arrival steps and a summer timetable for supervisors of summer interns; interpreted data from recruiting surveys (May 1995 to August 1995)

HONORS AND ACTIVITIES

- Honors Graduate, Penn State University, 1996
- Who's Who Among Students in American Universities and Colleges
- Student Government: Freshman Programs (Outstanding Freshman Aide)
- Parents' Weekend Committee Programming Sub-Chairman for 2 years
- Mortar Board, Inc./Cap & Gown (Publicity Chairman) - National Senior Honor Society
- Cardinal Key/Tau Kappa Chapter - National Junior Honor Society
- Freshman Program - planned activities to assist incoming freshmen with their transition from high school to college

GRADUATION   May 1998

Stacy R. Schmidt

LOCAL ADDRESS
24 Campus Road, #4-F
Raleigh, NC 13928
(415) 394-9584

PERMANENT ADDRESS
12 Sommers Lane
Chapel Hill, NC 18374
(705) 305-2948

EDUCATION

North Carolina State University, Master in Business Administration, emphasis in marketing, expected December 1997; current GPA 3.63

Clemson University, Bachelor of Journalism, emphasis in public relations and marketing, December 1995; Overall GPA 3.75

EXPERIENCE

Public Relations Intern, Gulf Pipeline Company, Houston, TX -- compiled a HAZWOPER cross reference list and researched all MSDS sheets for the area. Described the routing of Gulf pipelines through communities for inclusion in Gulf's Environmental Response Plan. Attended community meetings in which the plan was presented to fire and police personnel as well as community members (May 1995 to August 1995).

Advertising Intern, Sports Graphics, Inc., Chapel Hill, NC -- wrote copy and designed graphics promoting celebrity golf tournament and professional tennis event. Oversaw all stages of production for both projects. Used Macintosh computers (January 1995 to May 1995).

HONORS AND ACTIVITIES

- Graduate Assistant to Dr. Conrad Reicher, Journalism Department Head
- Recipient, Minority Merit Fellowship ($10,000 per year)
- MBA/MS Association-Mentors Program
- Graduate Women's Business Network
- American Marketing Association Student Chapter-Publications
- Member, Women in Communications, Inc.
- Public Relations Student Society of America-Attended the 1994 PRSSA National Convention
- Kappa Tau Alpha Honor Society
- Nordstrom Retailing Communications Competition - Outstanding Performance Award, January 1996

RELEVANT COURSE WORK

Consumer Behavior   Analyzing Consumer Behavior   Retail Concepts & Policies
Services Marketing   Research Marketing Decisions   Advertising Principles
Marketing Management   International Marketing   Media and the Community

GRADUATION   December 1997